Conscience in Crisis

Studies in Anabaptist and Mennonite History

Edited by
Cornelius J. Dyck, Ernst Correll, Leonard Gross, Leland Harder, Guy F. Hershberger, John S. Oyer, Theron Schlabach, J. C. Wenger, and John H. Yoder

1. Two Centuries of American Mennonite Literature, 1727-1928*
   By Harold S. Bender, 1929
2. The Hutterian Brethren, 1528-1931
   By John Horsch, 1931
3. Centennial History of the Mennonites in Illinois*
   By Harry F. Weber, 1931
4. For Conscience' Sake*
   By Sanford Calvin Yoder, 1940
5. Ohio Mennonite Sunday Schools*
   By John Umble, 1941
6. Conrad Grebel, Founder of the Swiss Brethren
   By Harold S. Bender, 1950
7. Mennonite Piety Through the Centuries*
   By Robert Friedmann, 1949
8. Bernese Anabaptists and Their American Descendants*
   By Delbert L. Gratz, 1953
9. Anabaptism in Flanders, 1530-1650
   By A. L. E. Verheyden, 1961
10. The Mennonites in Indiana and Michigan*
    By J. C. Wenger, 1961
11. Anabaptist Baptism: A Representative Study
    By Rollin Stely Armour, 1966
12. Lost Fatherland: The Story of Mennonite Emigration from Soviet Russia, 1921-1927
    By John B. Toews, 1967
13. Mennonites of the Ohio and Eastern Conference*
    By Grant M. Stoltzfus, 1969
14. The Mennonite Church in India, 1897-1962
    By John A. Lapp, 1972
15. The Theology of Anabaptism: An Interpretation
    By Robert Friedmann, 1973
16. Anabaptism and Asceticism
    By Kenneth R. Davis, 1974
17. South Central Frontiers
    By Paul Erb, 1974
18. The Great Trek of the Russian Mennonites to Central Asia, 1880-1884
    By Fred R. Belk, 1976
19. Mysticism and the Early South German-Austrian Anabaptist Movement, 1525-1531
    By Werner O. Packull, 1976
20. Conscience in Crisis: Mennonites and Other Peace Churches in America, 1739-1789
    By Richard K. MacMaster with Samuel L. Horst and Robert F. Ulle, 1979
21. Gospel Versus Gospel: Mission and the Mennonite Church, 1863-1944
    By Theron F. Schlabach, 1979

**Out of print. Available in microfilm or Xerox copies.*

STUDIES IN ANABAPTIST AND MENNONITE HISTORY

No. 20

CONSCIENCE IN CRISIS
Mennonites and Other Peace Churches in America 1739-1789

Interpretation and Documents

Richard K. MacMaster with
Samuel L. Horst and Robert F. Ulle

Herald Press, Scottdale, Pennsylvania, in cooperation with Mennonite Historical Society, Goshen, Indiana, is publisher of the series "Studies in Anabaptist and Mennonite History." The Society is primarily responsible for the content of the studies, and Herald Press for their publication.

Mennonites and Other Peace Churches in America, 1739-1789
Interpretation and Documents

Richard K. MacMaster with
Samuel L. Horst and Robert F. Ulle

HERALD PRESS
Scottdale, Pennsylvania
Kitchener, Ontario
1979

Library of Congress Cataloging in Publication Data

MacMaster, Richard Kerwin, 1935-
Conscience in crisis.

(Studies in Anabaptist and Mennonite history; no. 20)
Bibliography: p.
Includes index.
1. Mennonites in the Middle Atlantic States—History—Sources. 2. Friends, Society of—Middle Atlantic States—History—Sources. 3. Schwenkfelders in the Middle Atlantic States—History—Sources. 4. Church of the Brethren—Middle Atlantic States—History—Sources. 5. Moravian Church—Middle Atlantic States—History—Sources. 6. Nonviolence—Moral and religious aspects. 7. Pacifism—History—Sources. 8. Middle Atlantic States—Church history—Sources. 9. Middle Atlantic States—History—Sources. I. Horst, Samuel, 1919- joint author. II. Ulle, Robert F., 1948- joint author. III. Title. IV. Series.
BX8116.42.M33 261.8'73 78-27530
ISBN 0-8361-1213-X

CONSCIENCE IN CRISIS: MENNONITES AND OTHER PEACE CHURCHES IN AMERICA, 1739-1789

Published simultaneously in Canada by Herald Press, Kitchener, Ont. N2G 4M5
Library of Congress Catalog Card Number: 78-27530
International Standard Book Number: 0-8361-1213-X
Printed in the United States of America
Design: Alice B. Shetler

10 9 8 7 6 5 4 3 2 1

Dedicated to the memory of
Grant M. Stoltzfus,
who possessed the vision for this work but suddenly passed away before its beginning, and to
Melvin Gingerich,
whose long interest and competence in history was freely given until he, too, was called home.
May God be glorified.

CONTENTS

LIST OF TABLES

PREFACE

"One of the fascinations of history is that it is never finally written. Somewhere someone will discover new documents, new evidence, new light. The past can then be retold with fresh insights." Such were the words of the late Professor Grant M. Stoltzfus of Eastern Mennonite College, Harrisonburg, Virginia, in an article published in the January 1974 *Mennonite Research Journal.* He raised the question whether this can happen with regard to the Mennonite experience in the formative years of the United States of America. It is clear that Professor Stoltzfus thought it could. Indeed, as we read that article, "Waiting to Be Done: Basic Research on Mennonites in the American Revolution," we see that he was speaking for a growing number of persons who had some knowledge of the documents cached away in the state archives of the Eastern Seaboard states.

Various persons were verifying that such a rich lode of documents did exist. A substantial but modest foray into this material was made by James O. Lehman and Gerald Brunk of the Eastern Mennonite College faculty when they examined the militia records of Pennsylvania and Maryland and extracted many Mennonite, Amish, Moravian, and German Baptist (Tunker) surnames. Robert Ulle also was discovering numerous such documents in connection with his research as administrator for the Germantown Mennonite Church Corporation. Prior to this, indeed more than forty years ago, Wilbur J. Bender had published a booklet entitled *Pacifism in Colonial Pennsylvania* that was a commendable beginning in relation to this one topic. A scattering of perceptive church historians was becoming aware that this was only the "tip of the iceberg" and Stoltzfus acknowledged as much when he announced the publication of Brunk and Lehman's *Guide to Select Revolutionary War Records:* "It is clear that . . . [the collection of these names] . . . is only the first step in surveying, listing, and publishing source materials on the 'plain people' in the Revolutionary War period." He expressed fond hope that much more research might be done that would lead to fresh publication and a new understanding of this important period in the life of both nation and state.

This same sense of urgency was emerging in other circles also—in meetings of the Historical Committee of the Mennonite Church and specifically in a special interest group meeting held in connection with the August 1974 Assembly of Region V of the Mennonite Church at Christopher Dock Mennonite High School, Lansdale, Pennsylvania. It was following this latter unofficial meeting of persons interested in Mennonite history that the actual formation of a committee and the specific pursuit of this project was begun. The five Mennonite historical agencies serving the East Coast were each to select a representative and these five persons then constitute a committee to move the work ahead. The persons chosen were: Gerald Brunk for Eastern Mennonite College, later replaced by Hubert Pellman when Brunk went to Egypt for a sabbatical; Carolyn L. Charles for the (Lancaster, Pa.) Mennonite Historical Associates; James O. Lehman for Eastern Mennonite Associated Libraries and Archives; M. Virginia Musser for the Germantown Mennonite Church Corporation; and Gerald Studer for the Mennonite Historians of Eastern Pennsylvania. Studer was chosen to serve as chairman and Musser as secretary-treasurer for the newly formed Colonial Mennonite Source Book Committee. Lehman served as agent for the Committee in the Harrisonburg area and carried out with dispatch and sensitivity many of the details that were encountered during the course of the research and writing.

The Committee began by selecting an editorial team and a group of advisers. Already in the first meeting persons were suggested who were felt to be qualified for these tasks. These subgroups crystallized readily and the project was underway. As advisers to the project, the following were asked to serve and consented: Donald F. Durnbaugh of Bethany Theological Seminary, Oakbrook, Ill.; Leonard Gross, Executive Secretary of the Mennonite Historical Committee, Goshen, Ind.; Robert S. Kreider of Bethel College, North Newton, Kan.; John A. Lapp, Dean of Goshen College, Goshen, Ind.; and Melvin Gingerich of Goshen, Ind. The editorial team consisted of Samuel Horst, of the history faculty of Eastern Mennonite College; Richard MacMaster of Harrisonburg, Va.; and Robert Ulle of Germantown, Philadelphia. Horst was asked to serve as chairman. The team did a prodigious amount of work both in basic research and in writing the particular portions of the total manuscript which their expertise and available time would allow. MacMaster, whose personal schedule permitted the greater amount of time and attention to the research and writing, consequently wrote the greater part of the resulting manuscript. We are deeply indebted to these men for their painstaking and sacrificial efforts. The advisers provided an essential and varied perspective on the project and gave their critical reading and evaluation to early drafts of the manuscript.

Several questions remained throughout the preparation of the manuscript that defied easy resolution: the precise parameters of the source book, the target audience that was being addressed, whether to hasten to press for the celebrations of '76 or take more deliberate time, and the amount of interpretative and introductory material that should be supplied with the documents reproduced. The outcome will speak for itself as to how each question was resolved, and the committee along with the staff of *Studies in Anabaptist and Mennonite History* will take responsibility for any weaknesses that may remain.

From the beginning it was felt that Eastern Mennonite College occupied a particularly appropriate position with regard to both the needed leadership and expertise in directing the preparation of this source book. Throughout the several years that the manuscript was in preparation, EMC had generously cooperated both with funds and personnel. Editorial Team Chairman Samuel Horst had demonstrated his meticulousness in research and capability in writing with the publication in 1967 of *Mennonites in the Confederacy*. He provided the leadership and counsel needed for this project even amidst a heavy teaching load and the completion of his doctoral dissertation. Richard MacMaster, who later began employment with Mennonite Mutual Aid along with a part-time teaching assignment at James Madison University, Harrisonburg, Virginia, came onto the scene at a most crucial time bringing with him his considerable experience in both historical research and writing, not to mention his commitment to the Anabaptist Vision. Finally, it was Robert Ulle's pioneer work in collecting early documents related to his inter-Mennonite assignment in Philadelphia that sparked the launching of this whole project and, though he was neither related to EMC nor Harrisonburg nor of traditional Mennonite stock, yet it was he who introduced into the Mennonite historical mix just the element needed to enable the extraction and analysis of those earliest documents concerning us in the New World. We cannot express too strongly our indebtedness to the unique contributions of each of the editorial team.

The Committee wishes also to acknowledge with appreciation the help and counsel given to this project by SAMH Editor-in-Chief Cornelius J. Dyck and his editorial assistant (Mrs.) Suzanne Hilty Lind, as well as to Paul M. Schrock, Book Editor of Herald Press, and his staff for their professional help in bringing this book into print.

A word of thanks is due all who assisted financially in making this publication project possible: to the historical agencies represented on the Committee who each contributed to the extent of their abilities; to the Franconia Mennonite Conference and to Schowalter Foundation for their substantial support; and to a group of individuals whose personal interest prompted the giving of sums of money, some larger, some smaller, but all needed and most gratefully received; and last, to those individuals willing to loan money at no interest to carry us over the lean times.

We recognize with deep gratitude for their friendship and assistance, the contributions of Grant M. Stoltzfus and Melvin Gingerich, both of whom died before this project was completed, and to whom we dedicate this book. It is further our prayer that everyone in that large group of persons who contributed in a variety of ways will feel the deep thanks that each deserves but which neither space nor discretion allow our mentioning by name.

Gerald C. Studer
November 3, 1977

INTRODUCTION

The Sectarian Vision

Leaders of the Mennonite Church in Pennsylvania wrote in May 1742 to the Dutch Mennonite Committee for Foreign Needs to express their concern at the march of recent events in the colony and to acknowledge their own mistake in coming to America "without sufficient assurance concerning freedom of conscience." Although they were grateful for the peace and liberty of this free land after three centuries of intermittent persecution in Europe, these Mennonites saw reason to fear that Pennsylvania would enact a militia law and compel them "against our conscience to take up arms" in defense of the province. Before they wrote to their brethren in Holland, the Pennsylvania Mennonites had sought the help of the Quaker-dominated General Assembly. The members had been sympathetic to the Mennonite petition, to be sure, but there was little they could promise, for they were caught in the same dilemma.[1]

Mennonites and Quakers shared the sectarian idea of discipleship as a separate and distinct way of life. They regarded the New Testament ethic of love and nonresistance as binding upon the followers of Christ and they recognized no cleavage between the spheres of religion and daily life. Their whole life, not merely an occasional ritual on Sundays, was to them a service to God. In their following of Christ, they accepted William Penn's equation, "No Cross, No Crown." Dunkers, Schwenkfelders, and Moravians held similar views. But other Christians had a different attitude. The churches, unlike the sects, had never committed themselves to an imitation of Christ on all seven days of the week; and even those who believed most strongly in personal conversion and a new birth had no difficulty in separating religion and secular concerns.[2]

Tension between the sectarian and the secular viewpoint was inevitable. The Quakers had created in Pennsylvania a commonwealth in which "civil and religious liberty, social and political equality, domestic and external peace had reigned to a degree and for a length of time unexampled in the history of the Western world."[3] But a sectarian state is a paradox, and the instruments of political power had been in Quaker hands from the beginning of the colony.

The paradox became more apparent after Great Britain declared war on Spain in October 1739. When the news reached Philadelphia, Governor George Thomas called on the Assembly to do its part in the war effort by enacting a militia law. The Assembly responded that no act of the legislature was needed to set up a militia, since the governor was already authorized as captain general to recruit and command any military forces raised in the province. The Assembly, of course, would not be obliged to pay the expenses of any militia that Governor Thomas might summon.[4]

Political Dimensions

Many elements entered into the quarrel between the Governor of Pennsylvania and the elected representatives of the people. Other colonial governors bickered with their legislatures over military supply bills without the slightest hint of any scruples being involved. The wars against France and Spain in the mid-eighteenth century required larger forces serving for a longer time and traveling greater distances than any previous colonial militia had been asked to do. The old idea of a militia as the able-bodied men of the community summoned to stand guard for a few days against marauding Indians or rebellious slaves began to give way. Volunteer forces, paid and supplied, armed and clothed by the government, were needed for campaigns in Canada and the West Indies. The power of the governor to raise and command the militia accordingly came to mean less and less, as Governor Thomas had discovered, without the willingness of the legislature to pass bills to equip and pay them.[5] It was not just in Pennsylvania that assemblymen saw in this situation an opportunity to bring the governor under their own control.

The situation in Pennsylvania was complicated by the ongoing quarrel between the governor, as the representative of the Proprietors, and the Assembly, as the representatives of the people, and the change in the character and composition of the two factions. William Penn had lobbied energetically in England for full religious liberty while providing a haven in Pennsylvania for his persecuted brethren. Once Parliament passed a Toleration Act in 1689, Friends in Philadelphia enjoyed no greater security of person and property than Friends in London and they began to look at Penn less as a benefactor and more as the absolute landlord of Pennsylvania. The Quaker Assembly had pressed the Proprietor and his appointed governors thereafter for more liberty. The Charter of Privileges, which Penn granted in 1701, was a landmark in this struggle. Succeeding generations continued the effort and Pennsylvania politics revolved around two factions, one holding office or otherwise attached to the proprietary interest and the other seeing itself as the elected watchdog of the popular interest.[6]

Because they were Quakers, and not merely a group of well-to-do colonists who chafed at having too small a share in their own government, the Quaker Party was more than just a popular or anti-proprietary party. Its vision was a sectarian vision. It sought to protect and extend that liberty that made it possible for the nonresistant sects to *live* according to conscience and not just to *worship* according to conscience. This vision was enshrined in the First Article of the Charter of Privileges, where Penn had pledged that persons living peaceably in the colony should never be obliged "to do or suffer any other Act or Thing, contrary to their religious Persuasion" and that they should "be capable (notwithstanding their other Persuasions and Practices in Point of Conscience and Religion) to serve this Government in any capacity, both legislatively and executively." It was this broad definition of religious freedom, with its acknowledgement of the primacy of conscience, that allowed Mennonites and Dunkers, Schwenkfelders and Moravians, as well as Quakers, to participate on equal terms in the life of the colony.

That right was to be challenged again and again in the turbulent half-century that followed the opening of the war between Great Britain and Spain in 1739. The issue was put clearly by the Quaker Assembly when they replied to Governor Thomas in September 1740: "Though our Principles do not allow us to pass a Militia Bill, build Forts, provide Arms, So that therefore our Principles are inconsistent with the Ends of Government, is no self-evident proposition."[7] The governor's logic is not particularly compelling, but his successors, under the king and under the Continental Congress, renewed his argument in each succeeding crisis and the men who framed the 1776 Pennsylvania Constitution made military service, in person or by substitute, the obligation of every citizen.

But, if Mennonites and Quakers could only be citizens of a free commonwealth by compromising their principles, then the much-vaunted liberty of Pennsylvania was a sham. Religion would be reduced to a merely ceremonial function, for the price of religious liberty would be that religion has no practical consequences. Thus the overwhelming issue of these fifty years, so far as the sects were concerned, was the survival of the sectarian vision.

Nonresistance and Self-Government

It is little wonder that Mennonites, Quakers, Dunkers, Schwenkfelders, and others united in a common effort through what was for them a prolonged crisis and sought to elect representatives who would pledge to preserve the liberties guaranteed in Penn's Charter. They were consistent in opposing successive proprietary governors down to 1764 and in seeking to defeat the drive for a royal government in that year and for independence twelve years later. For they knew that any change in government could only mean that the Charter of Privileges would be abridged or abandoned and with it the rights they cherished.

Ironically, their participation in a freely elected government created another serious problem for the peaceable sects. It was a modern dilemma. In successfully asserting their control over the government, the Quaker legislators had simply carried forward at the Proprietor's expense the Whig principles of self-government that they had brought from England and that Penn himself had kept alive.[8] The constitutional principle on which the Quakers rested their case in all their disputes with the governor or the crown in the eighteenth century was that only the elected representatives of the people could decide on matters that related to affairs within the colony. If the Friends in the Assembly had appealed to the British government or to the Proprietor to defend the province in wartime, they would have had to abandon the basic principle of self-government. Yet to vote a militia bill was contrary to the conscience of each one.[9]

The plight of the Quaker Assemblymen who were called on by successive Pennsylvania governors to vote a militia bill or provide supplies for the army should not obscure the fact that it was the nature of representative government, not the accident of Quaker membership in the legislature, that created difficulty for the sects.

The writings of sixteenth-century Anabaptists and seventeenth-century Quakers had emphasized biblical nonresistance as the norm for the individual disciple in his following of Christ. The love of the nonresistant Jesus was the proper response to a persecuting magistrate or a hostile neighbor. Christians, who claimed to be His followers, could not take part in wars or lawsuits or coercion of any kind. The Swiss Anabaptist Conrad Grebel wrote in 1524 that "true Christians use neither the worldly sword nor engage in war since among them taking human life has ceased entirely, for we are no longer under the Old Covenant." The Old Testament law of an eye for an eye had given way to the New Testament ethic of nonresistance. The Anabaptists rejected the appeal of Luther, Zwingli, and other Reformers to the kings and princes to force Reformed Christianity on their subjects and defend Protestantism with military power. They believed that there was power enough in the gospel, illumined by the Holy Spirit, to bring men and women to personal conviction. They repudiated the idea, almost universal in their time, that the state had an obligation to foster true religion. "The Gospel and those who accept it are not to be protected with the sword, neither should they thus protect themselves."[10]

The early Friends were led to a similar attitude, after initial indecision. To Quakers who asked George Fox to advise them on service with the militia when a Royalist uprising threatened the peace of England in 1659, he wrote that Friends are dead to all carnal weapons, and stand in a power which takes away all occasions of war. They should pay taxes to the rulers, who are to keep peace. But they cannot bear carnal weapons under the several governments.[11]

Refusal to bear arms was always closely linked in Mennonite and Quaker writings, as in George Fox's letter, to support of civil government. They held that all true authority was from God. A Quaker petition insisted in 1683 "that God Almighty hath taught and engaged us to acknowledge and actually obey magistracy, as His ordinance, in all things not repugnant to His Law and Light in our consciences." While seeking to govern their own lives by a higher law, they followed the New Testament teaching to render to Caesar the things that are Caesar's.[12]

Although they refused personal military service, Dutch Mennonites and English Quakers readily paid taxes that went to build new warships for the British or Dutch Navy and helped protect the worldwide empires the two great powers had acquired in the seventeenth century. There is little indication that the nonresistant sects ever criticized the military policy of the nation and, as English Quakers were to insist in 1755, there is every indication that Friends had always taught the necessity of paying taxes that they knew would be used solely for warlike purposes.[13]

Yet Quakers had always refused to pay what was called "trophy money," a special tax levied in England to provide flags and drums for the militia. Among the queries that every Meeting of Friends in England and America put to their members each year was one that asked about payment of this specific tax.[14] Why was it wrong to contribute toward a drum that kept time for a rustic militia marching around the village on the annual training day and a Christian duty to help pay for cannons and regiments of light dragoons?

The Mennonite and Quaker attitudes on payment of taxes, obedience to civil authority, and nonresistance, like those of the early Christian community, had developed in a situation where the ruling powers and the individual Christian were totally separate and distinct from one another. The granting of money "for the King's use" was not a euphemism coined to salve nonresistant consciences, but an acknowledgement of a centuries-old reality. The king, prince, or elector did not consult his subjects on what use he might make of his revenues. Allow that the subject had an obligation in conscience to render to Caesar whatever taxes and custom duties were due him and the question of how the king might use this revenue had no place in the discussion. When a monarch could declare war or hire an army of mercenary soldiers at whim, the subject had no more right to object than if the royal caprice turned to building a new palace for a favorite or endowing a chair at a university. So long as wars were fought by professional mercenaries and recruits voluntarily enlisted from the poorest segments of society, nonresistance may have meant little more in practice, with regard to wars and fighting, than that the military profession was closed to Mennonites and Quakers.

When Oliver Cromwell tried to replace a hireling army with a citizen militia, seeing in its direct link to the local community a safeguard for English liberty, he was introducing into England the idea that military service is one of the essential elements of good citizenship. Friends could not accept this and went to jail rather than serve or pay an equivalent fine. The English militia laws required individuals to furnish their own weapons, but the cost of flags and drums was spread over the whole community. The payment of "trophy money" would thus be acknowledgment of an obligation to military service on the part of all and the equivalent of taking up arms. Caesar had the undoubted right to the tribute penny, even if it went to build pagan temples, but he had no right to command Christians to worship him by offering a pinch of incense at his shrine. The mere payment of taxes and custom duties could not involve any *direct* or *voluntary* approval of wars and fighting, but the payment of the "trophy money" would be just that.

The growth of representative government in England and America had much the same effect as the effort to create a citizen army. If the elected representatives of the people could determine government policy or the use to which tax revenue could be put, the responsibility for that use or that policy could not be shifted onto an arbitrary monarch. The distinction between the government and the sects had dissolved. Caesar wore a broad-brimmed hat and used plain speech. The Quakers in the Pennsylvania Assembly were not being asked to vote a sum of money for the king to use as he saw fit, but to apply to specific military needs funds raised from taxes paid by every landowner in the colony. As John Churchman and John Woolman realized, responsibility extended beyond the Assembly to every Quaker, Mennonite, and Dunker in Pennsylvania who would be compromised by paying an ordinary land tax as much as by paying the "trophy money." The very liberty and self-government they prized had cast them into a cruel dilemma. Did the New Testament teaching on support of civil authority oblige them to do military duty and contribute voluntarily to the prosecution of a war?[15]

The nonresistant sects in eighteenth-century Pennsylvania thus stand on the threshold of the modern world. The issues they faced of religious liberty and the sectarian ideal of a life governed by conscience, of nonresistance and the military obligation as a duty of citizenship, and of the responsibility of conscience in a democratic state, are all modern issues that could scarcely be understood in the context of sixteenth- or seventeenth-century Europe. Our understanding of these issues derives largely from this one generation.

A Continuing Crisis

But these problems were far too complex to be settled in a single legislative session or even formulated by an experience of one crisis. They stretched over half a century. The basic points at issue and the leaders who sought to grapple with them remained essentially the same through this long period. They can only be understood if the period from 1740 through the American Revolution is seen as one prolonged crisis for the sectarian view. The Militia Law that the Pennsylvania Assembly framed in November 1755 remained the only sort of militia act that the sects could accept twenty years later, just as the Pennsylvania Militia Act of 1777 embodied the same objectionable features as the law drafted in 1757, after the Quakers had withdrawn from the Assembly. The sects rejected any claim to a universal military obligation in the Revolution and in the Colonial Wars, seeking to make widespread relief efforts a sufficient pledge of their interest in the commonwealth. This continuity is hardly surprising, since leaders like the Mennonite Benjamin Hershey, the Schwenkfelder Christopher Schultz, and the Quaker Israel Pemberton were the chosen spokesmen for the sects in each successive crisis.

The American Revolution was merely the last act of a drama that began when Governor Thomas demanded a militia act and defense appropriations of the Pennsylvania Assembly in 1740 and it fully justified the fears expressed by the Mennonite community in the letter to Holland. The sects could only escape personal military service by payment of fines and double taxes as an avowed equivalent to bearing arms. The repeated demand that the Quakers in the Assembly step aside and let others, less scrupulous about raising troops and building forts, take their place had led to a voluntary withdrawal from office in 1756. Twenty years later, the demand was for Mennonites and Quakers to give up any share in the government. The Test Act of 1777 effectively deprived them of the right to vote as well as be elected to office. The sects could only live in accord with their consciences if they withdrew from public life altogether and became a world unto themselves.

In Maryland and Virginia, North Carolina or any of the other colonies, Mennonites, Dunkers, and Quakers had exerted no political power. The gentlemen who gathered in Williamsburg and Annapolis at the public times could scarcely have known of the existence of small Mennonite communities on their utmost frontiers if an occasional petition for relief from militia fines or exemption from the customary oath in court had not come before the General Assembly. If Friends were better known in business and social life, they were too few to influence the course of events anywhere outside of Pennsylvania.

What happened in Pennsylvania thus became the accepted pattern, normative for both the state and the sects. The Holy Experiment, involving full political participation by Quakers, Mennonites, Dunkers, Schwenkfelders, and other sectarians in shaping the institutions of Penn's colony appeared to be the ideal relationship in this free land. The isolated role of the sects in the other colonies, as the quiet in the land, seemed more appropriate to the European pattern they had left behind, with its state religion and intermittent persecution for all who dissented. Neither Anabaptist nor Quaker thought had envisioned a Christian state nor the tension that could develop between the biblical commands of nonresistance and submission to the ruling powers, between peace witness and support for government. It was a creative period for the peace churches as they faced the wider implications of faithful discipleship and nonresistance in a more democratic society than they had experienced in Europe. Yet by 1789 all of them had become, by choice as much as through the collapse of the Holy Experiment, once more the quiet in the land.

Revival and Renewal

The prolonged crisis forced the sects to plumb the depths of their own Christian commitment. It accelerated a movement in the Society of Friends toward renewal and spiritual revival.[16] James Logan and other critics of the Quaker refusal to vote a militia law charged Friends with being "as intent as any others whatever in amassing Riches, the great Bait and Temptation to our Enemies to come and plunder the Place," which they would not defend.[17] Wealth had hastened the process of assimilation for Friends and now appeared to be a source of weakness rather than strength for the sectarian community. Mennonites had a similar reaction. Lancaster bishops and preachers reprimanded Martin Mylin in 1742 for building "a palace of sandstone" and he was questioned about his motives, because "the appearance of it might strengthen their enemies in prejudicing the government against them."[18]

The wealth, prestige, and political influence of the Quakers in Pennsylvania in the early decades of the eighteenth century did not assist them in attempting to change the world around them or in bringing the light of the gospel to their neighbors. In the same period, Friends in England and in all the American Colonies began to grant membership automatically to their children, without having to meet any tests of personal faith. A gathering of believers united in their conviction that the inner light inspired them to give testimony to the truth in all their actions was rapidly taking the form of a territorial church.[19] Their experience in the next few decades enabled Friends to reverse the apparently inevitable drift from sect to church and to reassert the traditional sectarian values.[20] In its early stages, this reform movement sought to make Friends more consistent in their words and their acts. It was an extension of the evangelism of the religious Friends to the nominal members of the Society.[21]

When reform took a new direction the Quakers were less than enthusiastic about it. When John Churchman and John Woolman called the implications of faith for slave-owning and payment of war taxes to the attention of Friends in 1755-1757, most Quakers were not ready to accept these hard sayings. But after a generation of rethinking what it meant to be a people called out to be witnesses to Him whose kingdom is peace and truth, the Quaker community recognized "that such behavior was the occupation of Quakerism, to be maintained in preference to accommodation to the environment, and, as in the American Revolution, at the cost of suffering."[22] In their campaign to convince their own members of the evil of slavery, living principles complemented rules of conduct, and in their refusal to support war, partial in the 1750s and complete in the 1770s, the vision of a suffering church reappeared to Friends. The sense of alienation from society and its norms returned to a degree that Quakers had not known since the generations of persecution in England.[23]

Mennonites, Dunkers, and Schwenkfelders had the same experience of following the dictates of conscience, even at the cost of suffering, and of discovering that this period of trial made them open to God's will for them as revealed through His world. They, too, discovered that there were perils in freedom and that faithful discipleship dictated a strategy of withdrawal.

The Mennonite experience in these years was further complicated by the impact of the Great Awakening, with its emphasis on personal conversion and personal religion, which provided its own challenge to the Mennonite idea of community. While much of the power and direction of this challenge came from leaders within the Mennonite brotherhood, most notably Martin Boehm, and its emphasis on a believers' church coincided with traditional Mennonite doctrine, the form of the revival among German-speaking colonists made it a divisive factor. When the Mennonite Bishop Martin Boehm and the Reformed Pastor Philip William Otterbein publicly acknowledged that they were brethren, they pointed to the new standard of brotherhood that threatened to dissolve older bonds. If a common Christian experience could unite Reformed and Lutheran pietists, Dunkers, Mennonites and Moravians, then the sectarian values of the Anabaptist tradition necessarily took a secondary place, even though they might not be directly challenged. Some Mennonites in Pennsylvania, Maryland, and Virginia sought a deeper brotherhood in groups that drew apart from their own congregations and from other churches. Boehm himself found closer fellowship with English-speaking Methodists than with the other Lancaster bishops and preachers. The revival's separatist tendency reached a climax in the Revolutionary War years and thereafter whole congregations as well as individuals withdrew from the Mennonite Church. This strain, together with the tensions between church and state in these years, encouraged Mennonites to more sharply define and emphasize the basis for their own brotherhood. To some degree, this pointed to a separation from the Quakers with whom they had worked closely up to this time.

Nonresistance was not a point of contention within the Mennonite brotherhood during these years and militia and tax records clearly indicate that communities sharply divided by the revival movement responded to the challenges of wartime as completely as more stable ones. Very few young Mennonite men served in the army or militia during the American Revolution. The Mennonites as a whole were more united on the implications of nonresistance than were the Quakers. The only real challenge came from the Franconia bishop, Christian Funk, whose stand on the payment of war taxes and the oath of allegiance contrasted with the views of his colleagues in the ministry and led to the separation of the Funkites. This relatively small group acknowledged the United States by an affirmation of loyalty and paid taxes to the new government, but they did not believe that Christians should take up arms or serve in the military in any capacity. On this important point the Funkites did not at all resemble the dissident Free Quakers, who had no hesitation about joining the Continental Army or the state militia.

While the impact of the French and Indian War and the American Revolution on the Society of Friends has long held the interest of historians, the efforts of the Mennonites and the other peace churches to maintain and defend their sectarian vision in the face of challenges from the American view of society, of the state, and of the church has received far less attention than it deserves.

Mennonite Beginnings in America

On an autumn day in 1683, a ship docked at Philadelphia with thirteen Dutch and German families standing on deck to catch a first glimpse of the wilderness that would be their home. William Penn and the first shipload of Quaker colonists had landed there just a year earlier. These newcomers had left their homes in Crefeld and nearby towns on the lower Rhine to accept Penn's invitation to share in the colony which Quakers were building on the banks of the Delaware, a colony where every man and woman could live according to the dictates of conscience and where they would learn war no more. The preaching and the witness of visiting Quaker missionaries in their homeland had stirred them, and with a long history of persecution for Christ's sake in their background, they readily left their homes to share in the Holy Experiment. There was no ill feeling between Mennonite and Quaker. Together they worshiped and together they signed a ringing denunciation of slavery and the slave trade a few years later. The history of the Mennonite settlement in Pennsylvania begins appropriately enough with friendly cooperation between Mennonites and Quakers, for the two peace churches had many opportunities for close association and interaction in the decades that followed.

Reports from Pennsylvania that reached Crefeld had only good things to say of the Germantown settlement, and other Mennonite families soon followed their former friends and neighbors to America. Others came from Hamburg-Altona and from the Palatinate. In 1690 William Rittenhouse was ordained as the first Mennonite pastor in America. Land for a church in Germantown was deeded to the congregation in 1703 and the first log meetinghouse built in 1708.[24]

Mennonites from the Germantown settlement had begun taking up land on Skippack Creek as early as 1702. Succeeding generations had pushed the frontier steadily north along the Skippack and the Perkiomen to seek new homes in adjacent parts of present Montgomery, Berks, Lehigh, Bucks, and Chester counties in the eighteenth century.

Dutch Mennonites enjoyed full religious freedom at home and played a major role in the social, economic, and intellectual life of Holland. They had no pressing reason to fly to a refuge in the wilds of Pennsylvania. But Mennonites in regions further up the Rhine, in Switzerland, and in the Palatinate, where many Swiss Mennonites had fled as refugees, had known persecution and suffering. They needed no personal appeal from William Penn to appreciate the value of liberty of conscience.

The first settlement of Swiss Mennonites was made on the banks of the Pequea in Lancaster County in 1710.[25] Other large groups came in 1717 and 1727. Over the next few decades a steady migration of Mennonite families from the Palatinate and from Switzerland and Alsace enabled Mennonite settlements to fan out north, east, and west across Lancaster County, which then included the present Dauphin and Lebanon counties.

Some of these settlers were very poor, others were exceptionally well-equipped to buy land and start a new life along the Pequea and the Conestoga. The Dutch Mennonite Committee for Foreign Needs helped many hundreds of poorer brothers to settle in Pennsylvania in the eighteenth century.[26] English Quakers also contributed to help some of the first Mennonites from the Palatinate cross the ocean to the new world.[27]

The Hans Herr House, built in 1719, was used by Swiss Mennonite settlers as a place of worship for many years. It has been restored by the Lancaster Conference Mennonite Historical Society and is open to the public as a museum. (Photo by Earl B. Groff, 1977.)

The Lancaster County settlements were the starting point for further Mennonite migrations. The Shenandoah Valley of Virginia drew some Mennonites from Lancaster as early as 1733. They settled first in the present Shenandoah and Page counties, with some families later taking up land in the present Rockingham County by the eve of the Revolution. Other Mennonite families had moved across the Susquehanna to settle in the present Pennsylvania counties of York and Adams after 1735. Still others moved on to settle on both sides of the Maryland border in the present Franklin County, Pennsylvania, and Washington County, Maryland, area, where they organized the Conococheague congregation in 1743.[28]

The first Amish Mennonite settlers came to Pennsylvania in 1736 and concentrated in Berks County. They were also Swiss in background, although most of them had lived either in Alsace or the Palatinate before coming to America. There had been a division of opinion among the Swiss Mennonites on the way to preserve a disciplined brotherhood in 1693. Jacob Amman was the leader of a group who believed in the need for avoiding any contact with excommunicated members, a practice of the Dutch Mennonites that had been several times rejected by the Swiss brethren. The *Ammansch* or Amish congregations included most of those in Alsace and a few in Switzerland. The greater number of Mennonites in Switzerland and those in the Palatinate did not adopt Amman's views. After efforts at reconciliation broke down in 1697, the Amish and the Mennonites went their separate ways.[29]

Who were these people? Contemporary writers, and not a few modern scholars, have included the Mennonites among the many different Pietist sects that sprang up in Germany among the Lutheran and Reformed state churches. But they were neither German nor Pietist in origin. They were the Anabaptists of the Reformation, neither Catholic nor Protestant.

Their movement began independently in different European centers. The Swiss Brethren traced their origin to Conrad Grebel, Georg Blaurock, and Felix Manz, who had rejected the compromise the Reformation made in setting up a state church system. They wanted the church to be composed of believers only, men and women who had committed their lives to Christ. They wanted no half-Christian profession, maintaining an outward form of godliness but denying the power thereof. They completed what Luther and Zwingli and the other Reformers began. The martyrdom of many of their leaders did nothing to dispirit those who shared this vision. The Swiss Brethren cherished their faith in prison and in exile for centuries to come. Anabaptism rose in Holland about ten years later to be met with no less fierce persecution. The leading spirit among the Dutch Anabaptists was Menno Simons, a former Catholic priest from Friesland. From him, Anabaptists began to be called Mennonists or Mennonites.

For two centuries and more, Catholic and Protestant rulers alike persecuted the Mennonites. What threat did they pose to the existing order? To begin with, they understood the New Testament to require more than the experience of the forgiveness of sins through justification by faith. It demanded a new life in conformity to the teachings of Jesus Christ. This concept of discipleship characterized the faith of the Mennonites. The church was a fellowship of men and women committed to discipleship. It followed, then, that any territorial basis for a church was impossible. Equally impossible was the notion of baptizing infants into membership in the church. The Anabaptists were so called because they taught believer's baptism, following a mature profession of faith in a living Lord.

The nature of the Christian church made it different from merely human institutions. It had an obligation not to be conformed to the social patterns of the world, but to pattern itself on the life taught in word and example by Jesus. "The word of God was given to be put into practice," Conrad Grebel wrote. Inherent in that pattern is the nonresistant love that Jesus explained to His disciples.

Other Religious Refugees

The Mennonite families who came ashore in Philadelphia, grateful for a breath of fresh air and a cup of fresh water after the long voyage from Rotterdam, were not the only religious refugees to seek freedom in Penn's colony. The Quaker founders of Pennsylvania had tasted persecution in England, Scotland, Ireland, and Wales and on the Continent, although the Toleration Act of 1689 had put an end to their sufferings throughout the British dominions. No such legislation had eased the plight of religious dissenters in German-speaking lands.

Pietists from the vicinity of Heidelberg and from other parts of Germany had found temporary refuge in Crefeld, where Mennonites had also been sheltered from persecution. They called themselves simply Brethren, but they were commonly known as Tunkers or Dunkers from their belief in believer's baptism by triple immersion. Mainly of Reformed background, they had been influenced by Ernst Christoph Hochmann von Hochenau, who taught the need to separate from the state churches. When Hochmann was arrested after preaching at Alexander Mack's mill near Heidelberg in 1706, Mack and his family fled to Wittgenstein. Convinced of the necessity of a disciplined brotherhood, Mack baptized eight others in 1708. Their movement spread to Switzerland, the Palatinate, Hamburg-Altona, and other areas, but soon met with persecution on every hand. In 1715 many of these persecuted Dunkers fled to Crefeld; four years later the entire Crefeld congregation migrated to Pennsylvania. Mack and the rest of his followers left Wittgenstein for an isolated corner of the Friesland marshes in 1720, but in 1729 they crossed the Atlantic to join their friends in Germantown. By 1733 most of them had left Europe to settle in Pennsylvania.[30]

Few in number when they arrived in America, the aggressive evangelism of the Dunkers won them many converts. They sought out other German colonists and held revival meetings among them.[31] Hans Rudolph Nagele, a Mennonite preacher in the Groffdale section of Lancaster County, along with his family and members of the Landes and Mylin families, became the nucleus of the Conestoga congregation in 1724. Another early convert to the Dunkers in Lancaster County was Conrad Beissel. He later differed with his brethren on many issues, including the observance of Saturday as the Sabbath, the importance of celibacy, and other points of doctrine, and founded Ephrata Cloister. Both the Sabbatarians and the Sunday Baptists shared in the missionary zeal of the first Dunkers and organized congregations in many German settlements from New Jersey to South Carolina by 1750.[32]

Dutch Mennonites helped a band of harassed linen-weavers, merchants, and farmers from Silesia, who clung to the teachings of Caspar Schwenkfeld, cross the ocean in 1734. Caspar Schwenkfeld von Ossig, a contemporary of Martin Luther, had been the leading figure in the Silesian Reformation, but he had been driven into exile and his disciples scattered. By the beginning of the eighteenth century only a few families in the vicinity of Harpersdorf considered themselves to be Schwenkfelders and in 1719 the Jesuits began a campaign of alternate persuasion and violence to win them to the Roman Catholic Church. The Schwenkfelders looked to the Mennonites, with whom they felt a close affinity, for help and it was soon forthcoming from the Dutch Mennonites. The influence of Lutheran Pietism was also strong among eighteenth-century Schwenkfelders, most of whom worshiped with the Lutherans. They attracted the interest of the Lutheran Pietist Count Nicholas Ludwig von Zinzendorf, who invited them to stay on his estates in Saxony. Again with financial aid from Dutch Mennonites, the Schwenkfelders journeyed to Pennsylvania and settled along Skippack

Creek in the present Montgomery County.[33]

Count Zinzendorf, who befriended the Schwenkfelders, had invited the scattered remnants of the Moravian Church or Unitas Fratrum to settle on his Saxon estates in 1722. There they formed a new organization that was at once a denomination and an ecumenical brotherhood. From Herrnhut, their center on the Zinzendorf lands, the Moravians sent out missionaries to form new congregations in Europe and America. Their first effort in Georgia in 1735 proved unsuccessful and they turned to Northampton County, Pennsylvania, in 1740. Count Zinzendorf himself came to America to help in the establishment of Bethlehem the following year. The extensive Moravian missions to the Indians began at the same time and over the next few years daughter congregations were formed in Pennsylvania, New Jersey, and Maryland. In 1753 the Moravians purchased a large tract in the North Carolina Piedmont and founded the first of their Wachovia settlements as a center for mission work among both Indians and whites. The third of these North Carolina Moravian communities was Salem (the present Winston-Salem), which was established in 1766 and became the real center of Moravian influence in the South.[34]

If these religious refugees and others proved that William Penn's policy of granting the fullest liberty of conscience could draw persecuted people from many parts of Europe, the majority of the colonists, whether English or German speaking, had belonged to the state churches in their native lands, and they were looking for a fresh opportunity to earn a living, rather than a chance to live separated from the world in a community of believers. Mennonites, Quakers, and the other sectarians had no objection to acquiring land and accumulating wealth, but their basic understanding of the gospel message made them a people apart.

The quest for faithful discipleship amid persecution and flight strengthened the Mennonite sense of community. Could the same sense of community survive in this new freedom that the sects enjoyed in the American Colonies?

A Sense of Community

Community was a major element in the Mennonite experience in eighteenth-century America, just as it was for Quakers, Dunkers, Schwenkfelders, and Moravians. Their biblical faith found expression within a disciplined brotherhood. They saw themselves as a community (*gemeinde*) of brothers and sisters in Christ who came together for worship in a meetinghouse (*gemeindehaus*), unlike the church people who were their neighbors. Since they believed that the following of Christ was not limited to prayer and preaching on a Sunday morning, but that faithful discipleship should be the pattern for every day's work and rest, church membership was a commitment to a way of life. It was inevitably a commitment to one another as well.

Mutuality was an important part of Mennonite life. Indeed, a recent writer has seen "the discipline of hard work and mutual aid" as the outstanding characteristic of both Mennonites and Quakers in the eighteenth-century Lancaster and Chester counties.[35] The alms books that survive from many early congregations reveal one kind of mutual aid in gifts of money and clothes to needy brethren, loans to pay the passage of new arrivals and get their goods to their new home, and the like, but the community obviously shared with one another in many other ways that were never entered in ledgers, pooling labor for a barn- or house-raising or getting in a crop. Nor was concern for one another's welfare limited to times of economic need. Discipleship demanded that Christians be not conformed to the standards of the world around them and such a life could only be lived with the support of a caring and disciplined community. In practice, for Mennonites as for Quakers, many aspects of daily life were legitimate matters for community decision.

Community ties were threatened most directly by assimilation to the larger society around them. As it would be virtually impossible to follow the kind of life taught in the gospels without the support of the brotherhood, it would be impossible to share in the life of the brotherhood without a commitment to discipleship. As members chose to become more acculturated, the brotherhood suffered. Marrying persons who did not share the same commitment presented the most obvious threat and only marriages within the religious community were acceptable. As a result, community bonds were strengthened by ties of kinship. Within a generation or two of the first settlement, a complex network of family relationships undergirded the brotherhood. To some extent, this crossed and erased lines of nationality as men and women of Swiss, Dutch, and German background became identifiably Mennonite or Dunker or Moravian. In the same way, Quakers of Irish, English, and Welsh origin, with a few Friends from other parts of Europe, became blended in a recognizable Quaker "ethnic group."

It would be a mistake to think that the eighteenth-century sectarians lived in isolation as a world to themselves. Their sense of community was all the more important because they did not isolate themselves. Christopher Schultz, the Schwenkfelder leader, told friends in Silesia that they could hardly imagine how many denominations were mingled at funerals and social gatherings. "We are all going to and fro like fish in water but always at peace with each other; anybody of whom it would be known that he hates somebody else because of his religion would be immediately considered a fool; however, everybody speaks his mind freely." Schultz added that he was on friendly terms with the Mennonite preacher and the Catholic priest who were his closest neighbors in Hereford Township in Berks County.[36] There is ample contemporary evidence of friendly associations between Mennonites and Roman Catholics in this same Berks County community throughout the eighteenth-century.[37] In every place where they lived, Mennonites, Dunkers, and Moravians had daily contacts with neighbors of Reformed, Lutheran, Presbyterian, or Anglican background. The Lutheran Pastor Henry Melchior Muhlenberg described the inroads made by the missionary efforts of the Dunkers among the German settlers. While Mennonites did not share this enthusiasm, Muhlenberg noted that "the conversion to the Mennonites is also very easy, comfortable, and advantageous, and is one of the most quiet."[38] The Reformed leader John Philip Boehm wrote that the number of Reformed Church members who "have gone over to the Tumplers, Sabbatarians, Mennonites, and others is so large that it cannot be stated without tears in one's eyes."[39] If these worried pastors used rhetoric rather than statistics to make their point, extant registers of Lutheran and Reformed parishes make it evident that many families among the German settlers had Mennonites, Reformed, Dunkers, and Lutherans among their kindred. The Quakers fared no better, if as well. Marrying out of Meeting accounted for more losses of membership than all other causes combined, even in the years of most intense soul-searching from 1750 to 1799.[40]

The strength of the ties to the religious community did not prevent some members from marrying persons of different religious faith from themselves nor from uniting with other denominations. In the early days of the Conestoga settlement, the aggressive evangelism of the Dunkers appealed to some Mennonites and even a Mennonite preacher became a member of the first congregation of the Church of the Brethren in Lancaster County.[41] The Dunker congregations in York County, Pennsylvania, Washington County, Maryland, and Gaston County, North Carolina, absorbed other Mennonite settlers.[42]

Moravian missionaries had less success among Mennonites, although they began a rather intensive campaign in 1742, assigning Bernhard Grube to work among Pennsylvania Mennonites as he had earlier preached among Dutch Mennonites. These efforts were not productive. "In contrast to the large, amorphous Reformed and Lutheran churches, sectarians had formed small, tight-knit communities that did not welcome outsiders." The Mennonites, Amish, and Schwenkfelders resented the interference of the Moravians. Although some of them attended Count Zinzendorf's synods of all Christian bodies, they withdrew and resisted all attempts to draw them into the pietistic awakening.[43]

The failure of this German Awakening to reach more than a few members of the Mennonite, Amish, and Schwenkfelder communities has been explained by the greater success the sects had than the churches in establishing their religious institutions. One recent writer has seen this success in the better planning, organization, and financial support for the immigration of the sects and the assumption that "sectarian institutions were better adapted to the primitive conditions of the New World," in that they did not need a salaried pastor.[44] But the explanation is probably much simpler. As Philip Schaff observed in one of his first published comments on American church history, "a very small part of the German emigration sprang from persecution, or from aspirations after freedom of opinion and conscience, as was the case with the Puritans, Quakers, and others; it owed its origin mainly to material interest."[45] The loyalty of many German settlers to the Heidelberg Catechism or the Lutheran liturgy was probably no deeper than childhood habit. If a German-speaking pastor of their ancestral faith settled in their immediate neighborhood, they might be ready to identify with that denomination or they might not. For the sectarian, on the other hand, his religious faith was his primary loyalty and his primary identification. He was not a Swiss farmer who happened to be an adherent of the Reformed faith, he was a Mennonite who happened to be Swiss and a miller by trade.

While major migrations of Mennonites and Schwenkfelders were carefully planned in Europe and financed, in part, by Dutch Mennonites, great numbers crossed the Atlantic in family groups as part of the general tide of immigration. The Amish families of the Northkill settlement in Berks County drifted in individually or as small groups over a period of more than thirty years.[46] Mennonite genealogies reveal a similar pattern. Unlike their Lutheran, Reformed, or Catholic neighbors, their community already existed in Europe. Lutheran pastors and Catholic priests tried to establish churches in areas where their brethren had settled. Mennonite, Amish, and Schwenkfelder newcomers settled among their own brethren to be reunited with their community of faith.

Settlement Patterns and Community

Religious faith was thus the determining factor in settlement patterns. Mennonites, Quakers, Schwenkfelders, and Amish all tended to cluster together and to sell land by preference to one another.[47] Since they were generally better and more prosperous farmers than their neighbors, they had the ability to buy them out and townships became predominantly communities of one sect or another. The demand for land in the older established settlements, which were among the most successful farming sections of the colony, tended to push land prices higher and higher. The landless men in such an area had no opportunity to acquire land and no choice but to move out. As James T. Lemon has shown, only 7 out of 28 landless men on the 1772 tax list in Manheim Township in Lancaster County had become landowners by 1782 and the others had moved elsewhere. Five of the seven were sons of established farmers who had inherited their father's farms.[48]

Until the Revolutionary War years, there was apparently an adequate supply of land in the vicinity of Mennonite settlements in Pennsylvania. Sons took up farms within a few miles of the home place and the Mennonite neighborhood slowly radiated out from its original centers. The German settlers on the frontiers of Pennsylvania and Virginia were rarely Mennonite or Schwenkfelder. The drive that carried Mennonite pioneers to western Maryland and the Shenandoah Valley in the 1730s was quickly spent and no new centers developed. A few Amish families moved to the remote wilderness of the Glades in the present Somerset and Cambria counties just before the Revolution, and even into western North Carolina. The Brethren settlements in such distant places as Botetourt County, Virginia, and the back country of North and South Carolina were the results as much of evangelism as migration. Quakers had also migrated from southeastern Pennsylvania to western Maryland and the Shenandoah Valley in the 1730s. A second wave of Quaker migration, this time to Guilford County, North Carolina, led to the establishment of New Garden Monthly Meeting in 1754. New England Friends were a substantial element in this migration and it need not reflect a shortage of land in the established settlements.[49]

By 1775, however, land was clearly no longer within the reach of all in the older Mennonite settlements or their immediate surroundings. Migration into Rockingham and Shenandoah counties in Virginia began in earnest in the 1770s from Lancaster and from the older Page Valley settlement. Settlement of the Mahantango Valley in present Snyder County, Pennsylvania, began in 1774. Migrants from Lancaster

County formed the Rocky Spring settlement in Letterkenny Township in the present Franklin County about the same time. Several new settlements were made in Cumberland County between 1780 and 1790. The great migration of Lancaster Mennonites to Ontario began in the 1780s, as did Mennonite interest in frontier lands in western North Carolina. Other factors, such as the oppressive Pennsylvania Test Act clearly entered into this movement, but we may safely conclude that land prices and availability of good land were major elements both in the steady expansion of the first settlements in the early and middle decades of the eighteenth-century and the sudden movement to more distant regions in the closing decades of the century. The pattern familiar in Amish and Mennonite communities in more recent years was thus very likely at work in the very earliest settlements.[50]

Wealth and Community

The "rich Mennonites of Lancaster County" were a special target for the resentment of many Patriots during the American Revolution. As early as 1742, Rev. William Wappeler, S. J., the Catholic priest at Lancaster, noted, "The Mennonites are the wealthiest of the Germans. Some possess 1,000 acres." There can be no question that they were, in fact, better and more successful farmers than their neighbors.[51] Nor did the Franconia Mennonites or Schwenkfelders lag behind. A correspondent of the *Germantowner Zeitung*, who complained of the poor farming methods in eastern Pennsylvania, specifically exempted Mennonites and Schwenkfelders from his criticism.[52]

Several related factors would enter into any analysis of their success. Because they migrated for religious reasons and not for economic betterment, some of these settlers were able to buy good land and other farming needs as soon as they arrived. For all of them, the tradition of mutual aid was a significant factor. The community helped individuals get established and saw them through a bad season or disaster. Part of their European experience made Mennonites from the Palatinate and Switzerland leaders in agricultural progress, wherever they went. The law forbade land ownership by the Swiss Anabaptists. Dispossessed from productive lands in Switzerland, they were forced to develop marginal farmlands, usually as tenants, in both their original homeland and in southern Germany. They were forced to use new methods of fertilizing the soil, feeding their livestock and planting their crops. Their methods made them attractive to larger landowners seeking productive tenants. It was here that their agricultural abilities had full scope. Most Rhineland peasants were villagers, using traditional farming methods, but the Anabaptists farmed larger separate units and had a free hand to experiment and try new ways.[53]

They became the most prosperous and skillful farmers in Pennsylvania and carried these abilities with them to Maryland, Virginia, and other early settlements. Lewis Evans wrote in 1753 in his *Brief Description of the Province of Pennsylvania* of "how much we are indebted to the Germans" and called attention to "our back Settlements where the barns are large as pallaces, while the owners live in log hutts; a sign tho of thriving farmers."[54] Benjamin Rush went further in his enthusiasm for the contributions of German settlers to better agricultural methods, citing their use of fertilizer, their care for their livestock, and their methodical clearing of new land in contrast to "their English and Irish neighbours."[55] None of the early agricultural writers credited the Germans in general or the Mennonites in particular with a special sense for limestone soil. Franconia Mennonites and Schwenkfelders actually chose inferior red shales and not all Lancaster Mennonites chose limestone lands; some of the Mennonite settlement in Mount Joy and Rapho Townships was on inferior soil and in Donegal the Scotch-Irish farmed on limestone and the Mennonites did not.[56]

If hard work, better methods, mutual aid, good soil, and the ability to buy and equip a new farm contributed to making the nonresistant sects wealthy, wealth created problems of a different order. A Mennonite writer commented in 1770 "that parents who once accepted the Lord Jesus in faith to serve Him are glad when their children are very industrious and strive to become rich and highly respected in this world and provide for their children and grandchildren in this world, whereas they ought to be glad that the children strive to get rich in eternity." The same writer suggests that in the decade before the Revolution Mennonites were a prey to "pride and vanity" and "all manner of fashions" and "dress in all kinds of costly clothing and live splendidly." A similar strain within the Quaker community had led to a notable revival in the 1760s and 1770s. The testimony drawn up by the Lancaster bishops against Martin Boehm about 1780 declared that he had reconciled many people under the ban without requiring repentance, so there was evidently some degree of tension within the Mennonite community at this time.[56a]

Education and Community

Education strengthened community ties since all the sects believed in what the Quakers termed "a guarded education" in denominational schools. Mennonites and Schwenkfelders, in contrast to the churches, established educational systems of a high order from the beginning of their settlement. Their schools attracted Quaker pupils, while the teaching methods of Christopher Dock, the Skippack Mennonite schoolmaster, won sufficient interest to be published in his lifetime. John Brackbill and other Strasburg Township Mennonites employed a teacher of English and Latin and advertised for a successor in 1770.[57] Henry Boehm recalled that a Hessian prisoner, trained in the classics, was hired as a schoolmaster in Conestoga Township.[58] The older Mennonite meetinghouses in both the Lancaster and Franconia areas invariably had a schoolhouse built on the same lot by the congregation.[59]

But education could threaten the survival of the community, especially when it was deliberately chosen as a means of assimilating the Germans of Pennsylvania. The Reverend Michael Schlatter, a German Reformed minister, had visited Europe in 1751-1752 to recruit preachers and raise money for the struggling congregations of the Reformed faith in America. He had stressed the need for Reformed schools and the Synod of North Holland had collected a large sum for this purpose. Schlatter's *Appeal* was published in both Dutch and German and translated into English. Money was contributed in England and Scotland to further the cause. His proposal for free schools for German children attracted the attention of Thomas Penn and even the British King made a personal gift of £1,000.[60]

Thomas Penn and his political advisers subtly changed the Schlatter plan for denominational schools, planning a system "equally to the benefit of protestant youth of all denominations," and selecting trustees for the Reformed and Presbyterian endowment who were known for their attachment to the Proprietor. They included James Hamilton, William Allen, Richard Peters, Conrad Weiser, and the Rev. William Smith, a clergyman of the Church of England best known for his pamphlets attacking the Quakers. Benjamin Franklin's presence among the trustees of the charity schools was probably due to his involvement with every benevolent scheme in Pennsylvania, rather than to some sudden shift in his political allegiance.[61]

The trustees proposed printing "the several catechisms that are now taught among the Calvinists, Lutherans, and other protestant denominations" for the use of these free schools. William Smith established a press in Philadelphia to print not only catechisms but also a newspaper in the German language that would counteract the influence of the Quaker Party.

Smith went further. He proposed stripping the Quakers and their

German supporters of all political power. He forwarded to England proposals for an oath of office, by which all members of the Assembly would pledge "that they would not refuse to defend their country against His Majesty's enemies." He further urged that the Germans be forbidden to vote until they acquired "a competent knowledge" of the English language and the Pennsylvania Constitution. He wanted ministers and schoolmasters settled among them "to reduce them into regular congregations" and "instruct them in the nature of free government."

Christopher Sauer, Germantown editor and spokesman for the sects, exposed the motives behind the charity schools. He knew that the trustees "care little about religion" or the German settlers, beyond the fact that "the stupid Germans could be used as militia-men to protect their property." He saw that German voters would be encouraged to elect men who would pass a Militia Act, "establishing a regular soldiery," and he recognized Smith's plan for a fixed salary for ministers and schoolmasters as a clever way to force a religious establishment on the colony "in order to circumscribe the bounds of sectarianism."[62]

While Christopher Sauer used his newspaper to help defeat the charity school scheme, the Dutch Reformed learned that their donations had been misappropriated. A minister in Pennsylvania reported that the schools would be of no service to the Reformed Church, "for the only object of these schools is to extend the English language among the Germans, and so the object is a political one."[63] Reformed ministers and laymen turned against the scheme and sided with the sects. Schlatter's plan failed completely and his own reputation suffered.[64]

Their experience of the charity schools as a wedge to separate the German sects from the Quaker leadership of the Pennsylvania Assembly served rather to draw Mennonites, Dunkers, and Schwenkfelders even closer to their Quaker neighbors. The threat of assimilation, militarism, and interference with that religious liberty guaranteed by Penn's Charter had a lasting influence on the political attitudes of the German peace churches in the French and Indian War and in the subsequent political realignments in Pennsylvania.

Mennonites, Dunkers, and Schwenkfelders shared a genuine commitment to education, but they drew back from an educational scheme whose primary purpose was to weaken the ties that held their religious community together. The charity school proposals, in the end, served to increase their conservatism and make them more suspicious of change.

A Minority View

The nonresistant sects spoke for only a small minority of American colonists in seeking exemption from military service and militia fines. They made up no more than a fourth of the population in Pennsylvania and a much smaller proportion of the settlers in the other colonies. If Quakers had once been a majority in Pennsylvania, heavy immigration in the eighteenth century had greatly increased the numbers of non-Quakers in the colony. Mennonites, Dunkers, Schwenkfelders, and Moravians had come from Switzerland or Germany, but they were always outnumbered by Germans and Swiss of Reformed or Lutheran background, just as the steady stream of Irish Quakers to Pennsylvania was a mere trickle in comparison with the Presbyterian Scotch-Irish.

Official estimates of population in the eighteenth century were never more than educated guesses. "An Account of the Number of White Inhabitants in His Majesty's Colonies in North America" submitted in 1755 to the Board of Trade and Plantations in London estimated the Pennsylvania population at 220,000, with Germans and other foreign Protestants making up 100,000 of the total or slightly less than half the white inhabitants.[65] Benjamin Franklin supposed that there were 160,000 Pennsylvanians in 1766, a third of them Friends, and another contemporary guessed that the colony numbered 200,000 with Quakers forming about an eighth of the total population.[66]

Mennonites and Quakers took no census of their own members and outside observers could only hazard a guess at their total number. The sole exception is Philadelphia Monthly Meeting, where a census was taken in 1760 that disclosed a membership of 2,250. On the basis of this local census and the apportionment of funds to be raised in each Friends Meeting within the confines of Philadelphia Yearly Meeting in 1760, Jack Marietta was able to calculate that there were 9,207 Quakers within the limits of the Yearly Meeting in that year. Since this figure included members of meetings in New Jersey, Maryland, and Virginia, the total membership of Quaker Meetings in Pennsylvania in 1760 would be 8,345 according to Marietta's estimate.[67] These figures may be low, for there were 600 Quaker families in Philadelphia Monthly Meeting in 1760 and Frederick B. Tolles estimated the Quaker population of the city on this basis at 3,600.[68] The total Quaker population of Pennsylvania in 1760 might then have been as high as 23,149.[69] But the lower figure is probably closer to the truth. Although eighteenth-century families were large, mortality was high and it is unlikely that every Quaker family was large enough to give an average of six members.

Morgan Edwards, a Baptist historian, included his own estimates of the number of Mennonites and Dunkers in Pennsylvania in a book he published in 1770. He made every effort to obtain accurate statistics, but acknowledged that he was unable to get very full accounts of the Mennonites. His statement that his figures are "pretty exact, except the county of Lancaster hath introduced any error," since he had the greatest difficulty in obtaining information there, reduces his careful calculations to guesswork. He also excluded the Mennonite communities "which border on Maryland" from his figures, by which he apparently meant congregations in the present Franklin County area. With these exceptions, Edwards estimated that the Mennonite churches in Pennsylvania had 1,448 baptized adult members in 810 family units comprising 4,050 souls altogether.[70] In an unpublished work, fortunately preserved in manuscript, Edwards estimated that the Mennonite congregations at "Cunnecococheague" (in present Franklin County, Pennsylvania, and Washington County, Maryland) numbered 861 members in "about 400" family units.[71] This would give a total Mennonite population for this area of 2,402, using the same method as Edwards to calculate the ratio of baptized members to the total Mennonite community. Since the Maryland portion of this territory is believed to have included no more than 150 members in 50 families in 1770, the Pennsylvania portion must have numbered some 711 members in 350 families which amounted altogether to 1,984.[72] The totals given by Morgan Edwards for Pennsylvania should thus be adjusted to 2,159 members in 1,160 families or a total population of 6,034.

Even without the author's admission that he could obtain no certain information about Lancaster Mennonites, it is obvious that this figure is much too low. If Edwards did have access to accurate figures for the Washington-Franklin area, it is most unlikely that this small frontier community had more than half as many members as all of the older Mennonite population centers put together. On this ground alone, the estimate made in 1780 by Christopher Sauer III of between two and three thousand Mennonite families in Pennsylvania seems more probable than the figure given by Edwards. Since Sauer was actually correcting Edwards on the Mennonites and quoting his estimate of the Dunker population, his reliability is increased.[73] This would give a total Mennonite population of from 10,400 to 15,600 during the American Revolution.

The figures given by Morgan Edwards for the Dunkers are probably much more accurate than those he estimated for the Mennonites. He calculated a total of 763 baptized members in Pennsylvania in about 419 families containing in all 2,095 souls. Sauer thought they numbered 3,000 in 1780.[74]

The Schwenkfelders came closest of all the peace churches to an official census in a map prepared in 1767 for friends across the Atlantic in Saxony. It located the homes of 51 Schwenkfelder families, suggesting that there were no more than 300 Schwenkfelders in Pennsylvania in that year.[75]

By the most generous estimates, then, the peaceable sects together comprised less than a fourth of the Pennsylvania population. The Quakers, the largest group, may have amounted to 12.5 percent of the people in the colony on the eve of the American Revolution. The Mennonites may have represented 8 percent of the total and the Dunkers another 2.5 percent. The Moravians probably made up 1.5 percent. The numerically insignificant Schwenkfelders would hardly figure in the reckoning.[76]

But the sects were influential in Pennsylvania beyond mere numbers. Quaker leadership in the political life of the colony makes this a truism, but the influence of the Society of Friends in the Assembly depended in part on the political activity of Mennonites, Dunkers, Moravians, and Schwenkfelders. Like the Quakers, the German peace churches had a more developed political awareness and more natural organization than their neighbors. Religious structure served both groups admirably as political structure. Lancaster Mennonites met together to select candidates for the Assembly and to determine how many wagons they could provide for a military expedition. The sessions of the Philadelphia Yearly Meeting functioned as a caucus for Friends in the Pennsylvania Assembly to decide on many a course of action. After 1755, the Meeting for Sufferings of Philadelphia Yearly Meeting took over this role.

Lutherans and Presbyterians might share common interests or follow the advice of influential ministers, such as John Elder and Henry Melchior Muhlenberg, but there was no structured Lutheran voting bloc in the sense that a Mennonite vote existed from 1740 through 1776. Indeed, the peace churches had a disproportionate share of eligible voters down to 1765. It was necessary for foreign-born Protestants to be naturalized before they could take part in elections. By observing how many took an oath of allegiance and how many refused to take an oath, it is possible to know how many German church people and how many German sectarians were eligible to vote in a given year, as indicated in Table I.

Table 1

NATURALIZATIONS IN PENNSYLVANIA, 1740-1769[a]

	By Oath	By Affirmation	Jews
1740-1749	389	461	2
1750-1759	311	206	5
1760-1769	3,457	1,425	11
Totals	4,157	2,092	17

[a]Adapted from Henry J. Young, "Treatment of Loyalists in Pennsylvania," pp. 352-353.

Since 2,742 persons, nearly half of all those naturalized in the thirty year period, obtained citizenship in the single year 1765, out of fear that the Stamp Act would greatly increase the cost of qualifying, the total figure for 1740-1764 is no less illuminating. There were 2,257 who took the oath and 1,103 who affirmed their allegiance. Thus the Mennonites, Schwenkfelders, and Dunkers made up fully half of the qualified German voters through 1764, even though they comprised only a third of those naturalized between 1740 and 1769.

The influence of the Mennonites and the other German peace churches was also increased by their patterns of settlement in Pennsylvania. The Mennonite vote in Lancaster County was obviously crucial for the Quaker Party candidates and it is no less obvious that Francis Parvin, Clerk of Exeter Monthly Meeting, could not have been returned as a member of the Assembly from Berks County on Quaker votes alone. Some indication of the relative strength of the Society of Friends and the need to rely on Mennonite voters may be gathered from Table 2. The estimated number of members of the Society of Friends in each county includes females and males too young to vote so that the potential Quaker vote in Lancaster County in 1760 would not be 200 but 50. Thus the possibility of Quakers uniting to elect candidates by their votes alone existed only in Chester County and the City of Philadelphia. Although the Quaker population of Bucks and Philadelphia Counties was significant, Friends could not carry an election in either county without a good deal of assistance from German voters. In Berks, Northampton, Cumberland, and York counties, the number of Friends was far too few to influence any election by their votes alone. Only a handful of Mennonites and Dunkers lived in Chester County and the City of Philadelphia so that voters from the German peace churches were all but a very few concentrated in counties where they were able to give the maximum aid to the Quaker Party in an election.

Table 2

QUAKER POLITICAL STRENGTH, 1760

	Taxables 1760[a]	Estimated Voters 1765[b]	Estimated Total Quaker Membership 1760[c]
Philadelphia City	2,634	2,000	2,250
Philadelphia County	5,678	4,300	2,250
Bucks County	3,148	1,400	1,500
Chester County	4,716	1,100	2,450
Lancaster County	5,635	2,900	200

[a] Hindle, "March of the Paxton Boys," p. 463; [b] Newcomb, "Effects of the Stamp Act," p. 267; [c] Marietta, "Quaker Membership," pp. 42-43.

In the absence of voting registers and accurate census records for Colonial Pennsylvania, we cannot know how many persons were qualified to vote and how many of them exercised their franchise. There is every indication, however, that a large number of Pennsylvanians either could not or did not vote. A tally from Hereford Township in Berks County in 1772 indicated that only 6 persons of a total of 87 landowners in the township voted and all but one of the six voters can be identified as Mennonite or Schwenkfelder.[77]

In Virginia, where poll books are extant for some elections prior to the Revolution, Mennonites definitely voted for members of the House of Burgesses in significant numbers, but they formed such a minority of the population it is most unlikely that they sought to influence elections beyond casting their individual votes.[78]

The Pennsylvania situation was unique. There the Mennonites, Quakers, Schwenkfelders, Dunkers, and Moravians had settled in large numbers to enjoy the freedom of religion guaranteed by William Penn's Charter of Liberties. Only there did the peaceable sects have the potential for political action. And they responded to the threatened loss of their cherished rights by utilizing their political influence to the fullest extent possible. Whether political action is the most apt instrument for furthering the gospel message is a question for theologians rather than historians to decide. And yet the historical record makes it clear that in pursuing the politics of conscience in Pennsylvania, Israel Pemberton, Benjamin Hershey, and Christopher Schultz had answered this question to their own satisfaction. With the survival of the sectarian vision at stake, they made politics the vehicle for fundamentally religious concerns. They refused to be the quiet in the land. However strange a later generation might find a gathering of Lancaster Mennonites at Matthias Slough's tavern to choose candidates for the Pennsylvania Assembly, it is difficult to see what other course was open to them. The alternative could only have been a complete withdrawal from the world of men and women, for the changing circumstances of self-government had made them, together with governors and kings, the representatives of civil authority.

The sectarian vision is inevitably a minority view. The more seriously Quaker politicians like Israel Pemberton took their religion, the further they moved from the political realities of Colonial Pennsylvania. On an issue like taxing the Proprietary lands, the Quaker Party was truly a popular party, voicing the opinion of most Pennsylvanians regardless of ethnic or religious background. The expanded sense of the historic Quaker peace testimony that emerged from the deliberations of the Meeting for Sufferings, on the other hand, did not find ready acceptance even among Friends. Members of the Meeting for Sufferings labored for years without any apparent success in an effort to convince some prominent Quaker political leaders of the implications of their faith. The interests of the traditional Quaker Party and the sects diverged sharply and from the election of 1764 on the split was complete. The alliance of Mennonites, Schwenkfelders, and Dunkers with the religious Quakers was a natural one and, given the political situation, a necessary one. But it could not be a successful one. By the time the main currents of Pennsylvania politics had shifted into new channels and armed conflict between Great Britain and the American Colonies had become a real possibility, the sects had lost all possibility of influencing the course of events.[79] They could only react to policies determined by others—and they could suffer for their convictions. The experience of a nonresistant minority in the American Revolution brought them full circle from a political league based on religious principles to a new vision of the church as suffering servant in the world.

Notes for Introduction

1. Elizabeth Horsch Bender, tr., "A Pennsylvania Letter of 1745 to Mennonite Leaders in Holland," *Mennonite Historical Bulletin* (hereafter cited as MHB) XXXII (October, 1971), pp. 4-5.

2. Dietmar Rothermund, *The Layman's Progress: Religious and Political Experience in Colonial Pennsylvania 1740-1770* (Philadelphia, 1961), p. 62.

3. Frederick B. Tolles, *Quakers and the Atlantic Culture* (New York, 1960), p. 39.

4. Robert L. D. Davidson, *War Comes to Quaker Pennsylvania, 1682-1756* (New York, 1957), pp. 25-26.

5. John Shy, "A New Look at Colonial Militia," *William and Mary Quarterly* (hereafter cited as WMQ), 3rd Series, XX (January, 1963), p. 181.

6. Frederick B. Tolles, *Meeting House and Counting House: The Quaker Merchants of Colonial Philadelphia 1682-1763* (New York, 1963), pp. 12-15.

7. *Pennsylvania Archives*, 8th Series, III, p. 2656.

8. Tolles, *Meeting House and Counting House*, p. 14. Theodore Thayer, *Pennsylvania Politics and the Growth of Democracy 1740-1776* (Harrisburg, Pa., 1953), pp. 4-8.

9. Hermann Wellenreuther, "The Political Dilemma of the Quakers in Pennsylvania 1681-1748," *Pennsylvania Magazine of History and Biography* (hereafter cited as PMHB), XCIV (April, 1970), p. 158.

10. Harold S. Bender and C. Henry Smith, *Mennonites and Their Heritage* (Scottdale, Pa., 1974), p. 44.

11. William C. Braithwaite, *The Beginnings of Quakerism* (Cambridge, 1970), p. 462.

12. William C. Braithwaite, *The Second Period of Quakerism* (Cambridge, 1961), p. 600.

13. Henry J. Cadbury, "Nonpayment of Provincial War Tax," *Friends Journal*, XX (September 1, 1966), pp. 440-441.

14. Margaret E. Hirst, *The Quakers in Peace and War* (New York, 1923), p. 142. Kenneth S. P. Morse, *Baltimore Yearly Meeting 1672-1830* (Barnesville, Ohio, 1961), p. 14.

15. Jack D. Marietta, "Conscience, the Quaker Community, and the French and Indian War," *PMHB*, XCV (January, 1971), pp. 4-5.

16. Kenneth L. Carroll, "A Look at the 'Quaker Revival of 1756,' " *Quaker History*, LXV (Autumn, 1976), pp. 63-80.

17. "James Logan on Defensive War, or Pennsylvania Politics in 1741," *PMHB*, VI (October, 1882), pp. 402-411.

18. I. Daniel Rupp, *History of Lancaster County, Pennsylvania* (Lancaster, Pa., 1844), pp. 285-286. For Mylin's political career, see Alan Tully, "Englishmen and Germans: National Group Contact in Colonial Pennsylvania, 1700-1755," *Pennsylvania History*, XLV (July, 1978), p. 254.

19. Sydney V. James, "The Impact of the American Revolution on Quakers' Ideas about Their Sect," *WMQ*, 3rd Ser., XIX (July, 1962), p. 364.

20. Jack D. Marietta, "Wealth, War and Religion: The Perfecting of Quaker Asceticism 1740-1783," *Church History*, XLIII (June, 1974), pp. 230-241.

21. David R. Kobrin, "The Saving Remnant: Intellectual Sources of Change and Decline in Colonial Quakerism 1690-1810," PhD dissertation, University of Pennsylvania, 1968, p. 32.

22. Jack D. Marietta, "Ecclesiastical Discipline in the Society of Friends 1682-1776," PhD dissertation, Stanford University, 1968, p. 155.

23. *Ibid.*, p. 164.

24. John C. Wenger, *Franconia Conference History* (Telford, Pa., 1937), pp. 11-12.

William I. Hull, *William Penn and the Dutch Quaker Migration to Pennsylvania* (Swarthmore, Pa., 1935), pp. 387-388.

25. Martin G. Weaver, *Mennonites of Lancaster Conference* (Scottdale, Pa., 1931), p. 10.

26. A calendar of the papers of the Committee for Foreign Needs can be found in J. G. de Hoop Scheffer, *Inventaris der Archiefstukken* (Amsterdam, 1883), I, 176-463. The original manuscripts are housed in the Amsterdam Municipal Archives, but microfilm copies can be consulted at the Lancaster Mennonite Historical Society, Lancaster, Pa. and the Bethel College Archives, North Newton, Kan.

27. E. K. Martin, *The Mennonites* (Philadelphia, 1883), pp. 9-11.

28. Harry A. Brunk, *History of Mennonites in Virginia 1727-1900* (Staunton, Va., 1959), pp. 11-54. *History of Franklin County, Pennsylvania* (Chicago, 1887), p. 315. James O. Lehman, "The Mennonites of Maryland During the Revolutionary War," *Mennonite Quarterly Review* (Hereafter cited as MQR), L (July, 1976) pp. 201-202.

29. Grant M. Stoltzfus, *History of the First Amish Communities in America* (Harrisonburg, Va., 1958), pp. 31-51.

30. Donald F. Durnbaugh, *The Church of the Brethren Past and Present* (Elgin, Ill., 1971), pp. 12-14. Since 1908, the Dunkers or German Baptist Brethren have been known officially as the Church of the Brethren.

31. John B. Frantz, "The Awakening of Religion among the German Settlers in the Middle Colonies," *WMQ*, 3rd Ser., XXXIII (April, 1976), pp. 274-275.

32. Weaver, pp. 123-125. Donald F. Durnbaugh, *The Brethren in Colonial America* (Elgin, Ill., 1967), pp. 63-79.

33. Peter C. Erb, "Dialogue Under Duress: Schwenkfelder-Mennonite Contact in the Eighteenth Century," *MQR*, L (July, 1976), pp. 181-199. A convenient summary of Schwenkfelder doctrine and history can be found in Selina Gerhard Schultz, *A Course of Study in the Life and Teachings of Caspar Schwenkfeld von Ossig (1489-1561) and the History of the Schwenkfelder Religious Movement* (Pennsburg, Pa., 1964).

34. F. Ernest Stoeffler, ed., *Continental Pietism and Early American Christianity* (Grand Rapids, Mich., 1976), pp. 123-163.

35. James T. Lemon, *The Best Poor Man's Country: A Geographical Study of Early Southeastern Pennsylvania* (Baltimore, Md., 1972), p. 224.

36. Rothermund, pp. 190-191.

37. Edward H. Quinter and Charles L. Allwein, *Most Blessed Sacrament Church, Bally, Pennsylvania* (Bally, Pa., 1976), p. 40.

38. Durnbaugh, *Brethren in Colonial America*, p. 127.

39. *Ibid.*, p. 133.

40. Morse, pp. 51-58.

41. Weaver, pp. 123-125.

42. John Scott Davenport, "The Brethren in North Carolina During the Revolution," *Brethren Life and Thought*, XXII (Winter, 1977), p. 28.

43. Frantz, *WMQ*, 3rd Ser., XXXIII, p. 277.

44. Martin E. Lodge, "The Crisis of the Churches in the Middle Colonies, 1720-1750," *PMHB*, XCV (April, 1971), p. 197.

45. Philip Schaff, *Anglo-Germanism or the Significance of the German Nationality in the United States* (Chambersburg, Pa., 1846), p. 12.

46. Stoltzfus, pp. 34-44.

47. Lemon, pp. 43-45.

48. *Ibid.*, p. 93.

49. Hiram Hilty, "North Carolina Quakers and Slavery," PhD dissertation, Duke University, 1968, pp. 33-34.

50. George F. Dunkelberger, *The Story of Snyder County* (Selinsgrove, Pa., 1948), p. 648.

51. Lemon, pp. 20 and 188.

52. *Germantowner Zeitung*, July 24, 1787.

53. Stoltzfus, pp. 15-16.

54. Lawrence H. Gipson, *Lewis Evans* (Philadelphia, 1939), pp. 100-101.

55. Benjamin Rush, "An Account of the Manners of the German Inhabitants of Pennsylvania," *Columbian Magazine*, III (August, 1789), pp. 22-30.

56. Lemon, pp. 63-64.

56[a]. John F. Funk, who obtained this manuscript, identified it only as "by an old brother." Funk Papers, Archives of the Mennonite Church, Goshen, Ind. A similar theme is treated in Henry Funk's 1763 work, *Restitution or an Explanation of Several Principal Points of the Law* (Eng. tr. Elkhart, Ind., 1915) p. 269. On Martin Boehm, see John F. Funk, *The Mennonite Church and Her Accusers* (Elkhart, Ind., 1878), pp. 42-56.

57. *Pennsylvania Gazette*, February 15, 1770.

58. Henry Boehm, *Reminiscences, Historical and Biographical* (New York, 1866), pp. 11-12.

59. Weaver, pp. 438-439. Joseph Illick's suggestion that "Lutheran and Reformed Germans in the west resented the alliance of Moravians, Mennonites and Schwenkfelders with Quaker pacifists and became dissatisfied with the sectarian mentality that blocked the organization and education of Germans" is overstated. Cf. Joseph Illick, *Colonial Pennsylvania, A History* (New York, 1976), p. 244.

60. *Pennsylvania Gazette*, February 25, 1755.

61. Henry Harbaugh, *The Life of Rev. Michael Schlatter* (Philadelphia, 1857), pp. 261-263. James H. Hutson, "Benjamin Franklin and Pennsylvania Politics, 1751-1755: A Reappraisal," *PMHB*, XCIII (July, 1969), p. 368.

62. Harbaugh, pp. 288-295.

63. *Ibid.*, pp. 301-302.

64. Rothermund, p. 93.

65. Gipson, p. 99.

66. Rufus M. Jones, *The Quakers in the American Colonies* (New York, 1966), p. 524.

67. Jack D. Marietta, "A Note on Quaker Membership," *Quaker History*, LIX (Spring, 1970), pp. 40-43.

68. Tolles, *Meeting House and Counting House*, p. 68.

69. Isaac Sharpless put the Quaker population of Pennsylvania on the eve of the Revolution at 25,000. Jones, *op. cit.*, p. 524.

70. Morgan Edwards, *Materials toward a History of the Baptists in Pennsylvania both British and German, Distinguished into Firstday Baptists, Keithian Baptists, Seventhday Baptists, Tuncker Baptists, Mennonist Baptists. Volume I* (Philadelphia, 1770), p. 97.

71. Morgan Edwards, "Materials Towards a History of the Baptists in the Province of Maryland," Southern Baptist Theological Seminary Library, Louisville, Kentucky, Part IV, 1772, fol. 11.

72. Lehman, *MQR*, L (July, 1976), p. 201.

73. Durnbaugh, *Brethren in Colonial America*, p. 407.

74. Edwards, *Materials*, p. 64. Durnbaugh, p. 408.

75. Howard Weigner Kriebel, *The Schwenkfelders in Pennsylvania* (Lancaster, Pa., 1904), pp. 46-49.

76. There were an estimated 2,500 Moravians in the Colonies in 1775. William Warren Sweet, *Religion in Colonial America* (New York, 1949), p. 226.

77. Berks County Tax List, 1772, Hereford Township, Berks County Historical Society, Reading, Pa.

78. The original poll lists have been preserved among the Papers of George Washington, one of the successful candidates, in the Library of Congress, Washington, D.C., and were published in *WMQ*, 2nd Ser., VIII (July, 1928), p. 94. On the influence of religious dissenters in Virginia elections, see Charles S. Sydnor, *Gentlemen Freeholders:*

Political Practices in Washington's Virginia (Chapel Hill, N.C., 1952), p. 28.

79. Richard Bauman, *For the Reputation of Truth: Politics, Religion and Conflict Among the Pennsylvania Quakers 1750-1800* (Baltimore, Md., 1971), pp. 32-33 and 143. Alan Tully's analysis of German political weakness supports this view. *Cf.* Tully, *Pennsylvania History,* XLV (July, 1978), pp. 255-256.

Chapter 1

"IF A HOSTILE ATTACK SHOULD STRIKE THIS PROVINCE"

The First Crisis, 1740-1742

The long ordeal of the peace churches in Pennsylvania did not begin with settlers encroaching on Indian lands beyond the Blue Mountain, but with an English smuggler attempting to run a cargo to a tropical island in the Caribbean. Spain had far too small a navy to adequately protect its Latin American empire and enforce Spanish law. Her colonial governors relied instead on privateers and adventurers who were happy to use their authority to stop and search foreign merchantships for purposes that might otherwise require hoisting the skull-and-crossbones. As Captain Robert Jenkins told the story to a committee of the House of Commons in 1738, the Spaniards had not only plundered his ship but cut off one of his ears as a warning to other British sea captains. Neither government wanted war. Spain offered to pay substantial damages, but refused to drop the right to search foreign ships in Spanish waters. This was not enough. There was a good deal of interest in British business circles in revising the commercial clauses of the Treaty of Utrecht to give Great Britain a larger share of Latin American trade, especially the slave trade, and Jenkins' ear made as good an excuse as any for Englishmen to defend their country's honor. War was declared in October 1739. If some sort of argument could be made that British victory might increase the demand for Lancaster County wheat and give new ports of call to Philadelphia shipowners, the need for Mennonite farmers and Quaker merchants to join in defending their homes, their liberties, and the Protestant religion by attacking Cartagena in South America was not self-evident. It was an imperial war that concerned the American Colonies only insofar as they were elements of the British Empire. The reluctance of the Pennsylvania Assembly to appropriate large sums for defense, if unpatriotic, was not unreasonable.

The War of Jenkins' Ear was the first of a series of international quarrels that kept Great Britain and her American Colonies almost continuously at war until 1763. In each new crisis, whatever the occasion for war might be, the Colonies would be asked to contribute both men and money to the common effort. It was no longer a question of raising a few companies of militia to patrol their own borders, so the demand could not be brushed aside with the excuse that no hostile neighbors threatened the peace and security of the province. The friendly relations that Pennsylvania had enjoyed since William Penn's day with the Indians was simply irrelevant when all the Colonies were asked to share in a campaign that might directly touch all of them or none of them.

At the first session of the Pennsylvania Assembly after news of the declaration of war reached Philadelphia, Governor George Thomas asked that the colony be put in a proper state of defense. He demanded the establishment of a militia as a measure of military preparedness. He was stirring a hornet's nest that had been touched only once before in the colony's history. Benjamin Fletcher, royal governor of New York, had been ordered in 1692 to take over William Penn's colony for the "better defence and security of our Subjects Inhabiting those parts During this time of Warr." The Assembly, pressed by Governor Fletcher to comply with the demands for men or money, debated and finally defeated a militia bill.[1]

Militia laws requiring all able-bodied males within certain age limits, except for slaves and indentured servants, to turn out with such weapons and equipment as they could provide to defend the colony when their services were needed dated from the first settlements of the other American colonies. Later legislation had attempted to model the militia on the British system, which was itself neither efficient nor workable as a military force. One result of this effort was the universal requirement that anyone who failed to serve when liable or who neglected to attend militia training exercises should pay a fine. Men who had conscientious objections to military service were fined and sometimes imprisoned on this account.

Passage of the Toleration Act of 1689 gave Quakers the legal right to be exempt from militia duty, but the lawmakers in most colonies quickly imposed a heavy fine on all those who were exempt for religious reasons. In Virginia, for instance, Quakers petitioned the House of Burgesses in 1696 for relief from the fines which they had been condemned to pay for failing to attend musters and complained bitterly of the hardships this law imposed on them.[2] The Virginia Assembly granted relief to Quakers in 1766 and to Mennonites in 1772, but fines were again imposed in the Revolution. Quakers and Mennonites would continue to petition the Virginia authorities for exemption from militia fines without success throughout the eighteenth and early nineteenth centuries. Similar petitions went unread in other Colonies.

The Quaker Assemblymen could not be expected to vote for a law that Quakers in every other colony protested was an unfair burden on their consciences. Nor could they very well impose compulsory military service on all Pennsylvanians except themselves. Both solutions were politically impossible. Passage of a militia bill could not be had as long as Quakers dominated the Pennsylvania Assembly.

The renewed insistence on a militia bill in the Quaker colony came at a time when the colonial militia system had all but broken down. It was being replaced as the primary source of manpower by direct recruiting of volunteers, men who would be equipped and paid by the Colonial Assembly for long-term service often at a great distance from home. The militia ideal that saw every man of property turning out to defend king and country had given way in England and in the Colonies to a harsher reality, with regular army and volunteer regiments alike recruited from the very poor, landless, often homeless, laborers, unemployed weavers, and others without work, and, increasingly, the very indentured servants and apprentices excluded by the militia laws from military service.

While he was wrangling with the Assembly about the militia bill, Governor Thomas was beating for recruits for Admiral Edward Vernon's planned assault on the Spanish in the Caribbean. He raised 700 men in Philadelphia over the Assembly's objection that most of them were servants who still owed their masters one or more years of service. (Few of these runaways can have lived to enjoy their freedom, for Admiral Vernon managed to lose more than 20,000 of the 27,000 British and American soldiers and seamen who sailed with him for Cartagena in January 1741 to Spanish gunfire and malaria in a singularly disastrous campaign.) Governor Thomas thus gave the militia issue overtones of extended service in distant lands that would be distasteful to any independent farmer or shopkeeper in Europe, regardless of his religious convictions. The governor undoubtedly contributed to impressing on the minds of the peaceable sects that only the Quaker Assembly stood between them and military despotism.

When the Assembly refused to enact a militia law or to vote bounties for enlistment in His Majesty's forces, the governor countered with a fivefold argument. They represented all the people of Pennsylvania, he insisted, not just the Quakers. As Protestants they had an obligation to take up arms against Roman Catholics. Their refusal to bear arms only encouraged foreign enemies to attack Pennsylvania. Arguments for nonresistance were only valid against offensive war, not defensive measures. And finally William Penn himself had acknowledged an obligation to defend the colony.[3]

The Assembly responded in September 1740 with a point by point refutation, insisting that "to make any law against our consciences to bear arms would not only be to violate a fundamental in our constitution and be a direct breach in our charter of privileges, but would also" be the equivalent of "persecution."[4] For Mennonites and Dunkers, as well as Quakers, this would be a consistent stand for the troubled half century that followed.

Not only the military needs of the British Empire, but also the political climate in Pennsylvania itself underwent drastic change after 1739. The Proprietary Party had changed radically by this time. It had once been led almost entirely by Quakers, who differed from their brethren on the control that the governor, as the agent for the Proprietor, should exercise over an appropriation of money for some purpose or other, while agreeing with them on fundamental principles in both church and state. After 1739 politicians hostile to Quakerism itself began to take the lead in the Proprietary Party. They launched a campaign against the Quakers in the Assembly, centering on the peace testimony, that aimed at driving the Quakers altogether from political office.[5]

A week before the election of 1741, with governor and Assembly still at loggerheads, James Logan addressed a letter to the Philadelphia Yearly Meeting proposing that all "who for Conscience-sake cannot join in any Law for Self-Defence, should not only decline standing Candidates at the ensuing Election for Representatives themselves," but advise all who shared these scruples not to seek public office. Logan was satisfied himself that defensive war was lawful, but in any event the "Government at Home, and particularly the Parliament," appeared "to have this present War very much at Heart" and expected the Colonies to make the same exertions to equip armies and fleets. The Pennsylvania Quakers would do well to follow the example of their brethren in England who were "tolerated in their Opinions, as they interfere not with the Administration." If they did not demonstrate their loyalty by setting aside personal scruples and voting for the necessary defense appropriations or by stepping aside to let others do so, proceedings might well begin in England to revoke Penn's charter and make Pennsylvania a royal colony.

This was the advice of a Quaker, who had been Penn's secretary and the leader of the proprietary faction for many years. It was the sentiment of many conservative Philadelphia merchants as well. Friends attending the Yearly Meeting sessions refused to read Logan's appeal, although he later had copies of it printed.[6] Instead of following his advice, they looked to their natural allies among the German voters.

Thomas Cookson, a proprietary candidate for the Assembly in Lancaster County, found the Quakers had warned the Germans that if the governor's faction won the election they would have to pay high taxes and labor without pay in building fortifications. By reminding them of the tyranny of German princes, the Quakers "Raise very Dreadful Ideas in ye people."[7]

James Logan entered the political arena in Lancaster County by prevailing on Conrad Weiser, Pennsylvania's Indian Agent, to issue a circular letter addressed to the German voters. Logan actually wrote the letter, but it appeared over Weiser's name in a broadside printed just eleven days before the 1741 election. In this letter, published in both English and German as *A Serious and Seasonable Advice to our Countrymen ye Germans in Pensilvania (Ein Wohl gemeindter und Ernstlicher Rath an unsere Lands Leute, die Teutschen)*, Weiser appealed to his fellow Germans to help elect an Assembly that would put a stop to the differences between the governor and the legislature. He belittled the charges made by the Quakers "that if you took not Care to Choose Quakers you would be brought into the same Slavery you came hither to avoid." He urged them rather to turn out the Quakers who refused the legitimate requests of the British authorities. A war with France might break out at any moment and the frontiers of Pennsylvania would be open to the attack of a savage enemy, because of the obstructionist tactics of the Friends.[8]

Christopher Sauer, the Germantown printer, was the spokesman for the Quaker Party in this crisis. Three days before they went to the polls, he issued an address of his own to German voters. Sauer repeated the argument that the liberties and privileges the German settlers enjoyed in Pennsylvania would be imperiled by any change in the composition of the Assembly. Sauer insisted that the French were no menace, few in number, geographically remote, and blocked off from Pennsylvania by hostile Indians.[9]

The election of 1741 was an impressive victory for the Quakers in the Assembly. Thomas Cookson, whose appeal to Weiser and Logan led to the address to German voters, was defeated by the German voters of Lancaster County and other proprietary candidates fared no better. The Mennonite response to this election campaign can be gauged from the events narrated in the letter to Holland (*Document 1*) and the concern of the Lancaster brethren lest a "sandstone palace" bring the wrath of the government on them.

The Quakers gained another victory at the polls in 1742, marred by an election day riot in Philadelphia, where sailors clubbed "a great number of Dutch" voters and marched through the streets, crying "Down with the plain Coats and Broad Brims."[10] It is possible that the Quaker magistrates unintentionally provoked the riot themselves by ineptly handling a crowd of sailors on shore leave, but they were convinced themselves the sailors were paid by proprietary politicans to interfere with the voting.[11]

The first weeks of the 1742 session of the Assembly were taken up with a lengthy investigation into the riot, interrupted by the speedy passage of a bill providing for the naturalization of foreign Protestants, who were not Quakers but who had conscientious objection to taking an oath[12] (*Document 2*). The charge had been made that Germans who had no right to vote cast their ballots for Quaker candidates. The Assembly evidently took this charge at face value and framed a bill designed to give Mennonites, Dunkers, and Schwenkfelders the privileges of citizenship. They clearly considered this an important measure, since the governor's salary was used as a lever to force him to sign this particular bill into law.[13] The Quakers in the Assembly were honestly seeking compromise, for they traded passage of a long-contested money bill granting £4,000 to "the King's use" together with the governor's salary for his approval of the naturalization bill, which the Quakers had been trying in vain to force upon the governor in the previous two sessions.[14]

The first crisis ended on a conciliatory note, not because the Quaker political leaders had abandoned their principles but because of intense pressure from England to reach a compromise. They had not had to yield on the important question of a militia bill and many, probably most, Friends saw no inconsistency in rendering Caesar whatever taxes were due him, even for military purposes.[15] The lasting result of this crisis was a firm alliance between Mennonites, Dunkers, Schwenkfelders, and other nonresistants with the Quakers in defense of their liberties.[16]

The naturalization law was itself an important landmark in this alliance. Under its provisions, 278 men affirmed their allegiance in the year 1743 alone with only 89 persons taking the oath of allegiance in that year.[17] Penn had offered naturalization on liberal terms to all foreign Protestants in 1682, and for a limited time no further effort was required to obtain the rights of full citizenship. The 1682 legislation required the "renew'd Consent of the Governor and Freemen of the Province" for naturalization thereafter.[18] In 1706 Governor John Evans and his Council reacted favorably to a petition from "Joannes Koster, and about 150 other high and low Germans" requesting naturalization. The petitioners asked to be allowed to affirm, rather than swear, "some of the Petrs. being Mennists, who . . . could not for Conscience sake take an Oath."[19]

Despite this encouragement from Evans, it was August 1709 before a delegation of the petitioners came to his successor with a draft of a bill for the Assembly.[20] When the Assembly proposed a more extensive naturalization bill, Governor Charles Gookin objected. In its final form, the act signed by the governor gave the rights of citizenship to 85 named individuals in Philadelphia County and one in Bucks, many of them readily identifiable as Mennonites.[21] This was the second time that foreigners had been naturalized in Pennsylvania. The Assembly received petitions from time to time like that presented in 1721 by "a considerable Number of Palatines" asking not only for naturalization, but "to be exempt from swearing and bearing Arms." These petitions were invariably tabled without any further action by the Assembly.[22] Only ten persons were naturalized by Act of Assembly between 1709 and 1729. The Assembly had a change of heart in the following decade and naturalized 460 persons between 1730 and 1739, in every case by the cumbersome process of a special legislative act.[23] While sons and grandsons of early Mennonite settlers were rising to manhood with all the privileges of Pennsylvania-born British subjects, it is significant that only 555 European-born Pennsylvanians had acquired the right to vote by 1740. The liberal naturalization act passed in 1742 for the benefit of Mennonites, Dunkers, Schwenkfelders, and others who scrupled taking an oath had an obvious role in creating a German vote to redress the balance in favor of the Quaker Party.

New Wars and Old Demands, 1742-1748

Two distinct issues had emerged from the struggle between the governor and the Assembly in 1740-1742. One was the resistance of the Quaker-dominated Assembly to creation of a militia system and compulsory military service. On this point, Friends, Mennonites, and the other peace churches were in complete agreement. The other was the legitimacy of appropriating money for military purposes. The Assembly had at first refused and then given way to pressure and voted the money requested by the governor. The thought of the nonresistant sects had not yet crystallized on this point, for earlier Quakers and Mennonites had not imagined the possibility that individual Christians would be in the position of determining how Caesar was to use the taxes due him. Both of these issues came to the fore again and again in the next few years as new wars threatened the peace of Pennsylvania.

The conflict with Spain gradually drew in her ally—and Great Britain's major rival—France, as the European powers quarreled over Maria Theresa's right to succeed her father on the Austrian throne. The formal declaration of war came in March 1744 and news of the War of the Austrian Succession reached America two months later. The war was still far from Pennsylvania, but demands for Pennsylvania to carry its share were not long in coming. In January 1745 Governor Thomas asked the Assembly to make a contribution to the British effort in Nova Scotia.[24] The Assembly, more wary now, voted £4,000 "for the King's use," but carefully specified that it be put in the hands of two Quaker merchants who were authorized to draw on it only to buy "Bread, Beef, Pork, Flour, Wheat or other Grain," rather than arms and ammunition. The Assemblymen explained that their consciences did not "permit them to join in raising of Men or providing Arms and Ammunition, yet we have ever held it our Duty to render Tribute to Caesar," and they felt both principles were served by earmarking the money they voted for supplies of food for the army.[25] This was the distinction that Mennonite wagon masters made, when they refused to haul ammunition, only provisions and fodder, even though everything would be used by soldiers in the field.[26] When another call came in June 1746 for help in the campaign to take the French stronghold of Louisburg on the Gulf of St. Lawrence, the Assembly voted money for provisions and clothing as a demonstration of their loyalty to the king, "so far as our religious Principles will admit."[27]

Some men did not feel comfortable with this easy distinction between two kinds of military spending, but there was never any doubt about compulsory military service. No Quaker Assembly could pass a militia law. Benjamin Franklin, whose political star was just beginning to rise, saw a way out of the dilemma. In 1747 he published a pamphlet titled *Plain Truth* in which he described his own plan for defensive measures. He held that the only solution was an "Association," a voluntary agreement to serve and to get volunteer military units organized and to work out a plan to raise funds. Franklin appealed to the English and Irish settlers in Pennsylvania to rally to the cause and he did not neglect "the brave and steady Germans," appealing to those who had borne arms in the service of their respective princes "to unite with us in Defence of their newly acquired and most precious Liberty and Property," as they had once fought for "their Tyrants and Oppressors." Franklin was keenly aware of the influence of the German press and he had *Plain Truth* promptly translated and printed in German. In order to allay any criticism from Friends, since he was allied with the Quaker Party in the Assembly, Benjamin Franklin turned theologian for the occasion and quoted Robert Barclay and other early Quaker writers in his *Plain Truth* pamphlet to suggest that defensive warfare was not inconsistent with a profession of nonresistance.[28]

Franklin's Association was not only a great success as a military organization and, consequently, a spectacular entrance for Franklin himself onto the political stage, but it also put the Assembly on the defensive since private citizens had to join together to protect the lives and property of Pennsylvanians. Leaders of the Proprietary Party, who had been attacking the Quaker politicians for failing to provide a militia, now turned on them for taking away the governor's right to recruit and command any military force needed.[29]

The nonresistant sects were no better pleased. Although Franklin's Voluntary Association left military service to those who wanted to perform it and had no element of compulsion, Christopher Sauer's German newspaper attacked the plan in a series of articles and in pamphlets distributed free among German-speaking settlers. Sauer spoke for those who "do not love their goods so much that they would quarrel about them, let alone fight for them" and who saw this Association as a scheme to get misguided Germans to protect the property of men who cared nothing for their welfare. There was hardly an issue of Sauer's *Pennsylvanische Berichte* between December 1747 and November 1748 that did not include editorial blasts at defensive measures and companies enlisted under the Association. He urged his readers to drill with a flail in a barn instead. He criticized those Christian ministers who preached up warlike preparations and condemned efforts to raise money for fortifications below Philadelphia. But Sauer's fundamental point was a clear exposition of biblical nonresistance as the obligation of all Christians. This emphasis clearly attracted new readers and retained old ones, for Sauer's newspaper began to be issued every two weeks instead of once a month. The effect of Sauer's criticism was also evident in the vigorous counter-attack by supporters of the Association. He had stimulated Germans to become more involved in provincial affairs to help preserve the nonviolent policy of the Quaker Assembly; his opponents resorted to ridicule to try to undermine his influence.[30]

The news that Spanish privateers had been sighted in Delaware Bay made some Quaker merchants considerably less pacifistic than they had been when war was remote from them. They urged the governor to station a defensive warship within the Delaware Capes and some prominent Friends even signed a voluntary subscription pledging money for this purpose. In May 1748 the new governor of Pennsylvania, James Hamilton, laid before the Assembly the defenseless state of the province, asking them to appropriate money for a warship to patrol the lower reaches of the Delaware and to complete the battery being erected by private citizens below the city. John Churchman, a Quaker farmer from Chester County and a well-known minister among Friends, felt a deep concern at "the danger of departing from trusting in that divine power which had hitherto protected the inhabitants" and at the fact that many Quakers were willing to contribute to military preparations. He obtained permission from Speaker John Kinsey to address the session of the Assembly, urging them to beware of "acting to oppress tender consciences," since many of the people of Pennsylvania "would be greatly grieved to see warlike preparations carried on and encouraged by a law consented to by their brethren."[31] Churchman had hit on the crucial issue, which had somehow escaped others. How could Christians support war in the name of obedience to civil government when, in some measure, they were themselves the government?

John Churchman's understanding of nonresistance and the duty of Christians in public office emphasized the division that already existed among Friends. Like Christopher Sauer, he saw no way by which military adventures could be made compatible with the teachings of the nonresistant Jesus and he would not compromise conscience in the name of political expediency. Both Churchman and Sauer spoke for significant numbers within the peace churches, but few Quakers in the Assembly agreed fully with them.

The efforts of Thomas Penn, the Proprietor of Pennsylvania, to reform the colonial administration by reducing the power of the Assembly gave the Quaker Party a new and popular issue after 1746. The Assembly still articulated the attitudes and aspirations of Pennsylvanians and Quakers and Mennonites rallied to protect its influence against the Proprietary Party and its program of increasing the power of the governor. But the leadership of this Quaker Party included men like Benjamin Franklin, whose Association had given Pennsylvania some semblance of a militia, and Quakers who may have honestly believed that by voting for military appropriations they were protecting the liberties of all Pennsylvanians, for otherwise Penn's charter might be lost and a royal government substituted. How could such a party represent the ideals of a Sauer or a Churchman? This strain did not become immediately apparent, for the war ended in Europe in 1748, the voluntary companies were disbanded ("They may expect reward from neither God nor man," Sauer observed in a parting shot), and from 1749 to 1754 Pennsylvania was at peace.[32]

"The Heralds of the Judgment of God"

Differences within the Quaker Party might never have surfaced at all, if it had not been for an important change in Pennsylvania's Indian policy. William Penn had made his famous treaty with the Delaware Indians, the Lenni Lenape, who lived in the Delaware River Valley and along the Lehigh River. The peaceful Delawares had developed an admiration for Penn. Brotherhood with the Indians became the traditional Quaker policy, in contrast to most other groups in the English provinces, and all through the period of Quaker control of the colony an effort was made to treat the Indians fairly. Mennonites were in sympathy with Quaker ideals and also took a peaceful approach in their relations with their Indian neighbors.

As time went on, provincial leaders became less and less concerned to maintain friendship with the Delawares. They realized that the influential Iroquois must be reckoned with because they held the Delawares in subjection and initiated a series of conferences with the Iroquois to confirm previous agreements with the Delawares and other tribes. In 1736 the Proprietors of Pennsylvania made a duplicate payment to the Iroquois for lands previously purchased from the Delawares and pledged that henceforth all purchases would be through the Iroquois. At stake was the land between the Lehigh and Delaware Rivers. When the line of the "Walking Purchase" was run off in 1737 so as to take in all the lands of the Delaware tribe, the disaffection of these Pennsylvania Indians grew until it ended in open warfare, with relations embittered in the meantime by land problems, the rum traffic, and French influence.[33]

The Iroquois alliance had many advantages for Pennsylvania. In the war between France and England, the Iroquois acted as a shield for Pennsylvania by barring the way to the French and their Indian allies.

The Iroquois kept the peace among their tributaries and saved the Quaker colony from Indian disturbances for more than twenty years.

Yet when, on a June day in 1742, 160 Iroquois appeared at Conrad Weiser's house in Berks County on their way to impose a settlement of the "Walking Purchase" dispute on the Delawares, a Pennsylvanian gifted with a vision of the future might have wept at the success of the colony's Indian diplomacy. The conference held at Philadelphia in July of that year changed the temper of the Delawares. The Iroquois decided in favor of Pennsylvania and the aggrieved Delawares were more open than ever to French agents. Neither the Delawares nor the Shawnees who were compelled to cross the Poconos to Wyoming Valley ever forgot the sting of their displacement. Teedyuscung, the King of the Delawares, said in 1757, after war had broken out, that while "the Walk" was "not the principal cause that made us Strike our Brethren, the English, yet it has caused the stroke to come harder than it otherwise would have come." And this shabby treatment of old allies gave anyone—Indian, Frenchman, or Quaker—who wanted to discredit the governor and council ready ammunition.[34]

When British and French rivalry led to a new clash in 1754, the Iroquois alliance would not protect the Quaker colony and politicians and theologians could no longer ruminate on questions of military service and grants of tax money "for the King's use" in wars that were fought hundreds of miles away. With the frontier in flames from the Blue Mountains to the Blue Ridge, these questions were no longer issues for gentlemen in Philadelphia. They had a sudden, tragic immediacy for every man and woman in the colony. And wilderness diplomacy could no longer be safely left to the Logans and the Weisers who had left so much resentment behind them, not with Indian raiding parties—"the heralds of the judgment of God" on Pennsylvania's faithless policy, Sauer called them—threatening to destroy everything that William Penn had built.

Braddock's Defeat Brings a Militia Law

Rivalry over the Ohio Valley was the immediate cause of the conflict that erupted in 1754. The French had begun to exploit the fur trade of the tribes in the region south of the Great Lakes and had been methodically building a chain of forts across Western Pennsylvania to keep out traders from the English Colonies. When a large body of French arrived at the Forks of the Ohio to construct the last link in the chain—Fort Duquesne—they found the Ohio Company of Virginia already established at the juncture of the Allegheny and the

Monongahela rivers. A dozen Virginia planters with the financial backing of an English Quaker merchant had attempted to open the trade of a vast inland empire. They planned to assist German Protestants to move to the land beyond the Allegheny Mountains "as the most effectual method of promoting a speedy Settlement on the Ohio," promising them as full religious liberty as in Pennsylvania and a host of other advantages.[35] But, with limited capital and a late start, their enterprise was no match for the French. Major George Washington traveled to Fort LeBoeuf in present Erie County, Pennsylvania, to give the French commander an order from the governor of Virginia to stop trespassing on Virginia soil.

That was in the winter of 1753. Early in the following spring, Governor Dinwiddie sent a small force of Virginia volunteer militia to build a fort at the present site of Pittsburgh. When Captain Contrecoeur arrived with a thousand French regulars and Canadian militia, the 33 Virginians had no choice but surrender. Washington, coming up with reinforcements, met the retreating Virginians and decided to stand his ground. The French had no trouble in forcing the surrender of Fort Necessity, as Washington called his stockade, and on July 4, 1754, the Virginians were on the road to the Potomac. The Ohio Valley was indisputably French.[36]

The British Government decided at this point to assert their control of the Ohio with overwhelming force. Major General Edward Braddock sailed for America in the last days of 1754, before troop transports had begun to take on board the thousand British regulars he would command. From the moment he stepped ashore in Virginia, everything was bustle and confusion. Provincial troops had to be recruited to swell the ranks of Braddock's army. Food and drink for the men, hay and oats for the horses had to be found and made ready to be hauled behind the army on its march. Wagons, teams, and drivers had to be hired to carry the baggage, the arms and ammunition, supplies and fodder. Messengers were sent galloping to all the colonial capitals with new orders or demands.[37]

The Mennonite response to these military preparations can be seen in a petition Lancaster Mennonites sent to the Pennsylvania Assembly in May 1755 (*Document 9*) explaining their reasons for not "lending our Assistance against the Invader" and again expressing fear that their affirmation of loyalty to the king at the time of naturalization might require them to testify their loyalty "by defending him with Sword in hand." The Quakers of Pennsylvania and New Jersey issued an Epistle to all Friends in America in May 1755 reminding them of "our Duty to cease from those national Contests productive of Misery and Bloodshed."[38]

Mennonites did respond favorably to Benjamin Franklin's appeal at the end of April for wagons and horses for Braddock's army (*Document 10*). The Mennonite community provided about a fifth of the wagons, teams, and drivers used in the expedition. Several Dunkers and Quakers can also be found among the 144 contractors whose accounts were settled by the Commissioners in 1756 (*Documents 12, 13 and 14*). William Smith charged that the Mennonite teamsters refused to carry either arms or ammunition, accepting only provisions and fodder.[39] Mennonite willingness to provide food and hay and to serve as wagoners with the army continued throughout the French and Indian War, as a series of letters written in 1759 illustrate (*Documents 15, 16, 17, 18, 19*).

When Governor Robert Hunter Morris informed the Pennsylvania Assembly on June 17, 1755, that with Braddock's redcoats advancing toward the Forks of the Ohio, the French and their Indian allies might be expected to attack frontier settlements in Pennsylvania at any moment, he reminded them that this made passage of "a proper Militia Law" a necessity (*Document 20*).

Braddock's expedition came in the middle of a bitter wrangle between the governor and the Assembly over control of revenue. The Assembly had been in the habit of issuing paper money to meet specific needs and pledging certain specific taxes for a period of years to redeem it. (Paper money was used in the eighteenth century in a way that bears greater similarity to modern state and municipal bond issues than to modern paper currency.) By pledging the revenue for a longer term than was absolutely necessary, the Assembly had gradually gained control of most sources of revenue due to the Proprietor. One of Thomas Penn's aims was to reassert total control over all the Proprietary revenues and he instructed his representatives to authorize issues of paper currency only if the Assembly gave up any claim to control money raised by taxes or excise duties. This dispute had nothing to do with military appropriations or pacifism, but it effectively paralyzed the Pennsylvania legislature in the war emergency.

The oft-told tale of Quaker obstruction in 1755 from motives of conscience has been exploded by modern historians. It was the governor and the Proprietary Party who used obstructionist tactics, holding the lives of the frontier settlers to ransom for concessions from the Assembly.[40] In its special session in March, the Assembly came up with a bill to issue £40,000 in paper currency to meet various wartime expenses.[41] After days of wrangling with the governor over trifling points, they reduced the amount to £25,000 pledging the excise for ten years.[42] Governor Morris would not give his assent to any such measure, so Benjamin Franklin found a way through the morass by having the Assembly vote a loan fund to provide money to provision New England troops.[43]

Franklin's effort to find wagons for Braddock, an effort freely supported by the peaceable sects, brought firsthand knowledge of the degree to which Governor Morris had gone to poison the minds of the British commanders against Pennsylvania.[44] Following the 1754 elections, the Proprietary Party had drafted petitions to Parliament to disfranchise the Germans.[45] Publication of *A Brief State of the Province of Pennsylvania,* actually by the Proprietary politician-minister William Smith but widely believed to be by Governor Morris, disclosed an elaborate plan to destroy the Quaker influence by depicting them as refusing to protect the colony from the French and Indians.[46] It was a scenario that Morris seemed to be following to the letter.

The peace churches had gone as far as they could go in providing wagons and teams and in voting funds "for the King's use" earmarked for "peaceful" purposes. They refused to act on the governor's request for a militia law.

The magnitude of Braddock's disaster was not known until mid-July. Even so, it was Dunbar's decision to take the remnant of the army, still a mighty force by eighteenth-century standards, in full retreat across the Susquehanna and on through Lancaster and Chester counties to Philadelphia that left the Pennsylvania frontier open to Indian raids. And it was the rich plunder from the battlefield and from wagons unloaded to make room for the wounded that convinced many a wavering Indian council to throw in their lot with the French.

The first blow did not fall until October, when Indians killed or carried off 25 persons at Penn's Creek, near present Selinsgrove (*Document 21*). The alarm quickly spread to Lancaster County and women and children from the back parts of Cumberland, Lancaster, and Berks counties were streaming eastward before the month was out.[47] Delaware raiding parties followed swiftly on the first rumors of Indian troubles. Two men were killed on Swatara Creek late in October and Delaware raids were reported all the length of the frontier.[48] In November there was a massacre of settlers at Tulpehocken in Berks County.[49] Alarmed citizens were already standing guard in Berks; a Mennonite who brought a good gun with him joined Conrad Weiser's Tulpehocken company (*Document 22*). When news of the attack reached

Reading, some wanted to burn the homes of the few Quakers in town, blaming them for the Indian war *(Document 23)*. Petitions began pouring into the Assembly from all the exposed settlements asking for help. Mennonites who lived west of York signed one such petition (*Document 24*). John Elder, the Presbyterian pastor at Paxton in Lancaster County, complained that the frontier inhabitants had petitioned again and again. Forty settlers had been killed in a few weeks' time "and yet nothing but unreasonable Debates" had occupied the governor and Assembly.[50]

With this kind of pressure, the Assembly passed an act "for the better ordering and regulating Such as are willing and desirous to be United for Military Purposes" (*Document 33*). As the title of the act made clear, this was to be a purely voluntary military force, with all elements of compulsion deliberately excluded. The authorities in London later declared the act invalid, objecting among other things that it was "rather Calculated to exempt Persons from Military Services than to encourage and promote them."[51] Yet it served its purpose. Even before the act went into effect associated companies had been organized on the model of Ben Franklin's Association and others took the field afterwards.[52] And, as Governor Morris grumbled, "by appearing ready to pass one, however absurd," the Assembly had contrived "to turn all ye Odium on me" for Pennsylvania's defenselessness.[53]

When the Assembly passed a controversial Supply Bill, which will be treated in the next section, a week after voting the Militia Act, they authorized seven commissioners to use part of the £60,000 to maintain paid soldiers and to build and garrison forts. The commissioners had expected to employ 500 men, but by February 1756 they had 919 men on active duty along the frontier in forts and garrison houses.[54]

Other companies guarding the frontier were paid by private subscription and there is evidence that members of the peace churches took a willing part in paying for these forces. Many of the Indian raids fell on the most exposed frontier settlements, which were also some of the poorest communities in Pennsylvania, and thus the least able to arm and equip military units for their own defense. The land on the east side of the Blue Mountains, comprising Heidelberg and Lynn townships in Northampton County and Albany Township in Berks was known among the German settlers as "Allemangle." Jacob Levan, David Schultze, and others in more secure and prosperous Berks and Philadelphia (present Montgomery) county settlements began raising money to supply an independent company of volunteers to guard these outlying farms. At least some of the men behind the "Maxatawny and

Allemangle Independent Guard" were members of nonresistant churches, so their action may indicate the understanding of nonresistance in some of the German peace churches at that time. They agreed to contribute money to arm and equip other men, who would do the actual guard duty, and they considered this a charitable act. A circular letter signed by Schwenkfelder elder Christopher Schultz and the Dunker John Mack answered objections raised in Towamencin Township to the plan. Schultz and Mack wrote, in part, that such actions were necessary to avoid the need for a compulsory militia law and even for direct rule of the colony from England. "Things will undoubtedly come to such a pass that such governors will be chosen and sought out who will make the people come to help by force, who under a mild government out of good will and because the government has not yet required it by law have refused to give aid in this great need."[55] Contributions for the guard came from Perkiomen Valley communities, settled by Mennonites and Schwenkfelders, as well as from the Berks County frontier. Settlers in the exposed settlements in Albany and Maxatawny townships in Berks contributed less than half the cost of their own defense. The rest of the money came from Towamencin, Salford, Franconia, Hatfield, Worcester, Upper Salford, North Wales, and Upper Hanover townships in Philadelphia (present Montgomery) County.[56]

One of the trustees of this frontier guard was David Schultze, a Schwenkfelder, who wrote in January 1756 that the Assembly should have appropriated three times as much as it did to hire troops and build forts rather "Than to permit those Beast-like Creatures to turn the Province into its former State of Wilderness." He expected that little would come of the Militia Act, "by reason of the continual Disputes between those that are for and those that are or pretend to be principled against bearing Arms." Schultze saw its greatest weakness in the fact that "the latter are not obliged thereby to do at least Something to the Satisfaction of the former on that head."[57] If a Schwenkfelder could feel this way, his Lutheran and Reformed neighbors doubtless had less sympathy for scruples that stood in the way of defending their homes and families.

The Militia Act of 1755 was a one-year emergency measure that expired just about the time news reached Philadelphia that the law had been overruled in England.[58] The 1756 session of the Assembly was under pressure to pass a new, more comprehensive, militia law. In April 1756 there had been threats of a march on Philadelphia by a "great body" of back-country settlers "to make demands on the legislature."[59]

The governor played on frontier resentment in asking for a militia law, expressing fear that York and Cumberland counties would be evacuated at the next attack.[60] Nothing was done at that time, but the Assembly elected in October 1756 might be expected to comply. They did, in fact, frame a militia law that obliged conscientious objectors to pay a fine of 20 shillings in lieu of military service (*Document 34*). In March 1757 the Quakers sent a formal protest to the Assembly against the militia law then under consideration.[61] Friends had been giving serious thought to this "apparent Infringement on the religious Liberties to which we apprehend our Friends entitled by the Charter & Laws" and put their objections squarely on the issue of freedom of conscience.[62] To their surprise, the governor returned the bill to the Assembly as "even more anticonstitutional than their old Law repealed by the King."[63] The Assembly retorted that they were sorry to find that no militia law would satisfy the governor, "unless it is framed in such Manner as will enable designing Men to overturn the Constitution, subvert all our Rights and Privileges, and persecute several Sects of religious Societies and honest and loyal Members of the Community, whom the Governor is pleased to favour with the Appellation of 'the worst of Persons.' "[64] It was a stalmate again and Pennsylvania would have no militia law until 1777, when many of the features of the 1757 bill would be adopted.

Mennonites, Quakers, and Dunkers in the other Colonies lived under a militia law and paid fines as the price of exemption, while petitioning for a larger measure of freedom of conscience (*Document 72,73, 74*). When Indian raids threatened the Shenandoah Valley of Virginia, some Quakers joined their neighbors in standing guard. There is no evidence that any Mennonites did so.[65] Friends also expressed concern in 1758 about Quakers "voluntarily assisting with their Ships, waggons or other carriages" in transporting "Implements of War or military Stores" or giving money to hire wagons for the army.[66] There was a good deal of agreement among all the peaceable sects about military service, even with Indian attacks all around them. Paying for war, whether through contributions such as Schwenkfelders and others made to the frontier guard units or through taxes levied on all alike was still an issue that was open to discussion.

Taxes for Military Purposes

Amid the flurry of petitions to the Pennsylvania Assembly in November 1755 one was received from "some of the People called Quakers" urging them to provide money to "cultivate our Friendship with our Indian Neighbours" and to support those white settlers in distress, but not to impose taxes for military purposes (*Document 31*). John Woolman, John Churchman, and the 21 other signers of this petition acknowledged an obligation to pay taxes and otherwise support civil government, but they preferred to suffer the consequences "rather than consenting" to military spending "by the Payment of a Tax for such Purposes." They had clearly stated a point of immense consequence: the individual is responsible for the actions of his government in a free society. Woolman acknowledged in his *Journal* that "a scrupling to pay a tax on account of the application" was uncommon and many Friends in Pennsylvania could not see the force of his argument, "still there was a scruple so fastened upon the minds of many Friends, that nothing moved it."[67]

After the Supply Bill was passed by the Assembly, Woolman, Churchman, and others considered the matter with a committee of Philadelphia Yearly Meeting. They issued an epistle to Friends in Pennsylvania, signed by 21 Friends, reminding them that "as we cannot be concerned in wars and fightings, so neither ought we to contribute thereto by paying the tax directed by the said act, though suffering be the consequence of our refusal."[68] There had been no real agreement, but some who felt no qualms about paying "mixed taxes" had quietly withdrawn from the discussion. When copies of this letter reached England, British Quakers were uneasy with the advice it contained. In 1756 the London Meeting for Sufferings asked John Hunt and Christopher Wilson, who were about to leave for America, to express their concern to Pennsylvania Friends and to "explain and enforce our known principles and practice respecting the payment of taxes." Hunt and Wilson brought with them extracts from the minutes of London Yearly Meeting, running back to 1715, that made it clear that English Quakers felt obliged to pay taxes levied for carrying on a war. Their testimony convinced some Friends, while others felt convicted by John Woolman and John Churchman. The 1757 Yearly Meeting found so little evidence of consensus on war taxes that they preferred not to discuss it at all, but to recommend "fervent charity towards one another."[69]

If there could be no real distinction between paying war taxes and fighting in a war, how could a nonresistant Christian vote a sum of money for military purposes or serve on a committee authorized to use the money to build forts and pay soldiers? The Quaker Assemblymen who did both in November 1755 apparently saw no inconsistency in their acts and their religious profession. They were consistent in their politics, maintaining the Assembly's right to control the use of the money it appropriated, even when the grant was for the war chest. Had they done otherwise they would have abandoned the right of self-government.

One of the Quakers who drafted the petition to the Assembly about payment of war taxes was Israel Pemberton, Clerk of Philadelphia Yearly Meeting, a former member of the Assembly and one of the wealthiest men in Pennsylvania. Pemberton wrote in December, 1755, that the vote on the Supply Bill "struck a damp on many of our minds, & doubt, whether we could individually give our approbation to this measure by freely paying our assessments." The Quakers who voted for it had shattered the strength of the Society of Friends and proven themselves to be hyprocrites.[70]

The deep division in the Society of Friends that resulted from the revival movement led by Churchman, Woolman, and Pemberton himself had come to the surface. The religious Quakers thought that Friends should withdraw altogether from the Assembly and the six Quaker members who had opposed the Supply Bill resigned in May 1756. For completely different reasons, English Quakers recommended that their brethren should all resign from the Assembly. They were shocked by the stand some had taken on war taxes and feared that Quakers might lose all their privileges in the British Empire if they appeared to be unwilling to support their government. In October 1756 four more Quakers resigned. All the entreaties of their brethren had no effect on the remaining Quaker members. The Quaker politicians levied more taxes and raised the penalties for nonpayment, they ignored the advice of Friends on a militia law, and they opposed everything that Pemberton and the other reformers advocated for preserving the ethical teaching of Quakerism.[71]

The resignation of ten Quakers from the Assembly in 1756 has often been interpreted as an abdication by the Pennsylvania Friends of political responsibility, but the Quaker leadership was invigorated rather than weakened by the events of the war years. The deep division among Friends, which remained a difference in ideas within a broader unity, led the religious Quakers to despair of achieving anything through the secular Quakers in the political arena. Led by Israel Pemberton, they turned instead to the Mennonites and other German peace churches. Between 1756 and 1765 this wing of the Society of Friends worked closely with Mennonites, Schwenkfelders, and Dunkers in important projects and forged a political alligance that would last through the Revolution.[72]

The 1756 withdrawal from office turned out to be a turning point for the Quaker reformers in their drive to revitalize the Society of Friends. Far from the end of a period of cooperation between Mennonites and Quakers, it was really the beginning of a working partnership that was to influence both groups on many levels.

The Sectarian Response

The Quaker petition to the Assembly in November, 1755, had offered an alternative to defense spending and foreshadowed the response of the peaceable sects to the challenge of war. It had proposed efforts to regain the friendship of the Indians and efforts to assist refugees fleeing from raids on the frontier.

The Mennonites took the lead in bringing food and clothing to the war refugees. In November 1755 the Indians had attacked the Moravian mission at Gnadenhutten at the junction of Mahony Creek and the Lehigh River, killing all but two of the unarmed men, women, and children there.[73] The Moravians at Bethlehem appealed for help for refugees from their settlements at Christiansbrunn, Nazareth, Gnadenthal, and Friedensthal, all on the exposed frontier of Northampton County.[74] Skippack Mennonites sent "a train of wagons loaded with supplies" for the Moravian refugees (*Documents 48, 49, 50, 51*). Lancaster Mennonites came to the aid of their fellow Germans in Berks County sending wagon loads of wheat, corn, and pork to Tulpehocken (*Documents 52, 53*).

Quakers, Schwenkfelders, Dunkers, and Moravians shared in the relief effort, which became increasingly important as new raids devastated new sections of the frontier and sent more families fleeing to the safety of the older settlements. More than 600 refugees took shelter at Bethlehem, the Moravian center, where Quakers, Mennonites, and others sent food and clothing to them (*Document 52*).

This relief work, some of it organized, much of it spontaneous, continued until the Indian threat receded in 1758. It was renewed again in Pontiac's War in 1763, when Lancaster Mennonites responded to the need of settlers beyond South Mountain in present Cumberland County (*Document 53*).

Few Mennonites or Quakers lived on the frontiers most exposed to Indian attack in 1755-1756, but as the raids became more daring and more frequent, settlements that seemed secure in the first fury did not escape. The Lancaster County frontier communities in present Dauphin and Lebanon counties were the victims of bands of Delaware and Shawnee warriors from the beginning. Mennonites may have drawn the anger of their neighbors in this region for their nonresistant stand

(*Documents 35, 36, 37*). The Northkill Amish community in Berks County suffered from the Hochstetler Massacre in 1757 (*Documents 38-44*). The Mennonite community in the Shenandoah Valley of Virginia suffered from an Indian raid in May 1758. One family, probably that of Jacob Holtiman, was killed and 38 other families left their Valley farms, many for the safety of Lancaster. Benjamin Hershey wrote a letter on their behalf to the Dutch Mennonite Committee for Foreign Needs (*Document 45*). The Lancaster brethren obviously supplied their more immediate needs. The Eckerlin brothers, Dunkers from Ephrata, had pioneered in settlements on the New River in Botetourt County, Virginia, and on the Cheat River in Preston County, West Virginia. Both of these remote settlements suffered from Indian attack.[75]

The Delaware and Shawnee tribes had actually wavered for some time between French and English, even after the overwhelming defeat of Braddock's army. They were still smarting from the loss of their lands between the Lehigh and the Susquehanna. The final blow was the news that settlers from Connecticut were claiming the Delaware lands in the Wyoming Valley had been sold to them by the Iroquois in 1754. Pennsylvania's Indian policy was thus a complete failure in 1755. The Iroquois could not protect frontier settlements in Pennsylvania and the habit of dealing with the Iroquois had finally driven the Delawares to take up the hatchet against the white settlers.[76]

Pennsylvania also wavered for a time, long after Delaware bands were ravaging frontier settlements. In April 1756 Governor Morris declared war on the Delaware Nation, "earnestly inviting" the people "to embrace all Opportunities of pursuing, taking, killing, and destroying" them. Some Quaker leaders had appealed for further peaceful efforts before war was declared. When the governor and council met two days before the formal declaration of war, Quakers presented an address "bearing Testimony against War," but to no avail. They asked the authorities to allow time for friendly Indians to persuade the Delawares to bury the hatchet. After the declaration of war, Israel Pemberton and other Quaker leaders began their own effort to make peace with the Indians. With Governor Morris' approval and Weiser's assistance as interpreter, they held conferences with Delaware chiefs at Pemberton's house in April and with Teedyuscung, the "King" of the Delawares at Easton in the last days of July 1756. Thus was the Friendly Association for Regaining and Preserving Peace with the Indians born.[77]

Christopher Sauer enthusiastically endorsed the plan for the

Friendly Association in April 1756 and promised to write to the Germans, "especially the Menonists," about this Quaker initiative (*Document* 55). Andrew Ziegler, Mennonite preacher at Skippack, wrote to Pemberton about meetings to discuss Indian affairs and to gather money and about a Mennonite delegation calling on the governor (*Document* 58). In November 1756 the newly arrived Governor William Denny met with Teedyuscung at Easton. Israel Pemberton and dozens of Quakers were also present for the ten-day conference. Pemberton urged the Indians "to speak bold, and to be strong and fear nothing," according to Weiser. Teedyuscung insisted that the Indians had been deprived of their lands by fraud and, still worse, felt that they were despised by the whites for letting themselves be swindled.[78] Soon after the Easton conference, a meeting of Schwenkfelders resulted in "formation of a union to support the principles of the Friends Society" (*Documents* 58-63).

The Delaware Nation finally agreed to a peace treaty at Easton in October 1758. Teedyuscung's only real demand was that the Indians be given title to some piece of land that would not be subject to later trickery. The Friendly Association had a major part in ending the war, but so did the Iroquois who pressured the Delawares into accepting the peace offers. With the Delawares no longer allied to the French, the war was virtually over. General John Forbes marched a column of British regulars toward Fort Duquesne (Pittsburgh) and found the fort in flames when he got there, with the French falling back to Canada.[79]

The Friendly Association, in which Mennonites and Schwenkfelders now played a much greater part, kept up its activities in attempting to secure just treatment of the Indians and to ranson white captives until 1763 when it disbanded.[80]

The war years gave Mennonites and other peace churches a pattern of refusal to support war in any way, while undertaking both relief work and peacemaking efforts, as well as an experience of close cooperation that they would carry with varying success into the next wartime crisis in 1775.

DOCUMENTS
The Obligations of Allegiance

Letters to the Dutch Mennonite Church

Leaders of the Mennonite congregations in Pennsylvania wrote to the Committee for Foreign Needs *(Commissie voor de buitenlandsche nooden)* of the Dutch Mennonite Church in 1742, asking for guidance in a difficult situation. Although they had enjoyed full liberty of conscience in the Quaker commonwealth, they were afraid that the government might compel them to take up arms to defend the colony. Their letter indicates that they first appealed to the Pennsylvania Assembly, without obtaining the guarantee they were seeking. No record of such a petition can be found in the minutes of the Assembly, but it is not unlikely that, after consulting privately with sympathetic members of the legislature, they decided against formally presenting their request.

The original letter to Holland was also lost, but, in 1745, with the threat of war mounting, the ministers of the Skippack congregation wrote again in the name of all the Pennsylvania Mennonites. They repeated what had been said in the earlier letter and added a request for help in translating and publishing the *Martyrs Mirror*. This letter has been preserved, with other records of the Committee for Foreign Needs, and deposited in 1975 in the Amsterdam Town Archives.

Document 1

To all the ministers and elders of the nonresistant Mennonite congregations of God in Amsterdam and Haarlem and wherever this may be read, we, all the ministers and elders of the nonresistant Mennonite congregations in Pennsylvania, wish you as a greeting God's grace, love and peace from the fullness of Jesus.

Dearly beloved Brethren,

In the year 1742 on May 8 we sent a letter to you in which we presented our concern and out of sincere love, although in weakness and simplicity, informed you somewhat of our circumstances. First, that we have up to the present under the honorable crown of Great Britain been able to live unhampered in freedom of conscience. Further we told you about the state of the local congregation, how under divine direction it has propagated itself and has spread and grown.

In our earlier letter we also presented our concern to you that, although we have hitherto been able to live in peace and liberty, for which we give God sincere thanks, and have been tolerated; there is no guarantee that, if a hostile attack should strike this province, we would not, like all the other provinces, be compelled against our conscience to take up arms and meet the foe with weapons with a heavily burdened conscience.

Further we informed you in that letter that we, for the sake of assurance in freedom of conscience, have notified the present government and the Assembly, which to be sure received our petition kindly, but still declared itself toward us that such a matter is entirely beyond its authority, and that such freedom of conscience must be sought from the Royal Majesty of Great Britain.

When we now consider our own condition from our point of view, we find ourselves powerless, weak and incapable of seeking such a matter in our littleness at such a court and high power, and in this case see no course before us but to entrust it to the one eternal and almighty God, who has hitherto graciously protected our province from all hostile attacks, so that we can still live in peace. But because our old deceased brethren Hans Burckholder and Benedikt Brechtbiell and others, who came to this country 27 years ago, received kind consolation from the brethren of Amsterdam, in precisely such matters: that is, if we for the sake of freedom of conscience should suffer want, we should make it known to the brethren in Holland, that they would be inclined to the extent of their ability to come to our support with counsel and help, which caused us greatly to rejoice.

We acknowledge our misstep in coming to so distant a land without sufficient assurance concerning freedom of conscience.

This is in brief the content of our former letter; but because we have received no information whether it was received or accepted by the brethren, we were moved to let you know this by means of these lines, hoping that you will kindly accept this from us, and also, as far as you are able, to inform us of your advice in such troublesome circumstances.

We now want to elaborate further about our concern:

It cannot be known, now that the flames of war seem to be mounting higher and higher, whether cross and tribulation may not all the sooner fall to the lot of the nonresistant Christian. It therefore becomes us to arm ourselves for such cases with patience and endurance, and to make every preparation for the steadfast constancy in our faith. It was, therefore, unanimously favored by the Brotherhood in this land, to see if we could manage to have Dielman Jans van Braght's *Bloeding Toneel [Martyrs Mirror]* translated into German, especially since here in this country in our brotherhood many young people have grown up and greatly increased in number, so that our posterity may have before their eyes the traces of those loyal witnesses of the truth, who walked in the way of truth and have given their lives for it. Although we have greatly desired to have this work published for a number of years, it has heretofore remained unaccomplished. The establishment of a new German printing office has renewed the hopes, but the bad paper used here for printing has caused us to reconsider. Besides, up to this time, there has not appeared, either among ourselves or others, anyone who understands the languages well enough to make a faithful translation. We have for certain reasons not been able to entrust it to those who have volunteered and promised to do it, for however much we are concerned to have it translated, we are equally concerned that the truth remain unblemished by the translation.

Lately we agreed to commit this plan to the brethren in Holland for their counsel. To this all the ministers and elders have unanimously given their consent.

We therefore earnestly request that you accept our entreaty in love and reply as regards this case as soon as possible, sending an estimate and specification, what it would cost to print and bind one thousand copies, and whether they could be shipped to us here without high customs and other expenses, what they would come to with or without copper plates, whether you consider it better that they be shipped singly or all at once, however it seems most feasible to you to manage it.

This petition is made to you, dear brethren, because there is here a deep desire to have the above-mentioned book translated into German, so we ask you to take counsel in this matter to determine whether it can be carried out in these dangerous times with the war going on and what a copy would cost with translation, printing and binding, if we have one thousand printed. We hope you will accept this request in love and let us know as soon as possible your counsel and opinion.

In which hope we remain, Your brethren in willing service and fellow ministers in Jesus Christ.

Jacob Godschalk	*Heinrich Funk*
Marthin Kolb	*Gilles Kassel*
Michael Ziegler	*Dielman Kolb*

The above names of the leaders of the local congregation at Schiebach [Skippack] have been commisioned by the rest of the congregation to send this to you; done on October 19, 1745.

P.S. We inform you herewith that by reason of duty we should not have delayed with this letter. But because we have not yet received your reply to our previous letter the matter has been left thus. We are sending this in duplicate so that in case one gets lost in the disturbances of war we hope one copy will reach you safely.[81]

Election Day Riots and Resulting Legislation

An election day riot in Philadelphia on October 1, 1742, greatly alarmed the Quaker majority in the Pennsylvania Assembly. Sailors armed with clubs and sticks had roamed through the streets shouting "Down with the Broadbrims" and threatening to beat any Quaker or German who tried to vote. A recent study of the incident concluded that it was easily avoidable and stemmed from the overreaction of certain Quaker magistrates, but contemporaries saw it as part of a plot to drive Quakers from control of the Assembly.

The Assembly responded by conducting a thorough investigation into the riot, pausing in their hearings to pass a bill to make naturalization easier for foreign-born Protestants who could not take an oath of allegiance. No general naturalization act had been passed up to this time. The legislation passed in 1742 for the benefit of Mennonites, Dunkers, and others with scruples about oath-taking helped create a German voting bloc that shared many concerns with the Quakers. A bill that gave persons born outside the British dominions who died unnaturalized the right to pass property to their heirs was introduced the same day as the naturalization bill and carried to the same successful conclusion.

Document 2
[October 19, 1742]

Ordered, That *Thomas Leech, Isaac Norris, Robert Jones,* and *John Wright,* be a Committee to prepare and bring in a bill for naturalizing such foreign Protestants as are settled or shall settle, in this Province, who, not being of the People called *Quakers,* do conscientiously refuse the Taking of any Oath; then the House adjourned to Ten a Clock To-Morrow Morning.[82]

Document 3
[November 4, 1742]

A Petition from a considerable Number of *German* Protestants, setting forth, that being formerly Subjects to the Emperor of *Germany,* and other foreign Princes in Amity with the King of Britain, they had, by the Encouragement given by the late Proprietary, and in Hopes of enjoying the Privileges of *British* Subjects, transported themselves and estates into this Province; but being, tho' not *Quakers*, conscientiously scrupulous of taking any Oath, they cannot, as the Law now stands, be naturalized; and praying that a Law may be passed in their Favour on that Account; was read:

And some of the Petitioners attending without, and desiring to be heard on their Petition, were called in, and heard accordingly; And being informed that the House had already sent up a general Bill to the Governor, in Favour of all in their Circumstances, they withdrew; then the House adjourned to Three a Clock in the Afternoon.[83]

Document 4
[January 12, 1743]

The House met, &c.

The Governor, by his Secretary, sent down the Bill for naturalizing such foreign Protestants as are settled, or shall settle, in this Province, who, not being of the People called *Quakers*, do conscientiously refuse the Taking of any Oath, with a written Message, to the House, which was read by Order, and follows in these Words, *viz.*

GENTLEMEN,

As the Bill, intituled, *An Act for the Relief of the Heirs, Devisees and Assigns, of Persons born out of the King's Liegance*, &c. seems to me to affect the Rights of the Honourable the Proprietaries, I think myself obliged, in Duty and Justice, to make them acquainted with it, and shall therefore decline any Observations of my own upon it, until I receive theirs. Since they have not taken any Advantage hitherto of the Heirs of such Foreigners as have, *Bona Fide*, purchased and paid for Lands, and have died unnaturalized, future Severities are the less to be apprehended from them.

Upon a Review of the King's Attorney and Sollicitor General's Report on a supplementary Act, prescribing the Forms of Declaration of Fidelity, &c. passed since my Coming to the Government, and his Majesty's Disallowance of it, I am of Opinion, that a Naturalization Bill, in the Method usual here, or a Bill with a particular Designation of all the religious Societies of Foreigners that conscientiously refuse the taking of any Oath, will be more likely to receive the Royal Approbation, than the Bill now before me, as either of them will be less dangerous to Society in general, and be more conformable to the *British* Acts of Parliament.

George Thomas

January 12, 1742-3.[84]

Document 5
[January 13, 1743]

The House resuming the Consideration of the Bill, intituled, An Act for naturalizing such foreign Protestants as are settled, or shall settle, in this Province, who not being of the People called Quakers, *do conscientiously refuse the Taking of an Oath,* and the Amendment proposed to the same;

Resolved, That *Owen Evans* and *Samuel Lewis* wait upon the Governor with the said Bill, and acquaint him, that as the Indulgence granted by the Act for Advancement of Justice (approved of in *England*) to those who conscientiously scruple an Oath, is general, the House are of Opinion, that the Bill, in the Terms it is now conceived, will best answer the Purposes intended; and therefore they hope the Governor will give his Assent to the Bill as it is now formed; nevertheless, that if the Governor shall persist in his Sentiments that the Names of the several religious Societies ought to be inserted, rather than the Bill should miscarry, the House are willing to agree to the Amendment proposed.[85]

Document 6
[January 14, 1743]

A Message from the Governor by his Secretary, *viz.*

Mr. Speaker,

"The Governor commands me to acquaint the House, that the Act for the Advancement of Justice had been under his Consideration before he proposed the Amendment to the Bill for naturalizing foreign Protestants, &c. and he had observed that the Indulgence is general; yet he was and is of opinion, that the Inserting the Names of the religious Societies of Foreigners, will render the Bill less liable to Objection in *England,* as it will be more conformable to the *British* Acts of Parliament: Should the House, however, continue to think otherwise, he is willing to waive the Amendment, rather than the Bill should be postponed for such a Length of Time as it may require to inform himself of the several Religious Societies of Foreigners that conscientiously refuse to take an Oath."

Resolved, N.C.D., That the House adhere to the Bill.[86]

Document 7

The House, according to Leave given the Fourteenth past, resolved itself into a Committee of the whole House upon the Governor's Support. . . .

And the House taking the same into Consideration,

Resolved, That on the Passage of such Bills as now lie before the Governor, the Naturalization Bill, and such other Bills as may be presented to him during this Sitting, there be paid him the Sum of *Five Hundred Pounds.*[87]

Method of Naturalization

Christopher Sauer, the Germantown printer, gave a clear explanation of the method of naturalization in his *Pennsylvanische Berichte* for April 1, 1755. The use of the Lord's Supper to reinforce an oath of allegiance was to be expected in the State Church tradition common to both the British Empire and the German homelands of the newly naturalized British subjects. This requirement was waived for those who affirmed their allegiance. The exclusion of Catholics from citizenship was based on the belief that the pope could absolve them of allegiance to the king and the oath of allegiance included renunciation of both the pope and the Jacobite Pretender. Pennsylvania and Maryland Catholics owned land and had their churches open for public worship without any difficulty at this time.

Document 8

Germantown

Upon request it was reported in the preceding issue that Germans can be naturalized on April 10 and on September 25. In order that no one may come in vain and be rejected until later, they must know: 1) that one must have been in this country or within English borders for seven years without having been out for two months; 2) Everyone who gives the oath must have received the sacrament within the past 12 weeks; he must bring a certificate from the minister, signed by two witnesses, that he belongs to that faith and that they saw him take the sacrament at the time the preacher gave in the certificate, and its date cannot be over, but must be under 12 weeks old, or he will be rejected; 3) Those who refuse to render the oath and say they are Mennonites or Separatists must make the Quaker attestation, and vow with "Yea" to keep faithfully what the rest have sworn to do; 4) None can be accepted with the name of Catholic. Furthermore, the excuse that the pastor did not offer communion during the specified time is not valid, for he is obligated to give it if it is requested by the one seeking naturalization.[88]

Mennonites Face the Real Meaning of "Fidelity"

In 1755, with war clouds on the horizon, Lancaster Mennonites appealed to the Provincial Assembly of Pennsylvania, claiming that they had not been familiar enough with the English language to comprehend the real meaning of their declarations of fidelity. They were afraid that the pledge to defend the king might require them to take up arms, which, of course, they could not do under any circumstances.

Document 9

To the Honourable the House of Representatives for the Province of Pennsylvania in General Assembly conven'd in Philadelphia May the 15th 1755.

The Humble Petition of the Elders, and Presbyters of the Church which is called the Menunists in and about Lancaster and the parts there adjacent.

May it please the Honourable House to permit your Petitioners to lay before you Some of our Grievances we lye under at present: and as it will be impossible to represent the case, without being something tedious, We Humbly pray you would exercise your Patience with respect to it.

It is a matter of deep concern to your petitioners when we reflect on the Naturalization Oath, that was administered to us, when we first arrived in this Country; it being exceedingly repugnant to the Articles of our Faith, and our consciences not able to comply with the tenor of it. At the time we were qualified, when Naturalized, none of your Petitioners were acquainted with the English tongue; and we quickly found, the Translation of the Oath into Dutch, to be very wrong; which was done by some of our own people, who presumed to instruct us into the Nature of it, but was not capable themselves to conceive the meaning of the same by which means, we were Innocently brought into a Difficulty, which has occasion'd to your Petitioners much concern and Perplexity.

Therefore, we confess and acknowledge with Grief of Heart, that by so doing we have Transgressed against the Lord our God, by not more Strictly examining the nature of our Qualification before we were Qualified; and that we Omitted the compareing the Translation with the Original in a word by acting so Implicitly.

May it please the Honourable House to permit us to declare, what we are willing to be Qualified unto or rather that we would with the utmost Cheerfullness perform (for the taking of an Oath in any manner is what we are prohibited from in our Articles of Faith). We do with the utmost fidelity acknowledge George upon the British Throne to be our lawful King and Sovereign, we Gladly own him as such, and accounts our Selves faithfull & Loyal Subjects to his Majesty, being willing and ready to Submit and to be faithfull and obedient to him his Heirs and Successors. This we are willing to evidence by a Cheerfullness to pay the duty, Tax, &c. that the Laws of Great Britain, and this Province requires, and to comply with every other particular relating thereunto wherein our consciences are free and clear.

So far we have Divine Authority for, from the Injunction of Christ and his Apostles, Our Lord desires that we render to Cesar, the things that are Cesar's, and to God, the things [that] are God's. Therefore we conclude that it is our Incumbent duty to render what Tribute, Duty or Tax is required to our King and Sovereign. We are likewise Authorized from the Mosaic dispensation to acknowledge that the Legislative Administration is commited to the care of Kings, who if faithful are to be acknowledged as Servants of God, and as Paul Teacheth such Shall be honoured as a Protector, and as one that beareth not the Sword in vain, who is a Terror to evil doers, and a praise to them that do well. In this manner we are oblidg'd to revere his Majesty, and to endeavor according to our Stations, and agreeable to the dictates of our consciences, to render his administration as little Burthensome as possible, and this we think may be done without going Counter to the express prohibitions recorded in the Sacred Oracles, viz. of Testifying our Loyalty by defending him with Sword in hand. In those Divine Oracles we are injoin'd to Love our Enemies to bless them that curse us, and to pray for them that despitefully use us and persecute us, and those who follows these injunctions, are Characterized as Children of the most High. But how to reconcile this Sacred Text with the Tenor of the Naturalization Oath, is to us absolutely impossible, and cannot, without giving our Consciences the greatest violent Attempt to reconcile them. In this Oath, we are bound to help to maintain the Title and Reign of his Majesty, and to defend him with Heart, Hands and Life, not only against the Pretender, but likewise against all his other Enemies. But we must Humbly reply, that we cannot nor dare not, promise this in so extensive a manner. We are willing as far as we have the divine assistance, to pray for the King, that he may have a long and prosperous Reign, that his life may be one continued Scene of Peace and felicity that he and all his Royal Issue may live continually here under the Divine protection, and hereafter in the full fruition of Immortal Bliss; And more than this we dare not consistant with Peace of Conscience, comply with, it is our fixed principle rather than take up Arms in order to defend our King, our Country, or our Selves, to Suffer all that is dear to us to be rend from us, even Life it Self, and this we Think not out of Contempt to Authority, but that herein we act agreeable to what we think is the mind and Will of our Lord Jesus.

Your Petitioners not being willing to detain you any longer would only just obviate an Objection that perhaps might arise to what has been said. First some may be ready to Say that the Menunists, now hearing that an invasion is threatned by the French on this Colony, Therefore we would endeavor to Screen our Selves from lending our Assistance against the Invader. But to this we Humbly reply That God Who knoweth our Hearts, and the most Secret design therein knoweth that this is not the cause of this present procedure, but that it is only a Sense of command of God upon us forbidding us to take up Arms against any, And that it is out of obedience to the Divine precept, and consequently to the discharge of a Good conscience, that excites us to Address the Worthy Members, and would humbly intreat you would not once imagine that we have taken offence at the former Proceedings of the Assembly respecting our People, and the Qualification Administered to us, and taken by us out of Ignorance. No, we assure you we retain in no manner any dislike either to the Governor, or the worthy Members, but with the utmost Sincerity wisheth peace and happiness to you.

Your Petitioners therefore requests that the Honourable House may allow us the Priviledge Granted in William Penn's Charter for this Province, that all the Inhabitants (behaving themselves Honestly), that their Consciences be by no means molested, and the form of the Naturalization Oath with respect to the Menunists may have such Alterations, as they may in their Conscience be free to take, and this to extend not only to those in this Country who are not yet Naturalized, but also to Such who may yet arrive in this Province.

And Lastly, we intreat the Worthy Members, that your Sentiments with regard to this Important Point may be Sent to us at your next Adjournment. We Cannot but encourage our Selves that requests so reasonable, will obtain an Answer which will fill our Hearts with Joy and Gladness and Inviolably oblidge your Petitioners as in Duty bound to pray.

Hanss Schantz	*Hanss Meier*	*Jost Mosser*
Aberham Reist	*Christian Wenger*	*Benni Landiss*
Jacob Graft	*Ulerich Rott*	*Jacob Mardi*[89]
Benss Hirschi	*Carli Christofel*	
Jackob Böhn	*Mardin Behr*	

Wagons for the Army

Benjamin Franklin's Handbill

Virginia and Maryland had failed to produce the horses and wagons promised to haul baggage and supplies for General Sir Edward Braddock's army and Sir John St. Clair, Braddock's quartermaster, suggested that wagons be secured from the "Dutch settlers at the foot of the Blue Ridge." When he realized not enough teams could be found there, he threatened to impress teams in Pennsylvania. By April 1755, Braddock and St. Clair were angry at Pennsylvania's lack of progress in constructing a military road and accused the Pennsylvanians of disloyalty.

The alleged disloyalty of the Germans was proven false when Benjamin Franklin called for horses and wagons to carry provisions for the Braddock expedition. Franklin had visited the general in his camp at Frederick, Maryland, and promised to improve on the poor response of Maryland and Virginia. Proceeding to Lancaster, where the county court was in session, he prevailed upon the judge to make a speech to a large gathering, mostly German farmers, telling them that he had been commissioned to procure 150 wagons and as many horses as possible. By publishing a handbill with appeals to the farmers in Lancaster, York, and Cumberland counties and by using a blend of encouragement and threats of coercion, Franklin was able to get more wagons than requested within three days.

Document 10

After the governors of Boston, New York, and Pennsylvania, accompanied by several gentlemen, came to General Braddock in camp, he assigned to Mr. Franklin the arrangement for wagons and horses; this Mr. Franklin took upon himself and had the following advertisement posted in various places.

Lancaster, April 26, 1755

Since 150 wagons with 4 horses for each wagon and 1,500 saddle or work horses are wanted for the service of His Majesty's forces, which are now about to assemble at Will's Creek; and since it is the pleasure of His Excellency General Braddock to authorize me to pay for the horses and wagons, I herewith announce that I will stay in Lancaster until next Wednesday evening; in York from next Thursday forenoon to Friday evening, at which places I shall be ready to make an agreement on wagons and teams or single horses on the following terms:

1. For each wagon with four good horses and a driver the pay will be 15 shillings per day. And for every dependable horse with a pack, saddle and bridle, two shillings per day. And for every dependable horse without a saddle, eighteen pence per day.

2. Pay commences from the time of their joining the Forces at Will's Creek (which must be on or before May 20) and a reasonable allowance will be made over and above for the time necessary for travel to Will's Creek and home again.

3. Each wagon and team, and every saddle or pack horse, is to be valued by indifferent persons, chosen between me and the owner, and in case of the loss of any wagon, team or horse, recompense will be made according to such valuation.

4. Seven day's pay is to be advanced and paid by me to the owner of each wagon and team, or horse, at the time of contracting; and the remainder to be paid by General Braddock, or by the Army Paymaster, at the Camp, at the time of discharge.

5. No drivers or persons who take care of horses shall be obligated to perform military service or be employed in some other duty in addition to looking after and taking care of their loads and horses.

6. Oats, corn and other feed brought to the camp by the horses or wagons in excess of what is needed for the care of the horses will be taken for use by the army and a reasonable price will be paid for it.

Note. My son, William Franklin, is also authorized to make agreements with persons in Cumberland County.[90]

Document 11

What seems most remarkable is that all the Waggoners from Lancaster and York Counties, in this Province, who engaged in the Service of the Army, have returned safe but two, one of which died by sickness.[91]

Mennonite Participation and Compensation

Mennonites responded remarkably well to Franklin's appeal for wagons and teams for Braddock's army, making up perhaps 20 percent of the total number. Other Lancaster County farmers found that they had contributed pasturage to the army, when they discovered the horses and cattle of the retreating British column grazing in their meadows. Peter Swarr and John Brubaker petitioned the Assembly for damages. Both men were paid the full amount when accounts were settled for wagons and teams.

Document 12
[September 19, 1755]

A Petition from *Peter Schaur,* of the County of Lancaster, was presented to the House and read, setting forth, that when the Forces under Colonel [Thomas] Dunbar were at *Lancaster,* in their Way to *Philadelphia,* a considerable Number of Horses and Cattle belonging to them were put into the Petitioner's Meadow, and kept there for two Days, whereby the greatest Part of the Grass in the said Meadow was destroyed; that the Damage done the Petitioner by the said Horses and Cattle was valued by *Jacob Myer,* and others, at *Eleven Pounds Seven Shillings;* the Petitioner therefore prays that this House would pay him for the Damage aforesaid.

Ordered to lie on the Table.

A Petition from *John Brubacker,* of Lancaster County, was presented to the House and read, setting forth, that a Considerable Number of Horses and Cattle, belonging to the Forces under Colonel *Dunbar,* were put into the Petitioner's Meadow, whereby a great part of the Grass in the said Meadow was destroyed; that *Jacob Myer,* and others, have valued the Damage done the Petitioner by the said Cattle and Horses at *Eight Pounds Five Shillings;* the Petitioner therefore prays that this House would pay him for the aforesaid Damage.

Ordered to lie on the Table.[92]

Payment for Wagons

Christopher Sauer reported in his *Pennsylvanische Berichte* for November 1, 1755, that all those who had supplied wagons and teams for the army under Braddock would be paid.

Document 13

Germantown

It is reliably reported that the King has sent money to pay the war expenses for the Ohio Expedition. The money has come and is ready, waiting for a safe opportunity; and so the drivers are hopeful that their horses and wagons will be paid for; they must only have patience until it arrives in Philadelphia. One hears that a number of people because of poverty have offered their horses and wagons, also draft and work horses, in order to earn some money from the army, who now believe that they have lost their wages as wagoners as well as the wagons and horses, and have offered for sale at a low price the documents and bonds which they got from Mr. Franklin. But since it later became known, on October 16, that the drivers were to be paid, it would be quite unfair if greedy rich people were to buy the bonds from the poor for less money than they had hoped; such gain would receive no blessing for it would be deceitful dealing. People should have patience that long.

The day on which the money is to be paid will be announced in the newspapers so that anyone who has demands may be able to present himself at the designated time.

The above report was announced by General Shirley (who has now been appointed as the chief general over all the armies in America), and he also ordered that no servant or apprentice would be accepted as a soldier; those who had already been enlisted were to be released.

A report has recently arrived by a ship from England that General Braddock wrote a letter to his superiors in London in which he boasted how prompt and loyal the Pennsylvanians had been to aid the King's troops with horses, wagons and everything they needed; whereas, on the contrary, other colonies though to be sure promising much, kept few of the promises.

We also hear that the Germans, who had to pay 15 shillings for naturalization, shall get a Thaler back; but they will have to have patience until justice arrives.

Since the Germans in Pennsylvania have been painted so black in England, one might have supposed that the King would punish these obstinate rebels and rude boors with whips or discipline them with black scorpions; but, on the contrary, he is sending them so much money that the loyal and industrious Germans will get paid for their service as drivers, and for their wagons and horses, since General Braddock wrote to England so glowingly about the Pennsylvanians. He is indeed a good King![93]

Settling Claims

On January 31, 1756, Governor Robert Hunter Morris appointed Edward Shippen, Samuel Morris, Alexander Stedman, and Samuel McCall, Jr., as Commissioners to "audit, liquidate, and settle" the accounts of the owners of all wagons, teams, and horses hired for the expedition against Fort Duquesne. Edward Shippen kept a careful account of the 144 claims he and the others had to settle. Many of the men who went with their wagons and teams on Braddock's disastrous march were apparently Mennonite, as these claims settled at Lancaster on February 4 and 5, 1756, suggest.

Document 14

February 4.

J. CHRISTIAN HAIR, D[ebto]r.

To cash pd by Mr. Franklin	3	5	0
To ditto by Mr. Scott	1	2	6
To 5 days, a horse dying on ye journey		12	6
Bal[ance] due to Christian Hare	100	12	11
	£107	12	11

C[redito]r.

By waggon and team	66	0	0
By 51 days wagon hire, [at]15s	38	5	0
By expenses	3	7	11
	107	12	11

JACOB HARTMAN, Dr.

To cash pd by Mr. Franklin	5	5	0
Balance	99	7	11
	104	12	11

Cr.

By waggon and team	63	0	0
By 51 days waggon hire	38	5	0
By expenses	3	7	11
	104	12	11

MARTIN GROVE, Dr.

To cash pd by Mr. Franklin	5	5	0
To ditto pd by Mr. Scott	1	2	6
Bal. due to Martin Grove	83	10	5
	89	17	11

Cr.

By waggon and team	48	10	0
By 51 days wagon hire	38	5	0
By expenses	3	2	11
	89	17	11

February ye 5th.

VINCENT MYER, Dr.

To cash pd by Mr. Franklin	5	5	0
To the waggon	11	0	0
To a horse returned	12	0	0
Bal. due to V. Myer	76	2	11

Cr.

By waggon and team	49	0	0
By the hire of 3 horses fifty days at 2s.6d., with geers	18	15	0
By expenses	3	7	11
By the waggoner's service, 30 days	5	0	0
	£76	2	11[94]

Mennonites "Wholeheartedly" Supply Military Needs

Edward Shippen was authorized to obtain wagons and teams in Lancaster County for military operations against the French and their Indian allies in western Pennsylvania and to supply Colonel Henry Bouquet's forces with provisions and fodder for this 1759 campaign. Once again Mennonites cooperated wholeheartedly in meeting this military need, as letters that passed between Shippen and Bouquet indicate. They probably supplied wagons and teams for General Forbes' successful expedition against Fort Duquesne in 1758, as the fourth letter in this series speaks of farmers in Donegal Township in Lancaster County who had still not been paid for wagons provided for Forbes the previous year, but no specific records of this have been located. Quakers expressed concern about their members who furnished wagons for the 1758 campaign. Mennonites not only approved of supplying wagons and produce to the army in 1759, but were willing to "mention it at their Meetings next Sunday."

Colonel Henry Bouquet, a Swiss professional soldier, entered the British service in 1756 and served continuously in America until his death in 1766. His papers are in the British Museum, including the originals of Shippen's letters to him. The other side of their correspondence is in the Shippen Papers in the Historical Society of Pennsylvania.

Document 15

Lancaster 24th May 1759.

Sir

I informed you by the Post that there was no meeting of the Menists at Landis', according to appointment; this, I have understood Since, was owing intirely to a mistake, & not to their want of Zeal for his Majesty's service; however I am going amongst them this morning again, and make no doubt but I shall find them very hearty in the Cause.

I have written to our Magistrates about the Country, and inclosed an advertisement to each of them. Please to send me more advertisements, Mr. Ourrey having, brought me but a quarter of a hundred. He paid me £2116..00.06. I shall write you again next Monday of our Success in Sending off Waggons with forage. Bags are making of Ozenbrigs & Ticklinburgs & other Stuff & best I can find, tho' these Sorts are scarce. I mentioned the Article of Bagging in my Letter by the Post. I am

Sir

Your Most Humble serv[an]t

Edwd. Shippen.[95]

Document 16

Philadelphia 25th May 1759.

Dear Sir

I receiv__d your favours of the 23rd & 24th Inst. I was glad to See that the disapointment you met with from the Mennonists was not owing to their want of zeal for the Service, & I hope you have by this time Settled Matters with them to your Satisfaction.

I Send you more Advertisements, and wish they may have the desired Effect, being Supported by your Letters to the Magistrates of each Township. Please to forward to Mr. Stevenson at York 100 of the Advertisements not Signed, with the Stuff to make 400 Baggs. 400 hundret Should also be Sent to Col. Weiser at Reading, or more if they can collect forrage. 1,000 to Carlisle with 50 Advertisements, directed to Colonel Armstrong.

Forrage must be collected with all possible Speed, without raising the Price, either oats, spelts, or Rye. I beg you will employ without noise as many People as you think proper, allowing them a Dollar Commission for Every hundred Bushells they purchase. The £250 of Mr. Hubley have been payd, when I have the Pleasure to See you, We Shall include that Sum in your Receipts.

The old Landisville Mennonite meetinghouse was one of the places where Lancaster County Mennonite farmers met with British officials to hear of the need for wagons and teams and demonstrate their "zeal for his Majesty's service" by supplying horses, wagons, hay, and fodder. (Photograph by Carolyn Charles, 1977.)

The General waits only for Waggons to move the Troops forward, Therefore I beg that no means be left untried to dispatch a Brigade or two immediately with forrage. Flour will be carried for the present by Messrs. Scott, Stoner, Lesher & others.

I shall be glad to hear of your Success and remain

Your most obed[ien]t h[um]ble Servant
Henry Bouquet.

Document 17

Dear Sir 26th May 1759

The General has ordered that one hundred of the Waggon Horses bought by Capt. Hambright be sent to Bedford, with large Baggs of forrage, and no Saddles. They are to replace at Carlisle what they will consume upon the Road. A Waggonmaster will be sent to Lancaster to take charge of them, with Drivers. I beg you would give orders that these Horses be Shod, and if Drivers can be got in your County to engage them at 3 shillings per day, besides the Provisions. Mr. Price must see this is done and the Horses properly formed in Teams. The Geers and Waggons will be provided at Bedford. I Send you by Lieut. McDougall of the R[oyal] A[merican] R[egiment] £400 Currency, for which you will give him a Receipt. Money being wanted at Carlisle, I beg you will send £500 Curry. to Col. Armstrong; I shall forward more money by the first opportunity.

Henry Bouquet

The Baggs for oats are to contain Seven Bushells.[96]

Document 18

Dear Sir Lancaster, 30th May 1759

Your kind favour of the 25th Instant I received with Four hundred Pounds *P* Lieutenant [Mc]Dougal and according to your Orders have sent Col. Armstrong five hundred pounds by Jno. Hays. (Mr. Jno. Hays is a Commissr. for this County & is the Waggon Master and gone with this Brigade) And the Letters under your Cover I immediately sent away by Express, a lively Spry fellow, with the Advertisements, for Mr. Stevenson and Colo. Armstrong.

Twenty Waggons are gone off, Eighteen to proceed to Rays Town, & two only to Carlisle, and One to [Fort] Loudoun.

The Nine Waggoners who came first to Town where chiefly Menists, and tho', they were very willing to go, yet we had a good deal of trouble with them on one Acct., the getting them to take good Loads of Oats: and if Mr. Price (while I was absent) had not promised to be contented with their taking only about 36 bushels each they would not have gone without being prepar[ed?], which would have caused the greatest Confusion imagineable at this time; their Excuse was, want of room, as they had 35 bushels of Oats & a great deal of Cut Straw & several bundles of hay of their own to carry; & to take more of us, than ye Quantity above mentioned would have raised their Loads too high & so a part liable to fall off on ye Road. The two Waggons which are only to go to Carlisle carrying but little provender, took In 90 Bushels each, to be paid 4/-[shillings] per Cwt. gross weight, paying their Own ferriage: this is a very common price, so Mr. Price says. Stoner sent 2 Load of Flour, and there is 4 barrels in Pughs Waggon and the rest of the Waggons are well loaded, but all with ye Kings Stores, we being obliged to endeavour to please Every body as far as we could in order to make a Beginning.

We find great Difficulty in getting Forage, Bar & Slough having purchased but 1800 bushels Oats & I have rec'v'd None from anybody else. Stoner has been in quest of Spelts but could get None under 2/6 & upwards. Forage would come in fast enough would we give an extortionate price for it. A farmer within 5 Miles of this Borough has between two and 300 bushels of Oats by him; but it seems he cant, i.e. he wont Spare any at 2/- Per bushel without Compulsion.

I have employed four good Hands to buy Oats at 2/- [shillings] & Spelts &ca. &c. And Hans Bar is gone to Tulpehockin to try what quantity he can purchase there. . . .

I wrote last week to all our Magistrates to do their utmost to in procuring Waggons with ye greatest Expedition, but have yet had no Answer, except from Justice Galbreath in Dounogal [Donegal] Township, who only promises a Couple, he says the people are not able to provide Waggons and horses for want of Money & that most of the people thereabouts are in debt for ye Waggons & horses which they furnished out for General Forbes. How it is I cant say, but ye General Complaint of ye people is want of pay for past Services, which disables them from doing what otherwise they are willing to do; but however I expect more encouraging Acco[un]ts from other Quarters of the County but yet I apprehend We Shall be greatly disappointed in getting ye Waggons.

The Waggons already sent off are directed to the Care of Mr. Daniel Clarke at Carlisle by advice of his father In Law Mr. Hoops. You will please to give me full directions as to this, or any thing also which the General orders to be done.

The Express above mentioned is to go no further with ye Letters aforesaid than to Carlisle if Colo. Armstrong should have an Express ready to proceed On with them. If I dont hear from ye rest of Our Magistrates to Night I shall send Expresses to them to morrow to know what Waggons the General may certainly depend Upon; and at ye same time I shall not omit to Mention ye Article of forage. I shall also assure them that In Case the People do not exert themselves to the last degree at this Critical Juncture (making no more Excuses about things that cannot now be helped) for his Majesties Service, That Measures must be speedily taken to Compel them to their Duty.

I had not time to write you yesterday by Johny Piper ye Express who carried down the disagreeable News of ye Defeat of our large Party going between Ligonier & Pitsburg escorting provisions. I am deeply concerned to hear of this. Your Noble General & Self may depend upon it that my whole Attention Shall be on the Service I have ye honour to be employed about, & that I am with very great Esteem

His & Your most obedt. Humble Serv[ant].

Edw: Shippen

please to Excuse blots &c.[97]

Document 19

Lancaster the 17th August 1759

Dear Sir,

To Day I received the favour of your Letter of the 13th Instant being the same day I wrote you by an Express who came from Carlisle, & sent you a State of our Waggons and Said Something of forage. Just as your Letter abovementioned came to hand I was alighting from my horse having been part of these two days amongst the Menonists treating with them about Waggons & forage, in the former of which, they Say they have done their Share; but will do more; and as to the latter they are to mention it at their Meetings next Sunday & hope to be able to persuade one another to set about threshing out their Oats and Spelts immediately afterwards. Great part of the oats have not been in the Barns three days & the farmers Say it Should sweat in the Mow ten or 12 days; but I think I can persuade them to begin to thresh next monday. I can step out four or five miles now and then without being much missed at home by Waggoners going out, & coming home.

Inclosed is Mr. Prices Acco[un]t of the Waggons sent to Bedford Since the 10th Instant. . . .

Tomorrow I shall send Duplicates of General Stanwixs Letter to my Self and Others concerned in procuring Waggons, To all our

Magistrates; and Shall at the same time write to them in a very pressing manner to endeavour to induce the people to begin to thresh out their grain for forage for the Kings horses and to send it to me immediately. I am writing a few Lines to the General and Shall to the utmost of my Power endeavour to obey both Your Commands, being with great Regard

Dear Sir

Your Most Obedt. Humble servt.

Edwd. Shippen[98]

Indian Raids and Demands for a Militia

Militia Bill Proposed

With Braddock's army marching against the French at Fort Duquesne in June 1755, the governor of Pennsylvania called on his Assembly to appropriate money for defensive measures on the exposed frontier and to vote for a militia bill. The Quakers in the Assembly, like Mennonites and other nonresistants, had always refused to enact any form of compulsory military service and refused to act on this request for a militia act.

Document 20

[June 17, 1755]

The Governor, by the Secretary, sent down to the House a Message in Writing, which was read, and is as follows, *viz.*

GENTLEMEN,

"I have lately received Intelligence, and sent the same forward to the General, that several Bodies of Troops have passed from *Canada* over the Lake *Ontario* in their Way to the *Ohio,* to join the Forces already there; that the *French* are using their utmost Endeavors to engage the *Indians* to take Part with them in this Dispute, and are determined to oppose General *Braddock,* though it should require the whole Force of *Canada.* There is also great Reason to apprehend that when the *English* Army is removed to a considerable Distance, the *French* and their *Indians* will fall upon the Inhabitants of the Back Country, and either cut off or greatly interrupt the Communication between us and the Army, which will be attended with very fatal Consequences both with respect to our People and the King's Troops employed for our Protection. . . .

I must also recommend it to you, Gentlemen, by a proper Militia Law, to put this Province into such a Posture of Defence, that the Inhabitants may not be exposed to the cruel Incursions of the Enemy.

If a Number of Men should be raised and supported by this Province, as there are by almost every other Colony upon the Continent, they might not only serve as Escorts, but might join the General, if the Numbers brought against him should make such a Re-enforcement necessary. But if these Things be not done, and the Army, by being weakened, should be defeated, or rendered unable to perform the Service they are destined for, or, should they be distressed for Want of necessary Provisions, I am fearful the Blame will be laid principally upon this Province, as we are most immediately concerned, and best able to prevent these Mischiefs.

When I consider, Gentlemen, the Duty we owe his Majesty, and our Mother Country, who have sent these Troops to recover what we have suffered to be invaded: when I reflect on the Regard we ought to have for the Safety of those Men that are employed in that Service, how much the future Prosperity and Happiness of this Country depends upon their Success, and how easy it will be for this Province, rich and flourishing as it is, to contribute to that Success, by your doing what I have now recommended, I will not suffer myself to doubt but that you will enter immediately into these Matters, and without Delay take the proper Steps, and grant the necessary Supplies, for carrying them into Execution.

Philadelphia, June 17, 1755.

Robert Hunter Morris."[99]

First Indian Raid

The first blow fell on the Pennsylvania frontier on the Penn's Creek settlement near present Selinsgrove, where Delawares killed or carried off 25 persons on October 16, 1755. This settlement was on disputed land, for the Delawares insisted they had not sold the Shamokin area to the whites. An account of the massacre was included in a letter sent by three Swiss Mennonites to friends at home, indicating that some of the victims were personally known to them. Only a fragment of the original letter was published by Ernst Muller in 1895. He noted that this and other letters from Pennsylvania were then in the possession of a Mennonite family in the Canton of Bern, but their present whereabouts is unknown. Ulrich Engel, one of the three writers, was the father of Jacob Engel, the founder of the Brethren in Christ Church.

Document 21

Ulrich Engel, Christen Brechbühl and Isaak Neuenschwander

write on Dec. 7, 1755, from "Danigall" in Pennsylvania, that Hans Jakob König [LeRoy], or the dyer from Sonceboz, left his wife and the younger children with an Abraham Zerr in "Canenstoga," but he with his son and daughter and "Odina from Dramlingen" as servant went out and settled on the frontier towards the savages at a place called "Schamogen" along with several other households. The savages complained that "they come too far out into their land and often warned them to leave or expect misfortune, but they refused to be warned, then the savages fell upon them rashly, miserably destroyed six families, burned their houses, killed thirteen persons in all and took away the others, among whom the dyer, it is said, was pitiably killed and murdered; his son and daughter and the aforementioned servant they took away, meanwhile Hans Jakob Willar's daughter also escaped, and later towards the borders they committed several more murders, which aroused a great fear in the land." This letter is also to be shared with "our people at Rotenbühl."[100]

Defense Problems Increase

Conrad Weiser reported to William Allen about rumors of Indians and the readiness of Berks County settlers to fight, adding that even a Mennonite had turned out to serve with Weiser's volunteer company in Tulpehocken. When the Indians actually struck at Tulpehocken two weeks later, the alarm bells rang in Reading and frightened settlers turned their resentment against the few Quakers living there. Both of these letters were used by Governor Morris to increase pressure on the Assembly to vote for a militia bill.

Document 22

Reading, October 30th, 1755.

Kind Sir:

I have but just time to acknowledge the receipt of your Favours of the 27th, being arrived last Night in this town; as you will have the perusal of the Letter I wrote to the Governor, I need not repeat matters over, but only informing that I think all our Indians are gone off with the French, or rather joined them because they could not stand their Ground against the French and their Indians; and what is worse I am afraid the French are about Fortifying themselves this side of the Allegheny Hills, if not on Sasquehanna about Shamokin, where they will find and have found plenty of Provisions, as the Country is deserted by its Inhabitants, leaving their Corn and Cattle behind them. The reason of my fear is because Mr. Adam Read told me that a Young man lately arrived on Sasquehanna from Ohio, who said for positive that about 1, 500 French and Indians crossed Allegheny Hills at the Head of Rinacson River, and that actually a part of them had been at Shamokin, which last proves to be true as you will see in the Governor's Letter that the Young man I mentioned was taken Prisoner by the French last summer in the unhappy action, & some Delaware Indians got his liberty from the French, promising two scalps from Pennsylvania, and they the Indians set him at Liberty, or he made his escape as far as Adam Read's. He also gave out that the Enemy told the Delawares that if they would assist they would repossess them of their native Country and bring the people under their Command. The common cry of the People here is for Arms & Ammunition & Regulations from the Governor and Assembly. I believe the people in general up here would fight. I had two or three long Beards in my Company, one a Menonist who declared he would live and die with his neighbours; he had a good gun with him. I must conclude and subscribe myself.

Honoured Sir, Yours &ca.

Conrad Weiser[101]

Document 23

[November 16, 1755.]

My dearest Father:

I'm in so much horror and Confusion I scarce know what I am writing. The Drum is beating to Arms, and Bells ringing & all the people under Arms. Within these two hours we have had different tho' too uncertain Acc[oun]ts all corroborating each other, and this moment is an Express arrived dispatch'd from Michael Reis' at Tulpehoccon, 18 Miles above this Town, who left about 30 of their people engaged with about an equal number of Indians at the sd. Reis'. This night we expect an attack, truly alarming is our situation. The people exclaim against the Quakers, & some are scarce restrained from burning the Houses of those few who are in this Town. Oh my Country! my bleeding Country! I recommend myself to the divine God of Armies. Give my dutiful love to my dearest Mother, and my best love to Brother Jemmy.

I am, Honoured Sir, Your most affectionate & obedient Son,

E. Biddle[102]

Panic and Petitions

Panic was also spreading on the York County frontier. The county magistrates, including Herman Updegraff, a Quaker, petitioned the governor for arms and ammunition and money to pay men to guard the frontier. George Stevenson, one of the magistrates, bombarded the authorities in Philadelphia with letters and petitions to the same effect. One of the many petitions he forwarded was signed mainly by Mennonites, but as no copy of it is known to be extant we have no way of knowing what was said in their petition or even whether it was that presented on November 7, asking for arms and ammunition, although this seems most probable.

Document 24

May it please your Honour,

We receiv'd sundrie Accts, lately, all concuring in this, that a numerous Body of Indians & some French are in this Province, which has put the Inhabitants here in the greatest Confusion, the principal of whom have met sundrie Times, & on examination find that many of us have neither Arms nor Ammunition.

Herewith we send a Copy of an Express just arived from John Harris's Ferry, by way of James Anderson, with Intelligence that the Indians are encamp'd up Susquehannah within a Day or two's March of that Place and 'tis probable, before this comes to Hand, Part of these back Counties may be destroyed.

We believe there are Men enough willing to bear Arms & go out against the Enemy, were they supplied with Arms, Ammunition & a reasonable Allowance for their Time, but without this, at least Arms and Ammunition, we fear little to purpose can be done.

If some Measures, are not speedily fallen upon, we must either sit at home till we are butcher'd without Mercy or Resistance, run away, or go out a confused Multitude destitute of Arms & Ammunition & without Discipline or proper Officers, or any way fixed on to be supplied with Provisions.

In short we know not what to do, & have not Time to deliberate.

As the Company who go, from this Town & the Parts adjacent, to Morrow, to the Assistance of the Inhabitants on our Frontiers, will take almost all our Arms & Ammunition with them, We humbly pray your Honour to order us some Arms & Ammunition, otherwise we must desert our Habitations.

We have sent the Bearer Express with this Letter, and also a Petition to the Assembly, which our People were signing, when the Express came to Hand.

We humbly hope your Honour will excuse this Freedom, which our Distress has obliged us to use, and beg leave to subscribe ourselves,

Honoured Sir,

your most obedient Humble Servts.
Geo. Stevenson *Thos. Annor* *John Adlum*
Her. Updegraff *James Smith*

York Saturday 11 O'Clock, P.M.
1st Novr. 1755
[Endorsed] Letter from the Magistrates of York County to the Govr.[103]

Document 25

Dear Sir,

By the Expresses which, I suppose, more than Daily come to yr. Hand from the Frontier Parts of this Province, you can conceive the Confusion, Horror & Distress, with which every Breast is filled; All possible Attempts have been made here to Stockade this Town, but in Vain. . . . We have sent down a Petition by the Bearer sign'd in about a quarter of an Hour, whilst we were yet signing it We rec'ed the Express from Harris's, a Copy of which we have sent to the Governor, together with a Letter, five of us have made bold to write to him on this Important Subject. I beg you will use your Influence with the Governor and Mr. Allen, to whom I made free to write two days ago. I am so fatigued with the People, & 'tis now so late that I must conclude.

Dr. Sr.,
yr. most obliged
& obedient Servt.,
Geo. Stevenson

York, 12 O'Clock, Saturday Night, 1st Nov., 1755
Mr. Peters.[104]

Document 26

Dr. Sr.

Herewith you have a Copy of Ben Chamber's Letter, rece'd about an hour ago. We have formed a Counsil here of the Principal Inhabitants, who join with me in beging you to deliver the Petition & Copy of Letter herewith sent, to the Speaker of the Assembly, and pray them in our Names & behalf, for God's sake either to send us Arms, Ammunition & Blankets, and a Letter to encourage the People, & assure us of what we may expect, or else our Country will be deserted. The Bearer waits, I refer you to our Letter & other papers sent to the Governor. I am, Dr. Sr., in the greatest Distress,

Yrs most affectionately,
Geo. Stevenson

York, Monday, Nov. 3, ½ an hour past 11 A.M.
To Richard Peters, Esq., Secry. of the Province of Pennsylvania.[105]

Document 27
[November 5, 1755.]

A Petition from sundry Inhabitants of the Town and County of *York* was presented to the House and read, setting forth, that the Petitioners find Numbers in the said County willing to inlist, and bear Arms for the Defence of the Frontiers during the Continuance of the present Troubles, if they had any Assurance of Arms, Ammunition, and reasonable Pay: That three Fourth of the Petitioners have neither Arms nor Ammunition, and cannot supply themselves therewith, and are moreover without any proper Regulation for their Conduct: That there are no Forts to shelter their Wives and Families during their Absence, should they go forth against their Enemies. The Petitioners therefore pray that this House would take the Premises into Consideration and enact such Law or Laws as they shall judge best adapted to remedy the same.

Ordered to lie on the table.[106]

Document 28
Dr. Sir:

As the Bearer carries the same News to you which he brought to me, 'tis needless to say any thing about that.

We have sent 53 Men, well filed, from this Town last Monday, 2 o'clock P.M. & a Doctor, some Medicines & what Ammunition we could spare to Tobs. Hendrix's to join the main Body of English on the most needful Part of the Frontiers. Mr. Adlum is with them. Mr. Hamilton is gone towards Conigogeeg last Sunday with a Compy.

Mr. Bay yesterday with & at the Head of another. We are all aloft and such as have Arms hold themselves ready, but alas they are few in Number; 40 Men came here yesterday willing to defend, but had but 3 guns & no Ammunition, & could get none here, therefore went home again.

We stay all here yet, how long God knows, 6 Familys fled from their Homes, Dist[ant] about 15 miles viz: Canewago last Night, the last came into Town about Day Break This Morning. I am determined to stay & by the Assistance of Mr. Lispy & the other Justices on the spot Spirit up the People & keep 'em together (if possible,) till I hear from the Government.

A few of us have pledged our Credit for publick services, if we are encourag'd we will stand till we are cut off, if not or if no News comes to us (wch we shall construe as discouragemt.,) some of us are bound to the lower parts of Maryland immediately, if not scalp'd by the way.

Herewith you have another of our Petitions to the Assembly, all I shall say about it is that the bigest Part of its Signers are Menonists, who live about 15 miles westward of York.

Please to deliver it to the Assembly, the Express waits which hastens me to the only agreeable Part of my Letter, to my self & that is that in Peace or War, Comfort or Distress, I am, Dr. Sr., with great Esteem,

yr. most obedient Hble. Servt.

Geo. Stevenson

York, 11 o'clock, A.M. Wednesday 5th Novr.
Mr. Peters.[107]

Document 29

[November 7, 1755.]

A Petition from sundry Inhabitants of the Town and County of *York*, praying for Arms and Ammunition, was presented to the House and read, and

Ordered to lie on the Table.[108]

Document 30

[November 7, 1755.]

David M'Connaughy, returned a Representative for the County of *York*, appearing in the House, took and subscribed the Qualifications by Law appointed to be taken by Members of the Assembly, and then took his Seat in the House accordingly.

A Petition from a considerable Number of the Inhabitants of the Frontier Settlements, in the County of *York*, was presented to the House and read, setting forth, that a savage and cruel Enemy are at this Time upon our Borders, barbarously murdering our Friends and Fellow-Subjects, while the Petitioners are unable to afford them the wanted Assistance; that the Petitioners would have been in more unhappy Circumstances, were it not for the generous Supply of Arms and Ammunition sent them by this House, for which they beg Leave to return their hearty and most grateful Acknowledgments; that the said Arms and Ammunition are put into good Hands, by Means whereof those who have received them are spirited up to withstand the common Enemy. The Petitioners therefore pray, that the House would enable them yet more to shew with what Resolution they shall endeavor to defend their Lives and Properties, their King and Country.

Ordered to lie on the Table.[109]

Friends Refuse to Pay War Tax

Israel Pemberton, John Pemberton, John Churchman, and other weighty Friends signed a petition which they then presented to the Assembly on November 7, 1755. They were concerned about the bill for issuing £60,000 in paper currency to provide money for wartime expenses and sinking it by a tax of ten shillings a head on all taxable persons and sixpence in the pound on all taxable property. They bore their testimony that they could not in good conscience pay this tax, since it would involve giving their consent to military spending. They were aware that by insisting on the right to control all money raised and appropriated for government expenses, the elected representatives of the people in the Assembly would take on themselves the direction of the war effort and do it in the name of those they were chosen to represent. Granting the money "for the King's use" was an empty formula, since the king did not control its use, as at an earlier date he would have done. The twenty signers told the Assembly that they and others could not pay these war taxes and would be prepared to suffer the legal consequence of refusing to pay taxes. As soon as they withdrew, the Assembly passed the Supply Bill, so their petition had little effect. But it remains a major landmark in the development of the war tax issue among Christians.

Document 31

The House being informed, that sundry Freeholders of the City of *Philadelphia* were attending without, and desired Admittance, in order to present an Address to the House, they were called in; and they accordingly presented the following Address, signed by *Twenty-three,* of the People called *Quakers,* which was read by the Clerk, and they then withdrew, *viz.*

To the REPRESENTATIVES of the Freemen of the Province of *Pennsylvania,* in GENERAL ASSEMBLY met, at *Philadelphia, Eleventh Month* 7, 1755.

The ADDRESS of some of the People called Quakers, in the said Province on Behalf of themselves and others.

THE Consideration of the Measures which have lately been pursued, and are now proposed, having been weightily impressed on our Minds, we apprehend that we should fall short of our Duty to you and to ourselves, and to our Brethren in religious Fellow-ship, if we did not in this Manner inform you, that although we shall at all Times heartily and freely contribute, according to our Circumstances, either by the Payment of Taxes, or in such other Manner as may be judged necessary, towards the Exigencies of Government; and sincerely desire that due care be taken, and proper funds provided, for raising Money to cultivate our Friendship with our *Indian* Neighbours, and to support such of our Fellow-Subjects who are or may be in Distress, and for such other like benevolent purposes: Yet as the raising Sums of Money, and putting them into the Hands of Committees, who may apply them to Purposes inconsistent with the peaceable Testimony we profess, and have borne to the World, appears to us in its Consequences to be destructive of our religious Liberties, we apprehend many among us will be under the Necessity of suffering rather than consenting thereto by the Payment of a Tax for such Purposes, and thus the Fundamental Part of our Constitution may be essentially affected, and that free Enjoyment of Liberty of Conscience, for the Sake of which our Forefathers left their native Country, and settled this, then a Wilderness, by Degrees be violated.

We sincerely assure you we have no temporal Motives for thus addressing you, and could we have preserved Peace in our Minds, and with each other, we should have declined it, being unwilling to give you any unnecessary Trouble, and deeply sensible of your Difficulty in discharging the Trust committed to you irreproachably in these perilous Times, which hath engaged our fervent Desires, that the immediate Instructions of supreme Wisdom may influence your Minds, and that being preserved in a steady Attention thereto, you may be enabled to secure Peace and Tranquility to yourselves and those you represent, by pursuing Measures consistent with our peaceable Principles; and then we trust we may continue humbly to confide in the Protection of that Almighty Power, whose Providence has heretofore been as Walls and Bulwarks round about us.[110]

Document 32
[December 3, 1755]

The Report of the Committee on the Petition from *William Moore*, and others, of *Chester* County, the Address from *Anthony Morris*, and others, of the People called *Quakers*, and the Representation from *William Plumstead*, and others, of the City of *Philadelphia*, being again read and considered; *Resolved*, That the said Report be entered on the Minutes of this House. . . .

That the Petition, entituled, *An Address of some of the People called* Quakers, *in behalf of themselves and others*, signed by *Anthony Morris*, and Twenty-two others, so far as it engages for any more than themselves, and as it insinuates that many will be under the Necessity of suffering, rather than consenting to the Payment of Money to be raised and put into the Hands of Commissioners, who may apply it to Purposes inconsistent with the peaceable Testimony they profess and have borne to the World, appears to us (however decent the Language may be in respect to the House) assuming a greater Right than they were invested with, and an Indication that they had not duly considered what has been heretofore transacted in the Assemblies of this Province, particularly in relation to the Act for granting *Two Thousand Pounds* for the Queen's Use, passed [in] the Year 1711, and is therefore an unadvised and indiscreet Application to the House at this Time. . . .

James Pemberton, William Callendar, Joseph Gibbons and *Peter Worral* dissent to that Part of the Report which relates to *Anthony Morris*, and others, of the People called *Quakers.*[111]

First Militia Act Passed

The Pennsylvania Assembly passed the first Militia Act in the colony's history on November 27, 1755. The bill, as Governor Morris objected, appeared to be drawn more to protect the rights of conscientious objectors and to deny any right of the authorities to require compulsory military service than to create a military force. When the law was reviewed by the British authorities, they vetoed it in the king's name. The idea of a purely voluntary militia, with no obligation of military service or equivalent fines for those who believed in nonresistance, was again advocated by the peace churches in the early days of the American Revolution.

Document 33

An Act for the better ordering and regulating Such as are willing and desireous to be United for Military Purposes within this Province.

Whereas, this Province was Settled by (and a Majority of the Assembly's have ever since been) of the People called Quakers, who, tho' they do not as the World is now Circumstanc'd, condemn the Use of Arms in others, yet are principled against bearing Arms Themselves. And to make any Law to compel them thereto against their Consciences, would not only be to Violate a Fundamental in our Constitution, and be a direct breach of our Charter of Priviledges, but would also in Effect be to commence Persecution against all that part of the Inhabitants of the Province; And for them by any Law to Compel others to bear Arms and Exempt themselves, would be inconsistent and Partial. Yet, for as much as by the General Toleration and Equity of our Laws, great Numbers of People of other Religious Denominations are come among us who are under no such Restraint, some of whom have been Disciplined in the Art of War, and Conscientiously think it their Duty to fight in defence of their Country, their Wives, their Families, and Estates, and such have an Equal Right to Liberty of Conscience with others.

And Whereas, a great number of Petitions from the several Counties of this Province have been presented to this House, setting forth That the Petitioners are willing to defend Themselves and their Country, and desirous of being formed into Regular Bodies for that purpose, Instructed and Disciplined under proper Officers with suitable and Legal Authority, representing withall that unless Measures of this kind are taken, so as to Unite them together, Subject them to due Command and thereby give them Confidence in each other, they cannot Assemble to oppose the Enemy without the utmost danger of exposing themselves to Confusion and Destruction.

And Whereas, the Voluntary Assembling of great Bodies of Armed Men from different parts of the Province on any Occasional Alarm, whether true or false, as of late hath happen'd without Call or Authority from the Government, and without due Orders and directions among themselves, may be attended with Danger to our Neighbouring Indian Friends and Allies, as well as to the Internal Peace of the Province.

And Whereas, the Governour hath frequently recommended it to the Assembly, that in Prepairing and passing a Law for such purposes, they should have a due regard to Scrupulous and Tender Consciences, which cannot be done where Compulsive means are Used to force men into Military Service.

Therefore, as we represent all the People of the Province, and are composed of Members of different Religious Persuasions, We do not think it reasonable that any should thro' a want of legal powers be in the least restrain'd from doing what they Judge it their Duty to do for their own Security and the publick Good; We in Compliance with the said Petition and recommendations do offer it to the Governour to be Enacted. . . .

Provided also, that nothing in this Act may be understood or construed to give any Power or Authority to the Governor or Commander in Chief, and the said officers, to make any Articles or Rules that shall in the least affect those of the Inhabitants of the Province who are conscientiously scrupulous of bearing arms, either in their Liberties, Persons or Estates, nor any other Persons of what Persuasion or Denomination soever, who have not first voluntarily signed the said Articles, after due consideration as aforesaid.[112]

Proposed Second Militia Act Provides for Conscientious Objectors

When the king overruled the Pennsylvania Militia Act in 1756, the Assembly received new requests from the governor for a "proper militia law." The resignation of ten Quaker members by this time made it more likely that he would receive the kind of law he wanted. This second Militia Act was sent to the governor for his approval in March 1757, but he refused to sign it into law.

This rejected measure is of considerable interest for its provisions relating to conscientious objectors. The bill assumed a universal military obligation and imposed a fine of 20 shillings on all conscientious objectors. The methods of obtaining lists of men of military age, including members of the peace churches, and of collecting fines as an equivalent to military service were used again in the American Revolution. The provision for noncombatant service was not made part of any later militia legislation.

Document 34

Be it carried to the Governor. An Act for forming and Regulating the Militia within this Province.

Whereas, in this Time of actual War with the French King and his Subjects, and his Savage Indian Allies, it is absolutely necessary for the Service of our most gracious Sovereign, the Defence and Security of this Colony, and the Preservation of the Rights and Privileges of it's Inhabitants, that the Province be put into a proper Posture of Defence, and the Inhabitants thereof duly regulated, well armed and expertly Disciplined in the Military Art, whereby they may be enabled under the Favour and Assistance of Divine Providence to defend their Lives and Fortunes against the Hostile Invasion of his Majesties perfidious Enemies, to quell and suppress any Intestine Commotions, Rebellions or Insurrections that may happen therein, and to preserve those invaluable Rights and Privileges which they are entituled to under the present Constitution and Form of Government.

Be it therefore enacted by the Honourable William Denny, Esquire, Lieutenant-Governor, under the Honourable Thomas Penn and

Richard Penn, Esquires, true and absolute Proprietaries of the Province of Pennsylvania, and Counties of New Castle, Kent and Sussex, upon Delaware, by and with the Advice and Consent of the Representatives of the Freemen of said Province in General Assembly met, and by the Authority of the same,

That the Sheriff of each and every County of this Province by himself or his Deputy, shall, and is hereby empowered and required under the Penalty of Fifty Pounds within Fifteen Days after the Publication of this Act, to issue his Precept to the Constable of every Township, Burrough or Ward in his County, ordering and directing him within three Days after the Receipt of such Precept, to give Notice by publick Advertisements to the Freeholders of the Township, Burrough or Ward wherein he resides, to meet together, on a certain Day, not less than Three nor more than Five Days, after such publick Notice [has been] given, at some convenient Place by him to be appointed and named in said Advertisement, and then, and there, betwixt the Hours of Ten in the Morning and four in the Afternoon, by Tickets in Writing make choice of one discreet and reputable Freeholder of the said Township, Burrough or Ward, to be an Assistant to him the said Constable in performing the Duties required by this Act, who together with the said Assistant shall take down in Writing the Names and Surnames of every male person residing in the said Townships, Burroughs or Wards (Servants and Apprentices excepted) above the age of Seventeen and under Fifty-Five Years, noting against every Name to what Religious Society each Person belongs, especially such as are Papists, or reputed Papists; which said Lists the said Constables and their Assistants respectively shall, under the Penalty of Ten Pounds, make out and return to the Sheriff of the said County, who issued the Precept to him directed, within five Days after the said Assistant is chosen as aforesaid, and shall, upon Oath or Affirmation, declare the same to be a just and true Account to the best of their knowledge, which said Oath or Affirmation the said Sheriff is hereby authorized and enjoined to administer. And the Sheriff of every County within this Province, by himself, or his Deputy, with such reputable Freeholders, as he shall call to his Assistance shall, and he is hereby enjoined and required under the Penalty of Fifty Pounds, within three Days after the said Lists shall come to his Hands, as afores'd, to divide his County into Districts or Divisions, allotting so many adjacent Townships, Burroughs and Wards together, as they shall by the help of said Lists judge will furnish a Company of male persons capable of bearing Arms, consisting of not less than Sixty, nor exceeding an hundred men; exclusive of such

Persons as are noted in the said Lists to belong to, or frequent those Religious Societies or Congregations, whose Tenets and Principles are against bearing arms, and all Papists, and reputed Papists. . . .

And whereas there are in this Province a great number of Persons of different religious Persuasions, who conscientiously scruple to bear Arms, and yet in Time of Invasion and Danger would freely perform sundry Services equally necessary and advantageous to the Public, Therefore be it provided and enacted by the authority aforesaid, That all Quakers, Menonists, Moravians, and other conscientiously scrupulous of bearing Arms, who shall appear on any Alarm with the Militia, though without Arms, and be ready to obey the Commands of the Officers in the following Particulars, that is to say, In extinguishing Fires in any City or Township, whether kindled by the Enemy from without, or by traiterous Inhabitants within; in suppressing Insurrections of Slaves or other evil minded Persons during an attack; in carrying off and taking Care of the Wounded; in conveying Intelligence as Expresses or Messengers; in carrying Refreshments to such as are on Duty, and in conveying away to such Places of Safety as the Commanding Officer shall appoint, the Women and Children, aged, infirm and wounded, with the Effects that are in Danger of falling into the Hands of the Enemy; Such Persons so appearing on any Alarm, and performing the Services aforesaid, when required, shall, and they are hereby declared to be free and exempt from the Penalties of this Act, inflicted on Persons refusing to appear under Arms on such Occasions. . . .

And for as much as the Parliament of Great Britain has thought fit to exempt the Church or Congregation called Unitas Fratrum or United Brethren from bearing Arms, or personally serving in any Military Capacity upon their paying a reasonable Equivalent or Compensation for such Service; And there are divers other religious Societies of Christians in this Province, whose Conscientious Persuasions are against bearing Arms, who are nevertheless willing and desirous to promote the Public Peace and Safety: Therefore be it enacted by the authority aforesaid, That the Captain of the Company of each District in every County of this Province shall within Six Months after he receives his Commission, cause his Clerk to make out a fair Duplicate or true Copy of the Return made by the Constable and his Assistant, of each Township of his District which was delivered him by the Sheriff, marking thereon every Persons name that is on his Muster-Roll, and also distinguishing those who belong to such religious Societies whose conscientious Principles are against bearing Arms; which said Duplicate or Copy of Constable's Returns, after so marked and distinguished, the said Captain shall deliver or cause to be delivered to the Commissioners of his County, chosen by Virtue of the Act for raising County Rates and Levies: And the said Commissioners of each County of this Province, within Twenty Days after the Receipt of the Duplicates aforesaid, shall meet together and cause their Clerks to make out fair Duplicates of the Names and Sir Names of all and every Person and Persons in each District or Division, marked and distinguished as aforesaid to belong to such Religious Societies, whose Principles are against bearing Arms. And the said Commissioners of the respective Counties are hereby authorized and commanded, under the Penalty of One Hundred Pounds Current Money, to charge every such Person the sum of Twenty Shillings on the said Duplicate, and appoint Collectors for receiving the same, and cause their Clerks to deliver to the said Collectors fair Duplicates of the Names of the Persons so charged, with a Warrant annexed thereto under the Hands and Seals of two or more of the said Commissioners, requiring the said Collectors forthwith to Collect and Receive the several Sums in the said Duplicates respectively mentioned; And if any Person or Persons so charged by Virtue of this Act shall refuse or neglect to pay the same on demand, the said Collector or Collectors by Virtue of the said Warrant, shall call to their assistance, if occasion be, any Constable of his County, and levy the Sum so charged on the Goods and Chattels of the Person so refusing, and make Sale thereof, rendering the Overpluss, if any be, to the Owners in the same manner as Collectors are impowered and directed by the said Act for raising County Rates and Levies. And be it enacted by the Authority aforesaid, That the said Sum of Twenty Shillings that shall be so charged to any young Man under the Age of Twenty-One and above Seventeen Years, who belongs to any of the Societies aforesd. and shall reside with his Parent, shall be paid and recovered as aforesaid of and from his said Parent.[113]

Settlers Seek Greater Protection

More daring Indian raids in 1757 increased the need for the paid provincial troops who garrisoned forts at key points on the frontier. These new attacks also increased the bitter feeling against those who had not given the borderlands sufficient protection. Governor William Denny wrote to the Proprietor on June 30, 1757, that the mangled bodies of persons killed in present Lebanon County were taken to Lancaster and laid at the court house door and that the inhabitants of that section where the murders were committed petitioned him for some protection, since they had no militia or associated company and lived among Mennonites who would not defend them. The petitions came from Hanover and Derry townships and made no mention of Mennonites.[114] In a separate incident occurring at the same time a farmer named Isaac Sneveley was burned out apparently by his Hanover Township neighbors.

Document 35

In a Letter from Hanover Township, in Lancaster County, dated the Second Instant, it is said, that on the 29th ult. in the Night, the House of one Isaac Snevely was set on Fire; and with great Difficulty put out; and that the next Night his Barn was set on Fire, and intirely consumed, with 18 Horses and Cows &c. in it. The Writer of the Letter is positive that both House and Barn were fired on Purpose, and that it was not done by Indians.[115]

Document 36

Since our last we received Advice from Lancaster, that on the 17th Instant, five Men, and a Woman (who was big with Child) were killed and scalped by the Indians, about 30 Miles from that Place, and that the Bodies of three of the Men, and the Woman, had been brought down there [Lancaster] by some in the Neighbourhood where the Murders were committed.

We are likewise informed, that an Express arrived in Lancaster on Saturday Morning last, with an Account of seven People being killed in one House the Night before. And there are Letters in Town, which advise of more Murders being committed, the Number uncertain; but it is thought there are above Twenty destroyed, besides what may be carried off; and that the Frontier Inhabitants are in great Distress, and moving from their Plantations as fast as they can. The Number of the Indians that have done, and are doing, the Mischief is not known. These late Murders have been done in Hanover, Lebanon, Bethel and Paxton Townships, all in Lancaster County.[116]

Document 37

. . . . I had the further Mortification to hear of the Enemy Indians coming within Thirty Miles of the Place of Treaty, desolating a long Tract of Country, and killing and scalping many of the Inhabitants. Four dead Bodies, one of which was a Woman with Child, were brought to Lancaster from the neighbouring Frontiers, scalped and butchered in a most horrid Manner, and laid before the Door of the Court House for a Spectacle of Reproach to every one there, as it must give the Indians a sovereign Contempt for the Province. They were however removed by my Order, and the Treaty with an Intermission of a Day went on in its ordinary Course. The poor Inhabitants where these daring Murders were committed, being without Militia or Association, and living among Menonists, a numerous Sett of German Quakers, came supplicating me for Protection, and immediately with the Approbation of the Commissioners, who attended at the Treaty, I gave Lieutenant Col. Weiser a Warrant to raise Three Companies, of Fifty-Three Men each, for their Relief, and to enlist them for three Months; not doubting but in that Time, with proper Encouragements, the Forces wou'd be recruited to their full Number. . . .[117]

Delaware Raid in Berks County

A Delaware raid scattered the Amish settlement in Bern Township in Berks County in September 1757, killing the wife and child of Jacob Hochstetler and carrying his other children into captivity. John Hochstetler escaped in 1758. Their father was still trying to ransom Joseph and Christian in 1762.

Document 38

From Reading, in Berks County, there is advice, that on Thursday and Friday last, some people were murdered in Bern Township and others carried off.[118]

Document 39

On October 1 some Indians entered the home of Peter Wampler in Lancaster County while he and his wife were out in the meadow to get a load of hay. The Indians took five children, four girls and a boy; the smallest child was hardly a year old and could not walk yet; they took from the house all they could carry away. The rest they ruined, scattered the flour, poured out the honey, broke up the windows and cut up the beds. The same letter report that nearly all of the back border have fled and that on the same day and the next several head of cattle were killed by the enemy in Hanover Township, and that on the preceding Thursday in Berks County four persons were killed and four taken away by the Indians at the Northkill. It is thought there must have been fifty who did it.

Philadelphia, October 7

[Excerpt from a letter from Tulpehocken, September 30]

I am sorry that I cannot report anything better than that the Indians have again murdered many of the residents of our outlying border, not far from Nicolas Langen's place. They say there were 40 to 50 Indians around there. Those poor people who live in the back areas will now all have to move away. We are living in great fear; yesterday we heard nothing all day except about murder and killing, but no one goes out to fight the enemy.

On Saturday, October 1, in Heidelberg Township where the highway [crosses] over the Blue Mountain, Henrich Franz's daughter, between 15 and 16 years old, was a small distance from the house; when they looked for her they saw Indian footprints, and they saw by the footprints that she had resisted. Nothing has been heard of her since.

In the same week Indians came to the Hoffstetler home; the man called to his neighbors for help. Meanwhile the Indians killed his wife and took the children, and set fire to the house and barn. One boy escaped.[119]

Document 40

From Reading we have advice that last Wednesday the enemy burnt the house of one Hochsteller and killed Hochsteller's wife and a young man and himself and three children are missing.[120]

Document 41

Honoured Sir

According to your desire, to make out a List of the people, who are Murdered and taken [into] Captivity by the Indians, I send hereby so near as possible, I could get it/ to wit/

George Eberhard and his Wife and 5 Children Killed and scalp'd	in the Month of Octr. 1755, on the Shoemokee road over the Kittitiny hill
Baltzer Shefer Killed and scalped and his Daughter taken Captivity	
Henry Hartman Killed and scalp'd in his house over the Mountain	in Novr. 1755
John Leyenberger & Rudolf Kendel George Wolf & John Apple Caspar Spring & Jacob Ritzman Fredk. Wieland & Geo. Martin Bower are all killed	in Novr. 1755 as they where going on the watch on the Kittiting hill on Saturday at noon where Fort Henry is Built at present

Philip House	Killed the same Evening in his house
Henry Robels wife and 5 Children and a Girl of Wm. Stein are Killed and some scalped	on the next Day or Sunday
Baltzer Newfangs wife killed and his son taken Captivity	In March 1756 over the Mountain
Valentine Baumgartners Son Killed	In April 1756 over the Mountain
an old Men Caled Clous and his Wife are killed and scalp'd	
2 Children Killed and Scalp'd	in Bethel Township in May 1756
Martin Cappeler and his Wife are killed and scalped	in July 1756 Bethel Township
Philip Guinters Wife, Son in Law and a Daughter are Killed and scalped, And a Daughter & 2 Children taken Captivity	in Octr. 1756 over the Mountain
Two Men Killed and scalped and one Bernard Motzs taken Captivity	in Octr. 1756 on the plantation of Nicolaus Long in Tulpehokin Towns.
George Peter Gisingers Wife taken Captivity	in Decr. 1756 in Tulpehokin Township
Adam Miller Killed and scalped	in Aprill 1757 over the Mountain
George Peter Gisinger Killed and scalped	in Aprill 1757 Tulpehokin Township
Baltzer Smith's Daughter taken Captivity	the same day Bethel Towns.
Fredk. Myer and his Wife Killed and scalped; and 3 of his Children taken Captivity	in June 1757 in Barn Township
Highstealers Wife and one Child Killed and scalped, himself and 4 Children taken Captivity	in Septr. 1757 in Barn Township
Philip Summer Killed and scalp'd	

This is as near as I could Collecting the same, in the County of Berks on this side of the River Schuylkill

I am Sir — Your Most humble servt.

Tulpehokin, ye 28 Novr. 1757 — *Peter Spycker*[121]

Document 42

A man by the name of Hochstattler who had been a prisoner of the Indians for 8 months and escaped reported that because the French have very few provisions, the Indians are also in need, and that might be more of an inducement for making peace.[122]

Document 43

Examination of John Hocktattler

Intelligence given by John Hocktattler a Swiss by Nation; which was Settled in Bergs [Berks] County, Bern Township, near Kauffmans Cr]eek]; was taken by the Enemy Indians the 12th of October. 1757 and Escap'd from them arriving at Shamokin 5th May 1758.

Question: By What, and how Many Indians was you taken.

Answer: By the Delaware and Shawnese 15 in the whole.

Q: Which way did you pass before you came into the Enemys Country.

A: We Marched 3 Days before whe arrived at the E[a]st branch of Susquahanna 20 Miles from Shamokin where it was [fordable], from there whe keept intirely West all along the west Branch, till after 17 Days Journey we arrived on the Ohio.

Q: In What place on the Ohio do Jou arriv'd.

A: Where the French C[reek] emptys into Ohio there upon the Corner is a smal Fort Established Lately, of Logs, Framed together, there are 25 Men Garrison'd in it, without Artillery, there whe pas'd the Ohio for to come by it, the place is call Wenango [Fort Venango, present Franklin, Pa.]

Q: How do you proceded further.

A: Up the French Creek 3 Days traveling on Battoes at the end of it whe came to a fort built in the same manner as the other, and Garrison'd, with 25 Menn, [Fort de la Riviere au Boeuf, present Waterford, Pa.] from there the French Creek a Road to Presque Isle; wich is a Days Journey from it Distant.

Q: What became of jou affter that.

A: Affter 3 Days travel Est south Est, I was brought to Buxotons Cr[eek] where it emptys in the Ohio whe came to an Indian Castle wich lys upon the Corner of it, then I was kept Prisoner all that time.

Q: Do you ever heard anything of Fort du Quesne.

A: Ten Days before I Escap'd five Dutch Prisoners was brought up by the Indians from there wich told me that there was 300 Man garrisoned in Fort du Quesne, the Provision Scarce, so that the Indians was oblicked to bring away from thiere Womans and famelys.

Q: Do jou never heard what Cannons the French had There.
A: Yes I heard several but are Dismounted.
Q: Do jou never Learned if the Indians Receiv'd Order for Marching against us.
A: 5 Days before I did escape an old Indian was telling to me, shewing aginst all parts of the world, that Indians was coming from there and then he shew'd about Est south Est, telling that the [y] would attack the English there, wich I did Imagine that It was Intended for Chamakin.
Q: Do jou Ever could learn from how the French get intelligence of [the English].
A: 6 Weeks before my Departing there came 2 Delaware Indians telling that the came from Shamoking that the Commandant took thier arms from them not trusting [them], and that the English was Drawing together about Conistage, or Lancaster, laying up a great Deal of Cattle, that the was waiting till the grass was groan.
Q: How do jou Escap'd from there, how long and in what Manner do jou was coming, and where did jou arrive.
A: I got the liberty for hunting, one morning very soon took my gun finding a Bark Canoe on the River wherein I crossed it, traveling Est for 6 Days from there I arrvd. at the source of the west Branch, there I march for 4 Days further till I was sure of it, there I took several Bloks tying them together till I got a flott, there I flotted myself Down the River for five Days where I did arrive at Shamokin, Living all time upon grass. pass'd in the Whole for 15 Days.[123]

Document 44

To the Honorable James Hamilton, Esq.,
Lieutenant Governour of Pennsylvania,
The Humble Petition of Jacob Hockstetler of Berks County,
Humbly Sheweth:

That about five Years ago your Petitioner with 2 Children were taken Prisoners, & his wife & 2 other Children were killed by the Indians, that one of the said Children who is still Prisoner is named Joseph, is about 18 Years old, and Christian is about 16 Years & a half old. That his House & Improvements were totally ruined & destroyed. That your Petitioner understands that neither of his Children are brought down, but the Embassadour of King Kastateeloca, who has one of his Children is now here.

That your Petitioner most humbly prays your Honour to interpose in this Matter, that his Children may be restored to him, or that he may put into such a Method as may be effectual for that Purpose.

And your Petitioner will ever pray, &c.

his
Jacob X *Hocksteter*
mark

Aug. 13, 1762.[124]

Mennonite Refugees Appeal to Dutch Church

Indian raids caused many settlers in the Shenandoah Valley of Virginia in present Page, Shenandoah and Frederick Counties to flee for their lives. One of the most severe attacks was made in May 1758, when 50 people were killed and several hundred fled from their homes. The wives and children of Jacob Holtiman and John Stone were among the victims in the Massanutten settlement in the Page Valley. Many who fled from their homes returned to friends and relatives in eastern Pennsylvania. Martin Kauffman, Jacob Borner, Samuel Bohm, and Daniel Stauffer, who were among the Mennonite refugees from Virginia, sent an appeal to the Dutch Mennonite Committee for Foreign Needs through Johannes Schneyder and Martin Funck, their minister. Their letter and the Dutch response are now in the Town Archives at Amsterdam.

Document 45

The grace of God and the love and peace of Jesus Christ, is our wish to all God-loving souls and especially to our brethren in the faith in Holland. Greetings.

Today, the 7th of September, 1758.

Herewith we authorize our brother and co-fellow in the faith, Johannes Schneyder, who until now has been a good friend to the poor, and who contemplates a journey to the friends and brethren in Holland on account of the dark times in which we find ourselves at this time, owing to the tyrannical or barbarous Indians who have already killed so many people, and have taken many prisoners and carried them away; others were driven from their homes and lands, so that many people are now in great poverty and distress.

We were thirty-nine Mennonite families living together in Virginia. One family was murdered and the remaining of us and many other families were obliged to flee for our lives, leaving our all and go empty handed.

Last May the Indians have murdered over fifty persons and more than two hundred families were driven away and made homeless.

We come, therefore, with a prayer to you, brethren and co-fellows in the faith for help, by way of charitable aid, if your love will persuade you to show mercy to us, so that we may with God's help, and the aid of good friends, be guided through this Valley of Grief; the dear Lord will reward you for it, here in this life and finally in eternity for what you will do for us.

Further, I do not deem it necessary to write much, as our friend and brother will give you a better report than I could in my simple and imperfect writing, for, he too, has been in danger of his life with his wife and four children, and was compelled to flee and leave his all behind. He had been so situated that he could make a comfortable living. He had a nice little farm, and besides he had begun the distilling of [document damaged] and turpentine oil. He was always a good friend to the distressed in time of need.

Further we request you to remember us in your prayers, as we are likeminded toward you, that we may have the comfort of good old Tobias, with which he comforted his son, when he said, even though we are poor, but if we fear God, we shall receive much good.

P.S. This our friend desired a traveling companion from the congregation to accompany him on his journey, as he deems it best not to go alone. Upon our advice and with our Best Wishes, our minister and elder, Martin Funck, has consented to go. Until now he was found true and honest in all things by all. He is, however, still a single man, and by occupation a miller. He, too, was compelled to flee and leave all he had behind. This man was found by the grace and help of God, and will be a true traveling companion to our brother, Johannes Schneyder, on his journey to Holland.

Further, in my simple-heartedness, I do not know what more to write, only to give greetings from us all to all the brethren and congregation in Holland.

Signed by and many others.

Michael Kauffman *Samuel Bohm*
Jacob Borner *Daniel Stauffer*

Written by Benjamin Hirsche, one mile from Lancaster town, Mennist Minister.[125]

Document 46

Amsterdam, December 27, 1758.

Michael Kauffman, Jacob Borner, Samuel Bohm, Daniel Stauffer:

Dear Friends:

We have received your letter dated September 7th, but without denomination of the place out of which it is written, by the hands of your deputies, Johannes Schneyder and Martin Funck, who have given us an ample account of the calamities you had suffered, which moved our hearts with due compassion, and since we do not doubt but their narration of your troubles was true and faithful, we have opened our hands to your assistance with fifty pounds English Sterling which according to the value of your money amounted to the sum of seventy eight pounds, eleven shillings, and five pence, Philadelphia money, which you may receive upon the enclosed Bill of Credit from Messrs. Benjamin & Sam Shoemaker in Philadelphia.

We hope that this sum will be sufficient to help and assist you until it pleases the God of Peace to restore the desired peace in America, as well as in Europe; and that you get restitution of the lands and properties from which you are driven out and enjoy there the same prosperity as before for the sustentation of your families and the assistance of the poor, which the Almighty will grant you out of his all sufficient grace!

In the meanwhile we recommend you highly to keep fast the confession of your holy faith in our Saviour Jesus Christ, and be always thankful for the goodness of God bestowed upon you by our compassionate hands and hearts; for as we were unknown to you, it was only the good God who makes this impression on our bowels and gave us the power to assist you.

We hope the bearers of these, the above mentioned deputies, will return soon and in good health to you, and find you and other friends in a good condition. We have provided them all the necessities here and for their return till London.

We leave you to the Almighty Providence of God and our Saviour Jesus Christ, and we are with tenderest affection, dear friends,

Your well-wishing Friends,
The Committee

P.S. When occasion offers we desire your answer that we may be sure that you have duly received the above mentioned money, and please to direct your letter to Mr. Hendrick Kops at Amsterdam.[126]

Document 47

Williamsburg, July 7

Last Night a Messenger arrived from Augusta County, with Advice that the Indians had lately killed and captivated 26 People between Winchester and Augusta Court House [Staunton]; and that a large Body of the Inhabitants, to the Number of 300, were removing into Culpepper, and the other Counties on this Side the Blue Ridge.[127]

The Sectarian Response: Relief Efforts

Mennonites Initiate Relief Program

The Mennonite community responded to the first Indian raids in 1755 with a spontaneous program of relief work, sending wagon loads of food and clothing to the men, women, and children who had fled from their farms on the frontier, sometimes with Delaware and Shawnee warriors in close pursuit. The Mennonite relief program was quickly followed by Quaker, Schwenkfelder, Lutheran, and Reformed contributions to help the refugees.

Document 48

Tulpehocken, December 12

Our Free Party [Company of Volunteers] now consists of 100 men; they are stationed at four places and roam through an area of 8 miles along the Blue Mountains a whole day, but at night stay in houses built for the purpose at the four places. In the outlying townships of Lancaster County a similar arrangement has been made, and their Free Company also has about 100 men. But where no better arrangements have been made, that is as good as nothing. Some of the inhabitants who fled have moved back to their places, but they left their best furniture behind. But those along the mountains who fled and whose possessions were destroyed are still with us, as well as those on the other side of the mountains. There are a large number of poor people here. The Mennonites from the area of Lancaster County have sent several wagonloads of flour, meat, and clothing, &c. for the poor around here. On Monday a wagonload was distributed; but for each family hardly a bushel of flour and a small piece of meat came. The man who reported this is one of those chosen to make the distribution. He has on just his list some 30 families, some of which have six to eight children, and some with no clothing at all, just as they were when they fled. Alas, the misery is horrible! There is not a family that does not have some of these refugees. One of the boys, who was shot in the forehead, died, and also a scalped child. Still another is very sick and also the man shot in the heel. Sicknesses are spreading rapidly, much of it caused by the terror. May the Lord have mercy on these poor and wretched inhabitants and awaken some hearts that will follow the Christian and praiseworthy example of the Mennonites in Lancaster County.[128]

Document 49

The day before New Year the Mennonites of Skippack and those living farther up sent 7 wagons with flour and other provisions to Bethlehem and Nazareth for the impoverished people who had fled there from the Indians.[129]

Document 50

Philadelphia, January 8

The Quakers in this city have raised considerable sums for the support of the residents who were driven from the border by Indians.

And we hear that the Quakers in Bucks County are also collecting grain together with other necessities for such people.[130]

Document 51

Germantown, January 15

We hear that when it became known that a great mass of people fled to Bethlehem, not only the Mennonites, but also Lutherans, Reformed, and Schwenkfelders collected their gifts and sent up flour and other provisions for the support of the poor refugees.[131]

Moravians Aid Refugees

Many of the refugees from the Northampton and Berks frontier had fled to the Moravian settlement at Bethlehem. Joseph Spangenberg, the Moravian bishop, sent an appeal to Anthony Benezet, a Philadelphia Quaker best known for his devotion to the anti-slavery cause. Friends made contributions to the needy refugees, as did the Mennonites. Eighteen months later, there was evidently some talk that the Moravians had used some of these relief shipments for themselves. Bishop Spangenberg wrote to Benezet again, enclosing an enormously detailed list of the goods received at Bethlehem in December 1755 and January 1756 and the names of the refugees to whom they were given. Spangenberg's letter and one example from the lists in the Historical Society of Pennsylvania are reproduced here. From the lists it is clear that Mennonites in Franconia Township donated 22¾ bushels of rye, 7½ bushels of wheat, 3½ bushels of beans, 5 bushels of dried apples, 1½ bushels of salt, 382 bushels of meal, 85 pounds of meat (beef), and 60 pounds of pork. Skippack Mennonites provided 34 bushels of rye, 2½ bushels of wheat, 1½ bushels of Indian corn, 7 bushels of dried apples, 736 pounds of meal, 185 pounds of meat and pork, 4 pounds of butter, 21 pounds of salt, 12 quarts of beans, 6 yards of flax linen, 7 yards of tow linen, 4 ounces of thread, one coat and waistcoat, 4 pairs of children's shoes, one child's jacket, and one bed sheet.

Document 52

My Dear Friend Anthony:

Please to remember, that I once wrote you in that hard Winter, when more than six Hundred Men, Women and Children, in their utmost Distress, came to the [Moravian] Brethren's Settlements, in the Forks of Delaware, to find there a Shelter, and some Relief in their Wants and Nakedness; Many of them having had their houses, Barns, Cattle and all burnt and destroyed by the Savages and just having saved their Life.

You was so kind, to communicate my Letter to some Friends and they moved with Compassion, sent up some goods, Cloaths, etc., to relieve the said unhappy Sufferers; with Orders, that those, who had lost all they had at Gnadenhutten should by no Means be excluded from partaking of the said Charities.

I upon that, not being able myself to make the Distribution thereof, went to one of the Magistrates of this County residing in Bethlehem, and desired him, to appoint some Persons of a noted good Character, and to give them the Charge of a prudent and faithful Distribution of the just mentioned Charities; such Things of that Nature requiring great Exactness, that they may appear just and right, when examined into, before all the World, so as they are done in the Eyes of the Lord.

Mr. Horsefield, upon this my Request, appointed Joseph Powel, Samuel's Brother, to take the said Matter into Hand with the help of some other Brethren, who were to assist him, and he was Advised first, to inquire into the Circumstances of each Family, to take down the Number of their Children, to find out what Losses they had met with, and what were their Wants and Necessities; and then to look over the List of all the Goods He had received, and to make a proper Distribution, giving them most, who had lost most, and wanted most, and giving them less, who had something left unto them, and could help themselves yet.

He faithfully did so, to the best of his Ability (and He is a Valuable Man) and kept an Account of all things, making himself Debtor for all, He had received, and Creditor for all, He had given to the poor Refugees, taking at the same Time Receipts for all, He gave out; when this could be done; for in some Triflings it could not be.

When afterwards the said Joseph Powel was moving to Oblong, in Dutches County, Newyork Government, where He at present preaches the Gospel with Blessing; he had first all his Accounts enter'd into a Book, which He put into the Hands of a Magistrate of this County, to be inspected by any one, who has Reason to ask for it; viz: into the Hands of Timothy Horsefields, Esqr.

Now I hear, that some unkind People have spoken ill of the Brethren, as if they had not dealt faithfully with the said Charities; and that some of the Friends have spoken in the same Way. It is pity.

If I remember right, this is not the first Time, that I let you know, how we have acted in the said Circumstances; desiring you, to acquaint all the Benefactors with it. I hope, you have done so, but who can help against a wicked Tongue?

However, my Dear Friend, give me Leave to ask one favour of you, viz.

Please to lay this my Letter before the Benefactors, who sent up the said Charities for the poor Refugees?

Please to ask them, for Goodness sake, to send up two or three Deputies, to inspect the said Accounts of Joseph Powels, and to examine them.

This I hope will be the best way to satisfy every Body, who is suspicious about it; when He hath a Mind to be satisfied with the Truth. As for the Rest of the People, who don't care what they say wether right or wrong, wether true or false, wether good or bad; I think, we should beat the Air, in trying to set them to rights.

I have thought some Times; wether the said Accounts should not be published? But considering that the Names of poor honest people must be exposed to the public (: and many poor honest people would rather suffer the greatest Hardships than see themselves in their Poverty exposed) in so doing, have thought it best, to leave it in Mr. Horsefield's hands, for the use of all, who want to see it. When once it comes in that way, that it is rather a Shame for a Christian to be rich, then to be poor (for our Master was poor in the World) I then will alter my Opinion.

Thy affectionate
Br[other Joseph] Sp[angenberg]

Bethlehem, June 10 1757.

No. 3 Meal

1755 Decr.	From sundry People recd. in Nazareth 21 Bushe[l]s Rye Meal at 37 lb pr Bushl make 777 lb	
30	Saml. Folck in great Swamp	150 lb
31	Hanickel in Cushehoppen	1998 lb
1756 Janry 2	Frencon Township pr Chrn. Meyer	382 lb.

	Shippach pr Valentin Hussiger	736 lb
	Saccon Township pr. Bale. Lawr	422 lb
5	Lower Do. pr Gratius Lark	217 lb
Febry 12	The Friends in Worcester	2239 lb
18	The Friends in Lower Saccon Township pr John Nichs. Full	1705 lb
	Carried forward	8626 lb[132]

Renewed Efforts to Help Refugees in 1763

Relief efforts of this kind continued through the French and Indian War as new Indian raids devastated one frontier community or another. The peace achieved with the Delawares in October 1758 gave the Pennsylvania settlers a respite from marauding bands of warriors. But in 1763, when Pontiac's War sent Shawnees, Senecas, and Delawares on new attacks along the Pennsylvania, Maryland, and Virginia frontier, fresh efforts had to be made to help the hundreds of refugees who once again abandoned their outlying farms and fled toward the more settled areas.

Document 53

Lancaster, July 28

There are certain accounts that Indians have passed the South Mountain and are gone into York County, and that some of them have assuredly been near Carlisle. The wants of the distressed refugees have been greatly relieved by sums of money collected in the different congregations in Lancaster County. The Quakers and Mennonists have been very liberal on this occasion, having raised a considerable sum and having hired men to assist the poor people in gathering in as much of their harvest as possible—and we are told that several large parties have again attempted to go over the mountains for this necessary and laudable purpose, but the risk they run is so great we cannot think of them without dread.[133]

The Sectarian Response: The Friendly Association *Attempts to Work for Peace with Indians*

When Pennsylvania declared war on the Delawares in April 1756, Israel Pemberton and other Quaker leaders formed an organization to work at peace with the Indians on the basis of righting the wrongs done them by the whites. The Friendly Association for Regaining and Preserving Peace with the Indians by Pacific Measures involved Quakers, Mennonites, and Schwenkfelders in a common effort. A chronicle composed by Christopher Schultz gives a brief summary of its achievement from a Schwenkfelder point of view.

Document 54

1756. Since the Quakers as well as we and others who have scruples of conscience against taking up weapons against an enemy were accused of not being willing to bear their due share of the common burdens in a time of great unrest because of the Indian War (on whom the Governor has now declared war) and quarrels between the Governor and the Assembly and other party disputes in the land; inasmuch as these people regretted the pitiable condition of the inhabitants living on the frontier and have also known and understood that the Indian War arose because of the unjust treatment of the Indians and would be carried on with unholy purposes to the highest detriment of the province; therefore we have combined in a plan and have imparted it to others who thought the same way and have tried to persuade them to try their utmost that peace with the Indians be restored again and be maintained better from now on, although we realized that such an attempt and aim cannot be accomplished except with the utmost effort and expence.

1757. To further this plan our people have each contributed faithfully according to our abilities so that our people have subscribed to a sum of £215 and have paid this sum as the bills here submitted will demonstrate.

1758. The efforts and dispersements so applied have so thrived through God's blessing that even though it looked doubtful (because of internal divisions in the province) first an armistice and finally a peace with the neighboring Indians was achieved, as can be seen in the printed Conferences.[134]

The Friendly Association

Christopher Sauer, the Germantown printer, was one of the earliest supporters of the Friendly Association. He wrote to Israel Pemberton in April 1756 of his own interest in the Quaker effort and promised to write to Mennonites who would be most willing and able to assist in the work of the Friendly Association. Sauer also gave the Friendly Association's efforts to get the Delawares to agree to a peace treaty editorial support in his newspaper. The first news item in the *Pennsylvanische Berichte* for June 16, 1756, described preliminary maneuvers toward a conference with the Indians. Sauer's information about Thomas Pownall's appointment as governor of Pennsylvania was incorrect, but he was not mistaken in reporting the resignation of the six Quaker Assemblymen. His comments on their withdrawal from office are interesting, especially since he shared their nonresistant views. In his August 16, 1756, issue, Sauer gave a straightforward account of the conference at Easton in July and then made a direct appeal to the peace churches to join in the work of the Friendly Association.

Document 55

germantown 4 mo. 25th 1756

Friend Pemberton

I am glad to hear that friends have proposed for an accomodation with the Indians and as many ignorant as well as ill-minded people are enreached [enraged] towards friends, ascribing to them all mischief done by the Indians without any sound reason, I should be very glad and willing to assist in what manner I can and do believe that many friends who are against bearing arms will contribute towards a Peacible way and I think that among them by a voluntary way of subscription more will be geathered than what many will think and as I have correspondence with many friends among the germans I will write to them to conclude about it in their meetings especially to the menonists which are most able and willing to contribute to such a purpose. Let me know what is proposed to the Indians which are going to the discontented ones of their nations and as soon as it can be and if something is done that the publick may know let that be by itself and thee will oblige thy friend

Christopher Sower[135]

Document 56

Germantown

We hear that the Governor has not considered it advisable that private persons make peace with the Indians with such a large gift in a province where there is a governor; but because he has already declared war against them, he took both duties upon himself: to let the Indians know that although war has already been declared upon them, peace will also be offered to them, which they then willingly accepted. It is therefore in the Governor's hand at present to make a treaty of peace, if only avarice does not intervene, so that the poor Indians will not always have to complain that they have received too little and not what their land is worth, and that the French will easily offer and give them more, and thus the treaty will not be binding, or else the end will be worse than the beginning. But still it is certain that our Governor issued a proclamation on the evening of June 3—that for 39 days no one shall harm the Indians. We also hear that he will send them another delegation after he has taken the advice of his Council and the Assembly.

Certain reports say that because the Government in England took it ill of our Proprietor that he gave his Governor such instructions as have created great hindrances in Pennsylvania in a time of war; therefore the Proprietor left it to the King to appoint and install a governor himself in wartime; this was done. Thus, the Honorable Thomas Pownall, Esq. was appointed Governor of Pennsylvania, and he is to come with Lord Loudoun. It is reported that they would sail with their troops from Plymouth on the 20th or the end of April. All the reports indicate that he is a very intelligent man.

We hear that six members of the Assembly, of the Representatives of the free inhabitants of the Province of Pennsylvania have resigned; namely, from Philadelphia County James Pemberton, William Callender and Joshua Morris; from Lancaster County Peter Worral; from Berks County Francis Parvin; from Chester County Mr. [William] Peters. They know that they are only a hindrance in the House when in this time of war such matters are to be treated and legislated that are contrary to their conscience; they should and will leave it to such as are capable of serving in wartime; a special election will therefore be held before the Assembly can sit again. The wise will therefore be concerned with choosing such people in their place who can be trusted to promote the welfare of the land as well as they know how, and will not elect those who do not know or do not want to know how a poor countryman feels when he has to pay a heavy tax and bear a heavy burden.[136]

Document 57

Germantown

On Saturday, July 31, when the conference with the Indians had ended, our Governor traveled from Easton to New York; when he arrived war was commenced against the French.

Present at the conference were chiefly the King of the Delaware Indians Teedyuscung with his advisors and the Susquehannas with the exception of those who remained behind in the fortress. And on this side were besides the Governor and his Council and several members of the Assembly, also about 40 private citizens from among the Quakers, whose presence was demanded by the Indians; then because the Government had already declared war against the Indians, and the Quakers intervened between the Government and the Indians, the Indians expressed their pleasure several times that the same 40 persons would also be present at the treatymaking.

The King told the Governor and others that he came in the name of the Ten Nations; they offered peace to this province and promised to adhere faithfully to it; they would take no part in what the other nations, who were incited by the French, might do. Details can perhaps follow at some later time.

In brief, it was left to this: they would meet again in three months, when deputies from each nation would also be present.

We hear that they did not openly explain the cause of their displeasure; but since they know how expensively their land is sold and what they got for it, and the Delaware King had on one occasion said: The Delaware is mine! And so, honest men can easily imagine why they are dissatisfied.

Then, since the Delaware King offered to notify all the above nations that he had offered peace, and since all the Indians already know how much they could gain if they stay with the French and bring them scalps and prisoners, it is easy to imagine, that so many warriors would not be put off with empty words about peace in addition to some tobacco pipes, since the French freely offer, and would perhaps give them as a gift, guns, powder, lead, tomahawks and scalping-knives and also pay them well for prisoners; and because the Governor's hands are tied to such an extent that they cannot reach into the right pocket even if they wished, and the province is already burdened with a heavy tax, for these reasons the 40 private citizens have considered it wise to raise a considerable sum by voluntary contributions to satisfy the Delawares and bind them to the province by an annual income, and they would at least keep the peace in order to get their annual income and not forfeit it; and also in order that the remaining nations would be detached from the French and be brought into friendship with us and the English nation.

But since it is not only a principle with the Quakers but is also a tenet in the faith of various others that one should not let loose with the sword, but put the sword in its sheath, that one does good to the enemy, that one should seek peace and pursue it with the saints, that one closes the mouth of the malicious by good deeds and repays them in the manner of the Prince of Peace for what one has not taken, thus showing virtues in deeds; and since for a considerable time many Germans have offered a substantial sum according to their means if there could be prospects of a lasting peace with the Indians without bloodshed, that the lives of so many poor people on both sides could be saved.

And so it is herewith made known that all who are still or will be of that mind should hand in their voluntary contributions to people whom they trust to turn it over correctly.

But since there are among these people some who, to be sure, have the means and the good intentions, but no ready cash, arrangements have been made that they, indeed all, may pay in a year's time if they will guarantee to pay the interest to the lenders in the amount that they subscribe.

But let all well-intentioned children of peace declare within three months how much they are willing to contribute so that those who are in charge can make their plans accordingly.

The Indian chief did not give an affirmative reply to the demand of the governor that prisoners be released, because he did not have charge of all, and many may already have been sold among the French and will no doubt have to be bought back.[137]

Mennonites and Schwenkfelders Join Friendly Association

Mennonites and Schwenkfelders responded warmly to the idealism of the Friendly Association. Andrew Ziegler reported a meeting in his Skippack congregation and prospects of other Mennonite congregations in the Franconia area joining in the effort. Christopher Schultz drafted a subscription for Schwenkfelders and later he and Casper Kribel attended a meeting of the Friendly Association trustees to clear up a misunderstanding that many Schwenkfelders had. Andrew and Michael Ziegler also met with Israel Pemberton early in 1757. In an important letter to Michael Ziegler and Dielman Kolb, Pemberton explained the Friendly Association's need for money to convince the Indians of Pennsylvania's interest in their welfare by obtaining land for their settlements secure from any encroachment by the whites and sending them agricultural missionaries. He also indicated his hope to include Mennonites among the trustees of the Friendly Association and to have Mennonites attend the next peace conference at Lancaster in May 1757.

Document 58

This 14th day of October 1756

friend Is. Pempberton

Please to Let us know wether our Governor is at Home for some of our friends have a minde to see him, if thou thinkest it of any good in this present time. N.B. I let the know that we hat a meeting Do Day about the affairs of the Indians for geatering some money and more of our meetings will do the same. so much of this friend

Andrew Ziegler

[Endorsed] Abt. subscription among the Menonists.[138]

Document 59

It is the will of the within subscribers, that it may be known that they are a few families of a dispersed people in Silesia, who have always, under God's blessing, maintained themselves by the labors of their hands only, and have been forced to leave their estates behind in Silesia, on account of their confession, and who have already here, partly suffered by the incursions of the Indians, in relieving their poor distressed neighbors. Therefore, they hope that their contributions, small as it is, will not be contempted, for it may well be compared with the two mites which the poor widow *in Evangelio* cast in, for they have cast in their living. Nevertheless, they do it with cheerfulness and delight, to be assisting in the intended salutary endeavors, as also they are ready to satisfy their true loyalty to the King's government to which they have submitted.

Know all men by these presents, That, whereas, some of the principal members of the people called Quakers, within the province of Pennsylvania, do intend to raise a considerable sum of money by way of a public and voluntary subscription, to lay a fund in order to be thereby enabled to do some satisfaction to those Indians who have already done terrible damage and disturbances to the frontier inhabitants of this province, and therewith, if possible, to procure a peace to this country; and as the said members have also communicated their said scheme to us, the hereunto subscribers, so late emigrants of Silesia, and desired of us to assist them in the above mentioned purpose:

So know ye, therefore, that in consequence thereof, we whose names are hereunto subscribed, do, in the name of God, hereby voluntarily and of our own free will and accord, promise to pay and contribute to the above said fund, which is to be employed to so salutary an end, consistant with the Gospel of our Saviour, and with principles of the doctrine we profess, every one of us, all the respective sums of money as every one shall hereby promise and subscribe, on or before the 27th day of November next ensuing, after the date hereof, unto Caspar Kriebel and Christopher Schultze, as this day by us chosen and appointed trustees, for the term of two years from hence next ensuing, either in ready payment, or in case of non-payment, every one of us shall be at liberty to keep the principal sum in his hands, and to pay the interest for the same, after the said 27th of November next. To the true and punctual payment whereof, we do hereby oblige and bind our heirs, executors, and administrators, and every one of us and them, in the penalty of double the sum, as every one hereunto shall subscribe, firmly by these presents.

In witness and confirmation and for the true performance thereof, we have hereunto set our hands, together with the respective sums of money, as every one hereby promises to pay and contribute, to the purposes above mentioned.

Done at Lower Salford Township, in the county of Philadelphia, on this thirteenth day of November, Anno Domini, 1756.[139]

Document 60

That we the Subscribers were sent and come to Phila. to get ourselves better informed about the Fundamental views and Measures and Managements of the known subscription, of which the Subscribers in the Papers of yesterday by us Communicated to the general meeting has hitherto been partly much in the dark. So we must know in Discharge our Duty confess, that by what we have been able to learn as well in open Meeting as private conversation we are fully Satisfyed about the good intents and purposes as well Management of the Affair concerned, and that Therefor we, on our own Part, were readily willing to join our Subscription to have it entered by the Treasurer, but since it is now our Duty to look back upon our People whom we at present represent in this matter, we find that the Manner of application the money is somewhat otherwise, as a report prevailed amongst us at the Time of Subscription, that a Fund should be laid by of said money, and the interest which from Time to Time should arise of the said money should be applied to such uses as is by and would be by the pacifick minded friends intended, and on these terms some poor Subscribers were induced to subscribe more readily. Whilst they apprehended the money would not so directly be demanded, and could by paying interest keep it as long as were convenient for them in their own hands, therefor as we find the matter otherwise it will be but prudent to inform them of the circumstances wherin we find the matter, and convince them of the good purposes of applying the money as well as we are convinced, before we enter their subscription in the treasurers hand.

Casper Kribel
Christopher Schultz

2nd Dec. 1756[140]

Document 61

[An unsigned note in Israel Pemberton's handwriting]

On the 22nd 2 mo 1757 Andrew Ziegler & his bro. Michl. came to see me & in ye course of Conversation enquiring what late intelligence concerning ye Indian affrs. they told me they had heard an Express was come to Easton Jeremiah Trexler to inform ye govr. some Indians were come to Fort Allen upon which immediately went to ye Dutch tavern to enquire for him & presently Jerry Trexler came to see and informed me that he had brought letters. . . .[141]

Document 62

To M. Ziegler & others of the Menonists near Skippack

Philada. ye 8th 4 mo. 1757

esteemed Friends
Michael Ziegler & Dielman Kolb

As the endeavour used by Friends to promote Peace with the Indians have hitherto been singularly blessed and affords us a prospect that if proper methods continue to be pursued a lasting peace may be established with those Poor People and from our Bitter enemys they may be brought to become our Good Friends; and if Land is allotted them & proper persons encouraged to assist them in settling together not only a foundation may be laid for the future welfare of many of them by impressing on their minds by Precept & a corresponding conduct the great Truths of the Christian Religion, but they may be a Hedge to us to prevent ye Incursions of the French Indians, which we during the War shall in our present Circumstances be exposed to, as has already been experienced in a Neighboring Colony by the Good effects attending the religious care taken by some Christian People in thus settling some Indians near them, where the whole Neighborhood, tho' the most exposed was preserved from the French Indians, when other Places not so much exposed where no Indians, were settled suffered much from the enemy, some account of which will soon be printed, but as we cannot bring about those good ends proposed, nor convince the Indians of the Sincerity of our Intentions, without granting them such Assistance as may oblige us to be at a considerable expence, we thought it necessary to remind you of the expectation we have had given us from the beginning of this undertaking, that your several congregations will be willing to assist us in this good work. And as we believe that your not having done any thing therein does not arise from any unwillingness to contribute thereto according to your ability, but rather because your People are at a Loss how to proceed therein, we think it necessary

to request that you, our esteemed Friends Michl. Ziegler & Dm. Kolb & such others among you who are better acquainted with what has hitherto been done in this affair, [document damaged]
leading members of yr several Meetings at Skippack & Conestoga and desire that they may now take into their serious Consideration as a matter highly worthy of both their religious & civil regard and think of the most proper methods for raising Money amongst you for carrying on so good & necessary a work, and so well becoming both you and us who cannot for conscience sake be assisting in carrying on of war. The trustees appointed by Friends in this City will always be willing to acquaint any Person appointed by yr Meeting or any of yr Bretheren with the steps that have been or will be taken in the disposal of money. And if it should be any Particular satisfaction to yr Brethren I believe it would not be difficult to prevail upon the Contributors at their next Election to choose one or more of yr. Bretheren in the Number of Managers, & give their advice in what manner you may employ such sums as you may raise so as best to answer the End propos'd: a great deal of the difficulty we have been under in the first part of the work is removed by the free & generous manner we have been treated by the Earl of Loudon, with whom some Friends had several Conferences when he was in the City, & we are in hopes as there is likely to be a treaty held at Lancaster in abt two weeks if some of you would weightily consider the Matter, it will appear to you, as it does to us, that the Prince of Peace is graciously affording us an opp[ortunit]y of manifesting the Sincerity of our Desires for the extending of his Reign of Government in ye Earth & that the Heathen may become his Inheritance & the utmost parts of the Earth his Possession, & that all Nations, Kingdoms & People may come to serve him; let us not therefore be Slothful in this Business, but Fervent in Spirit as in the Service of the Lord. [Postscript written in the margin:]

There abt 170 Indians come in Lancaster chiefly of ye 6 Nations abt 200 daily expected of the Shawnese & Delawares, as soon as they are got together the time of ye treaty will be fixed. as a great many frds intend to go up to Lancaster, if ye Brethren in Lancaster could enter into a Subscription etc. where thru their meetings would appoint some to come to Lancaster might address to yrs[142]

Document 63

Dear Friend Isr. Pemberton

Several of you will remembrer that we were in Decr. last with you at your meeting and notifyed our concurrence to your scheme for the pacifick measures with the Indians, not [now?] the most part of the Subscribers amongst us are resolved to pay in at present the half part of their respective Sums, and if affairs can be settled with the Delawares they will pay the Rest about Next Fall, therefore we the hereunto Subscribers are resolved to come down to Philada at next Quarter Session Court and will consult with you wether this and others like Resolves will suit your plan and Measures, that then we might do accordingly. And you will please to inform us with the Bearer hereof wether the said mentioned time will be Convenient on your Part, that we can meet one or other of you, that the Money which we then should have with us, could properly be accepted and received. We have a little while since heard of severall murders committed on our Frontiers, we hope you shall better know what prospect there is of any hopes towards a well-grounded pacification than we do. Please to let us also somewhat know, and we shall always continue

your hearty friends

Caspar Kribel
Christr Schultz

Towamenson May 23 1757[143]

Lancaster Conference Unsuccessful

The conference at Lancaster in May 1757 proved to be a disappointment. A delegation of Iroquois had come down to attend the peace negotiations, but neither the Delawares nor the Shawnees were willing to attend. Even Teedyuscung, the Delaware "King" who had met with the Governor and the Friendly Association at different times before, sent word that he would not come. Pemberton noted that the Delawares had no love for the Iroquois, who had been brought in before to "chastise and oppress them" and "they were determined not to give them another opportunity of doing it." While Governor Denny was at Lancaster meeting with the Iroquois chiefs, Indians from the Ohio boldly attacked Lancaster County settlements and the resentment of the unprotected frontier increased greatly (*Documents* 35, 36, 37).

It was little wonder that the Lancaster Mennonites were dissatisfied with the progress made toward a lasting peace. But they did contribute £680 to the Friendly Association and planned to send a delegate to the next conference with the Indians. Since the Friendly Association had raised and spent less than £1,000 in its peacemaking efforts since 1756, the Mennonite contribution was a very substantial one.

Document 64

Lancaster the 11th of 7 mo 1757

Esteemed Friend Israel Pemberton

Being with Banj. Hersey [Hershey] this morning he desired me to acquaint thee that a many of their people was not well satisfy'd to subscribe towards the expenses and presents that might be thought needfull to be given in order to promote a peace with the Indians, until such time as a peace was more fully concluded—tho their is, he informs me, more than one half willing to contribute, so he desires to know by thee or some other friend whether It might not be as proper to wait while the next treaty be over. But if thou or friends thinks proper they will collect what is already subscribed. I further understand by him that those thats not willing has been persuaded by some people of other societys not to do anything towards any such thing, but if they had anything to spare to give it to the poor. I know their has been some in this town very busy in insinuating & spreading abroad that the late murders committed near us was done by the Indians that was at the late treaty (which hitherto has not been proved against them) and amongst other reports and wicked expressions is maid use of against them of which if kept in, would be more commendable as it is not more than conjecture, tho I believe it is too true that there has a many suffered laitly in this county by some Indians. I am with kind love to thee and all enquiring Frds.

thy Frd *Isaac Whitelock*[144]

Document 65

Lancaster 24th 8th mo 1758

Esteemed ffrd.

This week Benjn. Hersey was at my house and acquainted me that their people had collected the money Subscribed by them for the Indians, which amounts to about Six hundred & Eighty pounds and is to be taken down [to Philadelphia] by the persons appointed, to wit, John Hare and Jacob Myers and as I am requested by said people & appointed by their meeting to attend with the above sd. men, should be glad to have a Line from you to Inform if it might not be agreeable to thee to Let the bringing it down be whilst fifth or Sixth day before ye yearly Meeting; But if thou thinks it will be of more service to be brought Sooner I expect it will be complyed with likewise we hear that their is Likely to be a Treaty with the Indians Soon and as one of the above named Men is desirous to be there please to give me to understand where it is likely to be & wheather at Easton or Elsewhere. Thy answer to this will oblige me who am with kind Love to thee thy Assured ffrd.

Isaac Whitelock[145]

Continued Peace Negotiations

Governor William Denny had resisted the efforts of the Friendly Association, writing to England in 1757 that he "resented this in a Body of Men, who had no more Pretensions than any other religious Society to concern themselves in a Matter of Government."[146] Israel Pemberton's attempt to negotiate a peace based on justice for the Indians ran counter to the official policy at many points and the governor did everything he could to reduce the influence of the Friendly Association in treaty-making.

In July 1757 Teedyuscung and his eastern Delawares agreed to peace, provided they were given back their lands in the Wyoming Valley forever. In October 1758 the Iroquois imposed peace on the Delawares that left many of the most important land disputes unsettled.

The Moravian missionary Christian Frederick Post carried an invitation to the western tribes to join in the peace made at Easton in October and soon afterward a British army under General John Forbes marched to capture Fort Duquesne. They found the fort burned and the French forces gone. At this point, Israel Pemberton sought to make a just peace with the Ohio Valley tribes. He explained his purposes in a letter to John Hunt, Dr. John Fothergill, Richard How, Thomas Corbyn, Jacob Hagin, Jr., and Robert Foster, Friends in England.

Document 66

Philada. 10th. 12th month 1758

Dear Friends

By a Vessel for Liverpool yesterday I informed you we had received an acco[un]t of the Success of General Forbes, an Express is now arrived to our Government who came from fort du Quesne & confirms the good news. As another Express is just going to New York & on his Arrival there the Packet will be dispatched & may sail before the Post gets there, I herewith send you Copy of a Letter from Major Campbell (of ye highland Regim[en]t.) to Wm. Griffits & can just add to it that the General had by Return of one of the Messengers sent from Easton been informed of the friendly disposition of the Delaware Indians & that they were coming in to meet him. Delaware George who has during these troubles been our friend was come with four others before Apby (the Express) came away & said that a considerable Number would be there in a day or two. Honest Frederick Post with ye Indians sent from Easton was among the Indians ab[ou]t Log's Town & Bever Creek collecting them together & as the General intends to have a conference with them before he comes away & obtain their free consent to the repairing the Fort & keeping up that at Loyal Hannon, I hope the scandalous neglects & omissions of those who have hitherto transacted the Publick business will be remedied, for what men but themselves could have avoided, when they released back all Lands Westward of the Alegany Mountains stipulating for a right to maintain Trading houses &ca. in such places as would be most convenient? I have consulted our Steady friend Isaac Zane & my brothers & finding they approve it intend to morrow to send away a Waggon with 30 or 40 pieces of Matchcoats & Strouds for as the French have had no goods this Year such a supply will certainly be very seasonable & a satisfactory pledge of our friendship. We shall leave it to the General whether to present them from the Government or from us as Trustees for the Meninists & Swingfelders who deposited near £1,500 in my hands to promote the Work of Peace. The roads are yet very good but the Season considered it will not be prudent to delay doing this [which] is one reason for applying this Money to the present Purpose. We have reason to be thankful & you to be pleased that you sent us that Supply of Goods with [ou]t which the last Treaty nor the present Occasion could have been served.

I have purchased a bill for £500 Sterling which I am to receive next Week & intend to send you in part of ye Cargo in my Letters to John Hunt. I have desired him to send me on my Acco[un]t 40 p[ieces?] Striped duffels 40 pe. Matchcoats & 25 pe. Strouds & if you think proper to send the same quantity on your own Acco[un]t I have no doubt of your both serving the Publick interest & reaping some profit thereby for the Fund yet provided by Law & the timid disposition of the Commissioners will prevent so large & speedy a supply as will be necessary. The goods should come by two different Ships & if possible be dispatched early without waiting for a Convoy for besides what the Trade will require a Treaty early in the Spring may be expected which we should provide for.

And you may add the same quantity of half thicks, chiefly white some blue & a few purple & such an Assortment of other Goods as you sent before, only omitting the Drop Shott & putting up cheaper ribbons, fewer & better flints & at least 200 lbs. Vermilion, some brass Wire of several sizes, small brass kettles, a few fish hooks sorted, a few pocket compasses, gunhammers, artificial magnetts, Tobacco & snuff boxes, Beads, sleeve Buttons, Ivory combs of cheap sorts, Tobacco tongs, Morris bells, pistol Caped & lutto knives, small Taylors shears & scissers, 10 or 12 pe. printed Callicoes large figures & cheap strong cloths, 8 or 10 pe. midling y[ar]d wide Tandem, as many Tandem Silesias, a small quantity of bed lace, some brass Medals (ye kings head on one side) & 8 or 10 dozen small weeding hoes; such a supply may probably have the happy Effect in confirming the friendship of the Indians whose expectation is turned towards us but as a great deal depends on their coming early I would recommend your giving double freight for a vessel that will set out soon rather than wait till the Season be lost & other supplies sent; perhaps part of them may be sent soonest from Liverpoole from whence we have had a great many striped Blanketts this Year but [they] are much inferior to what you sent & much depends on our keeping our Credit in the quality of what we sell or give to the Indians.

As you will see I write in haste least I should lose this Opportunity. I rely on your excusing it. I am with true love & respect

Your assured friend[147]

Financial Questions

Other members of the Friendly Association were less enthusiastic about Pemberton's expanding plans and his use of the money from the "Meninists and Swingfelders" was overruled in a meeting in December 1758. Pemberton restored the funds to the Friendly Association and paid for the goods for the Indians out of his own pocket. This episode evidently left some uneasiness among Lancaster Mennonites, as Isaac Whitelock indicated in his letter to Israel Pemberton.

Samuel Lightfoot was busy hiring packhorses to carry the trade goods to Fort Cumberland in Maryland, where they would be transferred to small boats to float down to Pittsburgh. He included an account of a discussion of peacemaking with some York County Mennonites in a detailed report to Israel Pemberton.

Document 67

Lancaster 24th 2nd 1759

Esteemed frd.

I rec'd thine of the 14th of this Inst. and after observing the Contents I sent for the trader of whom I had bespoak us Saddles and he consented to send his Man, with his horse & I got the horse thy man brought up so that next morning sent of[f] the two horses and ye twenty sadles to York which got their that day. And since then have had an opportunity with Benjn. Hercey & several other of the Menonists and acquainted Benjn. of thy Intension of Writeing, and the reson of thy not doing it, so Soon as thou could have wish'd, and at the same time I tould him, thou desir'd thy kind wishes to be remembered to him & his Breathren, he likewise desired me to give his Dear Love to thee and further to acquaint thee that he & his Brea[thre]n should not be uneasy with any reports that might be Spread, without having it from a person or persons of whom they might safely Credit so that he desired thou might not be uneasy in the Least in that Respect.

Isaac Whitelock[148]

Document 68

York 23d 2 mo, 1759

Dear Friend

. . . . I have seen several of the Menists about Conewagoe (when in Search of Oats) some of whom I am sensible are well disposed considerate people which I was glad to observe and had my business permitted might have exchanged some satisfactory discourse with several of them brought on by informing them of my business that tho' we deemed it unlawful for us to fight and did therefore not go to war as others did yet we were greatly concerned at the Calamities and bloodshed which had happened and were anxiously desirous to do everything in our power consistent with our Christian profession to cause those broils to cease which visibly affected some of them and perhaps was what induced them to spare me what little oats they had as I believe they were really not plenty among them. . . .

Samuel Lightfoot[149]

Ransom for Prisoners

Although the western tribes had buried the hatchet, many men, women, and children captured on the frontier of Pennsylvania, Maryland, and Virginia still remained in the Delaware, Shawnee, Seneca, Ottawa, Chippewa, and Wyandot villages. The Mennonites preferred that their money be used to ransom these prisoners and in June 1760 Israel Pemberton made a formal proposal to the Commissioners for Indian Affairs in their behalf.

Document 69

If the Commissioners for Indian Affairs will agree to instruct their Agents to take every proper Opportunity of enquiring what Captives there are in each Indian Town & as near as they can their Ages & Sex,

& the disposition of the Indians, with whom they live, respecting the releasing them, it is thought the Minutes of all such intelligence may be of service, if transmitted in time, to be laid before the Governour at the time of a general Treaty. And if any of the Indians who have Captives are willing to release them before the Time of such a Treaty, in order to encourage them therein, Some small Presents might be given in Proportion to the distance they live from Pittsburgh, in consideration of their Journey in bringing them thither, the Value of w[hi]ch the Trustees of the fund raised by the Menonists will immediately pay to the Commissioners, their Agents or their Order, but as it may be very inconvenient to do any thing of this Kind in such a manner as to give the Indians cause to think we intend to ransom the Prisoners in general, great Caution is necessary in transacting the Affair.

Submitted to the Consideration of the Commissioners for Indian Affairs, the 7th 6th mo. 1760 On behalf of the Trustees for the Menonists

per Isr[ael] Pemberton.[150]

Papoonhank and the Wyalusing Indians

Later in 1760 the Schwenkfelders agreed that at least part of the money they contributed should be applied to ransoming captives from the Indians. Christopher Schultz, who replied to Israel Pemberton's request, added a word of caution about careful use of their funds.

Schultz included with his letter a German translation he had made of an article or pamphlet dealing with Papoonhank or Munsee John, who had established a Munsee Delaware village at Wyalusing in 1758. At first a prophet of the old ways and the old religion, he had been converted to Christianity by the Moravians. The Wyalusing Indians were a wonder to all for their fervent faith and their high moral code, including acceptance of a nonresistant ethic. Papoonhank later settled his people in the Moravian mission villages on the Tuscarawas River in Ohio, where he died in 1775.

Israel Pemberton sent a copy of the same account of the Wyalusing Delawares, possibly in Schultz's German translation, to Benjamin Hershey in January 1761.

Document 70

Hereford Decr. 1, 1760

Beloved Friend

Having consulted our Friends, concerning the Proposal lately made to us, for laying out of our Money now in thy Hands; they give these for their Opinion, as the Relief of the Poor Captives amongst the Savages is a matter of immediate Necessity to which Humanity as well as Christianity obliges to contribute, They are willing that in Conjunction what other Friends do contribute about the half part of the said money be applied towards the release of such poor prisoners late our fellow inhabitants, if it shall be found meet that something shall and may be done, and the future Circumstances continue to be such, that the Release of them be retarded, and not effected by the measures of our Government.

As there is now a Prospect of the Cherokees returning to their Alliance with the English it is probable our northerly Indians shall not so much hesitate as they hitherto have done, to accomodate themselves to reasonable Terms, especially as there is the giving up their prisoners; nevertheless, as we trust the Friends will act in that affair with all due circumspection, that when they have the immediate Relief of the Captives at heart to Effect the same, they will be not less cautious to prevent unnecessary charges upon private contributors as they are themselves.

The other part of the said money of about a Hundred Pounds could be left for further Purposes, necessity's or Considerations time and Occasion will furnish and bring on.

With these Presents I do return the Remarks on the Behaviour of Pawpunahoak having copied & translated the same into High Dutch; it hath been very acceptable to several of my friends, who rejoice in perceiving the hand of Grace to operate so strongly on the poor Heathen. I thank [you] for the communication of that Relation as well as for the Inquiry presented to me. If a high dutch Copy of the said Remarks should be of Service to thee, to shew them to some Friend, I would upon notice willingly furnish thee with one. I remain Thy most affectionate Friend

Christr. Schultze[151]

Freeing Captives and Making Treaties

Israel Pemberton sent a long letter to Benjamin Hershey detailing what little progress had been made in winning freedom for the captives still in the Indian villages. The decision to use the Mennonite fund for this purpose had evidently been reached when Israel Pemberton and Isaac Zane met with Lancaster Mennonite leaders sometime after February 1759 (*Cf. Documents* 67, 68.) General John Stanwix had succeeded to the British command on the death of General Forbes in May 1759 and negotiated treaties with the western tribes before leaving for

England in May 1760. George Croghan, as deputy to Sir William Johnson, Superintendent of the Northern Indians, was responsible for a policy opposed to that of the Friendly Association, when he was not diverting government trade goods to his own private interests.

Document 71

Philadelphia the 14th 1 mo 1761

Loving Friends

The Christian benevolent disposition of mind which engaged you to contribute towards the regaining and establishing peace with the Indians by pacific measures & the Confidence you were pleased to repose in me to apply your contributions to that purpose have fix'd in my mind an Earnest desire both to discharge the trust agreeable to your intention & to have you fully satisfied that this is my constant Endeavour—and with this view I have proceeded since I was at your meeting with my Friend Isaac Zane about two years since & have as I had opp[ortunit]y given some of you some information of what hath been done towards the perfecting this good work, but it being sometime having pass'd without any opportunity of conversing with any of you on this subject, I now think it expedient to send you in writing some account of these affairs.

The Generals of the King's Forces not being willing the Goods I sent to Pittsburgh should be apply'd in the manner I proposed towards the redemption of the Captives, some part of them were sold to the Indians at low prices & the rest were distributed at the King's Expence in presents at the Treaty which General Stanwix and the other commanding Officers held there, & as these Goods were ready there at a time, when no other supply could be had, the sending them proved to be of service tho' it was attended with greater difficulty & Expence, and the General was so sensible of it that when he paid me for the goods he had for presents he made me an allowance on that acco[un]t but not sufficient to make up the Loss I sustained. My agents were instrumental in obtaining the release of several captives while they were there, and since that time I have frequently renew'd my application to the General, to our Governor, the Provincial Commissioners & the Commissioners of the Indian Trade & offered if they would consent to have rewards given for the redemption of the Captives, to pay the same, but all I could expect to obtain from them was that the agents at the Trading Houses should be authorized to inform the Indians, that such as would bring them any of the Captives should be paid for their trouble in proportion to the distance they might bring them, and accordingly several have been since brought in, for which I have paid & I am in hopes this winter of several more, as I intend to use my endeavors to have the fullest use made of the Liberty allow'd for the benefit of those distressed people in captivity, since I find that seems to be the only method we can at present take for their relief.—Last winter by the Messages rec'd from the Indians & the information given us by others who had been among them, we had reason to expect there would be a general meeting of the Indians from the Northward & the Westward at this City sometime in the summer & as we were very desirous everything which remain'd unperform'd on the Part of the Proprietor of this Province should be compleated agreeable to the Expectations given them at the Treatys at Easton, in order that our Fellow subjects in Captivity might be Released & that Peace with them Indians might be established on a just foundation, we therefore (who are Trustees of the Friendly Association) thought it necessary to communicate to the Proprietor what appeared to us necessary to be done in order to effect those Good Purposes; this we did in an Address which we Sent to our Friends in London who delivered it to the Propr. & they Promis'd to consider it & return us their answer, but we have not yet receiv'd one from them.

The Indians were diverted in the summer from coming Hither as they Intended & tho a considerable number of them attended the General at Pittsburgh, & had several Conferences with Him, as George Croghan was employed to have the management thereof, there was little done there besides giving & receiving presents, & by words receiving their promises of Friendship to see each other. The Prisoners, as I am inform'd were not so much as mentioned, & the Indians before they came there had resolved not to enter into Deliberation on Matters of Consequence in a [conference?] stain'd with blood or with blood or with men who were employ'd in war, determining to leave all business of consequence till they should see their old Brethren at their old Council fire at Philadelphia. After their Conferences with the General the Indian Chiefs to prevent our treaty being impos'd on—by false accounts of what had pass'd mett together & employed a person they could confide in to write down the substance what had been said to them with their answers w[hi]ch they immediately ordered to be sent me, with an assurance of their intentions of coming next spring or Summer to see us & bring their captives with them.

But tho' we were disappointed of seeing the Indians in general, we had a very acceptable visit from about thirty sober religious Indians who are lately settled on the River Susquehanna about sixty miles above Wyoming. Their own behavior and weighty religious conversations very sensible satisfaction, for we found in them a sense of Religion more clear & better grounded than we had ever before mett with in any of these People which engag'd us to make a careful enquiry concerning them from other Indians who have since been here & from some white People who have been among them and having drawn up some account of what we have observ'd & been informed concerning them I herewith send you a copy of it, believing it will be cause of rejoicing to the serious & upright in Heart among you, *who are waiting for in faith for the fulfilling of the many glorious prophecies of the general spreading of the Gospel of our Lord & Savior in the back corners of the Earth, when the wilderness & the solitary places will be made to rejoice & become as the Garden of Heaven.*

When I am able to communicate any farther Material Intelligence concerning these Affairs, I intend to do it, in the mean time I remain

with much Love

Your Real Friend

I[srael] P[emberton]

To Benjamin Hersey & others the Menonists in Lancaster Co.[152]

Friendly Association Wanes

The Friendly Association continued to press the Proprietor and his agents in Pennsylvania to carry out the pledges they had made to the Delawares of returning their lands in the Wyoming Valley to them and they still worked at redeeming the captives, but the Friendly Association was gradually winding up its affairs. As the surviving account books show, funds for the Friendly Association came almost entirely from Mennonites in its latter years. Of £ 260 in the hands of the Friendly Association in 1763, £230 had been donated by Franconia Mennonites.

The degree to which Mennonites supported the Friendly Association was known to the general public and provided ammunition for political enemies of Israel Pemberton and the Quakers in the pamphlet war that followed the massacre of the Susquehannock Indians in Lancaster County in 1763. The Rev. Thomas Barton, Rector of St. James Episcopal Church in Lancaster, is generally considered the author of *The Conduct of the Paxton-Men, Impartially represented* (Philadelphia, 1764).

Document 72

2 mo 6 1762

By Cash of Israel Pemberton being part of the money Contributed

by Menonists residing in the Counties of Philadelphia & Berks
£ 200. .0. .0.

4 mo 19 1763

By Cash of Israel Pemberton being part of the Contributions of the Menonists in Philadelphia & Berks Counties £230. .0. .0.

19 4 mo 1763

We the subscribers in pursuance of the appointment of the board of Trustees of the Friendly Association for regaining and Preserving Peace with the Indians by Pacific Measures having Examined the above accounts of John Reynell Treasurer of the said Association do find that since the Adjustment of the Accts last year He hath rec'd from Sundry Members of said Association the Sum of Two hundred Sixty pounds ten shillings, including two hundred & thirty pounds *fifteen shillings & Six-pence halfpenny* paid by Israel Pemberton being money Contributed by the Menonists.[153]

Document 73

That whilst they were thus abused, and thus stript of their *Birth-Rights,*—ISRAEL and JOSEPH, two petty Fellows, who ought to have no higher Claims than themselves, were permitted to lord it over the Land; and in Contempt of the Government, and the express Orders of the Crown, forbiding them to hold private Treaties with the Indians, exchange Belts of Wampum with them—make them Presents—all this they have done, and in their own Name, without so much as including the simple MENONISTS, from whom they had extorted large Sums of Money to Support this Expence.[154]

Document 74

But all this they have done, sayeth this Writer, without so much as including the simple *Menonists*, from whom they had extorted large Sums of Money, to support their Expense. (The meaning of the Word Extort is this: to exact Illequally, or get, or take violently and by unjustificable Means, to abuse Authority) this must be a false Assertion.

Let the *Menonists* Answer for themselves. But the Truth is, that the *Menonists,* as a Society of good Religious people, by way of Simele collected Money and desired the Quakers to hand it to then suffering people on the Frontiers, to serve their Necessities. Is this extortion in the Quakers? Or doth it show the *Menonist* to be a simple people? No; it's evident that the Menonists were a compassionate people, not regardless of their fellow Creatures sufferings and willing to contribute to their Support.[155]

Conscientious Objectors on the Virginia Frontier

Militia Duty

Virginia, like most of the Colonies, already had a Militia Law obliging men of military age to turn out on muster days and learn the military act or pay a fine for their failure to do so. Few records of militia fines have survived. The Clerk of the Frederick County Court preserved a complete record for this Shenandoah Valley county, when he copied deeds into a book that had been used between 1755 and 1761 for the sessions of the court-martial that levied fines on reluctant militiamen.

The names of many Frederick County Quakers and Mennonites can be found in these records, as well as the names of men who had no apparent religious motive for their neglect of duty. Even in a frontier county, militia duty was never popular. Records of Hopewell Monthly Meeting show that Friends along Mill Creek in present Berkeley County, West Virginia, met for worship at the home of Morris Rees, Jr. Samuel Bohm was one of the signers of the letter from Virginia Mennonites to Holland in 1758 and David Kauffman and Henry Histand were also Mennonite pioneers in present Page County, Virginia. John Funkhouser, Jr., and Christian Crabell were among the Mennonite settlers in the Strasburg neighborhood of present Shenandoah County who paid fines in 1761 and signed a petition of Virginia Mennonites asking for exemption from the militia system on religious grounds.

Mennonites petitioned the Virginia House of Burgesses for exemption in 1769 and 1772 and renewed their request after the American Revolution.

Document 75

At a Court Martial held in the County of Frederick on Tuesday the 2nd Day of September 1755.

The Rt. Honble. Thomas Lord Fairfax County Lieutenant.

Ordered that Morris Reece senr. of the Troop Commanded by Capt. John Linsey be fined seven shillings & sixpence or seventy five ll. of Tob[bac]o for Absenting himself from One Private muster within twelve months last past.

Ordered that Morris Reece Junr. of the Troop Commanded by Capt. John Linsey be fined seven shillings & sixpence or seventy five ll.

of Tobo. for Absenting himself from one Private muster within twelve months last past. . . .

Ordered that David Coffman of the foot Company Commanded by Capt. William Bethel be fined ten shillings or one Hundred ll of Tobo. for Absenting himself from one Private muster within twelve months last past.

Ordered that Samuel Beam of the foot Company Commanded by Capt. William Bethel be fined ten shillings or one Hundred ll. of Tobo. for Absenting himself from one Private muster within twelve months last past.

Ordered that Henry Histand of the foot Company Commanded by Capt. William Bethel be fined ten shillings or one Hundred ll. of Tobo. for Absenting himself from one Private muster within twelve months last past.[156]

Document 76

At a Court Martial Held for Frederick County on Fryday the 9th Day of October 1761.

Ordered that Jacob Stover of Captain John Funks Company is fined Forty Shillings for absenting himself from three private and one General Musters within Twelve Months last past.

Ordered that John Funkhouser Jr. of Captain John Funks Company is fined Ten Shillings for absenting himself from the last General Muster.

Ordered that Christian Craebell of Captain John Funks Company is fined Twenty Shillings for absenting himself from one private and one General Muster within Twelve Months last past.

Ordered that John Martin of Captain John Funks Company is fined Forty Shillings for absenting himself from three private and one General Muster within Twelve Months last past.

Ordered that Christian Hockman of Captain John Funks Company is fined Forty Shillings for absenting himself from three private and one General Muster within Twelve Months last past.[157]

Document 77

Tuesday, the 14th of November 1769

A *Petition* of *Jacob Stricklor* and *Jacob Coughenor*, on Behalf of themselves, and their Protestant Brethren, of the Sect called Menonists, was presented to the House, and read, setting forth, that the Petitioners have retired to this Colony, in Hopes of enjoying the free Exercise of their Religion, and are willing to contribute a proportionable Part of their Estates, whenever the Exigencies of Government may require it, and desirous in every other Respect, as far as they are able, to promote the Public Good; but that they are forbidden by the Dictates of Conscience to bear Arms; and therefore praying that they may be exempt from the Penalties they are subject to for declining military Duty.

Ordered, That the Petition be referred to the Committee for Religion; and that they do examine the Matter thereof, and report the same, with their Opinion thereupon to the House.[158]

Document 78

Friday, the 17th of November, 1769

Mr. Treasurer [Peyton Randolph] reported, from the Committee for Religion, that the Committee had had under their Consideration the Petition of the Sect of Protestant Dissenters, called *Menonists,* and had come to a Resolution thereupon; which he read in his place, and afterwards delivered in at the Clerk's Table; where the same was read, and is as followeth, *viz.*

Resolved, That is is the Opinion of this Committee, that the Petition of the Sect of Protestant Dissenters, called *Menonist,* praying that they may be exempt from the Penalties they are subject to for declining military Duty, is reasonable.

Ordered, That it be an Instruction to the Committee of Propositions and Grievances, who were appointed to bring in a Bill, pursuant to the Thirteenth Resolution of the Committee of Courts of Justice, which was agreed to by the House on *Saturday* last, that they make Provision in the said Bill for exempting *Menonists* from the Penalties they are subject to for declining military Duty.[159]

Document 79

Monday, the 23rd of March, 1772

A Petition of *Jacob Strickley* [Strickler] and *Henry Funk,* in Behalf of themselves, and their Christian Brethren, of the Sect, called Menonists, was presented to the House, and read; setting forth that the Petitioners and their Friends are comfortably settled on the Frontiers of this Colony, where they can support themselves and their Families, if they may be relieved from the Payment of Fines for not performing military Duty, which their religious Tenets forbid them to exercise; and therefore praying that they may be exempt from such Penalties.

Ordered, That the said Petition be referred to the Committee of Propositions and Grievances; and that they do examine the Matter thereof, and report the same, with their Opinion thereupon to the House.[160]

Document 80

Monday, The 30th of March 1772

Mr. [Richard] *Bland* reported from the Committee of Propositions and Grievances, to whom the Petition of the Dissenters, called Menonists, praying that they may be exempt from the Penalties inflicted for not attending Musters, was referred, that the Committee had examined into the Matter of the said Petition, and had come to a Resolution thereupon, which they had directed him to report to the House; and he read the Report in his Place, and afterwards delivered it in at the Clark's Table, where the Resolution of the Committee was read, and it as followeth, *viz.*

Resolved, That it is the Opinion of this Committee that the said Petition is reasonable.[161]

Notes for Chapter 1

1. Wellenreuther, *PMHB*, XCIV (April 1970), p. 149.

2. Philip A. Bruce, *Institutional History of Virginia in the Seventeenth Century* (Gloucester, Mass., 1964), II, p. 8. The changing concepts can be traced in two excellent studies, L. G. Schwoerer, *No Standing Armies! The Anti-Army Ideology in Seventeenth Century England* (Baltimore, Md., 1974) and J. R. Western, *The English Militia in the Eighteenth Century: The Story of a Political Issue 1660-1802* (London, 1965).

3. *Pennsylvania Archives*, 8th Series, III, pp. 2529-2531 *et seq*. Davidson, pp. 25-26.

4. *Pennsylvania Archives*, 8th Series, III, p. 2656.

5. Tolles, *Meeting House and Counting House*, pp. 20-21. Wellenreuther, *PMHB*, XCIV (April 1970), p. 157.

6. "James Logan on Defensive War," *PMHB*, VI (October 1882), pp. 402-411. Frederick B. Tolles, *James Logan and the Culture of Provincial America* (Boston, 1957), pp. 154-156.

7. Thomas Cookson to Conrad Weiser, September 1741, Correspondence of Conrad Weiser, I, fols. 6-7, Historical Society of Pennsylvania, Philadelphia, Pa. (hereafter cited as HSP).

8. Paul A. W. Wallace, *Conrad Weiser, Friend of Colonist and Mohawk* (Philadelphia, 1945), pp. 112-114.

9. William Reed Steckel, "Pietist in Colonial Pennsylvania: Christopher Sauer, Printer 1738-1758," PhD dissertation, Stanford University, 1949, pp. 141-144.

10. Thayer, pp. 16-18;

11. Norman S. Cohen, "The Philadelphia Election Riot of 1742," *PMHB*, XCII (July 1968), pp. 306-319. *Pennsylvania Archives*, 8th Series, IV, pp. 2957-3009.

12. *Pennsylvania Archives*. 8th Series, IV, p. 2821.

13. *Ibid*., p. 2865.

14. Wellenreuther, *PMHB*, XCIV (April 1970), pp. 160-161.

15. Marietta, *PMHB*, XCV (January 1971), pp. 4-5. This was certainly the case with English Friends. Rufus M. Jones, *Later Periods of Quakerism* (Cambridge, 1923), p. 158.

16. Wilbur J. Bender, "Pacifism Among the Mennonites, Amish Mennonites and Schwenkfelders of Pennsylvania to 1783," *MQR*, I (July 1927), pp. 31-32.

17. Young, p. 352.

18. *Pennsylvania Archives*, 8th Series, I, p. 8.

19. *Colonial Records*, II, p. 250.

20. *Ibid*., p. 500.

21. *Ibid*., pp. 508 and 514.

22. *Pennsylvania Archives*, 8th Series, II, pp. 1383 and 1717.

23. Young, p. 351.

24. *Colonial Records*, IV, pp. 765-766.

25. *Ibid*., pp. 768-769. *Pennsylvania Archives*, 8th Series, IV, pp. 3017-3043.

26. Arthur Graeff, *The Relations Between the Pennsylvania Germans and the British Authorities 1750-1776* (Norristown, Pa., 1939), p. 81.

27. *Pennsylvania Archives*, 8th Series, IV, pp. 3093-3110.

28. Albert H. Smyth, ed., *The Writings of Benjamin Franklin* (New York, 1905), III, pp. 139-141. Steckel, pp. 154-158. Thayer, *Pennsylvania Politics*, pp. 21-23.

29. Theodore Thayer, *Israel Pemberton, King of the Quakers* (Philadelphia, 1943), p. 51. William S. Hanna, *Benjamin Franklin and Pennsylvania Politics* (Stanford, Calif., 1964), pp. 32-35.

30. *Pennsylvanische Berichte* (Germantown, Pa.), December 16, 1747; March 16, 1748. Steckel, pp. 159-167.

31. "An Account of the Gospel Labours and Christian Experiences, of that Faithful

Minister of Christ, John Churchman, Late of Nottingham, in Pennsylvania," William and Thomas Evans, eds., *The Friends' Library* (Philadelphia, 1842), VI, pp. 200-201. A reprint of the 1779 Philadelphia edition.

32. James H. Hutson, *Pennsylvania Politics 1746-1770* (Princeton, N.J., 1972), p. 6. Hanna, pp. 16-19. *Pennsylvanische Berichte*, November 16, 1748.

33. Davidson, pp. 68-69 and 77

34. Paul A. W. Wallace *Indians in Pennsylvania* (Harrisburg, Pa., 1970), pp. 142-43. Wallace, *Conrad Weiser*, pp. 277-285 and 333-349.

35. Lois Mulkearn, ed., *George Mercer Papers Relating to the Ohio Company of Virginia* (Pittsburgh, Pa., 1954), p. 145.

36. *Ibid.*, pp. 74-88.

37. Lee McCardell, *Ill-Starred General: Braddock of the Coldstream Guards* (Pittsburgh, Pa., 1958), pp. 135-142.

38. *An Epistle from our General Spring Meeting of Ministers and Elders for Pennsylvania and New-Jersey, held at Philadelphia, from the 29th of the Third Month, to the 1st of the Fourth Month, inclusive, 1755*, (Philadelphia, 1755), p. 1.

39. Graeff, pp. 87-88.

40. James H. Hutson, "Benjamin Franklin and Pennsylvania Politics, 1751-1755: A Reappraisal, "*PMHB*, XCIII (July 1969), pp. 332-335 and *passim*. Thayer, *Pennsylvania Politics*, pp. 43-44.

41. *Pennsylvania Archives*, 8th Series, V. pp. 3857-3859.

42. *Ibid.*, pp. 3869-3870.

43. *Ibid.*, p. 3901.

44. Hutson, *PMHB*, XCIII, pp. 349-350.

45. Thayer, *Pennsylvania Politics*, p. 37.

46. Hutson, *loc. cit.*

47. *Pennsylvania Gazette* (Philadelphia), October 30, 1755.

48. *Pennsylvania Gazette* (Philadelphia), November 6, 1755.

49. *Pennsylvania Gazette* (Philadelphia), November 20, 1755.

50. *Colonial Records*, VI, p. 704.

51. *Colonial Records*, VII, pp. 272-278.

52. William A. Hunter, *Forts on the Pennsylvania Frontier, 1753-1758* (Harrisburg, Pa., 1960), pp. 183-185.

53. *Pennsylvania Archives*, 1st Series, II, p. 561.

54. Hunter, pp. 194-200.

55. Andrew S. Berky, ed., *The Journals and Papers of David Schultze* (Pennsburg, Pa., 1952), I, 170-173.

56. *Pennsylvanische Berichte*, December 25, 1756.

57. Berky, I, pp. 163-167.

58. Hunter, p. 184.

59. *Colonial Records*, VII, pp. 87 and 91.

60. *Ibid.*, p. 120. *Pennsylvania Gazette*, January 16, 1756; April 16, 1756.

61. *Pennsylvania Archives*, 8th Series, VI, p. 4555.

62. Philadelphia Yearly Meeting Minutes of the Meeting for Sufferings, 1756-1775, fols. 53-54 and 73-79. Quaker Collection, Haverford College Library, Haverford, Pennsylvania.

63. *Pennsylvania Archives*, 1st Series, III, p. 115.

64. *Pennsylvania Archives*, 8th Series, VI, p. 4598.

65. *Hopewell Friends History* (Strasburg, Va., 1934), p. 496.

66. Philadelphia Yearly Meeting, Minutes of the Meeting for Sufferings, 1756-1775, fol. 128.

67. *A Journal of the Life, Gospel Labours, and Christian Experiences of That Faithful Minister of Jesus Christ, John Woolman (Dublin, 1794), pp. 80-86.*

68. *Friends Library*, VI, pp. 235-236.

69. Cadbury, *Friends Journal*, XX (September 1, 1966), pp. 440-441.
70. Thayer, *Pemberton*, p. 90 Marietta, *PMHB*, XCV (January, 1971), p. 17.
71. Marietta, *PMHB*, XCV (January, 1971), pp. 18-27. Ketcham, *WMQ*, 3rd Series, XX (October 1963), p. 436.
72. Rothermund, p. 96. Bauman, pp. 32-33.
73. *Pennsylvania Gazette* (Philadelphia), November 20, 1755; November 27, 1755.
74. *Pennsylvania Gazette* (Philadelphia), December 25, 1755.
75. Durnbaugh, *Brethren in Colonial America*, pp. 164-169.
76. Wallace, *Indians*, p. 146.
77. Wallace, *Weiser*, pp. 434-437 and 445-452. Peter Brock, *Pacifism in the United States from the Colonial Period to the First World War* (Princeton, N.J., 1968), pp. 149-150. Sydney V. James, *A People Among Peoples: Quaker Benevolence in Eighteenth-Century America* (Cambridge, Mass., 1963), pp. 178 ff. Theodore Thayer, "The Friendly Association," *PMHB*, LXVII (October 1943), pp. 356-376.
78. Wallace, *Weiser*, pp. 459-465.
79. Wallace, *Indians*, pp. 148-149.
80. Thayer, *Pemberton*, pp. 171-186.
81. Elizabeth Horsch Bender, tr., "A Pennsylvania Letter of 1745 to Mennonite Leaders in Holland," *MHB*, XXXII (October 1971), pp. 4-5.
82. *Pennsylvania Archives*, 8th Series, II, p. 2821.
83. *Ibid., p. 2835*
84. *Ibid.*, p. 2853.
85. *Colonial Records*, IV, pp. 628-629.
86. *Pennsylvania Archives*, 8th Series, II, pp. 2854-2855.
87. *Ibid.*, p. 2865. The Governor gave his assent the same day. *Ibid.*, p. 2866.
88. *Pennsylvanische Berichte*, April 1, 1755.
89. Guy F. Hershberger, "A Newly Discovered Mennonite Petition of 1755," *MQR*, XXXIII (April 1959), pp. 143-151.
90. *Pennsylvanische Berichte*, May 16, 1755.
91. *Pennsylvania Gazette*, August 21, 1755.
92. *Pennsylvania Archives*, 8th Series, V, pp. 4013-4014. The settlement of their claim can be found in Lewis Burd Walker ed., *The Burd Papers. The Settlement of the Waggoners' Accounts Relating to General Braddock's Expedition Towards Fort Duquesne* (Philadelphia, 1899), p. 70.
93. *Pennsylvanische Berichte*, November 1, 1755.
94. Walker, pp. 5-7. *Cf.* footnote 93.
95. Sylvester K. Stevens and Donald H. Kent, eds., *The Papers of Col. Henry Bouquet* (Harrisburg, Pa., 1940). VI^1, p. 146. Landis' probably refers to the still-standing Landisville Meeting House, built in 1752. Lieutenant L. S. Ourry was the assistant deputy quartermaster for Bouquet's forces.
96. Shippen Papers, Historical Society of Pennsylvania, Philadelphia, Pa. George Stevenson of York, Conrad Weiser of Berks, and John Armstrong of Cumberland were responsible for wagons and forage in their respective counties. Adam and Joseph Hubley were prominent in Lancaster.
97. Stevens and Kent, VI^1, pp. 168-171.
98. *Ibid.*, VI^2, pp. 38-39.
99. *Pennsylvania Archives*, 8th Series, V, pp. 3909-3910.
100. Ernst Muller, *Geschichte der Bernischen Taufer nach den urkunden Dagestellt* (Nieukoop, Netherlands, 1972), p. 365. The narrative of Marie LeRoy and Barbara Leininger, who were taken captive by the Indians and later escaped, was published by Christopher Sauer in German in 1759 and became a "best-seller." It was printed in English in *Pennsylvania Archives*, 2nd Series, VII, pp. 427-438. *Cf. Colonial Records*, VI, 645-648.
101. *Colonial Records*, VI, pp. 659-660.

102. *Ibid.,p. 705*
103. *Pennsylvania Archives*, 1st Series, II, pp. 448-449.
104. *Ibid.*, p. 449.
105. *Ibid.*, p. 461.
106. *Pennsylvania Archives*, 8th Series, V, p. 4096.
107. *Pennsylvania Archives*, 1st Series, II, pp. 514-515. The families who fled from Conewago and the signers of the petition *may* be the same people. Conewago Township in present Adams County may be meant; McSherrystown was formerly known as Conewago. The Conewago congregation of the Church of the Brethren (Dunkers) was established near East Berlin in Reading Township in present Adams County about 1741. Either location would be some 15 miles west of York.
108. *Pennsylvania Archives*, 8th Series, V, p. 4103.
109. *Ibid.*, p. 4105.
110. *Pennsylvania Archives*, 8th Series, V, p. 4102 gives no signatures. *Pennsylvania Archives*, 1st Series, II, p. 487 has 20 signatures, although the Assembly minutes say there were 23 signers. John Woolman had a hand in drafting it, but did not sign since he lived in New Jersey.
111. *Pennsylvania Archives*, 8th Series, V. p. 4173. The dissenters were Quakers. Pemberton represented Philadelphia County, Callender the City of Philadelphia, and Worral Lancaster County.
112. *Pennsylvania Archives*, 1st Series, II, pp. 516-519.
113. *Pennsylvania Archives*, 1st Series, III, pp. 120-137. Only those sections of the bill relating to conscientious objectors have been reproduced here.
114. *Ibid.*, pp. 158-159.
115. *Pennsylvania Gazette*, May 19, 1757.
116. *Ibid.*, May 26, 1757.
117. *Pennsylvania Archives*, 1st Series, III, p. 194.
118. *Pennsylvania Gazette*, October 6, 1757.
119. *Pennsylvanische Berichte*, October 15, 1757.
120. *Pennsylvania Journal and General Advertiser*, October 6, 1757.
121. "Lists of Pennsylvania Settlers Murdered, Scalped and Taken Prisoners by Indians, 1755-1756," *PMHB*, XXXII (July 1908), pp. 311-312. Original in Conrad Weiser Papers, HSP.
122. *Pennsylvanische Berichte*, July 8, 1758.
123. Sylvester K. Stevens and Donald H. Kent, eds., *Wilderness Chronicles of Northwestern Pennsylvania* (Harrisburg, Pa., 1941), pp. 119-121. The original is in the British Museum, Additional MSS. 21658, fol. 132.
124. *Pennsylvania Archives*, 1st Series, IV, p. 99.
125. H. Frank Eshleman, *An Authentic Background and Annals of the Swiss and German Pioneer Settlers of Southeastern Pennsylvania and of their Remote Ancestors, From the Middle of the Dark Ages, Down to the Time of the Revolutionary War* (Lancaster, Pa., 1917), p. 325.
126. *Ibid.*, p. 326.
127. *Pennsylvania Gazette*, July 27, 1758. No copy of a Virginia newspaper for 1758 is known to be extant.
128. *Pennsylvanische Berichte*, December 16, 1755.
129. *Ibid.*, January 16, 1756.
130. *Ibid.*, January 16, 1756. This item was translated from *Pennsylvania Gazette*, January 8, 1756.
131. *Pennsylvanische Berichte*, February 1, 1756.
132. H.S.P. *Cf.* H. M. M. Richards, "The Pennsylvania Germans in the French and Indian War." *Proceedings of the Pennsylvania German Society, XV (1906), pp. 199-202.*
133. *Pennsylvania Gazette*, August 4, 1763.
134. "Historische Anmerkungen was sich von Anno 1750 an folgentlich bisz 1775

mit den Schwenkfeldern, merkliches Verlauffen." Schwenkfelder Library, Pennsburg, Pa.

135. Papers of the Friendly Association, Quaker Collection, Haverford College Library, Haverford, Pa. Microfilm American Philosophical Society Library, Philadelphia, Pa.

136. *Pennsylvanische Berichte,* June 16, 1756.

137. *Ibid.*, August 16, 1756.

138. Papers of the Friendly Association, A.P.S.L.

139. Berky, pp. 188-189.

140-145. Papers of the Friendly Association, A.P.S.L.

146. *Pennsylvania Archives,* 1st Series, III, p. 109.

147. Pemberton Papers, H.S.P.

148. Papers of the Friendly Association, A.P.S.L.

149. *Ibid.*

150. Pemberton Papers, H.S.P.

151. Papers of the Friendly Association, A.P.S.L.

152. *Loc. cit.*

153. Friendly Association Account Book, HSP.

154. "The Conduct of the Paxton-Men, Impartially represented: with some Remarks on the Narrative," John R. Dunbar, ed., *The Paxton Papers* (The Hague, 1957), p. 272. The reason for the hostility towards Joseph Fox is unclear, as Israel Pemberton was the leading figure in the Friendly Association. Fox, a wealthy Quaker merchant of Philadelphia, had supported defensive efforts in 1755.

155. "An Answer, to the Pamphlet Entituled the Conduct of the *Paxton Men,* impartially represented," *ibid.*, pp. 321-322.

156. Frederick County Deeds, Liber 18, fol. 13. Frederick County Clerk's Office, Winchester, Va.

157. *Ibid.*, fol. 48.

158. John Pendleton Kennedy, ed., *Journals of the House of Burgesses of Virginia* (Richmond, 1906), XI, p. 256.

159. *Ibid.*, p. 267. The intention was evidently to amend the 1766 Militia Act, which exempted Quakers from military duty, if they provided a substitute or paid a fine of £ 10 each year. William Waller Hening, comp., *The Statutes at Large; Being a Collection of all the Laws of Virginia from the First Session of the Legislature in the Year 1619*. Richmond, 1821, 6, pp. 241-245. No such law was passed in the 1769 session.

160. Kennedy, XII, p. 266.

161. *Ibid.*, p. 280.

Chapter 2

"TO PREVENT THE DESTRUCTION OF RELIGIOUS LIBERTY"

Development of the Nonresistant Stance

The end of the French and Indian War began a new stage in the relationship of the Mennonites and the other nonresistant sects with their neighbors. The murder of the Conestoga Indians by the Paxton Boys in December 1763 and the march of armed frontiersmen on Philadelphia six weeks later led to an effort to end the proprietary government, entrusted to William Penn and his heirs, and substitute for it a governor and council appointed by the king and answerable to the authorities in London. To Benjamin Franklin and other leaders of the old Quaker Party in the Assembly, this appeal for royal government seemed the best guarantee of their liberty. Quakers, Mennonites, Schwenkfelders, and Moravians, at first enthusiastic, saw any change in government as a threat to liberty of conscience and united to defend their freedom at the polls.[1]

Thomas Penn's unpopular attempt to govern his colony more directly and tighten his control over the machinery of government had created a crisis within Pennsylvania politics from 1746 on and an appeal for royal government to take the place of the proprietary had been an undercurrent in the Assembly even in the calmest years. The need for military appropriations and frontier defenses against Indian raids had brought it to the surface in 1755. With the French and their Indian allies defeated and British arms everywhere triumphant by 1760, the fundamental issues between the Proprietor and the elected Assembly were left to simmer again, still unresolved, until Pontiac's War and the renewed demand for defensive measures again made the unwillingness of the Assembly "to submit to distant dictatorship or to any form of external control" the paramount issue in Pennsylvania politics.[2].

The supposed failure of the Quakers in the Assembly to protect their fellow subjects on the frontier had long been the principal argument advanced by those Pennsylvania politicians who aimed at taking away the right of Quakers, Mennonites, and the other sects to vote and hold office. The sufferings of the frontier settlers in 1755-1758 had left a great deal of bitter feeling against the Quakers and their German allies, who were supposed to be responsible for the wretched muddle of defense efforts. The withdrawal of some Quaker members in 1756 had done nothing to change this situation or to solve the deeper issue of conscience.

But these unresolved conflicts paled to nothing in comparison with the grievances of the Indians. The words of the white men proved to be empty air. White settlers had moved into the Wyoming Valley—the land that the Friendly Association had tried to secure for the Delawares forever—and brushed aside the protests of the Delawares and the Iroquois. Teedyuscung, who had warned away the first party of these Connecticut settlers, was burned to death in his cabin in April 1763 and the other Delawares fled from the Wyoming Valley with their houses blazing behind them. The Connecticut men claimed the Delawares had done it themselves, the Indians that the whites had murdered Teedyuscung. It was the same everywhere. In the forts and trading posts of the Ohio Valley and the Great Lakes, Sir Jeffrey Amherst's wrongheaded Indian policy seemed designed to send the tribes back on the warpath. Pontiac, a young Ottawa chief from the neighborhood of Fort Detroit, did no more than apply a match to the tinder.[3]

The savagery of the attacks and the panic that spread the length of the frontier were both surprising. An observer in Frederick, Maryland, reported that the number of refugees streaming from the frontier settlements far exceeded the panic after Braddock's defeat.[4] There was not a white settler left in Hampshire County, Virginia, and the Shenandoah Valley lay open to Indian raids. Fort Cumberland still held out, but an express rider from the fort to Winchester had passed scalped bodies on the road.[5] As the summer wore on, the Delawares and the western tribes struck deep into Pennsylvania. The *Pennsylvania Gazette* reported in July that "Carlisle was become the Barrier, not a single Inhabitant being beyond it" and "every Stable and Hovel in the Town was crowded with miserable Refugees." On both sides of the Susquehanna, the "woods were filled with poor Families, and their Cattle, who make Fires and live like the Savages."[6] Mennonites and Quakers from Lancaster risked their lives to get in the crops for some of these refugees and carried wagonloads of food and clothing to them (*Document 53*). All summer the smoke of burning barns and houses and the shadow of death hung over the Cumberland Valley.

The Assembly responded to the emergency by again authorizing volunteer companies and providing money to pay their expenses.[7] A militia bill would have taken months to be effective and the British army had rushed every man they could find in hospitals able to shoulder a gun as part of Colonel Henry Bouquet's force camped at Carlisle for a counterattack. Yet, after Bouquet had beaten the Indians at Bushy Run and the danger had subsided, Governor Hamilton harshly condemned the Quakers in the Assembly for doing nothing to protect the outlying settlements and caring not at all for the lives of the back-country inhabitants.[8]

The Paxton Massacre

On July 11, 1763, Governor Hamilton wrote to the Reverend John Elder, pastor of the Presbyterian congregation at Paxton in Lancaster (present Dauphin) County, informing him of an agreement "between me & the Assembly, that seven hundred men should be forthwith used for the defense of the Frontiers, against the Incursions of the Indians," and ordering Elder to raise two companies of 100 men in Lancaster County "to be immediately employed in protecting such parts of your Frontier, as may stand most in need of it." Hamilton planned for 400 men to be recruited on the west side of the Susquehanna to protect Cumberland and York counties and for 100 men each to be raised in Lancaster, Berks, and Northampton.[9]

The Cumberland Volunteers carried the war into the enemy's country, with Governor Hamilton's approval, attacking the Delaware villages on the West Branch of the Susquehanna. They went as far as the Big Island (present Lock Haven), where they "destroyed all the Houses, and above 300 Acres of fine Corn," but met with no Indians.[10]

The Paxton Volunteers, without waiting for orders or permission, mounted their own expedition to the Wyoming Valley, with the Christian Delawares of Wyalusing as their target. They reached the Wyoming Valley just two days after Captain Bull's Delaware war party had swept through the valley and left no white people alive in it. When the Paxton Volunteers returned home, Parson Elder informed Governor Hamilton of their grim discovery and blamed the Wyalusing band for sheltering the raiders, if not committing the murders.[11] The Wyalusings abandoned their village and, led by Papoonhank, arrived at Bethlehem three weeks later to warn the Moravians of hostile Indians.[12] They and other Moravian Indians remained at Bethlehem for the winter.

Much closer to Paxton than the upper reaches of the Susquehanna was the Conestoga Indian village in Manor Township in Lancaster County. Here lived a remnant of the Susquehannocks, with a few other Indians, dependents of the Proprietary government since their hunting grounds had been cleared and plowed. They sent an appeal to the newly arrived Governor John Penn, grandson of the founder of the colony. When it arrived in Philadelphia, they were dead (*Document 82*).

Two of their Mennonite neighbors, Benjamin Hershey and John Brubaker, heard that the Paxton Boys were planning to massacre those Indians who had been away from home and had then been taken to the Lancaster jail for their own safety. (*Document 84*). The authorities were unable or unwilling to act on this warning and the rest of the Indian men, women, and children were butchered (*Document 83*). Only two of the Conestogas escaped the massacre, since Christian Hershey hid them at his farm in Warwick Township (*Document 85*). Not all Mennonites had had friendly relations with the Conestoga village. Abraham Newcomer, a gunsmith, reported that he had been threatened by some of them because he refused to sharpen a tomahawk (*Document 87*).

The land of the dead Conestogas reverted, of course, to the Proprietor. Jacob Whisler, a Mennonite living in Manor Township, was commissioned by Governor Penn to take charge of the unsold portions of Conestoga Manor, including the Indian Town Land. In 1766 Whisler reported that some of the Paxton Boys were squatting on the Indian land and refused to be evicted (*Document 88*). Land hunger, as well as hatred of Indians, may have contributed to the massacre at Conestoga.

Confrontation in Philadelphia

The aftermath of the massacre was a confrontation between the frontier politicians and the representatives of the older settlements, particularly the City of Philadelphia, a renewal of the old debate between Proprietary and Quaker Party and an outpouring of resentment at the nonresistant sects. Frontier grievances were legion: unequal representation, unfair legal procedures, a muddleheaded Indian policy, and a general insensitivity to frontier sufferings. The Friendly Association seemed to be an outstanding example of Quaker preference for Indian murderers over their innocent victims and became a prime target for the aggrieved border settlers.[13]

The immediate cause for the Paxton Boys and their allies to march

The Friendly Association seemed to be an outstanding example of Quaker preference for Indian murderers over their innocent victims and became the prime target for aggrieved border settlers. In this cartoon, published in Philadelphia in 1764, a Quaker and an Indian are riding on the shoulders of frontiersmen along a path strewn with mangled bodies. The Indian's knapsack is marked I.P. for Israel Pemberton. The Quaker is accepting from a figure intended to be Benjamin Franklin a copy of the unanimous resolution of the Pennsylvania Assembly. (From a contemporary print in the Historical Society of Pennsylvania.)

on Philadelphia and put the city virtually under siege in early February 1764 was the presence there of the hapless Moravian Indians from Wyalusing, who had been hurried from Bethlehem to the comparative safety of the capital *(Document 89)*. Some Quakers felt that in such a case even nonresistants could take up arms to defend themselves and the Indians from another bloodbath *(Documents 90, 91)*. In this way, they gave the angry Scotch-Irish proof that they valued the life of a heathen Delaware over that of a Presbyterian. The resulting soul-searching among Friends about the meaning of their peace testimony served to bolster the position of those who would brook no deviation from strict nonresistance and had important consequences for Quakerism during the American Revolution.[14]

In their march on Philadelphia, many of their frontier neighbors, particularly German "church people," joined the Paxton men. The focus of the action had shifted, too. No longer the irrational act of a hotheaded mob, this was a concerted effort, colony-wide, to change governmental policies. The marchers camped in the Market Square at Germantown, where Benjamin Franklin and other representatives met with them and heard their complaints. After lengthy conferences, the marchers agreed to return peacefully to their homes, leaving two of their number to present a petition to the Assembly. They complained in their petition that Chester, Philadelphia, and Bucks counties and the City of Philadelphia elected 26 Assemblymen and the remaining counties chose only 10 altogether. Most of the petition went over the familiar ground of inadequate frontier defense, damned the Friendly Association and Israel Pemberton, and proposed driving the remaining Indians out of the settled parts of Pennsylvania. The Assembly refused to accept the petition.[15]

The massacre of the Conestoga Indians and the march on Philadelphia coincided in time with the renewed constitutional struggle between the Proprietor and the Assembly. John Penn, the nephew of the Proprietor, was the new governor and he showed no disposition to yield on any point in the dispute. In January 1764 he angered the Assembly by forcing them to accept a decision of the Privy Council in London that would exempt the Proprietor from the need to accept his own paper money, which always depreciated rapidly, in payment for lands, rents, or any other obligations due him from the colonists. When the vote came on this measure on February 1, Samuel Foulke, a Quaker member from Bucks County, was so exercised at seeing his colleagues put "their necks under the Tyrant's foot" that he proposed they immediately send a petition to the king for a change in government.

Others, no less incensed at Penn's action, counseled patience.[16]

Early in March, Governor Penn astonished the Assembly by again rejecting their money bill until they made still another amendment. The new demand required that the Proprietor's unimproved lands be assessed for taxation no higher than the lowest rate of any colonist's unimproved land, which, translated into practical application, meant that vacant lots owned by the Proprietor in the business district of Philadelphia would be taxed no more per square foot than the rocky acres owned by some pioneer on the upper reaches of the Juniata.

Once again the proprietary governor was holding the frontier settlers hostage to his own selfish interests. And once again the nonresistant sects served as scapegoat. While the Paxton Boys vented their rage on Indian-loving Quakers who left the frontiers unprotected, Governor Penn held up the bill providing money for frontier defense from December to March, sending it back with new demands each time the Assembly agreed to his last amendment.

This was the last straw. On March 10, 1764, the Assembly authorized eight members, including Benjamin Franklin and Joseph Galloway, to draw up "Resolves upon the present Circumstances of this Province and the Aggrievances of the Inhabitants thereof." Two weeks later the Assembly unanimously adopted their resolutions, including one proposing that the Assembly adjourn to consult with their constituents about asking the king "to take the People of this Province under His immediate Protection"[17]*(Document 105).*

Campaign for Royal Government

Franklin and Galloway wrote pamphlets to be distributed free to the voters and circulated blank petitions for royal government. When the Assembly reconvened in May, they received petitions signed by at least 3,500 persons, all asking for a change in government. Half of these petitions came from Philadelphia, the rest from the country. But this is only part of the story. At least one in three adult white males in Philadelphia signed a petition, but 3 percent of the eligible signers in the rest of the colony gave the petitions their support. The Presbyterian politician George Bryan observed that "in the country the petitions for a change in government are less liked, especially as you approach the frontier." Israel Pemberton noted that, in contrast to the Philadelphia Quakers, "very few Friends in the country had sign'd or Approved of these Petitions." The march of the Paxton Boys and Franklin's propaganda had helped swing city voters of every persuasion behind the drive for royal government.[18]

Contemporary observers as well as later historians have been in agreement that "great numbers" of Friends put their names on the petitions. It was a Quaker Party measure and the Assembly that called for a change in government by a unanimous resolution counted 16 Friends among its 36 members. When their Proprietary Party opponents began a vigorous campaign of their own, they collected some 15,000 signatures on petitions opposing a change in government and most of their support came from Presbyterians, Lutherans, and Reformed.

But it would be a mistake to think of the campaign for royal government only in terms of a Presbyterian-Quaker split or even an urban-rural division. Any change in government could endanger the liberties already secured to the people of Pennsylvania. Mennonites, Schwenkfelders, Dunkers, and Moravians were frankly alarmed at the prospect and many Quakers had serious doubts about it *(Documents 93-94; 95-97)*. The fears expressed by Quakers caused Philadelphia Yearly Meeting's Meeting for Sufferings to counsel against presenting an address to the king, if there should be any danger of abridging the rights and privileges already won.[19] *(Document 98)*.

In the 1764 elections, Franklin and Galloway were both defeated and the Quaker Party lost five of the ten seats it had held in the City and County of Philadelphia. The other counties returned the same Assemblymen, many of them Quakers, most of them Quaker Party politicians. The reason for this apparent paradox, defeat in their strongholds and victory in contests that should have gone to the Proprietary candidates, is not hard to find. "In the countryside, where royal government had never generated much enthusiasm and where it incurred more and more enmity as the summer advanced, Quaker party politicians saw that it was political poison, that to support it was to invite defeat. Therefore, they broke with their urban brethren, came out against it, and presented themselves to the electorate as patrons and protectors of proprietary government"[20] *(Document 103)*.

If the Quaker Party candidates changed their stand in the midst of an election campaign for political expediency, it would have been neither the first nor the last American election won on that basis. But this cannot be the whole story. Less than a month before the ballots were to be cast, the Meeting for Sufferings of Philadelphia Yearly Meeting officially discouraged Friends from "appearing in Support" of the change in government. In an epistle to London Yearly Meeting, they explained that many Quakers were to be found on each side of the issue and that, because of the fear that religious liberty might be curtailed, they thought it advisable for Friends not to give public support to the measure. What was at issue was the principle of nonresistance. *(Document 99).*

One of the offenses of Governor John Penn that the Assembly had denounced in the resolutions for a change in government was his refusal to pass a militia bill unless he was given authority to appoint all the officers. Some Philadelphia Quakers, who had stood guard when the Paxton Boys threatened the city, undoubtedly saw the governor's demand for a long list of patronage appointments in every county as the price for permitting a well-regulated militia as one more act of petty tyranny. The sects saw any militia bill as a far more threatening act of tyranny.

The "powerful Party" that the Quakers and Mennonites had made in the 1764 election broke with the Quaker Party leaders on the question of royal government out of principle. Israel Pemberton, so recently attacked by the Paxton Boys and their supporters as the archenemy of the frontier inhabitants, joined with John Dickinson in support of proprietary government, or rather in defense of the Pennsylvania Charter, the bulwark of the historic rights and liberties of the province. The Yearly Meeting held in September revealed that rural Quakers generally agreed with Pemberton, while comparatively few Philadelphia Friends supported him, but he was able to confidently declare that a majority of Quakers were opposed to a change in government lest freedom of conscience be imperilled.

Benjamin Franklin sailed for England in November 1764 to present the Assembly's grievances to the Proprietor. While he was there, he not only spoke in favor of the Stamp Act, but lobbied successfully for the appointment of his close associate, John Hughes, as Stamp Agent for Pennsylvania. The election of 1765 was overshadowed by the colonial reaction to the hated Stamp Act. Ironically, Christopher Sauer II, the Dunker elder who had succeeded his father as publisher of the Germantown newspaper and political adviser to the Pennsylvania Germans and who would one day be marched through the streets as "an oppressor of the righteous," made opposition to the Stamp Act and to the change in government major issues in the campaign against Franklin's party.[21]

Royal government was a real possibility until 1768. Since Franklin and the Quaker Party hoped to convince officials in London that the intensity of opposition to the Penn family was no indication of disloyalty to the king, they made every effort to reduce tensions over the bills passed by Parliament relating to the American Colonies. But as one set of issues began to fade in 1768-1769, new political alignments took shape. The old Quaker Party had broken up completely by 1770. Franklin and other leaders advocated resistance to the Townshend Revenue Act by boycotting British goods. They were joined by many of the proprietary political leaders and their Presbyterian, Lutheran, and Reformed constituents who had marched on Philadelphia with the Paxton Boys. Mennonites, Schwenkfelders, Dunkers, and Moravians had united with Quakers in political action and carried elections, not to save the proprietary government, but to preserve the liberty of conscience they prized. This was their one issue. Behind it was a commitment to nonresistance; a change in government would bring a militia law and other impositions on their right to live according to conscience. The very success of this peace church alliance in the royal government agitation limited its influence when not only issues but methods changed, from verbal protest and voluntary agreements to coercion and violence. Quakers were advised by Philadelphia Yearly Meeting in 1770 to have nothing to do with efforts to boycott British goods or other coercive measures. To the rapidly moving events of the next decade, the sects could only respond with a firm "No" at each step in the direction of change and violence.[22]

DOCUMENTS

Frontier Troubles in 1763

Peaceful Response to Warring Indians

When Indian raids threatened Pennsylvania in 1755, Christopher Sauer's newspaper counselled German settlers to offer food and drink to the Indians as a sign of friendship. William Smith mocked this advice in his pamphlet against the Quakers published in 1756. Yet there is evidence that Mennonites, Quakers, and other nonresistants did respond in this way. An account in the *Pennsylvania Gazette* described the ordeal of one Quaker family, who greeted a war party with Christian love in 1763.

Document 81

The same Day an Express arrived from Reading in Berks County, with the following Intelligence, viz.

"That on Thursday last, about two o'Clock in the Afternoon eight Indians came armed to the House of John Fincher (one of the People called Quakers) about three Quarters of a Mile distant from a Party of Captain Kern's, consisting of six Men, commanded by Ensign Sheffer, and about 24 Miles from Reading, over the Blue Mountains: That said Fincher, his Wife, two Sons, and Daughter immediately went to the Door, and asked them if they would eat any Thing, hoped they were come as Friends, and entreated them to spare their lives; That, however, after some Deliberation, they killed Fincher, his Wife, and two Sons, the Daughter said to be missing; but as she was heard screaming by some of the Neighbours, and crying Murder, it is feared she is likewise killed: That a little Boy made his Escape from the Savages, and came to the Ensign, who immediately went to the Place with his Party, but the Indians were gone, and finding, by their Tracks, which Way they went, pursued them to the House of one Nicholas Miller, where he found four Children murdered, the Enemy having carried off two others with them; but the said Miller, and his Wife, being at Work in a Field, saved their Lives by Flight, the Man being pursued near a Mile by one of the Indians, who fired at him twice: That our Party still pursued, and soon came up with the Enemy, and fired on them, which they returned; but the Soldiers rushed on them so furiously, that they quickly ran off and left behind them two Prisoners, two Tomahawks, one Hanger, and a Saddle; three of their Number being badly wounded: That the Two Prisoners recovered, were two of the above-mentioned Miller's Children, which they had tied together, and drove them before them: That the Persons murdered were all scalped, except a Child about two Weeks old, which they, in a most cruel Manner, dashed to Pieces against the Wall: That the Number killed over the Mountains was eight, and two missing: That the Inhabitants had all come on this Side and were in the utmost Distress."

That as the Express was setting off from Reading, certain Information was brought there, that the House of Frantz Hubler, in Bern Township, about 18 Miles from Reading, was attacked on Friday Evening last, by the Indians, when Frantz himself was wounded; his Wife, and three Children, carried off; and three others of his Children scalped alive, two of whom are since dead.[23]

The Paxton Killings

Massacres

The Paxton Boys, a group of men from Paxton and Derry townships, went to the village of the Conestoga Indians and murdered the men, women, and children they found there on December 14, 1763. Governor John Penn presented an address from these same Indians and a report of the massacre to the members of the Council, who then took swift action. At their next meeting, the governor had to report a second massacre, this time in the workhouse at Lancaster.

Document 82

At a Council held at Philadelphia, on Monday, the 19th December 1763. Present:

The Honourable John Penn, Esquire, Lieutenant Governor, &c.
Benjamin Shoemaker, Esq. William Logan, Esq.
Richard Peters, Esq. Benjamin Chew, Esq.

The Governor laid before the Board an Address from the Conestogoe Indians, congratulating him on his Arrival, praying the Protection of the Government, & complaining of some Encroachments made on the Lands reserved for them, & desiring that they might be furnished with Provisions as usual, which was read, and is as follows, viz.

"To the Honourable JOHN PENN, Esquire, Lieutenant Governor and Commander-in-Chief of the Province of Pennsylvania. Brother:

We (the Conestogoe Indians) take the present opportunity, by Captn. [Andrew] Montour, to welcome you into this Country, by this String of Wampum, and as we were settled at this place by an Agreement of Peace and Amity established between your Grandfathers and ours, We now promise ourselves your favour and protection, and as we have always lived in Peace and Quietness with our Brethren & Neighbours round us during the last & present Indian Wars, We hope now, as we are deprived from supporting our Families by hunting, as We formerly did, you will consider our distressed Situation, & grant our Women and Children some Cloathing to cover them this Winter. The Government has always been kind enough to allow us some Provisions, and did formerly appoint People to take care of us, but as there is no person to take that upon him, & some of our Neighbours have encroach'd upon the Tract of Land reserved here for our use, We would now beg our Brother the Governor to appoint our Friend, Captain Thomas M'Kee, who lives near us and understands our Language, to take care, and see Justice done us.

Sohays X his Mark
Ouyanguerrycoea X his Mark
Saguyasotha or John X his Mark

Conestogoe, Novr. 30th, 1763."

The Governor having received, on Friday last, a letter, dated the 14th Instant, from Edward Shippen, Esq. at Lancaster, acquainting him that a Party of Armed Men had that Morning murdered Six of the said Conestogoe Indians at their Town, laid the same before the Board, which was read, viz.

"Lancaster, 14th December, 1763, Evening.

Honoured Sir:

One Robert Edgar, a hired Man to Captain Thomas M'Kee, living near the Borough, acquainted me to-day that a Company of People from the Frontiers had killed and scalped most of the Indians at the Conestogoe Town early this Morning; he said he had information from an Indian boy who made his escape; Mr. [Matthias] Slough has been to the place and held a Coroner's Inquest on the Corpses, being Six in number; Bill Sawk and some other Indians were gone towards Smith's Iron Works to sell brooms; but where they are now we can't understand; And the Indians, John Smith, & Peggy, his Wife, and their child, and Young Joe Hays, were abroad last night too, and lodged at one Peter Swar's, about two miles from hence; These last came here this afternoon, whom we acquainted with what had happened to their Friends & Relations, and advised them to put themselves under protection, which they readily agreed to; And they are now in Our Work House by themselves, where they are well provided for with every necessity. Warrants are issued for the apprehending of the Murderers, said to be upwards of fifty men, well armed, & mounted. I beg my kind Complements to Mr. Richard Penn, & I am with all due Regards, Sir,

Your Honour's Obliged Friend & humble Servant,
Edwd. Shippen."

Whereupon the Council being moved with the cruelty & barbarity of the above action, & apprehending that the Indians who were settled at Conestoga were under the protection of this Government and its Laws, and that consequently the killing them without Cause or provocation, amounted in Law to the Crime of Murder, advised the Governor to write immediately to the Magistrates of the Counties of York, Lancaster, & Cumberland, to exert themselves on this Occasion, and issue Warrants, & do everything in their power for the Apprehending all the Principals concerned in the said Crime, & their Accomplices, and securing them, that they may be brought to Justice, and further, that a Proclamation be issued, ordering all Officers of Justice to be aiding & assisting therein.[24]

Document 83

At a Council held at Philadelphia on Thursday, the 29 December, 1763. Present:

The Honourable John Penn, Esquire, Lieuten't Governor, &c.

James Hamilton, Esq.	Richard Peters, Esq.
Benjamin Shoemaker, Esq.	Lynford Lardner, Esq.
William Logan, Esq.	Benjamin Chew, Esq.
Thomas Cadwalader, Esq.	

The Governor received last Night, by Express, the following Letter from Edward Shippen, Esquire, at Lancaster, which was laid before the Board for their Consideration, & is as follows:

"Lancaster, 27th Decemr. 1763, P.M.

Honoured Sir:

I am to acquaint your Honour that between two and three of the clock this afternoon, upwards of a hundred armed men, from the Westward, rode very fast into Town, turned their Horses into Mr. Slough's (an Inn-keeper) Yard, and proceeded with the greatest Precipitation to the Work House, stove open the door and killed all the Indians, and then took to their Horses and rode off, all their business was done, and they were returning to their horses before I could get half way down to the Work House; The Sheriff and Coroner, however, & several others, got down as soon as the Rioters, but could not prevail with them to stop their hands; some people say they heard them declare they would proceed to the Province Island, and destroy the Indians there. I am with great respect, Sir,

Your Honour's most Obedient humble Servant,

Edwd. Shippen."

The Council being of opinion that the Indians under the Government's protection on the Province Island, were greatly exposed in their present Situation to danger of being molested by the Rioters, & that it would be proper to contrive immediate Means for their defence, agreed that Three Flatts & 3 small boats should be sent without delay to the Province Island for the use of the Indians, that they might, on any intelligence of the approach of the Rioters, make their escape, till more effectual measures should be fallen on for their Protection.

The Council further advised the Governor to dispatch the Express back to Lancaster, with a Letter to Mr. Edward Shippen, desiring him to gain all the Intelligence in his power, respecting the further designs and motions of the lawless Rioters, and to endeavour to learn the Names of any of the Ringleaders or persons concerned in the murder of the Indians in the Work House, and to acquaint the Governor, from time to time, by Express, with every piece of Intelligence he should receive concerning them.

The Governor was also advised to write to Colonel [John] Armstrong, at Carlisle, and the Revd. Mr. [John] Elder, at Paxton, to exert themselves on this occasion, by using all means in their Power, to discover and detect the Rioters, and to suppress all such Insurrections among the People under their influence for the future.[25]

Document 84

Lancaster the 5th January 1764.

Dear Son,

On the evening of the 14th ult. I received a letter from Mr. James Wright acquainting me that a considerable [number] of the Conestogos Indians had been murdered that morning at their town, and desired me to see that a legal inquiry might be made by the Coroner the next morning, to know how they came by their ends; for that those Indians were put under his care by the commission to provide for them, and immediately I wrote him for answer, that I was very sorry for the occasion of his letter, but that I had an acc't of that murder early in the morning, and had just sent out the Coroner & Sheriff presently afterwards to hold an inquest over & bury the corpses and that they were just returned, & the Sheriff then with me, assured me that they had done their duty so far as to hold the inquest, and that the Coroner had given some men money to bury the dead, which they promised (he said) to do, the next morning, that being a stormy day, & a deep snow upon the ground; I acquainted Mr. Wright that some of the Indians who were far from home, being seen in this Borough were, by their own consent, confined in our Work house by the Magistrates, and I mentioned their names.

On Saturday the 25th ult. it came into my head to consult with Mr. Wright whether it would not be best on all accounts to remove the Indians from this Borough down to Philad'a., for by this time he had collected the rest of those who were missing, not that I had heard of any intention of the Peoples coming down to kill them. And going down to Mr. Slough's, I saw Johnny Lowdon there, and begged him to present my compliments to Mr. Wright and ask him whether he did not think it was advisable to order the Indians down to the Province Island. And the next evening hearing Mr. Wright was come to Town I waited on him at his lodging, and inquired of him whether he had received such a message from me by Mr. Loudon, and whether he approved of what the Justices had done in confining the few Indians; he said he did, but at the same time judged it most proper to consult the Indians on that head on Monday morning before he should set off for Philadelphia, after which, I had no opportunity of seeing him.

As to the report spread by somebody in Philadelphia that the Magistrates of Lancaster had certain information of the coming down of the Rioters to destroy the Indians in the Work House, the day or two days before they put their wicked design into execution, and that they had a meeting upon it, but took no measures to prevent that unhappy affair, which 'tis said was in their power to do, by applying to the commanding Officer of the Highlanders then in the town who would have given them his assistance with the King's Troops to preserve the lives of the Indians, who were under the protection of the Government. I shall communicate this heavy charge to my Brethren of which there are but three in the Borough, except the two Burgesses and myself, but as the Bearer is going down early in the morning I thought I would not omit the opportunity of saying every thing I could in our own vindication. On Tuesday night between 8 and 9 o'clock Donally the Prison Keeper came to my house, and said he was informed, a parcel of the Rioters who had killed the Conostogoe Indians at the Mannor, were collected together at the Tavern on the Donegal Road about four or five miles out who were to be joined by a larger number before midnight, & then they were to come in a Body, & break open the Work house, and kill all the Indians. — I asked him how he got his Information, he answered that two Dutchmen had assured him they had seen the Rioters, and overheard some of them say all this, but he had promised not to mention his authors, neither could I then persuade him to tell me their names, however as I considered it a very serious affair and the relation not improbable to be true, I went with him to Justice Thompson's and there I strenuously insisted upon knowing his authors, he answered he couldn't inform us. Well, then said I if you won't give us that satisfaction I will immediate return home, and coming away, he then told us they were Ben Horshe [Hershey] & John Bruebaker we then agreed to go to Justice Adams and to send for the Burgesses, And upon some consultation, we came to a Resolution to call the two Constables of the Borough, and to send them off as spies to a couple of Taverns about the distances mentioned and to bring us word as soon as possible, and if, on their return, we found the story true, we should immediately alarm the Borough, and do the best we could to prevent the Indians being killed, tho' God knows, the Inhabitants undisciplined, & unfavorably armed, could have made but a poor stand against 80 or 100 Desperadoes well armed at least, and in the dark too, the streets being full of ice and snow, and the weather excessive cold, and at that time I had not heard of any Commanding Officer with his Highlanders Soldiers being in the Borough. However the Justices Stay'd together till one o'Clock in the morning, when the Constables returned, almost perished with the Cold, and gave us the pleasure to hear that there were no Rioters at either of those Places, nor had any of them been seen thereabouts Since they came from the Conestogoe Town. After this we were in hopes we Should have no more disturbances from those People till they, Somedays afterwards, rushed into the Town at Noonday on horse back with their Muskets, Tomahawks, & Scalping knives, broke open the work house and killed the Indians, before we knew whereabouts we were; for it was said, they were not more than eleven or twelve Minutes perpetrating that Tragical scene. And I declare for my part, I never heard one word of it till it was just over, and the Rioters were returning from the bloody Place where the Indians were; So that if the Magistrates & Burgesses had thought of calling upon Captain Robinson for assistance, it could have been of no service; as his Men were mostly billetted up and down the town (as we understood) and quite off their guard. This is a faithful Account of the affair, and is the best excuse I can make for the Magistrates and therefore conclude.[26]

Two Indians Saved

Two Indians escaped the massacres because Christian Hershey hid them. In August 1764 Governor Penn took them under the protection of the proprietary government and issued them a passport, as he did to some of the Moravian Indians. This document tells nothing about them, but the recorded visit of two Lititz Moravians preserved the story of Hershey's part in saving their lives.

Document 85

Whereas, I am given to understand that the Bearers Michael and Mary his wife are friendly Indians who formerly resided with other friendly Indians in the Conestoga Manor, and have for upwards of fifteen months last past lived with Christian Hershey, at his plantation in Warwick Township in Lancaster County, Pennsylvania, during which time they have constantly behaved in the most friendly and peaceable manner to all his Majesty's subjects, I do hereby grant the said Michael and Mary my protection and do enjoin and require all officers, civil and military, as well as all other persons whatsoever within this Government to suffer to pass and repass on their lawful business without the least molestation or interruption, and they are hereby also desired to treat the said Indians with civility and to afford them all necessary assistance.

Given under my Hand and Seal at Philadelphia, the 17th Aug. 1764.

By his Honour's Command
John Shippen, Secretary.[27]

Document 86

May 21, 1767.

Brother [Bernhard Adam] and Sister Grube, visiting in the country, lost their way not far from Manheim and came to a house where abide the only couple of Indians remaining in this Province. The man was not at home but the woman was as happy as a child when Bro. Grube began to speak to her in the Delaware tongue, which she slightly understood—although she and her husband are Conestoga Indians.

At the time of the Lancaster Blood Bath, these two Indians were in some danger of being murdered, but the Mennonite with whom they were living for 15 years [?] hid them in his cellar, where they had to stay all winter until the excitement had somewhat abated.

The woman seems to be quiet and orderly but knows nothing at all of the Saviour, and that most familiar word "Potamaorinna" was unknown to her. She was glad to have Bro. Grube's promise that he would visit her again.[28]

Conduct of Paxton Boys Debated

Abraham Newcomer, a Mennonite gunsmith, related threats made against him by some of the Conestoga Indians. His testimony was included by the Rev. Thomas Barton of Lancaster in his pamphlet, *The Conduct of the Paxton-Men, Impartially represented.* The circumstances of Newcomer's testimony are unclear. Barton implies that affidavits were voluntarily prepared in February 1764 to answer some of the charges against the Paxton Boys, rather than part of any official court proceeding. The original affidavits have not been located.

Document 87

ABRAHAM NEWCOMER, of the County of *Lancaster* one of the People call'd *Menonists,* and by Trade a Gun-smith, hath personally appeared before the Chief-Burgess of Lancaster, and upon his solemn Affirmation hath declared, "That divers Times within these few Years, BILL SOC and INDIAN JOHN, two of the *Canestogoe Indians,* threatened to *scalp* him, the *Affirmant,* as soon as they would a *Dog.*"

He further affirms, "that a few Days before the Indians were killed in the *Mannor, Bill Soc,* aforesaid, brought a Tomahawk to him to be steel'd, which this Affirmant refusing to do, the said *Bill Soc* threatened, and said, *you will not! you will not! I'll have it mended to your Sorrow.* — From which Expressions this *Affirmant* hath declared, that he apprehended Danger from said *Soc.*"[29]

Paxton Boys' Intentions

Jacob Whisler, the Mennonite superintendent of the proprietary lands in Conestoga Manor, related an incident in January 1766 that indicated some of the Paxton Boys had an interest in taking the land of the dead Indians.

Document 88

On the 24th day of January 1766 Before the Honble. William Allen, Esq. Chief Justice of the Province of Pennsylvania personally appeared Jacob Whisler of Manor township in the County of Lancaster, yeoman, who is employed & appointed by Commission from the Honble. John Penn, Esq. dated the 15th day of June 1764 to superintend and take care of the unsold parts of Conestoga Manor particularly that part where the Conestogo Indians were permitted by the Proprietaries to reside called the Indian Town Land and being one of the people called Menonists & conscientiously scrupling the taking an Oath, did on his solemn Affirmation declare and affirm that on Friday last the 17th day of this Instant January in the Morning, he having occasion to go to Abraham Hare's Mill in the said Township saw there Robert Poke (who came to live on part of the said Indian Town land, soon after the said Indians were destroyed by the company of people called the Paxton Men as was generally reported and understood) and saw the said Robert Poke get from the said Abraham Hare a Kegg of Spiritous Liquor which this Affirmant understood and believes was for the use of a company of the said people called Paxton Men who met that day at the House on the said Indiantown Land which was built by the said Poke & the said Paxton Men at or near the site of the Cabbin late belonging to the Indian called Jo Hayes who was killed there & which now is possessed by the said Robert Poke.

That this affirmant on his return from the said Mill in the afternoon was told by his wife that Thomas Fisher (who this affirmant with the approbation of the Proprietors Agents had put upon a part of the said Indiantown Land to assist in taking care of it) had been at this Affirmants House to acquaint him that a great Company of the Paxton Men now were come to Robert Poke's & that he the said Fisher wanted this affirmant to come to his House, and thereupon this affirmant taking with him Martin Stouffer went to the said Fisher's house, there found a large Company of Men with Horses being about 25 or 30 as this Affirmant computes, many of them having poweder Horns and pouches and some of them Guns;

That on this Affirmant's going into the said Fisher's house where the said Men were, one of them, a young Man who called himself the Captain or leader of the said Company demanded of this Affirmant in a very angry, outrageous and menacing manner to know what authority he had to place the said Thomas Fisher on the said Indian Land, or to meddle therewith, to which he answered that he had the Governor's Commission or Written Order to oversee and take care of the Land; Whereupon the said young Man & several others of the said Company in the like angry and menacing manner insisted on his shewing them the said Commission or Orders to which he replied that he had them not with him and that he did not chuse to shew them to all that Company, least they should take or destroy them, but that if they would send 2 or 3 of their Company with Him to his House, he would there shew them his Orders; and thereupon the Young Man and Elderly Man who with the said young Man appeared to be the heads or chief Leaders of the said Company & another Man of the said Company whom this Affirmant had seen before and believes his sirname is Bayley joining the said two others, went with this Affirmant to his House, and he there produced to them his said Commission or Orders which when they had read they all said & insisted that the Governor had no power to give any such Orders & that [neither] he nor the Proprietors had any right to that Land, but that it belonged to the Indians that were killed, and that they (meaning the said Company) had now the best right to it, and would have it and keep it in spite of the Governor & Proprietors, and insisted in the like angry menacing manner that this affirmant should give up & concern himself no further with the said land and not let the Governor or Proprietors Agents know anything of their the said Company's Proceedings respecting the same, or to that Effect, and that on their returning to this affirmant his said papers the said Elderly Man called him aside & in a pretended friendly manner advised him by all means to have nothing to do with the said Land but quit it entirely, for that if he did concern himself any further with it, or offer to oppose the said company's taking and keeping Possession of it, he might depend upon it, they would do him some great Mischief, or to that Effect.

And this Affirmant further saith that he was not personally acquainted or knows the names of any of the said Company, save the Man, whose name he believes is Bayley, and to whom this Affirmant then said that he knew him & asked him if his name was not Bayley, to which he made no answer; and saith that the young man and Elderly Man who called themselves the Heads or Leaders of the said Company then told this Affirmant that all of the said Company had sworn to obey and stand by them, & would approve of every thing which they their said leaders should do with the said Land.

Jacob Whisler

Affirmed before me
WILL[IAM] ALLEN[30]

The March on Philadelphia

Some Quakers Take Up Arms

Governor Penn learned on February 4, 1764, that the Paxton Boys and their supporters were on their way to Philadelphia to deal with the Moravian Indians in the same way that they had with the hapless Conestogas. He put the city on guard and called on all the inhabitants able to bear arms to turn out to help defend Philadelphia.

A letter written by Sally Potts to her sister a few days later suggests the panic in the city and her own ambivalent feelings about Quakers taking up arms.

Edward Penington, a Philadelphia Quaker, defended his own violation of the peace testimony in a paper he prepared for Philadelphia Monthly Meeting. A prominent member of the Meeting and a trustee of the Friendly Association, Penington indicated that taking up arms was not the act of a few confused Quaker youths, but represented a significant minority view.

Document 89

At a Council held at Philadelphia on Saturday the 4th Febry. 1764.

The Commissioners acquainted the Governor that they had received Intelligence by a Letter from Lancaster County, & from Mr. Walne, a Member of Assembly, that a very considerable number of the people living on the Frontiers of that & other Counties, were actually assembling themselves with an intention of coming to this City to put to death all the Indians in the Barracks under the protection of this Government; & that to-morrow Morning was the time fixed on for the execution of their unlawful design.

The Governor thereupon desired the opinion of the Council as to the best measures to be taken on this occasion. They advised him to give written Instructions to Captain Schlosser to defend the Indians to the utmost of his power, by opposing, with the Detachment of the King's Troops under his Command, any attempts to destroy them, the riot Act being first read by a proper Civil Officer. To order Notice to be sent to all the Inhabitants of the Town to meet the Governor at the State House this afternoon at 4 o'Clock, to acquaint them there of the present Danger that threatened the Publick Peace, to desire they would immediately take Arms and put themselves under his Command in defence of the Government, and in Support of the Laws. To propose that 150 of the Gentlemen of the Town should assist the Soldiers in guarding the Barracks this night, and request that hereafter, upon any Alarm made by the ringing of the Bells, the Inhabitants would turn out with Arms and repair to the Barracks; or, if the Town should be attacked, that they would meet at the Court House, & defend the City.[31]

Document 90

By that time it was expected the Paxton Boys would be in Town and it was feared the Consequences wou'd be a Bloody Battle wherein a great many Innocent People might fall. They Indeavoured to put themselves in so good a Poster of defence as they cou'd and thinking the Attack wou'd be made at the Barracks where the Indians were, turn'd the most of their force there and we seem'd pretty still at our

End of the Town and Before Bed Time got better compos'd, the weather not being fit for 'em to March we hope to Sleep another Night in Security, did so and in the Morning finded all well until Meeting Time, went to Meeting, after meeting went up to Sister's, spent the remainder of the day in quiet, they was not come and we seem'd to think wouldn't come; home and went to Bed as usual but was Wak'd about 3 o'clock with the Ringing of Bells, the Alarm Guns and a Dreadfull Cry of Fire. Judge what could be more terrifying at such an hour.

Poor sister how I pity her when I think of it, with only her little Family about her, when in such Distress oblig'd to Conceal as Much as Possable her own Fright least it should heighten the Childrens. But when Day Appear'd it seem'd to Dispell the Melloncolly Gloom a little which had overcast the faces of all at least Females, we could now see each other and consult what was to be done. Sister Brought more dismal Accounts than we heard before that there was 900 at Germantown for Certain and it was expected they had a great Number of Friends in Town would Joyn 'em, that the Streets was so full of Arm'd Men she cou'd hardly Pass, Quakers not accepted [excepted], they seem'd as ready as any to take up Arms in such a Cause to defend their Laws and Liberties of their Country against a parcel of Rebels. Edward Pennington they say was at the Head of a Company and I am apt to think 2 thirds of the young Quakers in Town took up Arms. I believe its very Certain there was two or three Thousand Men Marching about Town two or three Days in Expectation of the Enemy's Coming. . . . The big Meeting House instead of having Meeting held as was expected was appropriated to the use of the Arm'd men to Shelter them from the Rain where the men was exercising and the Colours flying in the Gallary from whence there has so often Doctrain been Preach'd against that very thing of Bearing Arms &c &c.[32]

Document 91

To the Monthly Meeting of friends in the City of Philadelphia

Esteemed Friends—Having been frequently visited by divers Friends by appointment of the Meeting, on account of my having borne Arms contrary to the profession of the Society of which I am a member, I take this method to acknowledge your care and friendship therein; at the same time I request I may be permitted to relate some facts that may have a tendency to explain my motives in acting the part I did; for if my conduct appeared extraordinary, so did the occasion. It is well known a set of violent men had, in defiance of Government, killed a number of Indians at Conestoga Mannor, and the Indians that escaped their fury at that time and fled to Lancaster soon after shared the same fate. It is also well known that those men, not satisfied with the blood they shed in those places, formed a Design of killing the Indians then at the Barracks near this city, and for that purpose were on their march hither in an armed manner. To those they met on the way, they not only openly, avowed their said intention, but also threatened to kill several Friends, who had shown a desire that the natives be kindly treated. When intelligence was brought that these men were within a few miles of the city, and their designs such as I have related, [I] need mention the anxious concern of many who were friends to good government, that those disturbers of the peace should be brought to justice, or at least be prevented from committing further acts of violence; but by whom this was to be done, was on that day of distress a weighty question. Many of our society having scruples of conscience, could not bear arms on any occasion. Some of other societies, who make no such plea, I am sorry to say, seemed too indifferent what might be the consequences of those lawless proceedings. Matters thus situated, I considered them in the best manner I was capable, and thought it my duty to contribute all in my power to prevent those people from executing their bloody purposes: apprehending that no Government could long exist that only punished individuals for offending against its laws; while large bodies of men were suffered to commit the most horrid crimes with impunity. To prevent bloodshed and preserve good order in civil society, was my design in bearing arms. How far the conduct of those who had the same views might, (under Providence), contribute to answer those purposes, I leave. But be that as it may, I am truly thankful there was no blood spilt on the occasion. Having candidly related the motives of my conduct, permit me now to say, that notwithstanding my having thus deviated from the profession of Friends, I am fully convinced of the truth of their principles in general; and if, in the instance under consideration, I have done wrong, I hope it will please God to open my understanding, and that He will in the meantime enable me to live up to what I am already convinced is my duty. One part whereof, agreeable to the advice of the Apostle Paul, If it be possible, as much as lieth in me, to live at peace with all men.

I shall conclude with informing the meeting that I am very desirous of being continued a member of the Society, and in such unity as the nature of the case will admit. How far that may be, I leave to their consideration; but at the same time, I would first observe that I apprehend a good degree of unity may be maintained in a society whose members do not think exactly in every respect. I am equally desirous to clear Friends from any blame or reproach that may have been thrown on them by means of my conduct, which I hereby do, and take the same to myself.

I am with much esteem,
Your real friend
Edward Penington.[33]

Support for Paxton Boys

The Paxton Boys and their friends who marched on Philadelphia included many substantial citizens of the frontier townships and they had the warm support of many others, including most of the German "church people." John Harris reported on their progress to Colonel James Burd at Fort Augusta.

Document 92

Paxton March 1st 1764

Sir,

I Send you Some Letters & N[ew]spapers by Lt. Hunter. Colo[ne]l Boquet is Gone to N.York & at his Return We shall have Some European News as the Packet is Lately Arrived from England, the last Letter I Rec'd from Mr. Shippen he Desired me to Write to You. I cant well Describe the Commotions we have of late had Without Being too Tedious, but the Volunteers Caused Such a Pannick in Philada. during a late Conference or Treaty the Government held with them at Germantown, that Several Principal Persons of a Certain Society Left the City & Took Refuge in the Jerseys till Terms was Proposed, & Promises made on Both Sides. I Sent you by Lt. Hunter the Countrys Declaration With Part of their Grievances Printed in a Pamphlet, & the Five Frontier Countys are all now Petitioning for a Redress of their Grievances, & are at Present Uneasy, but I hope Every thing will be Settled Justly & Equitably, as a Number of the Head & Principal men of this Province now Supports the General Cause, the Assembly are all Summoned down & are now Sitting. the Good People of this Province will not suffer Tamely their Libertys & Priviledges to be Taken from them, By their Representatives. the Quakers took up arms in Philada. & made their Meetg. House a Place of Rendezvous. you would not thought Such a Conversion could be so soon wrought, the last time I saw you, by either Civil or Milatary Law, the Clergy or any Other Method. The Inhabitants of this province on all Roads from Paxton to Philada. used the Volonteers Well Particularly Lancaster & no Person Offer'd to Insult them, & they have a Good Character from Philada. Where abt. For[ty?]

of them did goe on Business, (& to see the City,) & [torn] an Acco[un]t of this Aff[ai]r on Both Sides the Question is already sent of to England & if no Redress is Got in this Province, Perhaps his Majesty & Parliament may be Apply'd too, in a Short time, I wish with all my Heart for an End to these things, for Such proceedings if Continued may Be Attended With Dreadfull Consequences. I am Sir with the Greatest Respects your Verry Hble Servant

John Harris[34]

Campaign for Royal Government

Two letters of Israel Pemberton to Dr. John Fothergill in London relate the aftermath of the Paxton Boys' march and the beginning of the campaign for royal government.

Document 93
To Doctor Jno. Fothergill
London

Philada 3 mo 7th 1764

Dear Friend:

There have been of late many occasions of public concernment w[hi]ch required thy receiving intelligence from hence, apprehending some others more capable would take care therein have concluded it was less necessary for me to undertake it, yet as something may occur to one which another may omit, the relation & sentiments of several may not be improper or unacceptable under our present Situation. . . .

I have taken notice there have been for some days past diverse Presbyterian priests passing the streets from whence have concluded they had something in agitation and am informed they are preparing a representation to be sent to London, the Contents whereof does not yet transpire further than if the Assembly overlook that part of the remonstrance for the five counties, it is intended to be prosecuted by an appeal to the King, &c., and as the Authority of the two persons who signed the remonstrance has been disallow'd by the House of Assembly, who think it beneath the dignity of the Government to take notice of such an application from a number of persons riotously assembled; there are great stirrings in the back counties to procure petitions to be Signed to the like purpose with which it is the opinion of some they are to attend in a body to present, & of others that a deputation only will come down on the occasion; Should this scheme take Effect, our Politicians expect it will be a great point gained, & enable them to return a majority of their Presbyterian friends for Representatives and the People of this City and County plead it as Equitable that an additional number should be allow'd them in proportion to the part they bear of the provincial taxes, which is reckoned near one third of the whole. This Object at present serves another purpose by diverting the public attention from the affair of ye riot to palliate the conduct of the persons concerned in it and fix a persuasion their only design in coming down in the hostile manner they did was for redress of grievances. Altho' the contrary appeared and was openly acknowledged by many of them while assembled at Germantown to several persons who went from this city to converse with them and that they had received repeated invitations from some here to prosecute yr. [their] scheme of destroying the Indians & Surprizing the Inhabitants with assurance of being joined by at least four hundred of their brethren here, in which finding they were much disappointed, & the great opposition they were like to meet with, & yr [their] own number less than was expected together with some providential interruptions, may have been the occasion of their being persuaded to desist from yr. Intentions & agreeing to return home, their Leaders at the same time pretending they did not know the Indians were under the protection of the King's Forces, otherwise yr. Loyalty would not permit them to have undertaken this Expedition.

B. Franklin was one of the persons who went to confer with them by the Governor's desire, to which he consented with much reluctance, & was induced to accompany the others fearing some concessions might be made them unworthy the Government; on the Rioters appointment of their deputies to represent them they requested B.F. & our mayor to assist them in drawing up their remonstrance to which they on terms consented, but the Deputies on arrival in truth soon found assistance of persons more suitable to their purpose that they have been excused from the trouble & it does not appear they were ever apply'd to on the occasion except to accompany the Deputies to the Government which B.F. rejected and has conducted thro' the whole of this affair with great firmness & resolution & a just detestation of the horrid proceedings.

On Consideration of the Remonstrance in the Assembly, the House proposed to the Government they should unite in an examination of the Remonstrants in hopes by that means to be able to make some discovery of the promoters of the Insurrection & to bring to Justice the perpetrators of the murders which was evaded thro' the influence of the Governor's Chief Advisors, so that there is no prospect at present of any measures being taken for this purpose, it rather appears probable the whole will be passed over.

There are many circumstances concurr to confirm the general Suspicion that the scheme has been conducted by some & countenanced by others whose Statures in the Government required a very different conduct; the supineness of the magistrates in Lancaster in omitting proper measures to prevent the murder of the Indians in that Burrough, the neglect of them & the other Justices of the County of sending intelligence of the motions of the Rioters afterwards, tho' some of them must be acquainted therewith puts it out of Doubt, the Expedition down here was intended to cover the two first massacres, & to defy the Governments calling the perpetrators to acco[un]t.

Great pains has been taken to extenuate the Crime, and to represent the Rioters to be men of Reputation, drove to this extremity by the severity of their distresses; others who have made it their business to inquire, insist on the contrary, that few among them have suffer'd by the Indians, & that they consisted chiefly of Idle Fellows, many of whom have been Soldiers in the province Service, who for want of Employment have been hired on this occasion. . . .[35]

Document 94

Philadelphia the 13th 6 mo 1764

My Very Dear Friend,

. . . . Our inveterate adversaries disappointed of fulfilling their Intentions have since been very Industrious in order to paleate their conduct in inventing pretended excuses for their madness by publishing and propagating the most scandalous & virulant pamphlets; in some of which not content with confining their abuses to our Society of the present time, they have not omitted to attack some of the writings of our ancient worthies by unfair quotations, which appear to be taken upon ye credit of the Old Adversary of Truth, the Snake in the Grass. Hitherto Fr[ien]ds have been content to bear with these reproaches unanswered, except what was early done in an address to the Governor, in answer to the Declaration & Remonstrance which was sent & delivered him in behalf of the Rioters; the minds of the people have been kept in such a ferment till lately that there did not appear any oppo[rtunity] of a fairer hearing which together with the weakness that attends us has prevented anything being as yet published in reply to their malevolent aspersions, as well as the occasion requires; whether there will be found strength enough among us I must leave untill our next meeting for sufferings.

Had the members of our Society more generally rejected the acceptance of stations & offices in civil Government which the extension of the times appeared to require & the repeated advice of their brethren frequently urged I can not but think these calamaties would not have been suffered so nearly to attend, but either a false opinion of retaining priviledges or a desire of honour has I fear been preferred by Some to what is more Essential & valuable that of bearing a faithful testimony to our religious profession, thus some by mixing temporal with Spiritual Concerns have become weak themselves, & undertake to reconcile [document torn] & involve their brethren in difficultys, & disable the honesthearted from assisting and vindicating the cause of Truth & our Antient testimony.

Our monthly meeting has now under notice the visiting those of our members who appeared under arms, & a hope appears of some benefit attending on ye labour. They were first collected together at a meeting at the schoolhouse, when about 140 were present chiefly the youth & a seasonable opportunity it proved, yet on this as well as many other occasions, a great want is experienced of more labourers qualified for religious services.

The rage & malice of our Adversaries seems at first somewhat subsided, tho' we have reason to think it is rather smothered than extinguished. It was remarked that without grounds upon the first Intelligence of the Proprietaries in London having expressed their abhorrence of the murders committed on the Indians in Lancaster, the Presbyterian party & their abettors became more silent, & since the arrival of the letter by the last packet of the sentiments of the [British] Ministry on hearing of the riot, they have become altogether so, & some begin to change their Language & pretend a detestation of the murders & it is thought they are fearfull their brethren will be called to an account for their conduct, a report prevailing that General Gage has rec'd such Instructions. I believe they find they began to put in execution too early their Aspiring Schemes. Should their numbers Increase on this Continent in future as for many years past, there is reason to apprehend the restless & aspiring temper of that people may prompt them to attempt a Revolution in the Government.

There hath been a long contest between our Assembly & Governor in Relation to a Supply Bill this winter, and as they attribute the occasion of their difficulties to Proprietary Views of encroaching on the Liberties of the People, they [the Assembly] formed several resolves protesting against the same, and adjourned in the 3 mo. [March] last in order to consult their Constituents about applying to the King to take this Government under his Immediate care and protection, in Consequence of which Pētitions to this Purpose have been handed about & signed by great numbers of the Inhabitants, and as I have been informed pretty Generally by the Members of our Religious Society, to which they have been induced by various considerations, on one hand tired with the repeated disputations between the Proprietary & the Assemblies & on the other the Riotous Conduct of the Presbyterians & the fearfull apprehensions of their getting the Legislative as well as the Executive part of Government into their hands, the latter of which they already possess in some counties & appear determined to mobbery & abuse to gain their point, have weighed with some to fall in with the proposal. The House mett again on 14th last month & after some further altercations with the governor they found themselves obliged to comply with all he demanded, & agreed to address the King to take the Government of their Province into his own hands, which I suppose are to be soon forwarded to their Agent in London. Should an alteration be made in the frame of our government in consequence of their Application, it may greatly affect our Society, but as our most material Charter Privileges are confirmed by Laws which have received the approbation of King & Council, some who profess knowledge in these matters undertake to assure us that we are not in danger on this account. It notwithstanding appears to be a very Critical Time for such an Application from the Proofs which the Parliament & ministry have given of their disposition towards the Colonies in the Act lately passed respecting trade. . . .[36]

The Royal Government Agitation

Fears Among the Peaceable Sects

Exasperated with Governor Penn's effort to force concession after concession from them, the Pennsylvania Assembly resolved in March 1764 to sound out their constituents on the possibility of petitioning the king to make the colony a royal province.

The change in government raised immediate fears among the peaceable sects that their cherished freedom of conscience would be endangered. Christopher Schultz, a Schwenkfelder, expressed his concern to Israel Pemberton. He reminded him that while British law recognized both Quakers and Moravians, no legal protection existed for Schwenkfelders, Mennonites, and Dunkers beyond the Charter given by William Penn. His fears of military obligations are understandable from the long agitation over a militia law; the then-current debate over appointing a bishop of the Church of England for the American

Colonies was behind Schultz's fear that royal government might bring episcopal jurisdiction.

Friends were no less concerned about implications of a change from proprietary to royal colony. The Meeting for Sufferings appointed a committee to see that Quakers' rights were protected.

Document 95

April 4, 1764

Beloved Friend Israel Pemberton,

I have been hindered by several circumstances to see Philadelphia (this last winter) and pay Thee a visit to inform myself how Friends bear up with the Care, Insurrections, and Diffamations from an unruly and wicked People in the Country who neither know nor understand what they do or say, acting in both parts against the Rules of God and man.

And now we hear that such a misunderstanding breaks out in our Legislature as threaten a Revolution in our Constitution that our Charter should be delivered up in the King's hands in which case if such as have transported themselves with their Families hither, in hopes for a full and free Enjoyment of the celebrated Privileges of the said Charter should be deprived of the same especially of the First Article of the Freedom of Conscience and instead of that be subjected to Episcopal Jurisdiction and Military Actions it would be very hard and striking to the Heart. It is true Quakers and Unitas Fratrum are protected in their Religions by Laws of the Realm of Great Britain, but what should be our Case and other Societies of the like Principles who have so far trusted themselves under the Wings of this Government erected and constituted for the best time by Quakers?* Therefore we earnestly desire and admonish you in brotherly love to use all possible means to prevent the Destruction and depriving of religious Liberty in any respect so laudably planned by your Fathers, for the Benefit of all settlers whose worthy Followers we hope you will approve yourselves in taking care that their Intention be not violated and what alterations should be made or agreed to it may be with Safety of Conscience for every Individual in this Province. And since you are the people who made the first agreement for the Settlement of this Province your Consent or non-consent to any alteration must consequently be of very great weight. And though we trust your best endevours in these critical circumstances will not be wanting nevertheless we thought to encourage you a little with these few Words, the freedom of which you will indulge from your Fellows in Sufferings.

Israel be so good and let me have more account how the above mentioned affairs stand, if it can be.

I am with true love they obliged Friend

C[hristopher] S[chultz]

[* *The following passage in Schultz's original draft was not included in the letter he sent Pemberton:*

that what Alteration should be made or agreed to, it might be with Safety of Conscience for every Individual in this Province. Your Consent or Nonconsent to any alteration must necessarily be of very great Wheight, And as the were done for the Benefit of all Settlers, we hope you will Readily follow the Footsteps of your Fathers in preserving their Intention for every Ones Benefit.][37]

Document 96
[June 21, 1764]

. . . And some hints being given that the Assembly of Pennsylvania at this last sitting have agreed to address the King to take the Government of that province into his own Hands, in order to be more particularly informed of their proceedings in this case, and to prevent any inconveniences to which Friends may be Subjected in respect to our Religious priviledges, Owen Jones, Abel James, Isaac Zane and James Pemberton are appointed to apply to the Speaker of the House requesting he would be pleased to give us the necessary Information.[38]

Document 97
[July 19, 1764]

Two of the Committee appointed to apply to the Speaker of the Assembly of Pennsylvania report that they were received kindly by him, and informed that directions were given to their agent, to proceed cautiously in the matter, and if there appeared any danger of not retaining the Religious & Civil priviledges the Inhabitants now enjoy, to decline presenting the Petition, until he had received further Instruction from the Assembly, but that there appeared no likelihood of any thing being done before the sitting of Parliament next Winter.[39]

The Election of 1764

The election of 1764 was inevitably a chance for the voters to express themselves on the proposed appeal to the king for a change in government. It was little wonder that "the Quakers & Menonists made a powerful Party" or that voter interest among all groups was extraordinarily high. The two major surprises in the election were the shift of Lutheran and Reformed Germans away from the Quaker Party to the Proprietary Party column and the decision of some important leaders of the old Quaker Party to campaign against any change in government. When the votes were counted, Franklin, Galloway, and others identified with the appeal to the king had been defeated and replaced by German "church people," but the Quakers won the election in most counties.

The alliance of Mennonites, Dunkers, Schwenkfelders, and Moravians with the religious Quakers was nowhere more significant than in Lancaster County. The first four of the following documents deal with the Lancaster elections from the point of view of the Proprietary Party, "the New Side," and their efforts to wrest control from the Quaker Party, "whom we call the Old Side." In understanding these letters, it will be helpful to know that the successful candidates were Emanuel Carpenter, James Wright, Isaac Sanders and James Webb for the Assembly, John Barr and James Webb, Jr., for sheriff, and Matthias Slough and George Stricker for coroner.[40]

Document 98

Philada. 10th Septr. 1764

Dr. Sir

The News which I brought from Lancaster of the Quakers & Mennonists having made a powerful Party to thwart the Measures your Friends have so vigorously pursued of late for thrusting out of the Assembly those men who have lately endanger'd our happy Constitution by their precipitate Measures, has given great Concern to all your Friends here, & very much dampened our hopes wh. were very Sanguine that there could be no danger of carrying the Election in yr. County to our Wishes. This unfavorable Prospect has induced several gentlemen here, to think that in order to prevent our being defeated at so critical a Time when measures are taken to bring about a general Change thro the whole Province It will be expedient to fall on some alteration of the Ticket lately proposed by a few leading Friends, & submitted to yr. Consideration, for Alteration or Amendment against the Borough Election, Vizt. to put in Emanl. Carpenter or Jacob Carpenter, Doctor Adam Choan [Kuhn], & Isaac Saunders & John Hayse or Andrew Worke. The design is by putting in two Germans to draw such a Party of them as will turn the Scale in our favor & tho by such a Measure we must reject Mr. [George] Ross, yet I'm persuaded he has too much regard for the Public Good to be offended at such a measure when taken purely to defeat the Views of our Antagonists & not thro' any disrespect to him. It would be equally agreeable If Mr. Ross came in place of any of the Irish but as their Interest must be much Stronger than this, it would be imprudent to offend them by rejecting one of their proposing. I wish the unhappy Contest ab[ou]t Sheriff could be reduced to two Competitors, on our side, (suppose Col. Worke & Jamy Anderson) it would unite our Friends to act with more Spirit & prevent their hurting the public Cause. Our Friends in Chester Co[unt]y are very sanguine in hopes of carrying the Election & we scarce admit a doubt of it here. We are this Day taking measures for Bucks Coy. & hope to make a strong Interest. Franklin & Galloway or at least one of them will be run in Bucks its said.

Last Night Jno. [John] Hunt a famous Quaker Preacher arrived from London in Order its believ'd to give Friends a Rap on the Knuckles for their late proceedings, & its said a Bro[the]r of the famous Docr. Fothergill will immediately follow on the same Errand, tho their great Sticklers have by numberless Falsehoods propagated a Belief that their Friends at home [in England] highly approv'd their Measures. you may communicate this to any of your Friends. I am respectfully Dr. Sir.

Your mo: Obedt. Servt.
Sam[ue]l Purviance Junr.
James Burd Esqu. at Lancaster.[41]

Document 99

Lancaster 17 Septem. 1764

Dr. Sir

I had the pleasure to Receive yours of the 10th Curr. ——— Saturday last being the Day of Election for Burgesses &c. for this Borrough we embrac'd the Opportunity to Settle a Ticket for our Representatives in Assembly &c., according to the Custom of this County ——— but I should have told you that previous to our Borrough Election we had an Interview with the People whom we call the Old Side, that was on Monday was week, we endeavoured at this Interview to Settle a Ticket with them in Generall for the County to prevent partys, we made severall overtures to them (which were rejected) the last was that Isaac Saunders & Eman'l Carpenter Should be Certain, & we would propose Six men to them out of which they should Choose one, and they should Name Six men too out of which we should choose One, which four men should be the Ticket. we accordingly Nam'd one out of their Six but they declined taking one of ours, upon which we broke up. at the same time we were inform'd they fixed the following Ticket which they sent out Amongst their People vizt. Isaac Saunders, Eman'l Carpenter, James Wright & James Web [b.] on Saturday last, the day of our Borrough Election we gave Publick Notice we were to meet at Crawfords Tavern in this Town to settle the Ticket. we met accordingly (that is the new side) we sent some of our People to find out the old side if they were met any where that if they were in any measure prepared to make a Genl. Ticket they might still have an opportunity on Reasonable Terms with this Exception only that Neither of the Two Men to be added to Saunders & Carpenter should be Quakers or men whose opinion was in any Degree known to be for a Change of our Present Government. But those Gentn. of the old side kept themselves so private that we could not find them; upon which we Resolved to stand upon our own Bottom and form a Ticket for ourselves which we did accordingly and you have it here Inclosed. There was some of our friends from every Township in the County with us who came to Town on purpose to Form a Ticket & they told us at the same time that what Ticket we settled they would carry home with them and that it should be unalterable and that we might depend all our friends in the County would steadily adhere to it.

I am inform'd to day that the old side met in Town unknown to us on Saturday evening and filled their Ticket thus Isaac Saunders, Emanuel Carpenter, James Wright, & George Ross, *& I am further inform'd that at this Settlem[en]t Messrs. [Thomas] Barton & Ross assisted. Mr. Barton was wt. us some part of the Evening & as I have not seen him since I can say nothing further.*

We have on our side all the Lutheran & Calvanist Dutch with many others of the Germans. we think ourselves strong Enough for the Task we have undertaken and I can only assure you that No stone shall be left unturn'd on my part to accomplish the Laudable Design. But at the same time I think if our friends in Philada. could prevail upon Mr. Henry Keply [Keppele] to write up Circular letters to his friends in this County to join me in the Ticket & those letters warmly wrote it would greatly help our Cause and if such a thing should be approved of by our Friends with you & done I should be glad to have a list of the Peoples Names that Mr. Keply writes to that I may talk to them upon the subject.

We Judge it most propper to leave the Sherriffs Blank. I am glad to observe by yours that there is a good prospect in Chester County, and more so that our affairs goes well in your County. I hope to hear good Accounts of Bucks. I wish friend Hunt good success in his Embassy if the purport of it is as you suspect. I wish he was here the 1st 8br. [October] so that Knuckles (only) may be rapt, for I am realy affraid the People will be too Warm, tho I will Endeavour all I can to prevent disputes going further than Words. I am most respectfully, Dr. Sir,

Your most obedt. Servt.
James Burd

Saml. Purviance junr.[42]

Document 100

The County of Lancaster contains upwards of 40,000 Souls; of this Number not more than 500 can be reckon'd as belonging to the Church of England; the rest are German Lutherans, Calvinists, Mennonists, Moravians, New Born, Dunkars, Presbyterians, Seceders, New Lights, Convenanters, Mountain Men, Brownists, Independents, Papists, Quakers, Jews, &c. Amidst such a swarm of Sectaries, all indulged and favored by the Government, it is no wonder that the National Church should be borne down. At the last Election for the county to choose Assemblymen, Sheriff, Coroner, Commissioners, Assessors, &c. [on October 3, 1764] 5000 Freeholders voted, and yet not a single member of the church [of England] was elected into any of these offices.[43]

Document 101

[October 3, 1764]

There was this day both great rejoicing and great exasperation in this city [Philadelphia] in the political sphere, since it was reported that the German church people had gained a victory, having elected our trustee, Mr. Henry Kepple, to the Assembly—A thing which very much pleased the friends of the gentlemen Proprietors, but greatly exasperated the Quakers and German Moravians. It is reported that, as old as Pennsylvania is, there was never such a mass of people assembled at an election. The English and German Quakers, with the Moravians, Mennonites, Schwenkfelders, formed one party, and the English of the High Church [the Church of England], the Presbyterian, and the German Lutheran and Reformed joined the other party, and prevailed in the election—a thing heretofore unheard of.[44]

Document 102

Philadelphia 6th Octobr. 1764

Dear Brother,

I received your Favour by Mr. Hay, and am extremely pleased to find, that you have succeeded so far in your Election as to keep in Mr

[Isaac] Saunders, having heard there was a great probability of his being left out.

I am in great hopes [James] Wright and [Emmanuel] Carpenter will acquiesce in the Measures of our New Assembly, since we have had the good Fortune to exclude [Benjamin] Franklin, [Joseph] Galloway, [document damaged] Rhodes and [Rowland] Evans; and in their Room, have put in Messrs. [Thomas] Willing, [George] Bryan, [Amos] Strettel & [Henry] Kepple. This Change in our Representative here has caused the greatest Dejection of Spirits in those of the Quaker party & their Friends.

Tho' [John] Barr and [Matthias] Slough may have acted a political part in the Election, that they might succeed themselves; Yet the Governor has been well assured by several Gentlemen, that they privately pushed Saunders in the Tickets of many of their Friends, by which Means alone he was kept in. However this may be, the Governor could not possibly think of appointing the Son of a Quaker to be Sheriff, who had taken infinite pains in riding about the Country to secure the Interest of the Germans in favour of the violent Measures of the late Assembly against his own Family & Government. Barr indeed has a better pretence to the Sheriff's Office, from his having been on the Return twice before & now highest in Votes; and if any Objections are made against him on Account of his favouring the old Ticket, the same are to be made against the other in a greater Degree. So that the Appointment of Barr is approved of by all the Governor's Friends here, without Exception.

Your Son Neddy returned here in good Health on Thursday Morning and joins with me in Love to my Sister, yourself & Children, being, Dear Sir,

Your very affectionate Brother
Joseph Shippen Jr.

Colonel James Burd.[45]

Document 103

Philad. Octo. 21st 1764

Honourable Sir

By two opportunitys since my arrival I have taken the freedom to pay my compliments to you, since the last time I have been employed in concerting matters with my friends for the elections, and in endeavouring to reconcile the different partys in the courts of Justice and Assembly, that, if I had not been of a strong habit of body the fatigue would have been too much for me.

No doubt you will hear that we have been to turn out the two grand incendiarys, in effecting which we had great help from the Lutherans and Calvinists among the Dutch, from their other sects we had great opposition: we had about half of the Church of England and the Presbyterians to a man. In the countys all but Northampton, the Quakers had the address, or I might say craft, to delude the Dutch by false storys so that they though well inclined to your Government were induced to oppose our friends, and carried the election against them. They were made to believe that, if they changed the Assembly, the Government would be changed.

The Grand Incendiary, Franklin, though he lost his Election both for the City and County of Philadelphia, being set up in both, yet is so far the Idol of the Quaker party, that he is like to come to England to be Joint agent with Mr. [Richard] Jackson under pretence that he may render his Country Service in opposing the Ministerial measure of taxing us internally, but the real design is to promote those of his wicked faction; you may expect him, fully freighted with rancour and Malice, determined to use every measure to injure the proprietary family. I hope you will be able so to Counter Act, as to defeat His Malevolent Designs.

You were pleased to desire me to give you an account of his Conduct after his receiving [Mr. Jackson's?] letter. I must therefore assure you that he has been for many years and still is the chief author and grand abbettor of all the seditious practices in this Government, and is continually infusing into the People's ears his Republican, Monarchical Notions. Being a printer, he frequently publishes the most virulent pamphlets against Government, among the rest, no doubt you have seen that which he calls your epitaph; he is a very artful man, and can colour the worst Designs with very specious Glosses. After I have said this much it will be needless to dwell longer on the character of that very bad man.

I must do the Presbyterians that justice that they are much devoted to your honourable family that they were early brought to pacifick measures. They, one and all, throughout the Province, said they would never give their votes for the last Assemblymen, as they seemed disposed to change the Constitution; But they were so far from desiring to differ with the Quakers that they were even willing they should name the Assemblymen, provided they were not of the last Assembly. I cannot say as much in behalf of the Quakers, a few, I might say, a very few, sober religious men excepted, their minds were so much inflamed that they would hearken to no terms of accomodation, and spurned at every offer of that sort, though I took infinite pains with numbers of such as I had the greatest hopes would bear cool reasoning. I assured them that the presbyterians had no desire to injure them, and would gladly compromise their differences, and could even join them in many commendable designs for the publick good, but nothing I could say could make any impression on them, they appeared to have so keen a sense of real, or imaginary, wrongs done them, that their anger was not to be assuaged. When I mentioned that Dr. [John] Fothergill, Messrs. [David and John] Barclays and other eminent friends advised us to pacifick measures, and to heal our Animosities, their sentiments seemed to have no more weight than my own. I am sure that I have carefully avoided entering into the contentions and have been so cautious as not even to go out of my house the day of the elections but to such who came to consult me, which were not a few, I gave my advice, and have, I hope, been not a little instrumental in preventing any tumults and riots at that time, having told all the people, particularly the presbyterians that I would not serve in the Assembly if they were guilty of the least breach of the peace, and these my sentiments I conveyed to all parts of the Province, and have the pleasure to tell you, that though the people's minds were so inflamed, the last was the most peaceable election that has been for many years as, no doubt, you will have a particular detail. . . .

William Allen

The Honble Thomas Penn, Esq.[46]

Document 104

[November 15, 1764]

Since our late yearly meeting a new assembly being chosen to Represent the Freemen of the Province of Pennsylvania, who have determined to prosecute the measures agreed on by the former Assembly respecting the address to the King, and have sent Benjamin Franklin to England to join with their other agent in the affairs of the Province, we have now concluded it necessary agreeable to what is mentioned in the Epistle to your yearly meeting to direct One hundred Pounds Sterling to be herewith remitted to our correspondents in your meeting, towards defraying such Expences which you may be subjected to in any application on our behalf, to prevent our being deprived of our Religious Liberties & privileges.[47]

Stamp Act

The Stamp Act overshadowed the 1765 elections. Delegates from eight of the American Colonies were to meet in New York City in October in a Stamp Act Congress to protest against this parliamentary measure. There had been a deep division in the Pennsylvania Assembly on the question of sending delegates to the Congress and the decision was made on a 15-14 vote. Many of the Quaker Party opposed sending delegates and the narrow victory was due to such men as Emanuel Carpenter of Lancaster voting with the proprietary side. Proprietary leaders made much of this and of Benjamin Franklin's supposed role in getting the Stamp Act passed in the first place. To their delight, Christopher Sauer II joined forces with them, publishing a lengthy address to the German voters "especially in Philadelphia, Bucks and Berks Counties" in which he urged them to elect members pledged to preserve the proprietary government and to defeat every man who opposed sending delegates to the Congress.[48]

Samuel Purviance, Jr., who had come to Philadelphia from Donegal in Northern Ireland in 1754, described the efforts of the proprietary leaders and their Presbyterian allies to get German voters to turn out the Quaker Party. He despaired of Lancaster County, but offered a bold plan to keep Mennonites from the polls at the risk of a riot. Mennonite opposition to Isaac Saunders had little to do with his support of the Stamp Act Congress or any other measure; Jacob Carpenter needed his seat and got it.

Document 105

Philada. Septemr. 20th 1765

Dr. Sir

You may possibly imagine from the general Silence with which our political Affairs have been conducted this year that perhaps we are relapsed again into the old passive humor of submitting the conduct of public Affairs to our former state Pilots & that if we at the Fountain head observe such a Conduct you at a distance shou'd follow the same nonresisting plan of your friends in town. Be assured that nothing is less thought of by us than such a Scheme, tho matters go on very quietly, yet every thing is preparing for making a vigorous Stand at the ensuing election, & every possible pains has been taken to strengthen & cement our interest—in such a manner as to afford us good hopes of carrying every man for both City & County. Our interest is greatly increased amongst several Societies who last year were divided in their views, & particularly strengthen'd by the Opposition lately made by John Hughes & his Friends against sending Commis[sione]rs to attend the Congress at N. York in order to remonstrate home against the Stamp

Act. This unpopular Action has greatly damp'd their Ticket, turn'd many of their warm Friends out of doors against them & even brought over some of their members in the house to our party by which means they carried the vote; there's great reason to hope this affair will produce the same effects thro' the Country & open the Eyes of many who blindly attach'd to them thro party, must now see what destructive measures these pretended defenders of Liberty & privilege are capable of pursuing. I met some of our Friends at Chester court & there concerted some measures for dividing the Q----r Interest in that County that our friends may join one party of them [;] this scheme promises good success, & will I hope be warmly push'd by our friends there. I went lately up to Bucks Court in order to concert measures for their Election in pursuance of which we have appointed a considerable meeting of the Germans, Baptists & Presbyterians to be held next monday at Neshaminy, where some of us & some Germans & Baptists of this place have appointed to attend in order to attempt a general confederacy of the three Societies in opposition to the ruling party [;] we have sent up emissaries among the Germans which I hope will bring them into this measure, & if it can be effected will give us a great chance for carrying matters in that County: cou'd that be carried it would infallibly secure our friends a majority in the house & consequently enable them to recal[l] our dangerous enemy Franklin with his petitions which is the greatest object we now have in view, & which shou'd engage the endeavours of all our Friends at the approaching election to make a spirited push for a majority in the Assembly without which all our struggles here will prove of little service to the publick Interest.

The general committee of our Society meet this day & on tuesday next & shall finally settle our Ticket, which is now ill fix'd, but only one.

Few of your friends here entertain any hopes of being able to change any of your members [from Lancaster County] this year after failing last year in your spirited attempt; however I think it mean to submit tamely, or without bearing the testimony against bad men & bad measures: was I to stand alone, I woul'd vote against the enemies of my Country. If you knew thoroughly the Methods Mr F---k--n is taking at home to blacken & stigmatize our Society, you wou'd perhaps judge with me that you never had more reason to exert yourselves in order to overset him, which we can only do by commanding a majority in the Assembly. I have seen a letter lately from a person of Character, that advises his wicked designs against us. The little hopes of Success, as well as the difficulty of engaging proper persons for the purpose, has discouraged me from attempting a project recom'd by some friends, of sending up some Germans to work upon their Countrymen. But that no probable means may fail, have sent up some Copies of a piece lately printed by Sowers of Germantown to be dispersed & which may possibly have some effect.

I have just rec'd certain advice of a project laid by the Menonists to turn Mr. Saunders out of your ticket the only good member you have, I hope it will inspire our people with more Industry to keep him in; the only plan I woul'd recommend to you to run Dr. Chune [Kuhn], or some other popular Lutheran or Calvinist in Webb's place.

You'll please to make a discreet use of this to any of our Friends; I am with best wishes for a successful Election
Dr. Sir Yr & the publicks sincere wellwisher

Saml. Purviance Junr.

Shall be glad to know what measures you resolve on as soon as possible.
I beg no mention may be made of the Author of the Inclos'd.
James Burd Esqr. In Lancaster.

[Enclosure]

As I understand the Menonists have Certainly resolved to turn out Isaac Saunders this Year tho' the only good Member your County has, I would beg leave to offer to you & other friends the following Scheme as the only probable Chance, I think you have to Carry the Election & keep Mr. Saunders. If the Scheme is properly executed & can be Conducted without danger of a Riot I think you Could infallibly Carry your Ticket by it.

Dont attempt to Change any of your Members save Webb. If you can run Doctor Chune [Kuhn] or some other popular German & can keep Mr. Saunders in you will do great things. As soon as your ticket is agreed on let it be Spread through the County that all your party intend to come well armed to the Election & that you intend if there's the least partiality in either Sheriff Inspectors or Managers of the Election that you will thrash the Sheriff every Inspector Quaker & Menonist to Jelly & further I would report it that not a Menonist nor German should be admitted to give in a Ticket without being Sworn that he is naturalized & worth £ 50 & that he has not voted already & further that if you discovered any person attempting to give in a Vote without being Naturalized or Voting twice you would that Moment deliver him up to the Mob to Chastize him, let this report be industriously spread before the

Election which will Certainly keep great Numbers of the Menonists at home. I would at the same time have all our friends warned to put on a wild face to be every man provided with a good Shilely [shillelagh], as if determined to put their threats into execution, tho' at the same time let them be solemly Charged to keep the greatest Order & peace. Let our friends choose about two dozen of the most reputable Men Magistrates &ca. who shall attend the Inspectors Sheriff & Clerks during the whole Election, to mount guard half at a time, & relieve one another in spells, to prevent all cheating & to administer the Oath to every Suspicious person & to Committ to immediate punishment every one who offers to Vote twice. I'll engage if you Conduct the Election in that manner & our people turn out with Spirit you can't fail of carrying every man in your Ticket, as I am well assured not a third of the Menonists are naturalized. I would Submitt this to your Consideration, if it's well thought of take your Measures immediately. I beg no Mention may be made of the Author of this. I see no danger in the Scheme but that of a Riot which would require great prudence to avoid.[49]

Political Problems

The 1765 elections brought few changes. John Hughes, made odious by his willingness to distribute the hated stamps, ended his career in the Pennsylvania Assembly. Joseph Galloway, Rowland Evans and Michael Hillegas won back three of the Philadelphia County seats taken from the Quaker Party the previous year. In Lancaster County Jacob Carpenter replaced Isaac Saunders.[50]

The issues raised in the campaign and particularly Christopher Sauer's bitter attack on Benjamin Franklin caused no little concern among the German peace churches. Israel Pemberton forwarded a letter from the Schwenkfelders, which raised questions about Franklin's involvement with the Stamp Act, to the British Quakers Dr. John Fothergill and Hinton Brown.

Pemberton's letter touches on other themes that concerned Friends and other nonresistants in 1765, the rise of a Presbyterian Party temporarily allied with the old proprietary interest and the growing American resistance to unjust actions of the British Parliament. The somewhat equivocal attitudes of the religious Quakers can also be seen. Pemberton opposed the Quaker Party policy of petitioning for a change in government, but regarded Franklin and his allies as guardians of the rights of the people against the proprietary-Presbyterian politicans. He was concerned for American liberty, but repelled by the riots and commotions.

Document 106

Esteemed ffriends Philada 12 mo. 17. 1765

I have been warmly sollicited by some ffriends of this Province to Send you the Inclosed Letter and to request that you would be so kind as to transmit me as early as you can, the best Intelligence you have or can obtain of the promoter of the Stamp Act, which is the present object of so much of clamour & tumult in most of these colonies.

This Letter is wrote on behalf of a Number of Sober and Religious disposed Germans of the Society called Swingfelders who are Settled in the upper part of the County of Philadelphia & other parts of the province, have allways conducted [themselves] with prudence and have a considerable influence among their Neighbours in preserving peace & the just rights of the People: the Calumnies wch are propagated against B[enjamin] F[ranklin] are the Effects of the Enmity of a disappointed party, not so much with an intent to injure him individually, as by that means to accomplish their wicked designs to the prejudice of the real Interest of the Inhabitants and thereby establish themselves in power, their exercise of which we have great reason to dread.

A Copy will very likely be sent to Benj. Franklin, but his great modesty & aversion to controversy make him negligent of care or labor in the reproaches wch he is conscious are unjustly cast on his own character and altho' there are letters from himself which shew he has not been active in promoting that Act yet it is apprehended your Confirmation thereof will be most Effectual in removing the doubts, and Satisfying the Request of the persons who are desirous of being inform'd, more especially as it is known you have lately interposed for the welfare of the province.

You must undoubtedly by this time have received Accounts of the Commotions & riotious proceedings of the people in the Eastern Colonies on the arrival of the Stampt paper wch may render it unnecessary to say much on that head tho' the papers every week continue to Supply us with painful occurrences of the same kind, that at present little but Anarchy & Confusion prevails.

The people here have not conducted with the same rage and violence, tho' a disposition of the like kind very early discovered itself, among numbers of the same principles of their Eastern Brethren but finding themselves too weak to commit such outrages & measures of more prudence & reason being proposed they have so far had an Effect as I hope will in some degree secure us from the Shame & Reproach in which with others we might have been involved.

The merchants & Traders of this City have united in a memorial to the merchants in London, solliciting the Interposition of their Influence, with the Parliament, for removing the burthens & restrictions to which the Colonies are subjected by some late Acts, & I shall be pleased to find they may be able to Obtain redress for us.

Unless we can have liberty for emitting a Sufficient quantity of paper currency as a medium of Trade, our commerce with Great Britain must certainly diminish, and in time utterly drop, and if liberty is given the Legislature to Issue Such a Sum as may be suff[icien]t to carry on the trade of the province, to be Lent out on Land security, the Interest arising therefrom may fully answer the common Exigencies of Government here as well as the requisitions wch may be made by the Crown, wch would be at once beneficial to the people & the most expeditious & easy method of complying with these demands [of the Crown]. Inclosed is a copy of the memorial a few of which have been printed off.

The Last Election in this province for representatives in assembly was the greatest ever known in this County, the Pre[sbyteria]ns notwithstanding the utmost exertions of their labor & influence, came so farr Short of success that they have not Since recovered Sufficient Spirit to attempt what their aspiring & pernicious temper & principles would otherwise have prompted them to, after the Example of their Brethren in the Eastern Provinces.

We shall be very sollicitious to hear from your side the resolutions of the Government in consequence of these provincial tumults. It may with pleasure be remarkd that ffr[ien]ds here & in New Jersey conduct with prudence & appear more united in ye preservation of Concord with each other than for many years past, avoid[in]g to Interest themselves in these Commotions; altho' we cannot but be very sensibly affected with observing the disorder & confusion so generally prevailing.

I am very respectfully
Your Loving ffrd
[Israel Pemberton]

To Hinton Brown & Dr. Jno. Fothergill, London[51]

Mennonites Active in Politics

Mennonites continued to be politically active in succeeding election campaigns and in Lancaster County, at least, their influence seems to have been decisive. James Burd received two letters about Mennonites meeting to select candidates for the Assembly and the county offices during the 1768 campaign. His father-in-law, Edward Shippen, reported their choice of George Ross for the Assembly, while William

Atlee told of differences over candidates for local office. Atlee's reference to the "Ch: Hare Ticket" may be an indication that Christian Herr had a prominent role in getting Mennonite endorsement for these candidates. John Carpenter, candidate for Commissioner, was probably the nephew of Assemblymen Emanuel and Jacob Carpenter.

Document 107

Dear Mr. Burd, Lancaster 16th Septr. 1768

Since I wrote the Inclosed, which I have sent for to Mr Litle's, I can tell you that on Mr. James Wright's resignation to serve as an Assemblyman the head Men among the Menonists have had a Meeting at Mr. Slough and have fixed a new Ticket with G[eorge] R[oss]'s name. Mr. Sanders was in town yesterday but never desired me to vote for him so that I dont know that he will set up a Candidate. I think you & I had best say nothing about the Election. I am with Love to You all in haste

Your Loving Father
Edward Shippen

My Boy is returned from Mr. Litles who tells him he had just forwarded my Letter above mentioned.[52]

Document 108

Sir Lancaster ye 20th Septr. 1768.

As I find Mr. Shippen writing to you, I thought it a good opportunity to forward you what is called the New=Ticket in opposition to the Ch: Hare Ticket.

Mr. Ross is fixed in both Tickets & will therefore doubtless carry his point this Heat.

The cheif alteration is in the Commissioner & one Assessor, the lower side have John Carpenter for their Commissioner & Be [original torn] Assessor & in their stead in this Ticket is Adam Ort Commissioner & James Keimer Assessor. If this Ticket carries we shall have the command at the board & (entre nous) I make no doubt but shall be able to give I[saac] S[aund]rs a lift at a future Day, but of that say nothing. I hope the Ticket will be agreeable to your part of the Country & if they give it the same assistance that they did the New Ticket last Year, I believe it will carry. Please tender my respects to Mrs. Burd & your good Family. I wish you great health & Joy & the New House & am sincerely

Your very hble. Servt.
Wm. Atlee

James Burd Esquire[53]

Notes for Chapter 2

1. Dietmar Rothermund, "Political Factions and the Great Awakening," *Pennsylvania History,* VI (October 1959), p. 331.

2. James H. Hutson, "The Campaign to Make Pennsylvania a Royal Province, 1764-1770," *PMHB,* XCIV (October 1970), p. 429.

3. Wallace, *Indians,* p. 156.

4. *Maryland Gazette* (Annapolis), July 13, 1763.

5. *Ibid.,* July 28, 1763.

6. *Pennsylvania Gazette,* July 28, 1763.

7. *Pennsylvania Archives,* 1st Series, IV, pp. 114-117.

8. *Pennsylvania Gazette,* November 3, 1763.

9. John Elder Papers, Dauphin County Historical Society, Harrisburg, Pa. (hereafter cited as Elder Papers).

10. *Pennsylvania Gazette,* October 20, 1763, where credit for Colonel John Armstrong's expedition is given to the Paxton Volunteers. This error was repeated in the issue for October 27 and corrected in large type in the November 3 issue. Did this newspaper mistake act as a challenge to the Paxton Volunteers to accomplish something like the Big Island raid?

11. Timothy Green to Elder, October 5, 1763. Elder to Penn, October 25, 1763. Elder Papers.

12. *Pennsylvania Gazette,* November 22, 1763.

13. David Sloan, "'A Time of Sifting and Winnowing:' The Paxton Riots and Quaker Non-Violence in Pennsylvania," *Quaker History,* LXVI (Spring 1977), pp. 3-4.

14. *Ibid.,* p. 22.

15. Hubertis M. Cummings, "The Paxton Killings," *Journal of Presbyterian History,* XLIV (December 1966), pp. 241-242

16. Hutson, *PMHB,* XCIV (October 1970), p. 432.

17. *Ibid.,* pp. 433-439.

18. *Ibid.,* p. 441.

19. Thayer, *Pemberton,* pp. 202-204.

20. Hutson, *PMHB,* XCIV (October 1970), p. 454.

21. Hutson, *Pennsylvania Politics,* pp. 174-175. The Stamp Act was unpopular among Pennsylvania Germans who feared naturalization would be so expensive as to be beyond their reach. Henry J. Young, "Agrarian Reactions to the Stamp Act in Pennsylvania," *Pennsylvania History,* XXIV (January 1967), pp. 25-30.

22. Hutson, *Pennsylvania Politics,* pp. 228-233. Bauman, p. 143.

23. *Pennsylvania Gazette,* September 15, 1763.

24. *Colonial Records,* IX, pp. 88-90.

25. *Ibid.,* pp. 107-108.

26. Edward Shippen to Joseph Shippen, January 5, 1764. Shippen Papers, Folder 314, A.P.S. A detachment of the 42nd Highlanders, the Black Watch, was stationed in Lancaster during the winter of 1763-1764.

27. *Pennsylvania Archives,* 2nd Series, II, p. 739.

28. C. H. Martin, "Two Delaware Indians Who Lived on Farm of Christian Hershey," *Papers Read Before the Lancaster County Historical Society,* XXXIV (October 1930), pp. 217-220. The document was translated by Martin from the Diary of the Lititz Moravian Congregation, Moravian Archives, Bethlehem, Pa.

29. Dunbar, p. 282.

30. Record Group 22-B, Pennsylvania Historical and Museum Commission, Archives Division, Harrisburg, Pa. (hereafter cited as P.H.M.C.).

31. *Colonial Records,* IX, pp. 132-134.

32. Sally Potts to "My very dear Sister," February 9, 1764. H.S.P.

33. Edward Carey Gardiner Collection, Penington Section, H.S.P.

34. John Harris to Col. James Burd, March 1, 1764. Shippen Papers, H.S.P.

35. Israel Pemberton to Dr. John Fothergill, March 7, 1764. Pemberton Papers, H.S.P.

36. Israel Pemberton to Samuel Fothergill, June 13, 1764. Pemberton Papers, H.S.P. Both of these letters are rough drafts with many blots and erasures.

37. Christopher Schultz to Israel Pemberton, April 4, 1764. Draft. Schwenkfelder Library, Pennsburg, Pa.

38. Philadelphia Yearly Meeting, Minutes of the Meeting for Sufferings, 1756-1775, fols. 236-237. Quaker Collection. Haverford College Library, Haverford, Pa.

39. *Ibid.*, fol. 238.

40. *Pennsylvania Gazette*, October 11, 1764.

41. Shippen Papers, H.S.P. Isaac Saunders had joined John Dickinson in protesting the resolutions of the Pennsylvania Assembly calling for a change in government. *Pennsylvania Gazette*, July 23, 1764. He was a resident of Bart Township and very likely a Presbyterian. Emanuel and Jacob Carpenter were brothers, sons of Dr. Henry Zimmerman, who settled in Germantown in 1698 and later in Earl Township. Jacob had married in 1746 Elizabeth, daughter of Emanuel and Maudlin (Brackbill) Herr, and sister of Mennonite preacher John Herr. "Our Carpenter Neighbors," *MRJ*, XVIII (January 1977), pp. 1-5. Dr. Adam Kuhn the elder was a Lancaster physician, as was his more famous son, but the latter did not receive his MD from the University of Edinburgh until 1767. Marion E. Brown, "Adam Kuhn, Eighteenth-Century Physician and Teacher," *Journal of the History of Medicine and Allied Sciences*, V (April 1950), 163-177.

42. Shippen Papers, H.S.P.

43. Rev. Thomas Barton to the Secretary of the Society for the Propagation of the Gospel, November 16, 1764, William Stevens Perry, ed., *Historical Collections Relating to the American Colonial Church* (Hartford, Conn., 1873), II, 366-371.

44. William J. Mann, *Life and Times of Henry Melchior Muhlenberg* (Philadelphia, 1887), pp. 397-398.

45. Joseph Shippen, Jr., was the son of Edward Shippen and brother-in-law of James Burd. He held the office of Secretary to the Proprietary Governor. Shippen Papers, H.S.P.

46. Penn Manuscripts, Official Correspondence, Vol. 9 (1758-1764), fol. 282. H.S.P. William Allen was Chief Justice of Pennsylvania from 1750 to 1774 and a staunch defender of the proprietary interest.

47. Philadelphia Yearly Meeting, Minutes of the Meeting for Sufferings, 1756-1775, fol. 250. QC, Haverford.

48. A translation of Sauer's election broadside of September 18, 1765, can be found in Durnbaugh, *Brethren in Colonial America*, pp. 380-386.

49. Shippen Papers, H.S.P. "The general committee of our Society" is apparently a reference to the Presbyterian Church.

50. *Pennsylvania Gazette*, October 10, 1765.

51. Unsigned draft, Pemberton Papers, H.S.P.

52. Shippen Papers, H.S.P.

53. Shippen Papers, H.S.P. Emanuel and Jacob Carpenter, James Webb and George Ross were returned to the Assembly from Lancaster County. Adam Ort was elected Commissioner, but James Keimer was not among the six Assessors chosen. One of the successful candidates for Assessor was Samuel Bare. *Pennsylvania Chronicle*, October 3, 1768.

Chapter 3

"WE ARE NOT AT LIBERTY IN CONSCIENCE TO TAKE UP ARMS"

Politics and Theology

Mennonites, Quakers, Schwenkfelders, Dunkers, and Moravians drew closer together as the disputes between Great Britain and the American Colonies reached a crisis in the 1770s. Mennonite leaders conferred with Friends at Gwynedd Meeting House and the Quakers published German translations of nonresistant writings at their request (*Document 109*). Other Mennonites met with Schwenkfelder elder Christopher Schultz, who took an active part with Berks County Patriots, in an effort to influence the deliberations of the first Pennsylvania Convention and decide on their own response (*Documents 110, 111*). But all of the historic peace churches found themselves reacting to situations forced on them by others, rather than themselves shaping the course of events. Christopher Schultz observed in a letter to Edward Burd in January 1775 that Pennsylvania Quakers did not take part in choosing delegates to the first Convention and that "Thousands amongst the Germans" had decided to "follow their example keeping inactive and watching the Event."[1]

It may seem strange that the nonresistant sects, who had never been reluctant to choose candidates or turn out in force on election days, should be without political power in the crisis of the 1770s. But Mennonites and Quakers had gone to the polls in the previous decade out of concern for a single issue—the preservation of those "renowned Privileges" that permitted them to live according to their consciences. If they had won elections in those years, they had, nevertheless, profound doubts about political action. The Quaker Meeting for Sufferings had continued to counsel Friends to withdraw from the Assembly, even when some of its own most active members were campaigning on the proposal for a royal governor for Pennsylvania.

When the public debate over the taxes imposed by the British Parliament became the major issue of the day, the attitude of the peace churches and that of the Franklin-Galloway wing of the Quaker Party coincided for a time, with both urging moderation and peaceful petition. But as the possibility of a change in government grew dimmer any political motive for currying favor with the British ministry also faded. With the total collapse of the campaign for royal government by 1770, the peace churches stood alone and isolated. It was at this point that the Meeting for Sufferings began to advise Quakers not just to follow a moderate course themselves, but to separate altogether from those who "manifest a disposition to contend for liberty by any means contrary to the peaceable Spirit of the Gospel."[2] By the time Paul Revere galloped into Philadelphia in May 1774 with news of the Intolerable Acts passed by Parliament to punish the Boston Tea Party rioters and Philadelphians responded by choosing men for a Committee of Correspondence and by calling for a Continental Congress, this attitude had taken firm hold. James Pemberton, one of those elected to the Committee, immediately resigned, pointing out the "impropriety of any Members of our Society meeting in such a Mixture to Confer on Affairs of this Kind." And the Meeting for Sufferings again warned Friends against "mixing with the people in their Public Consultations." As a recent writer noted, this was a confession that the peace churches "could not hope to influence the course of events in the direction they wished them to take. The Revolutionary movement was the most important domestic issue of the day, and circumstances were such that all the initiative and influence belonged to others."[3] It was an abdication of political power and, although the Quaker-Mennonite alliance continued to be a factor in Pennsylvania elections through 1776, a fatal step for a political party. But the constituency of the historic peace churches was not a political party and their reaction was not politically motivated.

The real significance of the wartime experience of the historic peace churches is theological, because the issues involved were theological issues. What was at stake in 1775 was not military service or an oath of allegiance so much as the sectarian concept of discipleship as a distinct way of life. War brought the essential conflict between the sects and the state into sharper focus, because in wartime the state necessarily makes far greater demands on the individual than in time of peace. But war merely created points of friction for two different views of society, as a community in active dissent from the larger society becomes inevitably a state within a state. Rhys Isaac's observations about Virginia Methodists in the era of the American Revolution are equally applicable to the Mennonites and Quakers. Religious commitment involved a radical rejection of the accepted way of life, with the introduction of a strikingly new set of models for moral conduct and moral authority. Order was symbolized in a strict code of conduct, and, in the close groups for sharing and confirming religious experience, a new focus of authority that operated at a popular level within the religious community. Fundamental shifts in values and organization that occur outside and against established structures are highly subversive in tendency. Isaac has raised the intriguing question whether the Patriot movement in Virginia, at least, with its vigorous reassertion of the cultural dominance of the elite may not be in part a defensive response from the traditional power structure.[4] Did the vehement reaction of Pennsylvania and Maryland Patriots to the sects stem from the recognition that religious community involved a different ordering of society and a separate source of authority?

The talk of militia laws and frontier defense over more than a generation had allowed the sects to see more clearly than ever before the creative tension between the Christian obligation to support civil government and the life of a follower of Christ in a disciplined brotherhood. It was never a question of casting off one allegiance in favor of the other, but of recognizing that the claims of the kingdom of Christ had to take precedence over the demands of any earthly sovereign. True to the teaching of the New Testament, they were prepared to obey the laws and pay the taxes required by civil authority. Where the tenor of the law conflicted with Christian teaching, they were prepared, in the words of a North Carolina Quaker petition, to submit passively and peaceably to such laws "by Suffering under them without Resistance or anything more than to Petition or Remonstrate against them," just as they would cheerfully obey "Good and wholesome Laws."[5] The Christian duty of submission to civil authority did not imply that the acts of government were necessarily good or divinely approved, only that the proper response to even a persecuting and tyrannical ruler is the nonresistant love of Jesus.[6]

Mennonites and Quakers shared an essentially negative view of government. They expected the civil power to provide the minimum peace and order that they needed to build their own communities, although they were prepared to survive if it failed to do so, and they expected it to remove those obstacles to their faithful discipleship that might be placed in their path incidental to some piece of legislation, although they were ready to pay the penalty if the authorities declined. Petitions to the Pennsylvania, Maryland, and Virginia legislatures from Quaker and Mennonite bodies in 1755-1785 deal with problems raised for their members by militia laws, court procedures, oaths of allegiance, and too restrictive manumission laws. Even when they had deep reservations about acknowledging the authority of the new government, Friends let their voice be heard against licensing theaters and applying tax money to the support of all Christian churches.

The men who made the American Revolution had no doubt that God intended government as a positive blessing for mankind. They were the heirs of the Reformation and Luther, Zwingli, Calvin, and the other Reformers had not hesitated to invest the state with the principal responsibility for cleansing the church and constructing a Christian society. In carrying out that mission, the rights of Roman Catholics had sometimes to be set aside. The Reformation had thus of necessity to invent a theology of revolution. As men of the eighteenth century, neither Patriots nor Loyalists were much concerned about the religious opinions of George III. They included secular blessings, like the protection of property rights, among the God-given duties of the state and secular sins replaced heresy as the ground for deposing a monarch. But they followed the Reformers in giving the state a very positive role in promoting the happiness of the whole community. When they read in the 13th chapter of Romans that "the powers that be are ordained of God," they interpreted the passage as God's provision for *just* and *equitable* human government. The higher powers could only claim the sanction of divine institution when they acted "to secure the property and promote the happiness" of society.[7]

By explicitly rejecting this Reformation tradition, Anabaptists and Quakers had no way of fitting a theory of revolution into their theology. No series of arbitrary laws or burdensome taxes could justify resistance that went beyond petition and remonstrance. Had George III closed their meetinghouses and ordered all their young men drafted into the British army, he would still have commanded the loyalty of the sects as their legitimate sovereign. Once protest passed beyond "proper respectful petition," the sects had little choice but to wait and watch the outcome.[8]

Events Conspire to Involve the Peace Churches

A revolution was in progress in the summer of 1774. The American Colonies responded to the news of the Intolerable Acts in a way that differed little from Boston to Charleston. The legislature or some of its prominent members called for a meeting of delegates from every part of the colony. Mass meetings, sometimes attended by fifteen or twenty, sometimes more representative of public opinion, drafted resolutions, elected a county or town committee, and chose delegates from among themselves to attend the colony-wide convention.

In Pennsylvania, where Quakers and other conservatives dominated the Assembly, the county committees chose to meet in provincial convention in July 1774 during a special session of the Assembly in order to reduce the influence of Assemblymen on the deliberations of the convention. The Assembly stole a march on the convention and elected Pennsylvania's delegates to the Continental Congress, assuring that Pennsylvania would be a bulwark of conservatism in the Congress. Despite careful attention to traditional forms, neither the special session nor the convention had any more legitimate authority than a gathering of sailors on a Philadelphia dock or a meeting of drovers at a tavern on the Lancaster Road. At this point, the sects began to take alarm.[9]

Opposition to the Stamp Act in 1765 had centered on a voluntary agreement to boycott British goods, a happy choice of weapons as it turned out. When Americans again had recourse to the same sort of voluntary association to protest the Townshend Revenue Act of 1767, it had proven far less successful. With this recent experience in mind, county and town committees proposed and the Continental Congress endorsed nonimportation and nonexportation agreements, binding on all, and enforced by local committees. By the autumn of 1774, these committees had begun to act very much like governing bodies and pressed this "Continental Association" on every citizen, at the cost of being branded "inimical to the liberties of America" should he refuse.

Quakers, Mennonites, Schwenkfelders were among the men elected to township, county, and even provincial committees in Pennsylvania and Maryland in 1774. Almost at once a tug-of-war began, as local meetings pressured their members to resign. Those to whom the religious community was primary, did resign, others, possibly more assimilated to the larger society, refused to withdraw from committee or convention. No pattern of social or economic differences separated the one group from the other. The division cut across family ties in some cases. Nor can we establish any pattern of future Loyalists drawing back at the brink of treason against the king. Evan Thomas, a Quaker who resigned his seat in the Maryland Convention, is typical of those who followed this course. One of the wealthiest men in his county, he abandoned many traditional Quaker ways in his youth, but then deliberately turned his back on the assimilative process and became a noted minister among Friends. He freed his own slaves and the records of Sandy Spring and Indian Spring Meetings show that he served on many committees dealing with members who refused to manumit their slaves or otherwise breached Quaker practice. Richard Thomas, a first cousin, served on committees, accepted a colonel's commission, and held on to his slaves. It would be logical to assume that Richard Thomas, despite Sandy Spring's dealings with him over a long period of years, wore his religion more lightly than his cousin did. In other respects, the two men can be shown to be virtually identical so we cannot have recourse to differences in acreage or education as an explanation. The fact that Colonel Richard Thomas took up arms, contrary to his Quaker upbringing, is proof not only that he was a dedicated Patriot, but that his first loyalty was to the wider community. Evan Thomas' refusal proves that his first loyalty was to the Quaker community, not necessarily that he was a "passive Loyalist" or "neutral." As Clerk of the Meeting for Sufferings of Maryland Yearly Meeting and a wealthy planter, Evan Thomas was harassed by the authorities during the Revolution. We have complete records from both sides of the charges levied against him and the fines he paid, but no hint that his "Toryism" was anything other than fidelity to Quaker principles. A sheriff who arrested a Quaker for preaching without a license would not have overlooked rumors that the same Quaker had spoken "words inimical to American liberty" or any other treasonable offense, if there had been any suggestion that Evan Thomas was a Loyalist. Of the persons, including both Patriots and Tories, dealt with by Philadelphia Yearly Meeting for violations of the peace testimony during the American Revolution, 420 chose to be disowned, rather than express repentance, indicating that the religious community was not central for them.[10]

The Mennonite experience is more difficult to chart, for the simple reason that we have no church records proving that a man was or was not a Mennonite. Jacob Wistler of Manor Township was among those elected to the Lancaster County Committee of Observation in December 1774. He was "one of the people called Menonists," as his 1766 statement proves (*Document 88*). Others chosen to the Committee on the same day included Valentine Brenneman of Hempfield, Martin Bear of Conestoga, Samuel Bear of Manheim, Jacob Erisman of Rapho, Jacob Erb of Warwick, Henry Light of Lebanon, John Brubaker of Earl, John Witmer, Jr., of Lampeter, and Jacob Bear of Bart.[11] In

1775 Abraham Newcomer was serving as a Committeeman for Conestoga Township. He can be identified as a Mennonite gunsmith from Document 87. Were Committeemen Michael Shank of Lancaster Township, John Breckbill of Strasburg, and others members of the Mennonite Church? Shank, Newcomer, Breckbill, and Witmer were all reelected in November 1775, along with Peter Brubaker and John Hoover of Hempfield, Henry Funk of Manor, Peter Good of Brecknock, and John Light of Lebanon.[12] All we can safely conclude is that a number of men from the Mennonite community did support the Patriot cause in 1774-1775, just as many Friends did. We cannot document Jacob Wistler's motives for resigning from the committee nor Abraham Newcomer's for continuing to serve. No more can we trace the decision of Moravian William Henry to accept a place on the Lancaster County Committee or of the Schwenkfelders Christopher Schultz and Melchior Wagner to attend the Pennsylvania Convention in January 1775 as representatives from Berks and Philadelphia Counties respectively. What is clear is that the peace churches had a fair opportunity to influence the Patriot committees and members of the sects were elected to these bodies in about the same proportion as any other group, but by early 1775 the greater number of them had resigned and Quakers and German nonresistants alike stood back from the march of events, nervously awaiting the outcome.[13]

In Pennsylvania, their last real victory was in holding the Pennsylvania Convention to a series of resolves in favor of home industry and greater emphasis on sheep and beef production, with no hint of coercive measures or armed defense. Quakers and Mennonites found the Convention's request for aid to the poor of Boston a project particularly appropriate for themselves to undertake.[14]

But events were moving too quickly. Soon after Lexington and Concord, the local committees were circulating a new kind of "association." The Lancaster County Committee of Observation, for example, resolved on May 1, 1775, that the inhabitants should immediately form military companies and circulated printed copies of "The Association of the Freemen and Inhabitants of the County of Lancaster," a voluntary enlistment paper (*Document 113*). These association papers were soon dog-eared from passing hand to hand for signatures and companies of farmers and shopkeepers were studying the art of war at every crossroads in the American Colonies. Joining these voluntary companies soon became a test of loyalty and "Non-Associators" were branded as enemies of American liberty.

Quakers and Mennonites were prepared to donate to the relief of the poor of Boston, and later to aid other war victims, without making any commitment to the cause of Parliament or Congress. Philadelphia Yearly Meeting adopted a plan for war relief, in cooperation with New England Yearly Meeting, and sent printed subscription forms to every Friends Meeting for contributions.[15] Mennonites and other peace churches contributed through the Committees of Observation (*Document 112*).

Contributing to the Common Cause

During the French and Indian War, Quakers and Mennonites had contributed generously to help refugees from the stricken frontiers and to the work of the Friendly Association. They left the task of guarding forts and blockhouses to those who voluntarily "associated" in military companies in Pennsylvania, where they had successfully blocked a comprehensive militia law. In other Colonies, they had personally refused to perform militia duty and accepted fines and imprisonment instead. But the sects could not be allowed to stand aloof from this struggle. The clamor began early for a fine on Non-Associators with conscientious scruples about bearing arms that would be an equivalent for turning out with the militia. Its purpose was to compel the Philadelphia Quaker and the Lancaster County Amishman to take his place beside his neighbor "in defence of the liberties of America" and no longer to be an onlooker in a struggle that did not concern him. Resentment against the sects flared into mob violence in some places. A Mennonite who talked about the folly of mustering at a barnraising in York County, Pennsylvania, was sentenced to be tarred and feathered (*Documents 114, 115*). The Lancaster County Committee, in the heart of the largest Amish and Mennonite community, issued a handbill, warning that "Persons, whose Religious tenets forbid their forming themselves into Military Associations, have been maltreated." The Committee sought to discourage such behavior as well as reported incidents of laughter and abuse directed at the companies of Associators learning the military arts (*Document 117*). The Lancaster Committee succeeded only in provoking a riot by their handbill and, amid rumors that they had accepted a bribe "to excuse the Quakers and Menonists from arming," the Committee resigned in a body and new elections were held (*Documents 118, 119*)

At its very first meeting, the new Lancaster County Committee received a petition protesting against those who would not associate (*Document 121*). The first item on their agenda was the method of involving the sects in the common cause.

A delegation representing the Mennonites, Amish Mennonites, and Church of the Brethren in Lancaster County met with the Committee to ask their permission for an appeal to Congress (*Document 126*). The text of the minutes was considerably edited for publication, as the several drafts in the Library of Congress attest, but in all versions the representatives of the peace churches agreed to "contribute towards the Support of the Rights & Liberties of their Country." The voluntary contributions of £3. .10. .0 and the unspecified sum equal to the provincial tax assessment were thus understood by the County Committee at least as the equivalent of mustering in support of American liberty. The funds raised in this manner were to be applied, moreover, to any public purpose that seemed good to the authorities, including the purchase of arms and ammunition.

The peace churches understood their contributions as charitable donations to the poor, although they were aware of ambiguities in their position.[16] However they labeled their contributions, the peace churches did contribute in Lancaster County. In one township, the only one for which a record is extant, five sixths of the peace church members and less than one sixth of the Presbyterian and Church of England Non-Associators gave to the cause (*Documents 133, 134*).

The Lancaster County experience was repeated in a short time in other Pennsylvania counties and in other colonies where Quakers, Mennonites, and Brethren were numerous. The Committee for the Upper District of Frederick County in Maryland suggested a tax on conscientious objectors. The Committee declared that this course would be acceptable to "a great number" of Dunkers (Church of the Brethren) and Mennonites in the Hagerstown area, with whom they had had conversation (*Document 145*).

Fines for Non-Associators

The nonresistant sects had fallen into a trap. Far from allowing them to stand aloof from the political conflict and contribute for the needy or war victims, the authorities had chosen to interpret their gifts as contributions to the war chest. In July 1775, the York County Committee learned from a delegation of nonresistants: that contributing to the "present measures carrying on" was as objectionable as mustering. They made it a matter of conscience, on the other hand, to pay the provincial tax, which was not used for military purposes. The obvious expedient of levying an additional tax on all the Non-Associators appealed to the York County Committee as a happy solution (*Document 129*).

Other county committees preferred to ride roughshod over the claims of the peace churches to conscientious objector status. In Berks County a meeting of Non-Associators argued that the earlier resolves of the Pennsylvania Assembly and the Continental Congress required only voluntary contributions, which they had cheerfully made. They agreed to voluntary subscriptions "for the Uses pointed out by the said Recommendations" of Congress and the Assembly, even though the money would be used by the Committee of Safety for whatever purposes "agreeable to the said Recommendations" it chose. By recourse to the original resolves, they could preserve some hope that the money would be used for "their needy brethren" and not for military purposes (*Documents 135, 136, 137*).

Time was running out on the peace churches by the autumn of 1775. Soon after the October elections in Pennsylvania, petitions began to pour into the Assembly from military Associators. In hastily arming the province and raising battalions in every county, the Committee of Safety for Pennsylvania as well as the local committees ran far ahead of available funds and the deficit had to be made up. The petitioners proposed a tax on all Non-Associators. If a need for additional revenue was at the bottom of it, these petitions were asking much more of the conscientious objectors than an increased tax assessment; every member of the community had an obligation to contribute to the common cause and the additional tax would be a concession to those who could not meet that obligation on the field of battle (*Document 138*).

The peace churches rightly put their case on the high ground of religious liberty. The Quakers argued constitutional law with the Assembly to no avail. The Mennonites and German Baptists (Church of the Brethren) simply set down the limits of what they could do in good conscience (*Document 141*). It made little difference to the course of events. The day after the Mennonite petition was read, the Pennsylvania Assembly voted to require all white male Non-Associators of military age "to contribute an Equivalent to the Time spent by the Associators in acquiring the military Discipline," and appointed a committee to draw up legislation.[17] On November 24, 1775, the Assembly imposed a tax of £2..10..0 on Non-Associators between the ages of sixteen and fifty, which would be remitted for those who joined a military unit.[18] The bill made no specific provision for the use of the money, other than that it was to be paid by the county treasurers to Michael Hillegas, who was treasurer of the Pennsylvania Committee of Safety. The military purpose of the tax might also be inferred from a resolution regarding the voluntary contributions made by conscientious objectors for "their distressed brethren." A committee appointed by the Assembly to adjust the accounts of the military Associators was further "directed to make particular Enquiry concerning the Contributions made by the People called Menonists, Omish Menonists and Sunday Baptists in Lancaster County, in pursuance of the Recommendations of the late House of Assembly on the Thirtieth of June last, and report to this House at their next Meeting, *how much of the said Contributions has been paid for the Use of any, and what Battalion or Company of Associators in that County.*"[19]

The Assembly clearly intended to make the peace churches pay the cost of the war and the tax on Non-Associators was an avowed equivalent to military service. Under this increasing monetary and social pressure, the vast majority of non-pacifist conservatives, including many future Loyalists, signed the Association and drilled with the militia. By the closing months of 1775, the Non-Associators, against whom the tax was directed, consisted almost entirely of Quakers, Mennonites, and other nonresistants.[20] A tax on conscientious objectors as an equivalent to military service and intended for military purposes was an infringement on the religious freedom enjoyed by the people of Pennsylvania under William Penn's Charter. The war tax issue thus arose in a context of liberty of conscience curtailed for those whose Christian faith forbade "giving, or doing, or assisting in any Thing by which Men's Lives are destroyed or hurt."

An Equivalent to Military Service

Deluged with fresh petitions for a heavier fine on Non-Associators, the Pennsylvania Assembly increased the tax on April 5, 1776, to £3..10..0. The changes they made in the military association satisfied some of the more substantial demands of the radical military element. The Pennsylvania Assembly raised the fine on Non-Associators, provided for speedy naturalization of German *Associators*, and introduced the death penalty for mutiny, sedition, and deserting to the enemy. The following day, the Assembly reluctantly voted to implement the March 14 recommendation of the Continental Congress to disarm all Non-Associators. These measures brought Pennsylvania abreast of the other Middle Colonies.[21]

The Convention that sat in Philadelphia through the summer of 1776 framing a Constitution for the free and independent Commonwealth of Pennsylvania had its sessions interrupted by the drums and fifes of companies of ill-trained Associators, half of them without muskets, marching off to join Washington's army at New York.

Scarcely a day went by without news of some success gained by Sir William Howe's British and Hessian regulars or of the difficulty some county committee was having in mustering its battalions. Angry at the failure of so many Pennsylvanians to turn out with the Associators, whether for reasons of conscience or not, the Convention "in a passion" increased the Non-Associator fine to £1 a month. More important, they incorporated the principle of taxing conscientious objectors as an equivalent to military service in the Declaration of Rights they adopted in September 1776 (*Documents 143, 144*). The contradiction did not escape comment. A writer who signed himself "Andrew Marvell" observed in the *Pennsylvania Packet* that "in one of the articles of the Bill of Rights, it is declared that men shall not be compelled to bear arms against their consciences, and in one of the ordinances of the Convention every man who declines bearing arms is fined Twenty Shillings a month and is taxed Four Shillings in the Pound." He added that even "A Committee of the Convention was struck with the enormity of the sum exacted from the Non-Associators."[22]

The Pennsylvania Assembly overruled the Convention and repealed the increased fine. It was actually collected only in Northampton, before the law was changed. But the demand for a heavier burden on Non-Associators became all the more strident. Taxes and fines on the unpopular conscientious objectors made up what could not be collected from nominal Whigs.[23]

Shifting some of the cost of war onto the shoulders of those who would not bear arms proved so popular a measure that other colonies followed Pennsylvania's example. The Maryland Convention, which had originally exempted "persons who from their religious principles cannot bear arms in any case," reversed its stand in the December 1775 session, making all adult males liable to militia duty and imposing a fine of not less than 40 shillings nor more than £10 to be assessed by the county committees "for the use of the Public" on those who refused to muster.[24] Even before the Maryland Convention acted, the Committee of Observation for the Upper District of Frederick County had decided on October 2, 1775, "that every person who enjoys the benefit of their religion & protection of the Laws of this free Country ought to Contribute either in money or Military service towards the defence of these invaluable Rights." The committee consequently determined to fine on a weekly basis "all those who are restrain'd by religious principles" from doing their part with their neighbors in the militia.[25]

The Virginia Convention ordered Quakers and Mennonites enrolled with the militia, but exempted them from musters as well as actual service (*Document 199*). In those counties where Mennonites and Quakers were numerous, petitions circulated in 1776 proposing that "Quakers and Menonists" be "subjected to the payment of a certain sum, to be annually assessed by the county courts" (*Document 150*).

North Carolina imposed a £25 fine "to defray the Expences of the War" on Quakers, Moravians, "Dunkards and Menonists," who were exempt from militia duty.[26]

Fines thinned the ranks of Non-Associators until only men with real conviction remained in that camp. As late as March 1776, only nine men in Brecknock Township in Lancaster County had signed the military association, while 105 of their neighbors chose to be Non-Associators.[27] An assessment of Non-Associators in August 1777 in Brecknock Township revealed only 42 Non-Associators and an undated return from the same township crossed off 14 of these names. By the end of 1777, the proportion of Associators to Non-Associators had very nearly reversed, with 86 Associators and 28 Non-Associators in Brecknock Township.[28] This process took a year and a half of war to complete, transforming those who were willing to shoulder arms in defense of American liberties from a tiny minority of Brecknock men and boys to a substantial majority. At the same time, the Non-Associators became the Mennonites of Brecknock Township under another name, as men with different backgrounds and other reasons for declining to join the militia signed the association. The failure of militia fines to have any real impact on the peace churches is just as obvious when we consider townships with a Mennonite majority. In Conestoga Township, for instance, there were 193 males between the ages of sixteen and fifty in 1776 and 139 Non-Associators in December 1777.[29]

As a way of involving Mennonites, Quakers, Dunkers, Schwenkfelders, and Moravians in the struggle, fines on the Non-Associators proved a dismal failure. The sects had more enthusiasm for the Patriot cause in December 1774 than they did in December 1775 or at any time thereafter. By insisting that personal military service was as essential an element of good citizenship as paying taxes and customs duties, the Pennsylvania authorities introduced a new element into the relations between the sects and the state.

DOCUMENTS

Friends Try to Calm Revolutionary Spirit

The rapid march of events in 1774 and 1775 disturbed Mennonites and Quakers, who sought to avoid any recourse to arms. In a letter to Dr. John Fothergill of London, the Quaker leader Israel Pemberton described the efforts made by Friends to calm the revolutionary spirit. Mennonites sent a "special deputation" of preachers to confer with Friends at Gwynedd Meeting in Philadelphia (Montgomery) County. The Meeting for Sufferings of Philadelphia Yearly Meeting had a doctrinal statement on nonresistance printed in German for distribution among them. Pemberton believed the Epistle and Testimony issued by the Meeting for Sufferings had a moderating effect on the first Pennsylvania Convention in January 1775 and the quite innocuous resolutions it adopted. Pemberton's letter is a rough draft, with many words crossed out and others inserted. A lengthy section dealing with an unnamed English woman minister among Friends has been omitted.

Document 109

Philada. 2 mo. 15th 1775

Dear friend

I wrote to thee last on the 6: 11 mo. and a few days before inclosing the Extracts of the proceedings of the American Congress, soon after the publication of which the spirit of party raged with redoubled malice & spread like a Contagion not only among those who have been active in these public Comotions, but infected others, so that they who could discern the sorrowful tendency of the measures recommended could do little more than lament without the power of interposing. At length the delusion catches our Assembly off their guard, being with great precipitation hurried into a resolve approving and recommending the Resolutions & Agreements of the Congress, which has since cost some of the members much trouble of mind & shame to themselves, especially part of the few of our Society who were present at this resolve of the house. this Step we had reason to fear might produce division of sentiment [and] Conduct among them but an opportunity taken as early as convenient of Conferring with such members of the Assembly as profess with us, some of them were soon convinced of the great Error they were drawn into, as we have reason to believe was the case with others, tho' averse to acknowledge it, and we have the satisfaction to find that the more the Resolutions of the Congress become known & maturely considered, the less they are held in repute. the several pamphlets which have been lately published have contributed much to allay the violent spirit which has prevailed & the minds of the people become daily more disposed to hearken to reason, so that in New York & this City it is greatly abated tho: there is a party who are yet very industrious to delude the people.

The Assembly of New Jersey has been so weak as to follow the Example of ours & plead the precedent as an Excuse, tho' their Governor gave them a favorable oppo[rtunity of] embracing more salutary measures, which the Assembly of New York have judiciously adopted. how our Govern[or] can reconcile his neglect of communicating the like Instructions to our Assembly we are at a loss to account for, but that he is of an inactive indisposition & has not the most judicious Advisors.

The proceedings of the Assembly, & the general State of things requiring the immediate attention & care of ffrds [Friends] our meeting for sufferings gave forth some fresh advice by an Epistle of the 5th Ulto., and finding a further duty incumbent on us, a testimony was also published by that meeting on the 24 of the same month, both which were Considered maturely & concluded with great Unanimity, and by the Effects we have reason to believe they were necessary & seasonable. the latter has been translated into German & dispersed among that people, the thoughtful part of whom have been so solicitous to have the advice of ffrds [Friends] that the Menonists sent down special deputation of three of th[ei]r preachers to ye mo[nthly] meeting of Gwynnedd for this purpose, abt. the time we were considering the Expediency of such a publication, and as great pains were taking to obtain a provincial Convention, with a design to engage the people to furnish themselves with warlike weapons & learn the Art of War, such a declaration on the part of ffrds appeared the more necessary, and with other circumstances we think has contributed to defeat that ill judged intention, so that this Convention soon finished their business & broke up after making some plausible resolves relating to domestic Oeconomy, among which there is one of a Military complexion.

Since this the King's Speech has reached us which has Struck a further damp on the Republican spirit, the advocates for which have been since at a great stand & sense their party daily to weaken. In Maryland there have been some unwarrantable Outrages but latterly the people are become divided. The Virginians remain warm & resolute. In the Massachusetts the moderate party gains ground. so that on the whole, & from the temper of parliament whose proceedings we have down the 17 12mo we have a faint hope, the state of things will soon give a more favorable aspect.

Our Assembly meets by adjournment the 20 Inst, when they may have an oppo[rtunity] of amending their late Conduct, if they have wisdom to see the mistake of ye last sitting and candour to own it; but there are some Inflammatory Spirits among them.[30]

Nonresistants Influence 1775 Convention

John Bechtel, pastor of the Mennonite Church in Hereford Township, Berks County, conferred with his neighbor Schwenkfelder elder Christopher Schultz about the implications of the upcoming Pennsylvania Convention for nonresistants. Their attitude is explained in an extract from a letter Schultz wrote to Edward Burd, a fellow member of the Berks County Committee and a fellow delegate to the Convention. William Reeser, another Committee member, urged Schultz and other concerned nonresistants to meet in Philadelphia before the Convention was called to order and adopt a common policy. As the Schultz letter indicates, they were particularly anxious to block any effort by the Convention to arm the people or create a militia. In this much, they were successful. When the Convention dissolved on January 28, 1775, it had passed a series of resolutions in favor of home industry and one prohibiting the slave trade.

Document 110

A virtuous Standing unto the last Extremity, to the peaceful Maxims, under which this Province hath been founded, and by which we have been till now safely protected and preserved by divine Providentz in several most imminent Dangers, would draw I hope a Blessing upon our innocent Endeavors, would endear and keep up good Confidence unto one another; we could all remain free, to do jointly and severally, what is most essential to our Preservation; and which I think we could well excuse to be not contrary or offending the Union with our Sister Colonies: Seeing whereas a peaceable opposition to the Ministerial oppression is resolved by the Continental Congress, Our erecting a Militia in our Circumstances at this Time of professing and Petitioning for Peace, would in us be a rash Attempt, and a very foremost Step towards War, before other Colonies, whilst we undertake now to do, what we never have done before, and what we on several pressing Occasions by all Means have avoided to do. When other colonies only go on and improve or continue with that which ever since their Foundation hath been a rule and custom with them.[31]

Document 111
January 13, 1775

Honored and dear friend Christopher Shultz:

I received your letter of yesterday through John Bechtel, and from it understand your thinking, as well as that of other well-meaning people. As far as the enclosed letter is concerned, I thought it over in a mature way (I believe), and it is my opinion that it should be retained. But the following suggestion came to me: if you, with several intelligent men, go to Philadelphia on time for the session of the convention, and go to Etzidal (?) (Eszidol?) and hear, in response to your presentation, his mind and opinion about such an important work, there he will, as I think, express himself more clearly than perchance by means of a short letter. I for my part do not let any opportunity pass by if I can instigate anything good with sincere people, in view of this more important work.

Nevertheless I still have hope that even though God may intend to discipline us thereby, he will not punish us in his wrath, requesting this as David did; but first we ought to confess our transgressions and humble ourselves before God; then he would still be merciful toward us, and as he says through the Prophet, Reform your lives, then I shall dwell with you.

Further I report that the Committee met yesterday and came to an agreement with the butcher that no sheep are to be slaughtered until the first of May, and no lambs from May to October.

As far as the affairs of the country are concerned, they are apparently getting worse daily; I wish that at the next meeting the Lord may govern your and everyone's heart that all may redound to his honor and glory and to the welfare and good of every inhabitant, so that even the wicked would have to desist from their plans and humble themselves under the mighty hand of the Lord. That we have sinned is a fact, without contradiction, and sin is followed by punishment unless true repentance and reform of life intervenes. But the same God who lived in Haman's time still rules today, who in all ages knows how to redeem his people out of tribulation if we call upon him from our hearts.

I will close herewith, wishing you prosperity, both temporal and spiritual. I remain a true friend of all those who love God and use their time for the benefit of the neighbor.

William Reeser[32]

Confusion and Suspicions

A brief note from William Reeser to Christopher Schultz gives the flavor of the days immediately after news of Lexington and Concord reached Pennsylvania. Both Schultz and Reeser served on the Berks County Committee of Observation, but both men had religious scruples about war. Their confusion and the suspicions they aroused by refusing to urge their neighbors to drill and learn the military art were common to all moderates in Pennsylvania.

Document 112

Reading, May 1, 1775.

First, a greeting to all acquaintances. With this opportunity I would like to report first that I and my family are still well and living in peace. But our general need seems to be increasing. Instead of having the opportunity as previously of hearing a lovely harmony of peace, we now have the discordant drum daily in our ears, with flags flying; to serve the war-god is for many now the greatest occupation, which in truth often saddens one's heart, because one becomes aware that virtue and honesty are declining. I must often be like one who is not heard and has no answer in his mouth, as David says. As far as the news from Boston is concerned, I think you may probably have heard it as well as we. I wrote to you several weeks ago, but the letter did not reach you; there is no danger even if it gets into the hands of others. One hears often with astonishment how men at the present time pretend to one's face to be friends, but behind one's back prove to be enemies; there is no better defense than patience. If at this time I could have my home at a lonely place as well as in Reading I would be spared many trials (as I believe).

About two weeks ago various members of the Committee met, which at the request of many I attended. Because without my presence there could be no majority, the proposals remained concealed until the end. Then Dr. P.° said it was necessary that each member encourage the brethren in his neighborhood to make armed resistance and so nothing further was done, for he said that I would not give my consent to such action, as he already knew.

William Reeser

Christoph Shultz in Hereford[33]

°Dr. Jonathan Potts of Reading, a member of the Berks County Committee.

Patriots Sign Association

When news of the fighting at Lexington and Concord on April 19, 1775, reached Pennsylvania, the county committees met to draw up associations, a voluntary pledge to join with others in a militia and learn military discipline. The Association adopted in Lancaster County on May 1, 1775, was drafted at a meeting attended by at least two men of probable peace church background, Samuel Bare of Rapho and John Whitmore, Jr., of Lampeter. They published the Association as a broadside, which was then distributed throughout the county to be signed by Patriots. Copies with many signatures can be found in several manuscript collections in the Pennsylvania Historical Society, the Lancaster County Historical Society, the Library of Congress, and other libraries.

Everyone who agreed to sign one of these papers became an "Associator." The difficulty for Mennonites, Brethren, Quakers, and others in signing a pledge to drill with a military company is obvious. It should be noted that the Association also asserted a duty to God to fight for their religious and civil liberties, which would require a formal denial of their own Christian faith.

Document 113

At a meeting of the Committee of Observation for Lancaster County, May 1st, 1775.

PRESENT

Edward Shippen, George Ross, Jasper Yeates, William Atlee, Adam Riegart, Casper Shaffner, Valentine Brenizen, Charles Hall, Samuel Bare, Sebastian Graff, Eberhard Michael, James Burd, Joseph Sherer, John Campbell, William Patterson, James Cunningham, Bartram Galbreath, Alexander Lowry, Thomas Clark, Curtis Grubb, Emanuel Carpenter, Alexander Martin, Zacheus Davis, David Jenkins, John Whitmore, Jr., Thomas Porter, John Snodgrass, William M'Entire, Thomas Whitsides, Robert Bailey, Joshua Anderson, Hieronimus Heckman.

George Ross, Esq. was unanimously chosen Chairman.

Upon Motion, Resolved, That it is the unanimous opinion of this Committee, that it be most heartily recommended to the Inhabitants of the County of LANCASTER, immediately to associate and provide themselves with Arms and Ammunition, and learn the art of Military discipline, to enable them to support and defend their just Rights and Priviledges, against all arbitrary and dispotic Invasions, by any Person or Persons whatsoever.

The following *Association* was then proposed, and being read paragraph by paragraph, was unanimously agreed to by the *Committee*, and follows in these words, *To wit.*

The *Association* of the Freemen and Inhabitants of the County of

Lancaster.

Whereas, the enemies of Great-Britain and America, have resolved by force of arms, to carry into execution, the most unjust, tyrannical and cruel edicts of the British Parliament, and reduce the free born sons of America to a state of vassalage, and have flattered themselves from our unacquaintance with military discipline, that we should become an easy prey to them, or tamely submit, and bend our necks to the yoke prepared for us.

We do most solemnly agree and associate, under the deepest sense of our duty to God, our country, our selves and posterity, to defend and protect the religious and civil rights of this and our sister colonies, with our lives and fortunes, to the utmost of our abilities, against any power whatsoever, that shall attempt to deprive us of them.

And the better to enable us so to do, we will use our utmost diligence to acquaint ourselves with military discipline, and learn the art of war.

We do further agree to divide ourselves into companies, not exceeding one hundred men, each so as to make it most convenient to our situation and settlements, and to elect and chuse such persons as the majority of each company shall think proper for officers, viz. for each company, a Captain, two Lieutenants, and one Ensign, who shall have the power of appointing the other officers under them, necessary for the companies.

That, when the companies are formed, and the officers chosen and appointed, an association shall be signed by the officers and soldiers of each company, for the good order and government of the officers and soldiers.[34]

[Blank space was left at the bottom for signatures.]

Tension Between Associators and Non-Associators

Tension grew between the Associators, who joined military companies in every township, and the Non-Associators, who refused for one reason or another to take up arms. In May 1775 a young Mennonite contradicted the captain of a York County company of Associators, who insisted that everyone must muster or be counted as an enemy to his country. This was in Manchester Township. The York County Committee ordered him tarred and feathered. The Rev. George Neisser, pastor of the Moravian congregation at York, recorded the incident in his diary. (*Document 114*). John Adlum included a much more detailed account in his memoirs, written some years after the event (*Document 115*).

Document 114

May 31, 1775.

To-day there was an excitement. In spite of all warning a German gave vent to his feelings in insulting Congress and its measures for instituting defensive warfare. In accordance with the usual mode of punishing such delinquents, he was seized, and tarred and feathered, for his insulting speech.[35]

Document 115

In one instance and the only one that took place in York County was an attempt to tar and feather a young Dutchman (German) for venturing to give an opinion with respect to the times contrary to Captain [Michael] Smyser* at a house raising. The captain was informing the people at the raising that they all must join some company or other to muster as it was called, and that anyone who refused would be ranked among the Tories, the name given to all who would not join our cause. This young man who was one of those called Menonists contradicted the captain and spoke against mustering and told them that the day might come when they would repent it. The captain immediately came down and entered a complaint to the [York County] committee [of observation] against the young man as being a Tory and enemy to his country, who immediately sent for him to appear before them. On his appearance Captain Smyser was requested to declare upon his honor what the young man had said. Colonel [Thomas] Hartley was the chairman and after the captain had given his evidence the young man was asked what he had to say for himself. He answered nothing, only that what he had said he believed there was no harm or injury to anyone, neither had he injured anyone. Colonel Hartley after a short consultation with the other members of the committee pronounced him an enemy to his country and a Tory and that he should be tarred and feathered. Some busy person had sent a tarbox such as is used for wagons, and a boy had a pillow of feathers. The young man was ordered in front of the court house where the tar box was standing, but no one was there to tar him, none of the boys would undertake it. One of the committee, a very violent man, said he must tar himself. The other part of the committee had sneaked off apparently ashamed of the business and themselves. The young man pulled off his shirt and put one hand in the tar box and applied it to his shoulder, when the boys interfered and told him to let the person who ordered him to tar himself, do it. He paused and looked about for a moment when some one of the boys told him to take up his shirt and jacket and go home. He immediately picked up his shirt and moved from the courthouse, when some mischievous persons ripped up the pillow and shook the feathers after him, but I do not believe any struck him. Some small boys followed him a short distance but by the time he got about one hundred yards on his way there was no mob after him, nor no one in the middle of the street but himself, nor did I hear that he was in anywise molested on his way home.

I was a witness of the whole proceedings until I saw the boys leave him, and so ended a very foolish and ridiculous affair and I have no doubt but that the principal actors were ashamed of. I have no doubt but that if the boys had joined in the business and tarred and feathered the poor man and mobbed him, there would have been more of it. But to their everlasting credit they put down the business at once by not taking part in it.[36]

Threats, Protests, Riots

Threats and violence were used against Lancaster County Mennonites who refused to join the military association. A Mennonite delegation asked the Lancaster Committee for protection on May 29, 1775. The same day, the Committeemen had heard complaints from Manheim and Rapho townships about rivalry for new recruits and incidents of name-calling as the untrained volunteers marched down country roads. The Committee attempted to settle the matter with a letter to the township committee and a handbill in English and German, calling on all parties to respect the rights of others. Before printer Francis Bailey of Lancaster had the handbill ready, rumors about it flew through the city and the county. The Lancaster Associators refused to drill in protest over the privileges given to conscientious objectors and, ignoring their officer's commands, stormed through the town as an armed mob, demanding the handbills from the Committee. The Committeemen resigned in a body, when their action provoked a minor riot, but not before sending a spirited defense of religious liberty to the Pennsylvania delegates to the Continental Congress.

°Captain Michael Smyser, a tavern-keeper in Manchester township, was wounded and taken prisoner at Fort Washington in November 1776.

Document 116

Lancaster May 29, 1775.

Gentlemen

It is represented to the Committee by Captn. Gantz & his Company, that Jeremias Miller* & his Son, Mr. Welsh** & Some others seem to take great Pains to break up that Company; That many Persons in the Parts through which the Company marches, either to recruit their Men or perform their Exercises, make it Their Business to insult the Company, calling them Black-Guards, Fellows who are lazy, & follow the Drum from an idle Disposition, with many other insulting & disagreeable Terms.

If there are any of the Inhabitants of those Parts, whose religious Principles will not suffer them to take up Arms in Defence of the Rights of themselves & their Countrymen, they ought to be satisfied that they are permitted to sit quietly, & ought not to insult or behave with Impertinence towards those who have Virtue to stand forth & risque their Lives in Defence of the Rights & Liberties of their Country. If they do, they must expect such Treatment, as may perhaps be disagreeable to them, as the Committee of the County will certainly take Notice of every Person who shall behave in that manner, at the Same Time that they shall use their Influence to prevent any Violence or Insults to those whose religious Principles persuade them that it is sinful to use Arms in Defence of their Properties.

If any new Companies are raising in these Townships, great Care should be taken that none of those who have already joined in one Company be persuaded to join in another. Something of this Sort we hear hath already created Uneasiness in that Part of the County, and in the above mentioned Company.

The Committee request that you, Gentlemen, will endeavour to accommodate & settle Matters amongst the Inhabitants, so that no further Disputes may happen amongst them. You will please to discountenance any Insult or abusive Language on either Side, & mention that the Committee will take Notice of it. You will mention their Disapprobation of any Officer drawing off the Men from another Company to complete his own, & assure those who shall associate for themselves & their Countrymen that the Committee of the County will do all in their Power to serve them & the Common Cause.

---

*Jeremias Miller was a druggist in Manheim in Rapho Township in 1775.

**Mr. Welsh was probably Neal Welsh of Rapho Township. Neither of these men was a Mennonite.

As Captn. Gantz's Company are to meet at Manheim on Saturday it might not be amiss, if some of you Gentlemen would attend there on that Day to mention to the Company & People, & especially to such as you shall have Reason to believe have taken any active Part in their Disputes, the Sentiments of the Committee. We are

Gentlemen
Your most Obedient Humble Servants

Edwd. Shippen	*William Bausman*	*Cas. Shaffner*
Adam Simon Kuhn	*William Patterson*	*Chrn. Voght*
J. Yeates	*Charles Hall*	*Eberhart Michael*
Will. Atlee		

To Messrs. Sebastian Graff
Samuel Bare
Patrick Hays &
Jacob Erisman*

Members of the Committee for the County of Lancaster in Manheim & Rapho Townships.

(A true Copy.)

Copy of the Committee's Letter to Messrs. Graff, Bare, Hays & Erisman, respecting the Disputes in Manheim & Rapho Townships. Lancaster May 29, 1775.[37]

Document 117

At a Meeting of the Committee of Inspection and Observation of the County of Lancaster, at Lancaster on the 29th Day of May, 1775.

Edward Shippen, Esq., Chairman

The Committee having received Information, that divers Persons, whose religious Tenets forbid their forming themselves into Military Associations, have been mal-treated, and threatened by some violent and ill-disposed people in the County of Lancaster, notwithstanding their Willingness to contribute chearfully to the Common Cause, otherwise than by taking up of Arms: This Committee duly considering the same, do most heartily recommend to the good Inhabitants of the County, that they use every possible Means to discourage and prevent such licentious Proceedings, and assiduously cultivate that Harmony and Union so absolutely necessary in the present alarming Crisis of Public Affairs. At the same Time they conceive it to be their indispensible Duty, to intimate to the Public, their intire disapprobation of any

*Jacob Erisman, Rapho Township Committeeman, belonged to a Mennonite family and may have been a church member.

abusive, opprobrious or insulting Expressions, that may be made Use of by any Persons whatsoever, against such of the respectable Inhabitants who may think proper to associate for the Defence and Support of their inestimable Rights and Privileges. The Committee will find means to bring all such imprudent Persons to a proper Sense of their Misconduct: Yet they ardently wish and hope, that no future Violence, Threats or Animosities may appear, but that every Member of the Community will readily use his utmost Endeavours to promote Peace, good Order and Unanimity amongst the Inhabitants of this respectable County.[38]

Document 118

Lancaster June 3d. 1775

Gentlemen,

With singular Regret & Concern are we compelled to address you. The good Order of this Borough & the very Being of its Government must depend on the wise & prudent Deliberations of the Congress upon an Incident of the most alarming Nature which lately happened here. We beg Leave to offer you a candid & faithful Narrative of the Facts, on which your Sentiments will be absolutely necessary.

On the 29th Ulto. the late Committee of this Borough met on a Complaint made to them that a Company formed in Rapho & Manheim Townships had been insulted by a few persons;—They thought proper on this Application to express their Abhorrence of that Conduct; & wrote to the Members of the Committee of those two Townships, to appear at the next Mustering of the Company, impress their Disapprobation of such improper Proceedings & Behavior, & conciliate Harmony & Friendship. We send you hereby a Copy of our Letter.

Just before the Committee broke up, they received a second Application from two of the chief Persons of the Menonists, complaining that Violence & Threats had been used by some People to Members of that Society, because they do not form themselves into military Associations, and that some of that religious Profession had deserted from their usual Work by Reason thereof, that their Members would chearfully co-operate in the Common Cause except in such Acts as were repugnant to their Consciences, & praying the Protection of the Committee from any future Outrage. We observed to them, that probably such Conduct had partly arose from abusive or opprobrious Language bestowed by some of their Denomination against Bodies of People then under Arms, & warmly pressed them to discountenance any such Expressions, that whilst they looked to us for Security, we should expect they would take an active Part in Prevention of future Bickerings & Animosities. They pledged themselves to the Committee for the Performance of those Duties, disclaimed such wanton & rude Terms, & further went so far as to declare that they objected not to any Member of their Society Taking up Arms, whose Consciences were free in this Particular. Upon mature Deliberation, It was unanimously resolved by the Committee, that a Number of Hand-Bills both in English & German (one of which we now inclose to you) should be struck off & dispersed through this County.

We flatter ourselves, Gentlemen, we need use no Arguments in Vindication of the Measure adopted. Our most excellent Charter of Privileges in the very first Paragraph was a plain Directory for the Conduct of the Committee. "No one shall be molested or Prejudiced because of his conscientious Persuasion or Practice, nor be compelled to do or suffer any Thing contrary to his religious Persuasion." The Act of 12 & 13 Gul. 3 [William III] confirmed a Doctrine so highly agreeable to the Spirit of Christianity. When one of the Chief Grounds of our Opposition to the late arbitrary Statutes was the impious Destruction of the Charter of Massachusetts-Bay, Could we sit tame Spectators of equal Violence to our own Country-Men? Or in the glorious Struggle for Freedom, could we deny to others their Liberty of Conscience?

But whilst we thought it just & reasonable to discourage Licentiousness, we judged it equally right & proper to guard & protect those reputable Inhabitants, who nobly appeared in Arms, in Defence of America, from Scoffs & Insult. The bringing such imprudent Persons to a proper Sense of their Misconduct, evidently pointed to the Directions of the last Congress, with Respect to the Violation of the Association.

We chearfully submit the Step we have taken to the Honble. Congress, for their Examination & Opinion, Conscious of having discharged the Duties of our Trust with Fidelity & Care, so far as our Judgments or Understandings directed us, & we shall rest satisfied & contented with their Determination.

On the Afternoon of the 1st Instant, when the five Companys in this Town were assembling, the Printer called on a Member of the Committee with the Hand-Bills. He said an Officer had threatened to take them from out of his House, with a Body of Men, by Force. In a few Minutes after, another Officer came in, who informed the same Member, that the Companies were greatly dissatisfied with the Committee's Proceedings, and would not muster, if any People whatever were excused from bearing Arms & Associating. He was sincerely sorry for what had happened, & desired to know what could be done to remove the public Discontent. The Member proposed to him, that those Persons who excepted against the Hand-Bill, should meet together peaceably, & appoint ten or a dozen of their Body to confer with the Committee. If on such Conference, the Committee were convinced of their Error, or that the Publication of the Hand-Bill would injure the Common Cause, they would deem it honourable to recede, and perhaps on a free Communication of Sentiments, all Matters might be set aright. The Officer took his Leave, having behaved throughout the whole Interview with the greatest Politeness & good Manners.

Two Minutes had not elapsed, when one of the Companies marched toward the Court-House. When they had arrived thither the Commanding Officer ordered them to halt, but the Soldiers cried out, March on! March on! The Officer then left them, & with their Firelocks in their Hands, they called at the House of another of the Committee grossly insulted him & demanded that all the Hand-Bills should be delivered up to them. The Member answered, he had them not in his Possession. He received for Reply, that the Company would have them at all Events. The first mentioned Member then came up and avowed his having the Papers. The Soldiers, who by this Time, were joined by many more, insisted repeatedly that they would have the Hand-Bills. They were informed that they should not be delivered up to a Body of armed Men, who demanded them in that Manner; that if one of their Officers required a Copy, it would be delivered to him with Pleasure. One of the Officers came into the House, & having received a Hand-Bill upon his Request, went out & delivered it to his Men, who immediately affixed it to the Whipping Post & then several of the Soldiers fired Guns at it & consumed it. By this Time, the Town was in a great Ferment & this Commotion was increased by some Persons who either wickedly or ignorantly took Pains to mislead the People. No Hand-Bills had been distributed by any of the Committee & very few Persons had seen any of them. The Tumult, after a Time, subsided somewhat, and the Companies proceeded to their Exercises, tho' they mustered but thinly. Some other Violences happened on their Return, after being dismissed by their Officers, but these Things we hope to be spared the mortifying Task of repeating. Many Threats were thrown out against the Committee that Evening & some Acts of Outrage were apprehended. A second smaller Party met before the same House, where the Soldiers had assembled, about 10 O'Clock at Night & insulted the Owner—& the Door of his House was found tarred & feathered next Morning.

Yesterday we fondly hoped, the popular Clamour would have abated, & Reason resumed her seat in the Minds of many. We most ardently wished for this Event, but we found on the most minute Inquiry that it was in vain to bear up longer against the Torrent. As we had unfortunately lost the public Confidence, & could no longer be useful as a Committee, we judged it most eligible & prudent to resign the Trust delegated to us, & to request a new Election. We accordingly met & after serious Consideration signed a Paper, which was affixed to the Court House Door, the Copy of which now follows:—

"The Members of the Committee having taken into Consideration their Situation with Respect to many of the Inhabitants of the Borough of Lancaster & that their well-meant Endeavours to serve the public Interests have not proved satisfactory to divers People resident in the said Borough, and that should they continue to act longer as a Committee their Proceedings may be productive of Dis-union & destroy that Peace & Good-Order which they ardently wish to cultivate & maintain, do unanimously resign the Trust formerly reposed in them by the worthy Inhabitants of the Borough, & decline serving as a Committee for the future. And it is recommended to the Inhabitants of the Borough that they proceed to the Election of a new Committee in their Stead & Room."

(Signed) "Edwd. Shippen, Adam Simon Kuhn, J. Yeates, Will. Atlee, William Bausman, Sebastian Graff, Chas. Hall, Christian Voght, Cas. Shaffner, Adam Reigart, Eberhart Michael."

In Consequence of the above Advertisement, we have the Pleasure of informing you that a new Committee for the Borough has been elected this afternoon. We flatter ourselves the Minds of those Inhabitants, who have been so strongly irritated, will now be made easy. Our chiefest Views, Gentlemen, in now addressing you, are by your salutary counsels to prevent any future Disturbances of the Peace of this opulent Town, to strengthen & support the Hands of the new Committee, & to avoid any Misconstruction of our Conduct. We profess ourselves warmly attached to the true Interests of our Country, but we deprecate the fatal Consequences of public Anarchy & Confusion. We wish never to see the Day, when the patriotic Spirit of our Countrymen shall be the Source of our greatest Misfortunes, when the Vigour of Government shall be relaxed, & the Arms put into the Hands of the People shall be perverted to Instruments of Ruin. Your Aid & Weight in the Continental Congress, we are confident, will not be wanting in securing to each individual his Liberty of Conscience & in promoting Peace, Harmony & Good Order so essentially necessary to the Well-Being of the Community.

We are, Gentlemen, with the greatest Respect
Your most Obedt. And very Humble Servts.

Edwd. Shippen	*Sebastian Graff*
Adam Simon Kuhn	*Christian Voght*
J. Yeates	*Cas. Shaffner*
Will. Atlee	*Adam Reigart*
Chas. Hall	*Eberhart Michael*

Mr. William Bausman, absent,
out of the County.

late Members of the Committee for the Borough of Lancaster To the Honourable the Delegates of the Province of Pennsylvania In the Continental Congress.[39]

Document 119

Reading 7th June 1775

Dear Sir,

One Criner a Shoemaker who lives near Mr. George Ross Junr. has been Spreading a Report here that the Lancaster Committee were bribed with £1500 to excuse the Quakers & Menonists from arming. Upon his being asked what Evidence he had of it, he said their excusing those Societies was sufficient Evidence. He mentioned Mr. Atlee, you & Mr. Bausman as the Persons Suspected by the People; It enraged me a great deal & I was determined to inform you of it. . . .*

They have made me their Secretary in the Committee for this County in Opposition to Dr. Potts, who strove eagerly for it. This happened while I was on the Road from Sunbury, without my Knowledge. There was a Meeting of 70 odd Members, being composed of Committees for each Township. I find ye office exceedingly troublesome & inconvenient.

I beg my kind love to all the Family. I am, Dear Sir,
Your affect. Brother
E. Burd

Jasper Yeates Esq.
Lancaster[40]

Document 120

At a Meeting of the Committee of Inspection, Observation and Cor-

*Two paragraphs dealing with Edward Burd's legal practice have been omitted.

respondence, of the County of Lancaster.
William Henry, Esq; Chairman.

The Committee taking into their serious Consideration, the present Uneasiness and Disquiet subsisting in the Minds of many of the respectable Inhabitants of this County, Do *unanimously agree,* That Notice be sent to the several Committees of the different Townships in this County, desiring and requesting their Attendance at the Court-House, on FRIDAY the sixteenth Day of this Instant, JUNE, at Three o'Clock in the Afternoon, to consider on Ways and Means to restore that Harmony, Peace, Unanimity and good Order, which the People of this County have hitherto enjoyed, and which is absolutely necessary in the present alarming Crisis of Public Affairs; and at the same Time to consider on such other Business as may at that Time be laid before them.

By Order of the Committee,
John Reily, Clerk
Committee-Chamber,
Lancaster, June 5th, 1775.[41]

Document 121

To the Comittee of the County of Lancaster when met at Lancaster June ye 16th 1775

The Petition of the first Associated Company of Monjoy Township Humbly Sheweth, That Whereas, Certain Persons, Inhabitants of said Township, inimical to the Liberties of America, make it their practice to Disswade Such as they have Influance with, from entering into Associations, for our Common Defence, and are Even so bold as to Insult, and brand with the Term of Rebellion our Associations, to learn the Military Art, we therefore pray the Committee to take the premises into Consideration, that such measures may be prosicuted as may have the most Imediate tendincy to put a stop to such proceedings, which if indulged, must prove highly Injurious to the Cause of Liberty, And your petitioners as in Duty bound Shall pray

Signed At the Request and in behalf of the Said Company by
Abrm. Scott 1st Lieut.
[and five others][42]

Document 122

June 16, 1775

It being moved whether the Committee at this Meeting should go into the Consideration, of a certain paper, "agreed on by the late

Members of this Committee who have resigned lately in the Town of Lancaster," the same carried in the Negative and therefore the Consideration is put off untill a futer day, if the same shall be thought proper to be inquired into.

It being moved whether every Person in the County of Lancaster and [torn] take up arms produce a good and sufficient Gun—their Ability to be judged of and determined by the Committees of the respective Townships in the said County—Carried in the Affirmative. And that every person whose religious Principles preclud them from taking up arms shall pay into the hands of the Committee Treasurer the Sum of £3..10..0 to be applied to such use as the Committee shall think proper.

Upon Motion, Resolved that those Persons in the County of Lancaster whose religious Principles preclude them from taking up Arms shall pay into the hands of the Committee Treasurer any Sum *they please, provided it be** not less than the *Sums laid** Provincial Taxes paid by such persons as laid by the County Assessors. Carried in the Affirmative.[43]

Document 123
[Resolution adopted by the Pennsylvania Assembly on June 30, 1775.]

The House taking into Consideration that many of the good People of this Province are conscientiously scrupulous of bearing Arms, do hereby earnestly recommend to the Associators for the Defence of their Country, and others, that they bear a tender and brotherly Regard towards this Class of their Fellow-Subjects and Country-Men; and to these conscientious People it is also recommended, that they chearfully assist, in Proportion to their Abilities, such Associators as cannot spend their Time and Substance in the public Service without great Injury to themselves and Families.[44]

Voluntary Contribution Imposed

The Pennsylvania delegates in Congress did not reply to the Lancaster Committee's letter until July 5, 1775. They refused to involve themselves in the local differences, but used the opportunity to effectively impose a voluntary contribution on all Non-Associators with religious scruples against military service. John Ettwein, the Moravian chronicler, believed that the poor response of Mennonites and Quakers

---

*These words are crossed out in the original.

to the voluntary subscription led to their later troubles. Ettwein was apparently misinformed about the date. The German broadside of the Assembly resolution and the letter from the Congressional delegation indicates that it was not even considered by the Committee until July 11, 1775. ("Bey einer Versammlung von der Committe von Correspondence and Observation von Lancaster County, in dem House des Matthias Slough, Esq. in Lancaster Borough, den 11ten July, 1775." Broadside 144-8, Rare Books Room, Library of Congress, Washington, D.C.)

Document 124

Gent.

While we received the highest Satisfaction from the patriotic Spirit prevailing in your County and your associating and arming for the defence of the liberties of America, We are sorry to hear that the friendship and harmony that formerly subsisted among the good people of your County has been much disturbed.

Without a very minute enquiry into the whole it would ill become us to censure or approve the Conduct of any person and therefore we shall not take upon us to do either.

We have only to say we doubt not you will exert your utmost abilitys according to the Trust reposed in you to restore and preserve confidence, harmony and affection between all your people. The assembly taking into consideration the situation of many conscientious people of this province with respect to Arms have on the 30th day of June last, by their Recommendations of that date, given to them as well as others, Advice which we hope all persons will most chearfully follow The Congress and your Assembly greatly to their honour have taken means for the protection of America and this Colony. And we would advise you, Gentlemen, to carry into Execution the Plans recommended by them that this Colony may unitedly act upon one and the same principle.

Those who contribute will put their Money into the Hands of a Person they shall choose to be paid over to such Treasurer as the Committee shall appoint for the Uses recommended by the Assembly.

We are Gent.

Your very hbe. Servants

Philadelphia, July 5, 1775.

The above is a true Copy.

Examined by *Chas. Humphreys*

Geo. Ross[45]

Document 125

The fruit of this soon became evident, for the Town Committees published, on July 6, 75, a resolution of the Assembly, dated the thirtieth of June, together with a recommendation of Congress. [Ettwein quoted the Assembly resolution and a portion of the letter sent by the delegates in Congress to the Lancaster Committee.] That the rich Mennonites in Lancaster County and the Quakers in Philadelphia displaid so little inclination to follow this advice, gave the first occasion to the subsequent bitterness against them.[46]

Peace Churches Discuss Voluntary Contributions

The Lancaster County Committee met with a delegation of representatives from the Mennonite, Amish, and "First Day Baptists" (Church of the Brethren) to discuss the voluntary contributions to be made by the peace churches. The "Form of subscription for the Menonists & c" preserved among the papers of Jasper Yeates was very likely drafted or presented at this meeting.

Document 126

At a Meeting of the Committee of Correspondence for the County at the house of Matthias Slough in the Borough of Lancaster on the first Day of July A.D. 1775.

Present William Henry Esqr. Chairman, Edward Hand, John Hopson, George Musser, Samuel Boyd, Edward Gruber and John Witmer Junr.

Benjamin Hershey senr., John Hare senr., John Witmer senr., Representatives of the Society of People called Menonists, Christian Rupp & Michael Garber, Representatives of the Society of people called Amisch Menonists, And Henry Snyder, Daniel Bollinger and Daniel Hollinger, Representatives of the Society of People called First Day Baptists Appear before this Committee in behalf of their Constituents and Report, That the Generality of the several Societies which they represent esteem it but just & equitable that they should contribute towards the Support of the Rights & Liberties of their Country, But as they apprehend that the mode of raising Contributions for that Purpose, recommended by the Committee of this County, cannot be carried into Execution with Respect to any Individuals in their Societies who may prove obstinate, they hope that this Committee will not object to their making Application to the Continental Congress in order that a Method may be fallen upon by them which may be thought more binding, and which may afford Satisfaction to all the Inhabitants of this County of every Denomination. And that if the Congress should not chuse to interfere in this Matter, they will then of themselves fall upon such Measures as they expect will give general Satisfaction.

Resolved that a Copy of these Minutes be sent to each of the Townships in this County.

Resolved that a Copy of this Report and also the Extracts from the Proceedings of the County Committee lately published be sent to the Continental Congress.[47]

Document 127

We the Subscribers Being Sensible of the Calamities now Hanging over the whole Continent of America and being on all Occasions Willing to assist the Common Cause otherwise than by Taking up arms, Respectively Promise to pay the Sums to Our Names Annexed under Such Regulations as We Shall at the Time of Paying the Same Request to be allowed us.*

We the Subscribers being highly sensible of the Calamaties & Misfortunes under which British America now labours, & being on all Occasions sincerely & chearfully disposed to contribute to the Common Cause otherwise than by taking up of Arms, which we hereby declare to be against our Consciences, do from the Sense of Duty to our Country, our Brethren, ourselves & Posterity respectively promise to pay the Sums to our Names annexed under the following Regulations—Vizt.**
Form of Subscription for the Menonists &c.*[48]

Petition Against Non-Associators

In predominantly Presbyterian Donegal Township, Lancaster County, resentment against "people of different persuasions" who refused to associate from conscientious or personal reasons was expressed in a petition for fines on Non-Associators and for guns to be collected from all inhabitants. The petition is undated, but a later hand has penciled July 12, 1775, on it.

Document 128

We part of the inhabitants of the Township of Donegall, having associated into a Company, and has signed an agreement for the regulation of the said Company, as well officers as soldiers, understanding that the Committee for this County is to meet in Lancaster in order to

---

*In the handwriting of an unknown person.
**In the handwriting of Jasper Yeates.

adjust and settle grievances, we Conceive the greatest grievances is by numbers of People of different persuasions who will not join in the sd. Association, some for Scruple of Conscience, some for the Loss of time, and expences, and others being disaffected at the Cause, which we associate for, Some of the said people being the wealthyest and best seated in the County. We imagine that there should be none of the inhabitants of this County exempted from joining the sd. Association or paying in *an equal** proportion *of every expence** for the finding of arms and other necessarys to those who are willing to do it, who are not of ability to Provide themselves with such. We request of you that it be allowed that all the Land-holders and farmers in the County of Lancaster be Obliged to find at Least one good gun each, and that every other person who is judged by the Committee to be of ability Likewise to find a good gun, whether they be joined in Association or not, this will put the County in a State of Defence. We request of you that such a sum as is Reasonably thought by you be Laid upon each and every person who will not join the sd. Association, exclusive of finding the arms aforesaid, in Restitution of the time which the people that has joined the sd. Association has and will expend, Learning exercise, and other duties necessary. And that Such Sums of money and Arms be paid and Received into the hands of the Committee of the different townships in the sd. County, or into the hands of any other persons which you shall appoint, to be Laid for the use and Support of the Associators of the Townships such sums and arms will be Received in, if the sd. proposals be not put into execution by you. We for our part do intend to Continue no Longer in the sd. Association, as it will be intirely useless for the greatest number of our Company to Continue in the Same, who are not of ability to find themselves in arms or other necessaries. But on the Contrary if no Partiality is or will be shewed by you or indulgence to the enemies of the Cause, but to have all persons in the sd. County equally concerned therein, according to their several abilities, we will, as we always had done, defend and protect the Cause of our Country, to the Extremity of our Power and ability.

Signed by part, and by order of the sd. Company by
Alexr. Mitchel [and 86 others]

Tax Rather Than Voluntary Contribution?

The York County Committee also had difficulties in raising voluntary contributions from conscientious objectors, who expressed as great

---

*These words are crossed out in the original.

a concern about paying for war as fighting in it. They believed that a tax on Non-Associators would be less objectionable.

Document 129

York 14th Sept. 1775

Gentn.

The Committee of York County on the 28th & 29th July last together with Militia Officers met and Divided the County into districts & Battalions (& the Steps taken in that behalf will be the subject of another Letter herewith Sent). It was Represented to the Committee by Many Associators, that it greatly retarded the Publick Service, and gave much dissatisfaction to the People who Mustered that others who scruple at Mustering had not Contributed nor Offered to Contribute any Thing to the Publick Service, tho' Recommended to them in the Strongest Terms by the Resolution of the Assembly of the 30th June and afterwards by the Honourable the Continental Congress the 18th July.

The Committee had Reason to Expect that some Proposal would have been offered by these People tending to shew, that they are friends to liberty and would Contribute in some way Consistent with their Consciences. After the County Committee separated, the Committee of Correspondance were informed by some who are People of that Persuasion, That it was equally against their Consciences to subscribe or pay any thing towards the Present Measures Carrying on, as to bear Arms. As many of them make it a Matter of Conscience to pay the Provincial Tax, and some favored us with the inclosed Proposals, as the only Expedient they Could think of, and which they were Confident would remove all uneasiness—The Committee thinking it a Matter too much Co[torn] for them to undertake of themselves, Applied to the Provincial Delegates for their Approbation but the Congress was Adjourned so that they Received no directions in that Particular.

The Committee beg leave to inform the Committee of safety, that the former uneasiness Still subsists and increases and threatens the Dispoliation of the Association in the County; and unless some Measures are speedily taken to Carry the Resolutions of the Assembly and Congress into Execution in this County, very Mischievous Consequences must follow, and those Consequences we are afraid may Extend further than to this County: the Glaring impropriety of one part of the Community defending the whole in a Strugle where every thing dear to Freemen is at Stake must Strike every thinking Person.

We are Gentn.

Your most obedt. hble. Servts.

Jas. Smith	*Will (?) Albright*
Rd. Mcalister	*Michael Schmyser*
Martin Eichelberger	*Archd. Mclean*
Thos. Hartley	*James Dill*
John Finlay	*Nichls. Buttinger*
Wm. Rankin	*Daniel Messerley*
Geo. Eichelberger	*David Grier*
Joseph Jefferies	*George Slake*
John Hay	

To the Committee of Safety of the Province of Pennsylvania[50]

Records of Subscriptions

The Lancaster County Committee of Observation heard reports on the money raised by voluntary contributions from the Non-Associators and ordered lists to be prepared in each township of Non-Associators who did and who did not subscribe to the collection. Only one such list is known to be extant. The record of subscriptions in Earl Township is doubly interesting as the only religious census of Non-Associators that has survived. Some names left without denominational identification appear to be of Mennonite origin and the identification of two Showalters as Amish has been questioned by family genealogists.

Document 130

It being moved, to put it to a vote, whether or no, the propriety of the Hand-Bill of the Committee of Correspondence, who resigned in June last, shall be inquired to at all, or not, carried in the Negative, and Resolved, that all further consideration of the same Bill be given up and no more notice be taken thereof.

Resolved that the Committee be furnished with a List of the Names and the sums annexed to them of those persons who have contributed towards the Service of their Country in Money by the Person or Persons in whose Hands the said Moneys were originally paid.

Resolved that Mr. Curtis Grubb wait on Mr. Mathias Slough and desire his attendance at the Committee's Chamber, to inform the Committee what Monies have been paid into his Hands, by the People conscientiously scrupulous of bearing Arms.

Mr. Mathias Slough appeared according to desire and reported that he had in his Hands the Sum of £532..1..0 likewise the Sum of

£26..12..0. Resolved that Mr. Slough pay the said Monies into the Hands of Mr. William Henry, the Committee's Treasurer, Subject to the Resolves & orders of the Committee.

James Burd Chairman.[51]

Document 131

August 4, 1775

Resolved, That every person who does not actually Associate, and who has not subscribed, and refuses to subscribe, the Genl. Associating agreed on the 1st May last shall be deemed a Non-Associator, and be returned as such, by *the respective* Borough or Township Committee where he lives, to the Standing Committee at Lancaster on or before the first Day of September next, agreeable to the resolve of yesterday, and that the said Committee *of the respective Townships* return to the said Standing Committee certified Copies of the particular Associations & Agreements entered into by the respective Companies, in their Borough or Township, for the perfecting themselves in the Art Military, &c., containing the date of the Agreement, and properly certified and attested, if required. That these Minutes be annexed to the Minutes or Resolves above referred to and that 400 printed Copies in the English & German Languages be Printed & dispersed through the County.[52]

Document 132

Extracts from the Minutes of the Committee of Correspondence, Observation and Inspection for the County of Lancaster, held in the Borough of Lancaster on the first and second days of September 1775.

Resolved, that the Members of this Committee in their respective Townships, make lists of the names of all non-associators of the Age of sixteen and upwards, and deliver the same to the Standing Committee, at Lancaster on or before the fifteenth day of this instant September.

Resolved, that all persons who have collected or received any sum or sums of Money within this County, from any person or persons agreeable to the recommendation of the Assembly of this Province, do, on or before the fifteenth day of this instant, pay the same into the hands of the Committee's treasurer; and at the same time furnish the said treasurer with a list of names of those who have contributed with the several sums annexed.[53]

Document 133

A list of the Non Associaters that has Subscribed and the Sums Annexed & their Religion in Earl Township Lanctr. County.

	Religion	£	S	D
Christian Burkhold precher	Ment.[Menonist]	1	2	6
David Martin & 2 Sons	"	3	0	0
Henry Rorrer	"	0	7	6
Peter Burkholder	"	0	15	0
David Grove	"	2	15	0
Abram Rife & Son	"	5	0	0
Mark Grove & Son	"	3	0	0
Joseph Horse	"	1	10	0
Jacob Carpenter & Son	—	1	10	0
Christian Graybill	Dunkard	3	0	0
Christian Meyer Junr.	Ment.	1	10	0
Martin Shafer	"	0	10	0
Samuel Shafer	"	0	10	0
John Shafer		0	10	0
Peter Diller	"	0	15	0
Christian Ruppe	Amist[Amish]	3	0	0
John Ruppe	"	3	0	0
Christian Winger	Ment.	1	10	0
Michl. Winger	"	2	5	0
Stofel Ryer	Dunkard	1	10	0
Christian Myer	Ment.	1	0	0
John Myer Distiller	Dunkard	3	0	0
John Myer Senr.	Ment.	2	0	0
Philip Spreicher	Church[of England]	1	0	0
George Clemer	—	0	15	0
George Hildebrand	Ment.	0	7	6
Abraham Huntbarger	"	0	7	6
Christian Smoker & Son	Amt. [Amish]	1	0	0
John Huber	Ment.	3	0	0
Martin Huver	"	1	0	0
Abraham Curts	Amt.	2	0	0
George Bare	Ment.	3	0	0
Christian Carpenter	Mennonist	4	0	0
Peter Senseney Doctr.	"	1	5	0
Henry Martin Creek	"	1	10	0
John Myers by Weavers	"	1	0	0
Michl Shirk Peters son	"	0	10	0
John Shirk " "	"	0	15	0
Henry Winger Creek	"	1	10	0

John Stunhard	Presbn. [Presbyterian]	0	7	6
Christian Carpenter Jno. son	Ment.	0	15	0
Henry Weaver at Carpenters	"	0	10	0
John Carpenter Snr.	"	1	10	0
Peter Carpenter Jno son	"	0	10	0
John Senseney	" 1 gun & Habert at	3	0	0
Adam Stock	Church	0	7	6
Peter Stofer	Ment.	1	10	0
Mathias Stofer Peters son	"	1	10	0
John Weaver Snr.	"	3	0	0
John Weaver Jno son	"	0	10	0
Michl. Raunk	"	0	10	0
Jacob Glaufer [or Glausser]	Church	1	0	0
Christian Rute	Ment.	2	0	0
John Weaver Fat	Ment.	—	—	—
Henry Weaver Stiller	"	1	10	0
Joseph Shirk Peters son	"	0	15	0
Ichart Snr.	"	0	15	0
Michl. Ichart his Son	"	0	10	0
Christian Ichart	Presbn.	0	10	0
Mich. Martin	Ment.	1	15	0
John Shallabarger	"	0	15	0
Jacob Huber	"	1	0	0
John Linder	Amist.	1	5	0
James Welsh	—	0	10	0
Michl. Witmer	Ment.	2	5	0
Jacob Senseney	"	1	10	0
John Brondrager	Aminist	0	15	0
Jacob Stofer	Ment.	0	10	0
Michl. Senseney & Son Jacob	"	1	0	0
Jacob Shuwalter	Amist.	1	0	0
Christian Shewalter	"	1	0	0
Henry Rute	Ment.	1	5	0
George Martin	"	1	10	0
Henry Martin Preecher	"	1	15	0
Martin Martin	"	1	10	0
Joseph Grove	"	1	0	0
Christian Weaver & 2 Sons	"	1	10	0
Henry Weaver & Son by Shirks Mill	"	1	15	0
Jacob Weaver at Shirks mill	"	0	10	0

Michl. Shirk Michl. Son	"	0	15	0
John Widmer	"	0	18	0
Jacob Krim	Church	0	5	0
Jacob Ringwalt	"	1	0	0
Jacob Weaver & Son John	Ment.	3	0	0
Balser Smith	—	0	10	0
Jacob Hold	Ment.	0	7	6
Christian Hold	"	1	0	0
Joseph Hold	"	1	0	0
Thos. Morgan	Church	2	0	0
John Winger & Son Chn.	Ment.	1	10	0
George Claper (?)	"	0	4	6
Vincent Myer & 2 Sons	"	2	10	0
John Kempfer	Dunkard	1	10	0
David Kemper	"	1	10	0
John Shallabarger	Ment.	0	10	0
Jacob Grove	"	1	0	0
Casper Shirk	"	0	10	0
Jacob Sumey	"	0	15	0
Peter Sumey	"	1	2	6
Henry Sumey	"	0	15	0
Daniel Grove	"	1	0	0
Christian Grove	"	1	0	0
John Linder	Amt.	1	5	0
Jacob Huver	Ment.	1	0	0
Christian Mussleman	"	1	13	9
Samuel Raunk	Moraven	0	7	6
Jacob Carpenter	Mt.	3	0	0
George Hildebrand	—	0	7	6
The Whole Amount of Suppscriptions		£ 141	18	9
		4	6	3
108 Subscribers[54]		£ 145	6	3

Document 134

A List of the Non Associaters and Non Subscribers and their Religion in Earl Township Lancaster County.

John Defendever	Church [of England]
William Good	Prestn. [Presbyterian]
Leonard Stone Senr.	Church
John Defendever	"

George Menser	"
John Pitser & Son	"
Jacob Adam	"
Martin Neer	"
John Swigart	"
John Gundey	Ment. [Mennonite]
Philip Rode	Prestn.
Christian Swatsmiller	Church
John Reme	Prestn.
David Shirk	"
John Geer	"
George Geer	"
Philip Weaver	"
Peter Rush	Ment.
Andrew Wise	Prestn.
George Wise	"
Henry Shults	Church
John Seiler	"
Philip Fense [st?]ack	"
Joseph Reme	"
Martin Bowman	Ment.
John Bowman	"
John Miller	
Jacob Rode Philips son	Prestn.
Henry Huber	"
Peter Baker M. Creek	Church
John Baker " "	"
Jacob Carpenter	
Henry Pinkerton	
Alexr. McClary	Prestn.
Thos. Hanley	
Henry Miller	
Henry Bowman	
John Weaver	
Henry Lauchshaw	
Soloman Herman	
Christian Hidely	
John Myer Chrtn. Son	Ment.
John Myer Stillers Son	
Christian Grove	
Jacob Grove	

Martin Grove	
Abraham Graybill	
Joseph Ru	
Christian Horsh	
Jacob Bare	
John Hildebrand	Ment.
George Burger	"
Saml. Graybill	"
Michl. Graybill miller	"
Peter Smith	
Michl. Graybill Senr.	Ment.
Peter Baker Snr.	Prestn.
Leonard Elmaker	Church
Michl. Rine	"
Michl. Raunk	Maravin
Martin Bare	Ment.
Martin Bare Junr.	"
Saml. Bare Geo. son	"
Christian Huver Mar. son	"
Christian Musleman Junr.	"
John Huver Jno. Son	"
Martin Huver " "	"
Vallintine Huver	Church
Ignatious Elmaker	"
Christophel Wyht	"
Casper Deal	"
John Stragleman	C
Evan Evans	Church
James McClary	
Joseph McClary	Prestn.
Thos. Gault	"
James Gault	"
Alexander Gault	"
James Keemer *Senr.*	Church
John Edwards	"
Charles Miller	"
Adam Diller Senr.	"
Francis Harvey	Church
Nathan Evans Snr.	"
Antoney Ellmaker	"

89 Non Subscribers & Non Associaters[55]

Conscientious Objectors Draft Petition

Conscientious objectors in Berks County met on September 1, 1775, to make their voluntary contributions and present certain grievances. William Reeser of the Berks County Committee forwarded their resolutions to the Committee of Safety. A draft of a petition to the Berks County Committee in the handwriting of Christopher Schultz of Gosenhoppen (Bally) in Hereford Township would seem to have been presented at this meeting or soon after. The loss of the minutes of the Berks County Committee makes it impossible to learn their reaction to it, or the exact date it was presented to them. It refers to a decision by the Berks County Committee to impose a fine on all those who refused to take up arms, a decision necessarily taken by the Committee in its own name before a similar fine was levied by the Pennsylvania Assembly in November 1775.

Document 135

To the Comittee of the County of Berks, the Remonstrance of Several Inhabitants of the Said County Respectfully Sheweth

That we the Said Inhabitants with hearts full of the highest Concern for the Preservasition of our Constitution and Liberties now attempted to be overthrown by the Enemies of the same, and tenderly affected for the Honour and Peace of this County and Province, and the Welfare and Happiness of ourselves and our Posterity, beg leave humbly to Petition and remonstrate against some late Resolves and Doings of the last Convention of the Committee of Berks County, whereby every Male Person between the Ages of Sixteen and fifty five Years is without Exception and without Regard of conscientious Scrupels obliged to take up Arms and Submit to their military Rules or be fined in such a Degree, whereby numbers of Families would be reduced to utter Ruin, and such Fines to be raised by distraint of their Goods, by military Force, Resolves which your Remonstrants conceive to be of very dangerous Tendency, pregnant with *Dishonour and Mischief** the greatest Mischief to ourselves and our Posterity, *and* highly derogatory to the Honour of this County and destructive of the established Rights of the Inhabitants of this Province, and a Grievance of the highest Concern for the following Reasons.

If any Priviledge may properly be called an established Priviledge the Priviledge of Conscience is One of the formost in the Dictates of humanity and sound reason and is indeed the formost amongst them all

*The italicized words were crossed off in the original.

that are established and mentioned in our Province Charter, unalterable by any People or Body of People whatsoever, except that Six parts out of Seven of the Freeman of this Province in General Assembly met do consent or make an Alteration. This Priviledge is a Sacred Right and Property to every Person inhabiting in this Province who Shall confess and acknowledge One Almighty God &c. whereby it is declared "That no Person or Persons . . . Shall be in any Case molested or prejudiced, in his or their Person and Estate, because of his or their conscientious Persuasion or Practice, nor be compelled . . . to do or Suffer any Act or Thing contrary to their religious Persuasion." *Now whereas* It is a divine and Sacred Right, *the Attempt of Depriving any Body of the Enjoyment of the Same must be deemed Sacrilege*° Therefore to wrest the Enjoyment of the Same from any Body must be Sacrilege [and e]xcite divine Vengeance, and must be void in Effect.

In good Conformity to this Established Charter Right the Wisdom of our worthy House of Assembly have lately made the following Ordonance running in a Stile as *becomes* dos Honour to Men of Gravity and high Station. "In Assembly June 30th 1775. The house taking into Consideration, that many of the good People of this Province, are conscientiously scrupulous of bearing Arms, do hereby earnestly recommend to the Associators for the Defence of their Country and others, that they bear a brotherly Regard towards this Class of their fellow Subjects and Country Men; and to these conscientious People, it is also recommended, that they chearfully assist in Proportion to their Abilities such Persons as cannot Spend both Time and Substance in the Service of their Country without great injury to themselves and Family."

Of the Same *pious*° Genteel Moderation is the Sense and Resolution of the Continental Congress of the 18 of July 1775, by which *the Same Priviledge of Conscience is*° these Great Politicians nobly Scorn to violate Peoples Consciences, and by which the sd. our first Statute Priviledge is guaranteed, further confirmed and safely preserved, in the midst of all the present publick Conflicts and warlike Operations and Ordonances.

Adding to these the Feelings of humanity and the Impulses of true Religion and if we *may*° are allowed the chief Precept of our Saviour; And in Politicks our Common Duty to be watchful to preserve entire our Charter and Constitution, Your Remonstrants cannot Sufficiently express their Astonishment, on finding such Resolves, of the said Convention, which are in direct Opposition and Violation to all the above cited Charter Rights and to the Recommendation both of our House of Assembly and the Continental Congress, and to the Principels of humanity and Religion, Assuming an unlimited absolute Power, Running in the high Tone of Precept, inflicting Mulcts and Fines whilst the free People of these Colonies have been accustomed to be addressed from the Continental Congress, their House of Assembly (as appears by the above recited Resolve) and in former Times even by the Ministers of State in the soft Stile of Recommendation.

Your Remonstrants beg Leave further to observe, that we cannot learn that any of the People in this County were disinclined or deficient in their Duty, to what hath been recommended to them by their Assembly and the Continental Congress, and what reasonably could be expected from them by the County Committee, but on the other hand, that a *good many** great number of such as have conscientious Scrupel to take up Arms, have publicly offered to Sacrifice all their Fortune for the Upholding of the common Cause.

And your Remonstrants impulsed by dire Necessity beg Leave further to Say, and declare, that they find themselves as in Duty bound to their Country, themselves, and their Posterity to protest against the said Resolves of the sd. last Convention, and that we are unwilling and cannot Submit to the same, as being unconstitutional and Subversive of our most dearest Rights of civil and religious Priviledges, tearing our Charters, taking our Property from us without our Consent, subjugating us under a *military** Despotick, arbitrary yea military *Government** Execution, depriving us of the *choisest** most precious Pearl of a free People, the Trial by Juries and of the protection of the civil Law.

Therefore your Remonstrants do humbly pray and request, to reconsider the aforesaid Votes Resolves and Doings, and make such Provision in the Matters and Premises, whereby our Security may be further established, Disunion prevented, Disgrace and reproach to this County averted and interior Peace, Harmony and good Order preserved, and Your Remonstrants as in Duty bound, Shall ever be willing, to do their utmost for the Welfare and Support of the common Cause.[56]

Document 136

Reading, September 11th, 1775.

Gentleman,

Inclosed is a Copy of the Resolves entered into by the Deputies of a considerable Number of such of the Inhabitants of this County as are conscientiously scrupulous of taking up Arms, though at the same time fully sensible of the Justice of our Cause and willing, as far as in them lies, to contribute to its support.

*The italicized words were crossed off in the original.

The sum now in my hands amounts to one hundred and fifty-two pounds, which you will observe by the Resolves is at the Disposal of your Committee, and I have the strongest assurances from the numbers of the Subscription that they will ever cheerfully contribute their proportion towards the Safety and wellfare of the Public.

I am,
Gentlemen,
with great respect,
your very humble servant,
William Reeser.

Directed.

To the Committee of Safety, for the Province of Pennsylvania, at Philadelphia.[57]

Document 137

At a Meeting of Deputies of divers Inhabitants of the County of Berks, being conscientiously scrupulous of bearing Arms, held at the Town of Reading on the first Day of September, 1775, The following Resolves were made:

1. That in Pursuance of the Recommendations of our House of Assembly of June 30th, and of the Continental Congress of July 18th, last past, the said Inhabitants hath cheerfully agreed to voluntary Subscriptions for the Uses pointed out by the said Recommendations.

2. That the Sums raised by such Subscriptions in this County be paid into the Hands of a Treasurer chosen by the said Inhabitants or their Deputies in Meeting convened, who shall keep a regular Account of all the Monies by him received and laid out, and render a just Account of his Doings herein when requested by the Deputies of the said Inhabitants, or by four joined Members of them; And that William Reeser of Reading, Gentleman, is chosen Treasurer for this Time.

3. That the Disposal and direct Appropriation of all such Monies be ultimately vested in the Committee of Safety appointed by our Assembly, as Part of a Share to be accounted for Berks County, that the said Committees may be enabled to act the more pertinently & uniformly in that Affair.

4. That the said Treasurer give Notice of these Transactions and Resolves unto the said Committee of Safety, as also to the Committee for Berks County, that the said Committees may be enabled to act the more pertinently and uniformly in that Affair.

5. That for the future the said Subscribers will always pay a due Regard to all such Requisitions as Necessity shall oblige the said Com-

mittee of Safety to make and signify to the said Treasurer, who is to give due Notice to the same to the Members of the said Subscription.

A true Copy from the Minutes,
William Reeser[58]

Associators Request Tax or Fine for Non-Associators

In September 1775 the Pennsylvania Assembly received several petitions requesting a tax or a fine on Non-Associators that would be equivalent to the burden borne by Associators.

Document 138
September 27, 1775

A Memorial from the officers of the military Association for the City and Liberties/ of *Philadelphia* was presented to the House and Read, setting forth, that the Memorialists/ with great Concern, perceive that fatal Mischiefs will arise to the Association from the/ Lenity shewn towards Persons professing to be conscientiously scrupulous against bearing/Arms;—that People *sincerely* and *religiously* scrupulous are but few in Comparison to/those who upon this Occasion, as well as others, make *Conscience* a *Convenience*;—/that a very considerable share of the property of this Province is in the Hands of People/professing to be of tender Conscience in military Matters;—that the Associators think/it extremely hard that they should risk their Lives and injure their Fortunes in the De-/fence of those who will not be of the least Assistance in this great Struggle;—that the/Memorialists therefore humbly conceive that some decisive Plan should be fallen upon/to oblige every Inhabitant of the Province either with his person or Property to con-/tribute towards the general Cause, and that it should not be left as at present, to the/*Inclinations* of those professing tender Consciences but that the proportion they shall con-/tribute may be certainly fixed and determined;—that in order to give strength and/ Permanency to the Association, the Memorialists thought it absolutely necessary that/some general regulations should be formed to be offered to the Associators for their Go-/vernment,—that under this Idea the Memorialists concurred with the Members of the/Committees for the City, Liberties, and County, and the Officers of the County Bat-/tallions, in requesting the Committee of Safety, who appeared to be vested with exten-/sive Powers in the Recess of the Assembly, to form Rules and Regulations adequate to/the Occasion;—that those Rules being formed and recommended by the Committee of/Safety, and by the Memorialists offered to the Associators, they refused to sign or agree/to them, for the Reasons contained in the Papers herewith presented to the Honourable/House, in Pursuance of their Request,—that the House will perceive the Reason, which pervades almost the whole of their Objections, is the Partiality and inequality of the Association, which/being once obviated, the Memorialists respectfully offer it as their Opinion, that the Associators will chearfully put up with many Inconveniences and/that all jealousies and Suspicions about Forms will cease—that the Memorialists there/fore pray the Honourable House will take the Premises into their Consideration and/fall upon some effectual Plan to remedy the Inconviences attendant on their present/Situation, and to preserve together and properly divest the Associators, who express/every wish to defend their Country in this Season of Difficulty and Danger/*ordered to lie on the Table.*[59]

Document 139

To the honorable the Representatives of the Freemen of the Province of Pennsylvania in General Assembly met, the Memorial of the Committee of Safety respectfully sheweth. . . .

The Committee having thus laid before the House the Steps they have already taken & their Opinion of some Measures which appear proper to be adopted, beg Leave before they conclude this Report, to submit to the House a Matter interesting to the Public Welfare. The Military Association entered into by Numbers of the good People of this Province has received the Approbation of the House, & undoubtedly deserves every Encouragement as a Body of Freemen animated by a love of Liberty & trained to the Use of Arms afford the most certain & effectual defence against the Approaches of Slavery & Oppression. It is to be wished therefore that this Spirit could have been more universally diffused; but the Associators complain & with great Appearance of Reason that while they are subjected to Expences to accoutre themselves as Soldiers, & their Affairs suffer considerably by the Time necessarily employed in acquiring a knowledge of the Military Art, very many of their Country Men, who have not associated, are entirely free from these Inconveniences. They conceive that where, the Liberty of all is at Stake, every Man should assist in it's Support, & that where the Cause is common, & the Benefits derived from an Opposition are universal, it is not consonant to Justice or Equity that the Burthen should be partial.

The Committee therefore would submit it to the Wisdom of the

House whether at this Time of general Distress & Danger, some Plan should not be devised to oblige the Assistance of every Member of the Community. But as there are some Persons who from their religious Principles are scrupulous of the Lawfulness of bearing Arms, this Committee, from a tender Regard to the Consciences of such, would venture to propose, that their Contributions to the common Cause should be pecuniary, & for that Purpose a Rate or Assessment be laid on their Estates equivalent to the Expence & Loss of Time incurred by the Associators. A Measure of this Kind appears to be founded on the Principles of impartial Justice, calculated to appease the Complaints which have been made, likely to give general Satisfaction & be of Course beneficial to the great Cause we are engaged in. . . .

Sign'd B. Franklin
Septr. 29, 1775.[60]

Document 140

A Representation from the Committee of Privates of the Association belonging to the City of Philadelphia, and its Districts, was presented to the House, and follows in these Words, *viz.*

To the Honourable the REPRESENTATIVES of the
FREEMEN of the Province of Pennsylvania, in
GENERAL ASSEMBLY met.

We the COMMITTEE of the Privates of the ASSOCIATION belonging to the City of Philadelphia and its Districts,

Humbly beg Leave to Represent,

That it is with no small Degree of Reluctance that we are obliged either to approach this Honourable House with this our Representation, or by our Silence in some Measure to acknowledge the Claims and admit the Charge of those Men who, in their late Address to this Honourable House, stile themselves the People called Quakers, a Copy of which we have seen.—

In this extraordinary Address we find ourselves and others represented as Men who endeavour to induce this Honourable House to enter into Measures manifestly repugnant to the Laws and Charter of this Province, and which, if enforced, must subvert that most essential of all Privileges, Liberty of Conscience, which they apprehend will not only increase the Public Distresses, but occasion the grievous Sufferings of many conscientious People of divers religious Denominations, and also as Persons who now forget the Equity and Justice of their Laws and Government of this once peaceful Province, and, by preferring our own Schemes, overlook the Importance of inviolably maintaining and supporting the Principles of Civil and Religious Liberty.—

We beg Leave to assure this Honourable House, that we are far from wishing to do any Thing which would have the remotest Tendency to increase the public Distresses, or to occasion the grievous Sufferings of any conscientious People of any Denomination whatever, and are utterly at a loss to comprehend how the Prayer of our Petition could interfere with the Consciences of Religious Men.

In our Petition we prayed the Honourable House in their Wisdom to recommend to their Constituents some general Plan of a Militia Law, which should equally extend to all the good People of this Province, and that any Indulgence which might be thought necessary to be granted by the Honourable House to any of the Freemen of the Province might be equally open to all, and granted upon such Terms as this Honourable House might think adequate to the many difficult and dangerous Services of those who were willing to hazard their Lives and Fortunes in the Defence of their Country.

How this Prayer, founded on the most certain and evident Principles of Equity and Justice, could be construed into an Endeavour to induce this Honourable House to enter into Measures manifestly repugnant to the Laws and Charter of this Province, and which, if enforced, must subvert that most essential of all Privileges, Liberty of Conscience, surpasses all the Ideas we had ever formed of the Power of religious Prejudices.

That Religion which teaches to deny the Demand of Justice and Equity, cannot be of God; nor will the Conscience which is influenced thereby meet with his Approbation. Those who believe the Scriptures must acknowledge that Civil Government is of divine Institution, and the Support of it enjoined to Christians; and it is not consonant to the divine Wisdom to enjoin and forbid the same Thing at the same Time. As your Adressors have not pointed out any Law of the Province to which the Prayer of your Petitioners is so manifestly repugnant, we beg to be indulged with the Liberty of doubting the Existence of any such; and as to the Thirty-fifth Section of Laws agreed upon in England the Fifth Day of the Third Month, One Thousand Six Hundred and Eighty-two, we would pass it over as a Section which we apprehend none but your Addressors would apply to the present Purpose.

With Regard to Arguments drawn from our Charter we would observe, that the great Law of Self-preservation is equally binding with the Letter of written Charters; nor can it be supposed that a People will be reasoned out of their Liberty, and every Thing they hold dear, by an over-nice scanning of them.

Nevertheless, with Regard to that Clause of the Charter of Privileges on which they ultimately found their Claim to a total Exemption from contributing their just Proportion towards the public Expence incurred in Defence of our Privileges.

We would, with all due Submission and Deference, represent to this Honourable House, that the Honourable and Worthy Proprietor William Penn had no Right, Power or Authority to grant Privileges further than was granted to him by the Royal Charter, and that the Royal Prerogative of the King of Great-Britain does not comprehend any Right or Authority in the Crown to grant any Exemption from supporting the Constitution and Government to any Man or Set of Men, on any Pretence whatever. This is a Power unknown to the Crown, and therefore could never be granted by the King to the Worthy Proprietor who granted the Charter of Privileges,

Liberty of Conscience is so sacred a Thing that it ought ever to be preserved inviolate, and we will always rejoice to see any Body of Men assert their Right to it. But when, under Pretence of this Liberty the very Existence of Civil Government is struck at, we beg Leave to represent that either the Liberty claimed must be given up or the Government dissolved; and this we apprehend to be the Case when any of the Members of a Community, from a Claim of Religious Liberty, refuse to support the Society to which they belong, and under which they claim this very Privilege.

That the Clause, which they quote, never did, nor could, extend to such Exemptions on any Pretence whatever, is plain from itself, because the Persons, who have a Right to claim the Liberty granted therein, are by that very Clause made to "profess themselves obliged to live quietly under the civil Government," which cannot possibly be when they refuse to support the Measures often necessary to its very Existence.

Moreover, it is plain that the worthy Proprietor, who granted this Charter, never meant nor intended any such Thing by the Liberty of Conscience therein mentioned, inasmuch as it would have been contrary to the 16th Section of the Royal Charter granted by the King, and accepted by the Proprietor, who, as they inform this Honourable House in their Address, was united with them in religious Profession and Principle, which is as follows: "And because in so remote a Country, and situate near many barbarous Nations, the Incursions, as well of the Savages themselves, as of other Enemies, Pirates and Robbers, may probably be feared; therefore we have given, and for us, our Heirs and Assigns, by themselves or their Captains, or other their Officers, to levy, musster and train all Sorts of Men, of what Condition soever, or wheresoever born, in the said Province of Pennsylvania, for the Time being, and to make War, and to pursue the Enemies and Robbers aforesaid, as well by Sea as by Land, even without the Limits of the said Province, and, by God's Assistance, to vanquish and take them, and being taken, to put them to Death, by the Law of War, or to save them at their Pleasure, and to do all and every other Thing, which unto the Charge and Office of a Captain General of an Army belongeth, or hath accustomed to belong, as fully and freely as any Captain General of any Army hath ever had the fame."

This Section of the Royal Charter, together with the Clause in the Charter of Privileges, which the Addressors hath quoted, shew evidently that the Proprietor, WILLIAM PENN, never intended to grant an Exemption from paying their just Proportion towards the Support of any Power necessary for the good Government of the Province, whether Civil or Military, and therefore can, with no Degree of decent Modesty, be pleaded in the present, or any other Case of the same Kind. Besides it is well known, that no such Claim of Exemption, from contributing their just Proportion towards the Support of any Civil or Military Measures entered into for the maintaining of the Government against their external or internal Enemies, has ever been granted the Society, on account of any such Scruple of Conscience, in any Part of the British Empire, though, as the Addressors alledge, the Society has existed for upwards of an Hundred Years, during which Period it has been obliged to, and still does, pay Taxes, levied for the Purpose of defraying the Expences of Military Expeditions, both here and in Europe; nor do we recollect to have found the Payment of such Taxes on the List of Grievances annually made out by the Society, though they duly commemorate those to which the Clause in the Charter of Privileges is evidently directed.

Thus their own Practice becomes a strong Proof against them, and shews at least that, if their religious Principles are abridged, we are not the Authors of the Abridgement.—Our Petition is, that the Scale of Justice may hang even, and if there are such Consciences as scruple to have impartial Justice administered, we pray that this Honourable House may, in their Wisdom, discountenance them; for if such Scruples once obtain Favour from government, it is plain who are most likely to claim and reap the Benefit of them.

We desire to conclude by assuring this Honourable House, that we are determined, to the utmost of our Power, to support the Liberties of America, and to inform them, that, as we ask no partial Favour for ourselves, so we request that it may not be granted to others: We therefore beg, that the Prayer of our Petition may obtain the most serious Attention of this Honourable House.

Signed by Order of the Committee,

William Adcock, President[61]

Document 141

[The Short and Sincere Declaration of the Mennonites and Church of the Brethren informed the Pennsylvania Assembly of the limits of their conscience in paying an equivalent to military service.]

A short and sincere Declaration, To our Honourable Assembly, and all others in high or low Station of Administration, and to all Friends and Inhabitants of this Country, to whose Sight this may come, be they ENGLISH or GERMANS.

In the first Place we acknowledge us indebted to the most high God, who created Heaven and Earth, the only good Being, to thank him for all his great Goodness and manifold Mercies and Love through our Saviour Jesus Christ, who is come to save the Souls of Men, having all Power in Heaven and on Earth.

Further we find ourselves indebted to be thankful to our late worthy Assembly, for their giving so good an Advice in these troublesome Times to all Ranks of People in Pennsylvania, particularly in allowing those, who, by the Doctrine of our Saviour Jesus Christ, are persuaded in their Consciences to love their Enemies, and not to resist Evil, to enjoy the Liberty of their Conscience, for which, as also for all the good Things we enjoyed under their Care, we heartily thank that worthy Body of Assembly, and all high and low in Office, who have advised to such a peacefull Measure, hoping and confiding that they, and all others entrusted with Power in this hitherto blessed Province, may be moved by the same Spirit of Grace, which animated the first Founder of this Province, our late worthy Proprietor William Penn, to grant Liberty of Conscience to all its Inhabitants, that they may in the great and memorable Day of Judgment be put on the right Hand of the just Judge, who judgeth without Respect of Person, and hear of him these blessed Words, *Come, ye blessed of my Father, inherit the Kingdom prepared for you, Ec. What ye have done unto one of the least of these my Brethren, ye have done unto* e, among which Number *(i.e., the least of Christ's Brethren)* we by his Grace hope to be ranked; and every Lenity and Favour shewn to such tender conscienced, although weak Followers of this our blessed Saviour, will not be forgotten by him in that great Day.

The Advice to those who do not find Freedom of Conscience to take up arms, that they ought to be helpfull to those who are in Need and distressed Circumstances, we receive with Chearfulness towards all Men of what Station they may be—it being our Principle to feed the Hungry and give the Thirsty Drink;—we have dedicated ourselves to serve all Men in every Thing that can be helpful to the Preservaton of Men's Lives, but we find no Freedom in giving, or doing, or assisting in any Thing by which Men's Lives are destroyed or hurt.—We beg the Patience of all those who believe we err in this Point.

We are always ready, according to Christ's Command to Peter, to pay the Tribute, that we may offend no Man, and so we are willing to pay Taxes, *and to render unto Caesar those Things that are Caesar's and to God those Things that are God's*, although we think ourselves very weak to give God his due Honor, he being a Spirit and Life, and we only Dust and Ashes.

We are also willing to be subject to the higher Powers, and to give in the manner Paul directs us;—*for he beareth the Sword not in vain, for he is the Minister of God, a Revenger to execute Wrath upon him that doeth Evil.*

This Testimony we lay down before our worthy Assembly, and all other Persons in Government, letting them know, that we are thankful as above-mentioned, and that we are not at Liberty in Conscience to take up Arms to conquer our Enemies, but rather to pray to God, who has Power in Heaven and on Earth, for US and THEM.

We also crave the Patience of all the Inhabitants of this Country,—what they think to see clearer in the Doctrine of the blessed Jesus Christ, we will leave to them and God, finding ourselves very poor; for Faith is to proceed out of the Word of God, which is Life and Spirit, and a Power of God, and our Conscience to be instructed by the same therefore we beg for Patience.

Our small Gift, which we have given, we gave to those who have Power over us, that we may not offend them, as Christ taught us by the Tribute Penny.

We heartily pray that God would govern all Hearts of our Rulers, be they high or low, to meditate those good Things which will pertain to OUR and THEIR Happiness.

The above Declaration, signed by a number of Elders and Teachers of the Society of Menonists, and some of the German Baptists, presented to the Honourable House of Assembly on the 7th Day of November, 1775, was most graciously received.[62]

Petition for Taxes

The Bucks County Committee drew up a petition to the Pennsylvania Assembly in February 1776 to ask for an increased tax on Non-Associators and a tax to be paid by men between 50 and 60 years old "who are entirely exempt from Military Duty and Expence."

Document 142

In Committee at John Bogarts Feb. 27th 1776 present

Joseph Hart	*Adam Lowdesleger*	*Benjamin Fell*
Richard Walker	*John Coryel*	*James McNair*
Robert Patterson	*Samuel Smith*	*Benjamin Sigle*
James Wallace		

Resolved that the following petition be presented to the Assembly relative to the military Association.—

That as a general uneasiness prevail's among the Associators in this County, on Account of the late Military Resolutions of this Honourable House and many persons have signed them under a full persuasion that Amendments would be made therein; And as there are many able-bodied Men, between the Age of fifty and sixty years, possessed of large estates, who are entirely exempt from Military Duty and Expence, Your petitioners therefore humbly prays that the Association may be extended to the Age of Sixty.—

And as the Tax upon Non-Associators is considered merely as an equivalent for personal Services, and the Associators have no Compensation for their Arms and Acoutrements, not to mention the Dangers they will be exposed to when called into actual Service, Your petitioners pray, that an Additional Tax be laid upon the Estates of Non-Associators proportionate to the Expences of the Associators necessarily incured for the general Defence of Property.

And as by marching whole Battalions or Companies of Militia, large tracts of Country will be left destitute of Men, except those who either hold all Resistance unlawful, or such as are disaffected to the present Measures, Your petitioners therefore beg leave to submit to the Consideration of the House, whether it would not be better to direct the Colonels to draught from their Battalions such Number as shall from time to time be requisite, thereby affording an Opportunity for those whose Circumstances will not always admit their going to get Volunteers in their stead, and at the same time leaving sufficient force in every part of the Country to quell any local insurrections.—

All which your Petitioners humbly pray may be taken into the

Consideration of the House and such Amendments made as you, in your Wisdom shall see meet.——[63]

Mennonites and Government

Christian Funk recalled the attitude of Mennonites to the question of separation from Great Britain in his recollections of a meeting in Franconia Township, Philadelphia (now Montgomery) County, Pennsylvania. His comments are important as documentation of the Mennonite concern "that our liberty might be endangered," since a change in government could imperil the religious freedom guaranteed in William Penn's Charter. His statement that Mennonites "neither could institute or destroy any government" was frequently echoed in the discussion of the oath of allegiance. While Funk wrote many years after the events, the Franconia meeting was probably held in response to the call for a convention to meet in Philadelphia on June 18, 1776. The process is described in this extract from the Bucks County Committee minutes.

Document 143

In Committee at John Bogart's May 22d 1776

Messrs. David Jones and Joseph Watkins having produced A Letter from the Committee of Inspection of Philadelphia requesting this Board to nominate a certain Number of their Members to meet Deputies from the Other Counties at this Province in Philadelphia on Tuesday the 18th day of next month, in Order to agree upon and direct the Mover of electing Members for a provincial Convention, to be held at such time and place, as the sd. Conference of Committees may appoint, for the express purpose of forming and establishing a new form of Government.

The sd. Letter together with some other papers to the same purport having been read and considered.

Resolved, that as this is a Matter of very great Consequence and ought to be considered with the utmost Deliberation, the same be held under Advisement until Monday the 10th of June when this Committee will meet and give an Answer to the said Letter, in the Mean time every Member of this Board will collect as much as possible the sense of his Township on this important Subject.—

The Committee then adjourned to monday ye 10 June.[64]

Document 144

In the year 1776, a meeting was held in Indian Field township, (now Franconia) for the purpose of choosing three men, who were to attend a delegation from other parts of this province, to deliberate whether Pennsylvania should join the other provinces, which were already fully engaged in the war, and to consent and acknowledge the independence from England. This naturally brought me into an unnecessary reflection—that our liberty might be endangered—and although I never before attended a township meeting, I resolved to attend this. On my arrival, I saw that nearly the whole township had assembled, composed of nearly two-thirds Menonists, and the remainder church people. I enquired if anything had been done, and was replied to in the negative. I expressed my opinion, that we could not interfere in tearing ourselves from the king—that he was the head or protector of Pennsylvania—and that we ought to submit to the three acts; for that we acknowledged ourselves a defenceless people, and neither could institute or destroy any government.[65]

Non-Associators Provoke Ill Will

In Washington County, Maryland, the refusal of Mennonites and Brethren to muster with the Associators also caused considerable ill feeling. Jacob Stull wrote from Elizabethtown (modern Hagerstown) in August 1775 to Colonel Samuel Beall, Jr., a member of the Maryland Convention, to request a fine on Non-Associators.

Document 145

E. Town Augt. 5, 1775.

Sir,

Many disorders are likely to arise in this settlement from some religous Sects refus[in]g to muster. Some Companies threaten to go to their houses & pull them out by force, others declare the[y] will lay down their Arms without proper notice is taken of these sects.—at this time when the authority of the Civil Magistrates is much relaxed the most alarm[in]g consequences are to be dreaded from the Irregular conduct of the people & the Committees are at a loss how to act.—I am therfore desired by the Committee of this district to represent the matter to you in order that it may come before the Convention in case you think it necessary—it is the opinion of the Committee *that any resolution of the Convention lay'g a fine on those who did not muster wd. be readily submitted to & wd. give Satisfaction to both parties*[*] that if the

[*] The portion in italics was crossed out in the original.

Convention wo[ul]d pass a resolve that all those who are restrained by religious Principles from mustering wod. pay a certain sum for each day that others muster it wod. give satisfaction to both parties & the Committee has good Authority for this opinion from the Sentiments of a great number of Dunkers Menonists &c. in this settlement.

I am wth. much respect
Yr. obt. H. St.
J. Stull Chairman

To Col. Saml. Beall Junr.

At a meeting of six Members of the Committee at Elizabeth Town on the 5, Augt. 1775, the above Letter was write & sent to Coll. Beall.[66]

Substitutes and Fines

The Virginia Convention exempted Quakers and Mennonites from military service in July 1775, without requiring them to pay any fine or other equivalent. The Committee of Observation in Frederick County, Virginia, suggested a fine on all Quakers and Mennonites who refused either to serve or provide a substitute. The Virginia Assembly responded by enrolling Quakers and Menonists in the militia, while still exempting them from musters. This action made them liable to be drafted and required them to furnish substitutes or be fined.

The Virginia Mennonites and Quakers did not cooperate by providing substitutes, so in October 1777 the Assembly authorized the county sheriff to seize their goods to pay the cost of hiring a substitute.

Document 146

At a Convention of Delegates for the Counties and Corporations in the Colony of Virginia, held at Richmond town, in the county of Henrico, on Monday the seventeenth day of July, in the year of our Lord one thousand seven hundred and seventy-five.

An ordinance for raising and embodying a sufficient force for the defence and protection of this colony.

And be it further ordained, That all quakers, and the people called Menonists, shall be exempted from serving in the militia, agreeable to the several acts of the general assembly of this colony made for their relief and indulgence in this respect.[67]

Document 147

A Petition of the Committee of the county of Frederick was presented to the Convention, and read; setting forth, that, by an Ordinance passed the 17th of July last, the people called Quakers and Menonists are exempted from serving in the militia; that they have a tender regard for the conscience scruples of every religious society, but at the same time beg leave to represent the injustice of subjecting one part of the community to the whole burthen of government, while others equally share the benefits of it; that they suggest, that, if, in lieu of bearing arms at general and private musters, the said Quakers and Menonists were subjected to the payment of a certain sum, to be annually assessed by the county courts at laying the levy, and, in case the militia should be called into actual service, they should be draughted in the same proportion as the militia of the county, and, on their refusal to serve, or provide able bodied men to serve in their places respectively, that they were liable to the same fines as other militia men in the like cases are subject to, it would be more equal; and that they submit it whether it would not be reasonable to allow any person who should choose to contribute to the support of the public, in lieu of attending musters, the same indulgence as to those who refuse from consciencious principles.[68]

Document 148

July 6, 1776

Whereas by an ordinance, intituled An ordinance for raising and embodying a sufficient force for the protection and defence of this colony, all overseers residing on a plantation, and all millers are exempted from being enlisted into the militia of their respective counties, which said exemption of overseers and of millers residing in the counties of Accomack and Northampton, on the eastern shore, hath been found inconvenient and unnecessary:

Be it therefore resolved, by the delegates and representatives of the several counties and corporations of Virginia, in general convention assembled, and it is hereby ordained by the authority of the same, That all overseers, and all quakers and menonists, in Virginia, and all millers residing in the counties of Accomack and Northampton, shall be enrolled into the militia by the commanding officers of the respective counties, and be subject to the same rules and regulations, and liable to the same fines, penalties, and forfeitures, as the rest of the militia, and the said overseers, quakers, and menonists, shall be immediately alloted to the several divisions of militia in their respective counties, in the manner prescribed by a former ordinance respecting the division of the militia in this colony, except in the counties of Accomack and Northampton; but the said quakers and menonists shall not be obliged to attend general or private musters.[69]

Document 149

Dunmore County Committee Chambers 23d July 1776

To the Honorable the President and Gentlemen of the Convention of Virginia

The Humble Petition of the Committee of the County of Dunmore Sheweth

That by an Ordinance passed at a Convention held at the Town of Richmond on the 17th of July 1775, It is ordained that all Quakers and the People called Menonists shall be exempted from serving in the Militia agreeable to the several Acts of the General Assembly of this Colony made for their relief and indulgence in this respect, Your Petitioners have a tender regard for the conscientious scruples of every Religious Society, but at the same time beg leave to represent the Injustice of subjecting one part of the Community to the whole burden of Government, while others equally share the Benefits of it. Your Petitioners consider the above exemption is extremely impolitic as well as unjust in the present unsettled state of the Country. They apprehend it will greatly discourage the People in general from discharging the duties of a Militia and other necessary impositions. Your Petions (*sic*) therefore humbly suggest that in lieu of bearing Arms at General and private Musters, the said Quakers and Menonists may be subjected to the payment of a certain Sum to be annually assessed by the County Courts at laying the Levy on each of them, and in case the Militia shall be called into actual Service that the said exempts be draughted in the same proportion as the Militia of the County and if they refuse to serve or provide able bodied Men to serve in their places respectively, that they be liable to the same Fine as other Militia Men in the like cases are subject to and to render the said Fines and Assessments as little injurious as may be, in case the said exempts shall refuse to pay the same, or receive the overplus arising from the Sale of Goods distrained for default of Payment, that the Collector of the said Fines and Assessments shall as soon as conveniently may be, after the sale of any Goods distrained for the purpose aforesaid, where any overplus shall remain in his hands, render the same to the Person whose Goods were sold, or leave notice in Writing at his usual place of abode of the amount of such overplus, and that he has the same ready to pay when demanded, and in case of refusal to receive or neglect to apply for the same within a limited time, that the said overplus be applyed to such publick uses as the Court of the County shall direct, and that the Person or Persons so refusing or neglecting shall be intitled to Credit for the Amount thereof out of such Fines, Assessments or Taxes as shall be thereafter levied him or them by the Court of the County in which he or they shall respectively reside. And Your Petitioners submit to the Consideration of your Honorable House, that it might be reasonable to allow any Person who should chuse to contribute to the support of the Publick in lieu of attending Musters the same Indulgence as to those who refuse from conscientious Principles. May it therefore please your Honorable House to reconsider that part of the Ordinance above referred to, and adopt some mode to oblige those who conscientiously scruple the use of Arms to make an adequate Contribution towards the public expence in lieu thereof. And your Petitioners shall ever pray.

Joseph Pugh Chairman
Francis Ravenhill Clerk

[Endorsed]
Dunmore Committee
their Petition
1776
Oct: 16: ref'd to
Propry. and Grievances
Ref'd
Reasonable[70]

Document 150

That Quakers and Menonists who shall be so draughted shall be discharged from personal service, and that the field officers and justices who attend the draught shall, and they are hereby empowered to, employ any two or more discreet persons to procure, upon the best terms they can, proper substitutes to serve in their stead, and to adjust and divide the charge thereof among all the members of their respective societies of quakers and menonists in the county, in proportion to the number of tithables in the family of or belonging to each member, and to authorise the sheriff of the county, by warrant under his hands, to levy such charge by distress, in case of any member refusing or neglecting to make payment thereof within ten days after the same shall have been demanded, upon the goods and chattles of the member so refusing or neglecting.[71]

Notes for Chapter 3

1. Elmer E. S. Johnson, "Christopher Schultz in Public Life," *Schwenkfeldiana,* I (September 1940), p. 17.

2. Arthur J. Mekeel, "The Relation of the Quakers to the American Revolution," *Quaker History,* LXV (Spring 1976), pp. 6-8. On the relation of the royal government to these developments, see Hutson, *PMHB,* XCV (January 1971), pp. 41-49. *Cf.* Marietta, "Ecclesiastical Discipline," pp. 90*ff.*

3. Bauman, p. 143.

4. Rhys Isaac, "Preachers and Patriots: Popular Culture and the Revolution in Virginia," Alfred F. Young, ed., *The American Revolution, Explorations in the History of Radicalism* (DeKalb, Ill., 1976), pp. 127-156. *Cf.* Rhys Isaac, "Evangelical Revolt: The Nature of the Baptists' Challenge to the Traditional Order in Virginia, 1765-1775," *WMQ,* 3rd ser., XXXI (October 1974), pp. 345-368.

5. Dorothy Gilbert Thorne, "North Carolina Friends and the Revolution," *North Carolina Historical Review,* XXXVIII (July 1961), pp. 323-324.

6. *Cf.* John Howard Yoder, *The Politics of Jesus* (Grand Rapids, Mich., 1972), pp. 201-205.

7. David Jones, *Defensive War in a Just Cause Sinless. A Sermon Preached on the Day of the Continental Fast at Tredyffryd in Chester County* (Philadelphia, 1775), p. 5. This was a common theme in sermons on public affairs in 1775.

8. Some recent writers have confused the rejection of political ends with the refusal to use political means. David Hawke, *In the Midst of a Revolution* (Philadelphia, 1961), p. 65, misunderstands the attitudes of the sects, assuming that "from the time of the French and Indian War it appears they refused even to vote." Peter Brock, too, writes of the "increasingly withdrawn character of Quaker pacifism" and of "the simple German-speaking farmers" in the other peace churches "who wished to live withdrawn from all affairs of state." Brock, pp. 159 and 191. They were, in fact, contending for a state in which they *could* participate.

9. David Ammerman, *In the Common Cause: American Response to the Coercive Acts of 1774* (Charlottesville, Va., 1974), pp. 43-44. Bernhard Knollenberg, *Growth of the American Revolution 1776-1775* (New York, 1975), p. 231.

10. "Memorial of Evan Thomas," Memorials, Baltimore Yearly Meeting, Friends Historical Library, Swarthmore College, Swarthmore, Pa. Montgomery County Court Minute Book, August Court 1780, fol. 12. Montgomery County Deeds, Liber D, fol. 680. Montgomery County Judgment Record 1786-1795, fol. 296. Montgomery County Court House, Rockville, Md.

11. *Pennsylvania Archives,* 2nd Series, XIII, pp. 283-286.

12. *Ibid.,* p. 294.

13. *Pennsylvania Gazette,* January 11, 1775; January 25, 1775.

14. *Ibid.,* February 1, 1775.

15. Henry J. Cadbury, "Quaker Relief During the Siege of Boston," *Colonial Society of Massachusetts Publications.* XXIV (1943), pp. 39-179.

16. *Pennsylvamia Gazette* (Philadelphia), November 15, 1775, Supplement. *Votes and Proceedings,* VI, 639-640.

17. *Votes and Proceedings,* VI, 646. Ministers of the Gospel and indentured servants were to be exempted.

18. *Pennsylvania Gazette* (Philadelphia), December 6, 1775. "This penalty was deemed too low, but worse still was the fact that non-associators over fifty years of age were not obliged to pay anything." Thayer, *op. cit.,* p. 172. This objection underscored the purpose of the tax as a direct equivalent of military service.

19. *Pennsylvania Ledger* (Philadelphia), December 2, 1775.

20. Henry J. Young, "The Treatment of the Loyalists in Pennsylvania," PhD

dissertation, Johns Hopkins, 1955, p. 88.

21. *Votes and Proceedings,* VI, 712-715. John A. Neuenschwanger, *The Middle Colonies and the Coming of the American Revolution,* (Port Washington, N.Y., 1974), p. p. 179. See also Document 192.

22. James T. Mitchell and Henry Flanders, eds., *The Statutes at Large of Pennsylvania 1682-1801.* (Harrisburg, Pa., 1897) IX, 538. *Pennsylvania Packet and General Advertiser* (Philadelphia) November 26, 1776.

23. Young, *op. cit.*, p. 90.

24. *Proceedings of the Conventions of Maryland, Held at the City of Annapolis in 1774, 1775 and 1776* (Baltimore, Md., 1836), pp. 21 and 74.

25. "Proceedings of the Committee of Observation for Elizabeth Town District," *Maryland Historical Magazine,* XII (June 1917), pp. 144-145.

26. Roger E. Sappington, "North Carolina and the Non-Resistant Sects in the American War of Independence," *Quaker History,* LX (Spring 1971), p. 37.

27. "A List of the None Associators," and "The Associators, March 22, 1776. Brecknock Township Tax Lists, Lancaster County Historical Society, Lancaster, Pa.

28. "Brecknock Township Assessment of Non Associators, August 20, 1777." Brecknock Township Tax Lists, Lancaster County Historical Society, Lancaster, Pa. A second copy of the same document has names eliminated and dates from December 1777.

29. "Conestoga Township Assessment of the Non Associators," 1777. Conestoga Township Tax Lists, Lancaster County Historical Society, Lancaster, Pa.

30. Pemberton Papers, Historical Society of Pa., Philadelphia, Pa.

31. Christopher Schultz to Edward Burd, January 12, 1775, Quoted in Elmer E. S. Johnson, "Christopher Schultz in Public Life," *Schwenkfeldiana,* I (September 1940), p. 18.

32. Schwenkfelder Library, Pennsburg, Pa., Translated from the German by Elizabeth Horsch Bender.

33. *Ibid.* Translated from the German by Elizabeth Horsch Bender.

34. Curtis Grubb Papers, H.S.P., Philadelphia, Pa.

35. "Items of History of York, Penna., During the Revolution," *Pennsylvania Magazine of History and Biography,* XLIV (1920), p. 309.

36. Howard Peckham, ed., *Memoirs of the Life of John Adlum* (Chicago, 1968), pp. 7-10. Reprinted with permission. The original manuscript is in the William L. Clements Library, Ann Arbor, Mich.

37. Yeates Family Correspondence, H.S.P., Philadelphia, Pa.

38. Peter Grubb Papers, H.S.P., Philadelphia, Pa.

39. Yeates Family Correspondence, H.S.P., Philadelphia, Pa.

40. *Ibid.*

41. Printed Handbill, Col. Peter Grubb Papers, H.S.P., Philadelphia, Pa.

42. *Force Collection Series IX,* Library of Congress, Washington, D.C. (Hereafter cited as L. C.)

43. Lancaster County Committee Minute Book, fol. 34, Force Collection. L. C.

44. *Votes and Proceedings,* VI. Also printed in *Pennsylvania Gazette,* July 5, 1775.

45. Force Collection, IX 13, L. C. An identical manuscript copy is in Yeates Family Correspondence, H.S.P., Philadelphia, Pa.

46. Kenneth G. Hamilton, *John Ettwein and the Moravians in the American Revolution* (Bethlehem, Pa., 1940), p. 234.

47. Lancaster County Committee Minute Book, fol. 45, Force Collection, L. C.

48. Yeates Family Correspondence, H.S.P.

49. Force Collection, L. C.

50. Records of the Supreme Executive Council, Pennsylvania State Archives, Harrisburg, Pa. The enclosed proposals are not with the extant papers.

51. Lancaster County Committee Minute Book, fols. 56-57, Force Collection, L. C.

52. *Ibid.*, fol. 57.

53. Broadside 144-10, Rare Book Room, L.C.

54. Peter Force Collection, L. C.

55. *Ibid.* German Reformed are probably designated "Presbyterian" and Lutherans included in "Church."

56. Schwenkfelder Library, Pennsburg, Pa.

57. *Pennsylvania Archives*, 1st Series, IV, 653.

58. *Ibid.*, 649.

59. *Votes and Proceedings*, VI, 599.

60. *Ibid.*, 600-601.

61. *Ibid.*, 640-642.

62. Broadside, Printed in English and in German by Henry Miller of Philadelphia.

63. "Minutes of the Committee of Safety, Bucks County," Bucks County Historical Society, Doylestown, Pa.

64. *Ibid.*

65. Christian Funk, *A Mirror for All Mankind* (Norristown, Pa., 1814), pp. 7-8.

66. Force Collection, L. C. See also, Documents 193 and 194.

67. W. W. Hening, comp., *Virginia Statutes at Large* IX, 935.

68. Journal of Virginia Convention, June 19, 1776, Virginia State Library, Richmond, Va.

69. W. W. Hening, *Statutes*, IX, 139.

70. Religious Petitions, Virginia State Library, Richmond, Va.

71. W. W. Hening, *Statutes*, X, 261, 334.

Chapter 4

"MILITARY SERVICE WILL BE EXACTED OF MANY OF OUR PEOPLE"

Failure of the Volunteer Association

In the first year of the American Revolution, a British army kept inside its entrenchments in besieged Boston while a force of Continental soldiers and New England militia, commanded by George Washington, camped on a chain of hills overlooking the city. In Canada, during the autumn and winter of 1775, a much smaller British force defended Quebec against American invaders. A handful of British regulars, captured in outposts on the road to Quebec, arrived in Lancaster and other inland towns as prisoners of war; now and again a company of riflemen, on the march to Washington's camp, caused a stir as they passed through the same towns with drums beating and children running alongside. It hardly mattered in 1775 if half the able-bodied men in Bucks or any other Pennsylvania county signed the military association while the other half, for reasons of conscience or political alignment, ignored the summons to learn the military art. Associators paraded along farm lanes in their own townships or swaggered about the county courthouse, more as a political demonstration to overawe wavering neighbors with the strength of support for a defense of American liberties than as a military force.

A year of armed conflict made certain unpalatable truths obvious. There would be no peaceful accommodation between the British government and the insurgent Colonies. The drift toward independence, denied time and again in those early months, was now an irreversible current, carrying along even Pennsylvania and New York, the most reluctant rebels among the Colonies. Under these circumstances, no armed demonstration by Massachusetts farmers could impose a solution. Both sides would need men and weapons sufficient for a long and bitter struggle.

The British government began pulling regiments out of garrison towns in Ireland and marching them to Cork to embark on transports. They dispatched recruiting sergeants to the Scottish Highlands and sent diplomatic couriers to the courts of the German princes to hire whole regiments from the colonel to the band. The Continental Congress had no need to go so far afield. Every able-bodied man in the Colonies from 16 to 50 years old was already obliged by a resolve of Congress to military duty. Inadequately trained and sketchily armed and equipped, voluntary Associators in every one of the thirteen United Colonies would be called on to defend American independence in 1776. These units would be utilized as a stopgap, while the states recruited and equipped regiments for service in the Continental Army and developed a more adequate militia system for short-term service.

In July 1776, a mighty armada of troop transports and warships crowded into New York Harbor, and Sir William Howe began disembarking 34,000 British and Hessian soldiers on Staten Island and Long Island. Washington and his veterans of the siege of Boston were already throwing up entrenchments to defend New York before the first British sails appeared over the horizon, for an attack on New York was long anticipated. But the Colonies were slow in fitting up regiments for the Continental line, and battalions of Associators from New York, Pennsylvania, and Maryland, formed into a Flying Camp, filled the depleted ranks of the American army. The Flying Camp was composed of volunteers from the regular Associator units, with each battalion assigned a quota of men for the Flying Camp.

When the first call for men came in the summer of 1776, the Associators responded with some enthusiasm. It was a burden for farmers to leave their fields with the crops coming in, but they did march. Local officials were hard pressed to find guns and blankets for their men and money to buy provisions enough to feed them. The Lancaster County Committee had to borrow money from merchants and farmers.[1] Continental officers complained of the slowness of the militia to march and the excuses offered for the delay. If the Associators could not march because they had no weapons and they were needed at home in harvest-time, one Pennsylvania officer suggested, the Non-Associators should give up their rifles and take their place on their farms (*Document 158*). The Pennsylvania Convention determined on one of these courses in July 1776 with the passage of an ordinance for disarming the Non-Associators. An express rider galloped into Lancaster late one July night with copies of their resolve and orders to speed the Lancaster County battalions on the road to New York (*Document 157*).

If there was no great resentment in the summer of 1776 at the Non-Associators who remained at home, the military defeats suffered by the American forces increased animosity against them. When news of Washington's defeat at Long Island reached them, the Pennsylvania

Table 3
BUCKS COUNTY NON-ASSOCIATORS, SEPTEMBER, 1775

Township	Associators[1] 1775	Non-Associators[2] 1775	"Signed, but do not associate"
Bedminster M	67	56	14
Bensalem	106	39	
Bristol[3]	65	118	26
Buckingham	43	193	
Falls	57	102	
Hillton M	65	89	
Lower Makefield	46	36	
Lower Milford	122	46	
Middletown	75	99	
New Britain M	110	89	
Newton	51	77	
Nockamixon	110[4]	9	
Northampton	123	30	
Plumstead M	85	115	
Richland	65	82	
Rockhill M	57	-	
Solebury	28	179	
Southampton	79	36	
Springfield M	56	-	
Tinicum	84	-	18
Wrightstown	29	55	

1. *Pennsylvania Archives*, 2nd Series, XIV, 147-179.
2. *Pennsylvania Archives*, 2nd Series, XIV, 221-243.
3. Borough and Township.
4. Includes 15 Associators under military age.

Convention "in a passion" increased the fines on Non-Associators fourfold to over £12 early in September 1776. The Assembly later overruled their action and repealed the fines.[2]

The Battle of Long Island on August 27, 1776, decided the fate of New York City, although Howe's dilatoriness prevented it from deciding anything else. The British tried unsuccessfully to trap Washington in a series of pincer movements, but by the end of November the

American army was across the Hudson and the war had shifted to New Jersey. Morale had never been lower. As the British pressed closer to Philadelphia, the Pennsylvania Committee of Safety demanded harsher penalties against Non-Associators.[3] The Assembly responded with increased fines.[4]

Resentment against the Non-Associators flared in every part of the Colonies where conscientious objectors were concentrated. In Dunmore (Shenandoah) County, Virginia, where Mennonites and Quakers were numerous, the County Committee protested against the exemptions granted them by the Virginia Assembly (*Document 149*). The Washington County, Maryland Committee also reacted harshly toward the Non-Associators. In December 1776 the Committee resolved: "that the Dunkards and Menonists be advertised, to pay their respective fines, to the Committee, on Tuesday next, otherwise, they may depend, that rigorous Measures will be immediately taken to Compel Payment."[5] (*Documents 197-199*)

Washington abandoned Trenton and crossed the Delaware on December 7, 1776. A few days later, General Charles Lee's leaderless, dispirited army tramped into Easton, after their commander blundered into a British patrol who captured a general by accident. With the British on their borders, many Pennsylvania Associators suspected that they were being summoned as a final reserve before the cause of American independence went down to defeat. The newspapers, at the urging of Congress, kept up a steady barrage of atrocity stories about the British advance across the Jerseys and appealed to the patriotism of Pennsylvanians. But all fell on deaf ears. The militia turned out poorly in Bucks and Northampton, as the British army advanced to the Delaware. Colonel Joseph Hart of Bucks County shamefacedly sent General Washington a list of 189 men in his regiment of Associators who "refused or neglected" to march to Philadelphia. Only six men in Captain William McCalla's company "marched, agreeable to his Excellency's orders," while 67 others, including all the officers, stayed at home in Plumstead Township.[6] In Berks County less than fifty men in Colonel Hunter's battalion turned out to draw bounty and rations and as quickly returned home. It was the same in Northampton, where men formed an association of their own to refuse militia duty.[7] (*Document 200*).

When the Associators, who once had rallied to the Patriot cause, had no stomach for military service, ill feeling increased against the Non-Associators. The Committee of Observation in Washington County, Maryland, urged "such of the young Dunkards & Menonists as have not enroll'd nor associated" to march with the Associators for entrenching, helping with the sick and other noncombatant duties and promised to remit the fines of those who volunteered to go. The Committee also directed needy families of soldiers "to apply to the Dunkards and Menonists residing nearest" for whatever they might want.[8] Fines on Non-Associators were at the discretion of the County Committee in Maryland and fines levied in December 1776 in Washington County were raised to the legal maximum of £ 10 in many cases.

The Pennsylvania Assembly, earlier inclined to be lenient with Non-Associators, reimposed the £ 3 . .10 . .0 Non-Associator tax and increased their maximum fine to £ 20 in February 1777, but this new tax was not always collected. County Commissioners found it difficult to levy, because they could not readily obtain lists of Non-Associators from township assessors and constables.[9] The Assembly took this into account in June, 1777, when it passed a new law giving the Commissioners thirty days to obtain the lists from township officials.[10] They also passed an act "for rendering the burthen of the defence of the State more equal" at this session. It provided "That all the estates real and personal of every person or persons not subjected by the Militia Law to military duties shall pay yearly and every year a sum of money equal to the sum that the estates of the persons are or shall be charged with in the States taxes." This meant double taxation for conscientious objectors.[11]

Enforcement of the £3 . .10 . .0 tax and the double tax on Non-Associators began in the summer of 1777. Lancaster County tax lists indicate that the Non-Associator Tax was collected between August and December 1777; a similar demand in Berks, Philadelphia, and Northampton caused great concern among Franconia Mennonites.[12]

Pennsylvania Adopts a Militia Law

A more sweeping change in the situation of Pennsylvania conscientious objectors came with passage of a Militia Act in March 1777. The new law required all white males from eighteen to fifty-three years old to enroll in the militia and exempted only members of Congress, the Pennsylvania Supreme Executive Council, judges of the Pennsylvania Supreme Court, masters and faculty of colleges, ministers of the gospel, and indentured servants.[13] This action brought Pennsylvania in line with the other states in asserting the legal obligation of every able-bodied male of appropriate age to be a part of the miltary forces of the state. This legal obligation was taken for granted everywhere in the Colonies, except in Pennsylvania, although military needs were actually met more often by enlisting volunteers than by drafting from the militia.[14]

Quakers and Mennonites had always dreaded any form of compulsory military service and had blocked an effective militia law throughout the period of proprietary government in Pennsylvania. The new measure did not have universal support, but any bill that shifted more of the wartime burden onto the shoulders of the unpopular Non-Associators was bound to receive considerable support. As one Philadelphia newspaper observed, "A militia law, which puts all upon an equal footing," would put a stop to special privileges for "those who by one means or other have hitherto screened themselves from every trial, hardship and danger to which the associators were exposed."[15] There would no longer be any grounds for claiming that military service was a voluntary option, to be taken or refused for personal reasons.[16]

The Pennsylvania militia law provided for the appointment of a lieutenant and sublieutenants in each county and gave them responsibility for embodying the militia and enforcing the new law. The county lieutenant and his subordinates were required to divide their county into battalions of equal strength, composed of companies located in neighboring townships. These companies were, in turn, subdivided into eight "classes"; when a given battalion was mobilized for active duty, the men in the first class of each company would be called on to march, while the others remained at home, and then each of the other classes would be drafted in their turn. This was also the system used in Maryland, Virginia, North Carolina, and other states throughout the war.

The lieutenant and sublieutenants received authority to sit as a court of appeals for persons who had been fined under the new law for failing to appear for drill or refusing to march with their class or provide a substitute. They heard a variety of excuses, religious scruples, illness, poverty, and family obligations in these periodic appeal days and had final authority in determining the amount of the fines levied or in remitting them altogether.

The Assembly chose men long active and enthusiastic in the Patriot cause in each county for these important posts. In March, 1777 they appointed Colonel Bertram Galbraith as Lancaster County Lieutenant, Richard M'Callister for York, John Armstrong for Cumberland, Jacob Morgan for Berks, John Wetzel for Northampton, William Coates for Philadelphia, Joseph Kirkbride for Bucks, and Robert Smith for Chester. For Pennsylvania conscientious objectors these men represented military authority most directly. Since they formed the vital link between the central government in Philadelphia and the county militia organization, the Council filled these posts with political qualifications in mind. The county lieutenants were thus "the local henchmen of the Radical leaders in Philadelphia."[17]

If the Pennsylvania Assembly had hoped to have the new militia system in operation for the next military campaign, their hopes were dashed even before the new county lieutenants had received their commissions. Every Continental private and every apprentice boy in the city knew perfectly well that Sir William Howe's advance on Philadelphia would begin with the end of winter. On April 9, 1777, Thomas Wharton, Jr., President of the Supreme Executive Council, called on the militia to repel the enemy. He acknowledged that "The Militia of this State, it is feared, cannot be arranged under the law in time for the present emergency," but he promised those who answered the present call that they would "not be called upon again until the whole Militia of the State shall have served in turn, agreeable to the spirit of the militia law."[18]

With the need for men critical, the Continental Congress urged the states to allow indentured servants to enlist and to require "all such persons as are by laws exempted from bearing arms or performing militia duties, to furnish such a number of able-bodied soldiers as the said legislatures shall deem a proper equivalent for such exemption."[19] A committee of the Pennsylvania Assembly reported favorably on this resolve in May 1777. Virginia and North Carolina modified their militia laws in 1778 to compel the nonresistant sects to provide substitutes when any of their members were called to active duty with their class.[20]

Difficulties of Mustering the New Militia

Under the threat of imminent British invasion, the new county lieutenants hastened to complete their formidable task. Early in April, Philadelphia County was organized as the law directed, with the Mennonite townships in modern Montgomery County falling by chance or design into one battalion.[21] Colonel Jacob Morgan, the County Lieutenant in Berks, divided the county into battalions later in April, but officers could not be elected until May, he explained, "as the County is so very extensive, half the Inhabitants would not have timely Notice," if he chose an earlier date.[22] As it happened, 18 of the 48 Berks County companies failed to muster and choose their officers.[23] Their lack of enthusiasm was by no means singular.

Lancaster County, with a large concentration of conscientious objectors, proved difficult to fit into the new militia system. County Lieutenant Bartrem Galbraith sent orders to battalion commanders to have the first class of each company ready to march to Chester early in May. The first class of the Paxton battalion turned out "tolerably well except the Germans, who seem chiefly all to stand aloof." The County Lieutenant urged immediate action in reporting men in that class with scruples about military service, so that he could find substitutes to take their place.[24] Colonel Galbraith complained of the serious problems he had in forming battalions in all the Mennonite townships.[25] He found it difficult to find substitutes to fill up the ranks where so many men refused to serve on religious grounds.[26] The nature of his problem can be readily seen from the figures in Table 4 on page 286. The Eighth Battalion of Lancaster County Militia in 1777 was composed of three Hempfield, three Manor, and two Conestoga companies. Of 279 men eligible for service in Hempfield Township in 1777, there were 196 Non-Associators, leaving only 83 men to serve when their own class was called or as substitues for conscientious objectors. In Conestoga Township, of 193 eligible men, only 54 had no objection to militia duty. Unless Colonel Galbraith drew men from other battalions, the Eight Battalion would never be able to take the field in full strength.

In the last week of May George Washington shifted his Continental soldiers to Middlebrook in an effort to block Howe's advance to the Delaware River. The call for militia to swell his ranks grew more insistent. The first class of Lancaster militia got their orders to march on May 29.[27] Two weeks later, orders came for the second class to be on the road to Philadelphia and for the third class to muster and await further orders.[28] The reluctance of Pennsylvania farmers turned to stubborn resistance. Galbraith had a full-scale rebellion on his hands early in June when men enrolled in the next militia class threatened to prevent the drafted men from marching. Galbraith reported that some men with religious scruples about bearing arms had joined the rioters.[29]

Tempers were already frayed on both sides when, later in June, Colonel Galbraith began collecting fines from those who would not serve with the militia. The law gave the County Lieutenant and his subordinates authority to seize livestock or household goods from anyone who refused voluntary payment. The Moravian community at Hebron (near present Lebanon) heard rumors of armed bands plundering neutral farmers under pretense of collecting fines. The feeling was so bitter that Galbraith's officers needed the protection of a squad of militiamen on their rounds. In the colonel's own neighborhood in Donegal Township, a mob assembled in Michael Albright's farmyard when the soldiers came to collect fines levied against his sons. Angry words led to violence, although Albright claimed he did his best to calm both

Table 4
LANCASTER COUNTY NON-ASSOCIATORS

Township	Males 16-50 1775	Males 16-50 1776	Males 16-50 1777	Non-Associators 1776 105	Non-Associators 1777 42(28)[2]
Brecknock		114			3(0)[2]
Coleraine	67				139
Conestoga		193	279		196
Hempfield					37
Lancaster Tp.		49			68
Leacock		262			34
Salisbury		247			

1. Lancaster County Tax List, Lancaster County Historical Society, Lancaster, Pa.
2. The figures in parentheses are the number of Non-Associators on a duplicate return for 1777.

parties. His eldest son grabbed the coulter of a plow and split the skull of Cornelius Boyle, a Donegal Township neighbor. The militiamen panicked, fired into the crowd, and Samuel Albright fell, mortally wounded. Later, Michael and John Albright and John Nicholas were jailed for their part in the riot. In his reports, Colonel Galbraith blamed the Mennonites for the Donegal affray, although one of the men accused of abetting Boyle's murder proudly claimed service in Galbraith's own regiment of Associators in 1776 and the Albrights did not affirm the statement of their property on Donegal tax lists (*Document 169*).

Table 5
LANCASTER COUNTY NON-ASSOCIATORS

Township	Taxables 1775	Taxables 1777	Taxables 1778	Non-Associators 1777
Bart	115		117	22
Brecknock	97		128	61
Caenarvon	97		121	67 (44)[1]
Cocalico	343		449[2]	259 (222)
Colerain	67	84	114	3
Conestoga	117		165	139
Donegal	204		204	147
Drumore	170	229		N.A.
Earl	354	384		239
Elizabeth	68	85	85	84
Hempfield	206	196		196
Lampeter	172	215		175
Lancaster Tp.	40		64[2]	37
" Borough	548	616		N.A.
Leacock	198	266		68
Little Britain	148	136	208	58
Manheim	105		142	106
Manor	137			N.A.
Martic	141		215[2]	31
Mount Joy	106	117		82
Rapho	214	208		175[3]
Sadsbury	70		107[2]	40 (34)[1]
Salisbury	154			34
Strasburg	206	240		136 (129)
Warwick	271	310		265

1. Figures on a duplicate return for 1777.
2. Figures from 1779 return.
3. Includes eleven marked "refractory."

Table 6
PHILADELPHIA COUNTY NON-ASSOCIATORS

Township[1]	Taxables[2] 1779	Non-Associators[3] 1779
Douglass	200	151
Frederick	104	97
Franconia (M,L)	81	72
Hatfield (M)	88	66
Limerick	156	130[4]
Lower Salford (M,B,R,S)	87	72
Marlborough	97	101
New Hanover (L,R)	—[5]	177
Skippack (M)	110	97
Towamencing (M)	88	64
Upper Hanover (S,L,R)	139	124
Upper Salford (L,R)	117	97

1. Returns of Non-Associators exist for only these twelve townships of Philadelphia County. Letters in parentheses indicate the presence of Brethren (B), Lutheran (L), Mennonite (M), Reformed (R), or Schwenkfelder congregations in the township.
2. *Pennsylvania Archives*, 3rd Series, XIV, 471-838.
3. *Pennsylvania Archives*, 2nd Series, XIV, 25-40.
4. These appear to be two separate lists of 52 and 78 names.
5. Included with Frankford tax assessment.

Colonel Galbraith's anger was more reasonably directed at certain other Mennonites who made the task of enrolling in the militia more difficult. The law required the constable of each township to prepare a list of able-bodied men from eighteen to fifty-three years old as the first step in apportioning the militia. Mennonite and Quaker constables refused. In July 1777, John Newcomer of Hempfield, David Eshelman of Conestoga, Joseph Wenger of Manor, and Abraham Whitmore of Lampeter were arrested and jailed in Lancaster. Abraham Hare, who took Abraham Whitmore's place as constable of Lampeter Township, was indicted in August 1777 for refusing to serve in that office. Jacob Hartman of Lampeter faced the same charge in November 1779.[30]

Enforcement of the militia laws bred widespread disaffection in the spring and summer of 1777, ranging from armed resistance to the levying of fines in Baltimore County, Maryland, to an armed rising under the British flag on the eastern shore of Maryland. Officials put responsibility for the Maryland troubles at the door of the Methodists, who were allegedly preaching nonresistance at the request of John Wesley and Lord Dartmouth, just as they blamed Quakers, Mennonites, and Germans generally for disaffection in Pennsylvania. Even without the influence of the peace churches, the first large-scale military draft in American history was bound to cause resentment as men were dragged from their homes to fight for a cause that many did not really support and that many more believed could not succeed. Quakers, Mennonites, and Methodists, each a readily indentifiable minority, provided an easy excuse for the lack of enthusiasm that spread through every religious, ethnic, and economic group in the newly independent United States on the first anniversary of the signing of the Declaration.

Sir William Howe Invades Maryland and Pennsylvania

After weeks of marches and countermarches across New Jersey, Sir William Howe embarked his redcoats on troop transports in New York harbor, intending to take Philadelphia by a seaborne invasion. The summer of 1777 was a season of rumors and alarms that called militiamen from their farms and sent them marching off to Philadelphia and Chester.[31]

On Sunday, August 25, a "distressingly hot, close morning," the British fleet dropped anchor off Cecil Court House at the head of Chesapeake Bay. All day sailors ferried British and Hessian soldiers, sweltering in their heavy uniforms, from the ships to shore, along with the horses, cannon, officers' tents, and all the paraphernalia of war. Militia officers interrupted church services in Harford and Baltimore county communities with news of the British landing and orders for able-bodied men to assemble. According to a Methodist preacher who held the opposite view, many Methodists refused to obey because they believed Christians could not take part in war. He noted in his diary that Colonel Richard Dallam, a Methodist, found substitutes for these conscientious objectors, but that officers treated them with extreme cruelty, even flogging them, "trying to force 'em by stripes to obey."[32] These Methodists remained faithful to their convictions, as did others on the eastern shore who were brutally beaten for refusing to fight.[33] As a result of draft resistance in 1777, Methodists were branded as Tories in Maryland; several preachers suffered from mob violence and an attempted lynching almost took the life of another.[34] In Pipe Creek Hundred in Baltimore County (now Carroll County), men who refused military service on conscientious grounds fled into the woods, while others prepared to resist the militia officers by force.[35]

Disaffection was rampant in Pennsylvania, too, in the summer of 1777 and it was scarcely confined to the nonresistant sects. Richard M'Callister, the York County lieutenant, reported that 200 Germans in the Hanover neighborhood had taken a pledge to refuse military service (*Document 180*). In Berks County, as in York County, Germans opposed the militia law with the same sort of counter-associations as had cropped up with the previous winter. In Berks County 4,000 men were called to militia duty between August 1777 and December 1778, but 2,003 of them were fined for refusing to muster or furnish a substitute. Only 1,781 personally reported for duty and another 310 men provided substitutes.

Stories circulated in Lancaster County of an elaborate conspiracy involving Sheriff John Ferree and two Church of England clergymen who were allegedly plotting to support the British army with a rising in Lancaster and Cumberland. Discovery of the supposed plot led to a rash of arrests.[36]

With an advancing British column in Chester County, the authorities nervously sent the British and Hessian prisoners in Lancaster County to the Lebanon area. Some militia officers were suspicious that Mennonites would interfere (*Document 175*).

It was apparently taken for granted that Mennonites and Quakers were behind every incident of draft resistance, but the actual records of persons indicted for these offenses do not substantiate this charge. Henry Skyles, who was charged with speaking publicly and deliberately "against the public Defence of the said States" in July, 1777, was an Associator and a militia officer in Leacock Township. Martin Heller and Jacob Shearer of Leacock Township, indicted in September for discouraging a neighbor "from Going to Serve in the first Class of the Militia," may possibly have been of Mennonite background, but no one indicted in Lancaster for similar offenses can be positively identified as a member of one of the peace churches.[37] The records of county courts in the Shenandoah Valley of Virginia reveal the same pattern.

The military situation did little to encourage wavering Patriots. On September 11, 1777, Washington's men made a stand on the Brandywine, hoping to halt the British advance on Philadelphia; that night, as badly beaten as an army can be without being totally annihilated, the whole American force streamed down the road toward Chester. A mob of defeated men, infantry colonels and artillery sergeants, Continental soldiers and militiamen, pressing on together without any semblance of brigades, regiments, or even companies was in full retreat toward Philadelphia. The next day Lancaster was in a panic. The Lancaster Jewish merchant Joseph Simon wrote, "We are all in Confusion here, reports every moment in Town that the Enemy are advancing toward this place."[38] Militia moving up to fill the gaps

The fighting on October 4, 1777, swirled around the Germantown Mennonite meetinghouse. British General James Agnew and other casualties are buried in the churchyard. The meetinghouse, still standing, was built in 1770 and is shown in this 1880 drawing as it appeared when the 1775 adjoining building still stood next door.

passed the flotsam of the broken army.

The British gave Washington a brief respite before they followed up their advantage. On September 18 the Continental Congress packed up its papers and set off down the Lancaster Road. Congress made York its temporary capital. The Pennsylvania Assembly settled on Lancaster.[39] On September 26 Sir William Howe's redcoats paraded down the streets of Philadelphia. As Washington regrouped and shifted his battered army to keep key roads open and block any new British advance, peremptory orders went to nearby counties for blankets, food, and men. "A company of soldiers came to take those belonging to the third class" of drafted militia, the Lititz diarist noted on September 27, 1777. "We, however, were spared this time. The young people in our neighborhood have run away, and are hiding themselves in the woods."[40] Draft calls for the fourth, fifth, sixth, and seventh classes followed in rapid succession in October.[41] Before the 1777 campaign was over, every man of military age in Pennsylvania had either marched with his company or had a heavy fine levied on him. Conscientious objectors joined the crippled and the sick in appealing fines that exceeded their ability to pay, usually to no avail.

Even total mobilization could not salvage the military situation. Drafted militiamen from Maryland, Virginia, Pennsylvania, and New Jersey straggled in uneven ranks into Washington's camp on the Skippack Road in the last days of September—reinforcements enough to justify a bold counterattack on the British advance post at Germantown on October 4, 1777. It was a shambles. Not even George Washington's personal courage could stem the rout. The whole army swept past him in full retreat, holding up their empty cartridge boxes to show him why they ran. The defeated army withdrew to Perkiomen Creek, then shifted its base first to Towamencin and finally to the old campsite on the Skippack Road. Every move devastated neighboring farms. The army itself was rapidly disintegrating. Public executions of deserters did little to slow the tide of men slipping away from their encampments, and savage floggings failed to reduce the incidence of drunkenness and looting.

By December the ragged army was totally ineffective. Washington thought of withdrawing to Reading or Lancaster or Wilmington, but the Pennsylvania Assembly and the Supreme Executive Council urgently requested Congress to keep the army close enough to Philadelphia to keep the British from ravaging the state. The army made its final move to Valley Forge in Chester County and camped there through the winter of 1777-1778.

Harsher Penalties on Non-Associators

The long chain of defeats added to the pent-up hostility many people felt toward the nonresistant sects. A militia riot in Lancaster County gave vent to this smoldering anger (*Document 175*). Colonel Galbraith and his sublieutenants had evidently taken it upon themselves to parade conscientious objectors through Lancaster and lock them up until they agreed to serve in the ranks, hire a substitute, or pay their fines. The Supreme Executive Council and other officials of the state government were in Lancaster when this took place, so it is likely that the militia had at least tacit approval for the harassment of the plain people.

Forcible induction into the militia was not common, but fourteen Quakers from Frederick County, Virginia, were compelled to march with their company to the American camp near Philadelphia. Some of the militia officers "with drawn swords pushed the Friends into Rank, threatening they would have their blood if they did not comply." When they refused to shoulder muskets, the captain ordered guns tied to their backs. The Quakers thought it inconsistent to accept food and water from the army while refusing to join its ranks, so they marched 200 miles without drinking or eating. Half of their number dropped from exhaustion on the road, some in Maryland, one in Reading. Seven survived the march to be discharged at Washington's headquarters on the Skippack Road on October 18, 1777.[42] The harsh treatment meted out to them was part of a more general reaction against Quakers in the Shenandoah Valley.

Virginia Mennonites may have suffered at the same time, since "Quakers and Menonists" were invariably linked in the protests from Frederick and Shenandoah County Committees against their military exemption. Mennonite preacher Peter Blosser and Martin Kauffman, a former Mennonite who was pastoring a Baptist congregation, cooperated in strengthening the resolve of conscientious objectors in Shenandoah County. According to tradition, a militia officer named Painter forced Blosser into hiding and generally harrassed the Mennonites.[43] A similar tradition in the Hottel family records that Jacob Hottel (d. 1813) hid in the mountains east of his Page Valley home to escape the draft.[44]

Records of the Meeting for Sufferings of Philadelphia Yearly Meeting give a few instances of individual Quakers drafted into the militia and others imprisoned in jails in Winchester, Virginia, and Lancaster and Chester, Pennsylvania, for refusing to perform militia duty.[45] Individual Mennonites might have had similar experiences.

This monument at Ephrata Cloister marks the burial place of American soldiers who died in the improvised hospital there after the Brandywine Campaign. The Ephrata chronicler noted the death on April 15, 1778, of "John Baer of disease contracted at the hospital. He was a Mennonite preacher." The same record listed the death of "the wife of Johann Baer" on March 20, 1778 "of camp fever" as typhoid was then called.

Mennonites and the Militia System

To what extent did Mennonites and other sectarians participate in militia units during the American Revolution? As can be seen from Table 4, there is an apparent correlation between the number of persons fined as Non-Associators and the relative concentration of Mennonites in a given Lancaster County Township. A comparison between Conestoga Township, where virtually all the males of military age paid fines as Non-Associators, and Salisbury Township, where Non-Associators were a small minority, will make this much evident. But from Tables 5 and 6 it is no less evident that some townships with a very small number of members of the peace churches within their boundaries often had substantial numbers of Non-Associators on their tax rolls. Is this relationship between Non-Associator fines and the historic peace churches real as well as apparent?

In Earl Township, the only one for which we have a religious census in 1775 of Non-Associators, 70 of the 208 persons are listed as "Church" or "Presbyterian" or have no church membership after their names. The larger number of Earl Non-Associators are identified in this list as "Menonist," "Dunker," "Amist," or "Moraven" (*Documents 133, 134*). What proportion of the nonresistants in Earl Township do these 138 names represent? A comparison with the tax lists for the township makes it safe to conclude that virtually *all* the Mennonites, Dunkers, Amish, and Moravians in Earl Township were Non-Associators. The only probable member of one of the sects on the tax lists, but not on the Non-Associator list is John Brubaker, the member of the Committee of Observation from Earl Township. If he was a Mennonite, and there is no evidence that he was or was not, he would be the only member of one of the peace churches who signed the Association in this particular township.

But men may have refused to sign the Association for any number of reasons. The Presbyterian and Reformed Non-Associators are not likely to have claimed conscientious objection to military service.

The 1777 Militia Act put military service on a totally different footing, requiring every man between the ages of 18 and 55 to be enrolled in a class and company, regardless of his politics, his religion, or his lack of enthusiasm for the American cause. All of the Earl Township Associators and all the Non-Associators were thus included in the muster rolls of companies commanded by Martin Bowman, George Rees, James Watson, Emanuel Carpenter, and William Crawford in the Tenth Battalion of Lancaster County Militia. Slightly more than a third of the men in these Earl Township companies actually mustered for training days and drills or responded to the call for service in the field. The others were fined for their failure to comply with the law.

Three men identified in the Ms. list as Mennonite Non-Associators appear on muster rolls as actually doing militia duty. All of the others are listed among the "Delinquents" who incurred fines. Captain Martin Bowman, who accepted a commission at the first organization of the militia in 1777 and commanded a company through 1782, was one of the three Mennonites who chose to serve. Martin Bowman (1730-1816) owned a gristmill and sawmill and 200 acres of good land, ranking him in the upper half of township taxpayers. At a time when many of the Lancaster County justices, both Scotch-Irish and Germans, scrawled letters in their own approximation of spelling and grammar, Bowman wrote excellent English in a copperplate handwriting, carefully crossing out "sworn" and inserting "affirmed" on printed muster rolls, indicating that he had received a better than average education. Nothing can be gleaned from his routine reports that would indicate why this one Mennonite chose to fight for American independence. Peter Burkholder and Jacob Summey were both frequently fined for failing to turn out with the militia, but both men mustered with Captain William Crawford's company three times in 1780. Peter Burkholder owned no land and appealed his fines on the ground that he was too poor to pay them. Economic pressure may have been too much for him. Summey owned a 200-acre farm and paid taxes well above average, so we cannot even guess at his motives for drilling with his neighbors. The names of both men appear regularly on lists of militia fines in 1781 and 1782. These three men are the exceptions that prove the rule. Despite appeals to patriotism and heavy fines, only one man among 138 Earl Township Mennonites, Amish, Dunkers, and Moravians accepted personal military service.

The law permitted men who could not or would not serve personally to hire substitutes. Jacob Carpenter was one of a number of Mennonites who "Refuse to go or to find a Subsidut." John Weaver, on the other hand, appealed his militia fines on the grounds that he had a man serving for him in the army. John Carpenter and Jacob Shirk, who could be Mennonites, but cannot be positively identified as such, also hired substitutes. Casper Shirk and John Showalter asked to be excused from militia fines because they had done a tour of duty in the wagon service and John Weaver, Jacob's son, protested that he was performing an important public service by grinding flour and meal at his mill. A few other delinquents noted that they had always paid the fines for failing to muster, implying that most did not. Among this group were

Mennonites Christian and Jacob Grove, Christian Graff, Sr., and Jacob Summey, Amish John Rupp and Dunker David Kempfer. Committeeman John "Brubagher" also neglected to do duty with his class of militia, explaining that he had served instead as Court Martial man.[46]

Mennonites, Amishmen, Dunkers, and Moravians in Earl Township did not comply with the Militia Act by personally serving their turn or drilling on training days or by hiring substitutes to take their place. Militia and tax records make this evident. Was Earl Township typical of the sectarian response? It is the only Pennsylvania township in which we can identify individuals as Amish or Mennonite or Dunker, but the sects can be recognized in other townships by persons who affirmed rather than swore to the truth of their tax assessment. In Donegal Township of Lancaster County tax and militia records reveal a pattern very much like that in Earl. The Donegal affirmants can all be identified as Non-Associators. Four of them, Daniel Longenecker, John Brenneman, Christian Musselman, and Christian Heagey later provided substitutes or attended one or more drills personally although all four were regularly fined. The rest paid fines. David Leman and George Barr explained to the Appeals Court that they were "conscientiously scrupulous of bearing arms" and asked to be excused the fine as well as military service.[47] In Hereford Township, in Berks County and in Franconia Township in Philadelphia (Montgomery) County the same Mennonite names occur again and again on the lists of absentees and none of them mustered in person or by substitute.[48] Maryland, Virginia, and North Carolina militia records are too fragmentary to permit us to follow the men of a predominantly nonresistant community through each year of the war. "A List of Alexander Machir's Company in the Strasb[ur]g District" of Shenandoah County, Virginia, has this significant annotation in Captain Machir's handwriting: "There are Severall in this List that never appear'd at Musters they Pretending to be in Communion with the Menonists." Ten of the names on this list are of men who signed the petition of Virginia Mennonites to the General Assembly in 1785 and seven others have the same surnames as signers.[49] The pattern is clear. Mennonites refused to serve in the militia and refused to provide substitutes with so few exceptions that they only prove the unanimity of the Mennonite response.

Mennonites in the Wagon Service

Some Mennonites assisted the Patriot cause in various ways that escaped the censure of military service. When barracks and a stockade were built in Lancaster in 1776 to house British prisoners, George Horst and Abraham Hare sold them lime for the barracks.[50] Andreas Bear and Christian Musselman were paid "for billeting and providing for the Militia on their March to Jersey" in November 1776.[51]

The need for horses and wagons was as imperative for the American army as the ammunition and flour barrels they hauled. Commissary officers looked first to the famous Conestoga wagons of Pennsylvania and the powerful draft horses that drew them. That these teams belonged to Non-Associators made it all the more appropriate to press them into service. Mennonite farmers went along to protect their property and bring it safely home. Eve Yoder and Esther Bachman protested in 1778 that their husbands had served as teamsters, along with others in the Northampton County community. The Lancaster County Committee had difficulty obtaining wagons in November 1776 to take British prisoners to Elizabeth, New Jersey, for exchange because of the shortage of fodder in the Jerseys and agreed to pay thirty shillings a day for them.[52] At least some of the wagoners who went with the prisoners and their militia guard were Mennonite, Amish, or Dunker. The 28 teamsters paid by the Lancaster County Committee on their return in January 1777 included John Stauffer, Christian Haldiman, Jacob Witmer, Christian Baughman, Andrew Smith, Christian Huffman, Henry Histand, Benedick Eschelman, Nicholas Bauer, Benjamin Landes, Henry Musselman, Adam Shaller, John Kauffman, Joseph Gingerich, John Erb, Philip Swartz, Adam Kindig, Melchior Brenneman, Abraham Hostetler, Christian Whisler, Peter Miller, and John Musser.[53]

Mennonites as Gunsmiths

Supplying Continental regiments and militia companies with muskets and powder and the other necessities of an army in the field—from bread and beef to shoes and canteens—put no little strain on the resources of the Thirteen Colonies. As in every other aspect of the war effort, the Continental Congress called on the Committee of Safety in each of the Colonies, and the Committee of Safety directed the county Committees of Observation to find whatever was needed.

In the first days after Lexington, the local committees scoured the stores and warehouses and bought up whatever powder and lead was on the shelves in their neighborhood, relying on voluntary contributions to pay for it. The Lancaster County Committee determined to make an immediate census of powder and lead available on May 3, 1775, and the next day agreed to buy it all from the merchants of the borough.[54] The Committee in Frederick County, Maryland, found powder and lead enough to equip Maryland's rifle companies on their march to General Washington's camp near Boston and still leave 276 casks of powder in the Frederick magazine. They bought powder, flints, and lead from the stock of nine Hagerstown, Georgetown, and Frederick storekeepers, but most of it came from the warehouse of the Vandalia Company, a syndicate interested in Indian trade and settlements on the Ohio River.[55] Contributions, many of them in very small sums, met the cost of some of these purchases, but in October 1775 the Frederick County Committee directed their treasurer to pay whatever money was in his hands "towards the discharge of the Bond passed by a former Committee of this County to the Vandalia Company for Ammunition."[56] The same story was repeated with slight variations from colony to colony. Local resources could outfit a company or two, but once the storekeeper delivered his half-dozen fowling pieces and a cask or two of gunpowder there was nothing left to supply an army and no money to pay for the supplies on hand.

The gunsmiths of Lancaster County had made the Pennsylvania rifle famous for its accuracy wherever men and boys gathered to shoot at targets for a turkey or a side of beef. The Pennsylvania Committee of Safety looked to these skilled craftsmen to turn out arms enough. On July 22, 1775, they resolved: "That a Messenger be sent to Joel Ferree of Lancaster County with a Letter from this Committee requesting him immediately to compleat the Guns wrote for as patterns," and to know how many he can furnish of the same kind and at what price.[57] In November 1775 the Lancaster County Committee encouraged all the gunsmiths in the county to produce weapons for Washington's recruits.[58] They appointed a subcommittee to supervise the arms industry and forbade any gunsmith to take any contract from a civilian until he had supplied the needs of the army.[59]

Martin Mylin, a Mennonite, was the first gunsmith to see how the standard German hunting gun could be improved into the Pennsylvania rifle, and many of the craftsmen who fitted gleaming steel rifled barrels to carefully polished stocks were Mennonites of a younger generation. They made rifles that could pick off a deer nibbling on the far side of a cornfield. If a Scotch-Irish frontiersman took one of their rifles from a peg in his cabin and shot an Indian, they need not be concerned; a hammer or a shovel could kill a man in anger. But a military contract was a different matter. Rifles made for the army could have only one purpose. On November 27, 1775, the Lancaster County Committee summoned John Newcomer, a Mennonite gunsmith of Lampeter Township, "he having refused to enter on the work of making muskets." The Committee told Newcomer that he could not continue at his trade, and let him go.[60] Other gunsmiths were less concerned about arming soldiers. William Henry, the Lancaster gunsmith and merchant, and other Moravian riflemakers filled government contracts throughout the war, and a Mennonite gunsmith was given an exemption from the militia because of his contribution to the war effort. The Lancaster County Committee determined in July 1776, when militiamen were marching off to swell Washington's ranks, "that Christian Wenger of Leacock Township Gunsmith and his apprentice Martin Micksell ought to continue at home at that Business and ought not to be marched with Capt. Bare's or Capt. Roland's companies to the Camp in the Jerseys.[61]

Members of the historic peace churches refused to accept military service, to hire substitutes, or to provide weapons for others to use with a degree of unanimity that would never be matched again in any American war. Among Mennonites and Amish, it would be safe to conclude that 95 percent or better supported the traditional teachings on nonresistance in 1776. Violations of the peace testimony were probably related to the degree of secular community pressure on the individual nonresistants, with slightly higher cooperation with the authorities where the religious community had a weaker claim on the loyalty of the individual or was itself disintegrating. The burdens of militia fines added new pressure on both the individual and the religious community. Heavier taxes, some intended solely for Non-Associators, increased that wartime pressure and forced the sects to reexamine the biblical command to render taxes to whom taxes are due.

DOCUMENTS

Disarming the Non-Associators

Rifles and Clothing

If Mennonites and others with conscientious scruples about war could not serve in the companies of Military Associators, Patriots believed they should be willing to furnish rifles and clothing to the Associators. George Ross, a Lancaster County member of the Pennsylvania delegation in the Continental Congress, made this proposal to the Lancaster County Committee in 1775.

Document 151

Gent.

I fear the Military Ardor in our County may in some Measure cool without the Assistance of our Committee in its support. I am informed that the Want of arms will prevent many persons from associating who might be supply'd by those whose Consciences are scrupulous on the Occasion. If therefore the Committee could come to a Resolve to Recommend to Such Persons to lend their Arms to those who are not able to purchase for themselves and take the Capt.s rec[eipt] for them to be returned unless lost in Actual Service, I think it would be of the Greatest use to the Cause and if it could be recommended also to furnish in the Respective townships the poor persons in the Compys. with Hunting shirts many Clever fellows would engage who can't now afford to pay the Expence & bear the loss of time. I have just thrown out these hints & leave them for the Consideration of the Committee.

We have heard of a Detach[men]t of 400 Men sent by Genl. Carleton to retake Ticonderoga whose Garison Consists of 150 Men but a Reinforcement of 400 from Connecticut I hope will arive before Carltons. And we have Ordered another Reinforcement from Connecticut of 1000, being determined to keep the [Fort.] I am with great Esteem

Your very Hble Servt.
Geo. Ross
Philada. 1: June 1775.

P.S. The Quakers & others of scrupulous Consciences here are takeing the Steps I have mentioned to you as to Arms & Cloathing.[62]

Gunsmiths

The Lancaster County Committee, like committees elsewhere in the Colonies, encouraged gunsmiths to produce weapons for the army. Riflemakers who refused to comply with military orders were not to make guns for civilian use. John Witmer, Jr., a member of the subcommittee entrusted with supervision of the Lancaster County gunsmiths, was of probable Mennonite background in Lampeter Township.

Document 152

At the request of the Committee of Correspondence for Lancaster County we the Subscribers went to the Houses of the Diferent Gunsmiths residing in the Borough of Lancaster and made enquiry in what Forwardness the were in making the Muskets which the have undertaken to make, and report as Follows to Viz—

John Graeff has got 15 Musket Locks finished and will Continue Making Locks till he has finish'd 30, which will take him about 2 weeks more and then he'll finish Muskets, has 3 Barrels ready for proof, and was at making a Rifle at the time of inquiry.

John Henry has 12 Musket Locks, 1 Barrell and will now be able to go on with Speed, but was at Rifle work when inquiry was made.

Fred: Veynot at making of Musket Locks has 14 nearly finish'd and the Stocks prepared, but Complains for want of Barrels, no Rifle work appeared when inquiry made.

Peter Roeser making Locks, has but 3 in Hands was not able to do more for want of Tools, which he has provided himself with, and will now be able to be more Speedy—no Rifle work appeared here.

Jacob Kraft has nearly finished 6 Muskets and appears that he has laid all kind of other Gunwork aside but that of making Muskets.

Christ. Breindenhard has not done or prepar'd himself with any thing towards making Muskets

John Miller & Peter Ganter have one Musket Compleatly finish'd (except firing the Bayonet) and have a Number of Musket Locks nearly finish'd, and appear to be in earnest making of Muskets but some Rifle work appear'd here.

Christ: Ish has been at Hewing out Stocks for Muskets has forg'd Some Barrels, is waiting for them to be Bored and Ground by Joel Ferree, no Rifle work appear'd here.

Jacob Deckert & all his Hands but one at Rifle Work, he has 4 Muskets nearly finish'd, is putting old Crown Locks on them, and Says the Locks are as good as those that are made here.

Lancaster Dec. 30th 1775.

Sebastian Graff *Michael Musser*
George Moore *John Witmer Jr.*

Return of Subcommittee respecting the Gunsmiths 30th decr. 1775.[63]

Seizure of Non-Associators' Guns

Congress directed the attention of hard-pressed local committees to the Non-Associators, recommending that guns owned by them be seized for the use of the army. County authorities were not slow to take this hint, as a resolution of the Lancaster County Committee and a letter from the Cumberland County Committee indicate. The minutes of the Bucks County Committee make clear what is implicit in the other documents: at this stage the Non-Associators were to be given a fair price for their guns. (*Documents 153, 154, 155*). Non-Associators refused to cooperate in some instances, requiring the Bucks County Committee to use force in disarming them (*Document 156*).

Document 153

In Congress, March 14, 1776.

Resolved, That it be recommended to the several Assemblies, Conventions and Councils or Committees of Safety of the United Colonies, immediately to cause all persons to be disarmed within their respective colonies, who are notoriously disaffected to the cause of America, or who have not associated, and refuse to associate to defend by arms these United States against the hostile attempts of British fleets or armies; . . . That the arms, when taken, be appraised by indifferent persons, and such as are applied to the arming of Continental troops to be paid for by Congress; and the residue by the respective Assemblies, Conventions or Councils, or Committees of Safety.[64]

Document 154

In Committee at John Bogart's March 27th 1776

A Letter from the Committee of Safety Dated March 19th 1776 requesting that the Associators in this County be properly equiped so as to be in Condition to march at an hours warning and that a strict attention be paid to their Arms and Accoutrements, as there is the greatest reason to apprehend that General How intend's an attack upon this Province.—

Also another Letter from that Committee dated March 23d 1776 requesting this Board to appoint proper persons to purchase such Muskets in this County as are in the Hands of Non-Associators or can be spared, for the use of the Battalions raised in this Province for the Continental Service, and the Batallion of Musketters raised for our provincial defence.

Said Letters having been read and considered RESOLVED that every Member of this Committee do as soon as possible purchase all the

Arms within his respective Township which he shall Judge fitt for service and are not made use of by Associators or their owners shall be willing to part with upon reasonable terms and that the same be delivered to Henry Wynkoop James Wallace or Samuel Smith who are hereby appointed to receive them & sent them to Philadelphia agreeable to the request of the Committee of Safety.[65]

Document 155

At a Meeting of the Committee of Inspection, Observation & Correspondence of & for the County of Lancaster at the House of Adam Reigart the 29th March 1776.

Resolved that it be Recommended to the Non Associators in this County to deliver up their Arms to the Captains of the respective Battalions, on their giving Receipts for said Arms with their Marks and Numbers the Captains aforesaid to be accountable for the said Arms to the Congress, Assembly and Committee of Safety when called upon.[66]

Document 156

In Committee at John Bogart's monday Junly ye 1st 1776

The Committee being informed that sundry persons had refused to surrender the Arms in their posession to the Collectors of Arms, appointed agreeble to A late Resolve of the Assembly of this Province.

Resolved, that, where such Refusal shall hapen in any township, the Militia be called upon for enforcing sd. Resolve, and that the Collectors of the Arms apply to the Colonel or in his absence the next in Command, of the Batallion to which the Associators of that Township belong who shall thereupon give Orders for that purpose to such Officer & such number of Men as he shall aprehend proper and sufficient to enforce the sd. Resolve of Assembly. . . .

The Committee appointed Solomon Gruver & Phillip Sheets, in the room of Theophilus Foulke & Peter Wikle, as Collector of Arms in the Township of Richland. The Collectors of Arms in Rockhil reported they had received 39 Guns.

The Committee adjourned to 10th July 1776.[67]

Disarmed Non-Associators Gather in the Harvest

The Pennsylvania Convention decided that seizing all the guns owned by Non-Associators would be the quickest way to get weapons into the hands of the battalions of Associators. Daniel Roberdeau urged the Convention to disarm the Non-Associators and let them take the place of Associators who were needed to gather in the harvest.

Document 157

July 12, 1776

The following Representation was this day drawn up approved, and Copies directed to be sent to the Committees of Inspection & observation of the Different Counties of this State.

Whereas the Assembly, in one of their late Sessions, did authorise and direct the Committees of Inspection & Observation to collect all the Arms from Non Associators within the Province, which there is great reason to believe has not, in many places, been executed with sufficient care and diligence,

And as there is a pressing and immediate necessity of arming all the Associators in this Province, our Lives, our Fortunes and Liberties, depending probably on the Efforts made this Campaign, the respective Committees of Inspection & Observation are reminded of this Important part of their Duty.[68]

Document 158

Honble. Sirs,

For the Good of the Service, I conceive it my duty to inform you, that the Pennsylvania Militia do not arrive so fast as the urgency of Affairs require. Prior to the meeting of the Convention, and in Compliance with a direction from Congress, I sent off Expresses on the 14th Inst. to the several Counties to hasten their March, and enclosed the request of Congress therein; since which, I received a letter from Northampton dated July 18th containing reasons for their delay which, I presume will be offered generally by the other Counties, i.e. "*Their Harvest, and the Want of Arms*" However pressing and reasonable the first of these may seem, it is, nevertheless, an Illjudged Prudence when duly reflected on, for unless Men turn out to defend the Soil, they run the danger of reaping an Harvest, not for themselves, but their Enemies; who will no doubt be better pleased to find it in the Barn than in the fields. The Convention will render essential Service, could they devise some Mode, that such as are not Associators should get in the Harvest for those who are, and cannot march on that account. All, must bear their part in some line or other, and those who make a Conscience of using the Sword, can offer none against using the Sickle.

The Second Reason, "the Want of Arms," shew the Absolute necessity of disarming the non-associators; which, perhaps, will be best effected, by issuing a Proclamation for all those who are possessed of any to bring them in, Levying a fine on those who do not.

I have ventured to suggest these hints, as the weight and multiplicity of Business before the Convention must greatly engross their Time and Attention, and shall be happy should they tend ever so little to facilitate the March of the Militia; A Circumstance which I cannot Press too often nor too earnestly.

We are unacquainted with the Number of the Enemy who are every day parading in Sight, in parties, on the opposite Shore. Should an Attack, by us, be judged necessary, it undoubtedly ought to be before the Enemy be reinforced, otherwise, it is probable they will attack us, and in either Case our Strength is insufficient. The Men are hearty and orderly, cheerfully disposed to whatever may be for the best, and uneasy for nothing but their Companions.

I am Honble. Sirs,
Yr. most obt. & very humb. Servt.
Daniel Roberdeau

Amboy July 24th 1776.

P.S. Gun Screws to draw the Ca*tr*idges of the Guards are greatly wanted, the want of which occasions a great waste of Ammunition.[69]

The Failure of the Military Association

Bounty Money

County Committees of Observation made every effort to get the Associators in the field in time to help Washington defend New York against the British. A bounty paid to each volunteer was a common method. In Northampton County, Pennsylvania, the bounty money was raised by a special tax on all the inhabitants.

Document 159

At a Meeting of the Standing Committee held at Easton the 9th day of July Anno 1776 Present Lewis Gordon, Chairman, Jesse Jones, Abraham Berlin, Jonas Hartzel, Cornelius Weygandt and Robert Matthews.

Resolved with the concurrance of the Commissioners and Field Officers of this County, that in order to encourage a sufficient number of Volunteers to turn out to serve in the defence of their County to Form a Flying Camp, a Bounty of £3 be given to every able bodied man to enlist in the said Service to the first day of December next, unless sooner discharged by Congress the said Bounty to be raised by Tax on the Inhabitants of this County. . . .

Ordered that the several Battalions in this County find the following Quota of Men to compose said Flying Camp, viz:

1st Battalion to find 92 Privates incl'g non Commissioned Officers
2d Battalion 120 do.
3rd Battalion 57 do.
4th Battalion 49 do.
318

At a Meeting of a Majority of the whole County Committee held at Easton the 17th day of July 1776

resolved. that the Tax agreed upon the 9th Instant to be raised to defray the expences of a Bounty of £3 to be given to those men who are now raising to compose the Flying Camp, be laid on the inhabitants of this County according to the last County Rates at 9d. per pound and that Single men pay at the rate of 6s. per head.[70]

Demands for Service or Fines

The Council of Safety, entrusted with the military preparedness of Pennsylvania, petitioned the Assembly in November 1776 for realistic fines on Non-Associators and for a militia system that would obligate all citizens to personal service or payment of equivalent fines. David Rittenhouse, the renowned scientist, drafted a somewhat emotional statement of the critical need for Assembly action. The legislators responded with a promise to pass the necessary laws. Rittenhouse was the grandson of the first Mennonite minister in the American Colonies and his immediate family included Mennonites and Quakers, so his harsh opinion of the Non-Associators is doubly interesting.

Document 160

To the General Assembly of the State of Pennsylvania.

The Council of Safety beg leave with the utmost respect,

To lay before this House their proceedings in consequence of divers resolutions laid before them by a Committee of Congress, and of several Resolutions since passed by that Honble. House.

In addition to these proceedings contained in the papers now before you, the Council beg leave to say that they have called together such of the Field Officers of the several Battalions, in and near this City as cou'd be Convened on a Short notice to consult their opinion on the best mode of calling forth the Militia of the City and the four Counties mentioned in the Resolve of Congress—they have expressed the utmost readiness to do their duty—but they with us lament the present Situation of our Militia as a public Calamity—it is unsupported by Law—the people are disgusted at the Inconveniences, hardships and Losses which they Suffered in their late Service, while Non Associators were permitted to remain at home in the peaceable Enjoyment of their possessions, and many of them increasing their Wealth by grasping the Trade of the absent Associators, whose patriotic Exertions have been Sneered at, and their hardships & fatigues, and the distresses of their families, insultingly made a jest of—and above all their just & reasonable expectations of seeing the Non Associators obliged to pay something for the indulgences which had been granted them, wholly disappointed. It has been proposed to call out the Battalions of the City and Liberties tomorrow morning, but under these circumstances, with the hardships of a Winter Campaign and the dread of leaving their Families to perish from the want of the necessaries of Life, what can we Expect from the Class of Men, who live from day to day on the produce of their Industry—Mechanicks, Tenants & Laborers, of which to the Scandal of Men in more easy circumstances, the Associators of this State are chiefly composed? Can it be expected, under these discouragements and Insults, that they will Consent to bear the whole Burthen, and face alone the dangers of defending the State? What shall we say to them when they are called together? Shall we depress their Spirits by describing the vast number of our Enemies and assuring them of the certainty of their intention of invading this State? Shall we trace out to them the footsteps of desolation, marked by the feet of insulting Conquerors? Shall we paint to them Cities in Flames, with the wretched inhabitants flying naked before their Enemies? Shall we Remind them of the the heartrending Cries of abused Infants, and the Shrieks of Violated Virgins, their Sisters, their daughters, when no relief can be given them? Shall we describe the Chains which will be heaped upon us, if we are conquered, by men who have lost every Character, but the form of human nature? such things may chill their Blood with horror or produce a rage of momentry Madness, but will it induce men to leave their tender Connexions unprovided for, or to forget the unequal Burthens which have been laid on them? No—They will demand Justice, and we are Convinced that, unless this is granted them, it is in vain that we call on them in this hour of danger.

The Council, therefore are constrained to address this Honorable House, while we may yet do it as Freemen, to unite to us, and to our Bleeding Country, to Postpone all other Business and every other Consideration, however necessary, proper & important in any other Situation of our Affairs it might be and aim at the Single Object of saving your Country from that destruction which will inevitably be the Consequence of the least delay. And they beg leave to intimate, that it wou'd be attended with many Salutary Effects if a fine of ____ Pounds were ordered to be Levied immediately on every able Bodied Man from the age of 16 to 50 years, who shall refuse or Neglect to go into Service when called upon to do so, and that a reasonable assessment be made on the Estates of those above that age ____ proper Persons may be appointed in each Ward of the City and in each Township in the respective (four) Counties to Enrol the Men and to Collect the Fines of Delinquents, with power to levy the same on the goods and Chattells and to make Sale thereof, returning the Surplusage if any, after paying the Charges &c., the Money so raised to be divided among those who shall be in actual Service as Militia — or some other Effectual Plan, adapted to the present Emergency, of making the Burthen of those who stay at home, in some degree equal to that of those, who go into the Field to meet the Enemy. But it is to the Wisdom of their Representatives that the People look up for Remedy of the Evils of which they Complain and from the Vigour of their Counsels, expect to derive that Confidence which is necessary to enable them to Exert themselves in the Common Cause.

As to this Council it shall be their Glory to exercise with a persevering firmness every power they are [document damaged] People to distinguish themselves and do honour to their Country, by seizing with a manly and patriotic Spirit the present glorious opportunity of signalizing their Courage in the defence of Liberty. And they have no doubt but that this Honble. House will on the present occasion, prove to the World, that dangers do not intimidate Freemen but on the Contrary will urge them to do all that is possible for Men who ask the Blessing of God on their Endeavors, and leave Events to him who governs the Universe.

Signed By order of Council
D. Rittenhouse V.P.

Copy.
Representation to House of Assembly
Novr. 26, 1776.[71]

Document 161

November 29th 1776

On motion, resolved unanimously,

That this house will take immediate measures to make effectual the provisions of the late house of Assembly, respecting the Collection of Fines imposed by that house on all Non Associators.

Resolved unanimously,

That this house will, as soon as possible, enact a Militia Law, and take such other Measures as will put the defence of their country.

Extract from the Minutes.

T. Matlack Clk.[72]

December 1776

The desperate situation of the American cause in December 1776, as Howe pressed nearer to Philadelphia, is described in contemporary accounts. The Lutheran pastor Henry Melchior Muhlenberg noted the reaction of the sectarians to news of the British advance.

Document 162

December 17, [1776], Tuesday

The strong spirits among the Independents had now lost everything they had and the Dependents took off their masks and let themselves be seen and heard. The credit of Continental paper money already began to sink in the country. In the city and the country persons busied themselves praising to the skies the extraordinary virtues and unusual courtesy of the British officers and their troops and declaring that everything that had been published about their actions and abuses in Jersey was a lie. The virtue that made the deepest impression, especially upon the sectarians, was the report that the British army had gold and silver and paid cash for everything.[73]

Berks County Associators Reluctant to Join Washington

Richard Tea reported the difficulty of mustering Colonel Daniel Hunter's battalion of Berks County Associators and ascribed some of the reluctance of the men to joining Washington to the influence of "one Abraham Latchar, who calls himself a Menonist." Both Tea and Latschar appear on Berks County tax lists as residents of Hereford Township, so the township meeting was probably in the strongly Mennonite neighborhood of Bally, Pennsylvania. Colonel Hunter's battalion was composed of companies from Hereford, Oley, Ruscomb Manor, Colebrookdale, and West District townships in 1777.

Document 163

Feb'y 21st, 1777

Gentlemen:—

I have been at a great deal of pains and trouble to draw out Colonel [Daniel] Hunter's Battalion (who is absent at the Assembly) in order to join General Washington, when it was the duty of every Man to show his attachment to the general cause: but the influence of the

Torys, (for I can call them nothing else,) in his Battalion, is such, that not Fifty ever met. Agreeable to your orders of the 18th January last, I have sent down one Abraham Latchar, who calls himself a Menonist, and that his conscience will not let him take up Arms. But his conscience does not prevent him from riding to a Township Meeting, when they were called together, in order to make themselves ready, to declare publickly that the Col. had no orders for doing what he did; nay, he went so far as to say that the present Assembly were no legal Body. As to myself, he has made it his Business to go to a publick House, and there declare he would use me ill, if any opportunity offered, for detaining his Gun, which was taken from him as a Non-associator. I have sent the witnesses with the party, and make no doubt the Council will deal with him in a proper manner. There is a number of others, but for want of evidence and people to take them, I am afraid they will escape, who deserve to be confined.

I have a letter from the Speaker of the House, requesting me to go down and take my seat in the Council of the State, but cannot think of leaving my family in the humour the People are in at this time. If some method is not taken to make this Battalion do their duty, I must resign.

I am, Gentlemen,
Your most obedient humble Serv't,
Rich. Tea

The Hon'ble Council of Safety.
Testes v. A. Latschar
John Miller
Peter Zell
Sebastian Lentz
Test. v. Den'l Berlick
Conrad Leffler[74]

Pennsylvania Adopts a Militia Law
Reaction of the Peace Churches

Passage of the Militia Act of March 17, 1777, caused great consternation among the peace churches. Two brief documents in the handwriting of Christopher Schultz of Goshenhoppen (Bally), Hereford Township in Berks County record the reaction of the Schwenkfelders. The original documents in his handwriting are in the Schwenkfelder Library in Pennsburg, Pennsylvania. This English translation by Henry W. Kriebel is reprinted with permission.

Document 164

A candid declaration of some so-called Schwenkfelders concerning present militia affairs, May 1, 1777.

We who are known by the name Schwenkfelders hereby confess and declare that for conscience' sake it is impossible for us to take up arms and kill our fellowmen; we also believe that so far as knowledge of us goes this fact is well known concerning us.

We have hitherto been allowed by our lawmakers to enjoy this liberty of conscience.

We have felt assured of the same freedom of conscience for the future by virtue of the public resolution of Congress and our Assembly.

We will with our fellow citizens gladly and willingly bear our due share of the common civil taxes and burdens excepting the bearing of arms and weapons.

We can not in consequence of this take part in the existing militia arrangements, though we would not withdraw ourselves from any other demands of the government.

WHEREAS at present through contempt of the manifested divine goodness and through other sins, heavy burdens, extensive disturbances by war and divers military regulations are brought forth and continued.

WHEREAS, we on the first of this month made a candid declaration concerning present military arrangements to the effect that we can not on account of conscience take part in said military affairs and

WHEREAS, it seems indeed probable that military service will be exacted from many of our people and that on refusal to render such service heavy fines will be imposed.

Therefore, the undersigned who adhere to the apostolic doctrines of the sainted Casper Schwenkfeld and who seek to maintain the same by public services and by instruction of the young have mutually agreed, and herewith united themselves to this end that they will mutually with each other bear such fines as may be imposed on account of refusal for conscience' sake to render military service in case deadly weapons are carried and used. Those on whom such burdens may fall will render a strict account to the managers of the Charity Fund in order that steps may be taken to a proper adjustment.

Coschehoppe, May 2, 1777.[75]

Substitutes

The refusal of conscientious objectors to serve in the militia made it necessary for the County Lieutenant to provide substitutes.

Document 165

Lancaster, May 15th 1777.

Sir,

In consequence of your late Orders from me to hold the first Class of each Company in your Battalion in Readiness, with Arms and properly Equipt with every other Necessary for your Immediate March to Chester on the Delaware, I Desire that such who fall into that Draught, and Conscienciously scruple the bearing of Arms, may be reported to me by you, or your Order Immediately, that I may find Substitutes in their Room and Stead, and at the same Time make me a list of such who may be willing to serve as Substitutes within your Bounds. Which orders, you'll on all Occasions of the kind, observe.

I have the Honor, Sir, to be your Humble Servant,

Bartrem Galbraith

Col. John Rogers, of the Sixth Battalion
of Lancaster County Militia.[76]

Recruiting

Colonel Bartrem Galbraith, the Lancaster County lieutenant, found it difficult to muster battalions in Mennonite townships.

Document 166

Donegal, May 19th, 1777.

May it please your Excellency,

Sir,

By this I'm to inform you that I have hitherto lost no time in endavouring to embody the Militia of this County, since my appointment, but find it an arduous task—I have got Six Battalions out of Nine formed, the three yet to form, are in the heart of the Mininists Settlements in our County, who tamper with the Constables & prevent them of making their Returns, by which I'm rendered unable to do any thing with them; I have heard it reported that they mean to withstand the measures, but as our Magistrates have been lately Qualified into Office hope to see matters have a different Complection.

Should they withstand the Measures, would be glad of some Instructions from your Excellency how to Proceed. Our Treasurers have refused answering any Draughts as directed by the Militia Act—I have given orders for the Quota of Men demanded from this County to March this week (from the Battalions formed) but as yet have not received an acct. from the different Colonels what arms & accoutriments may be wanting, yet I hope by the time the first division marches, I shall be able to give an account that your Excellency may order them Equipt at Chester. If your Curiosity should lead you to enquire further into the State of this County, I refer you to Col. Lawry who will be with you and can inform you particularly.

I have the honour to be your
Excellencys most Obedient
Humble Serv't,
Bartrem Galbraith.

To His Excellency Thomas Wharton, jun r, Esq., Philadelphia[77]

Document 167

To his Excellencie, Thomas Wharton, ju., Esq., President of the State of Pennsylvania.

Whereas, in Pursueance of your Excellencies appointment to me, directed as Lieutenant for the County of Lancaster, I called a meeting of the Sub Lieutenants appointed to my Assistance, divided the County into nine districts, & issued my Warrants on the 5th day of April last to the Constables of the different Townships for returning to me the Names of all the Male white Persons between the Ages of Eighteen & fifty three Years, as directed by the Militia Law; after the time allowed them for the takeing in those returns of their respective districts, waited at Lancaster for the receipt of them, & rec'd returns for the Borrough and Twenty-four Townships out of Thirty-three; Eight Townships yet remain Unreturned, & seem to give a Violent Opposition to the measures; I believe owing to the poisoned minds of a few Individuals amongst us. I sent a Guard for two Constables within those Townships, (having paid no regard to the Constable's Second Visit) and has oblidged them to give their Bonds and Security by two Sufficient surities in 200£ each, for their appearance at the first Court of Record to be held at Lancaster for the County of Lancaster, for their neglect of duty.

Your Excellencies demand for 600 men from the County of Lancaster, to march to Chester, turned my views another way. I appointed days for the choice of Field Officers within the Several districts returned to me, as well as Company Officers, & drawing the Classes of each Company. Immediately on the appointment of the Colonels transmitted to them a Copy of your Excellencies Letter, as well as the Resolve of Congress, with Instructions to hold the first Class of each Company, in their respective Battalions, in readyness for their March to Chester, at the same time pledging myself to them, that Notwithstanding some part of the Militia of the County remained unembodied equal Justice should be don to them in a Future Day; observing to them, that the backwardness of a few Individuals ought not to be the means of endangering the State. As Officers, they have don their duty; but the backwardnes (or rather Opposition) of a few, exceedingly Impede their March. A number of People, who hitherto have declared against bearing of Arms on Acc' of their Religious Principals, as well others, who have lifted Arms in defence of their Country, have Assembled (as I'm told) in different parts of the County, in order to prevent the March of those ordered to Chester; openly saying, if the first Class marches, we'l be obliged to March in our turn; but if prevented, the matter will be Settled. I therefore thought it my duty to wait of your Excellencie for particular Instructions in this matter, as well as a General rule for the line of my Conduct throughout that department, not being willing to undertake any thing that I was not able to go through with, or receive all necisary Aid. The Militia Law points out to me, that I'm to find Substitutes for all men without exception who refuse to March three days after being called; is this the Case, few men you'll find to Say, it Answers me to stand my draught two Months in the Militia. I have offered ten Pounds per month for Substitutes, but can't procure them for that money, and at the same time a Sufficient number of People Offering their Service. I would be glad to have that part of the Law explained, as to finding Substitutes on as reasonable terms as may be, that I might know the lengths I might Venture to proceed.

Your Excellencies Attention to this Matter, will Oblidge Friends to their Country, & particularly your Excellencies most Obed[t]

Humble Servant,

Bartrem Galbraith, Col. on Com[d.]

Lanc Co'ty.

Philad[a], 2[d] June, 1777[78]

John Newcomer Disobeys Orders

John Newcomer, Mennonite constable of Hempfield Township, was one of several constables who refused to carry out the repeated orders of the county lieutenant to prepare lists of men of military age eligible to be drafted into the militia. This was almost certainly the same John Newcomer as the Hempfield gunsmith who refused to make rifles in 1775.

Document 168

Lancaster County ss. August Term 1777

The Grand Inquest for the County of Lancaster upon their Oath and solemn Affirmation respectively do present that Bartram Galbreath Esquire Lieutenant duly and lawfully appointed and commissioned of and for the County of Lancaster did on the first Day of July in the Year of Our Lord One Thousand Seven Hundred and Seventy Seven at Lancaster County aforesaid issue his Warrant under his Hand and Seal directed to John Newcomer Constable of the Township of Hempfield in the said County com̄anding him in the Name the Com̄on Wealth of Pennsylvania within Ten Days from and after the Date thereof to make a just & true Return to him or the next Sub Lieutenant upon Oath or Affirmation of the Names and Surnames of each and every Male white Person usually inhabiting and residing within the said Township between the Ages of Eighteen and Fifty Three Years capable of bearing Arms—Delegates in Congress, Members of the Executive Council, Judges of the Supreme Court, Masters and Faculty of Colleges, Ministers of the Gospel or Clergy of every Denomination, and Servants purchased bona fide and for valuable Consideration only excepted; And that the said Warrant was on the Day and Year aforesd. at the County aforesd. delivered to the said John Newcomer and the Inquest aforesd. upon their said Oath or Affirmation aforesd. respectively do further present that the said John Newcomer of the said County of Lancaster Yeoman Constable of the said Township of Hempfield on the Twentieth Day of July in the Year aforesd. at Lancaster County aforesd. and within the Jurisdiction of this Court did neglect to Execute the said Warrant against the Form of an Act of General Assembly of the Com̄on Wealth of Pennsylvania in such Case made and provided, to the evil Example of all others in the like Case offending, and against the Peace and Dignity of the same Common Wealth.

John Morris Jr.
Atty. for the Com̄on Wealth

Test. p. Respublica [Witnesses for the State]
Bartram Galbreath
Sworn JMjr
Christopher Crawford[79]

Resistance to Militia System

Resistance to the new militia system exploded into violence in Donegal Township in June, 1777 when Samuel Albright killed a militiaman named Cornelius Boyle in a scuffle that began over an attempt to collect militia fines.

Document 169

Donnegall, Lancaster County, June ye 27th, 1777

To His Excellency *Thomas Warton,*
Comander and Chief in and over the State of Pennsyla.

Dr SIR:—I have been in a very poor State of health ever since I came Home, the cold and Cough I had when in Town, hath increas'd by the wet weather I had Coming home, which hath put me in a Slow fever, But if it please God I get any better in health, I Shall go to Town to the Council and give what assistance I can. the oposition given to the laws, by the Dutch, at Lenth hath Broken out into open Rebellion, they had threatned so much and bound themselves to each other, that any Constable that would levey on their Goods, for the fines impos'd by the Melitia law, accordingly on the 25th Instant, Colonel Lowrey Sent an Officer and Six men with the Constable, by order of a Magistrate, to Levy for the fines due by one Saml. Albright, who had got entiligance of their coming, and got together Twelve men and a number of women Armed with Sithes, Coulters, & Pitch forks, and the first stroke given struck one of the guard with a coulter, behind his back, which split his skul a bout 4 or 5 Inches, the rest of the guard thought they were all in danger of their Lives, were forsed to fire on the rebels, and Shot three of the ringleaders, but having no more Amunition, but what first loaded their Pieces, and some had none at the first, was Obliged to flee for their lives till the would git Amunition, yesterday we got evidence against the Twelve that were at the rescue, Likewise 23 More that were in League with them, we are Obliged to keep the Militia that were on marching orders, till we suppress this Rebelion these three that are Shott ar of these Consientious People menonensts who Preten non resistance, and persive Obedience, and there is about 15 or 20 More of the Same sact in the publick Cabal. But I think the greater part of that sact together with Zealous friends, are Secretly fomenting the whole. Persuading these other silly People of the Dutch, that if they resisted, and stand out that we are not able to put the Laws in Execution against them. Think it would be advisable when these 12 are taken that were in the riot, Should be taken to Philadelphia Goal, for Lancaster Inhabitats for the most part as you may see, by their Opositions of the Laws, and having such a large number of the British Prisoners Like wise such a large number of the hesians who are Chiefly out amongs't those Disaffeted Jermans, your Excellencies advice in this would be of much service, Lietenant Galbraith, Colonel Lowrey, & the rest of they Fild officrs of his Battalion, and what few Magistrates are here, Get Little rest night or day, endavouring to enfrce the Laws, but I hope if we had those Twelve sent to Philada, and the Heads men of the others in oposition, put under Bail to Answer the nex Court, I think our Affairs would go on afterwards with more regularity. I have sir the honour of being your excelencies Sincere friend and Humb'l Ser't.

John Bayly.[80]

Document 170

May it please your Excellency. Donegal, 27th June, 1777.

Sir—In consequences of your Sundry orders to me relative to the embodying & Marching the Militia of the County of Lancaster to Chester on Delaware, I have used my utmost efforts. I find in a General way that it must be substitutes chiefly who are to march from this County, and am unhappy in finding an Opposition in Various parts of it (as to putting the laws in execution) which I believe owe's to the backwardness of the leading People of the Borough of Lancaster; Notwithstanding I bro[t] up Commissions, when last in Philad[a] for them, not one yet Qualifyd; which is a means of preventing me from carrying the Militia Law into its proper force there as well as in the adjacent parts thereto. Such parts of the County as have Magistrates, I have made my application to them & have set the matter properly on foot. I'm under a needcessity of detaining such who I have as yet employ'd Substitutes, for the Protection of the Civil Authority untill I receive your further Instructions.

On the Twenty fifth Inst., James Bailey, Esq., one of ye Magistrates for this County, & who lives within the Neighbourhood of those Opposers reported to you by me when in Philad (upon application from me) proceeded to recover fines on delinquents for days of Exercise, The Constable declaring himself unwilling to Serve in that Capacity unless protected by a Guard of men which was granted by Col. Lowry, on request of the Magistrate; went to the House of Michael Albright, father of Samuel Albright, a person who was one of the delinquents (& had been summoned before, with others, as directed, but refused to appear and damning the Constable, saying who made such Magistrates & such Laws,) the Constable, reading to him his Execution & telling him that he must have Body or goods & requested him to goe peaceably along to the Magistrate, during which conversation there assembled a number of Riotous persons to the amount of 12 or 13 (the constables guard was 6 men) when the said Samuel refused going, and at the same time desireing the guard to stand off, the first man who touched him should be a dead man, upon which the guard surrounded him, when one of those Rioters fellows who had assembled to his Assistance, struck one of the Guard with the Coulter of a Plough, & knocked him down (who died in a few hours) began the Fray.

The Guard wounded three of them badly, among which was Albright. The Magistrate proceeded, held an Inquest on the dead Body and the Jury found it murder—there is as yet but one of them taken, who is sent to Goal; the others are fled or secreated by their friends & not yet taken. Special Warrants are out & I'm determined to have them taken, as well as enforce the Law at all events, but will be obliged to goe slowly on for want of peace Officers. I have on the examination of the evidences on oath, on the Inquest, found the names of a number of people who were the first exciting of the present Opposition, against whom I expect to proceed immediately & have them bound over; I shall wait with patience your answer to this & expect you'l send me Some, & am obliged to give most of the Substitutes £50 for the draught of two months. I have at the same time inclosed you the deposition of Thomas McArthur, a reputable man of Paxton Township against one Davis Hatter who lives next door to the Sign of the Bare in Market Street, Phila. Sir, it is with regret I behold the people in general with us and among us, in that Carracter of Contractors, Qr. Masters, & who are from every thing that appears, disaffected & cannot be entituled to the Carracter of friends to their Country, as conduct of this kind is productive of jealousys & doubts to many people of this State, I could wish that such matters were enquired into, in justice to the Continent, and for the future suppress such Villanies.

I have the honour to be your Excellency's
most obedient H'le Serv't,
Bartrem Galbraith,[81]

Denunciation of Nonresistants

Thomas Wharton, Jr., president of the Supreme Executive Council, responded to the reports from Bayley and Galbraith with a denunciation of the nonresistant sects, who seemed to him to be denying the grounds of their exemption from personal service.

Document 171

Jno. Bayley, Esqr., In Council, July 5, 1777.

Yours of the 27th of June came to hand, by which I was informed of the violent conduct of those people who make such loud declarations against the lawfulness of repeling the open and professed Enemies of our Natural and civil rights as freemen, and the dangerous length they have carried their resentment to, denying by their cruel and Illegal conduct (in this case) that pacifick disposition under which they have hitherto screened themselves, and been exempted by the laws of their Country from personal service under the military population. The daring opposition given to Government by these people in this unhappy instance, ought to stimulate every officer in the civil department to vigorous exertions of his duty in the preserving of peace and good order in his Neighbourhood, to convince our internal Enemies that the laws of the state must and will be supported, and as well to strengthen the hands of the honest and upright that they have a place of security to fly to for protection in all cases. Your opinion with respect to sending the most notorious leaders in the late riot to Philad. jail appears to be founded in reason, as it may be attended with good effects on several accounts. By strictly pursuing the wholesome regulation the late acts of Assembly has provided for the preservation of our free and Independent state, I make no doubt of soon seeing peace & good order restored. I have wrote more fully to Col. Galbreath on this subject, as your attendance in Council is greatly wanted, having as yet only a bare quorum of members; this being our present situation, I need not use any further argument to excite your speedy return.

I am Sir, your &c.[82]

Desire to Suppress Resistance

The county lieutenant appealed to the Lancaster County Committee for ammunition to be used in suppressing "some dangerous combinations which appear in the upper parts of the county."

Document 172

At a meeting of the Committee of Observation and Inspection at the House of Mr. Baker, the 28th of June 1777.

Present, Jasper Yeates, Christopher Crawford, John Miller, Michael Musser, George Moore, Adam Reigart, William Bowman, William Atlee.

William Atlee in the chair.

On the application of Colonel Galbraith for a quantity of ammunition out of the publick stores here to enable him to suppress some dangerous combinations which appear in the upper parts of the county in opposition to the Laws of the Commonwealth, It is the unanimous opinion of the Committee that it be recommended, and it is recommended to the Commissioners of the county, and such other persons as now have the custody or charge of the publick ammunition in this

County to deliver to Colonel Galbraith such a reasonable quantity of powder and lead as shall be thought necessary for him for these purposes, Mr. Galbraith here in committee engaging to place such ammunition into the hands of some one or more of the Civil Magistrates of this County, to be by him or them placed in the Hands of such prudent Persons as he shall appoint to assist the Civil officers in the execution of their Duty, and the utmost Caution is recommended by the Committee to be used by the Magistrates in the disposition thereof.

By order

Will. Atlee, Chairman.[83]

More Arrests

Michael and John Albright, father and brother of the accused murderer, were arrested as accomplices three days after the riot.

Document 173

Lancaster County ss.

Whereas there was on the twenty sixth Day of June last proof made by a variety of Evidences upon Oath that Michael Albright and John Albright the Prisoners now in Custody of the Constable is charged to be accomplices or Abettors in the Death of a certain Cornelius Boyle and also resisting the Laws of this State,—

You are therefore hereby commanded in the Name & by the Authority of the Common Wealth of Pennsylvania to receive into your Custody the said Michael Albright & John Albright and them safely keep until regularly discharged for which this shall be your sufficient Warrant given under my hand & Seal this 28th of June 1777.

James Bayly

To the Keeper of Lancaster Goal

A true Copy. *Michael Immel Golar*[84]

Petitions for Clemency

Michael Albright and John Nicholas, both imprisoned as accomplices to the murder of Cornelius Boyle, petitioned for clemency. The Nicholas petition is of interest as proof that he was not a conscientious objector.

Document 174

To His Excellency the President and Supreme Executive Council of the Commonwealth of Pennsylvania

The Petition of Michael Albright late of Donnegal Township in the

County of Lancaster now a Prisoner in the Gaol of Lancaster County aforesaid

Humbly Sheweth

That your Petitioner is confined in the Gaol of the said county of Lancaster by virtue of a Mittimus of James Bayly Esquire on a charge of being an Accomplice or Abettor "in the Death of a certain Cornelius Boyle, and also resisting the Laws of this State," a Copy of which Mittimus is hereto annexed.

That your Petitioner hath long resided in the said County of Lancaster, hath a Wife and seven Children, & hath always endeavoured to conduct himself so as to merit the good Will of his Neighbours & sustain the Character of an honest Man & useful Member of the Community.

That the unhappy Affray which occasioned the Death of the said Cornelius Boyle also deprived your Petitioner of his eldest Son, who was there wounded and is since dead of his Wounds. And tho' your Petitioner is charged with being an Abettor, yet he hopes on his Tryal to show to the Satisfaction of his Country, that he used every means in his Power to prevent mischief and hinder the effusion of Blood.

That the imprisonment of your Petitioner added to the death of a Son, grown capable of assisting him in the decline of Life, hath brought his Family into the greatest distress—to alleviate which would in some sort lighten his own Griefs, which now lay heavy on him.

He is therefore anxious, as well for the sake of his distressed Wife and surviving Children, as for his own Ease, to be with his Family, untill the time which shall be appointed for his Tryal—if he may be admitted to Bail—but as there are no Judges yet commissioned to whom he can apply or by whom he can be bailed, he is constrained to look up to the Honourable the President and Council

And prays that he may be released from his confinement & suffered to assist his unhappy Family, on giving Security to appear and answer the Charge against him, at such time and place as shall be appointed for that purpose.

In the mean time he will demean himself as a good subject of the Commonwealth ought to do.

And will ever pray &c.

Michael Albrecht

Lancaster Gaol July 25th 1777.

We the Subscribers beg leave to recommend the above named Petitioner to the Notice of the Honourable the President & Executive Council.

Jas. Bayly
Alexdr. Lowrey
Bartrem Galbraith
William Henry
John Hubley
Will. Atlee
A. Hubley[85]

Document 175

To his Excellency the President and Supreme Executive Council of the Commonwealth of Pennsylvania

The Humble Petition of John Nicholas Late of Donnegal Township in the County of Lancaster now a Prisioner in the Goal of Lancaster County Aforesaid Humbly Sheweth

That your Pettr. is confin'd in the said Goal by virtue of a Mittimus granted by James Bailey Esquire on a Charge of being an Accomplice or Abettor in the death of a Certain Cornelius Boyle, and also resisting the Laws of this State.

That Your Pettr. has long resided in the said County of Lancaster and has a Wife and three Children, has served last Campaign *in the Flying Camp* as a Militia Man under Coll. Galbraith and has always endeavour'd to conduct himself so as to merrit the Goodwill of his Neighbours and sustain the character of an honest Man and useful member of the Community, but notwithstanding your Pettr. is charg'd with being an Abettor, yet he hopes on his Tryal to show, to the satisfaction of his Country, that he is utterly innocent of charge alledg'd against him.

That your Pettrs. confinement is greatly distressing at this time on Acct. of his Wife and Children and the business of his *Plantation* trade which requires his immediate Presence at home untill a time shall be appointed for his Tryal, and hopes his being enlarg'd from confinement will be no inconveniency to the Laws and Governmt. of this State as he is ready and willing to give undeniable Security, for his future Appearance on any Tryal that may be hereafter apointed to try him touching the Premises.

That as there are no Judges yet commission'd to whom your Pettr. can apply or by whom he can be bail'd he is constrain'd to look up to the Honourable the President and Council relying on their Justice and Compassion in the Premisses.

May it therefore please the Honoble the President and Council to take the distrss'd circumstances of your Pettr. into consideration and Order him to be discharg'd from confinemt. on giving Security for his future Appearance and he as in duty bound will Ever Pray.

Johannes Nicholas

Lancaster Jail
July 27th 1777

We the Subscribers beg leave to recommend the within named Pettr. to the Notice of the Honourable the President and Executive Council.

Jas. Bayly *Cas. Shaffner*
Alexdr. Lowrey *William Henry*
J. Hubley *William Baussman*[86]

Draft Resistance

Draft resistance was widespread in 1777 as Pennsylvania's new militia system took shape. The York county lieutenant reported threats to militia officers.

Document 176

Hanover Town, July 4th, 1777.

Sir,

Altho I have don Everything in my Power, there still Remains severall Parts in this County I Cant Get arrainged, they will not meet to chuse ofesers, nor will any that we make Choice of serve, in som parts they Carry the matter so farr as to threaten the lives of the officers that have Excepted, there is now some w t me for arms and amonition, & say they must Leave there Dwellings if not suported, men they can Raise they are threatened there houses & windoes drove to shatter in the Night, this County is Quite Destitude of arms, & not many Places in more need. I hope y[r] Honour will be pleased to send a suply of the Above Artickles as soon as Posable.

As soon as I have Got a Return of the offusers I shall send them, which shall be as speedily as posable. Indeed I Expect nothing less than when this long tailed oath is to be imposed on the People in many parts of this County we shall have som truble on hand, as many are of opinion it is Verry Impolitick at Present. I am w th

Due Respect y Honours most obedient h'le Servent,

R[d] M[c]Calester.

To The Honorable Thomas Wharton, Esq'r, President, Philadelphia.[87]

The Militia Act

The Militia Act adopted by the Pennsylvania Assembly in 1777 required every adult male to be enrolled in a military company. The companies were then subdivided into classes, each to serve in turn when the company was called to active duty. Under the 1777 law, conscientious objectors were supposed to furnish substitutes or pay a heavy fine. The law provided for an appeals board to meet periodically at different places in each county to hear and adjudicate appeals against militia fines. An Appeals Docket for Lancaster County 1777-1779 in the Pennsylvania State Archives is typical of the many extant documents of this type. It is a record of courts of appeal held at Elizabethtown, Blue-Ball, Weylands Mill, and at the Court House in Lancaster, beginning July 28, 1777. The following extracts are from appeals from Warwick Township companies commanded by Captains John Gingrich, George Volck and George Feather and attached to Colonel John Huber's Ninth Battalion of Lancaster County Militia.

Document 177
[December 3, 1777]

John Miller 5th Class Feathers Co[mpany]

Says that he makes Matter of Conscience of bearing Arms, but at the same time is willing to render his Services in any other way, for the protection of his Country that may be Loocked upon Equitable & Just in Lieu of his Military Service, *Taylor*

Judg[men]t—to Serve his two months in making Cloaths for the Continent or pay Twenty pounds fine—

David Merkey 8th Faulk Says that he has a bad rupture, & is also lame in his

Arms by times, Conscientious—*Plantation*—

Judg.[t]— to do two months garision [sic] duty or pay thirty pounds—

Jacob Risaire 1st Ginghey Says that he is not Sick. But aledges he is
not able to pay his fine, has a plantation from his father paying
him the third Bushel as rent
Conscientious—

Judg.[t]—to perform two months tour of duty or pay the Sum of thirty five pounds—

Jacob Blickenderfor 2[d]. Feathers hearty & in good health but is Scrupulous of

bearing arms from religious principals has a small family, &
not able to pay the fine—*Labourer*—

Judgt— to perform two months duty or pay fifteen pounds

Leonard Shartzer 3d Feathers, Says that when he gets Cold he is Subject to

the Collick but appears well, Scrupulous Bearing arms, complains
of Poverty has a Small Plantation from his Father rented

Judg.[t]—to do two months duty in garrision or pay Twenty pounds—

Dec. 4, 1777 appeals
Christian Blickensderfer 3.[d] Feather, Apealed for by his father, who says that
he has got his leg cut with an Ax, that he cant walk is poor and not able, Conscientious
Judgt.—to find a substitute for two months duty or pay fifteen pounds—
John Henry Baugh 2[d] Feather, Says his principles will not admit his bearing Arms, has made considerable Improvements and
yet is in debt, think the Battalion fine beyound
his ability, but willing to
pay as adjudged
Auger maker
Judg.[t]—to find a Substitute for two months duty or pay twenty pounds
David Tannenberger 2 d Feather, his prinsiples forbids his
bearing of arms an Organ-Maker to trade, no Bussiness
done in that way, thinks he would not be able to pay the
fine but willing to pay as adjudged—
Organ Maker
Judg. t—to find a Substitute for two months duty or pay thirty pounds—
Daniel Kristt 3[d]*do* Principals as above, a poor man and is not
able to earn any more than what maintains his family, but
willing to pay according to his Ability—
Judgt.—to Serve two months garrision duty—by Substitute, or pay fifteen pounds
John Shank 6th or 7th *do* Principled as above, Says he is a
single man has nothing but what he Earns by his trade,
willing to pay as adjudged.
Nailer
Judgt.—to do two months duty by substitute or pay twenty pounds.[88]

Sir William Howe Invades Maryland and Pennsylvania
Nonjurors Disarmed

The imminent threat of British invasion led Pennsylvania authorities to order the nonjurors disarmed.

Document 178

In Council, July 31, 1777

Sir,

As the enemy is approaching this state and arms are wanting to pu into the hands of the militia to defend it—it becomes absolutely necessary that those who have not taken the oath of allegiance should be disarmed, and their arms made use of by those who are willing at the risque of their lives to defend their liberties and property.

I therefore, in compliance with a law of this state, request you will instantly disarm all those who have not taken the oaths aforesaid.

I am with respect, Sir,
Your very humble servant
T[homas] W[harton] Prst.

To Col. William Henry, July 31, 1777.[89]

Hessian Prisoners

With the British landing at the head of Chesapeake Bay, the Hessian prisoners in Lancaster County had to be removed to a more secure area. Joshua Elder feared that Mennonites would attempt to conceal these prisoners.

Document 179

Paxtang, 24th August, 1777.

SIR: I this Moment by Express from Col. Galbraith at Lancaster, have Intelligence that the Enemies Fleet have come far up Chesapeek-Bay, & are landing their Troops above Baltimore—he orders me to have the Militia in my District in Readiness to March in a Moment's Warning with such Arms as can be procured, those who have no Arms must march without them & will be supplied at Lancaster, he does not mention any particular Number of Classes but seems to Intimate the whole of the Militia. Now as your Battalion has always been understood to be in that District I expect you'll pay particular attention to the above orders & have your Battalion duly Notified & in the utmost Readiness until further orders—He & Mr. Atlee likewise Inform me that it is the orders of the Board of War to have the prisoners removed from Lancaster to Reading & Lebanon. You'll therefore have all the Hessian Prisoners (& others if any) in ye Battalion Collected as soon as may be & sent to Lebanon under a proper Guard where Messrs. Ort, C. Grub & Thom will Receive them & take Charge of them, you'll take Care to keep a List of the Prisoners & let the officer of the Guard take these gentlemen's Rect for them & how many when Delivered & forward the List to me. I imagin the Prisoners, if any in your Bounds, are Chiefly among the Menonists, which will require you to be very particular in Collecting them as no Doubt many of them will Endeavour to Conceal them if possible.

I am Sir with the utmost Regard,
Yr very Humble Servant,
Joshua Elder.
Col. *John Rogers.*[90]

Pennsylvania Germans Continue Opposition

The threat of invasion did little to remove the objections to the militia system among Pennsylvania Germans. Resistance in York and Lancaster was not limited to the refusal of conscientious objectors to serve in their battalions, but represented the German church people as well.

Document 180

Lancaster County ss.

To Alexr. Moharry

Whereas Complaint hath been made Upon oath by Henry Folts, Before me, one of the Justices of the Commonwealth of Pennsylvania, Assign'd to keep the Peace for the County of Lancaster,

That Martin Heller Yeoman & Jacob Sheerer Yeoman Both of Leacock Township Did Greatly Strive to Discourage him the sd. Henry Folts from Going to Serve in the first Class of the Militia of the Company to Which he Belongs According to Law, by asking him How much Wages he Would Receive pr. Month, Telling Him at the Same time that General How Would Do Better for him then that, and at the Same time Said that he Was the Only Buisy Body that was in all that Neighbourhood, Against the Peace, Safety and Dignity of the Commonwealth.

These are therefore in the Name of the Commonwealth To Command an Require You to take the Bodys of the said Martin Heller and Jacob Sheerer And them Bring before me or the Next Justice to Ans: the Premises, of this fail not.

given Under my hand and Seal this first day of Septr. Anno Domini 1777

Henry Slaymaker[91]

Document 181

York, Septr 3d, 1777

Sir,

My former Letter under all its Gloom, hath set forth but a small part of the Conduct of some of the leading Men in some parts of the County; And hath been entirely silent in Respect of what may unles timely prevented be yet feared from Combinations actually set on Foot, (tho' conducted with such Secrecy and Caution that we cannot so fully get at the Bottom of them as to deal with the Subjects thereof in a legal way). In Order to oppose the Operations of Government, particularly in Respect to the Collecting of the Fines, incurred by the Non-associators, under the Resolves of the late Assembly, and appointed to be levied by Acts of the present Assembly, and the Substitution Monies made payable under the Regulations of the Militia Law, by those who are the Subjects thereof and who do refuse their personal Service.

A Meeting it is certain hath been held amongst the Germans near M^c^Callister's Town, (properly Hanover) whereat as some do say One Hundred Persons were present, and it is reported the Party in the Secret are composed of 500 Persons, who either are or will become bound together to resist even unto the shedding of Blood and taking the Life, of any Officer or Person, who shall or may attempt to distrain or otherwise use any coercive means for Recovery of the Fines so incurred, and I am farther told, they have threatened the Lives of Messrs. M^c^Callister and Slagle, but upon strict Enquiry I cannot be informed of any one Person who will avow to be of the Party, and as the Matter hath not yet been put to Trial, cannot determine to what Height it may be carried. But in my humble Opinion, it will be difficult to get either Collector or Constable to do and perform their Duties, without having at the Beginning a sufficient Force to protect them.

I am,
Sir,
with due Respect,
your most obe^t^ h^ble^ Servt,
Arch^e^ M^c^Clean

To The Honourable George Bryan, Esquire, Vice President of the Supreme Executive Council, &c.

Pr. Favour of Michael Hahn, Esq'r.[92]

Motives for Resistance

An anonymous writer in a Baltimore newspaper described the various motives that led men in Pipe Creek Hundred in modern Carroll County, Maryland, to resist the militia draft and hide in the woods.

Document 182

To the lawless Banditti of TORIES lately assembled in Pipe-Creek Hundred, Baltimore County.

When you were requested to defend that cause, in which every honest man is warmly interested, your answers were, "*Conscience forbids us to take up arms, we cannot leave our plantations untilled, nor our wives and children to mourn in our absence.*" You had numberless objections, some of you were too old, others too young, some too deaf, and many of you lame, yet in your own sweet cause even miracles revived. The lame were made whole—the deaf heard the smallest whisper of sedition—time took away years from *fifty* and gave them to *fifteen*—wives, children, and plantations were of little consequence, and even CONSCIENCE (that insolent intruder on mankind) was "seared with a red hot iron"; happy men! to whom conscience is so gracious. . . .

News arriving that the English were near Philadelphia, you industriously circulated a report that the Continent was lost. This was the time to perpetrate your horrid design; you imagined the insurrection would become general. Providentially, for the innocent, as well as for yourselves, a universal cowardice prevailled in your camp—the very sight of a small party of militia effectually struck a panic through the whole—some were taken and put under confinement, some retired to their homes in confusion, and others are intirely gone off. Thus will heaven ever defeat the base schemes of wicked, ungovernable men. . . .

AMERICA.

October 10th, 1777.[93]

York County Units Lack Men

County Lieutenant Richard M'Callister reported his efforts to embody the remaining classes of militia, despite the number of Quakers, Mennonites, and Brethren in York County, who made it hard to fill up these units to the required strength.

Document 183

Hanover, Nov[r] 12th, 1777.

Sir,

Your Excelency Menchened in y[r] Last Letter to me that if the 4th & 5th Classes dident turn out pritey Generally then the other 2 Clas[ses] should be sent forth also.

These 2 Classes have turned out Past Expectation, som parts the Class made up a Company, but for the Greatest Part I threw two Classes together where they were like to be small Companeys, all made one large one & made the ofesers cast lots who should go.

But in the whole I belove about one half or som better is gon; those two Classes perhaps 3 parts in 4, the Grate Number of Quakers

Mananest & Dunkers in this County ocations the Companey to be so hard to be filled up, the others in the uper end of the County which is mostly Irish People and Low Dutch goes Prette-Generall; the People Complain much of being hurryed out in such Grate Numbers as they say, Indeed maney will not beleve it is the orders of Council but my own doings; However I shall comply with my orders as far as Posable, & should be glad to know if the other two Class is to have orders to march, which shall be don Imedity. I have purchased all the good arms I could git since I Rec[d] y[r] orders & put them into the hands of good men, there one arms & blankets appraised &c. So many scrupolis people as we have ocation much hiring and deter the busiess much.

I am,
Y[r] Excellencies Most ob[t]s[t]
Rd M[c]Calester.

Directed,
To His Excelency Thomas Wharton, Esq[r], President of the Exe[c] Council[94]
Lancaster.

Virginia Militia Act

Virginia enacted a comprehensive militia act at the May 1781 session of the General Assembly. Its provisions included one dealing with the case of Quakers and Mennonites who refused to serve and refused to obtain substitutes.

Document 184

And be it enacted, That where any quaker or menonist shall be allotted to any division of the militia, who is to perform the succeeding tour of duty, he shall not be compelled personally to serve the same, but it shall and may be lawful for the commanding officer of the militia of said county, to cause to be levied on all the society of quakers and menonists in such county according to their assessable property, by warrant under his hand directed to the sheriff or any person or persons whom he shall appoint, such sum or sums of money as he shall think sufficient to procure a substitute for each quaker or menonist whose tour of duty it is, and the money when collected s..all be deposited in the hands of the commissioners of the money tax, who shall pay the same on a warrant from the commanding officer of the said militia, to such substitute or substitutes as may be employed for such quaker or menonist, and the overplus (if any) shall be returned to the said quakers or menonists in equal proportion to their different advancements or credited in their next money tax; and in case the money so collected shall not be applied as above directed before the next assessment, the said commissioners shall allow the same in discount of their several taxes. Any sheriff or collector failing to perform his duty as above, shall forfeit and pay five thousand pounds of tobacco, and each of the said commissioners who shall fail to perform his duty, to be recovered on motion by the said commanding officer of the militia in any court of record, giving ten days previous notice. The fines thus recovered shall go towards satisfying the quakers or menonists who shall be aggrieved thereby, and the overplus toward enlisting a soldier to serve in the continental army.[95]

Wartime Petitions

Two petitions from the Shenandoah Valley, one from Rockingham County Mennonites and Dunkers and one from members of the Mennonite Church in Virginia, relate their wartime experience. The first of these petitions is damaged, but still readable and the entry in the Assembly Journal makes its meaning clear.

Document 185

Also a petition of the Societies of the people called Menonists and Dunkards, in the County of Rockingham, setting forth, that the tenets of their religion forbidding them to take up arms, they have failed to attend the musters and other military calls in the said County, and have been compelled to pay fines for such neglect, and praying that an Act may pass exempting them from all military duty.[96]

Document 186

To the Honorable the General Assembly of the State of Virginia The Petition of the Societies of the People called Mennoneists and Dunkards in the County of Rockingham Humbly Sheweth

That while we pay the greatest Respect to so Venerable a Body and wishing to Support Government and Comply with the Laws of so good a Legislative Body as far as we possibly can Suppose them consisting with the principles of our Christian Religion, but as it is well known we have long time laboured Under the incumbrance and Grievance of a Military law requiring us to lift up Arms and perform Military duty contrary to the dictates of our Consciences and the principles of our Religion and often tending almost to the Ruin or at least greatly to the prejudice of many poor Familys amongst us; while Fines are exacted off of us [ ]* non compliance with Military Orders, which we can in [ ]

voluntarily comply with as has been evident [ ] late war; rather wishing to enjoy Peace of Conscience [ ] we purchase it at the Expence of our whole Esta[ ] Humbly pray, the Honorable the Generall Assem[ ] take our case into their serious Consideration and [ ] Cause of our Grievance by Granting to us the [ ] & indulgences as have already been granted to [ ] called Quakers in the same case, And your Pet[ ] in duty bounds shall Pray &c.
November ye 2nd 1784

Henrich Shang	*Peter Crumpacker*	*Christian Fry*
Benjamin Bowman	*Nicholas Biri*	*Nicholas Beare*
Joseph Bowman	*John Maschberger*	*Henrich Wissler*
Jacob Bowman	*Michael Sheng*	*Ulrich Kessler*
John Crumpacker	*Abraham Brenneman*	*Jacob Ebersole*
Peter Cede	*Jacob Hight*	*Jacob Miller*
Abraham Miller	*Henrich Gaderman*	*Henrich Roth*
	Jacob Bauman	*David Brenneman*
	Jacob Reiff	*Jacob Kauffman*[97]

Document 187
To the Honorable the General Assembly of the Commonwealth of Virginia

The petition of the Subscribers Members of the Menonist Church in behalf of themselves and their religious Brethren

Respectfully sheweth

That an Article of Faith established by the said Church, forbids the bearing of Arms or sheding of Human blood which Article they conscientiously believe it is their duty to obey. In this scruple of Conscience *Only* they trust they have been short in being dutiful and Obedient Citizens. They have wished at all times to be faithful to the Laws that hath given them protection, and ever wish so to be, when consistent with the dictates of their religious Profession. There forefathers and Predecessors came from a far Country to America to Seek Religious Liberty; this they have enjoyed except by the Infliction of penalties for not bearing Arms which for some time lay heavy on them. But on a representation, and their situation being made known to the Honorable the Legislature, they were indulged with an exemption from said penalties untill some few years past, when, by a revisal of the Militia Law they were again enrolled and are now subject to the

° Empty brackets indicate that the document is damaged at this place

penalties aforesd. Therefore your Petitioners pray that the Honorable the General Assembly will take their Case into their Wise Consideration and so exempt them from bearing Arms or indulge them with such Militia exemptions as any other of the Citizens of the Commonwealth are indulged with for Conscience Sake and as far as their Fidelity and good Example shall merit, and your petitioners as in duty bound shall pray, &c. [December 10, 1785.]

Jaebez Shuh
Benjamin Stickli
Samuel Bohem
Peter Stauffer
Jorg Westerberger
Johannes Hodel
Isaac Kauffman
Christian Andrich
Abraham Beydler
Abraham Stauffer
Tobias Meili
David Stauffer
Ulrich Stauffer
Daniel Meily
Jacob Ruff
Nicholas Biery
Abraham Biery
Johannes Rieff
Jacob Ebersole
Andreas Christ
Henry Wissler
Johannes Maschberger
Abraham Branaman
David Brannaman

Valendin Faber
Johannes Faber
Peter Faber
Henrich Kagi
Matthia Snutz
Abraham Gochnaer
David Funkhouser
Johannes Fundhouser
Abraham Funkhouser
Christian Grabeel
Johannes Heisi
Jacob Gochnauer
Jacob Kauffman
Johannes Gochnauer
Abraham Schnitz
Jacob Neff
Jacob Kagi
Henrich Brumbaugh
Gorg Rothgeb
Jacob Bar
Peter Blaser
Christian Megert
Hans Megert

Abraham Rothgeb
Isaac Rothgeb
John Strickler
David Coffman
Jacob Ruffner
Christian Graff
Jacob Boehm
Christian Neff
Gabriel Seeger
Conrad Seiger
Christian Frey
Andreas Eby
Jacob Caufmann
Johannes Caufman
Jacob Bingerman?
Abraham Neff
Balser Hupp?
Peter Gut
Michael Gauffman
Henrich Scheng
Abraham Breneman
Heinrich Roth
Michael Scheng
Peter Zedty[99]

Church Membership Certificates

Members of the peace churches carried certificates of their membership. This document was drawn up by the pastor and deacon of the Mellinger Mennonite congregation in Lancaster County, Pennsylvania, for the son of members moving to North Carolina. Jacob Hartman (1714-1796) had served as pastor since 1760 and Tobias Greuter (Kreider) (d. 1791) was the first deacon known to have served in this congregation.

Document 188

This is to Certify that Jacob Jorde Now Living in North Carolina in Burcks County upon the South Fork of Cotabe river is a Son of peter Jorde and Magdalene Jorde Deceased wich Said peter Jorde and magdalena his wife has always being members in the Society Called menonist in pensylvania and never was Exempted and that the said Jacob Jorde never Ded any Crime while he lived with us So far as we Know. Given under our hands this 5th Day of Octbr. 1782.

Jacob Hartman
Minister of that Society
Tobias Greuter[98]

Peace Churches and the Militia System

The Pennsylvania Militia Act exempted all ministers of the gospel, regardless of denomination. Henry Funk, who had once been a minister in the Mennonite Church and joined his brother, Christian Funk, in the dissident Funkite group, was nevertheless drafted and fined. His protest led to a formal investigation that sheds light on the Funkite movement as well as on the workings of the militia system.

Document 189

Skippack Township
October 4th, 1781

To Dr. Joseph Gardner,
Member of Council,
Sir:—

The bearer hereof, Mr. Henry Funck, is going to Council with a complaint respecting a Demand of Substitute Fines made on him by Frederick Limback, Esqur., one of the Sub-lieutenants of Northampton County. The complaint, I confess, appears to me of a new Kind and Mr. Funck states it thus, that he (Mr. Funck) is a preacher and has been for many years among the people called Menonists, but having taken the test of the State and done a great deal of Business for the publick in the purchasing and milling way, was read out of the society, and as he is not now acknowledged a preacher by the Body of the society, Mr. Limback says he can not consider himself such, and consequently Fines him for neglect of duty in the militia, altho he favors many non-juror preachers of the same people. Mr. Funck can inform you more particularly of the circumstances, but this I know that he and his brother Christian Funck (a remarkably strong Whig) are preaching to the few well affected of that society, because of his attachment to the cause of this country). and that he has done much publick Business. Upon the whole, I think it a new Doctrine that he should be unprivileged, because he is disowned by the people for his complying with the Laws of his country, and beg you will be kind enough, if you find his complaint reasonable, to see him justice done as far as possible.

I am with real Esteem, Sir,
Your very H'by,
Daniel Hiester, Jr.[100]

Document 190

Gentlemen, Easton October 27th 1781

By Col. Balliet's Brother I received this day an order dated the Eighteenth Instant, from the Supreme Executive Council, directing me to answer to a complaint against me made by Frederick Limbach & Peter Burkholder Esquires, Two of the Sub Lieutenants of this County and also a copy of their letter to council dated the 15th instant. . . .

With respect to the paragraph in the letter of the Sublieutenants, wherein they say, "that Judgements was passed by the Courts of appeal against several persons in the districts under our care, who seemingly are disaffected, and having sent out executions for the fines, many obstructions have been thrown in our way by the Lieutenant and others in opposition to that Judgement," &c. As the Gentlemen have only thought proper to speak in general terms, I can only answer generally and guess at what they mean. When I had the honor to receive from council, by Mr. Henry Funk, a copy of a letter to the Honorable Joseph Gardner Esquire from Col. Daniel Heester, relative to Mr. Funk, with an order from council, requesting me to inquire into the Complaints of Mr. Funk, which papers Mr. Funk delivered me about the eleventh of this month, he, Mr. Funk, introduced a Person to me, whose name I do not recollect, and desired I would hear him a few words, the purport of which were, that he thought himself aggrieved at the last appeal held by Cols. Burkholder and Limbach, because, he having appealed thro' some bodily infirmity, had, I think, Eight Pounds Fine to pay, when others more able of body than himself, and equal, at least, in substance, had little or nothing to pay; at the same time [he] seemed to wish it might not be known he had complained; I replied, if he spoke the truth, what could he have to fear; if he did not approve of my mentioning what he said, why did he complain, it could answer no purpose—adding that I should mention it to the Sub lieutenants. Accordingly, when I wrote to Col. Limbach, in consequence of the order of council, by Mr. Funk, and appointed the nineteenth instant a day of hearing, I requested Col. Limbach would bring with him the appeals wherein Mr. Funk was included, and also those wherein certain persons were included which this complainant had mentioned; and upon this the Sub Lieutenants complaint must be founded. Col. Limbach attended on the nineteenth, but as the man did not, I enquired not much into the matter; but Col. Limbach assigned reasons which I suppose were well founded. This if I mistake not the matter, and I think I do not, was all my Interference. I cannot but take notice of the conduct of Col. Limbach when with me on the nineteenth, after the Letter to council was sent, that he neither in the most distant manner,then, or at any time before, had mentioned any of the matters complained of in the letter, or hinted that the Sub Lieutenants conceived they had cause of complaint against me, and had referred the consideration thereof to Council. The Affair of Mr. Funk I will beg leave to refer to another letter, this having extended to a much greater length than I expected, when I sat down to write, but I judged it necessary to shew my whole conduct to the Supreme Executive Council.

Were the good people of the county to apply to me as Lieutenant, and to request a hearing of any grievances they might think they laboured under, and to be rejected and denied a hearing, on complaint, I should be censured by council, and justly. If I do hear them and represent their complaints calmly to the Sub liutenants, they alledge, I am encourageing the disaffected opposing them, and creating Dissatisfaction among the people. Where shall I find a medium.

In obedience to a commission that the Supreme Executive Council were pleased to honor me with, which my fondness of retirement and speculative knowledge could not lead me to wish for or expect, I have, to the best of my abililties, endeavoured to execute the trust reposed in me with fidelity. From the irregular proceedings with the militia heretofore, I was not insensible of what would follow, if I attempted to go out of the beaten way of my predecessors; at the same time, I judged it expedient and most for the public utility, however disagreeable to myself it might be, or *seemingly* distressing or disgustful to the Inhabitants, to endeavour to form the Militia into discipline, upon the line of the Law, as quick as possible.

I am with the greatest veneration and respect

Gentlemen

Your Honours most obedient Servant

Robert Levers

The Honourable William Moore Esquire
Vice President and the Supreme Executive Council[101]

Document 191

Easton October 31st 1781.

Sir,

Yesterday Frederick Limbach, John Hays & Peter Burkholder Esquires, Three of the Sub Lieutenants were at this Place, and as the time of the First Class of Militia now in Service on the Frontiers will soon expire, it was their opinion, that the Second Class should be called out on the Frontiers, to relieve the First. We judged it proper to prepare to call out the said Second Class, as there might be some Indians skulking on our Borders, Waiting for the approbation of the measure from council.

For want of cash there has been great perplexity in supporting the militia with Provisions hitherto, and as the taxes begin to come in, tho' slowly, and the order received on the Treasurer for this County of One Hundred Pounds [is] much inadequate to the Sum necessary to enable Col. Balliet to keep up his credit with those he has already purchased from, I beg Council will be pleased to give an order for such additional sum as they may think proper.

Respecting the affair of Mr. Funk the Parties attended yesterday. John Witzel Esquire one of the former County Lieutenants says, that there was an Execution against Mr. Henry Funk, signed October 12th 1777 for Fifty Three Pounds Six Shillings, a Substitute Fine, signed by Justices Morry and Limbach, directed to John Jennings Esquire the then Sheriff, which was never served by him, and he dying in the Spring 1778, Mr. Henry Funk was again summoned on the eighteenth of June 1778 to shew cause why he should not pay the said Fine, and which Mr. Witzell says was after the Call of the 3d Class, and at the Time of the Appeal of the said Class, wherein Mr. Funk was likewise fined Forty Pounds, and for which an execution issued by Mr. Shoemaker, as appears by the Papers now enclosed, which were intended to be sent in the former letter on this Subject, so that by Mr. Witzel's account they are two distinct fines, which ought to have been paid long ago.

Philip Geisinger, Jacob Mayer, John Heestang, Jacob Weis & John Schons all of the Menonist Society likewise appeared, and say, that Henry Funk about the Year 1770, was put in to be a Preacher in their Society—That he preached among them and with their approbation and consent about Three Years—That he was frequently quarrelling with the Society, and therefore forbad, and not permitted, to preach any more among them—That he never had been authorised, according to the Rules of that Society, to baptize, or to administer the Lord's Supper among them. Upon Mr. Henry Funk's asking about what they had quarrelled, it was answered, that it principally was, that Mr. Henry Funk was too absolute, and that he wanted the whole Society to be subject to him. Jacob Scleip another Evidence brought, agreed in the same, and added that Mr. Henry Funk had been forbid to preach, because he was a horse swapper. Peter Myer, another Evidence, besides the above reasons why he was not permitted to preach, advanced, that because in a conversation some years ago under the late Government, he, Mr. Henry Funk, before Justice Klutz, in the presence of Jacob and John Yoder, did not stick to the Truth. Each of the Witnesses being asked, if they knew any thing of Mr. Henry Funk's having been forbad to preach, because he had applied to a Lawyer to clear him from serving as a Supervisor of the Road some years ago, they all declared they did not remember any such matter.

Upon the whole, it was agreed on all sides, that Mr. Henry Funk had been a Preacher in the Menonist Society about Three Years, from the Year 1770, that he was silenced by the Society who had first permitted him to preach—That he had ceased to preach for upwards of Five Years, in which Term the Two before mentioned Fines had been laid—That about Two years ago, his Brother Mr. Christian Funk had called him to assist him, and that he has since continued to preach for and with him, but not to baptize &ca. The Sublieutenants Messrs. Limbach and Burkholder are desirous to know, if these two Fines are to be paid by Mr. Funk, in what money they are to be received, and if it shall be adjudged by Council, whether he is to do duty in future as a Militia Man.

Respecting other Preachers of the same denomination being excused from Militia duty according to Mr. Henry Funk's Complaint, the persons alluded to it appears are John Newcomer of Upper Saucon, a Preacher about Four Years, and Christian Bare a Preacher about Eight Years, neither of these as the Sublieutenants say have ever been enrolled to their knowledge, and therefore have not been called out in the Militia; they likewise do not baptize or administer the Lord's Supper.

I am, Sir, Your Honors
most obedient Servant

Robert Levers

The Honorable William Moore Esquire
Vice President[102]

Document 192

[February 23, 1776]
Rough Heads Of Military Plans

All persons who do not associate (not being within the Exceptions in the Plan recommended by the Continental Congress) to be deemed Enemies to the Liberties of this Country whatever their Professions of attachment to it may be; & Quere? Sho'd not some Tax be imposed upon them more than on those who associate and do duty?

An Association to be subscribed to obey officers, & specifying what Service every Associator means to do. Every Person refusing to sign this to be held as an Enemy to the Service.

Things to be Recommended

That no national Distinctions be observed in forming Companies or Battalions, but that all join in every Corps as Americans.

That an Association be recommended to the Conscientious, suitable to their Principles.

Suppose a Clause that every Person tho' he be Conscientiously scrupulous of bearing arms, shall permitt his Apprentice to associate & appear on Duty & all Fines & company expenses incurred by the s'd apprentice shall be paid by the said Master, & charged to said apprentice on his coming of age, but if any Fine incurred thro' the Master's means, he to pay it himself?[103]

Document 193

A Petition from the Menonists & German Baptists was laid before the Committee praying their Interposition with the Convention that they may be indulged with giving Produce instead of Cash for their fines.

Ordered that Col. [Samuel] Beall and Captn. [Joseph] Chapline form a Letter to that Purpose. Col. Beall & Captn. Chapline brought in the following Letter.

Upper District of Fred'k County
3d July 1776

Honble Sir,

Whereas the inclosed petition was laid before the Committee of this District praying their Confirmation of the facts therein recited, & their interposition with your Honble. house, the Committee has therefore taken the Liberty (being truly sensible of the Justness thereof) to recommend the Prayer to your Consideration & that you will take order therein, and grant such relief as your Honble. house may think proper. I am with due respect,

Your most obedt. Servant
Signed by order of the Committee
Samuel Hughes Chairman

which is accordingly to be sent to the Convention[104]

Document 194

Upon the Society of Menonists and German Baptists prefering their Petition of the 3rd of July last to the Hble. the Convention of Maryland and Hble. Convention entered into the following Resolve

In Convention Annapolis 6th July 1776

On reading a Petition of the Society of Menonists and German Baptists,

Resolved, that the several Committees of Observation may in their discretion prolong the Time or take security for the Payment of any Fine, by them imposed, for not enrolling in the Militia, and may remit the whole, or any part of the fines by them assessed; and it is recommended to the Committee to pay particular attention and to make a Difference, between such Persons as may refuse from religious Principles or other Motives.

Extract from the Minutes
G. Duvall Clk.[105]

Document 195

Minutes of the Council of Safety

Dec. 7, 1776

Whereas, The safety and security of every State depends on the virtuous exertions of individuals in its defence, and as such exertions can never be mere reasonable and necessary than where a people are wantonly invaded by a powerful army, for the avowed purpose of enslaving them, which is at present the unhappy situation of our neighbouring States, and which may be hourly be expected in this: therefore,

Resolved, That no excuse ought to be admitted or deemed sufficient against marching of the Militia at this time, except sickness, infirmity of Body, age, Religious Scruples, or an absolute order from authority of this State.[106]

Document 196

Decem'r 22d, 1776

Resolved, That all able bodied men of the Townships of Moyalusing & Passyunk, those who have religious scruples against bearing arms alone excepted, are ordered to wait on General Putnam at 2 o'Clock tomorrow afternoon, with what arms and accoutrements they may have in their possession, to receive his orders, and the officers of the Militia in said Townships are directed to deliver into the Council a list of all persons as neglect or refuse to comply with this resolve.[107]

Document 197

On Motion resolved, that the Dunkards and Menonists be advertised, to pay their respective fines, to the Committee, on Tuesday next, otherwise, they may depend, that rigorous Measures will be immediately taken to Compel Payment.

The Committee being calld on extraordinary business met on Saturday 22d December 1776. Present

Joseph Sprigg in the Chair

William Baird	Doct[r] Hart
Dav. Hughes	Sam[l] Hughes
Col[l] Rench	Nicholas Smith
Capt[t] Sellars	Cap[t] Foglar

A letter from the Committee of Frederick County inclosing a Resolve of Congress requesting the assistance of the Militia, was read & it was thereupon order'd That a Copy of the same be sent to Coll Smith requesting his most earnest Attention thereto, & that he will send the same to Capt Joseph Chaplain & Capt Butler—

On motion to Coll Rench & seconded by J Hughes Resolved Unanimously that such of the young Dunkards and Menonists as have not enroll'd nor associated, shall immediately be requested to march with the Militia, in order to give their Assistance in intrenching and helping the sick and all such as will turn out voluntarily agreeably to the above Request, shall have their fines remitted.

It is further unanimously resolved, that on the marching of the Militia from this County, that all they that are well affected to this State and not capable of marching with the Militia, shall be formed into Companies, with proper Officers for the Protection and relief of such families, as shall be left without Assistance and that the officers of the Companies so formed shall divide the Settlement into certain Circuits and ride around such Circuits as shall be assigned them once a fortnight, and make particular enquiry into the Distresses of the Inhabitants, and order them such relief, as they shall think necessary, and should their Companies not be sufficient for giving such Relief; in that Case, they are required to apply to the Dunkards and Menonists residing nearest to give their Assistance, and in Case of Refusal or neglect they shall take down their names and return them to the Committee, on the Return of the Militia, that proper notice be taken thereof.[108]

Document 198
Tuesday, December 24th 1776.
The Committee met according to Adjournment.

On Motion resolved that Col^{n} Stull and Col^{n} Rentch Mr Baird and M$_{r}$ Lentz be a Committee to receive the several Fines from the Dunkards and Menonists, and any one of said Members are empowered to pass Receipts for the same—

Whereas the Congress have required the Militia of this County to march to Camp immediately, and as there is no Provision therefor—Resolved that the Money in the hands of the Treasurer for this County be apply'd to the above Purpose, and also to Defray the Expenses arising for apprehending Tories, and repairing a house for a Tory Goal—

The Committee for receiving Fines from the Dunkards and Menonists, report that they have received the sum of Two hundred and six pounds ten Shillings which is paid into the hands of Col$_{n}$ [John] Stull who has been appaointed Treasurer in the Room of Col$_{n}$ [Samuel] Beall.[109]

Document 199
Friday, the 27th December 1776

On Motion ordered, that Mr George Cellar, Doct^{r} Schnebley Mr Conrad Hogmire, George Shaver, Charles Swearingen, Captn James Wallen, Delashmet Wallen, Stophel Burket, Christian Lentz, Maj^{r} Christ^{n} Orindorf be impowered to collect from the Dunkards and Menonists, or from any other Person, all the Waggon Cloaths, that can be got, and make Return thereof to this Committee, who will appraise them and pay for the same—[110]

Document 200
In Council of Safety,
Philad'a, January 12th, 1777.

Orders were given to Colonel Morgan to have the 2nd Batt'n of Militia in Berks County, which he is to command, to make all necessary preparations, and to hold themselves in readiness to march on the Shortest notice, and wait until further orders from this Board.

The Council being informed that a number of the Country Militia are returning to their respective homes, disgusted at the precipitate orders they received this day, to march when they were not supplied w'th provisions, and in want of many other necessaries, which orders were given without the approbation of this Board.

Resolved, That John Hubley, Esq'r, a member of this board, be directed to endeavour to prevail on such of the Militia to return, and to assure them that this Council have, and ever will warmly interest themselves in behalf of their Countrymen, the Militia of this State, And will exert their authority to the utmost to preserve to them the rights of Freemen; and further, that this Council will, as far as possible, furnish such as shall return, with all proper equipment, And by no means consent to their being compelled to join the Continental Army until they are so supplied.

In Council of Safety, January 14th, 1777.

Resolved, That the officers of the first Battalion of Lancaster County, and the few men who remained with them when they were deserted by the greater part of the Battalion on the 12th instant, deserve the warmest acknowledgments of this Board for their endeavors to prevail on their Countrymen to stay, though those endeavors proved unsuccessful; and that the conduct of those who basely deserted, at that time, without applying to this Council, and waiting for redress, if they thought themselves aggrieved, is highly reprehensible.

In Council of Safety, PHILA, January 18th, 1777.

WHEREAS, This Council is informed that many of the principal Associators of Col. Hunter's Battalion of Berks County, refuse to march, to join General Washington's army at this Important Crisis, when so glorious an opportunity offers of Crushing the enemy, and thereby have prevented and discouraged the rest, and proceeded even to dare them to enforce the resolves of this Council upon them; therefore

Resolved, That Colonel Hunter be directed forthwith to Collect all the well affected in his Battalion, and to seize upon the ringleaders in this defection, and send them under guard to Philadelphia, and that he do execute the Resolve; the resolve of this Council of the seventh of December last, upon all who refuse to march without favour or affection, and that they do Collect Blankets and other necessaries for the use of those who are to march paying a reasonable price for the same; and should any person refuse to deliver such necessaries as they can spare, the Colonel is directed to take and pay for the same. Those that turn out are to march the most direct road to Head Quarters.[111]

Peace Churches Provide Supplies

Military service was not the only area where government officials pressed the sects to take a more active role. Wagons and teams, first provided voluntarily by both Associators and Non-Associators, had to be requisitioned by the law. So too were cattle, clothing, farm produce, and blankets and the peace churches provided more than their share.

Document 201

The Council Met. *Lancaster*, Friday, March 13, 1778.

James Patton, Deputy Waggon Master for the township of Conestoga, represented to Council that divers persons in the said Township who were duly summoned according to Law, to attend with their Waggons for the service of their Army, had neglected, & still continued to neglect to attend; and that on application by him made to Colo. Michael Haberstick, for assistance from the Militia, that he had not been supplied therewith; thereupon,

Ordered, That Col. Michael Haberstick be commanded forthwith to furnish a sufficient Guard to the said James Patton, to bring in the said delinquents.[112]

Document 202

In Council of Safety. Wednesday, November 26th, 1777.

It being represented to Council by Major George Ross, D.Q. Master General that Jacob Stakes, Christian Bauchman, Peter Witmer, Christian Hershey and Benjamin Miller, who were employed with their wagons in public service, have not performed their Agreement, *Ordered*, that the said Jacob Stakes, Christian Bauchman, Peter Witmer, Christian Hershey, and Benjamin Miller appear before this Council tomorrow Morning, at Eleven O'Clock, to answer the complaint of Major Ross. . . .

WHEREAS, many Farmers and others inhabiting the Neighbourhood of Lancaster, have been deterred from supplying the Inhabitants with Wood and provisions, through fear of having their Waggons impressed; therefore,

Resolved, That no Waggons or Horses by which Wood or Provisions shall be brought to Market in the Borough of Lancaster, shall be seized or liable to be impressed, coming to or going from Market.[113]

Document 203

In Council, June 21, 1780

Resolved, That in case of difficulty or delay in making up the said Teams the said Waggon Masters and their Deputies do apply to any Officers of the Militia for their assistance, and that they impress any Horses, Waggons or Gears distinguishing between such as have taken the oaths or affirmations of Allegiance, and those who have not, and saving always to every plantation at least two working Horses.[114]

Document 204

Lancaster, July 5th, 1780

Honble Sir,

Your favour of the 24th Ultimo Inclosing a Resolve of Council In Consequence of General Washington's Regulation to Raise Teams for the Immediate Support of the army I Recd the 2d Instant and am busely imployed in Engaging A. W. M. and am obliged to leave a blank in their Commissions with Respect to their pay, they absolutely Refuse to Raise the teams until they are Certain of their wages and the wages of those Conductors that the appoint to go out with the teams, and likewise the pay of the Militia that may be Called upon to assist as the whole teams will have to be impressed am not able to promise the waggon Masters more than twenty dollars pr day which is faur Inadquate to the Service, I can get no person to under take this Disagreeable task but those that have all along been Stench friends to their Country and have generaly Served Chefly out their own pockets; it will be merely imposoble for me to proced any further in this business if the above Request is not Generally Complyed with, as the Militia are Generaly men (or less: those we get to do this Service) that works for their living the will not go without their days pay what the Can earn at work which I have no authority to promise them. please to Excuse haste as the Gentleman who Carys this is waiting for it.

I have the Honor to be your Excellencys

most obedient and very Humble Servant

James Bayly, W. M. L. C.

To The Honble Joseph Reed Esqr Philadephia[115]

Document 205

Lancaster County, ss:

Personally appeared before me, Charles Hall, one of the Justices of the Peace for the County aforesaid, John Long, in the Township of Manheim, and Adam Weaver, in the Borough aforesaid, and was duly sworn according to Law, that they and each of them will Impartially Value and appraise between the owners and the United States of America, such horses, wagons & Tacklings thereunto belonging, as shall be brought before them by John Flieger, Ass't Waggon Master of Col'l James Ross's Distri't of the County aforesaid.

Adam Weber
John Long

Sworn and affirmed before me this
22d day of August, 1780.
Cha's Hall.

1. Michael Shriner, a waggon & Cloth Feeding trought, lock Chain, watter Bucket and tar pot £1,080.0.0
Benjamin Landis, to one black horse, hind geers & two bags . . 1,800.0.0
Henry Landis, to one black horse, hind geers and two bags, . . 1,300.0.0
Christian Myer, to one grey horse, fore geers & two bags 1,080.0.0
2. John Brubaker, a Waggon and Cloth, Tar pot, watter Bucket, feeding trought & lock Chair 1,260.0.0
Jacob Kaufman, to a black horse, hind geers & 2 bags 1,260.0.0
Henry Brubacker, to a black horse, hind gears & two bags £540.0.0
Jacob Pfeifer, to a bay horse, fore gears & two bags 1,080.0.0
John Kneisly, to a black horse, fore geers & two bags 1,500.0.0
3. Jacob Hare, a Waggon & Cloth, Tar pot and feeding trought 1,080.0.0
Jacob Kortz, to a black horse, fore geers & one Cask, ... 1,320.0.0
Daniel Ruty, to a bay horse, fore geers & one Bag, ... 1,800.0.0
George Bugh, to a black horse, fore geers 1,400.0.0
Martin Myer, to a grey horse, fore geers & one bag, ... 1,200.0.0
4. John Myer, a Waggon & Cloth, feeding trought, tarpot, watter Bucket, and hand screw 2,280.0.0
Christian Brubaker, to a black horse, fore geers & one bag 1,500.0.0
Jacob Myer, to a bay Mare, fore geers & one bag 1,080.0.0
Abram Myer, to a black Mare, hind geers & one bag, ... 1,500.0.0
Michael Shenck, to a Sorrel horse, fore geers & one bag . . . . . . 1,800.0.0[116]

Document 206
Shenandoah County, s.s

I hereby certify that I have received for public use of Jacob Strickler one steer weight judged by two men four hundred & sixty-eight pounds for which payment at the rate of Twenty-four Shillings p[er] Cwt shall be made according to the assurance contained in the resolution of Assembly of November 15, 1780. Given under my hand the sixteenth day of December 1780.

£5 . . 6 . . 12[117]

Document 207

Lebanon, June 16th, 1780.

Sir,

A Packet from your Excellency, inclosing a Number of Certificates, The Act for procuring an immediate Supply of Provisions for the Army, and an Appointment as one of the Commissioners, came duly to Hand on the Evening of the 7th Inst. I must confess however willing and ready I am to serve my Country, nothing less than so brave Soldiers in Distress as those of the United States, could ever have induced me to undertake so weighty and troublesome a Task in my present declining State of Health; but considering what Time would be lost should I decline this Service, until your Excellency should have Notice thereof, and make another appointment, I sat out the afternoon of the Day following, and have since purchased 31 and seized 13, amounting in the whole to 44 Head of Cattle, as you will observe by the inclosed Account. All of them eatable and Fit for immediate use. The 13 Head of Cattle seized I took from a certain Adam Rickard, a noted Drover and Dealer in Hard Money, from Chester County, who has taken the greatest Pains to represent our Cause and the Continental Money in the blackest Dye imaginable, in order to dispose of the Metal he was dealing in to the greatest advantage to himself, therefore, was very glad to embrace this Opportunity to curb his pernicious Designs in some Measure.

Cattle fit for immediate Use are exceedingly scarce and hard to be had under the Rule Established and laid down in the Law, nevertheless, it is with Pleasure I inform your Excellency that the whole of this Drove, (except the 13) I procured with the Consent of the Owners without Colour of Seizure; from the well disposed People out of affection and good Will, and from the Disaffected out of Fear.

And hope, if necessary, to be able to in about 10 or 12 Days to send about 40 or 50 more, without scouring the North and South Mountains, which must be done in Case of any further Demands. Your Excellency will please to observe that many of the wealthy Menonists and others who live in the Neighbourhood of Lancaster, Manheim and Conostogoe, drive Flocks of Cattle over the Mountains in the Spring Season, to the great Distress of the poor Inhabitants; Those Men undoubtedly have them to spare, otherwise they would keep them on their own Farms, and therefore ought to be taken from them; but this can not be done without the Assistance of 10 or 12 Men to drive them together, which would be attended with Extra Charges. Therefore wait your Excellency's particular Instructions in the Premises.

The Expence of collecting and driving the Cattle is so very high, (being out of money and shall not be able to pay for the Expence of those already procured) should therefore be glad that some Money would be sent by the Bearer to defray the Charges, otherwise can Send no more Cattle.

In a former Letter your Excellency has been pleased to request me to have my old Accounts, as Pay Master, in Readines for a Settlement; in Answer to which I would beg Leave to mention That my Accounts are fully settled, excepting Five Thousand Pounds, being the last Monies drawn in Consequences of an Order from the Hon'ble Council; which I shall settle by the very first Opportunity, finding a small Ballance due to Your Excellency's meet

Obed't humble Servt.,

P. Marsteller.[118]

Notes for Chapter 4

1. George Ross to Continental Congress, July 11, 1776. Papers of the Continental Congress, 83/LXIX. National Archives, Washington, D.C.

2. *Pennsylvania Packet and General Advertiser* (Philadelphia), March 18, 1777.

3. *Ibid.* David Rittenhouse to the Pennsylvania Assembly, November 26, 1776. Executive Correspondence. P.H.M.C.

4. "Extract from the Minutes, November 29, 1776." Executive Correspondence. P.H.M.C.

5. "Proceedings of the Committee of Observation for Elizabeth Town District (Washington County)," *Maryland Historical Magazine*, XII (December 1917), p. 341.

6. Peter Force, comp., *American Archives*, 5th Series, (Washington, D.C., 1833), III, 1472-1473.

7. Minutes of the Committee of Observation and Inspection of Northampton County, Pennsylvania," fols. 57-60. Easton Public Library, Easton, Pa.

8. "Proceedings of the Committee of Observation for Elizabeth Town District (Washington County)," *M.H.M.*, XII (December 1917), pp. 341-342.

9. *Pennsylvania Gazette* (Philadelphia), February 26, 1777. *Pennsylvania Packet and General Advertiser* (Philadelphia), February 25, 1777.

10. *Pennsylvania Packet and General Advertiser* (Philadelphia), June 10, 1777.

11. *Ibid.*, July 22, 1777.

12. Beck, "Extracts," *Penn-Germania*, I (1912), p. 451.

13. *Pennsylvania Packet and General Advertiser* (Philadelphia), March 25, 1777; April 1, 1777.

14. Charles A. Lofgren, "Compulsory Military Service under the Constitution: The Original Understanding," *W.M.Q.*, 3rd Series, XXXIII (January 1976), p. 63.

15. *Pennsylvania Packet and General Advertiser* (Philadelphia), March 18, 1777.

16. *Pennsylvania Evening Post* (Philadelphia), March 13, 1777.

17. *Pennsylvania Packet and General Advertiser* (Philadelphia), March 25, 1777. Robert L. Brunhouse, *The Counter-Revolution in Pennsylvania 1776-1790* (Harrisburg, Pa., 1971), p. 81.

18. *Pennsylvania Evening Post* (Philadelphia), April 12, 1777. *Pennsylvania Packet and General Advertiser* (Philadelphia), April 15, 1777.

19. *Pennsylvania Evening Post* (Philadelphia), April 19, 1777.

20. *Ibid.*, June 12, 1777.

21. *Pennsylvania Packet and General Advertiser,* (Philadelphia), April 15, 1777.

22. Jacob Morgan to Thomas Wharton, April 27, 1777. Autograph Collection. H.S.P.

23. Jacob Morgan to Thomas Wharton, Jr., May 16, 1777, Gratz Collection. H.S.P.

24. Joshua Elder to John Rogers, May 11, 1777, *Pennsylvania Archives*, 2nd Series, XIII, 474. There were 198 Non-Associators in Paxton Township in August 1777 and 56 in Upper Paxton, both in present Dauphin County. Tax Lists, Lancaster County Historical Society, Lancaster, Pa.

25. Bartrem Galbraith to John Rogers, May 15, 1777, *Pennsylvania Archives*, 2nd Series, XIII, 475.

26. Bartrem Galbraith to Thomas Wharton, Jr., May 19, 1777, *Pennsylvania Archives*, 1st Series, V, 342-345.

27. *Ibid.*, May 19, 1777, 352-353. Joshua Elder to John Rogers, May 29, 1777, *Pennsylvania Archives*, 2nd Series, XIII, 475.

28. Bartrem Galbraith to Joshua Elder, June 18, 1777, *Pennsylvania Archives*, 2nd Series, XIII, 475.

29. Bartrem Galbraith to Thomas Wharton, Jr., June 2, 1777, *Pennsylvania Archives*, 1st Series, V. 352-353.

30. Lancaster County Indictments, Records of the Court of Quarterly Sessions, Lancaster County Historical Society, Lancaster, Pa.

31. The first three classes of Lancaster County militia were ordered to Chester at the beginning of August. Bartrem Galbraith to John Rogers, August 3, 1777, *Pennsylvania Archives, 2nd Series, XIII, 479.*

32. Christopher Marshall to Children, August 25, 1777, Christopher Marshall Letter Book, fols. 243-244. H.S.P. John Littlejohn Journal, August 24—August 30, 1777. Typescript copy in United Methodist Church Commission on Archives and History Library, Lake Junalaska, N.C., 64-65.

33. *Thomas Rankin Journal, August 10, 1777 and passim.* Typescript in United Methodist Church Commission on Archives and History, Lake Junaluska, N.C.; Thomas Rankin to John Wesley, September 17, 1777. Methodist Research Centre, London; Richard K. MacMaster, "Thomas Rankin and the American Colonists," *Proceedings of the Wesley Historical Society*, XXXIX (June 1973), pp. 3-26.

34. Gordon Pratt Baker, ed., *Those Incredible Methodists* (Baltimore, Md., 1972), pp. 49-51.

35. *Maryland Gazette and Baltimore Advertiser*, December 2, 1777.

36. Henry J. Young, "The Treatment of Loyalists in Pennsylvania" (PhD Dissertation, John Hopkins University, 1955), pp. 99-101. Hubertis Cummings, *Scots Breed and Susquehanna* (Pittsburgh, 1964), pp. 227-230.

37. Lancaster County Indictments, L.C.H.S., Lancaster, Pa., Skyles, far from being a pacifist, was later indicted for murdering a Patriot.

38. Joseph Simon to Patrick Rise, September 12, 1777, William Henry Papers, H.S.P., Philadelphia, Pa.

39. The Philadelphia newspapers also migrated to Lancaster with the exception of Christopher Sauer's German-language paper, but a German paper printed by Francis Bailey briefly filled the gap and countered Sauer's Loyalist viewpoint with its own Patriot propaganda.

40. Beck, ed., "Extracts," *Penn-Germania*, I (1912), 491.

41. Bartrem Galbraith to John Rogers, October 1, 1777, October 25, 177, *Pennsylvania Archives*, 2nd Series, XIII, 481-483.

42. "A Narrative of the Sufferings of Thomas McClun," 3rd 8th month, 1778. Papers of the Meeting for Sufferings of Philadelphia Yearly Meeting, Quaker Collection, Haverford College Library, Haverford, Pa. Arthur Mekeel, "The Society of Friends (Quakers) and the American Revolution" (PhD dissertation, Harvard, 1940), p. 293. Copy in Haverford College Library. Thomas Gilpin, *Exiles in Virginia* (Philadelphia, 1848), p. 181. John Smith to John Hancock, October 1, 1777, Papers of the Continental Congress, 78, XX, 155. National Archives, Washington, D.C.

43. John W. Wayland, *History of Shenandoah County, Virginia* (Strasburg, Va., 1927), pp. 207-208. Harry A. Brunk, *History of Mennonites in Virginia 1727-1900* (Staunton, Va., 1959), pp. 37-38.

44. W. D. and L. M. Huddle, *History of the Descendants of John Hottel* (Strasburg, Va., 1930), pp. 14-15.

45. Philadelphia Yearly Meeting, Minute Book of the Meeting for Sufferings, 1775-1785, fols. 287-289, 430, Quaker collection, Haverford College Library, Haverford, Pa.

46. Appeal Docket for Lancaster County, Records of the Office of the Comptroller General, R. G. 4, Military Accounts, Lancaster County, Pennsylvania State Archives, Harrisburg, Pa.

47. Record Group 4, Boxes 23 and 29, P.H.M.C., Harrisburg, Pa.

48. *Ibid.*, Boxes 2 and 3.

49. Twyman Williams Papers, Virginia State Library, Richmond, Va.

50. "The United States of America to the Committee of Lancaster County, Dr.,

August 10, 1776—October 10, 1776," Lancaster County Miscellaneous Documents, H.S.P.

51. Lancaster County Miscellaneous Documents, H.S.P.

52. Lancaster County Committee Minute Book, fol. 167. LC.

53. Lancaster County Miscellaneous Documents, H.S.P.

54. Lancaster County Committee of Observation Minutes, fols. 21-22, Force Collection, L.C., Washington, D.C.

55. "Journal of the Committee of Observation of the Middle District of Frederick County, Maryland," *Maryland Historical Magazine*, XI (March 1916), pp. 60-63.

56. "Journal," *M.H.M.*, X (December 1915), p. 306.

57. Records of the Supreme Executive Council, Committee of Safety Minutes July 3, 1775—July 22, 1776, fol. 15, P.H.M.C.

58. Lancaster County Committee Minutes, fols. 28-30, L.C.

59. *Ibid.*, pp. 31-33.

60. *Ibid.*, fol. 78.

61. *Ibid.*, fol. 126.

62. Force Collection, Series IX, 12, L.C.

63. Force Collection, L.C.

64. *Pennsylvania Ledger* (Philadelphia), March 23, 1776.

65. "Minutes of the Committee of Safety of Bucks County," Bucks County Historical Society, Doylestown, Pa.

66. Lancaster County Minute Book, fol. 96. Force Collection, L.C.

67. Minutes of the Committee of Safety, Bucks County," Bucks County Historical Society, Doylestown, Pa.

68. Committee of Safety Minutes, 1775-1776, fol. 425, Records of the Supreme Executive Council, P.H.M.C.

69. Executive Correspondence, P.H.M.C.

70. "Minutes of the Committee of Observation and Inspection of Northampton County, Pennsylvania, December 21st 1774 to August 14th 1777," fol. 31-33, Easton Public Library, Easton, Pa.

71. Executive Correspondence, P.H.M.C.

72. *Ibid.*

73. *Journals of Henry Melchior Muhlenberg*, II (Philadelphia, 1945), 765.

74. *Pennsylvania Archives,* 2nd Series, III, 706-707. See also Document 200.

75. Schwenkfelder Library, Pennsburg, Pa.

76. *Pennsylvania Archives,* 2nd Series, XIII, 475.

77. *Ibid.*, 1st Series, V, 343-344.

78. *Ibid.*, 353-355.

79. Lancaster County Indictments, Lancaster County Courthouse, Lancaster, Pa.

80. *Pennsylvania Archives,* 1st Series, V 405-406.

81. *Ibid.*, 407-408.

82. *Ibid.*, 413-414.

83. *Lancaster County Historical Society Papers,* V (1901), 20-22.

84. Records of the Supreme Executive Council, Clemency File. P.H.M.C.

85. *Ibid.*

86. *Ibid.*

87. *Pennsylvania Archives,* 1st Series, V, 768-769.

88. Appeal Docket for Lancaster County, Records of the Office of the Comptroller General, R.G. 4, Military Accounts, Lancaster County. P.H.M.C. David Tannenberger of Moravian community at Lititz was one of the great American organmakers. His career is sketched at length in Orpha Ochse, *The History of the Organ in the United States* (Bloomington, Ind., 1975), pp. 51-55.

89. *Pennsylvania Archives,* 1st Series, V, 472.

90. *Ibid.*, 2nd Series, XIII, 480-481.

91. Lancaster County Indictments, Lancaster County Courthouse, Lancaster, Pa.
92. *Pennsylvania Archives*, 1st Series, V, 575-577.
93. *Maryland Gazette* & *Baltimore Advertiser*, December 2, 1777.
94. *Pennsylvania Archives*, 1st Series, V, 767-768.
95. Journal of the House of Delegates, December 3, 1784, V.S.L., Richmond, Va.
96. W. W. Hening, *Virginia Statutes at Large* (Richmond, Va., 1823), X, 416-441.
97. Religious Petitions, V.S.L., Richmond, Va.
98. Hartman Family Account Book, Lancaster County Historical Society, Lancaster, Pa.
99. Virginia State Library, Richmond, Va.
100. *Pennsylvania Archives*, 2nd Series, III, 463.
101. Northampton County, Military Affairs, 1779-1782, Pennsylvania State Archives, Harrisburg, Pa.
102. *Ibid.*
103. *Pennsylvania Archives*, 2nd Series, I, 578.
104. "Proceedings of the Committee of Observation for Elizabeth Town District (Washington County)," *M.H.M.*, XII (December 1917), p. 328.
105. *Ibid.*, p. 335.
106. Record Group, 27B, P.H.M.C.
107. *Colonial Records*, XI, 59.
108. Proceedings of the Committee of Observation for Elizabeth Town District (Washington County)," *M.H.M.*, XII (December 1917), p. 341-342.
109. *Ibid.*, 343. Colonel Stull "rec'd from the Dunkers & Menonist for their Fines" £206..10 collected from Christian Newcomer, Henry Avey, John & Jacob Hoover, Joseph Bowman, Jacob Root, Jacob Stover, Adam Shoop, David & Joseph Funk, Joseph Byerly, Christian Coogle, Jacob Lesher, Abraham Miller, Samuel Bachley Junr., Isaac Bachley, Adam Pifer, Abraham Good, Christian Good, John Hoover Junr., Olerich Hoover, Martin Funk, John Good, Christian Hoover, John Rohrer, Jacob Rohrer, Martin Rohrer, Paul Road, Jacob Road, Samuel Vulgamet, Chrisley Weldy, Abm. Houser, John Bomberger, Jacob Hess, Michael Garber, Jacob Studebaker, David Miller, Matthias Stauffer, Jacob Coughinour, Christian & Jacob Thomas, John Miller turned in £ 54 paid to him by Jacob Broombaugh Junr., John Broombaugh, Abraham Gansinger, Christian Shank, Micht. Shank, Abraham Lidey, Andrew Postalor, John Mashabaugh, Jacob Huffer, John Bowman, David Miller Son of Philip, Jacob Herr and Henry Calglesser.
110. *Ibid.*, 344.
111. *Colonial Records*, XI, pp. 94-95.
112. *Ibid.*, 438.
113. *Ibid.*, 349-350.
114. Papers of the Continental Congress, Pennsylvania State Papers, 83/69/II/227, National Archives, Washington, D.C.
115. *Pennsylvania Archives*, 1st Series, VIII, 390-391.
116. *Ibid.*, 2nd Series, III, 375-377.
117. Harry M. Strickler, *A Short History of Page County, Virginia* (Richmond, Va., 1952), p. 392.
118. *Pennsylvania Archives*, 1st Series, VIII, 328-329.

Chapter 5

"I'D AS SOON GO INTO THE WAR AS PAY THE TAX"

A Question of Allegiance

The question of paying war taxes is ultimately a question of allegiance, of rendering to Caesar the things that are justly Caesar's. It has never admitted of an easy solution, because it is a question of discerning the limits of complementary allegiances, never of shaking off obligations to one in the name of the other. The biblical injunctions to render tribute and custom to whom they are due underscore the attitude of the New Testament church that accepted even the tyrannical Roman ruler as the representative of legitimate civil authority.

Anabaptists, their faith deeply rooted in the Bible, considered it their religious duty to "display our subordination in humility and obedience to the authorities" and "never to refuse to pay the taxes, tributes, and tolls which are its due, as we are taught." Of the many groups within the Anabaptist movement, only the Hutterites took a consistent stand by saying that there was no difference between participating in war personally and paying indirectly for its prosecution.[1] Quakers developed a similar tradition of actively supporting civil government. From the beginning, they made payment of taxes and customs duties an integral part of the queries sent to every local Friends' Meeting.[2]

But both Anabaptists and Quakers agreed in placing limits on the authority of civil government. In the face of a general European acceptance of established churches, they denied the government's right to coerce them into attending the church it favored. They refused to serve in its armed forces. (Logic would be on their side if they questioned the right of their rulers to tax them to support an established church or an army.) The severe persecution both groups suffered from the authorities undoubtedly made them reluctant to raise issues that could easily be construed as marks of disloyalty; if they were to suffer, it would be as Christians and not as revolutionaries. A later generation of Quakers, more concerned about the use to which their taxes would be put, accepted the contrary practice of early Friends as the result of their difficult situation.[3]

A careful discrimination about the payment of taxes would be a great deal to expect from any people whose very right to exist was questioned by their government. Such a concern would be no more likely to arise, even without persecution, until some clear division between "war taxes" and "taxes" was apparent. The biblical texts would normally be read as enjoining payment of taxes and this would be decisive, unless the tax collector himself made some distinction in the purpose for which the tax was levied.

The Problem of "Trophy Money"

Trophy money provided the first real challenge on war taxes. It was a specific military tax, devoted to equipping the militia and for no other purposes. Payment of trophy money involved some voluntary cooperation and, like hiring a substitute to serve in the militia in one's place, some acknowledgement of a personal obligation to military duty. English Quakers responded to this direct challenge. Robert Barclay, the Quaker apologist, wrote in 1676 that "we have suffered much in our country, because we neither could ourselves bear arms, nor send others in our place, nor give our money for the buying of drums, standards, and other military attire."[4]

Quakers on both sides of the Atlantic thus had a long tradition of refusing direct military taxes, such as trophy money. When in 1758 London Yearly Meeting rewrote the queries sent annually to English Friends, they asked: "Do you bear a testimony against bearing arms and paying trophy money or being in any manner concerned in privateers, letters of mark or dealing in prize goods as such?" Maryland Yearly Meeting, Philadelphia Yearly Meeting, and Friends in New England, New York, and Virginia adopted the identical query the same year.[5] It is worth noting that trophy money is bracketed with completely voluntary contributions to the war effort such as enlisting, fitting out privateers, and buying or selling goods captured by privateers; only the refusal to pay trophy money could require personal confrontation with government. Both the Quakers and the British government expected Friends to refuse voluntary cooperation but to permit the authorities to take the equivalent in goods under a writ of distress, and the law provided for this concession to the conscientious objector.[6]

Some English and American Quakers were uneasy with the military use to which a portion of their ordinary taxes was put, and they questioned whether "their distinction between a Fine or Tax, in lieu of personal serivce, to be applied to warlike purposes, and a Tax immediately for the pay of men hired to perform the same service, between a Tax to purchase Drums, colors, &c., and the common Taxes to arm, cloath, victual [soldiers] &c., was not too great a refinement?" They believed, nonetheless, that they had to pay these other taxes. As an English Friend explained to Rhode Island Quakers, they found "no way to avoid the thing, that Tax being mixed with other Taxes."[7] The Quaker testimony on war taxes is quite clear down to 1755. A Friend could not voluntarily pay to hire a substitute for militia service or voluntarily pay any tax solely and directly intended for military purposes. He was obliged in conscience to pay every other tax, even "mixed" taxes, which would be used in part for the military budget.

Mennonites and War Taxes

The Mennonite attitude is much more difficult to trace, but it was constructed of the same elements. Support of civil government and payment of taxes was an obligation in conscience, explicitly enjoined by the New Testament. Voluntary participation in warfare by personal service or otherwise was forbidden.

This attitude had taken deep root by the time of the American Revolution. The rumor that Christian Funk permitted payment of the £3..10 tax on Non-Associators was enough to cause dissatisfaction in his congregation.[8] This particular tax was levied as an avowed equivalent to military service and was intended wholly for military purposes. Mennonite statements in the crisis of 1775, particularly the address to the Pennsylvania Assembly in November, repeated their sense of obligation in conscience to pay taxes, but insisted that they found no freedom "in giving, or doing, or assisting in anything by which men's lives are destroyed or hurt." As noted in a previous section, the context of this petition makes it clearly a statement of conscientious objection to any tax that would be an equivalent to military service. The Mennonite position on voluntary hiring of substitutes for militia duty was so well known that Pennsylvania and Virginia lawmakers incorporated a provision into the militia laws for levying substitute fees and militia fines by distraint on "quakers and menonists," eventually on the community as a whole, rather than on individuals.[9]

The Dunkers Hold Similar Views

The Church of the Brethren held similar views on payment of substitute fines as a means of buying personal exemption from militia duty. The Brethren annual meeting of 1780 forthrightly condemned payment of substitute fees. The following year they reaffirmed this decision.[10]

The concern expressed by a Lancaster County congregation of the Church of the Brethren in 1775 that voluntary contributions should be "for the needy" rather than "protection money" (*schutzgeld)* was noted in a prior section. We might reasonably conclude that at least by 1775 the Church of the Brethren taught that voluntary payment of *schutzgeld* ran counter to the Gospel of Jesus Christ.[11]

A New Challenge to Consistency on War Taxes

John Woolman introduced an entirely new element into the thought of the historic peace churches on the payment of war taxes. Before he expressed his concern about paying taxes that would be used in part for military purposes, no one seriously challenged the assumption that Christians were bound in conscience to pay taxes to whom taxes are due, regardless of how the money was later apportioned. Woolman was interested in the consequences of actions, not their ritual purity.

Even if all Friends did not share Woolman's conviction, they were prepared to actively support those who felt they could not pay war taxes. In 1757 Quakers reminded the Pennsylvania Assembly that they "cannot be concerned in Military Services nor in paying *an Equivalent or Compensation* for such Services without violating that Liberty of Conscience" which they prized. Friends had not advanced beyond acknowledging that this scruple existed among some of their brethren. The Society of Friends had no official policy of discouraging payment of war taxes, and the weight of tradition was in favor of paying taxes without questioning the use to which they would be applied.[12]

The concern about war taxes surfaced again in the crisis of 1775. Many Friends had serious doubts about meeting not only the demands for militia and substitute fines, but the ordinary provincial taxes that would now be used to arm the military associators. Others questioned the legitimacy of accepting paper currency issued specifically to fund a war.

Timothy Davis of Sandwich, Massachusetts, published anonymously *A Letter from one Friend to some of his Intimate Friends on the subject of paying Taxes* (Watertown, Mass., 1775) in which he gave a strong argument for paying war taxes.[13] New England Meeting for Sufferings expressed fear lest it "subject those who have tender Scruples respecting paying Taxes towards supporting War to Sufferings."[14] The war tax issue split New England Yearly Meeting, with Davis and others who took a militant patriotic stand withdrawing to form a separate Free Quaker meeting.[15] Even after their withdrawal, the New England Yearly Meeting contained a substantial number of Friends who felt obliged to pay all their taxes.[16]

As the war dragged on, many Quakers had a heightened sense of the inconsistency of refusing to fight or hire a substitute while their tax dollars supported the war effort. Conscientious objection to war taxes became more general among American Friends.[17] Some Quakers were concerned, nonetheless, with the different motives that seemed to be behind some of this tax resistance. Moses Brown of Providence, Rhode Island, was convinced that Christians ought not contribute in any way to war by paying taxes, but he had difficulties with the arguments advanced by some Friends who refused to pay war taxes on political grounds, "more on Account of the Authority that demands the Taxes than because they are used for War," and others who "refuse all taxes, even those for Civil Uses," and who appeared to disregard "our Testimony of Supporting Civil Government by readily Contributing thereto."[18] It was easy to cross the line that separated refusal to pay war taxes from disloyalty, and for some in the peace churches, who favored the old regime or found the new one burdensome, this was a real temptation.

The Quaker testimony against war taxes rested on a much firmer foundation than the shifting sands of political belief. It assumed that the Scriptures are to be taken seriously and that Jesus Christ has set us free to lead a new kind of life. Samuel Allinson of Burlington, New Jersey, the ablest Quaker writer on war taxes, understood that to refer the prophecies of Isaiah and the hard sayings of the gospel to some future age was to deny their power.

If war belongs to a fallen kingdom over which Christ has already triumphed, Christians should not pretend that war is a legitimate function of civil government. It is less a question of supporting war with our taxes than of supporting war with our minds and hearts, while seeking personal exemption.[19]

Samuel Allinson, Job Scott, and other Quaker writers on the war tax issue perceived that the more traditional claims for conscientious objection led logically to the refusal to pay taxes for war, for if war is admitted to be a legitimate function of civil government and the Christian is obliged to support civil government in its legitimate functions by

Table 7
SUFFERINGS FOR TAXES AND FINES
MARYLAND YEARLY MEETING[1]

	1777	1778	1779	1780	1781	1782
Militia and Substitute Fines	6	11	2	4	3	—
Triple Tax[2]	-	17	10	8	-	-
Assessment Fine[3]	-	-	6	18	13	7
County Tax	-	-	—	1	5	-
Mixed Tax	-	1	-	-	-	-

1. Minutes of Meeting for Sufferings of Maryland Yearly Meeting, Quaker Collection, Haverford College Library, Haverford, Pa. Microfilm in Maryland Hall of Records, Annapolis, Md.

2. Similar to the nonjuror tax in Pennsylvania, this was imposed on all who refused the oath or affirmation of allegiance.

3. Imposed on all those who refused to hand in a list of real and personal property for tax purposes.

Table 8
SUFFERINGS FOR TAXES AND FINES
PHILADELPHIA YEARLY MEETING[1]

	Chester M.M.[2]	Concord M.M.[3]	Pipe Creek M.M.[4]
Militia and Substitute Fines	12	35	19[5]
Taxes for Military Purposes	29	5	14
Fines for Refusing to Collect Taxes	10	2	-

1. Philadelphia Yearly Meeting, Minutes of Meeting for Sufferings, 1775-1785, fols. 285-290. Haverford College Library, Haverford, Pa. Other meetings failed to enumerate suffering cases.

2. Chester Monthly Meeting, Chester County, Pa.

3. Concord Monthly Meeting, Chester County, Pa.

4. Pipe Creek Monthly Meeting, Frederick County, Md.

5. Includes 7 identified as "non-associator fines."

his taxes, it would seem to follow that he has an equal obligation in conscience to support it by personal service as a soldier in the ranks.

Refusal to pay taxes destined in part for the Continental Army or the state militia was not to involve any insubordination; Friends who refused these taxes were instructed to "quietly suffer the distraint of our effects for those uses also." Since the law already provided for levying taxes by seizing property of both conscientious objectors and ordinary delinquents, it is difficult to tell how widespread was refusal to pay "mixed" taxes. Accounts sent by local Quaker meetings to the Meeting for Sufferings give a hint, but many meetings failed to send in anything like a complete record of goods seized from their members, and some who did failed to give enough details to determine what were the circumstances of the seizure of so many bushels of wheat or a mare valued at so much. Inconsistency in use of terms compounds the difficulty. The overall impression gleaned from the records is that this particular form of war tax resistance was still a minority opinion.

Mennonites and Dunkers Accept the Challenge

To what extent the German-speaking peace churches shared this Quaker testimony is an even thornier question. At their 1781 annual meeting the Church of the Brethren decided that militia and substitute fines could not be paid voluntarily (*Document 210*). A majority evidently felt that the example Jesus gave in paying the temple-tax was to be the model for Christians in paying all taxes demanded of them. On the other hand, a creative minority in the Church of the Brethren felt obliged to refuse to pay certain taxes. The context makes it obvious that these are war taxes. But it is by no means clear whether they meant specifically the tax imposed on conscientious objectors or all war taxes. The definite article makes the first a distinct possibility, but it does not rule out the other. If the Brethren generally paid the Non-Associator tax, while a lesser number refused it, they would have differed from the Mennonites on this point. The Non-Associator tax, moreover, had been regularly collected since 1777 and the Franconia Mennonites took a position on it in that year; why would the Brethren take it up only in 1781? Quaker concern about paying "mixed" taxes reached a peak in 1780 and might have found a response in the Church of the Brethren.

The crucial document on Mennonite payment of war taxes is Christian Funk's *Mirror for All Mankind.* The payment of taxes figured prominently in his deposition from the ministry in 1778, and his attitude was apparently different from that of other Mennonites. Funk composed his account in 1809 and wrote from a highly partisan viewpoint, but his memory of events so significant in his own life would probably suffer less from the passage of time than from a natural desire to justify his own course of action.

According to Funk, his difficulties began when his congregation was preparing to celebrate the Lord's Supper in 1777. The rumor that he had taken the affirmation of allegiance, repeated by two of his accusers, would necessarily date the events sometime after June 1777, when the Pennsylvania Assembly passed the Test Act.

The major accusation against Funk, made by twelve members of his congregation, was that he *allowed* payment of the tax of £3. 10s. He was not accused of paying the tax and, indeed, as a minister, he was exempt from it. What was the tax in question? A tax of this amount was levied by the Lancaster County Committee on all Non-Associators in 1775 and other committees followed their example. The first general tax of £3. 10, again on Non-Associators, was passed by the Pennsylvania Assembly on April 5, 1776. The Pennsylvania Convention replaced it in September 1776 with a much higher fine, which the Assembly later repealed. On February 14, 1777, the new Assembly revived the £3. 10 fine on all Non-Associators, with the passage of "An Act, Directing the mode of collecting the Fines imposed on persons who did not meet and exercise, in order to learn the art military." As the title of the law made clear, it was intended that the £3. 10 Non-Associator tax be a direct equivalent for military service, paid only by men from 15 to 50 years of age. This was the tax that Christian Funk and his accusers discussed.

Since Non-Associators had faced similar obligations for two years, it is curious that the morality of paying the tax was a live issue among Franconia Mennonites in the latter part of 1777. Had Mennonites generally refused to pay the earlier exactions? The September 1776 legislation was enforced only in Northampton County, and enforcement of the April 1776 law may have been more spotty than we realize. But even if the authorities enforced none of these fines on Non-Associators, the threat of enforcement would require some policy or decision to pay or refuse to pay. The fact that twelve of Christian Funk's congregation thought that the mere suspicion of countenancing payment was grounds for excluding him from the Lord's Supper is suggestive that Mennonite opinion considered payment immoral and that Funk was deviating from the norm.

Christian Funk implied that the principal objection to the tax was either that it was payable in Congress money, which it was, or paid to the Continental Congress, which it was not. The argument that the government exacting the fine was not legitimate needs some consideration, for the Pennsylvania Assembly that passed the law was the first under the new Constitution of 1776. The objection that "we should not pay this tax to the government, considering it rebellious and hostile to the king" is thus plausible, but it does not explain why Funk's accusers settled on the Non-Associator tax and not all taxes laid by the Assembly in 1777, or all taxes payable in Congress money. He makes it clear throughout his account that only the tax of £3. 10 was thought objectionable or even discussed.

A man is likely to remember a pithy statement, particularly if it is his own, far better than more abstract issues. Christian Funk doubtless quoted Luke 20:25 and held a piece of Continental currency in his hand to prove the lawfulness of paying the tax, but that need not mean that "Congress money" was the real issue. If that were the case, Andrew Zeigler's equally pithy remark seems pointless. "I would as soon go into the war, as to pay the £3 10*s*. if I were not concerned for my life," Funk recalled the Skippack bishop saying. If the real objection to the tax was that it was an equivalent to military service, Zeigler's remark makes a great deal of sense.

This account of Christian Funk's difficulties is thus a strong indication that for many Mennonites payment of war taxes was refused on conscientious grounds.

The confessional statement drawn up by the River Brethren in 1780 points in a contrary direction. Three of the five early versions of this document make a specific reference to *protection money* or *schutzgeld* as among the duties of the Christian to the state: "We are also exhorted to pay tribute, or protection-money unto the governments, because Paul calls them God's ministers, Romans 13." This would apparently indicate that payment of war taxes was considered an obligation binding in conscience.[20]

War Taxes Add New Burdens

Taxes proved increasingly difficult to collect throughout the Revolution, whether the delinquent taxpayer was a militant Patriot or a member of one of the peace churches. The more new taxes the Assembly voted, the further behind the townships fell. The special assessment on Non-Associators and men over military age in 1777 was intended to make up the deficit, but it was no sooner announced than new problems arose. In April the Lancaster County commissioners met with the assessors, "but many of the constables neglecting to bring in their returns agreeable to the warrants," they could not lay a county tax.[21] The commissioners met regularly through the summer of 1777 with no better results. Several township constables, identifiable as Mennonites, were fined that summer for failing to fulfill the duties of their office, and others faced similar charges as late as 1779.

Between war taxes and the test oath, many nonresistant officials found it impossible to hold township offices after 1777. Upper Salford, Lower Salford, Franconia, and Towamencin townships in Philadelphia County failed to elect any local officials at all in 1777, despite protests from the authorities.[22] In Byberry Township a largely Quaker population bypassed elections throughout the war and provided for the care of the poor and the upkeep of the roads without reference to either king or Congress.[23] A similar situation is implied by court cases in Lancaster County (*Document 236*).

Tax resistance could be the result of conscientious scruples, of pro-British sympathies, or simply an indication of war weariness on the part of an overburdened civilian population. Whatever the cause, it was widespread in 1780. Fully 149 German settlers in Bern, Tulpehocken, and Bethel townships in Berks County were convicted in November, 1780, of signing a formal agreement to refuse payment of monthly taxes and fines.[24] Since these townships were Lutheran and Reformed strongholds, it is unlikely that the morality of war taxes was at issue here. The Berks County Court fined 24 township collectors and assessors for refusing to collect taxes in 1780 and ten in 1781. In addition, seven men refused to collect militia class fines. Six of these men were probably Mennonite, one a Schwenkfelder, and one a Quaker, but 33 had no obvious peace church affiliation, so the incidence of tax resistance was much greater than the possible war tax resistance.[25]

If it was immoral to pay taxes for the support of war, could one accept the paper money issued by the Continental Congress and the individual states to meet wartime expenses? The problem was a vexing one for Quakers and Mennonites. Friends meetings from New England to the Carolinas discussed whether they should refuse the new currency and refuse to pay the taxes used to redeem it. Quakers universally left it to individual conscience, but substantial numbers of Friends did reject the Continental bills. In some places, notably the Shenandoah Valley of Virginia, great resentment built up against them for that reason. Surviving alms books, with sums identified as "hard money" and "Congress money," indicate that both Amish and Mennonites did accept the paper bills.[26] But some Mennonites did have scruples about using paper money, refusing to sell produce for Continental bills, and at least one Lancaster County Mennonite was prosecuted for his objection.

Table 9
DISAFFECTION IN BERKS COUNTY, PA.

Township[1]	Taxables 1779[2]	"Tories" 1779[3]	Tax Problems 1779-82[4]
Albany	120	-	-
Alsace	170	-	1 case
Amity (Q)	160	-	-
Bern (A, B)	327	13	2 cases
Bethel (B)	139	2	5 cases
Brecknock (M)	49	2	1 case
Brunswick	151	-	-
Caernarvon (A, M)	90	-	-
Colebrookedale (M)	100	-	-
Cumru (A, M)	249	3	-
Douglass	103	-	-
East District	129	-	1 case
Exeter (Q)	173	-	-
Greenwich	153	-	-
Heidelberg Mor.)	340	1	2 cases
Hereford (M, S)	139	-	1 case
Long Swamp (M)	147	-	1 case
Maiden Creek (Q)	99	-	9 cases
Maxatawny	161	-	-
Oley	156	-	1 case
Pine Grove	144	-	1 case
Reading (Q)	459	-	-
Richmond	110	-	-
Robeson (Q)	115	6	7 cases
Rockland	146	-	1 case
Ruscomb Manor (B)	97	-	1 case?
Tulpehocken (B)	290	4	1 case
Union	118	-	2 cases
West District	74	-	1 case
Windsor (A)	152	1	-

1. The letters in parenthesis indicate the presence of Amish (A), Brethren (B), Mennonites (M), Moravians (Mor), Quakers (Q), or Schwenkfelders (S) with the township.

2. The number of taxables is taken from the tax lists in the Berks County Historical Society, Reading, Pa.

3. This indicates the number of persons in each township who are designated by this term on the 1779 tax lists.

4. This indicates the number of cases prosecuted in the Berks County Court between March 7, 1780, and February 12, 1782, and listed in "An Acct of Fines on Refusing Collectors 1780 and 1781" in the court records on deposit in the Berks County Historical Society, Reading, Pa. This record begins with "The Commonwealth v Martin Shuy for Refusing to Collect Taxes [document damaged] the Additional Supplies for 1779. Fine £500." The township to which each assessor or collector belonged could be readily identified from the tax lists, with the exception of Standly Kirby, who owned land in both Maiden Creek and Ruscomb Manor townships.

DOCUMENTS

Mennonite Position Debated

A Chester County Presbyterian minister attempted to refute the Mennonite position on paying war taxes in a sermon preached in Lancaster in 1775. The Reverend John Carmichael preached on "A Self-Defensive War Lawful" at the Presbyterian Church in Lancaster on June 4, 1775, in the presence of Captain Ross' company of Lancaster County militia. The Scottish-born pastor said, in part:

Document 208

That a self-defensive war is lawful, I will prove from the conduct of Jesus Christ himself. If civil government is necessary to self-preservation, and war is necessary, at times, in government, as has been already proved; then it will follow, that those who support civil government, do support war, and so of consequence approve of war. But Jesus Christ did pay his tribute money, to the Emperor Tiberius, Matthew xvii, 27. And those who are acquainted with the life of Tiberius Caesar know that he had frequent wars. Our Lord did here, as in several other places, draw a line of distinction between church and state; the church was his own kingdom, and spiritual in its nature and government, and was not of this world; but the state was a distinct constitution, was of this world, was purely civil, and it was not essential to the being of an emperor, of what sort of religion he was of, or whether of any, as was the case of Tiberius, Tiberius was a pagan; but as the Jews were tributaries to the Romans, and our Lord was a Jew by birth, he paid his tax as a peaceable member of the commonwealth; *but had our Lord been a Mennonist he would have refused to pay tribute to support war, which shews the absurdity of these people's conduct.* . . . . In Rom. 13, from the beginning, to the 7th verse, we are instructed at large the duty we owe to civil government, but if it was unlawful and anti-Christian, or anti-scriptural to support war, it would be unlawful to pay taxes; if it is unlawful to go to war, it is unlawful to pay another to do it, or to go to do it: *What a foolish trick these people put on their consciences, who for the reasons already mentioned will not pay their taxes, and yet let others come and take their money, where they can find it, and be sure they will leave it where they can find it handily.*[27]

Some Mennonites Defend Tax Payment

Christian Funk, bishop in the Franconia congregation since 1769, was excommunicated in 1778 for advocating the payment of war taxes to the revolutionary government and refusing to take a stand against the declaration of allegiance to the same. He and his brother, Henry Funk, a former Mennonite preacher in the Swamp congregation, led a small group of Mennonites who had no difficulty in paying taxes or pledging allegiance to the new government. Christian Funk composed a defense of his conduct in 1785 and incorporated it in a longer account of the division that he published in 1809.

Document 209

A tax of £3. 10*s*. was now laid, payable in congress paper money—my fellow ministers were unanimously of opinion, that we should not pay this tax to the government, considering it rebellious and hostile to the king; but I gave it as my opinion that we ought to pay it, because we had taken the money issued under the authority of congress, and paid our debts with it. As yet this caused no manifest dissatisfaction between us, until about the year 1777, when, as usual, I invited my eight fellow ministers together, and observed to them that the time was at hand to break the bread with the congregation, and to see whether we were in peace, and further remarked, "I am in peace with you and the congregation," for no brother, nor minister, hath revealed anything of a contrary nature to me. On this day the great calamity had commenced without my knowledge; for Christian Meyer answered to my declaration of inward satisfaction, "I cannot at this time break the bread — I am not satisfied with myself" — the other seven said the same. I replied, if this is the case, you may all depart to your homes — if you are not fit to break the bread, neither are you fit to preach — the seven answered, that it was not meant so — that they were willing to go along, but Meyer would not. Whether they had been displeased at the Americans who had taken our horses, wheat, and provender, or no, was unknown to me, it however will manifest itself. As these ministers had recalled their first obscure answer, and outwardly exhibited signs of peace towards me, I was not disturbed, and conducted myself so as if I had not heard it.

A day was at length agreed upon, when we should hold an examination for the three congregations: I at Clemens's, Meyer at the Plain, and [Henry] Rosenberger at Baechtel's. But in the mean time [John] Baechtel came to me and said, none of the ministers and elders should put the usual questions, but that private members should interrogate — I replied that it was strange the ministers and shepherds were appointed for the purpose of giving counsel, help, and comfort to troubled members — And as there was no complaint against me and my fellow ministers, I was as yet no way disturbed at this dark effort; I put the questions at Clemens's, and found the congregation to be in peace. — Meyer and Rosenberger proposed to the other two congregations, that private members only should make the necessary inquiries, and that the congregation should state what they had against their ministers. This I considered as directly pointed at myself, and now that the congregation should state what they had against their ministers. This I considered as directly pointed at myself, and now they had what they sought for. Fourteen accusations were exhibited against me, and behind these they sought to shelter themselves. On Tuesday evening following, Rosenberger and [Jacob] Oberholzer came to my house — Rosenberger remarked, that the whole congregation were in peace except with me; and that I could not celebrate the Lord's supper. I enquired what complaints were alledged against me; but could not be informed of any. On this my wife observed, that they were always creating contentions before the breaking of bread — Oberholzer replied, that he would tell her of an hundred sins, and departed in anger.

Early the next morning I went to Rosenberger, and enquired of him, who had been at the examination; but he refused to inform me. I told him that I must know who was not in peace with me; on which he replied, that Isaac Dierstein and Samuel Detweiler would give me the names of my accusers, which they accordingly did. I first went to twelve who informed me, that they had nothing further than that I had allowed payment of the tax of £3. 10*s*. and that I had not expressed myself opposed to congress; on an explanation, however they were all satisfied, except the wives of Samuel Baechtel and Abraham Gehman, who being asked whether they had complained against me, at the time of the enquiry, the mother answered in the affirmative; and on my asking her the reason, she replied with some warmth, "because the Hertzils say you have taken the (affirmation) allegiance:" — at this, however, I was not disturbed, but remarked, that I sought no offering, but peace, and asked her whether it was not a shameful act to go to the examination and falsely accuse her ministers — at this they began to weep, and shewed the most peaceable dispositions towards me — whether their husbands were concerned with them, I cannot pretend to determine.

The whole congregation was now again in peace, except Oberholzer and Rosenberger, who about three days before, came to my house, and endeavored to prevent me from discharging my functions, and did what lay in their power to retard the celebration of the Lord's supper: In consequence of this, I went to Oberholzer and observed, that I had been with the fourteen, and that from appearance the bread would be broke; and further asked how matters stood with him and my wife — he replied, "do you go home and tell your wife that I was in a wild-fire that evening." Afterwards I went to Rosenberger, who likewise appeared in peace; and in consequence of this appearance of a perfect understanding, a large supper was held. — Immediately after which I became indisposed.

While thus situated, my fellow ministers proposed to the congregation not to pay the tax of £3. 10*s*.; a division however respecting the payment existed in the congregation. After I had become somewhat better, Andrew Zigler waited on me, and said, that he and Meyer had been in the congregation at Goshenhoppen, and that they had proposed that no person should pay the tax of £3. 10*s*. to which I replied, "I think we can pay it," not knowing that Zigler was opposed to me. Shortly after, Andrew Zigler and myself again met, and in the presence of Abraham Schwartz and Christian Meyer he said, "We cannot pay the £3. 10*s*. tax;" but notwithstanding all their interdictions, very few were influenced thereby. Andrew Zigler, after this, with six ministers, came to my house — On seeing them approach I went towards them to salute them in peace: On my salutation, Zigler flew back, saying, "I do not give you the kiss;" which example they all followed — this I considered against all christian charity. I by no means knew what they wanted, and said, "Doth the thing stand so bad?" You may, however, come into my house. Andrew Zigler said they had come to see whether they could pay the £3. 10*s*. tax; to which I replied, you already know my opinion. He then expressed a wish that I should examine whether, according to the gospel, we might pay the tax or not. I observed that it was my opinion we could pay it; and he asking me with what propriety, I replied, that Caesar had not been considered by the Jews as their legitimate sovereign, and thought they owed him no tribute, and that they had tempted Christ to find a cause against him. (What did these six men want but to tempt me? It was impossible that their intention was to obtain evangelical advice, when, before they entered into my house, they had refused me every evangelical peace.) — But Christ demanded a piece of their money, and asked what image and superscription it bore, to which they answered Caesar's; he then replied, "Render unto Caesar that which is Caesar's, and unto God that which is God's." — I remarked further — were Christ here, he would say, Give unto congress that which belongs to congress, and to God what is God's. This displeased Andrew Zigler, and rising, said, I would as soon go into the war, as to pay the £3. 10*s* if I were not concerned for my life; and departed in anger.

The foundation was now laid by Ziegler and his fellow ministers, upon which (at a meeting held without my knowledge) they decided that I should no longer preach the gospel.[28]

The Church of the Brethren Considers the Issue

The Church of the Brethren dealt with the question of militia and substitute fines at their annual conference in 1780 at the Conestoga church in Lancaster County. No record of that meeting has survived. In 1781 they returned to the problem of "substitute money" and took up the issue of paying "the tax."

Document 210

Article 1. Inasmuch as at the great meeting at Conestoga last year, it was unanimously concluded that we should not pay the substitute money; but inasmuch as it has been overlooked here and there and some have not regarded it, therefore we, the assembled brethren, exhort in union all brethren everywhere to hold themselves guiltless and take no part in war or bloodshedding, which might take place if we would pay voluntarily for hiring men; or yet more if we become agents to collect such money. And inasmuch as some brethren have received written orders to tell their people and afterwards to collect (such money), accompanied by the threat of a heavy fine, we fervently exhort not to be afraid to do that which is right. Still, we exhort also that if a brother is fined, there should be provision made for such brethren, and assistance rendered as far as money is concerned. In case a brother or his son [is] drafted that he or his son should go to war, and he could buy himself or his son from it, such would not be deemed so sinful, yet it should not be given voluntarily without compulsion. But where this has been overlooked, and the substitute money has been voluntary, and (the brother) acknowledges his mistake from the heart and repents it, the church shall be satisfied with him.

If a brother bears his testimony that he cannot give his money on account of his conscience and would say to the collector: "If you must take it, then use your authority, I shall not be in your way"—with such a brother we should also be satisfied. But concerning the tax, it is considered that on account of the troublesome times and in order to avoid offense, we might follow the example of Christ (Matt. 17:24-27). Yet, if one does not see it so and thinks perhaps, he for his conscience sake could not pay it, but bear with others who pay in patience, we would willingly go along inasmuch as we deem the overruling of the conscience to be wrong.[29]

The Quakers Consider the Issue

American Quakers had no settled policy on payment of war taxes in 1775, but a concern about the morality of supporting war was expressed by Friends from New England to North Carolina. Virginia Quakers sought the advice of the Meeting for Sufferings of Philadelphia Yearly Meeting. The original minutes of this meeting makes clearer some of the concerns that troubled Friends in considering the problem of war taxes. A letter from William Matthews, a minister in the Society of Friends from York County, Pennsylvania, indicates a desire to await consensus on this issue on the part of the Virginia Yearly Meeting rather than make a hasty decision.

Document 211

At a meeting of the Yearly Meeting Committee held at John Harrison[torn] at Cedar Creek the 22nd of the 12 mo. 1775

Present 15 of the members likewise Mason Janny, John Hough, Joseph Janny & Saml. Canby a Committee appointed by Fairfax monthly meeting & sundry other Friends —

After a Time of solid waiting in Silence in which the Calming influence of our heavenly Father's Love was measurably witnessed among us, we took under our weighty Consideration the following matters respecting the Society —

1st. Concerning Friends Receiving or Paying the paper Bills of Credit that are or may be Issued for the Purposes of (*procuring Arms & Ammunition &*) Carrying on (*the*) War (*against the Parent State*) & after duly considering the matter it was unanimously agreed to adopt & recommend to the notice of Friends the advice given by the last yearly meeting in Philada.

2ly. Respecting the propriety of Friends Voluntarily Paying or refusing to Pay the Taxes that may be laid for Sinking or redeeming the above paper Bills of Credit, after some Time spent thereon & many Friends having expressed their sentiments, it is concluded that it would be best to Correspond with the Meeting for Sufferings in Philada. on the occasion before we come to a decisive Judgment.[30]

Document 212

I feel a freedom to inform thee that on the 2 of Last month I set of for the Yearly Meeting in Virginia (having for my Companion William Jackson Jur.) it began on the 17 & held untill the 22d & thro' mercy was a time of favour & near uniting of the Honest in heart, the business was Carried on in much Condescension & divers matters of weight

Considered therein, Especially the Case of the oppressed negroes, & that of friends paying taxes for the Carrying on the war &c.; and as Some of us apprehended that it might in this time of tryal be of use for friends of the different Provinces to unite in a Consideration of the State of our Society it was proposed to that meeting to appoint some Suitable friends to attend our next Yearly meeting, which was readily agreed to & a committee of 6 or 8 friends appointed for that purpose.[31]

Samuel Allinson's Ideas

The most developed Quaker thought on war taxes in the period of the American Revolution came from the pen of Samuel Allinson, a young Friend from Burlington, New Jersey. This brief excerpt develops two of Allinson's key ideas, that war is not a legitimate aspect of civil government and that each generation must apply biblical truths to the issues of its own time. Allinson's "Reasons against War, and paying taxes for its support" was written in 1780 and apparently circulated in manuscript copies.

Document 213

It is true that until the instance of John Churchman, John Woolman & others in 1756, and since, Friends have generally paid their Taxes, except those in lieu of personal service, and for the purchase of Drums, Colors, &c., called Trophy Money in England. It is as true also that for many Years Friends bo[ugh]t and Sold Negro's, held them as Slaves, and took the profits of their Labor, which is condemn'd now. While evil remains in the World it is probable War may be suffered to continue and rage at times, but whether those who profess to be and are in a good degree redeem'd from the causes whence it proceeds, and from the spirit with which it is supported, should voluntarily contribute thereto in any respect is the Question. It looks most consistent, even in the eyes of the degenerate World, and it feels sensibly so at times to a remnant who desire to be clear of a business so dark and destructive, that we should avoid the furtherance of it in any and every form. This therefore seems to be the criterion; whenever an act strikes the mind with a religious fear that the voluntary performance of it will not be holding up the light of the Gospel of Peace, or be a *stumbling block* to others it ought carefully to be avoided, thus being faithful to every manifestation of Grace, righteousness would rise higher and higher, and the light thereof would not only open the path of its true votaries, but be seen by others, to the advancement of the Kingdom of the Messiah, that it may be established, and his will be done on *earth* as it is done in heaven; a state possible, I presume, or he would not have taught us to pray for it. And nothing, perhaps, will more contribute to the hastening of this kingdom than a patient suffering for well-doing, or for a refusal to do ill, *mediately* as well as immediately. . . .

We have never entered into any contract express or implied for the paym[en]t of Taxes for War, nor the performance of any thing contrary to our Relig[iou]s duties, and therefore cannot be looked upon as *disaffected* or Rebellious to *any* Gov[ernment] for these refusals, if this be our Testimony under *all*, which many believe it will hereafter be. Some may indeed say, that the Sword of War is as necessary to be unsheath'd against a foreign enemy, as the Sword of municipal justice is sometimes against an internal Malefactor, but there is a manifest difference. Municipal justice is conducted by known rules agreed upon in stillness and quiet, and may be done without injury to anyone; War makes no distinction, proceeds by Violent arbitrary measures, and makes havock of the innocent peaceable inhabitant as well as those who are in the spirit of it—the rights of all where it comes are trampled upon. If the most inoffensive subject of either power sends his Vessel abroad on the most necessary occasion, it is liable to be captured and the property confiscated tho' he has been in no fault. Civil Justice is an innocent dispassionate remedy; this cannot be said of War. And without asserting that War is not necessary but to the Pride of man let it be considered that it is for want of a due regard to the Christian Virtues, mostly on both sides, that the Amicable means of treaty & accomodation are not heartily adopted or they would effectually settle every difference. War generally springs from known causes w[hi]ch might be remedied and both sides are generally in fault; Civil wrongs happen to the most innocent on whom no blame could be fixed, and as the sufferer did not foresee so he could not prevent them. Hence there appears to be a wide distinction between the *Military* part of Government and the *civil*, the former springing out of evil, and it seems to be a general punishment for evil, the other may be compared to the various regulations or powers of a machine, each tending to keep the whole in order, and may be executed in harmony and good will; or to the Governm[en]t or authority of a Parent over his Children and Family.

It is not to be wondered at, or an argument drawn against a reformation in the refusal of Taxes for War at this Day, that our Brethren formerly paid them; Knowledge is progressive, every reform[atio]n had its beginning, even the disciples were for some time ignorant of many religious Truths, tho' they had the Company and precepts of our Savior, and they continued so for some time after his ascension; instance the conversion of the Gentiles, for they could not at first believe they were to preach the Gospel to and initiate them in the Christian Church, until a miracle was wrought to convince them of it; the doctrine of circumcision is another instance, to which rite as well as Water Baptism Christ submitted, but we do not argue thence that they ought to continue. Our Savior told his disciples he had many things to say to them which *they could not then bear*, but he promised, that when he left them he would send them the *Comforter*, and he should *teach them all things, guide them into all truth*, and *shew them things to come*. John XVI.[32]

Refusal to Provide List of Tithables

Members of the historic peace churches in the Shenandoah Valley of Virginia sometimes refused to cooperate with the tax collector by giving a list of their taxable property or even providing the number of "tithables" (persons subject to taxation) under their roof. Jackson Allen, Joseph Allen, and Mary Mowrer were presented for this offense at the Shenandoah County Court in 1778. The first two were Quakers. On September 5, 1780, sixty-six persons, many of them Quakers, were summoned to the Frederick County Court for the same offense.[33] In 1783 Joseph Allen, Frederick Alderfer, and Michael Coffman were ordered to appear in Shenandoah County Court for refusing to hand in a list of tithables. Allen was a Quaker, Alderfer a Dunker, and Michael Coffman was probably the Mennonite minister of that name. Two Quakers charged with a similar offense in Berkeley County, [West] Virginia, explained that their action was not contemptuous.

Document 214
October 29, 1778

On an information by the Deputy Attorney in behalf of the Commonwealth agt. Jackson Allen, Joseph Allen and Mary Mowrer for refusing to give in their taxable property on oath, Ordered that they may be sum[mone]d to the next Court.[34]

Document 215
[February 27, 1783]

Ordered, that Process issue against Jackson Allen, Frederick Alderfer, Michael Coffman, Adam Zeller to cause them to come here at the next Court to answer an Information filed against them respectively for failing to give in the number of their family according to law.[35]

Document 216

May it please your Excellency

On the 16th instant a judgment pass'd in the Worshipful Court of Berkeley against your Petitioners on an Information for not giving in upon oath or affirmation an account of their property liable to a tax or pound rate. Your petitioners were then present; & upon being permitted to defend themselves with many others,—They observed to the Court that the fact was true; but they humbly conceived, they were not within the law, nevertheless. They conceived that the *oath* or *affirmation* was intended to extort a just render of all taxables, & that, if this were done, it mattered not by what means soever. They proved to the satisfaction of the Court that a just inventory was given in; that the omission of an oath or affirmation was not contemptuous, that their conduct if wrong was influenced by a wrong interpretation of the law, & that they were then willing to affirm that their render to the Assessors was just & true. Upon this, the Court was of opinion, that their case was peculiar & merited compassion; & thereupon came to a resolution, that the fine should not be levyed immediately & that your petitioners shou'd have three months, in order to solicit & obtain a remission of the same. Your petitioners do therefore now apply to your Excellency & intreat a remission thereof, & do promise & assure you, that they never have & never will act in contempt of the authority of any court or the laws of the Commonwealth.[36]

Jacob Moon *Benjamin Thornburgh*

Tax Problem Greatest in Pennsylvania

The problem of persons refusing to hand in an account of their taxable property was naturally most serious in Pennsylvania, where the peaceable sects were concentrated. Attorney General Jonathan D. Sergeant gave his opinion on their liability under an Act of Assembly passed in 1779. A different opinion came from Nicholas Waln, an eminent Quaker attorney and veteran of many years in the Pennsylvania Assembly. On February 3, 1780, the Meeting for Sufferings of Philadelphia Yearly Meeting petitioned the Assembly, citing instances of oppression under both the tax laws and a Supplement to the Test Act passed in 1779, requiring those who did not take the oath of allegiance to pay double taxes.[37] The Supreme Executive Council responded with a promise to investigate and an insistence that payment of war taxes was an indispensable duty of every citizen. Correspondence with the Berks County Commissioners indicated that this was a real difficulty in their area.

Document 217

S[r],

The Commissioners unacquainted with Law, are at a Loss what Construction to put 7th Section of the Act of General Assembly for raising the supplies for the year 1779,

Suppose A Assessor of a Ward or Township calls on B to take a return of his Taxable property, B refuses to give any Account; Is that considered an intention to screen his property from Taxation, and in that Case ought B to pay fourfold for the whole of his Estate. If not, what penalty does B incur.

I think in this Case according to the words of the Law B ought to be assessed fourfold for the whole. The Legislature could never intend to punish a partial Concealment & let a total Concealment go unpunished.

Jona. D. Sergeant.°

16 Dec., 1779.

Indorsement.

1780, Rec[d] January 10th, Opinion of Attorney Gen[l] on the 7th Section of the 15 Million Tax Law.[38]

Document 218

Case

In the Act of Assembly which grants the four Million of Dollars Cap 105 is the following Clause.

#7 If any person shall wilfully conceal in the Return which he makes to the Township or Ward Assessor any part of his taxable Property within such Township or Ward with Intent to screen the same from Taxation, the person so concealing shall pay four fold Taxes for all such Property so concealed, &c.

Under this Act the following Case has arisen: A. Number of Persons, who apprehend they are called upon to bear a Testimony against Wars and Fighting, not through Obstinancy, Fraud or Deceit, but from a real Scruple of Conscience decline giving an Account of their Estates, as they cannot actively pay a tax to carry on War, tho' they do not use any Device to screen their property from Taxation, but expect passively to pay their Proportion.

Qu. Are such persons within the meaning of the said Section and liable to the heavy Penalty of a four-fold Tax upon all their Estate?

A. Penal Laws which affect particular persons are to be strictly construed and not extended beyond what the clear Words will bear; it would be very unsafe to trust those who are to execute Laws with Power to create Offences by strained Implications, otherwise they might become as Gins and Snares to entrap innocent people and be prostituted to Purposes very different from what the Legislature intended. The Assembly have been very plain in describing the Fraud or Offence which they mean to have punished, and I apprehend not one of the Characters which go to make up the Offence is to be found in the Case stated. I know not by what Train of Reasoning it can be made out, that a person who consienciously declines making any Return at all for the Reasons stated and who expects passively to pay his full Tax, is one "who in the Return he makes willfully conceals a part of his taxable Property, &c," with Intent "to screen the same from Taxation." The two Cases are as distinct in Nature and Description as Light and Darkness; the Act of Assembly has Reference to something done with a covinous or fraudulent Intention, the Case stated has not the least Mixture of Fraud or criminal Intention, in the one is a Design to screen the Property from Taxation, in the other no such View. In short to constitute the Offence mentioned in the Act three things are necessary. 1st, there must be a Return made. 2dly, a wilful concealing of a part. 3dly, With Intention to screen the same from Taxation—But it may be objected that giving no Account, must be a greater Offence than giving a partial Account, to this I oppose (upon the Case stated,) a well known Law Maxim, that the Act does not make a Man guilty, unless the Mind be guilty, and where a person of sober Life and good Morals does declare he acts from a mere Motive of Conscience in Matters of this kind, Charity which is the Perfection of Christianity forbids to deny him Credit and would induce to proceed in the most lenient Manner. And besides as the Act of Assembly makes no provision in the Case stated, it is Casus omissus and it is as I apprehend out of the Power of the Commissioners and Assessors to impose the Penalty; neither would such a Clause & accumulate Suffering upon consciencious Men have been just, confounding the innocent and guilty together. I therefore conclude that the Assembly intended to leave Matters of this sort to the reasonable Discretion of the Commissrs and Assessors, who may fall upon easy Means of doing what will obtain a proper Proportion of Tax from such persons without any public Disadvantage and more consistent with Equity, which is all that ought to be desired. For the above and other Reasons I am clear in Opinion, that the Penalty referred to in the Question can not by the said Act or by any law that I know of existing in Pennsylvania, be imposed upon the Persons stated in the Case.

Being requested to give my Sentiments upon the foregoing Subjects, which being as above, are submitted, &c.

Nicholas Waln.

Philadelphia, 1st Mo. 10th, 1780.

Note.—There is another part of the same Paragraph, which clearly shews the present Case was not intended by the Assembly respecting the Qualification of the Witness to prove the Concealment which a Case of a Refusal officially known to the Collector, would be superfluous, but it is proper for the purpose intended.*[39]

Document 219

In Council,

Philad'a, Feb'ry 5th, 1780, Saturday.

WHEREAS, Sundry persons of the Society called Quakers, have represented that divers hardships and oppressions are exercised in the collection of Public dues, Militia and other fines, by the persons employed in those services; Whereupon, the same being deliberately considered.

Resolved, That this Board doth highly disapprove of all practices tending unnecessarily to distress and impoverish any inhabitants of this State, and as the laws in force afford a sufficient remedy against all such abuses, this Board doth earnestly recommend to any persons so injured by public officers to exemplary punishment, being assured of the utmost countenance and assistance of the public authority in so doing.

Resolved, That the several particular Cases of complaint arising in the Counties of Philadelphia, Chester and Bucks, and enumerated in a paper delivered to the President, be transmitted to the Attorney General of the State, in order that the same may be prosecuted in the Courts of Justice, if the complaining parties will attend and make the necessary proof.

Resolved, That the collection of Publick Taxes, and supporting a competent force to repel the designs of the common enemy, are indispensible duties, which we owe to ourselves and posterity, and that therefore, it is highly incumbent on public authority to execute the necessary laws for these purposes with firmness and resolution, & to support and countenance every Officer of Government therein while discharging his office with fidelity and uprightness.[40]

Document 220

Reading, March 8th, 1780.

Sir.

We beg leave to lay the Inclosed Letter of Ja^{s} Biddle Esqr before the Honble Council, and beg their advise thereon, as Several very Obstinate Inhabitants in this County have positive refused to make any return for raising the Supplies for 1779 which this Board took as an Concealment of the Effects in fact and accordingly Taxed them fourfold. And now the Attorneys of Law think to make a Handle thereof, to the great delay of Collecting future Taxes and Irritating the good people, (for if the Money must be returned to those by them Called Tories,) they will be very dissatisfyed. We are Sir

Your most Obt
Humble Servants,

John Kirlin,
Adam Witman,
Thos. Jones, Junr.

Commisrs.

His Excellency, Joseph Reed, Esqr President Of the Supreme Executive Council of the Commonwealth of Pennsylvania, Philadelphia.[41]

Document 221
Philade, March 13, 1780.
Gentlemen;

Your letter of the 8th Inst, has been duly received & laid before the Council. As the Difficulties you have met with in the execution of your Office, we believe originated here it becomes easier to give you a full & clear Answer. Our Advice & Direction therefore is that you proceed upon the Act of Assembly agreeable to the Opinion of the Atty General which is enclosed & which was obtained in Consequence of a like Objection made here by Persons who have manifested little Attachment to the great Cause we have been and are yet supporting. When Gentlemen of the Law give their Opinion to their Clients they are acting in their Profession & if any Person chooses on such an Opinion to enter into a Contest with the public Officers he must abide the Consequences, but then Opinions are generally too interested to be a safe Guide to public Officers & we recommend to you not to pay any Regard to them in the execution of your Office, but in cases of real Difficulty to apply to the Board as you have now done, to the Supreme Court or Attorney General when Alone.

We therefore have only to repeat to you what we have already said to the Commissioners of the County that you ought to proceed with Firmness and Temper in the Collection of the Taxes, leaving to Individuals to avail themselves of the Laws of the Country for Redress if they apprehend themselves injured & while acting with impartiality & Integrity you may rely upon our fullest Support & Assistance.

I am Gentlemen,
Your Obed^{t} Hbble Servt,
Jos Reed,
President.[42]

Document 222

Reading, June 5th, 1780.

Sir,

By one of the Commissioners of the County of Lancaster, one of our Board was informed that they did not Continue the double Tax on those that have not taken the Oath or Affirmation to their Returns for the Monthly Supplies. Jona. D. Serjeants, Esq., Council to us was that the double Taxes are to be Continued, on which we have Issued our Duplicates to the Collectors, but should we act Contrary to what other Counties do, evenly, should it be the perfect meaning of the Law, we think we are not able to Support it. We therefore beg your advice thereon if Possible by this Post.

We are, Sir,
Your mo. Obt. H'ble Servt.,

Adam Witman,
Thos. Jones, Junr.

P.S.—We are likewise Informed that it is discontinued in Chester County.

Public Service.

His Excellency, Joseph Reed, Esqr., President Supreme Executive Council, Pennsylvania.[43]

Amount of Tax Questioned

Schwenkfelder Christopher Schultz and Mennonite Michael Ziegler joined in a respectful protest to the Berks County Commissioners over the "enormous Sum" required from Hereford Township for the 1779 Supply Tax. Schultz carried the Hereford protest to the Supreme Executive Council, who promised to have a full and impartial inquiry. The County Commissioners, ignoring Schultz's appeal to the Council, ordered the taxes collected and began legal proceedings against Schultz for failing to do his duty. At issue was the amount of the tax and not any use to which it might be put.

Document 223

To the Board of Commissioners

Gentlemen

By the above it will appear that we have obeyed your order and assessed the Township of Hereford to raise the Sum of £5667, as we were directed, but being apprehensive that the said Sum far exceeds our just Quota as your Board was not provided with our Returns to fix them and having great cause to presume if the Quantity and Quality of the Taxable articles of our Township were legally compared with the same in the Townships of the County equity wou'd in that case exonerate us perhaps of a third part of the Sum and to enable you to judge the better, we give, in a summary way, the Quantity of Acres with the Horses and Cattle in our Township, viz. 12,712 Acres of Land of which there is four fifths hilly and stoney and of the same Quality with the District [Township] Land and the remaining fifth is of a tolerable good condition. Horses there is the Number of 191 and Cattle 349 Heads. We must therefore insist in behalf of the Township to have justice done, according to a lawful investigation of the matter, and hereby solemnly Protest that our proceedings shall not be construed as allowing or submitting to this injury. We have gone on with the Assessment that we might not by any means obstruct the furtherance of the Taxes, under confidence your Board will in Consequence of this our Remonstrance duly rectify that great Error, and in your Duplicate to the Collector, cut off that proportion of each Taxable persons assessment as the said Township will appear to be over rated by that enormous Sum, whereby the Clamours of Injury may be prevented, and the thought of seeking other Redress happily suppressed.

We are Gentlemen

Your humble Servts.

Christr. Schultz

Richard Tea

Michael Ziegler[44]

Paper Currency Refused

Other Friends refused the paper currency issued by the Continental Congress to pay for the war.

Document 224

John Cowgill, having a religious Scruple against circulating the paper Currency emitted by the Continental Congress, was taken before a body of men called a committee of Inspection, on, or about the 12th of the 12th month 1775, and not being free to give them the assurance they required, that he would take it in future, he was by their directions advertised in the public News papers and declared to be an "Enemy to his Country," and all persons warned against having any dealings with him, so that some millers became unwilling to Grind his Corn for the use of his family, and the Schoolmaster who taught his Children sent them home for a time; and on the 1st day of the 2nd month 1776, as he was going to a weekday meeting with his family, he was seized on the road by a number of Armed Men, who told him that the said Committee had sent for him, and they conveyed him in their own Cart to Dover, beating a drum before him to the town, and through it, with a paper fixed to his back inscribed "On the Circulation of the Continental Currency depends the fate of America;" after which he was drove out of the town and dismissed, not being permitted to warm himself, tho' the day was very cold; all which hard usage he appeared to bear with patience and resignation, having the reward of peace in his own mind, for his faithfulness to what he apprehended to be his religious duty.[45]

Document 225

Dear General, Cross-Roads, Dec. 21, 1776.

I hope the subject of this letter will serve as a sufficient apology for the liberty I take in writing you. I think it my duty to inform you of the strange and perverse change in politics which hath taken place through a great part of this county. Even some quondam associators, as well as conscientiously scrupulous men, totally refuse to accept Congress money as payment for old debts; and there are some so maliciously averse to our support of liberty that they refuse to part with any commodity whatsoever, even the necessaries of life, unless they get hard money, or the old paper currency of this province. Most of the tavern-keepers (who are Friends) on the Lancaster road have pulled down their signs, and refuse the soldiery provisions or drink; they will assign you no reason for such conduct. The reason, however, is too evident: they are afraid to receive Congress money. The other day a man offered the sum of £300 Congress for £150 Pennsylvania currency. While people are suffered thus to depreciate that money by which we carry on the present war, and are passed by, unnoticed and with impunity, I cannot hesitate a moment in pronouncing the contest near an end, and, what I dread, an inglorious one, too.

What officer or soldier will enter into the service in future if the common and immediate necessaries of life are denied them, because they have it not in their power to lay down any other than Congress money? Inclosed, I beg leave to send you a Resolve, which, in my weak judgment, (if adopted by Congress), would remedy every inconvenience. If you should like it, you no doubt will exert your influence with that august body to have it passed as soon as possible.

I am dear sir, etc.

F. Johnston

Resolved, That all persons, to whom debts are now, or shall henceforth become due, who shall refuse to accept Continental money, from his or their debtors in discharge of such debts (it being first properly tendered them in the presence of two witnesses), shall be, and they are hereby forever debarred from the recovery of such debts, and are hereby ordered to deliver up any bond, bill, or note, upon which such debt may have become due, unto the said debtor or debtors, under the pains and penalties of fine and imprisonment.[46]

Document 226

The following resolution of Congress was directed to be inserted on the Minutes of this Council:

"In Congress, December 27th, 1776.

"*Resolved,* That the Council of Safety of Pennsylvania be requested to take the most vigorous and Speedy measures for punishing all such as shall refuse Continental Currency, and that the General be directed to give all necessary aid to the Council of Safety for carrying their measures on this subject into effectual execution.

"By order of Congress.

"Sign'd *John Hancock,* President."[47]

Document 227

The Petition of the Subscribers Inhabitants of the County of Frederick, Most Humbly Sheweth, That sundry Persons have and do refuse to receive the present Circulating Currency in Payment of Bills, Bonds and Mortgages for Debt, to the great inconvenience and injury of many, and the depreciation of the Currency in General, which they Consider as a weighty Grievance, and therefore Earnestly beg that a Law may Pass for relief of all Persons who are desirous to pay off their respective Debts, as they conceive it Strictly just that each Individual should have the care and risk of their own money.[48]

Court Cases

Caspar Sauder of Manor Township in Lancaster County was convicted in 1777 of refusing to accept the money issued by the Continental Congress. In a similar case Frederick Koble was jailed by the Berks County Court in 1779.

Document 228
Lancaster County ss.
July 3d. [1777] The Common Wealth of Pennsylvania
v.
Caspar Sauder . . . . £200. .0. .0
Christn. Wirtz & Bail in £100 each is 200. .0. .0
Willm. Henry Esq.

To be & Appear at the next Court of General Quarter Session to be held for the County aforesd. on the first Tuesday of August next to answer unto such matters & things which shall be laid against him by Christina Miller, for refusing the Continental Bills of Credit in pay of a debt of £10 due him by her Husband, & said the Money was not good and that they Rebelled against the King.
Christina Miller bound in the Sum of £20. .0. .0

A. Hubley[49]

Document 229

Christopher Schultz to "his Excellency the President of the Supreme Executive Council," May 30, 1780

Having had the Favour of a Hearing in Council on the 19 Instant, on presenting my Petition for Protection against the Oppressions of the Board of Commissioners & Assessors of Berks County against me and my fellow Inhabitants of Hereford Township in the sd. County, when your Excellency was pleased, to assure me of a just Inquiry into the Premises, by the Judges of the Supream Court at Reading, which was expected shortly to commence, and that mean while the sd. Inhabitants Should rest Still and easy, as I understood. I now beg leave Sir, to inform you, that since That Time the sd. Board has proceeded, to overset all my Doings as Assessor in the Business of raising the Taxes in Hereford aforesaid, by appointing Georg Moll Collector, to be now Township Assessor, with Orders and Powers as if never an Assessor had been in the Township for raising the Tax, or any part of the Business done. And have likewise sent their Summons to me by the Sheriff, to appear personally before the Board, on the 5th of June next, to shew Cause why Execution shall not Issue against me for the fine to be recovered from a Township Assessor who neglects his Duty or any of his Duty &c. Dated the 20th May 1780 Signed Adam Witman Thoms. Jones jur.

And whereas several Magistrates of Reading whom to see I had an Opportunity on the 26th last, have told me, they could not know, neither when or whether a Supream Court would be held at Reading this Spring Time, and Execution for Fines undoubtedly will soon be Issued against me and fines laid upon the newly appointed Assessor and other Inhabitants of our Township, whose Confidence is directed to Your Excellencies Protection in their just Cause and are unwilling farther to Submit to the injurious Proceedings of the sd. Board, but ready to comply with the Assessment notified to them by the Collector by which the full Quota unjustly settled upon them by the sd. Board will be raised; when on the other hand it now will require a Length of Time before the Taxes in their arbitrary Way (were it even without Opposition) can be collected. Therefore I humbly hope your Excellency will not be offended, when I take the Liberty, to lay these Matters open before You, that your Excellency may take such Measures in the Premises, as in Your Wisdom you shall find best Suit for the common Welfare & Prosperity, and the Protection of such as in their Station have faithfully Served the Commonalty, among which Number if fairly counted, will be found,

Sir, Your Excellencys
most obedient humble Servant
Christopher Schultz

P.S. The high Sheriff of Berks lately told me, that being charged by the Board to Serve an Execution to recover a Fine on a Collector whom the Board knew beforehand he could and would not Serve, he was, charged to seize besides the Fine and all the Costs of Execution, the Sum of One hundred and fifty four Pounds merely for their Trouble in ordering that Execution. A Number of like Extortions the sd. Sheriff could and I think would tell if properly asked, and which in my opinion could Serve to the public Tranquility. Your generosity Sir will make Allowance for my Defects in Language, and will be pleased I hope to favour me with our Pleasure and Commands by the Bearer hereof Michael Ziegler.[50]

Conspiring to Obstruct the Collection of Taxes

The heavy tax burden imposed by the war, rather than any conscientious objection to war taxes, was clearly the motivating force behind tax resistance in Bern, Bethel, and Tulpehocken townships in Berks County. In November, 1780, the Supreme Court convicted 149 persons from these three townships of conspiring to obstruct the collection of taxes. Since there were a total of 756 taxpayers in the three townships, this would mean that one of every five taxpayers was convicted of this conspiracy. Although Bern Township included a number of Amish families, none of them took part in this refusal to pay taxes.

Document 230

Tulpehoccon in Berks County Sept. 18th 1780.

Know all Men by these Presents that this Day an Agreement hath been settled between us the Subscribers Inhabitants of the said Township and of Bethel Township as follows to wit: Firstly.—The Subscribers bind and engage themselves together as one Man that they will not by any Means pay the Fine imposed upon them for refusing to qualify to their Returns Upon this Condition that if the property of any one of us should be seized for the said Fine then the others are bound upon the first Notice to deliver his Goods to him again and so each and every of them in Case their Goods should be seized shall receive Assistance from us as far as this Agreement between us extends. And if one or other of us should not appear upon the first Call at the Place where it may be necessary, in Case he shall be at Home and in Health, he shall at the Discretion of the Associated Company have his Goods seized without bail and shall be deemed an Enemy to the Liberties of his Country. And for the true Performance of this Agreement we have signed the same with our names.[51]

Document 231

Berks ss.

Philip Reeser of Bern Township yeoman bound in £10,000

William Reeser of Reading & John Althaus Jr. of Bern bound each in £5,000

To and for the Use of the Commonwealth of Pennsylvania

Upon these Condition that if the above bounden Philip Reeser Shall be & appear before the Judges of the Supreme Court to be held at Reading in & for the County of Berks the sixth day of November next then & there to answer a charge of having entered in to a treasonable association to oppose the Laws & Such other things as shall be objected against him and not part from sd. Court without Leave that then the above Recognizance to be void otherwise to be & remain in full force & virtue.

Signed & Acknowledged	*Philip Reeser*
the 21st October 1780	*William Reeser*
before me	*Johannes Althaus*[52]
	Henry Christ

Document 232

Berks Oyer & Terminer
Novr. Sessions 1780.

Berks County ss.

The Jurors for the Commonwealth of Pennsylvania upon their Oaths & Affirmations do present that David Bright, John Scheffer, Jacob Ruth, Peter Lebo, Valentine Mayer, Philip Read, Henry Moyer, Jacob Lingel, Michael Wolfard, Jacob Read, Adam Brown, Nicholas Kinsecker, Jacob Decker, William Goodman, Michael Paffenberger, Jacob Lebo, Jacob Bettleman, George Gebhard, Andrew Saltzgaber, Christian Bardorff, John Albert, John George Read, Nicholas Read, Frederick Read, John Light, John Hubler, Henry Kiplinger, Michael Koppenhaver, Henry Scheffer, Windle Kieffer, Casper Read, Nicholas Gouker, Andreas Schott, John Riegel, Michael Will, Robert McCann, Conrad Wert, George Hawk, Charles Bamberger, George Goosman, John Roan, Adam Petreicher, Anthony Fitzler, Conrad Gissler, Christian Shell, Peter Ritzman, Michael Kuhns, John Sweitzer, Peter Mohn, Peter Kreitzer, George Woolf, Nicholas Hawk, Casper Ruth, Joseph Gissler, John George Weil, Martin Brown, Michael Read, Christopher Wolfard, Philip Gundm[an?], George May, Adam Riehm, Jacob Artzt, Henry Holtzman, John Brown, Michael Walborn, Peter Liep, Leonard Strip]Striss?], Peter Schwartz, Michael Troutman, Thomas Kurr Junior, Simon Kern, Jacob Weiser, Henry Lebo, Peter Kridzer, Christian Walborn, Jacob Bortner, John Nicholas Dock, John Wirtz, Jacob Butzins, George Mayer, John Swartzhaubt, Philip Clane, George Windle Woolf, Adam Albright, Christian Badorf, Christopher Kern, George Kremer, Henry Goodman, Abraham Kissinger, Albright Hoy & Godfried Rohrer all late of the County afd. Yeomen, on the Eighteenth Day of September in the year of our Lord one thousand seven hundred & Eighty being Subjects of this State & owing Allegiance to the same & owing obedience to the Laws thereof; but not being content to submit to the Laws afd. & falsely & seditiously resolving to oppose the Execution thereof on the same Day & Year at Tulpehocken in the County afd. unlawfully & seditiously did assemble & meet together and so being assembled & met did then & there unlawfully & seditiously conspire combine & agree among themselves that none of the sd. Conspirators, after the sd. Eighteenth Day of September in the Year afd. would or should pay the Fines & Penalties nor any of them which now or should be imposed according to Law upon them or any of them for refusing or neglecting to make a Return of their taxable property upon Oath or Affirmation according to the Form of the Act of Assembly in such Case made & provided And then & there being so assembled & met together did further unlawfully & seditiously conspire combine & agree that if the property of any one of the sd. Conspirators should be seized according to Law for the sd. property out of the Hands of the Officers appointed by Law for seizing the same & that they would so rescue the same & redeliver it to the sd. Conspirator who had been the Owner thereof and that each & every of the sd. Conspirators in Case their Goods should be so seized as afd. should receive Assistance from the other Conspirators pursuant to the Terms of the Agreement and that if any one or more of the sd. Conspirators should not appear upon the first Call at the place where it might be necessary to give such Assistance he or they so not appearing in Case he were at Home & in Health, should at the Discretion of the other Conspirators have his Goods seized without Fail & be deemed an Enemy to the Liberties of this Country, in manifest Contempt of the Laws and Government of this State & to the Obstructing of the Execution of its Laws to the evil Example of all others in the like Case offending & against the Peace & Dignity of the Commonwealth of Pennsylvania.

Jona. D. Sergeant Atty. G.

Witnesses, Thos. Kurr
Henry Christ
Peter Spiecher

Berks Oyer & Terminer
Novr. Sessn. 1780
Respublica
Conspy.
v.
David Bright & others
A True Bill
per John Ludwig foreman
Defts. plead guilty & Fined £300 each & Costs commd.[53]

Document 233

To His Excellency Joseph Reed Esqr. President of the Supreme executive Council of the Common Wealth of Pennsylvania

The Petition of the Subscribers Inhabitants of the Townships of Tulpehoccon & Bethel in the County of Berks

Humbly Sheweth

That your Petitioners imprudently had signed a certain Treasonable paper, which at that time they were made to believe had no other Tendency, than to withhold payment of the Fines incurred on the

Monthly Taxes, until such time they could be informed what their Sister Counties were doing in that case. And that your Petitioners have always been uniformly and strongly attached to the Liberties of America but were then by some Ill designing means taken with them, unwarily led into that unwarrantable act, of which they sincerely Repent. And whereas the Fines and Penalty they thereby incurred, and which they were sentenced to pay by a supreme Court held in Reading the 6th day of November 1780, if rigurously exacted from them, will reduce your Petitioners and their innocent Families to distress and Want. Your Petioners therefore Humbly pray, that the Mercy of Government might be extended towards them, and their respective Fines and Penalties be remitted. And your Petitioners as in duty bound will ever pray Tulpehoccon January 11th 1781.[54]

Document 234

To the Honorable the President and Council of the State of Pennsylvania

The Petition of Conrad Schneider and Jacob Faust both of Bern Township in the County of Berks in the said State

Humbly Sheweth

That your Petitioners were fined at the last Court of Oyer and Terminer held for the said County in the Sum of Three hundred Pounds each for conspiring (as was supposed) to prevent the Payment of the Fines for not making their Returns in the manner appointed by Law. When in fact neither of your Petitioners ever signed the Association entered into for that Purpose or any wise countenanced such Measures; the Names of Both of the Petitioners having been signed to the said Association without their Knowledge or Consent by Persons unauthorized so to do, as neither of them attended the Meeting or ever saw the Paper signed by the Conspirators as aforesaid.

That the said Petitioners have since duly paid the double Tax imposed on them to the Collector of the said Township. They therefore humbly pray that under the Circumstances aforesaid, your Honors will be pleased to remit the Fines set upon them by the sd. Court. And they will pray &c.

Reading Jany. 21st 1781

Conrad Schneider
Jacob Faust[55]

Self-Imposed Tax for Local Needs

In Lampeter Township in Lancaster County, a public meeting was held at the home of Jacob Houser to apportion a tax for the relief of the poor "without any orders from Justices or any other authority." The fact that the tax was laid so openly and that no effort was made to hide the identity of the self-appointed assessors and tax collectors makes it obvious that this was not a case of a simple swindle. Rather, Lampeter taxpayers, like the Quaker tax collectors in some eastern Pennsylvania communities, were meeting local needs without reference to either king or independent Commonwealth.

Document 235

Jno. Christy of Lampiter Township says—

That about ten Days agoe John Rohrer came to him & demanded a poor Tax from him. Christy asked him how much it was. Rohrer sd. it was £13. .0. .0 continental or 4/- hard money. Christy demanded a sight of his duplicate. Rohrer showed him a Paper wherein the Inhabitants of the Township were rated & signed by some Persons. Christy asked him who laid the Tax. Rohrer told him it was laid by Jacob Houser, Christian Hartman, Abraham Buckwalter & some others. Christy observing by the List that John Grove was taxed but £9. .0. .0 he paid that Sum to John Rohrer. Christy says that John Grove told him that he had paid Rohrer 3/- hard Money for his Tax. That David Grove told him that he Grove was at Jacob Housers when the Tax was laid & that it was laid without any orders from Justices or any other authority. That David Grove told him he had paid Rohrer 5/6 hard Money for the Tax of himself & his Brother. That John °a Distiller who lives with Martin Mellinger told him he had paid £9. .0. .0 to Rohrer for poor Tax. That Rohrer & Nicholas Meck (who joins Rohrer) were collectors of the Tax on this side Pequea, but dont know the others.

9 May 1780.

Examn. of Jno. Christy respecting the Lampiter Tax gatherers.[56]

Document 236

Pennsylvania, to wit

Whereas I have received information that Jacob Houser of Lampeter Township in the County of Lancaster Yeoman, Christian Hartman of the same Township Yeoman, and Abraham Buckwalter of the same Township Yeoman have without any authority from or under the Government of the State of Pennsylvania and in contempt of the

°Left blank in the original.

authority of the Government aforesaid assessed and levied divers Sums of Money by way of Taxes on the Inhabitants of the said Township of Lampiter And that John Rohrer & Nicholas Meck of the same Township of Lampiter Yeomen by and under the direction, appointment & authority of the said Jacob Houser, Christian Hartman & Abraham Buckwalter have collected and received divers Sums of Money so assessed from divers Inhabitants of the same Township, These are therefore in the name of the Commonwealth aforesaid to require and command you forthwith to apprehend the said Jacob Houser, Christian Hartman, Abraham Buckwalter, John Rohrer & Nicholas Meck and bring them before me to answer the Premisses and that they may be dealt with according to Law. Given under my Hand & Seal at Lancaster the ninth Day of May in the Year of our Lord One thousand seven Hundred & eighty.

Thos. M:kean

To the Sheriff of the County of Lancaster
in the State of Pennsylvania and to all and
every the Constables in the said County.

Commonwealth — Sur charge abovesaid.
v.

Jacob Houser, Christian Hartman, and Nicholas Meck

Partes ipse—each is held in £40,000 sub conditione to appear and ansr. at next court of Oyer & Terminer & General Goal Delivery at Lancaster for the county of Lancaster, and in the mean time to keep the peace & be of good behavior &c.

Peter Miller of the Borough of Lancaster in said County Butcher and Jacob Klotz of Do. Hatter, and Abraham Whitmore of Lampeter township Yeoman tent. each in £20,000 as sureties &c.

Taken May 10th 1780

Before *Thos. M:Kean*

Respublica
v.
John Rorer

Pars ipse tent in £20,000 sub conditione &c.* to appear & answer &c. at next court of Oyer & Terminer & General Goal Delivery to be holden at Lancaster for the county of Lancaster, & in the mean time to be of good behavior &c.

*The party himself bound in £20,000 on condition &c.

John Whitmore of the Borough of Lancaster in the said county Yeoman tent. in £10,000 as surety.
Acknowledged May 11th 1780 Before *Thos. M:Kean.*

Respublica
v.
Abraham Buckwalter

Pars ipse tent. in £20,000 sub conditione ut supra.*
Christian Vert of the Borough of Lancaster Gentleman tent, in £10,000 as surety &c.
Acknowledged May 11th 1780
Before *Thos. M:Kean*
Warrant for apprehending Lampiter Tax Gatherers & Assessors And their Recog.[57]

Notes for Chapter 5

1. Donald D. Kaufman, *What Belongs to Caesar?* (Scottdale, Pa., 1969), 71-74. Walter Klaassen, "Anabaptism and Church/Government Issues," Paper read at Inter-Mennonite Conference on War Taxes, Kitchener, Ont., October 30—November 1, 1975. Walter Klaassen, "Mennonites and War Taxes," *Pennsylvania Mennonite Heritage,* I (April, 1978), 17-23.

2. Samuel Allinson, "Reasons against War, and paying Taxes for its support," dated 13th 6th month, 1780. Quaker Collection, Haverford College Library, Haverford, Pa. *Cf.* William C. Braithwaite, *The Second Period of Quakerism* (Cambridge, 1961), 601.

3. Anthony Benezet to George Dillwyn, n.d., endorsed "7 mo. 1780," George Brookes, *Friend Anthony Benezet* (Philadelphia, 1937), 345-347.

4. Margaret E. Hirst, *The Quakers in Peace and War* (New York, 1923), 142.

5. Kenneth S. P. Morse, *Baltimore Yearly Meeting 1672-1830* (Barnesville, Ohio, 1961), 14.

6. Hirst, 195.

7. Allinson is quoting from the Journal of John Richardson, an English Quaker who visited Rhode Island in 1702. Allinson, "Reasons against War," Q.C., H.C.L.

8. Christian Funk, *A Mirror for All Mankind* (Norristown, Pa., 1814), 10-15.

9. Hening, *Virginia Statutes at Large,* X, 314-315, 261-262, 334-335, 416-419.

10. This evidence is examined in "The Historical Tradition of the Brethren Regarding Payment of Taxes for War Purposes," which accompanied the statement on "The Christian's Response to Taxation for War" adopted at the 1973 Church of the Brethren Annual Conference.

11. Durnbaugh, *Brethren in Colonial America,* 353-354.

12. Jack D. Marietta, "Wealth, War and Religion: The Perfection of Quaker Asceticism 1740-1783," *Church History,* XLIII (June 1974), 237n.

13. Mack Thompson, *Moses Brown, Reluctant Reformer* (Chapel Hill, N.C., 1962), 139.

14. New England Yearly Meeting, Meeting for Sufferings to Philadelphia Yearly Meeting, 12th 3rd month, 1776. Philadelphia Yearly Meeting, Minutes of Sufferings, 1775-1785, fols. 74-76, Q.C., H.C.L.

15. Arthur Mekeel, "The Free Quaker Movement in New England During the American Revolution," *Bulletin of Friends Historical Association,* XXVII (1938), 72-82.

16. Moses Brown to Anthony Benezet, 2nd 10th month, 1780, Brookes, *Friend Anthony Benezet,* 429-435.

17. Philadelphia Yearly Meeting, Minutes of Meeting for Sufferings, 1775-1785, fol. 309. Q.C., H.C.L.

18. Brookes, *Friend Anthony Benezet,* 429-435.

19. Samuel Allinson, "Reasons against War," Q.C., H.C.L.

20. Martin H. Schrag, *The First Brethren in Christ Confession of Faith.*

21. Lancaster County Commissioners Minute Book, April 7, 1777, *et seq.* Lancaster County Historical Society, Lancaster, Pennsylvania.

22. *Pennsylvania Evening Post* (Philadelphia), August 12, 1777.

23. *The Friend,* V (June 23, 1832), 290. Samuel J. Atlee to Supreme Executive Council, June 22, 1780, Continental Congress, Pennsylvania State Papers, 83, 69, II, 233. National Archives, Washington, D.C. "The Deficiencies of Paxtang Township 1780," William Henry Papers. H.S.P.

24. Records of the Supreme Court: Courts of Oyer and Terminer, I, fols. 82-85. Petition of Tulpehocken and Bethel townships, January 17, 1781, Petition of Conrad Schneider and Jacob Faust, January 26, 1781, Clemency File, Records of Supreme Executive Council. P.H.M.C.

25. "An Account of Fines on Refusing Collectors 1780 and 1781, Berks County Historical Society, Reading, Pa. The relevant court minute books for Berks County are either lost or inaccessible; at least a diligent search by the librarian of the Historical Society failed to turn up any earlier than the May 1781 session.

26. Northkill Amish Congregation Alms Book, in possession of Miss Catherine Miller, Grantsville, Md.

27. Rev. John Carmichael, A.M., *A Self-Defensive War Lawful* (Philadelphia: John Dean, 1775), 17-18.

28. Funk, 10-15.

29. Durnbaugh, 353-354.

30. Brock Collection, Henry E. Huntington Library, San Marino, Calif. Italicized words were crossed out in the original.

31. William Matthews to Israel Pemberton, June 16, 1776, Fairfax, Va., Pemberton Papers, H.S.P.

32. Samuel Allinson, "Reasons against War, and paying taxes for its Support," Q.C., H.C.L.

33. Frederick County Order Book, XVII, 1778-1781, fols. 372-373, Frederick County Court House, Winchester, Va.

34. Shenandoah County Order Book, 1774-1780, fol. 82. Shenandoah County Court House, Woodstock, Va. Jackston Allen, a miller, had been called into court in 1776 because he freed his three slaves.

35. Shenandoah County Court Minute Book, 1781-1784, fol. 150. Shenandoah County Court House, Woodstock, Va.

36. Legislative Petitions: Berkeley County, Virginia State Library, Richmond, Va.

37. Philadelphia Yearly Meeting, Minutes of the Meeting for Sufferings, 1775-1785, fols. 253-254. Q.C., H.C.L.

38. *Pennsylvania Archives*, 1st Series, VIII, 49.

39. *Ibid.*, 81-82.

40. *Colonial Records*, XII, 244-245.

41. *Pennsylvania Archives*, 1st Series, VIII, 124.

42. *Ibid.*, 133-134.

43. Ibid., 303.

44. Hereford Township, Berks County, Tax Assessment for 1779, Berks County Historical Society, Reading, Pa.

45. Philadelphia Yearly Meeting, Minutes of Meeting for Suffering 1775-1785, fol. 176. Q.C., H.C.L.

46. J. S. Futhey and Gilbert Cope, *History of Chester County, Pa.* (Philadelphia: 1881), 615.

47. *Colonial Records*, X, 70.

48. April 5, 1779, Legislative Petitions: Frederick County, V.S.L.

49. Lancaster County Indictment, Lancaster County Court House, Lancaster, Pa.

50. Letters of Members of the Provincial Congress, I, 68. H.S.P.

51. Records of the Supreme Court. P.H.M.C.

52. *Ibid.*

53. *Ibid.*

54. Clemency File, Records of the Supreme Executive Council, P.H.M.C.

55. Clemency File, Records of the Supreme Executive Council. P.H.M.C.

56. Records of the Supreme Court. P.H.M.C.

57. *Ibid.*

Chapter 6

"WE CANNOT KNOW WHETHER GOD HAS REJECTED THE KING"

The Problems of Allegiance and Obedience

War taxes, militia fines, and the obligation to provide substitutes for drafted men were all devices to draw members of the peace churches into alignment with the Patriot cause. Their refusal to give the rebels a serious commitment and their insistence on paying fines under duress continued to make them suspect and, early in 1777, Patriots adopted a new plan to force neutrals to choose sides once and for all.

Until they signed the Declaration of Independence, even delegates to the Continental Congress could protest a firm and unwavering loyalty to King George III and insist that their quarrel was only with the king's ministers in Parliament. But a new nation was born on July 4, 1776, and its citizens could no longer claim to be at one and the same time loyal subjects of the British crown.

Only a minority of Americans welcomed independence in 1776. Even more alarming was the readiness of Patriot leaders to accept British pardon and protection. After Sir William Howe's troops occupied New York City in September, 1776, the president of the New York Convention and a host of lesser Patriots took formal oaths of allegiance to King George. The offer of an unconditional pardon to all who renewed their allegiance to the king, announced by Howe in November, 1776, was no idle gesture for propaganda purposes. Washington countered with a proclamation in January, 1777, requiring everyone who had sworn allegiance to the king to affirm his loyalty to the United States or be regarded as an enemy. The oath of allegiance was needed "to distinguish between the friends of America and those of Great-Britain," General Washington said. An oath would also make clear that "every man who receives protection from and is a subject of any State (not being conscientiously scrupulous of bearing arms) should stand ready to defend the same against any hostile invasion."[1]

Radical Patriots saw the necessity for an oath to identify friends and enemies beyond the comparative few who had received a pardon from a British general. They demanded that every adult male take a loyalty oath. In the February, 1777, session of the Maryland General Assembly, the House of Delegates passed legislation intended to curb the active Loyalist and smoke out the covert Loyalist or neutral, but the Maryland Senate modified the sweeping provisions of the Tory Bill, eliminating a proposed general test of allegiance and requiring a loyalty oath only of officeholders.[2] No sooner was this bill enacted into law than a new proposal for a test oath passed the House of Delegates in June 1777. This bill stopped short of a general test oath, but authorized justices of the peace to require any suspicious person to take the oath and empowered the county court to exile anyone who refused.[3] Again the Maryland Senate blocked action on the bill, so radicals carried their case to the people. Debate on the proposed test act filled the columns of the Maryland newspapers in the summer of 1777.[4]

While Marylanders debated, the Pennsylvania General Assembly followed the radical lead. In May, 1777, the Philadelphia Whig Society addressed the Assembly on the subject (*Document 237*). There could be no neutrals. Anyone who was not an active Patriot was an enemy, and those who held back because of religious scruples "or peculiarity of sentiment" should be treated in the same way as the man who shouldered a musket alongside Sir William Howe's redcoats.

The Assembly on May 22, 1777, considered the Whig Society petition "for the encouragement of those who are supporting the independence of those who are supporting the independence of the United States and for the suppression of those who are not," and began debate on a test oath for all adult male Pennsylvanians. A bill "obliging the male white inhabitants of this state to give Assurances of Allegiance" became law on June 13, 1777.[5]

The act declared that allegiance and protection are reciprocal and that "those who will not bear the former, are not (nor ought not) to be intitled to the benefits of the latter." Every white male over the age of eighteen was obliged to swear or affirm allegiance to the free and independent state of Pennsylvania and to renouce the king of Great Britain, but taking the oath was a voluntary act. There was no power to coerce anyone to subscribe to the test, except for suspicious persons traveling from one county to another, who could be brought before a justice and tendered the oath. Those who failed to take the oath were declared incapable of voting, holding office, serving on juries, suing for debt, or transferring real estate by deed.

The Pennsylvania Assembly's swift action gave little time for public debate on the wisdom of a test oath. One critic thought the penalties too light, since many who would not take the oath would prefer exclusion from jury duty and the ballot box to defending American liberty.[6] A groundswell of public opinion favored higher taxes for the nonjurors, as those who refused the oath were known. The test act under consideration in Maryland that summer went beyond the Pennsylvania legislation as "they intend laying taxes afterward on all persons who shall neglect or refuse to take the test." The editor of the *Pennsylvania Evening Post* endorsed this plan and thought "it probable something of the same kind may be done hereafter in this state."[7]

Speedy passage of the test act allowed too little time for Patriots to prepare their constituents to accept the new measure. A Moravian diarist in Lancaster County noted in June 1777 that "Much excitment has recently prevailed concerning the taking of the test oath, to which people are strongly opposed."[8] A York County Patriot anticipated that as soon as "this long tailed oath is to be imposed on the People" in his county, "we shall have som truble on hand, as many are of opinion it is Verry impolitick at Present."[9] Few Cumberland County men took the oath voluntarily, a Patriot reported from Carlisle, although the others "must soon see the necessity of Complyance."[10] Indifference, hostility, and conscientious objections made Pennsylvanians slow to carry out the demands of the Assembly, although the peace churches formed the core of opposition to the test act.

Mennonites and Quakers refused to affirm their allegiance, although they were ready, in the words of Henry Funk, a Northampton County preacher, to "Qualify to be true to the State according to the Doctrine of S. Paul Rom. 13, be subject to the higher Powers."[11] They made a distinction between subjection to the powers and unqualified allegiance. Their consciences were also troubled by the unsettled status of the new government. The revolutionary leaders did not clearly represent the powers established by God, "because it is so uncertain upon what side God almighty will bestow the Victory."[12] An oath of allegiance seemed to them a form of taking sides during a war, of setting up and pulling down kings. A Lancaster County Mennonite saw the test as "an oath of enemity" which his religion and his conscience forbade him to take.[13] The numerous doctrinal statements issued by the Society of Friends agree with Mennonite sources in their appeal to these closely related motives for refusing the test oath. The same points were made by some Dunkers and Schwenkfelders.[14]

The central objection raised by Moravians, Schwenkfelders, and some others presented a different motive for refusing the oath. Many German-born Pennsylvanians had sworn or affirmed their allegiance to King George III when they became naturalized British subjects. They did not have to abjure the ruler of their native state when they were naturalized. They now argued that the test required by the Pennsylvania Assembly went further and asked them to perjure themselves. The Moravians expressed concern lest a formal abjuration of the British king make it impossible for them to function as missionaries within the British dominions.[15]

Sir William Howe's decision to invade Maryland and Pennsylvania brought the war closer to home in the summer of 1777, and fear of imminent invasion raised hostility to British sympathizers and neutrals alike to a new pitch. Christopher Marshall wrote from Lancaster late in August that "our place is in a great fermintation what with this News and the Calling upon all people of the other Countys and States for to take the Test without Distinction, so that it will not be Safe for any of you to come here except you can produce a Certyficate of your having taken the Test."[16] Several Quakers who refused to take it were lodged in Lancaster jail.[17] In Northampton County, an overzealous justice of the peace jailed a Mennonite and a Schwenkfelder who had conscientious scruples with the test oath, but the Pennsylvania Supreme Executive Council reprimanded the justice and ordered his prisoners released. Prosecutions under the 1777 act were few, because the law itself limited prosecution to suspicious persons traveling outside the county or state where they lived.

Since the Pennsylvania legislature met in Lancaster so soon after Sir William Howe's redcoats marched into Philadelphia, the members were in no mood to temporize with men who could not commit themselves to one side or the other. In November 1777 the Pennsylvania Assembly imposed special obligations on nonjurors to furnish food and clothing for the army.[18]

The Maryland Assembly began debate in October, 1777, on the harsh "Act for the Better Security of the Government" that it had rejected in the previous session. Under its provisions, persons who failed to take the oath or affirmation of allegiance, for whatever reason, would have to pay three times their regular state and county taxes and were forbidden to practice law or medicine or to "preach or teach the Gospel" or to teach in a school. The Assembly rejected an amendment in favor of "quakers, menonists and dunkers" on November 14, 1777, and sent the bill to the governor for his signature on December 3, 1777.[19] This Maryland act served as a model for legislation in Virginia, North Carolina, Pennsylvania, and other states.

Pennsylvania followed Maryland's example with a crushing supplement to the test act on April 1, 1778. The new law denied nonjurors the right to engage in trade, commerce, law, medicine, surgery, pharmacy, or education, but wisely avoided penalizing nonjuring preachers. Those who failed to take the oath had to pay double taxes and lost nearly all the rights of citizens; they could not go to civil or criminal courts to demand any right in law or equity and were declared incapable of receiving a legacy or deed of gift, of acting as guardian, executor or administrator, or of making a will. Nonjurors had already lost the right to vote or hold office. The April, 1778, law set a deadline for swearing or affirming loyalty. Nonjurors had until June 1, 1778, to subscribe their names to the test. Otherwise all of these disabilities would follow them for life, even if they later took the oath.[20]

The greatest concern about the new legislation came from the peace churches. The Pennsylvania Assembly received petitions from the Moravians and from the Schwenkfelders in May 1778. The Mennonites and the Quakers hesitated to petition the Assembly, lest they acknowledge the new government.

The Moravian and Schwenkfelder petitions sought suspension of the clause requiring formal renunciation of the British king. Many prominent members of the Assembly and the Council favored their request and Timothy Matlack, secretary of the Council, assured Ettwein that, "If we alone were involved, our request would have been granted at once; but the Quakers and Mennonites stood in our way, 'an irresistible Resentment prevails against them.' "[21] The resolutions adopted by the Assembly on the Moravian and Schwenkfelder petitions clearly indicate that, even without this "irresistible Resentment," the Assembly could not allow the changes in the law that they requested.[22]

Resentment did have a great deal to do with the harsh treatment meted out to nonjurors in the summer of 1778. Despite express instructions from Vice-President George Bryan and the Council that the test act be invoked only against persons suspected of being active Tories, local magistrates imprisoned inoffensive Mennonites, Quakers, and Moravians and, in Northampton County, confiscated their property and gave them thirty days to leave the state.

Christopher Marshall, a Quaker disowned for his somewhat unorthodox opinions, was an Assemblyman in 1778 and apparently friendly to the Lancaster County Mennonites. Chrisley (Christian) Musselman and John Carryle were among his Mennonite visitors in June, 1778, and, at different times, each "spent some considerable time in religious and political conversation respecting the test required to be taken throughout this state." On June 12, 1778, Marshall noted in his diary: "Dined with us Peter Swart and his wife; had a good deal of conversation respecting taking the test; A day or two past, it's said, that ten of the Menonists were brought from the back part of this county to this jail, refusing to take the test; committed by Curtis Grubb."[23] The identity of the ten Mennonites jailed by Curtis Grubb, ironmaster at Hopewell Furnace, militia captain, and justice of the peace, is not given; Grubb's associations would suggest they came from the Lebanon area. They were still in Lancaster jail, apparently, when Christopher Marshall, on August 6, 1778, "spent some time in conversation with some of the Justices and Assemblymen respecting the Menonists in prison in order for their enlargement and respecting the signing of two petitions that were intended to be presented to the Assembly."[24] Six Quakers also went to prison in Lancaster in June 1778 for refusing the test oath.[25]

Harsh Enforcement Leads to Repeal of Some Provisions

Frederick Limbach, the Northampton County justice whose harsh enforcement of the 1777 test act drew a reprimand from the Pennsylvania Council, applied the letter of the law in forcing the test oath on Mennonites and Moravians and jailing them when they refused. His excesses led finally to repeal of some of the harsher provisions in the 1778 act.

Sheriff John Siegfried and Stephen Balliet and Jacob Miller, commissioners of confiscated property, sold the cattle, horses, farm implements, books, and furniture of George Bachman, Casper Yoder, and Abraham Geisinger to the highest bidder on August 24, 1778. Relatives and friends recovered some household goods. Others sold at low prices to neighboring farmers and even Sheriff Siegfried and Justice Limbach loaded farm tools into their wagons when the sale was over. Over the next few days auction sales disposed of the property of Henry and Peter Zell, John Geisinger, Henry Geisinger, Abraham Yoder, Christian Young, Jacob Yoder, and John Newkommer. The sales brought a total of £6,455..7..5 into the coffers of the Commonwealth.[26]

With the first hint of autumn in the air, these destitute Mennonite families faced a winter without food, bedding, or even the warmth of the iron stoves unbolted from the floor and sold by the sheriff's order.

Eve Yoder and Esther Bachman sent a petition to the Pennsylvania Assembly in September telling them of their plight.[27] Quakers tried to win the support of powerful and influential people. The French Minister to the United States reported that Anthony Benezet and other Quakers appealed to him "to exercise my good offices in behalf of some Mennonites affiliated with them, who had been imprisoned and fined for not taking up arms." Minister Gerard informed them "that it was not in my mission to arrest the energies of the American government, and that when the Quakers had performed their duties they would no longer be in fear of persecution."[28] In the end, the simple eloquence of Eve Yoder and Esther Bachman's petition made the Assembly reconsider. Shortly before adjourning, the Assembly asked the Council to investigate and take action to right the wrong done in Northampton County.[29]

Reports reached Philadelphia of other excesses in Justice Limbach's neighborhood. Preacher Henry Funk brought complaints of property confiscated from Michael Myer and Abraham Meyer for refusing the test oath.[30] Limbach had also begun to move against the Northampton County Moravians, offering the test to all the adult males in Bethlehem, sending all the men from Emmaus to jail, and preparing to confiscate the extensive Moravian property in Northampton County.[31]

The Pennsylvania Assembly repealed the laws that permitted such gross injustice on December 5, 1778. They voted to restore all the rights and privileges of a citizen to anyone who took the test oath at any time. They also limited the penalties on those who refused the oath to double taxation and the loss of the right to vote and hold office.[32]

The severe penalties of the April, 1778, legislation and the efforts of men like Frederick Limbach to enforce the letter of the law thoroughly frightened and divided the opposition. Any Pennsylvanians who, from a lingering loyalty to the British crown or insufficient enthusiasm for the Patriots, had not taken the test oath had long since subscribed. The Schwenkfelders and Moravians abandoned their scruples and took the test. Only three Schwenkfelders affirmed their allegiance in 1777, but in the summer of 1778 all of the Schwenkfelder community, including their pastor Christopher Schultz, yielded to the pressure.[33] The Moravians, under the pressure of fines and imprisonment, also capitulated in the course of 1778. As early as May, 1778, the Lititz Moravian community in Lancaster County split over the test oath when "to our pain and grief, we heard" that a majority of adult males "had, all warning unheeded, taken the Oath of Allegiance and forsworn the king."[34] The Emmaus Moravians broke down in Easton jail and took the test oath.[35] The great majority at Bethlehem, Nazareth, and other Moravian colonies soon followed their example.[36]

Peace Churches Deal with Those Members Who Took the Oath

The Dunkers dealt with the problem of reconciling those who had already taken the oath at their annual meeting at Pipe Creek in Frederick County, Maryland, in the summer of 1778. They returned to the subject when they met at Conestoga in Lancaster County in 1779 and determined that preachers who had taken the test should "not baptize or administer the breaking of bread."[37] York and Lancaster County tax rolls indicate that a great many Dunkers chose to pay the penalty of double taxation as nonjurors, but a significant number did take the test. In Cocalico Township in Lancaster County, for instance, slightly more than half were nonjurors.[38]

Some Mennonites and Quakers also took the test oath in the difficult summer of 1778, but members of these churches remained the core of the nonjurors. The test act was an element in the division within the Mennonite churches in Northampton County. Christian Funk and his brother, Henry Funk, both Mennonite preachers, were the central figures in this "Funkite" schism. In 1781, Henry Funk declared that he had been a Mennonite preacher "but having taken the test of the State and done a great deal of Business for the publick in the purchasing and milling way, was read out of the society."[39] Investigation by Northampton County authorities established that several other factors entered into Henry Funk's withdrawal from preaching from 1773 to 1778 when he began assisting his brother.[40] If not the only issue, the test oath precipitated the division. In 1781, Daniel Hiester, Jr., of Skippack observed that Henry Funk and "his brother Christian Funck (a remarkably strong Whig)" were preaching "to the few well affected" Mennonites and we know from other sources that few Mennonites, apart from the Funkites, took the affirmation of allegiance.[41]

Most Peace Church Members Refuse to Comply

The savage penalties imposed on nonjurors in April 1778 frightened waverers, even among the peace churches, but, paradoxically, they had little real effect in rallying support to the Patriot cause. In Donegal Township, Lancaster County, for example, fully 168 of the 183 men who ultimately took the test oath subscribed to it before December 1777. The 80 Mennonites and River Brethren in Donegal Township who paid double taxes as nonjurors clung to their position, despite the fresh burdens imposed by each session of the Assembly. In all, only 15 persons *affirmed* their allegiance in Donegal Township during the American Revolution, indicating that they were Mennonites, Brethren, River Brethren (Brethren in Christ), or Quakers. So high a number affirming allegiance was unusual in Mennonite areas. In sections of Lancaster County where Mennonites predominated, the overwhelming majority refused the oath; scarcely any defectors can be found from the general Mennonite position. In Earl Township there were 214 nonjurors and only 77 men who took the test oath. Only one person with a possibly Mennonite surname took the oath, while 106 nonjurors can be positively identified as Mennonite. A comparison with other Lancaster County townships readily leads to the conclusion that nonjurors were simply the members of the historic peace churches, Mennonites, Quakers, and Brethren, under another name, and that threats and harsh laws did little or nothing to thin their ranks. Religious affiliation was the single significant element determining whether a man took the oath or refused it. The solid ranks of Mennonite and Quaker nonjurors included wealthy farmers and millers and landless men; the very small number of Mennonites and Quakers who took the oath reflected the same broad range from wealth to poverty. No less significant is the fact that Mennonites who did take the affirmation of allegiance almost without exception came from communities that were not predominantly Mennonite, where it would be possible to avoid conformity to the opinion of the Mennonite community. The Pennsylvania test oath identified by name and imposed penalties on a definite class of people known as nonjurors, a class composed after 1778 almost exclusively of Quakers, Mennonites, and Brethren in full fellowship with their churches. On these obviously inoffensive people fell the crushing burden of double taxation. As the war became ever more costly and inflation ran unchecked, the tax burden was simply insupportable and taxes became uncollectable in many communities. Township assessors and other local authorities had grave difficulties performing their duties and county officials apologized for ever larger deficiences in their returns. Under these circumstances, the unpopular nonjurors paid their full double assessment and, where they refused war taxes, their goods were seized and sold, frequently far in excess of the amount of the tax.[42]

Political Implications of the Test Act

The test act also eliminated the political alliance of Mennonites and Quakers, the backbone of the old Quaker Party, from Pennsylvania

Table 10

LANCASTER COUNTY NONJURORS

Township	Taxables 1778	Taxables 1779	Jurors 1777-9	Nonjurors 1779	Non-Associators 1777
Bart	117	127	125[1]	29	22
Brecknock	128	120	—	61	42 (28)
Caernavon	121	107	—	76	67 (44)
Cocalico	—	449	284[1]	133	259 (222)
Coleraine	114	114	—	1	3 (0)[5]
Conestoga	165	162	—	77	139
Donegal	—	204	196[1]	80	147
Drumore	—	206	59[1]	31	—
Earl	—	291	—	214	239
Elizabeth	85	—	—	34	84
Hempfield	—	252	109[1]	—	196
Lampeter	—	202	—	112	175
Lancaster					
Borough	616	—	—	29	—
Township	—	64	111[1]	21	37
Leacock	266	—	—	82	68
Little Britain	208	215	143[1]	38	58
Manheim	141	142	70	76	106
Manor	—	309	62	185	—
Martic	—	215	—	—	31
Mount Joy	—	139	—	—	82
Rapho	—	286[2]	—	111	175
Sadsbury	—	107	43	41	40
Salisbury	—	218	182[3]	82 (22)[3]	32
Strasburg	241	271	—	—	136 (129)[5]
Warwick	310	334[4]	—	284 (280)[5]	265

1. Taken from the lists in *Pennsylvania Archives*, 2nd Series, XIII, 453-472, which may include persons from other areas who took the oath before a justice in this township and exclude local person who affirmed alleignace before a neighboring justice, so these figures must be used with caution. All other figures are from the original tax lists in the Lancaster County Historical Society, Lancaster, Pa.

2. Includes 68 taxpayers in Manheim-Town.

3. The list of jurors and nonjurors for Salisbury Township is dated 1781. No earlier list is extant. Although 82 names are listed as nonjurors, only 22 paid double taxes.

4. This list includes 13 taxpayers identified as members of the Lititz Moravian community.

5. The figure in parentheses is drawn from a duplicate list with names crossed out, *possibly* indicating these persons were no longer refusing to associate.

Table 11
NONJURORS IN YORK COUNTY, PA.[1]

Township	Taxables[2] 1781	Nonjurors[3] 1781
Berwick	269	39[4]
Hamiltonsbann	162	5
Heidelberg	205	46
Hellam	306	57
Manchester	324	59[5]
Reading	188	108
Straban	168	1
Windsor	214	22
York-Town (Borough)	382	30[6]
York (Township)	216	6

1. No nonjurors are listed for Dover, Monaghan, Tyrone, or Warrington townships. Returns for other townships are not available.
2. *Pennsylvania Archives*, 2nd series, XVI, 327-492.
3. Taken from a copyrighted compilation of nonjurors in the Library of the Historical Society of York County, York, Pa. and published with permission.
4. From an undated return, probably 1779.
5. Includes Herman and Samuel Updegraff, not listed as nonjurors, but assessed double taxes.
6. Includes George Leh and William Norris, not listed as nonjurors, but assessed double taxes.

politics. As late as 1776, heavy voting by Lancaster County Mennonites threatened to defeat the call for a Revolutionary Convention.[43] The 1777 test act and the later supplements to it excluded nonjurors from voting or holding public office. After 1777, Mennonites no longer participated in the political life of Pennsylvania. John Hubley, a Lancaster County Patriot, repeated the common view that the test act "was intended for naught but to hinder substantial, good disposed People to be ellect or be ellected."[44] George Bryan, acting president of the Supreme Executive Council, acknowledged that this charge was not far from the truth when he cautioned a friend about encouraging Moravians, Schwenkfelders, and Mennonites to take the oath, since "if many of these people should be found to qualify themselves for enjoying all privileges, they might by appearing at elections disturb the plans layed for the defense of the State."[45]

Taking the right to vote from members of the nonresistant sects was an issue in the 1778 elections. A writer, using the pseudonym "Hampden" raised the question in articles in the *Pennsylvania Packet*, charging that the test oath was intended to keep a single faction in power. Replies to "Hampden" agreed on the need to keep Quakers, Mennonites, Brethren, and Moravians from the polls.[46]

Repeal of the Test Act

The Pennsylvania Assembly had modified the law in December 1778 but it had retained the provisions that barred those who did not take the oath from voting or holding office. It reduced the penalties against nonjurors to the loss of political rights and set no deadline for taking the oath. This gave the neutrals, especially the Quakers, Mennonites, and other sectarians, an opportunity to pursue their professions, conduct their schools, preserve their property, and await the outcome of the war without prejudice. The Assembly rejected by an overwhelming majority a proposal to further liberalize the Test Acts in March 1779 and in October passed a new Test Act which required all citizens to take the prescribed oath by December, 1779, or be forever barred from political participation in the Commonwealth of Pennsylvania. From an analysis of the votes in the Assembly on the Test Acts, Owen S. Ireland concluded "that the alignment on the Test Acts was a more intense manifestation of the ethnic-religious dichotomy" than had emerged on any other of the wartime issues. His figures support the inference that the Test Acts were an effort by Scotch-Irish Presbyterians to eliminate Quakers and Mennonites from Pennsylvania politics. Better than 90 percent of the votes for the Test Act came from the Presbyterian bloc and better than two thirds of the opposition from Quakers, Episcopalians and Germans.[47]

No further effort to repeal or modify the Test Act was made until 1787, when the Assembly gave favorable consideration to a petition from Chester County, signed by Quakers and others.[48]Although the Assembly debated possible modification of the Test Act in the 1787 session, no action was taken until two years later.[49] Thomas Mifflin, president of the Supreme Executive Council, included repeal of the Test Act in his message to the Assembly and, with this pressure, the Assembly repealed the wartime acts in 1789.[50]

Mennonites, Brethren, Quakers, and others who refused to take the oath or affirmation prescribed by law were thus deprived of their civil rights for almost a decade after the surrender of Cornwallis. A writer in the *Pennsylvania Gazette* blamed the harsh provisions of the Pennsylvania Test Acts for the migration of Mennonites and Quakers from Pennsylvania to Virginia and Canada in the 1780s.[51] The committee of the Pennsylvania Assembly that considered the repeal of the Test

Acts in 1789 expressed concern that the laws had alienated "the affections of tender, though perhaps mistaken, minds from a government, which, by its invidious distinctions, they are led to consider as hostile to their peace and happiness."[52] This experience undoubtedly colored the attitude of the sects on the relationship of church and state in the new republic.

The Pennsylvania test act was thus the final act of a drama that began when six Quaker members of the Assembly resigned their office rather than share in appropriating money for military purposes. The peace churches were now totally excluded from the political process, and generations of Mennonites, Brethren, and Quakers were to grow up without the slightest doubt that a Christian could not vote or hold political office.

The story of the test act in the other Colonies can be briefly told. The Maryland act of December 3, 1777, imposed a triple tax rate on nonjurors and barred them from the legal and medical profession, school-teaching, and preaching. Brethren and Mennonites in Washington County together with Brethren in Frederick County, paid heavy taxes, rather than take the oath; the treble tax on nonjurors made up better than a third of the total Washington County revenue in 1778.[53] Maryland Quakers suffered for refusing the oath, but a significant number were disowned or under care for yielding to the pressure to affirm their allegiance. A Quaker preacher visiting meetings in Montgomery, Prince George's, Ann Arundel, and Calvert counties in 1782 found only one or two adult males in full membership in all these meetings.[54] Maryland's unique provision making it a criminal offense for a nonjuror to "preach or teach the Gospel" was invoked in the case of only one Quaker, Evan Thomas of Sandy Spring, Clerk of the Meeting for Sufferings, but dozens of Methodist preachers were jailed, fined, and subjected to mob violence for refusing the test oath.[55] Methodists bore the brunt of the struggle for religious liberty in Maryland until the legislature repealed this section of the test act in 1782.[56] The Maryland Assembly tried to avoid a confrontation with the Quakers and the other peace churches, offering to modify the test act in their favor in 1778. Evan Thomas informed a legislative committee that no modification of the test would be acceptable to Friends, since they objected to pledging allegiance to a government not yet established beyond doubt.[57] The Assembly suspended the treble tax in 1779 and repealed it altogether in February 1781 for those who had refused the test oath from religious scruples and in November 1781 removed the restriction on "quakers, menonists and tunkers" preaching without first taking the test oath.[58]

Virginia adopted a very moderate test act in 1777, essentially a voluntary pledge. In November, 1778, when the General Assembly considered adopting penalties for nonjurors such as Pennsylvania and Maryland imposed, Virginia Quakers petitioned for relief.[59] The measure failed to pass.[60] Quakers and Mennonites were politically insignificant in Virginia, and, consequently, there was little need to harass them.

In North Carolina the legislature imposed a test oath of allegiance and abjuration in 1777 and strengthened it the following year with confiscation and banishment amendments. The North Carolina Assembly listened to the serious objections raised by Moravians, Quakers, Mennonites, and Brethren and early in 1779 offered a more acceptable form to the peace churches.[61] Friends thanked their representatives, but reminded them that no affirmation of allegiance could be palatable to them.[62] The Moravians, on the other hand, were overjoyed, and readily took the test in the new form.[63] Mennonites and Brethren apparently held the same position as the Quakers. In 1780 the North Carolina Assembly enacted a law to protect the land titles of nonjurors, since "numbers of persons under pretence that the people called Quakers, Moravians, Menonists, and Dunkards, have not taken an affirmation to the State, have entered and taken up lands which the said denominations of people have remained in quiet possession of for many years."[64]

DOCUMENTS

Whig Society Requests Oath of Allegiance

The Philadelphia Whig Society asked the Assembly to require some form of oath or affirmation of allegiance of all Pennsylvanians.

Document 237

We know, Honorable Sirs, but two characters of men throughout this extensive continent, *those who are for supporting the independence of the United States as declared by Congress, and those who are not;* and however fame, fortune, or peculiarity of sentiment, may distinguish the individuals of the former, we proudly call them FRIENDS; and regardless of the same distinctions among the latter, we call them ENEMIES. Therefore our prayer to this Honorable House is that they will provide some effectual means for the protection and encouragement of the former, and for the detection and suppression of the latter.[65]

Document 238

An ACT obliging the male white inhabitants of this state to give assurances of allegiance to the same, and for other purposes therein mentioned.

WHEREAS by the separation of the Thirteen United States from the government of the Crown and Parliament of Great-Britain (who by their acts of oppression and cruelty, as set forth in the Declaration of Independence by Congress, bearing date the fourth day of July, 1776, had rendered such separation, on the part of the said States, absolutely necessary for their own happiness, and the happiness of succeeding generations) the good people of this state of Pennsylvania are become free and independent of the said Crown and Parliament.

And whereas from sordid and mercenary motives, or other causes inconsistent with the happiness of a free and independent people, sundry persons have, or may yet be induced to withhold their service and allegiance from the Commonwealth of Pennsylvania as a Free and Independant State, as declared by Congress; And whereas sundry other persons, in their several capacities, have, at the risk of their lives and the hazard of their fortunes, or both, rendered great and eminent services in defence and support of the said independance, and may yet continue to do the same; and as both those sorts of persons remain at this time mixed, and in some measure undistinguished from each other, the disaffected deriving undeserved service from the faithful and well affected: And whereas allegiance and protection are reciprocal; and those who will not bear the former, are not (nor ought not) to be intitled to the benefits of the latter: Therefore, be it enacted by the Representatives of the Freemen of the Commonwealth of Pennsylvania in General Assembly met, and by the authority of the same, That all male white inhabitants of this State, except of the counties of Bedford, Northumberland and Westmoreland, above the age of eighteen years, shall on or before the first day of July next, take and subscribe the following oath or affirmation before some one of the Justices of the Peace of the city or county where they shall respectively inhabit; and the inhabitants of the said Counties of Bedford, Northumberland and Westmoreland, above the said age, shall, on or before the first day of August next, take and subscribe the said oath or affirmation, before some one of the Justices of the said three counties last mentioned, in which they shall respectively inhabit; and the said Justice shall give a certificate thereof to every such person; and the said oath or affirmation shall be as followeth, viz.

"I do swear, or affirm, that I renounce and refuse all allegiance to George the Third, King of Great-Britain, his heirs and successors; and that I will be faithful and bear true allegiance to the Commonwealth of Pennsylvania as a free and independant state; and that I will not at any time do, or cause to be done, any matter or thing that will be prejudicial or injurious to the freedom and independance thereof, as declared by Congress; and also that I will discover and make known, to some one Justice of the Peace of the said State, all treasons or traitorous conspiracies, which I now know or hereafter shall know, to be formed against this or any of the United States of America."

And the form of the said certificate shall be as followeth, viz.

"I do hereby certify, that hath voluntarily taken and subscribed the oath or affirmation of allegiance and fidelity, as directed by an act of the General Assembly of Pennsylvania, passed the thirteenth day of June, A.D. 1777. Witness my hand and seal, the day of A.D.

(L.S.)"

And be it farther enacted by the authority aforesaid, that the Justice or Justices of the Peace, before whom such oath or affirmation shall be subscribed, shall keep fair registers of the names and surnames of the persons so sworn or affirmed, and the time when, and shall, on or before the first day of October in every year, transmit in writing, under his or their hands and seals, to the office of the Recorder of Deeds for the said city or county, a true list of the names and surnames of those who, within the same year, have so sworn or affirmed before them respectively; and the said Justice or Justices shall lay their accounts before the county commissioners, or any two of them, from time to time, to be examined and allowed; and the said commissioners shall draw orders on the County Treasurers for such sums as shall be so allowed, which orders the said Treasurers are hereby authorized and required to pay out of the state taxes; and the Recorders of Deeds, in the city and several counties of this state, are hereby enjoined to record the said lists, in books to be prepared for that purpose and shall be paid for the same, in the same manner as the Justices, at the rate of five shillings for every hundred.

And be it farther enacted by the authority aforesaid, that every person above the age aforesaid, refusing or neglecting to take and subscribe the said oath or affirmation, shall, during the time of such neglect or refusal, be incapable of holding any office or place of trust in the state, serving on juries, suing for any debts, electing or being elected, buying, selling or transferring any lands, tenements or hereditaments, and shall be disarmed by the Lieutenant or Sub-Lieutenants of the city or counties respectively.

And whereas there is a danger of having the seeds of discord and disaffection greatly spread by persons, whose political principles are not known, removing or travelling from one part of the state to another, and it is well known that this state is already become (and likely to be more so) an asylum for refugees flying from the just resentment of their fellow citizens in other states: For remedy whereof, be it enacted by the authority aforesaid, That every person, above the age aforesaid, who shall travel out of the county or city in which he usually resides, without the certificate aforesaid, may be suspected to be a spy, and to hold principles inimical to the United States, and shall be taken before one of the Justices nearest to the place where he shall be apprehended, who shall tender to him the said oath or affirmation; and upon his refusal to take and subscribe the said oath or affirmation, the said Justice shall commit him to the common jail of the city or county, there to remain without bail or mainprize until he shall take and subscribe the said oath or affirmation, or produce a certificate that he had already done so.

And be it farther enacted by the authority aforesaid, That all persons coming from any of the other United States into this state, are hereby required to apply to one of the nearest Justices after he enters this state, and take and subscribe the said oath or affirmation, under the penalty of being dealt with as in the case of persons travelling or removing out of the city in which they usually reside, unless he can produce a certificate that he hath taken an oath or affirmation of the like nature in the state from whence he came.

Provided always nevertheless, That Delegates in Congress, prisoners of war, officers and soldiers in the Continental army, merchants and mariners trading in the ports of this state from foreign powers in amity with the United States, and not becoming resident, are declared not to be within the intent and meaning of this act.

And be it farther enacted, That if any person shall forge such certificate, as by this act is to be made out and given by any one of the Justices of the Peace of this state; or shall cause or procure others to forge or counterfeit the name and seal of the Justice of the Peace to such certificate, or shall, by erasing or otherwise taking out, or covering or putting over, a man's name that was wrote in a true and genuine certificate, knowing it to be forged or altered, every such person and persons so offending, and being thereof legally convicted before any Court of General Quarter Sessions of the Peace of the city or county where such offence shall be committed, shall be fined the sum of fifty pounds, and be committed to jail, until he pays the fine and cost of prosecution: And if he shall not, within the space of thirty days, satisfy the judgment of the Court, he shall be whipped with any number of lashes not exceeding thirty-nine, on his bare back, well laid on.

John Bayard, Speaker.

Enacted into a law, June 13, 1777.

John Morris, jun. Clerk of the General Assembly.[66]

Quakers Oppose Oath

Philadelphia Quakers wasted no time in registering their opposition. The Meeting for Sufferings referred Friends to the advice given in their *Testimony of the People Called Quakers* in December 1776 to "withstand and refuse to submit to the arbitrary injunctions and ordinances of men, who assume to themselves the power of . . . imposing tests not warranted by the precepts of Christ, or the laws of the happy constitution under which we and others long enjoyed tranquility and peace."[67]

Document 239

The Persons who now act as Rulers of Pennsylvania having framed & Published "An Act Obliging the Male Inhabitants to give assurances of allegiance to the same" & to renounce their allegiance to the King of Great Britain & One of like tenor being made in New Jersey, which strikes at Our Religious Testimony, & by which it is very likely great Sufferings will be brought upon Friends, the Consideration of which affects our minds & produced at this time many suitable Observations, tending to excite a steady attentive care over ourselves & the members of our Religious Society, and the Epistle Issued from this Meeting 20th 12 month last Containing Suitable advice on the present Occasion it is desired may be again Read in Our Several monthly meetings of Discipline.[68]

Moravians Uncertain What to Do

The Moravians, for reasons of their own, had scruples about the oath. The question of abjuring and refusing allegiance to King George III was a significant issue for many Moravians and other Germans, since they had taken an oath of allegiance to the king when they were naturalized. Many of them hesitated to take a new oath denying their earlier pledge, but the sectarian view that God alone established governments and overturned them was equally important to the Moravians.

Document 240

Thorough discussions were held in the settlement congregations as to what decisions could be reached in this matter, without sacrificing a clear conscience or acting unworthily of our name and calling. Each Brother was interviewed individually and his opinion sought. It developed, almost without exception, that they were unwilling to take the oath and would rather face some suffering. Answers like these were given: "I promised loyalty to the King when I was naturalized; how can I withdraw that and abjure him, without first being assured that God has taken this Province from him?" "The Test Act is a restraint upon conscience; were I to abjure the King through fear, contrary to the promptings of my heart, I should suffer from a bad conscience, bear false witness against myself, and cause the Justice to bear false witness." "I should give great offense to my Brethren and to many other good people in my neighborhood." "I should consider it shameful ingratitude for the Brethren voluntarily to renounce the English Government, since they have enjoyed so many benefits under this rule and still do enjoy them in all English lands." "Why, I should act contrary to our congregational rules were I to cast my lot with this party and join in the contest!"[69]

Enforcing the New Law

Enforcement of the new law proved to be uneven, with some local authorities far more harsh than others. In Northampton County, Frederick Limbach, a justice of the peace, made the test oath a requirement for taking a statement from the Schwenkfelder George Kriebel about the age of his drafted son and then committed him to jail when he refused.

Document 241

The Substance of what has passed between John Wetzel Frdk. Limbach Esqurs. and George Kriebel when they tendered the Oath of Allegiance unto him. Mr. Limbach had granted a Warrant for my Son Abraham Kriebel who being but 17 Years of Age the 26th of May last past for Fine for not Exercising which I refused to comply with they send George Welder the Constable and had him the sd. Abraham arrested and ordered me to come along with him to the said Limbach Esqr. Justice of the Peace and told me also that Mr. Wetzel Esqr. Lieutenant was also there; when we came there Mr. Limbach called my Son: Abraham! come here, So he went to him, Mr. Limbach asked him, Says he, here is a Warrant against you for £ 1..12..6 have you anything to say against it? The Boy made no Answer at all, for he never had been before any Magistrate before: Then Mr. Limbach said unto him: The Meaning is this: whether you be 18 Years old or not? The Boy answered, No. are you sure of it? Yes. Have you any Evidence? Yes. Who is it? my Father. Then Mr. Limbach called me to come nigh, and asked me: How old is your Boy? he was 17 the 26th of last May I answered. Can you prove it said Mr. Limbach? Yes Sir! I can prove it by a Qualification or by writtings. Just as you Please. Well Says Mr. Limbach your Words may be well enough, but here is an Act of Assembly so that we can't take your Evidence before you take the Test prescribed in this Act. Then I Stopt a litle, and then said: I can not take this Test for the Present Time. Mr. Wetzel said: Why can't you take this Test now. I said: there are a few Words in it which keep me backwards: Mr. Wetzel said which Words? I said: To renounce & refuse all allegiance to the King his Heirs & Successors. Wet[zel asked] Why can't you give up the Allegiance to George the III &c.? I said: I have promised allegiance to him when I was naturalized and I am afraid I might be guilty of Perjury before God and in my Conscience, and moreover it is very uncertain upon which side the Victory will fall and therefore I can't do it for the Present Time. Then Mr. Wetzel said: So do you declare yourself for George the III of Great Britain? No Sir! I don't declare myself for him; But because it is so uncertain upon what side God allmighty will bestow the Victory. Mr. Wetzel said: Then you won't take that Test? No Sir! not at Present, I said. Mr. Wetzel: Then I do command the Justice that he shall imediately committ you to Goal and I will not depart from here untill I See you Secured, and you Shall not come clear from imprisonment, at no rate, even if you do pay me £ 1000 Cash upon the Nail. Mr. Limbach said: well George You see I can't help it. I must draw a Mittimus for you and sent you to Goal, you better take the Test and stay at Home. I said: I can't do it yet but I will consider the Matter and consult my Friends about the same, and a great many more passed between us to the same purpose, among other things Mr. Wetzel said: I will do my utmost to have all those that will not take this Test droven out of the Country. But Sir! where shall they go unto? I said: They may go unto Lord Howe or whereever they Please leaving their Estates behind but shall never come back again amongst us, This he spoke in a very haughty manner, besides a great many more, which all to relate would be troublesome. But these is the most material of our discourse, which happened on the 18th Day of July 1777.

George Kriebel[70]

N.B. I Promised Mr. Wetzel & Limbach That I would be true to the State as much as were in my Power in Paying any Lawfull Taxes or other Charges and in Carting or any thing they Should want Except in bearing Arms which was against my Conscience but all the rest what ever I could do with the consent of my Conscience I were willing to do it.[71]

Henry Funk Jailed

Justice Limbach also jailed the former Mennonite preacher Henry Funk on suspicion of spying for the British when he refused the test oath.

Document 242

The Substance of what has passed between me Henry Funk, and Philip Walter & John Laub when they took him up on the 8th of August 1777

I The said Henry Funk went the same Day unto one Michael Smith and pay'd Some Money unto him for Wheat which I had bought of the sd. Mich: Smith, and from there I went unto one Nicholas Klotz a black Smith where I have a new Waggon to see wheter it was done or not. From there I went back again with an Intent to go home. But when I was come about half a Mile back to a Tavern, I was to go past but said Philip Walter seeing me through the window called me to Stop, he had some thing to say unto me: I Stopt; and he came out of the House and asked me: where you come from: I said from Klotz's. He said: have you a Pass? I said no! Then said he: you are my Prisoner and took my Horse by the Bridle, and called for the Tavernkeeper to take care of my Horse, and I should go with him unto the next Justice, and told the Tavernkeeper either he or John Laub must go with him to the Justice, but the Tavernkeeper refusing to go he had not Time John Laub should go with him. I asked Walter: For what do you take me up what is the Reason—Walter said: because you will not take the oath of allegiance, and therefore it is our Duty to take such People up, and so they brought me before Mr. Limbach. When we came there they said unto Mr. Limbach: They had some Mistrust upon me because I would not take the Oath not to Day nor if I could not be better convinced to morrow neighter. Mr. Limbach asked me: why I could not take it? I said: It is against my Conscience, because we shall be at Peace with every body and forgive all Men etc.: Mr. Limbach asked these Men, Walter & Laub: Wheter I had Spoken any Thing against the State. They answered No! Limbach asked me again: Wheter I would take the oath? I said no, not at Present without I be more convinced by further Consideration. So he gave me Time unto the ninth of this Instant to consider the Matter. When we all had met at the said Day at Mr. Limbachs: He asked me what I would do now? I said: that I had considered the matter well all this Time and the more I consider it the less Liberty I can find in my Conscience to take that Test. Then Mr. Limbach said If you can't take the oath I must Qualify these Men. I answered that I would Qualify to be true to the State according to the Doctrine of S. Paul Rom. 13, be subject to the higher Powers, &c. Then Mr. Limbach asked Walter & Laub: If they could Swear that they were convinced in their Hearts & Consciences that they mistrust me to be a Spy. He asked them what Reason they [had] for such a Suspicion. They said, because he travels forwards & backwards and for refusing to take the oath. Then Mr. Limbach Swore them upon the holy Evangelists of almighty God And after they had Sworn Mr. Limbach said: now you are Qualified to say the Truth the whole Truth & Nothing but the Truth. What reason have you to suppose that Henry Funk is a Spy. They made the same Answer as before for traveling forwards & backwards. Then Mr. Limbach asked them again: If they were convinced in their Conscience that Henry Funk might be a Spy, they said Yes. Then Mr. Limbach asked them If they had any other Thing to say against sd. Funk, they said no. upon this Mr. Limbach committed me to Goal. This is the Substance of my Trial before Mr. Limbach.

Henry Funk.[72]

Christopher Schultz Opposes Test Act

Christopher Schultz, Schwenkfelder minister in Hereford (now Bally) in Berks County, explained his difficulties with the test act to his friend Sebastian Levan, a member of the Pennsylvania Assembly. Schultz and Levan had served together on the Berks County Committee of Observation and in the 1775 Pennsylvania Convention, so the arguments of a staunch Patriot nonjuror carried considerable weight. Schultz declared that "we are unwilling to take oath concerning things that are of utmost uncertainty whether we can remain true to the same and yet we are to bind ourselves by oath," repeating the objection commonly made by Mennonites, Brethren, and Quakers. He also sensed the Assembly's hostility toward the sects, "the most worthless sweepings which you wish to suppress to the utmost and crowd out of the land."

Document 243

My dear old friend Sebastian: For some time it has often been in my mind that I ought in writing to remind you of a few necessary points, since for a long time we have been upright friends so far as I know in order that I on my part may fulfill the duties of true friendship and free myself guilty and that at the same time if possible I may be serviceable to you in your erring conduct. Without further detailing to you many particulars, receive therefore what is held before you mirror-like in the following lines as coming from an old friend out of a sorrowing heart.

I wish to speak with you as with a member of a House which gives laws to the citizens of a once free Pennsylvania and also without taking counsel of their consciences forces these laws upon the said inhabitants by force of arms, fines, imprisonments, exclusion from all civil rights as the recent Test-Act and the proceedings against innocent, conscientious people with us here shows. If you would be looked upon as representatives of the citizens of Pennsylvania and would act in their behalf, you inevitably have the duty resting upon you to take to heart the true welfare of each and every class of said inhabitants as well as your own and not to lift up one party through the suppression of the others in so far as they have not occasioned it through malicious unfaithfulness or wickedness. Since you indeed know quite well that Pennsylvania was originally the property (both in regard to the land as to the right of government) of those people who on account of scruples of conscience have misgivings against killing other people and who also consider very carefully before entering, in the place of an oath, upon a course concerning which they can not be fully assured that they can continue in the truth and steadfast in it, and as you at the same time know that of these people a large number are still here and constitute a great part of the most respectable, the well-established, and irreproachable citizens. A necessary question when one considers your acts and feels how they are applied is this:—Have you in your hearts at any time put yourself in the place of these people and viewed and represented their matters of conscience as your own? Or is it not shown that you consider them the most worthless sweepings which you wish to suppress to the utmost and crowd out of the land? If this is not the case why is my cousin George Kriebel imprisoned in the Easton jail and must let himself be told that if he does not swear the way you want him to, he can not be set free until his own are delivered to his enemies with abandonment of all his property. Why do you rob us of all civil liberty and freedom of conscience in so much that we are to hold nothing as our own, we are not allowed to trade on God's earth, or move about or even to live—merely because we take into consideration what may be helpful to the rest and peace of our souls and minds; because we are unwilling to take oath concerning things that are of the utmost uncertainty whether we can remain true to the same and yet we are to bind ourselves by oath. This is the sum of the whole matter that you expect things of us in this respect and impose them upon us with loss of all that one holds dear in the world, things that no tyrant, nor tartar nor turk much less a Christian government in former times demanded, namely that in the midst of the hottest warfare and before the conclusion of the matter a former lord is to be denied under oath. Consider the history of former times and you will not be able to show a like tryanny over conscience. If action indeed was necessary with respect to spies, traitors or the like malefactors as the preamble of your Test Act declares, why do you implicate innocent people in their punishment? Or where is he who can justly accuse us of such things? let him step forth. Have we not always been willing to bear our full proportion of the public burdens as far as might be done consciously, that is without preparation for manslaughter. Why is it that you are continually speaking of fines or, that what is demanded of us must be paid under the name fine? Are you here our true representatives?

O my dear friend! I beseech you for God's sake, consider while it is yet time. You may indeed now think, you are a nice friend that you come to me with such uncivil questions. But, but you will indeed not escape, and I heartily wish for the sake of your soul that it may not be too late that you will have to answer dearly before him before whom we must all render account, whether you have oppressed God's own who place their hope and trust in Him, who are afraid to offend Him and who fear his word. . . .

Concerning the Test Act, experience and sentiment show that by it door and gate are opened wide to all manner of vanity, robbery, iniquity and mischief to carry out the same on quiet, innocent, conscientious people without fear or shame in this our worthy land, yea, several of the executives of the laws publicly encourage in such conduct those who with them are equally inclined to wrong-doing. May God have mercy and restrain the iniquity. Shall not the government here take the place of God to whom virtue is well-pleasing and all vice an abomination. Yea, is it not established to protect the good and to punish the evil? For this their souls will be called to account at the great day in all strictness by him who is the judge of the whole world in righteousness.

We are freeholders no more; as witnesses we are accepted no more; we are not to step from our land lest we be driven to Howe or into the wild sea; Every one may beat, scourge, deride, abuse us as Satan can inspire him and we shall receive from the present government no help nor protection other than that we are placed in secure imprisonment there to languish. And all this because we will not by public oath or its substitute promise or vow that which we do not know whether we are able to fulfill and hence can not be done without pollution of conscience. O, consider these things and for God's sake reflect what you have done and change it before the hand of the Highest overtakes you and fearlessly punishes you. Were I even to lose my own, I would not for ten such rich estates as yours be partaker in these unrighteous actions. To-morrow I shall go to Philadelphia to see whether from that quarter restraint of this iniquity may be had for thus we can not live. In the meantime I wished in this way to call your attention to these things. If you think I have earned in any respect in friendliness show me what is better and I shall accept it in love.

I remain

your friend and well wisher

Chr. Schultz

Hereford, Aug. 12, 1777.

P.S. If it be agreeable to you, send with the messenger who delivers this, David Meschter, my two books again which I brought you at one time by way of a loan when we were still free people, but according to present rights I may not ask them again of you. Hearty greetings to you and your wife. Vale.[73]

Petition to the Supreme Executive Council

Funk and Kriebel jointly petitioned the Supreme Executive Council, charging that Justice Limbach had exceeded his authority in imposing penalties on them as nonjurors beyond those provided in the act passed by the Assembly. Their petition is in the handwriting of Christopher Schultz, the Schwenkfelder preacher. The Council saw their case in the same light and administered a reprimand to the over-eager justice.

Document 244

To his Excellency the President and Council of the State of Pennsylvania

The Petition of Henry Funk of ye Society of Christians called Menonists and George Kriebel belonging to the Society of Christians called Schwenkfelders and Inhabitants of the County of Northampton in the State afsd. humbly sheweth

That by the Test Act of this State, Non-jurors labour under certain Disabilities in the sd. Act mentioned, but in every other Respect are lawful Men, and entitled by the Laws of the Land to all the other Rights Liberties and Priviledges which other Subjects enjoy; That of these Rights and Priviledges, it is not in the Power of any Magistrate to divest them, or to inflict on them any other Penalties than the sd. Act warrants; That one of your Petitioners having heretofore at the Time of his Naturalization taken the Oath of Allegiance to his Brittanic Majesty, cannot without wounding his Conscience abjure the sd. King, concieving that would be contradictory to his former Oath, but both of them have ever lived in a peaceable inoffensive Manner, paying due Obedience to the ruling Powers, and are ready to testify their Fidelity to this State: Notwithstanding which, they have lately been apprehended in the County of their Residence, and committed to the Goal of the sd. County by Frederick Limbach Esq. for refusing to take and subscribe the Test by the sd. Act required, being considered by the sd. Justice as inimical to this State and a Spy barely for refusing so to do; That in the Opinion of your Petitioners, it is clear, that the Conduct of the sd. Justice was highly culpable, and a daring violation of the Principles of the Constitution, of the known Law, and of his sworn Duty.

Wherefore your Petitioners humbly pray, that a day may be appointed for the hearing of the Complaint of your Petitioners, when they may be permitted to attend in Person or by Council, in Order to be restored to that Liberty, which they concieve themselves to be most unjustly and illegally deprived of.

And yr. Petrs. shall &c.

Augt. 12th 1777

Christopher Schultz

(Endorsed)
Petition of Henry Funk & Geo. Kriebel
Read in Council August 15 1777
Ordered, That the Secretary do write to F. Limbach Esqr. and inform him of the sd. petition & explaining the law respecting the foundation on which suspicion of a Spy is to be founded & also to desire the sd. Magistrate not to extend the law in the execution thereof beyond what it will fully justify.

T[imothy] M[atlack] Secy.[74]

Document 245

The Council met.

Philad'a, Friday August 15, 1777.

The Petition of Henry Funk & George Kriebel, complaining that they have been for some days past, confined in the Goal of Northampton County, by commitment of Henry Lumbeck, Esq'r, because they had refused to take the Test of Allegiance directed to be taken by the Act of Assembly passed the 13th day of June last, & praying a day might be appointed for the hearing of said complaint, was read, & thereupon.

Ordered, That the Secretary write to the said Frederick Lembach, Esq'r, & inform him of the said Petition, and explaining the law respecting the foundation on which a Commitment on a suspicion of a Spy is to be founded, & also to desire the said Magistrate not to extend the said Law in the execution thereof, beyond what it will justify, & to recommend to the said Magistrate, in case any difficulty should arise in the discharge of the Petitioners, to take some other Magistrates to his assistance, & re-consider the case; And, if any difficulty shall prevent the enlargement of the Petitioners, Tuesday the ninth of September is appointed for hearing of the Parties.[75]

Document 246

Philad [a], August 15, 1777.

Sir,

The Petition of Henry Funk & Geo. Kreibel was this day laid before the Council representing that they have lately been apprehended in the County of their residence and committed to the goal of this County by you, for refusing to take and subscribe the test required by the laws of this State to be taken, and praying that a day may be appointed for the hearing of this complaint in order that they may obtain that liberty to which they apprehend they are entitled.

The Council, having taken the said petition into their consideration, have directed me to write to you on this subject, and to remind you that the law is clear and express as to the circumstance which shall justify the commitment of a person refusing or neglecting to take the test—to wit, travelling out of the County or city in which he usually resides, without the certificate, &c. But, from the representation of the petitioners they were not found travelling out of the County in which they usually reside, nor does the contrary appear by the commitment, it will, therefore, be highly proper for you to reconsider the case of the petitioners, and if you find any difficulty arise therein, it will be adviseable to call to your assistance two other Justices, and if, after such conference, you shall still find any difficulty arise to prevent the enlargement of the petitioners Council appoint the 9th of September for hearing both parties, but there is reason to hope will not be found necessary. I am disposed by the Council to desire you to be careful not to extend this further than the words of it will fully justify, and it will therefore, &c.

Directed,

To Frederick Leimback, Esqr.[76]

Document 247

The Schwenkfelders, Separatists, and many others agreed, by means of deputies, in a gathering held at Oley, upon a protest against the test, which they planned to present to the Assembly. They sent it to the Brethren, also, asking them to subscribe to it. Since, in our opinion, it was both moderate and well-founded, we had no misgivings in adding our names to it, thus pleading for a change in the Test-Act among a large group of others, without focusing attention upon ourselves. It was signed by about 1500 people from Berks County, Northampton, and Philad. County. But just when it was to have been presented to the Assembly in Philadelphia, the latter was chased out of the city; the petition, or protest, lay in Germantown when the Eng. came thither and was not presented.[77]

Wendel Bowman's Refusal to Affirm Allegiance

Wendel Bowman of Lampeter Township, a member of a well-known Lancaster County Mennonite family, explained why he could not take an "oath of enmity against any party." He had raised suspicions by making a trip to British-occupied Philadelphia to settle his father's estate and was imprisoned when he refused to affirm his allegiance.

Document 248

To the Honorable Council of Safety the Humble Address of Wendel Bowman

Humbly Sheweth that my Circumstances are the most miserable immaginable, Confind in a Common Goal, Subject to all manner of inconveniency, Melancholy Sickness, and in Short, death it Self, I am afraid will be the Consequence of my miserable Confinement, Now your Honorable Board is to Know; that I am innocent of any thing illegal, or Criminal, and that my Character together with the evidence of all those that are Acquainted with me, Can make it appear, that I never acted in word or deed against the proceedings of the Honorable Congress, or the united States of America, I am charged with going to Philadelphia, it is true, I acknowledge I have been there, upon, a Lawfull and urgent business, which I hope will not Appear Criminal to your Honours; my father departed this Life lately, which left my poor mother a widow, and no Body left to take care, or do business but myself; I was oblidged to undertake a journey to Philadelphia, tho' against my Will, to bring Some Papers, of Consequence, that were left in the hands of John Wiester [Wistar], I got in to the Citty at nine of the Clock in the morning, and Came out the Same Day and without making the least delay pursued my journey whome, after my arrival, I tould all my neighbors that I came from Philadelphia, thinking as I was guilty of nothing Criminal, that I had nothing to fear. This is the State in fact of my Crime and the Cause of my Confindment. I was of offered my Liberty on Condition of takeing the Oath, but I being bred in a religion, whose Principles together, together, with my Conscience, prohibits my taking an oath of enemity against any party, or individual whatsoever, therefore I must abandon my religion my conscience, and all that is, and Should be dear to me, before I am free to take the oath proposed, which I hope Your Honorable Board will not oblidge me to do, but I am willing to give Sufficient Bail or Security, for my Good behaviour, or forfeit so much money together with my liberty if I act in Word or deed against the united States of America; now I with the Greates Humility and defferrence immaginable, Make my application to your Honorable Board, to accept my terms, and extricate me out of this miserable Confindment; otherwise, I am inevitably lost, and my poor mother ruined. If Your Honours does not think it convenient to grant me liberty, I hope you will have no objections against my writing to his Excellency General Washington.

I am Buoyed with hopes the Honorable Board will answer my expectation and as in Duty bound I will allways pray
(Endorsed)
1778 March 23rd
Petition of Wendel Bowman a prisoner in the goal of this borough.[78]

Moravian Leader Calls Act Ineffective

John Ettwein, the Moravian leader, believed the 1777 test act was generally ineffective, even with the amendments made by the General Assembly in the autumn of 1777.

Document 249

Since very few people had conformed to the Test Act, a Supplement to it was passed on the 12th of October [1777]. In it the age was fixed at 16 years instead of 18. Moreover, should one or more witnesses denounce an individual as being hostile to the freedom and independence of the country, he was to be summoned by warrant before a justice and by him required to take the test; should he refuse, he was to be imprisoned, even though he had not left the county, in which he resided. But when even this had little effect, it was proposed to confiscate the estates of all who would not take the test.[79]

Document 250

And since this had too little effect, though it was rigidly enforced in some places, therefore the Assembly passed a new law on April 1, 1778, by means of which it sought to bolster up and support its unstable, violent rule. According to it, all male white persons above 16 years were to abjure King G[eorge] III and all his heirs and successors prior to June 1, 1778, swearing allegiance to the Republic of Pennsylvania. Whoever should fail to do this, should be excluded from all the rights and privileges enjoyed by the Freemen of the State and forfeit all legal rights; schoolmasters, merchants, apothecaries, doctors, surgeons were not to be allowed to carry on their professions. Nonjurors were to pay double taxes. After the 1st of June, two or more justices of the peace could summon by any constable or officer any individual who had not taken the test and require the oath of him. Should he refuse to take the same, he could be imprisoned for 3 months or be bound over to the next court and fined, though not above £10. The court could then again require such a prisoner, or one so bound, to take the oath, record his refusal, and banish him from the country within the space of 30 days. This would entail the loss of his personal property. His real estate, i.e. fixed goods and landed property, would pass to his nearest heir, provided the latter would take the oath.[80]

Document 251 [October, 1777]

To the Honorable Delegates of the free people of the State of Pennsylvania, meeting in the General Assembly;

The petition of the members of the brotherhood known as Schwenckfelders, resident in the counties of Philadelphia, Berks and Northampton,

Who humbly testify:

That we, said members, and our forefathers lived for 200 years in Silesia under the Empire and the constant protection of the Emperor of the Holy Roman Empire. There we were finally severely pressed by the Jesuits to adopt the Roman Catholic creed, with which our conscience could not agree, and we were therefore compelled to leave our possessions and seek asylum where we can obey the dictates of our conscience. This was the only reason for our journey over the great ocean, and we have happily become partakers of the benefits of the just and well-known religious freedom as well as civil liberty in Pennsylvania.

It has at all times been the accepted principle of our faith to conduct ourselves harmlessly, quietly and submissively toward the higher powers under which we live. Our forefathers always had the reputation of being good and useful subjects; this testimony was made repeatedly by their rulers, and it frequently hindered the Jesuits in their proceedings against our people; the Imperial court viewed our departure from our homeland with great unhappiness and tried to prevent it.

That was the reason that caused the present king of Prussia, when he became the ruler of Silesia, to call us to come back from America by a public document in which he guaranteed his royal protection and promised to repay our losses and to assure our civil as well as religious liberty. But we considered ourselves to be well protected under this freedom here in Pennsylvania. We therefore decided not to go back over the ocean, and were well content that our brethren in Silesia could enjoy their benefits.

On the basis of this same principle we never assumed that we would remain exempted, in view of the present difficulties, from bearing our share in the present disturbances, and we have with patience and silence suffered much at the hands of certain people who said, "they are destroying the militia law because they do not perform military duty," which for conscience' sake we can by no means perform.

It is therefore a serious concern for us that in consequence of several recently enacted laws and amendments which contain the oath known as the "Test of Abjuration," which oath every white male over eighteen years of age must render (removing from those who cannot sincerely take this oath the benefits of all the other laws). We therefore find ourselves compelled to present this petition to the Honorable House, that you may be willing to calm our thoughts, because we must confess that according to our Christian and ecclesiastical principles such a deed would deeply violate our conscience, because it is not in harmony with those principles. We fear the consequences of undertaking such a decision, which the "Highest Council" has preserved unto Himself as a divine privilege to put into positions of authority whomever He will.

Meanwhile, in accord with our principles, we are very sincere about our intentions in promising to render our loyalty to the state when it is required of us, and that in accord with the teachings of our Savior our yea must be yea and our nay nay, and that our heart, mouth and deed must be in agreement; and we consider that such an affirmation includes all obligations for preserving the welfare of our church, and refraining, by the grace of God, from all deceitful acts—this will be our intent at all times.

Further, we sincerely affirm that if anyone in our brotherhood falls short in his loyalty, then he shall be dealt with according to the law in such cases.

And since we humbly believe that the House is convinced of the need to spare the conscience because of its divine character, and that mercy from above has always come upon such countries which have established such clemency because it follows the precedent of our Blessed Lord,

we therefore trust and beseech the Honorable House most humbly to grant this request, and to take into earnest consideration our reasons, and to find therein whatever exemption seems feasible in your wisdom, so that your petitioners may not be forced to violate their consciences, and that the glorious freedom may shine forth in full view, and that Pennsylvania may continue to be a place of true liberty for the oppressed and innocent. This your petitioners will always request.[81]

John Ettwein Carries Petition to Assembly

John Ettwein, who carried the Moravian petition to the Assembly, wrote of his stay in Lancaster:

Document 252

Four of the leading Mennonites visited me several times and would have liked to have made a petition. They were reluctant chiefly to address the Assembly as the Representatives of the Freeman. I told them I, too, had long been reluctant on the same point, but that they were the true and actual representatives of those who had elected them; whether they were many or few was immaterial to us, for we and they had none, because we had been excluded from the election; and, after all, no other Assembly existed for the time being. However, they soon learned that the proposal to repeal or suspend the Act had been rejected by a majority of the House.[82]

Document 253

Extracts from the minutes of the third sitting of the second general assembly of the commonwealth of Pennsylvania, which met at Lancaster, on Wednesday the 13th of May, 1778.

Wednesday, May 20.

The petition of the Moravians and Schwengfelders, praying relief from such hardships which (they apprehend) they suffer from the test and militia laws of this state, was again read and considered, and, after considerable debate thereon, it was resolved, That Col. Lollar, mr. Lauman, col. Lowrey, mr. Rhoads, and col. Dill, be a committee to draw up and assign the reasons which induced this house not to grant the prayers of the said petition, and report the same to the house.

Monday, May 25.

The committee appointed to set forth the reasons which induced the house not to grant the petitions of the Moravians and Schwengfelders societies, so far as the said petitions relate to the dispensing with the abjuration of allegiance to the king of Great Britain, contained in the test of allegiance, required by law of the inhabitants of this state, beg leave to report, that the house appears to your committee, to be influenced by the following reasons:

First, Because the honourable the Continental congress, in their declaration of independence, have declared, "That these united colonies are, and of right ought to be, free and independent states, and that they are absolved from all allegiance to the British crown, and that all political connection between them and the state of Great Britain is and ought to be, totally dissolved."

Secondly, Because though the present glorious struggle for liberty and the natural rights of mankind against the tyrannical power of Great Britain is, at this time, well understood, yet many persons amongst us preferring a slavish dependence on the British king, from prejudice, expectations from lucrative office, or the most unworthy motives, and screening themselves from the notice of government, by a professed neutrality, have, nevertheless, as soon as opportunity offered, declared themselves in favour of our enemies, and become active against the liberties of America; it is therefore absolutely necessary that, whilst the good citizens of this state are freely exposing their lives and fortunes to protect what is still dearer to them than either of these, a proper discrimination be made, that may distinguish our friends from our enemies.

Thirdly, because it cannot be conceived that any person can bear true allegiance to the united states of America, and at the same time refuse to renounce his allegiance to that power who, without any just pretence, is now carrying on an offensive and cruel war against us, laying waste, burning, plundering and destroying our country by his fleets and armies, and committing every outrage that refinement or savage barbarity can invent.

Fourthly, Because the petitions on this subject make it evident, that the people, on whose behalf they are presented, do consider a general test of allegiance to the state to be, in some sort, consistent with a reservation of allegiance to the king of Great Britain, and that an alteration in the test required by law, upon the present petitions, would be an acknowledgment, by this house, of the propriety and justice of such a construction of a general test.

Fifthly, Because the Germans, in particular, have the less reason to the oath of allegiance as directed by law, as they have heretofore generally renounced allegiance to a royal family which had forfeited its pretensions to the British throne, by acts not less outrageous and insulting on the rights of the subject than those which the present king has been guilty of towards the people of America.

Sixthly, Because the house, in all their deliberations and proceedings, have carefully avoided giving offence to any religious society, by granting any indulgence or preference to another; and as many of the good people of the Moravians, as of every other society, have freely and voluntarily taken and subscribed the oath or affirmation of allegiance and fidelity as directed by the laws of this state; this circumstance affords a just ground to infer, that the objections made are really the objections of individuals only; but were it otherwise, this house cannot grant relief to the petitioners, without giving just grounds of suspicion and offense to those who have already taken the oath or affirmation as aforesaid.

And thereupon it was resolved, That this house do adopt the said report, and that the house is, nevertheless, ready and willing to grant to the petitioners every encouragement and protection in their power, which may appear consistent with the duty they owe to their constituents, and the welfare of the united states of America.[83]

Authorities Reject Harsh Measures

George Bryan, vice-president and acting president of the Supreme Executive Council, informed Northampton County Lieutenant, Colonel John Wetzel, that the Pennsylvania authorities did not want the oath of allegiance forced on the Moravians and Schwenkfelders or other harsh measures taken against them.

Document 254

Sir, Lancaster, May 22d, 1778.

The Moravian and Swenkfelders have been very urgent with Assembly to relax the Test, and free them from the abjuration part. The claim of the King of Great Britian forbids any thing like this being done at present. When that prince shall renounce his claim it will be time enough to reconsider the Test. However, as these people are not to be feared, either as to numbers or malice, it is the wish of government not to distress them by any unequal fines, or by calling them, without special occasion happens, to take the oath at all. The disabilities ensuing upon their own neglect are heavy, and will without further pressing (which may be termed rigor by people in general, and persecution by themselves) operate strongly upon them.

On these grounds, we wish it to be understood, that Council and Assembly desires to avoid any noise from the people above mentioned, and to have them dealt with, as others, in regard to the delinquency in the Militia. Your prudent advice to your friends and deputies, without exposing these lines to the knowledge of the petitioners, will serve the public interest and oblige,

Your very obed't serv't,

G. B.

P.S. The president is very sick.*[84]

Directed.—To Col. Weitzel, Northampton.

*Thomas Wharton, President of the Pennsylvania Executive Council, died soon after.

The Government's Intentions

George Bryan explained the government's intentions regarding the Test Act in a candid letter to John Thorne. He thought only active Tories should be brought before a magistrate to take the oath and he was sure "no Moravian, Sweinkfelder or Menonist will be found" in that category. The peace churches should not be distressed by "well meaning but over-zealous & imprudent" Patriots or the jails would soon be overcrowded. The Dublin-born Patriot correctly saw that the nonresistant sects hestitated to take sides in a civil war and that time would gradually remove their objections to affirming their allegiance as the Patriot cause became more clearly established. For the present time, Bryan acknowledged, the test oath would serve to keep Mennonites, Quakers, Moravians, Schwenkfelders, and others from voting. His comments suggest that this was the main purpose of the Test Act and its supplements. Bryan also alluded to a petition from the Rev. Thomas Barton of Lancaster County in behalf of the Church of England clergy sent to Pennsylvania by the Society for the Propagation of the Gospel, asking that they be exempt from taking the test oath. It was, of course, rejected.

Document 255

Lancaster, 25th May, 1778.

Sir,

During the late Session of Assembly the Moravian Society & the Sweinkfelders applied to the Legislature to be freed of the test, so far as the renouncing of the British King. Allegiance they declared themselves ready to attest, but this certainly includes the denial of all other authority. Their scruple therefore, proceeding from ignorance of the duty of subjects, shews the necessity of supporting the express disowning of the prince who actually claims authority over us, being a new argument for insisting on the full words of the Test. They were denied. You will perhaps think it extraordinary that the Rev'rd Mr. Barton, for the missionaries, asked a total exemption, on the ground that they were itinerants, subjects of England, sent over on the sole business of preaching the gospel, alledging the example of Christian missionaries elsewhere. But tho' the Assembly refused to relax this pledge of fidelity, it is not the wish of Government that the delinquents after the first of June next should be called on to swear at all without special cause. Our goals might soon be crowded, and the imputation of cruelty brought on the State. The disabilities & difficulties which follow their neglect are very compulsive, & if the enemy remove out of the State, & these ignorant people become better satisfied of the establishment of our cause, it may be expected that their objections will gradually wear away. On the other hand, should measures be taken to press them severely, they may assume the complaint of persecution, & become fixed in stiff opposition to us, a situation of the most inconvenient nature, as consistency in conduct will dispose them to persevere.

It is hoped, therefore, that the power of calling delinquents before a justice will be reserved for persons whose character & conduct shall threaten active mischief against the State. Among these, I trust no Moravian, Sweinkfelder or Menonists will be found. Such has been the practice in England in the execution of a like Law enacted after the revolution. Perhaps, too, if many of these people should be found to qualify themselves for enjoying all privileges, they might by appearing at elections disturb the plans layed for the defense of the State.

In these views I hint to you that the private interference of prudent persons with the magistrates and others, to soften the harsh councils of some well meaning but over-zealous & imprudent men, may be very useful, & acceptable, particularly to, sir,

Y'r most obed't humble Serv't,
George Bryan, V. P.[85]

Direct Tax Suggested

The Reverend Alexander McDowell explained the difficulties that Mennonites and Quakers had with the test act and suggested to Vice-President George Bryan that modifying the act in their favor would be more advantageous than enforcing it. McDowell did not understand all of the objections made by the peace churches, but he was on target when he suggested that a direct tax, rather than a military fine, be imposed on conscientious objectors.

Document 256

June 1 st, 1778.

Honoured Sir,

You will forgive these hints, which will give your weightier affairs but little interruption, to be used as you think they deserve. I have been in several parts of three Counties of this State, and find in all, great complaints made by Menonists & Quakers, of the oath of allegiance now required of its Subjects, as including an obligation to fight, contrary to their known principles. They say, a good many at least, that they would affirm to be faithful Subjects to the State, endeavour nothing to its hurt, but discover all they knew doing so, &c., in consistence with their principles against bearing arms; to require more of them, they say, is persecution; and tho' the Constitution promises the rights of Subjects to all denominations, presently oaths are required, which they cannot take unless otherways qualified without renouncing their principles: and that such are not trials who are friends to the State, but who are Sincere in their profession. I find some of our sensible Whigs say, an oath of allegiance, suited to these people's known Sentiments, might increase the friends of the State and lessen the warm discontents of many; and then levy more from them than others under the name of a Tax, for the use of the State, but not of fines; as they would enjoy greater advantages by not bearing arms. And such as refuse qualifications, so framed, would have no excuse, but appear plainly to be enemies.

Wishing direction to all our public Councils, a speedy issue of war and happy establishment of these States,

I am, Sir,

Your humble serv t,

Alex'r McDowell

Directed,

George Bryan, Esq'r, Vice-president of Pennsylvania State.[86]

George Bryan Responds

George Bryan replied to the Rev. Alexander McDowell's statement of the Mennonite and Quaker case against the test act in a letter published in the Lancaster *Pennsylvania Packet* under the pseudonym "Candidus." He did not respond to the central problem that any pledge of allegiance represented taking sides in a civil war.

Document 257

Mr. Dunlap,

By inserting in the Packet the following answer to a real letter, you may perhaps help some mistaking persons to a better opinion of the Test of Allegiance, required of the subjects of Pennsylvania, and you will oblige.

Sir,

Your very humble servant,

Candidus.

Lancaster, June 6th, 1778.

Reverend Sir,

I was favoured with your letter of the first instant. Your apology for writing was quite misplaced. Besides the pleasure of hearing from you, the subject is of great and public importance. The cause of religious liberty has numerous advocates among us; I trust that I am accounted one of them.

You observe, "that on a late visit to several parts of three counties of this State, you found great complaints made by the Menonists and Quakers, of the oath of allegiance, required of its subjects, as including an obligation to fight, contrary to their known principles. You say, that many of these people declare their willingness to *affirm* to be faithful subjects of this State; do no injury to it; and discover all they know to do it." The objection you state, would I allow, be weighty, if it were founded in truth. But the matter is plainly mistaken. Ever since the revolution in 1688, when William the Third ascended the throne, the subjects of England have been holden to give assurances of allegiance, and to abjure the pretended descendants of the *Stuart* race, in the very terms prescribed by the new Legislature of Pennsylvania. To convince you of this, I shall copy some sentences of a form established by an Act of Assembly of the Province, passed in the eleventh of George the First, for accommodating the declaration of abjuration, enjoined by the English Parliament, to the use of Quakers, viz. "And I do renounce and refuse any allegiance or obedience to him (the Pretender) and I do solemnly promise, that I will be true and faithful against all traiterous conspiracies and attempts whatsoever &c. and that I will do my best endeavour to disclose and make known to King George and his successors all treasons &c." To this the Quakers never objected. Nay, their ancestors drew up this very form, and imposed it in all cases wherein the like declaration was directed by the laws of England. Now in England, two Justices are impowered to call before them any person, and require him to make this declaration on oath, (or if a Quaker, to affirm the affect of it) on pain of imprisonment, till he comply. (1st George the first, Statute 2. Cap. 13. Sect. 10,11.) The words of the State test of allegiance and abjuration complained of, are these: "I A.B. do swear (or affirm) that I renounce and refuse all allegiance to George the Third, King of Great Britain, his heirs and successors; and that I will bear faithful and true allegiance to the Common Wealth of Pennsylvania as a free and independent State, and that I will not at any time do, &c. and that I will discover all treasons, &c." You will easily see that no obligation to bear arms and fight is deducible from the latter form, and that it is as indulgent to Quakers and others, scrupulous of defending their country by force, as the form heretofore established by the Quakers themselves. As to the Menonists, it may be observed, that the

Germans (and these people are, I believe generally such) at their first arrival, and on naturalization, have conformed to the declaration first mentioned, and consequently can not consistently, on pretence that it obliges them to fight, refuse the present form of attesting allegiance and abjuration. It must be allowed, that the test now insisted on is much the clearest for a conscientious man to take, for the English form, even as modified by the Quaker Assembly, is embarrassed with reference to two acts of Parliament, which, perhaps, not one in a hundred, called to adopt it, ever read.

You add, from these complainers, "That the constitution promises the rights of subjects to all denominations; presently, oaths are required, which they cannot take, without renouncing their principles." But nothing new, or affecting religious principle is now required. If Menonists and Quakers could and did comply with the oaths established under the late government, without renouncing or violating their principle of non-resistance, they may, it appears, give the assurance now called for without scruple. Their construction of the constitution is not fair. It is indeed declared by one article, that no farther or other religious test than that provided by the frame of government shall ever be required. But do not these very words imply, and reserve to Legislature, a right to demand reasonable assurances of fidelity from the subjects of the State, especially at a time when disaffection is, we well know, very common; and when a contest is now actually carried on within the State, for the sovereignty of it, in which many of the inhabitants have joined the invading enemy. Hereafter, perhaps, the form may be simplified without inconvenience, but the safety of the people requires, that at present a test, which makes a proper discrimination, be demanded. All must confess, that the authors of it have been very honest and explicit, so that doubt and evasion are precluded. I would willingly hope, that this clearness in expressing what is meant, is no objection. If it were, a farther and important reason would be thereby afforded for its continuance.[87]

Test Act Called "Nothing New"

A similar claim that the test act represented "nothing new" appeared in a German-language paper published at Lancaster.

Document 258
Lancaster, June 6, 1778

Concerning the affirmation of fealty which was required during the first year of the reign of George I this was submitted especially to the Quakers of this state, and now it is being submitted to all the inhabitants of this state. We want to put these two affirmations side by side, so that everybody can see that they are quite similar; that it is nothing new, but an old custom; that a government not only swears in its inhabitants but also forswears them.

Affirmation during the reign of George I, required especially of the Quakers in Pennsylvania:

And I renounce all fealty to him (the pretender), and promise faithfully that I will be true and upright, and will conduct myself as a true and faithful subject toward King George, and I will prove myself against any treasonable conspiracies, etc. And that I will try to discover any acts of treason etc. and that I will make them known to King George and his successors.

Affirmation for our present government:

I, A.B., affirm that I deny George III King of Great Britain, his heirs and successors, all fealty and obedience; and I will prove myself as a true and faithful subject of the Commonwealth of Pennsylvania, as a free and independent state; and that I will discover any treason, etc.

In England two justices of the peace can force a person to take this oath or affirmation, and to put him in prison until he will do so.[88]

Quakers' Motives Termed Political

The Patriotic newspapers insisted that the reluctance of Quakers to take the affirmation of allegiance stemmed from purely political motives.

Document 259

It is said, that the people called Quakers have determined to *disown* all persons of their society who have taken or who shall take the oath of allegiance to this State, or to any other State in North-America, as a free and independent State; or who shall, by paying taxes or otherwise, acknowledge any authority of Government in any of the United States, but what is derived from the crown of Great Britain; and that great numbers have already been disowned both in this State and in Maryland, in consequence of this determinaton. If this be *true*, what must be the consequences of such a measure to *that part* of this people who have adopted it? If it is *not true*, it is surely of great consequence to them to have the matter explained to the satisfaction of the public.[89]

Quakers Study Reasons for Refusal

The Meeting for Sufferings of Philadelphia Yearly Meeting decided that even Quakers needed instruction on the reasons for refusing the test oath and accepting whatever penalty might follow.

Document 260

And on Consideration of what is necessary to be proposed to Friends in general on the Subject of the Declaration of Allegiance and Abjuration required by some late laws passed by the Legislatures who now preside in Pennsylvania and New-Jersey having several times met and deliberated thereon, we have the Satisfaction to find we are united in Judgment that consistent with our religious Principles we cannot comply with the Requisitions of those Laws, as we cannot be instrumental in setting up or pulling down of any Governments but it becomes us to shew forth a peaceable and meek Behaviour to all Men, seeking their Good and to live a useful, Sober, and religious Life without joining ourselves with any Parties in war or with the Spirit of Strife and Contention now prevailing, and believe that if our Conduct is thus uniform and steady and our hopes fixed on the omnipotent Arm for Relief, that in time he will amply reward us with lasting peace which hath been the Experience of our Friends in times past, and we hope is of some who are now under Sufferings; and in order to communicate this Union of Sentiment in so important a Subject and to preserve our Brethren in religious profession from wounding their own Minds and bringing Burthens upon themselves and others, we think it expedient to recommend to the Committees appointed in the several Monthly Meetings to assist in suffering Cases in pursuance of the Advice of our Yearly Meeting with other faithful Friends speedily to appoint a solid Meeting or Meetings of Conference with each other in the several Quarters in which the Grounds of our Principles on this head may be opened, and our Objections against complying with those Laws fully explained, and a united Concern maintained to strengthen each other in the Way of Truth, & Righteousness, & to warn and caution in the Spirit of Love and Meekness those who may be in danger of deviating.[90]

Church of the Brethren Struggles with Test Act

At their annual meeting held at Pipe Creek in Frederick County, Maryland, in the summer of 1778, the Church of the Brethren grappled with the problem of the test act. Some Brethren had evidently taken the affirmation of allegiance and the church required them to not only acknowledge their error but also to return their certificate to the justice of the peace and have their name stricken from the list in the county records. This was also the practice of Quakers.

Document 261

After much reflection, in the fear of the Lord, it has been concluded in union, that the brethren who had taken the attest should recall it before a justice, and give up their certificate, and recall and apologize in their churches, and truly repent of the error. If they cannot do this, and instead justify themselves, the apostle exhorts us that we should withdraw ourselves from every brother who conducts himself wrongly, and such a brother will be deprived of the kiss of fellowship, of the council, and the breaking of bread, until he becomes obedient again. Ministers and elders who have taken the attest, and are sorry and grieved about it, who confessedly recall the matter before the justice of the peace and in the public church, counsel shall be held about them in their churches in the presence of one or more ministers or overseers to consider, in the fear of the Lord, whether he or such as before mentioned could serve again in their office. But if such minister or elder should stubbornly defend himself and justify his course, yes, even teach the same, then we cannot comprehend how he can be obedient to the spirit of truth, which teaches we shall not touch an unclean thing, nor be unequally yoked together with unbelievers, because Christ has no concord with Belial. Therefore, we decide that such laborers are unfit in the Lord's vineyard, and also unfit to be members in the church of the living God, until their minds are changed and they speak again with new tongues, or find their hearts with David. May God have mercy upon us![91]

Continued Discussion in Church of the Brethren

The Church of the Brethren returned to the thorny problem of the test act at the 1779 annual meeting at Conestoga in Lancaster County, Pennsylvania.

Document 262

Regarding the taking of the attest, it has been concluded in union as follows: Inasmuch as it is the Lord our God who establishes kings and removes kings, and ordains rulers according to his own good pleasure, and we cannot know whether God has rejected the king and chosen the state, while the king had the government; therefore we could not, with a good conscience, repudiate the king and give allegiance to the state. And it seems to us that those who have done so have committed a fault, on account of which we could not break bread with them, but bear with them in love. But, if they would come moved by their own conviction, and would make acknowledgement, being truly repentant, then we will forgive them, and we believe God would also forgive them, and we will break bread with them. But in regard to the ministers, we think that they should stand still in their labor, and not baptize or administer the breaking of bread. Should they, however, become convinced in themselves that they have erred, and show contrition, saying: "We are sorry," then we will forgive them and be in full fellowship with them, yet so that the churches to which they belong are satisfied with them when they should continue in their offices. But if such go still further in this matter, as holding office, and so forth, show no sorrow, and rather continue in such course, then they should also be deprived of the church council and holy kiss, and *nota bene*, not only the ministers but all who have taken this course."[92]

Prisoners Need Support

Mennonites and Quakers were reluctant to petition the Pennsylvania General Assembly, lest they seem to acknowledge them as more than just one party to a still unsettled conflict, but in August 1778 Friends asked for some measure of relief for their members in prison because of the Test Act.

Document 263

In general assembly of Pennsylvania, Friday, August 7, 1778, A. M., the following representation was presented to the house, viz.

To the assembly of Pennsylvania, the Meeting for Sufferings for Pennsylvania and New Jersey, on behalf of the society of the People called Quakers,

Respectfully represent,

That the government of the consciences of men is the prerogative of Almighty God, who will not give his glory to another; that every encroachment upon this his prerogative is offensive in his sight, and that he will not hold them guiltless who invade it, but will sooner or later manifest his displeasure to all who persist therein.

These truths, we doubt not, will obtain the assent of every considerate mind.

The immediate occasion of our now applying to you is that we have received accounts from different places that a number of our friends have been and are imprisoned, some for refusing to pay the fines imposed in lieu of personal service in the present war, and others for refusing to take the test prescribed by some laws lately made. The ground of our refusal is a religious scruple, in our minds, against such compliance, not from obstinacy, or any other motive than a desire of keeping a conscience void of offence towards God, which we cannot without a steady adherence to our peaceable principles, and testimony against wars and fightings, founded on the precepts and examples of our Lord Jesus Christ, the prince of peace, by a conformity to which we are bound to live a peacable and quiet life, and restrained from making any declarations or entering into any engagements as parties in the present unsettled state of public affairs.

We fervently desire you may consider the generous and liberal foundation of the charter and laws agreed upon in England between our first worthy proprietary William Penn and our ancestors, whereby they apprehended religious and civil liberty would be secured inviolate to themselves and their posterity, so that Pennsylvania hath since been considered as an asylum for men of tender consciences, and many of the most useful people have resorted hither in expectation of enjoying freedom from the persecution they suffered in their native countries. We believe every attempt to abridge us of that liberty will be a departure from the true spirit of government, which ought to influence all well regulated legislatures, and also destructive of the real interest and good of the community; and therefore desire those laws, which have a tendency to oppress tender consciences, may be repealed, so that those who live peaceably, may not be farther disturbed or molested, but be permitted to enjoy the rights and immunities which their forefathers purchased through much suffering and difficulty; and to continue in the careful observation of the great duty of the religious instruction and education of the youth, from which, by one part of the said laws, they are liable to be restrained.

We hope, on due consideration of what we now offer, you will provide for the discharge of such who are in bonds for the testimony of a good conscience, which may prevent others hereafter from suffering in like manner.

Signed in and by desire of our said meeting held at Philadelphia, the 5th day of 8th month, 1778.

Nicholas Waln, clerk.

Which, being read, was ordered to lie on the table. Extract from the minutes, *John Morris, Jun.* C[lerk] G[eneral] A[ssembly][93]

Banishment Order Produces Partial Repeal of Test Act

The arrest of ten Northampton County Mennonites and their subsequent banishment by the court when they refused to affirm their allegiance followed the letter of the act passed by the Pennsylvania Assembly on April 1, 1778. Their cruel treatment at the hands of the

Northampton County justices led to the repeal of the worst features of the test act. The petition sent to the Supreme Executive Council by George Bachman and the others on July 4, 1778 as well as Jacob Bachman's petition to the Assembly in August 1778, had little effect. Both the Council and the Assembly were well accustomed to petitions from imprisoned Tories and suspicious persons by the summer of 1778. Eve Yoder and Esther Bachman's straightforward account of the banishment order and the forced sale of even the stoves and beds from their houses touched a different response. The Assembly ordered the Council to investigate and to right this obvious wrong.

Document 264

In June, Mr. Limbach and [Jacob] Morey, two Justices in Saucon and Upper Milford, summoned a number of their neighbors to take the test and, since they refused, sent them to jail. Many did not appear; these got off successfully. But 9 Mennonites and 2 others were very harshly dealt with, in accordance with the latest Test-Act; they were notified to leave the country within 30 days; all their movable property was taken from them and sold at public auction; their children's flour was taken out of the sack and even the women's spinning wheels.[94]

Document 265

To the Honorable, the Supreme Executive Council of the Commonwealth of Pennsylvania

The Petition of George Bachman, Jacob Yeoder, Casper Yeoder, Abraham Yeoder, Henry Sell, Philip Geisinger, Henry Geisinger, Abraham Geisinger, & Christian Young, & John Newcomer of Upper Saucon in the County of Northampton & State of Pennsylvania

Humbly Sheweth,

That your Petitioners having received Sentence of Banishment at the last Court of Quarter Sessions held at Easton, for no other cause but that we could not with freedom of Conscience comply with the Law of this State Imposing a Test on the Inhabitants, & being deeply afflicted with the complicated distresses, our unhappy Families are thereby involved in; beg leave, in all humility to lay before you, our deplorable case, not destitute of some hope of obtaining Your merciful Interposition, as we believe none can Justly Charge any of us with having ever done any act, that can be Construed inimical to the State, or Government we live under, but have always been peaceable Subjects, ready & willing to contribute our full proportion towards the support of it, Except going into military Service, it being contrary to our religious principles to bear Arms in any case whatsoever, and if ever we are found Guilty of any thing contrary to these Our peaceable Principles, may we Suffer the Severest Penalties;

Your Petitioners believing the Supreme Council to be invested with a dispensing Power to mitigate the severity of our sentence as we humbly conceive the process against us, has not been according to the Spirit of the Law, or the intention of the Legislature with regard to the peaceable Industrious part of the People, which Error is Imputed to the Magistrates not Clearly understanding the full meaning of the first & third Clauses of the Act for the further Security of Government, past the first of April last;

Your Petitioners not being able yet to get over their religious Scruple about taking the said Test, it appearing to us like Joining our hands to Military Service, and being very desirous to Continue to be, not only peaceable, but useful Subjects to this State; do humbly request the Honorable Supreme Council to take our distressed Case into Consideration, and grant such relief therein as to You in Your Wisdom Shall Seem meet and Your Petitioners Shall as in duty bound pray &c.
4th July 1778

Philip Geisinger · *Jacob Yoder* · *Peter Sell*
Christian Jung · *Casper Yoder* · *Heinrich Geisinger*
Johannes Neukommer · *Abraham Joder* · *Johannes Geisinger*
Georg Bachman · *Heinrich Sell* · *Abraham Geisinger*

We the Subscribers, Freeman of the County of Northampton &ca. being duly qualified according to Law, beg leave to Certifie the Honorable Supreme Council of this Commonwealth, that we are Neighbors to, & well acquainted with the petitioners above named and have ever known them to be men of unblemished reputation for uprightness & Integrity in their Conduct, conversation & dealings amongst Men, & are convinced that their present blindness to their own Essential interests, proceeds from an unhappy bias in their Education, & not from any disaffection to the present Government.
Witness our hands the 5th July 1778

Felix Lynn · *Adam Lukenbach* · *Matts. Gangwar*
Nicholas Kooken · *Jorg Schaffer* · *Johannes Bair (?)*
Johannes Lukenbach · *Felix Rosenberger* · *Peter Fuchs*
Georg Rauschenberger · *Michael Zigler* · *Mattes. Muller*[95]

[The entire petition is in the handwriting of Dr. Felix Lynn of Northhampton County, except for the signatures of the other petitioners.]

Document 266

Friday, August 14, 1778.

A petition from Jacob Bachman, of Northampton County, setting forth, that he had leased from his father a plantation, together with the stock thereon, situated in the said county, which have since been seized by the agents for confiscated property to his great damage, and praying the house would order them to be returned to him, was read, and ordered to lie on the table.[96]

Document 267

To the Honorable the Representatives of the Freeman of the Common Wealth of Pennsylvania in General Assembly met

The Petition fo Eve Joder, Wife of Jacob Joder of Upper Saucon Township in the County of Northampton in this State, Yeoman, and Esther Bachman, Wife of George Bachman of Upper Saucon Township aforesaid, Yeoman, As well on Behalf of themselves and their said Husbands as also on Behalf of John Keisinger, Abraham Keisinger, Henry Sell, Jasper Joder, Abraham Joder, Jacob Joder, Henry Keisinger, Christian Joung, John Newcomer and George Bachman, all of them Freeholders and Men of Reputation of the sd. County, who have always beheaved peaceably & quietly and never intermedled in State Affairs But paid their Taxes & Fines, furnished Horses & Teams for the continental Service when ever demanded, and some of them have gone with their Teams as Drivers to carry Provisions to the Army of the united States for which Services they have hitherto received no pay;

That the said Freeholders were summoned to appear at the Court of Quarter Sessions held at Easton in June last past, where they appeared accordingly and the Test being tendered to them, by the said Court, which said Test they conscientiously scrupled to take (being of the Religious Society called Menonists) Whereupon the sd. Court sentenced them to be banished out of this State within thirty days after the said Court and that all their personal Estate be confiscated to the State;

That afterwards all their said personal Estate even their Beds, Bedings, Linen, Bibles & Books were taken from them and sold by the Sheriff to the amount of about forty thousand Pounds;

That from some of them all their Provisions were taken and even not a Morsel of Bread left them for their Children;

That all their Iron Stoves were taken from them out of their Houses, tho' fastned to the Freehold, they are deprived of every Means of Keeping their Children warm in the approaching Winter especially at Nights being obliged to lye on the Floor without any Beds;

That some of the said Mens Wifes are pregnant and near their Time of Deliverance which makes their Case more distressing and

That by Reason of the said Proceedings ten of the most respectful and considerable Familys in the said County of Northampton are become destitute and very much reduced:

May it therefore please this Honorable House to take the Premisses into Consideration and to mitigate the Severity of the Sentence of the said Court, and that some Reguard be had to the Command of God laid down in the Scriptures of Truth, to witt, "What God hath joyned together let not Men put asunder" and that our Husbands may be permitted to continue to dwell with us, and that our Children may not be taken from us,

And your Petitioners as in Duty bound will ever pray. September the 9th 1778.

her
Eve E *Joder*
mark
her
Esther E *Bachman*[97]
mark

Document 268

The Petition of Eve Joder and Esther Backman in behalf of themselves, their Husbands and other Inhabitants of Northampton County being read.

Resolved that the Petition be referred to Council and it is recommended to them to inquire into the facts set forth in the said Petition and if the same are found to be true to grant such Relief in their present Distresses as they may think proper by a Draft on the State Treasurer.

Extract from the Minutes

John Morris Jr.
Clk. of Genl. Assembly[98]

Document 269

Philadelphia 17th Septemr, 1778.

Gentlemen,

The Honourable House of Assembly were addressed, just before their late adjournment, by Eve Yoder and Esther Bachman in behalf of themselves, & their Husbands, & the families of divers others inhabitants of Upper Saucon in the County of Northampton whose heads or husbands had been sentenced to be banished by the Quarter Sessions of the County, their personal Estate to be forfeited to the Commonwealth, & their real property to descend to their heirs respectively, as if they were naturally dead, for refusing assurance of allegiance according to an Act of Assembly, entituled "An Act for the further security of Government." They set forth that the personal Goods of these persons were all seized & sold by the Sheriff, & their families left destitute of the necessaries of life, & pray for some mitigation of the sentence & so forth.

The House on considering of this petition, recommended the Case of these people to Council, & that if the facts therein set forth be found on enquiry to be true, such relief as may be thought proper, may be granted, by a draught on the State Treasurer.

As it would be only adding to the difficulties, which these people already complain of, to expect they should support the Allegations contained in their petition before this board, & as their condition can be much better opined & understood on the Spot, you are requested by Council to take an early opportunity of enquiring into the matter, that on your report & advice an order may be sent by the State Treasurer to the Sheriff of yr. County to relieve their present difficulties. For this purpose, you have enclosed Copies of the petition above—mentioned, & the vote of Assembly thereupon. Doubting not of your good disposition in favour of distress in whatever shape, I remain,

Gentn.,

Yr. most obed. Servt.,

G. Bryan Vice President

To John Ralston and Peter Roads Esqr. and Doctor Linn.[99]

Document 270

May it please your Excellency,

In Pursuance of your Request, Dated Philada. Sept. 17, 1778, We Have inquired into the Facts set forth in a Petition signed Eve Yoder and Ester Bachman, in behalf of themselves & others.

And Beg leave to Report that most all the Personal Estates of the Persons named in the Petition was taken from them in consequence of an Act of the General Assembly, Intituled an act for the further security of the Government, and Likewise their Stores, yet we Learned from the Petitioners themselves, that they have Grain anough for the support of their Families for one year, as their crops of the Last Harvest, both Grain and Hay, was wholly Left them for their own use, but as the seizure was made Just before harvest, Probably some of them Might have been in want for a few days; Likewise we find that Abraham Geisinger's wife had not a bed left her although she was Near her Time of Delivery, and also one of the most Necessitous; And that Henry Sell was Robbed of all his Cash shortly before his goods were seized, and is likewise at times somewhat Delirious; That by what we could Learn the sum arising from the sales of said Estates Amounts only to about Nine Thousand Pounds.

We are with Great Respect,
Your Excellencys
Most Humble Servants,
John Ralston
Peter Rhoads
Felix Lynn

Upper Sacon, Oct. 2d, 1778
His Excellency George Bryan, Vice Pres't[100]

Other Judicial Excesses

While the Pennsylvania Supreme Executive Council investigated the case of the Upper Saucon Mennonites, they learned of other excesses by the Northampton County justices. The former Mennonite preacher Henry Funk went to Philadelphia to intercede for Abraham and Michael Meyer, probably Mennonites, whose property had been seized when they refused the test oath.

Document 271

Philadelphia, 2d September, 1778

Sir:—One, Henry Funk, of your county, is come here, & alledges that you have seized the real & personal Estate of Abraham Meyer & Michael Myer, for refusing to take the oath of allegiance & abjuration appointed by law. Perhaps there may be some mistake in your proceedings. I shall therefore state to you in short the business you are called to. By the Act of Assembly under which the agents of Council act, the Estates in land & goods of persons charged with Treason in the Act, or by Council in proclamations since issued, who have not come in & surrendered themselves for Trial, are put under their care & disposal, & no other. Should any person called on by the magistrates to take the said Oath, refuse it before them and persist in such refusal in the Court of Quarter Sessions, afterwards he would forfeit his goods to the State, not his land, or anything fixed to or growing on it, but even in this Case the Sherrif, not the agents, would take care of the forfieture.

I write these lines by direction of Council, as well in behalf of these men, that nothing unlawful be done to them thro' mistake, as to caution you to keep yourself within your Duty, for be assured you may expect that the doings beyond what is warranted by the Act of Assembly would bring you under severe Censure & heavy Damages, recovered by the party affected.

I am, sir, Your very hum'l Serv't.

George Bryan.[101]

To *Jacob Miller*, Esq'r, one of the agents of N'n co'y

Intercession for Moravian Prisoners

The Northampton justices had also begun legal proceedings against the Moravians. John Ettwein wrote from Bethlehem asking Vice-President George Bryan to intercede for the Emmaus Moravians imprisoned by the Northampton County Court of Quarter Sessions.

Document 272

To His Excellency George Bryan, Vice President of the Supreme Executive Council of the Common Wealth of Pennsylvania

Honoured Sir,

You will excuse me that I trouble you again with the Concerns of a few Individuals belonging to the United Brethren. We gave great Offence to the Justices who had issued a summons for all the inhabitants of Bethlehem, Nazareth and Emmaus, in laying it before Government, and disobeying it on Account of its Illegality. But they have hitherto done nothing further against Bethlehem, &c a, but have issued an other Summons for the male Inhabitants at Emmaus, mentioning their Names, to appear before them at Bethlehem, September 18 th. On their Appearance, and refusing to take the Test as it stands, and also declining to give Security for their Appearance before the next Court, the Justices wrote their Commitment, and the Constable granted them Leave to return home and to appear at Court on Tuesday next. Esq r Levers, who was accidently here last Night, is much afraid that the Court might act with these poor People with the same Rigour last Court has done with the Mennonists in Saucon, and therefore advised me to send to your Honour an Express, to beg the Favour of You, to recommend it to the President of the Easton Court, M r Silleman, in a few Lines, if possible, to postpone the Prosecution against the Reverend M r Francis Boehler, and the others named in the said Summons, most of who have suffered a Month's Imprisonment before. I believe they would be willing to give security for their Appearance before the December Court, and apprehend their refusing to give security now, and choosing rather to go to Goal, was from a Notion that this present Court could not, in that Case, pass Judgment upon them, and they might gain Time to see what an other Application to the new General Assembly might effect. I do, therefore, most humbly pray that Your Honour would please to write a few Lines in their Favour to the Court, or to give some other Advice for their Relief. I can assure Your Honour that all the above Persons so summoned, are quiet, good, and faithfull subjects of the state.

I am, with high Esteem,
Your Honours
most humble Servant,
John Ettwein.
Bethlehem, Septemb r 19 th, 1778.[102]

Moravian Petitions

The threat to the existence of their settlements at Bethlehem and elsewhere in Northampton County led the Moravians to again petition the Pennsylvania legislature.

Document 273

Extracts from the minutes of the first sitting of the third general assembly of the commonwealth of Pennsylvania, which met at Philadelphia on Monday the 26th of October, 1778, A. D. and in the third year of the independence of America.

Monday, Nov. 9, 1778

A memorial from a very considerable number of the respectable members of the church called Unitas Fratrum, vulgarly Moravians, setting forth that they did in May last petition the late general assembly (for the subject of which they refer to the said petition) — that the said assembly in answer thereto declared, "that they were ready and willing to grant them every encouragement and protection in their power, consistent with the duty they owe to their constituents and the welfare of the United States of America," — that they confided in that declaration, and would not now have troubled this house, had it not been for some late rigorous examples, under the act for the further security of government, in the county of Northampton — that now the fruits of all their toil and labour in Bethlehem, and their other settlements in that county, are threatened and endangered — that they are willing to promise faith and allegiance to the state — And praying "for the benefit and effect of the above mentioned resolve of the late house of assembly," was read and ordered to lie on the table.[103]

Supplement to Act

On December 5, 1778, the Pennsylvania Assembly repealed the harsher provisions of the earlier legislation and substituted a new law that excluded nonjurors from voting, holding office, or serving on juries and continued the double tax. The relevant paragraphs of this "Further Supplement to the Act Intituled 'An act for the farther security of the government' " provided:

Document 274

And be it farther enacted by the authority aforesaid, That every person, who hath not taken the oath or affirmation, directed to be taken by the said laws, on or before the said first day of June last (except the persons before excepted) and who shall refuse or neglect to take and subscribe the oath or affirmation of allegiance herein prescribed, shall be, and is hereby declared to be excluded from, and incapable of electing or being elected into, or holding any office or place of trust under this government, and of serving on juries, during the time of such neglect or refusal, but that all other penalties, incapabilities and disabilities, imposed by any former acts of assembly, shall from henceforth cease and determine.

Provided always, that nothing in this act contained, shall extend to discharge any person who has incurred a forfeiture of double taxes, from the payment thereof, in such assessments as have been made or which shall be made by virtue of the laws of this state heretofore passed.[104]

Newspaper Comment I

"A Freeman" asked rhetorically in the *Pennsylvania Packet* for October 8, 1778:

Document 275

How can this act secure to the present Members their seats in Assembly? You have not undertaken to tell us, and indeed you generally content yourself with a bare *ipse dixit*, knowing that argument must fail you. There are some thousands in almost each county, and a great majority of the freemen of the State, who have taken the prescribed oath or affirmation, on or before the first of June last; and a great majority of those who have neglected it, (a few whigs only excepted, who will, no doubt, soon be relieved from any disabilities, incapacities or penalties on that account) are chiefly of the people called Quakers, and those sects who have been generally under the influence,

I mean the Menonists, German Baptists and Moravians. And are these the men you would have us intrust with carrying on the war against Great-Britain? I believe they are; but we have had *sufficient evidence* of their *want* of attachment to the community and to the liberties of mankind, to trust them in such a contest.[105]

Newspaper Comment II

A correspondent of the *Pennsylvania Packet,* who used the pseudonym "DeWitt," made some uncomfortably close comparisons between the British ministry and "the present Rulers of Pennsylvania," asking among other things:

Document 276

Whether the test imposed upon the Freemen of the state previous to their exercising the right of voting for Rulers, was not designed to keep the whole power of the state in the hands of a small faction?

Whether any power on earth has a right to deprive a Freeman of the privilege of chusing his Rulers, except in cases of *proven* incapacity or guilt?

Whether all laws throwing obstacles in the way of Freemen voting at elections, are not infringements of the *constitution* of the state?

Whether the test law of Pennsylvania, which not only has a retrospective operation, but dives into the *hearts* and consciences of all who take it, is not the most absurd, tyrannical and wicked law that ever was passed in a free country?

Whether *political* is not as bad as religious *persecution* for conscience sake?[106]

Law's Harshness Blamed for Mennonite Migration

The disabilities imposed on those who did not swear or affirm their allegiance remained in force until 1789, although an unsuccessful effort to modify the Test Acts had been made in 1787. A correspondent of the Philadelphia *Pennsylvania Gazette* blamed the law for the migration of Mennonites, Quakers, and others to Virginia and Canada and said that thirty Mennonite families were about to leave Lancaster County for Niagara "on purpose to avoid the disagreeable consequences of our ridiculous and tyrannical test law."

Document 277

March 3, 1787

The Committee on the petition from a number of inhabitants of Chester County, praying for an alteration of the test-laws, report

That having well considered the prayer of the said petition, they are of opinion that it will consist with good policy to satisfy the scruples of the petitioners respecting the test; for in the judgment of your committee it appears, that a government so well established as ours the security of an oath cannot be wanted, in the form prescribed by the existing laws.

The objections which have been made to the oath of allegiance are not of the petitioners only; they have occurred to many others who have considered the subject.

It has been remarked by them, that besides the declaration of attachment and fidelity, present and future, it contains a clause of retrospective aspect, conceived in words of too uncertain & indefinite import; and that the abjuration ingrafted on it implies a doubt of the fidelity of the citizens, few of whom can have the desire, as none can have an interest, to subvert our independence.

This being the case, and as the state stands in need of all its citizens to supply its various services, it must be a public injury to keep up a form, which has the effect to disqualify any number of them.

They therefore offer the following resolution

That a committee be appointed to bring in a bill to modify the oath of allegiance, in such manner as to reduce it to a simple declaration of attachment and fidelity to the government.[107]

Document 278

It is hoped, says a correspondent, the present Assembly will do away with the present disgraceful test-law. There are many thousands of good foederalists who never will vote at our elections while that weak and unnecessary law is in force. Virginia, and the governor of Canada, have already taken advantage of our folly; they invite Quakers, and other sects who are opposed to oaths, and promises of fidelity to government to come and settle among them, and assure them of perpetual exemption from those disgraceful badges of tyranny, which were invented at a time when kings and priests shared between them the dominion of mankind. It is said, that thirty families of the people called Menonists are about to emigrate from Lancaster county to Niagara, on purpose to avoid the disagreeable consequences of our ridiculous and tyrannical test law.[108]

Document 279

February 16, 1789

The committee to whom was referred that part of the message of the Council respecting the test law, read February 9th, was read the second time, and unanimously adopted, viz.

The committee, to whom was referred that part of the message from his Excellency the President and the Supreme Executive Council, which relates to the laws requiring from the citizens of this commonwealth certain tests of abjuration and allegiance beg leave to report—

That however proper such laws might have been during the late war, when, by the division of a powerful nation, it became necessary for individuals to make a solemn declaration of their attachment to one or the other of the contending parties, to your committee it appears, that in times of peace and of well established government, they are not only useless, but highly pernicious, by disqualifying a great body of the people from exercising many necessary offices, and throwing the whole burden thereof on others, and, also, by alienating the affections of tender, though perhaps mistaken, minds from a government, which, by its invidious distinctions, they are led to consider as hostile to their peace and happiness.

Your committee therefore beg leave to offer the following resolution, to wit.

Resolved, That a committee be appointed to bring in a bill, to be passed into a law, to repeal all the laws or acts of General Assembly, which require any oath or affirmation of allegiance to the commonwealth from the citizens thereof, and of abjuration and renunciation of any foreign power whatever, and to remove all disabilities created by a non-compliance therewith.

Ordered, That Mr. Lewis, Mr. Wynkoop and Mr. McLene be a committee to bring in a bill agreeably to the foregoing resolution.[109]

Test Oath and Military Service

Maryland Methodists saw the test oath as a pledge to defend the state against an invader, which undercut any existing exemption for conscientious objectors. For Jesse Hollingsworth, Baltimore businessman, personal military service was the issue.

Document 280

Baltimore March 10 1778

Dear Sir,

I have Been Much Consern'd Since I Came home from Anopolis I have Been Told that I had Declar'd My Avertion to this Oath in Generall, and Would not take it, I Declare Sir, I only Clame What is My Right, as I think, I had Desires to keep Out of the Army Or to Be

Oblig'd to March With the Militia, When they Ware Order'd Out to Prevent Which, I Desir'd the Recruting Sargant When he Met With a man, To high Pris'd for his Bounty, to Purchase him of his Master for Mee, Which he Did, and I have got a Discharge under that Law, (Without I had a nesety or of My own free Will) I Declare to you that I only Clame that Right, as I think the Words in the Oath Cuts up, Every Other Law On Exemptions, by the Words, I Will, Maintain, Support, & Defend, to the utmost of My Power — Sertainly these are Plain and Intilagable Words, and Can Convay no Meaning But What the[y] Expres, if so I am Oblig'd to March When Cal'd On, Or not, if Men are Wanted. But if to the Contrary I may Stay at home, When I Wish, and Be usefull, Why May not these Words Be Left Out, if the are to have no Influence on the Person taking the Oath, I Beleve that hundreds Would Take the Oath if them Very Words Were Left Out, or Chang'd into Softer Terms — as I Veryly Beleve, there is a great Number that Woud Serve their Cuntry, in any thing in their Power But Sheding Blud, and that Part of the Oath Binds them to do What their Religious Prinsipals is a Vers to — Pleas Excuse this Troublesum Letter I am Raly Willing to Serve you or My State Or the States in generall and hope I Shall Be Excus'd for Claming What the Law has Give Me a Right as to all the Other Parts of the Oath I have No Obiection to and Will Come before you to Confirm it if you Pleas from Sir your Humble Servant

Jesse Hollingsworth

To his Exelensy Thomas Johnson at Anopolis[110]

Document 281

William Lux wrote to Governor Thomas Johnson, March 3, 1778, that:

On the whole, I expect about one third of the County have taken the Oath of Fidelity, but its only guess work. Several good People have refused, every one of the Methodists, & all the Quakers, their objection is the compulsion to bear Arms, many of them I believe would have affirm'd, with that exception. — I feel Concern for some and among the rest Mr. Hollingsworth, who has been always a most industrious & useful Member of Society, he comes down to see you and have some Conversation, I wish you wou'd have a Chat with him at Night, because I think it probable that you may remove his Scruples, as I know he entertains the highest Opinion of you.[111]

Virginia Test Act

The first test act passed in Virginia restricted only the civil rights of nonjurors.

Document 282

July 8 [1777] They passed an Act for a General Test for all free male Inhabitants above 16 years of age; to be taken before the 10 of October next. They must swear to renounce all Allegiance to the King of England & his Successors for ever; swear Allegiance to Virginia, as a free & independent State, & to do nothing prejudicial to its interests; to reveal all treasons, conspiracies, &c. against the State &c &c. The penalty of a refusal to take this Oath is to be disarmed, rendered unable to serve on Juries, to elect or be elected, to sue for the recovery of debts, to purchase Houses, lands or Hereditaments.[112]

Quakers Prevent Passage of Harsh Virginia Law

Virginia Quakers were able to turn aside a proposed bill before that state's General Assembly, imposing harsher penalties on all who refused the oath of allegiance.

Document 283

A memorial of sundry inhabitants of this State, of the society of people called Quakers, was presented to the House, and read; setting forth, that not to engage in war is a fundamental tenet of their religion; that they have refused to take the test from motives of conscience, and have understood, that a bill is now depending before the House, which, if passed into a law, will subject them to great difficulties and sufferings; and praying such relief as may be thought just and reasonable.[113]

North Carolina Quakers and the Test Act

North Carolina Quakers acknowledged the effort made by their legislature to make the test act more palatable, but let the General Assembly know that any form of pledging allegiance would be equally objectionable.

Document 284

The Comitte met at Wells's in Perquimons the 9th day of the 1st month 1779 and propose Josiah White the Clerk at this time, and taking under their solid consideration the present Situation of affairs among us relative to the refusing of the affirmation of allegiance to the state of North Carolina (so called) it was unanimously concluded that it might be Necessary to Address the present Assembly on the acct. and an essay being prepared was deliberately read and some alterations proposed and agreed to, and ordered to be signed by the Clerk and is as follows, Viz:

To the General Assembly of the State of North Carolina Now Sitting

The Address and Petition of the people called Quakers from their Yearly meeting Committee in Perquimons County the 9th of the 1st month 1779 — Humbly Sheweth

That nothwithstanding we are in duty bound Gratefully to acknowledge your Lenity in suspending the Execution of the act of Assembly requiring the Test of Fidelity and Abjuration, and altering the word Allegiance to Fidelity to soften the former act and make it easier to us, yet we think it remains the same in substance, and being enjoined by our peaceable Principles to Live as much as in us Lies a Quiet Honest and Inoffensive Life and to keep clear from Joining with any party Engaged in dispute that are to be Determined by Military force as our reasons therefore doth not arise from the Least Intention of taking or persuing any steps against the state. If our Conscientious and tender Scruples in them Respects should have a tendency to bring Great sufferings upon us and terminate in the Ruin of many Honest Families we submit, but ardently desire that you will not consider us Enemies to our country because we Scruple taking the aforsd. Test. We [illegible] do Humbly request that you would be pleased to Grant us the priviledges that we have hitherto Enjoyed until proof be made that our behaviour manifests us to be unworthy thereof, and we hope our conduct will always Demonstrate our Gratitude.

Signed by order and behalf of the Committee aforesaid

By Josiah White Clk.[114]

Document 285

The Committee met at the Old Neck the 23rd of the 10th month 1779.

Two of the Friends appointed to present the above Address to the Assembly report that they attended & presented it which to Appearance met with a favourable Reception & a Committee was appointed to consider thereon who made some alteration in the Affirmation.[115]

Notes for Chapter 6

1. *Pennsylvania Gazette* (Philadelphia), February 5, 1777.

2. *Votes and Proceedings of the Senate of the State of Maryland. February Session 1777* (Annapolis, 1777), 40-42. William Kilty, *Laws of Maryland* (Annapolis, 1798), February 1777, Chapter XX. Richard A. Overfield, "A Patriot Dilemma: The Treatment of Passive Loyalists and Neutrals in Revolutionary Maryland," *Maryland Historical Magazine*, Vol. LXVIII (Summer 1973), 143.

3. *Votes and Proceedings of the House of Delegates of the State of Maryland. June Session 1777* (Annapolis, 1777), 110. *Maryland Gazette* (Annapolis), July 10, 1777.

4. *Maryland Gazette* (Annapolis), July 17, 1777, July 31, 1777. *Pennsylvania Evening Post* (Philadelphia), June 21, 1777.

5. *Pennsylvania Evening Post* (Philadelphia), June 7, 1777.

6. *Pennsylvania Packet and General Advertiser* (Philadelphia), June 10, 1777.

7. *Pennsylvania Evening Post* (Philadelphia), June 21, 1777.

8. Hebron, near Lebanon, was then in Lancaster, now in Lebanon County. "Extracts from the Records of the Moravian Congregation at Hebron, Pennsylvania, 1775-1781," P.M.H.B. vol. XVIII (1894), 451.

9. Richard McAlester to Thomas Wharton, July 4, 1777, *Pennsylvania Archives*, 1st Series, V, 412.

10. William Lyon to Thomas Wharton, July 7, 1777, *Pennsylvania Archives*, 1st Series, V, 416.

11. Statement of Henry Funk, August, 1777, Clemency File, Records of the Supreme Executive Council, P.H.M.C.

12. Statement of George Kriebel, August, 1777, Clemency File, Records of the Supreme Executive Council, P.H.M.C.

13. Petition of Wendel Bowman, March 23, 1778, Clemency File, Records of the Supreme Executive Council, P.H.M.C.

14. *Minutes of the Annual Meetings of the Church of the Brethren 1778-1909* (Elgin, Ill., 1909), 5.

15. John Ettwein, "A Short Account of the Disturbances in America and of the Moravian Brethren's Conduct and Suffering in this Connection," Kenneth G. Hamilton, *John Ettwein and the Moravian Church During the Revolutionary Period* (Bethlehem, Pa., 1940), 253 and 281-287.

16. Christopher Marshall to his children, August 25, 1777, Christopher Marshall Letter Book, fols. 243-244, H.S.P.

17. Philadelphia Yearly Meeting, Minutes of the Meeting for Sufferings, 1775-1785, fol. 214, Friends Historical Library, Swarthmore College, Swarthmore, Pa.

18. Young, "Treatment of Loyalists," 163.

19. *Votes and Proceedings of the House of Delegates of the State of Maryland October Session 1777* (Annapolis, Md., 1777), 11. William Kilty, comp., *Laws of Maryland* (Annapolis, Md., 1799), October 1777, Chapter XX.

20. Hamilton, *Ettwein*, 275.

21. *Ibid.*, 292.

22. *Pennsylvania Evening Post* (Philadelphia), July 23, 1778.

23. Christopher Marshall, Diary, June 2, 1778, H.S.P.

24. If these petitions were presented, they are no longer extant. Christopher Marshall, Diary, August 6, 1778. HSP.

25. Philadelphia Yearly Meeting, Minutes of the Meeting for Sufferings, 1775-1785, fol. 153, Q.C., H.C.L.

26. *Pennsylvania Archives*, 6th Series, XII, 429-448.

27. Petition of Eve Yoder and Esther Bachman, September 9, 1778, Clemency File,

Records of the Supreme Executive Council, P.H.M.C.

28. Conrad Alexandre Gerard de Rayneval to Comte de Vergennes, September 18, 1778, George Brookes, *Friend Anthony Benezet* (Philadelphia, 1937), 449-451.

29. *Pennsylvania Evening Post* (Philadelphia), October 21, 1778.

30. *Pennsylvania Archives*, 2nd Series, III, 210.

31. Preston A. Barba, *They Came to Emmaus* (Emmaus, Pa., 1959), 125-127.

32. *Pennsylvania Evening Post* (Philadelphia), December 9, 1778.

33. Montgomery, *Berks County in the Revolution*, 70.

34. Abraham Reincke Beck, ed., "Extracts from the Brethren's House and Congregation Diaries of the Moravian Church at Lititz, Pa., relating to the Revolutionary War," *Penn-Germania*, I (November-December 1912), 857.

35. Hamilton, *Ettwein*, 302-303.

36. *Minutes of the Annual Meetings of the Church of the Brethren 1778-1909*, 5.

37. Tax Lists, 1778, 1779, Cocalico Township, Lancaster County Historical Society, Lancaster, Pa.

38. *Mennonite Yearbook and Almanac*, 1919, 24.

39. Robert Levers to William Moore, October 31, 1781, Northampton County Military Papers, P.H.M.C.

40. *Pennsylvania Archives*, 2nd Series, III, 463.

41. Tax Lists, 1778, 1779, Lancaster County Historical Society, Lancaster, Pa.

42. Young, "Treatment of Loyalists," 103-105.

43. E. Wickersham to James Burd, November 6, 1776, Burd Papers, H.S.P.

44. *Pennsylvania Archives*, 1st Series, V, 427.

45. *Pennsylvania Archives*, 2nd Series, III, 169-170.

46. *Pennsylvania Packet*, October 3, 1778.

47. Owen S. Ireland, "The Ethnic-Religious Dimension of Pennsylvania Politics, 1778-1779," WMQ, 3rd Series, XXX (July 1973); 432-434.

48. *Pennsylvania Archives*, 2nd Series, III, 85-86.

49. *Minutes of the First Session of the Eleventh General Assembly of the Commonwealth of Pennsylvania* (Philadelphia, 1787), 133-134.

50. *Minutes of the First Session of the Twelfth General Assembly of the Commonwealth of Pennsylvania* (Philadelphia, 1789), 75, 63 and 73-74.

51. *Pennsylvania Gazette* (Philadelphia), February 4, 1789.

52. *Minutes of the First Session of the Twelfth General Assembly* (Philadelphia, 1789), 74.

53. Overfield, "Patriot Dilemma," 150.

54. William Matthews, Journal, May 4, 1781, Matthews Papers, Maryland Historical Society, Baltimore, Md.

55. Prosecution under the Act for the better security of the government began on May 22, 1778, with the indictment of eight Methodist preachers. Records of the General Court for the Western Shore, May Term 1778, fols. 506-507. Maryland Hall of Records, Annapolis, Md. At the October 1778 session of the court, 25 indictments were handed down, all Methodists, except for Evan Thomas. In the first case actually tried, the court fined Joshua Cromwell £13 . . 14 . . 6 and costs for "preaching and teaching the Gospel" as a nonjuror. *Ibid.*, October Term 1778, fols. 351 and 357.

56. Gordon Pratt Baker, ed., *Those Incredible Methodists: A History of the Baltimore Conference of the United Methodist Church* (Baltimore, Md., 1972), 46-51. Kilty, *Laws*, November 1781, Chapter LIV.

57. Minutes of the Committee for Sufferings of Maryland Yearly Meeting, 1778-1841, fols. 3-4. Microfilm in Maryland Hall of Records, Annapolis, Md.

58. Kilty, *Laws*, November, 1781, Chapter CXVII.

59. Journal of the House of Delegates, Commonwealth of Virginia, November 17, 1778, V.S.L.

60. Edward Stabler to Israel Pemberton, January 26, 1779. Pemberton Papers, H.S.P.

61. Roger E. Sappington, "North Carolina and the Non-Resistant Sects During the American War of Independence," *Quaker History*, LX (Spring 1971), 39-41.
62. Minutes of the Standing Committee of North Carolina Yearly Meeting, fols. 39-42. Quaker Collection, Guilford College Library, Guilford, N.C.
63. Sappington, *op. cit.*, 41.
64. *Ibid.*, 45.
65. *Pennsylvania Evening Post* (Philadelphia), May 16, 1777.
66. *Ibid.*, June 28, 1777.
67. Philadelphia Yearly Meeting, Minutes of the Meeting for Sufferings, 1775-1785, fols. 123-124, Q.C., H.C.L.
68. *Ibid.*
69. John Ettwein, "A Short Account of the Disturbances in America and of the Moravian Brethren's America and of the Moravian Brethren's Conduct and Suffering in this Connection," translated from the German in Kenneth G. Hamilton, *John Ettwein and the Moravian Church During the Revolutionary Period* (Bethlehem, 1940), 253.
70. Pennsylvania Supreme Executive Council Records, P.H.M.C.
71. *Ibid.*
72. *Ibid.*
73. Original draft in Schwenkfelder Library, Pennsburg, Pa., translated by Howard W. Kriebel, *The Schwenkfelders in Pennsylvania* (Lancaster, 1904), 207-219. A lengthy section on the militia law has been omitted here.
74. Pennsylvania Supreme Executive Council, Clemency File, P.H.M.C.
75. *Colonial Records*, XI, 269.
76. *Pennsylvania Archives*, 1st Series, V, 524-525.
77. Hamilton, *John Ettwein*, 262.
78. Records of the Supreme Executive Council, Clemency File, P.H.M.C.
79. Hamilton, 261.
80. *Ibid.*, 275.
81. Schwenkfelder Library, Pennsburg, Pa. Translated by Elizabeth Horsch Bender.
82. Hamilton, 290-291. Petitions "signed by a large number of the inhabitants of Berks County" also asked for modification of the test act. *Pennsylvania Evening Post* (Philadelphia), August 4, 1778.
83. *Pennsylvania Evening Post (Philadelphia), July 23, 1778.*
84. *Pennsylvania Archives*, 1st Series, VI, 541.
85. *Ibid.*, 2nd Series, III, 169-170.
86. *Ibid.*, 1st Series, VI, 572.
87. *Pennsylvania Packet* (Lancaster), June 17, 1778.
88. *Pennsylvania Zeitungs-Blat* (Lancaster), June 24, 1778.
89. *Pennsylvania Packet and General Advertiser* (Lancaster), June 17, 1778.
90. June 30, 1778, Philadelphia Yearly Meeting for Sufferings Minutes, 1775-1785, fol 154.
91. Durnbaugh, *Brethren in Colonial America*, 353-354.
92. *Ibid.*
93. *Pennsylvania Evening Post* (Philadelphia), August 13, 1778.
94. Hamilton, 296.
95. Records of the Supreme Executive Council of Pennsylvania, Clemency File, P.H.M.C.
96. *Pennsylvania Evening Post* (Philadelphia), August 22, 1778.
97. Records of the Supreme Executive Council, Clemency File, P.H.M.C.
98. *Ibid.*
99. *Ibid.*
100. *Pennsylvania Archives*, 1st Series, VI, 772.
101. *Ibid.*, 2nd Series, III, 210.
102. *Ibid.*, 1st Series, VI, 751.
103. *Pennsylvania Evening Post* (Philadelphia), April 9, 1779.

104. *Pennsylvania Packet & General Advertiser* (Philadelphia), December 9, 1778.

105. *Pennsylvania Packet and General Advertiser* (Philadelphia), October 3, 1778. The "Hampden" correspondence appears in the same paper, September 26, October 6, October 8, 1778. Benjamin Rush used the pseudonym "Hampden" at one time, but none of Rush's biographers identify this correspondence with him. The ideas are contrary to known opinions of Benjamin Rush in 1778 and one reply to "Hampden" warns him against using the name, lest the real "Hampden" respond, which indicates that the author was known *not* to be Benjamin Rush.

106. *Pennsylvania Packet* (Philadelphia), March 11, 1779.

107. *Minutes of the First Session of the Eleventh General Assembly of the Commonwealth of Pennsylvania* (Philadelphia, 1787), 133-134.

108. *Pennsylvania Gazette* (Philadelphia), February 4, 1789.

109. *Minutes of the First Session of the Twelfth Assembly of the Commonwealth of Pa.* (Philadelphia, 1789), 73-74.

110. Executive Papers, Box 10, Maryland Hall of Records, Annapolis, Md.

111. William Lux to Thomas Johnson; March 3, 1778, Red Book XX, 79, Maryland Hall of Records, Annapolis, Maryland. His assessment of the situation in Baltimore County is important, for this Baltimore merchant was in the front rank of radical Patriot leaders in Maryland. If William Lux had even a strong suspicion that those who refused the oath were secret Loyalists, he would have no reason to shield them. When he noted that "several good People" had declined, he obviously meant men sympathetic to or active in the Patriot cause. Jesse Hollingsworth, a Baltimore merchant and a Methodist, would fit this definition, as a prominent Patriot with conscientious objection to military service.

112. Robert Honyman, MD, "Journal fols. 135-136. L.C., Washington, D.C.

113. Journal of the House of Delegates Commonwealth of Virginia, November 17, 1778, V.S.L.

114. Minutes of the Standing Committee of North Carolina Yearly Meeting, fols. 39-42. Quaker Collection, Guilford College Library, Guilford, N.C.

115. *Ibid.*, fol. 43.

Chapter 7

"THE MOST LOYAL PEOPLE IN THE WORLD"

Few British Supporters Among Peaceable Sects

Mennonites, Quakers, Dunkers, Schwenkfelders, and Moravians may have lacked enthusiasm for the Revolutionary cause, but they did not give active support to the British effort during the war. Friends violated their traditional peace testimony to take up arms or serve in civil offices on the American side in significant numbers, but only a handful of Quakers joined the British forces. Among the German peace churches even fewer members took sides in the conflict, with a higher proportion engaged on the Patriot side than directly aided the Loyalists' efforts.

In the early stages of the Revolution, Patriots put great pressure or their nonresistant neighbors to join in Committees of Observation, sigr Associations, and drill with the irregular military units that were soo assembling from New England to Georgia. The British authoritie asked for nothing of the kind, but rather that all loyal subjects refuse t cooperate with these self-appointed Committees or enroll in the arm that the Continental Congress was assembling. When Sir Willian Howe occupied New York City and Long Island in 1776, the larg Quaker population was not drafted into the Royal Militia. The me who had until then fought for Congress more than filled its ranks. Th British took over several meetinghouses for temporary use as hospita and barracks and requisitioned wagons, farm produce, firewood, an fencing from local farmers without respect to religious or politica preference. The presence of so many soldiers inevitably led to inciden of theft of money and other valuables and barns and hen house ransacked. But with these exceptions, unavoidable in wartime, Britis respected the neutrality of the Friends within their lines. Much the same thing happened when Howe captured Philadelphia and held it through the winter of 1777-1778. Some hotheaded young Quakers from Philadelphia and Bucks counties acted as guides for the British Army or accepted commissions in the Loyalist units that Howe raised and a few more Friends continued as officials of the city or county government, but no "long-tailed oaths" or double and triple taxes were used to force the peacable sects to declare themselves openly for king and Parliament.

Loyalists or Nonresistants?

Under these circumstances, a fine line divided neutrality from a species of covert Toryism. Christopher Sauer III, who published a pro-British newspaper in the German language during the British occupation of Philadelphia, claimed in his Memorial to the Royal Commission on Losses and Services of American Loyalists in 1785 that "He was a Member of a religious Society who excommunicated all those who took part ag[ains]t G[reat] B[ritain]."[1] Abraham Pastorius confirmed that none of the Germantown congregation of the Church of the Brethren had taken an active part with the Americans. Does this imply that the Dunkers of Pennsylvania were Loyalists or no more than that they were nonresistants?

As far as Sauer himself is concerned, the answer is self-evident. In a 1784 Memorial he said that he and his father "freely published many political pieces in favor of the British government" by which both Sauers "became so obnoxious to the rebel rulers that they were obliged several times to secret themselves from the fury of their mobs."[2] The younger Sauer also declared that he had served as a guide with British units operating in the vicinity of Germantown, where he was wounded in action, captured, and exchanged for a prisoner of war held by the British.[3]

After Sir William Howe's redcoats took the city, Christopher Sauer III continued to publish a newspaper in Philadelphia, *Der Pennsylvanische Staats-Courier,* and, like his more famous father and grandfather, sought to shape the political attitudes of Pennsylvania Germans. His Loyalist sentiments led to his being proclaimed a traitor by the state authorities in 1778, and Sauer fled to New York with the retreating British army. He issued an *Address to all Germans in Pennsylvania and neighboring provinces* in April 1780, urging them to refuse to serve with the militia, pay taxes, or accept Continental currency as a mark of their loyalty to King George III.[4] How much mischief this advice from a self-proclaimed Tory created for Mennonites and Brethren is unknown.

By his own account, Sauer served as a link between "his friends in Pennsylvania, Maryland and the Delaware counties" and the British commander in New York. On September 1, 1780, Sauer transmitted a brief report to Major Oliver DeLancey, Jr., of Sir Henry Clinton's staff. It was based on an interview with Christian Musselman, a Lancaster County Mennonite, who had come to New York with a petition to the king. Sauer's report is still extant in the Sir Henry Clinton Papers in the William L. Clements Library at the University of Michigan, but no other reference to it or to any of the persons involved could be located in these files from the British headquarters in New York.

According to Sauer, Mennonites and Brethren in Lancaster County had several meetings to consult together on wartime problems. Sauer himself was present at one of these gatherings, almost certainly prior to the British occupation of Philadelphia in 1777. He had no contact with his friends after he left Philadelphia other than by correspondence.

Some Dunkers and Mennonites in Lancaster County had discussed an address to the king as early as the spring of 1780; at least rumors of this reached Sauer in New York. The arrival of Christian Musselman in New York, if not totally unexpected, was not necessarily the result of any of Sauer's activities.

Christian Musselman the courier was either a substantial farmer in Earl Township or one of two small landowners in Warwick Township. One man of this name was an acquaintance of Christopher Marshall and urged him to moderate the Test Act in 1778.

By Sauer's account, their address was drafted by "some of the ministers and leading men of those two societies," but only one man can be identified as a preacher among those named by Sauer as the authors of the petition. Michael Kauffman, Sr., was most likely Bishop Michael Kauffman (d. 1791) and Michael Kauffman, Jr., can probably be identified with either Michael Kauffman (1714-1788), a Virginia pioneer who returned to the Landisville area in Hempfield Township, or his nephew, Dr. Michael Kauffman (1746-1816), who lived nearby.[5] Philip Shoemaker of Warwick Township has been identified as a member of the Conestoga (Ephrata) congregation of the Church of the Brethren.[6] Two possibilities exist for identifying Melchior Brenneman. He could be Melchior Brenneman (1718-1794) of Conestoga Township, but Sauer's reference to ministers makes it more likely that he was Melchior Brenneman (1726-1809), a Mennonite preacher, farmer and miller in Donegal Township.[7] Both Brennemans appear on tax lists as nonassociators and nonjurors. The sons of Melchior Brenneman, the preacher of Donegal Township, all affirmed their allegiance to the state and served in the militia, as did members of Dr. Michael Kauffman's family. This was an unusual division in Mennonite families, but it gives an added poignancy to Sauer's observation that the older generation of Brethren and Mennonite families were conscientiously scrupulous of bearing arms while the younger generation were "less contracted."

Tory Plots in Pennsylvania

Christopher Sauer had been busy hatching plots with Loyalists in Pennsylvania almost from the moment he reached New York City with Howe's retreating column. The Rev. Daniel Batwell testified at Sauer's hearing before the Loyalist Commissioners in 1785 that the Dunker printer had sent "a person into the heart of York County Pennsylvania" in 1778 "to encourage the Loyalists to stand forth & the Messenger returned with an offer of their Services." Colonel William Rankin, who had held a commission in the York County Militia, testified that Sauer had carried on a correspondence with him about "a matter of considerable Consequence."[8]

Colonel William Rankin and the Rev. Daniel Batwell had both been implicated in an alleged plot in the autumn of 1777 to destroy the American military supplies at Carlisle and Lancaster and even capture the Continental Congress while they were in session at York. Charles Wesley, whose hymns are deservedly better known than his patriotic poetry, asked in one of his verses:

> Who has not heard of Rankin's proffer
> To bring the rebel Congress over,
> At little York to take them napping
> Without a mother's son escaping?[9]

George Stevenson of Carlisle gave the Supreme Executive Council information about this plot on September 15, 1777, and named William Willis of Newberry Township and James Rankin of Manchester Township, both in York County, and John Ferree of Strasburg Township in Lancaster County as the main instigators.[10] Both William Willis and James Rankin were Quakers. Daniel Shelly of Shelly's Island in the Susquehanna, a poor man who could neither read nor write English or German, gave evidence against the plotters in return for a promised pardon. His testimony implicated the Rev. Daniel Batwell, Church of England minister at York; and the Rev. Thomas Barton, his colleague in Lancaster; Dr. Henry Norris, who lived near Warrington Quaker

Meeting House in York County; and Alexander McDonald, who lived near Carlisle and claimed he had already enrolled enough Scotsmen in Cumberland County to take Carlisle without additional help. At least three of these prominent Tories can be identified as Quakers and Shelly himself affirmed the truth of his evidence against them. All of the people named by Shelly had actually taken up arms in favor of the British cause, but premature discovery of their plot left the Loyalists leaderless at a crucial moment.[11]

The direction of the Loyalist cause fell thereafter to William Rankin of Newberry Township in York County. Although of Quaker background, he had received a commission as Captain in the Pennsylvania Rifle Battalion in March 1776, but almost immediately resigned his commission.[12] There was no question of his devotion to the Patriot cause at this time, for he received a commission as colonel under the 1777 Militia Act and commanded the 2nd Battalion of York County Militia made up of companies from Newberry, Manchester, and Hellam townships.[13]

In December 1778 Andrew Fürstner of Allen Township in Cumberland County, Rankin's brother-in-law, arrived in New York City with a pledge from the colonel to assist the British with an unspecified number of Tory recruits in York and Northumberland counties and indicated that an officer of the Lancaster County Militia was also prepared to support the king's troops. Fürstner and John Roberts, a Quaker, made many secret trips carrying messages between Colonel Rankin and Christopher Sauer III outlining plans to destroy the arsenal at Carlisle and to cooperate with the Loyalist Colonel John Butler in raids on the Pennsylvania frontier. Sir Henry Clinton had accepted the fact that there were Loyalists in York and Lancaster prepared to rise on behalf of the Crown and had recognized Sauer as their agent and William Rankin as their accepted leader. From 1778 on, Rankin had "administered an oath abjuring the Congress and the rebel states" to each of his recruits and regularly enlisted them "under their respective officers" in the king's service.[14]

The British commander did nothing to encourage these Pennsylvania Loyalists because experience had shown that Tory risings could only be helpful to the British war effort if properly supported by British regulars. Abortive risings in North Carolina and New York in 1776 and on the eastern shore of Maryland in 1777 had only served to expose and disarm the Tories. In other words Rankin's Tories, like those in other Colonies, were useless to Sir Henry Clinton unless he could send an army into their neighborhood.

The Loyalist Myth Enters into British Planning

A new element had to be considered in any plan for a campaign in America after 1778. France had entered the war and the French, unlike the Americans, had a navy. The British had hastily abandoned Philadelphia in the summer of 1778 for just that reason, and no British commander could feel secure in launching an expedition that might be cut off from reinforcement or evacuation by a French fleet. But the French alliance with the Colonists had another effect. A strong element in Parliament wanted to make peace with the Americans so as to concentrate on the old enemy, France. Concessions were made in 1778 that might have saved the Empire, in 1774 or 1775. Parliament abandoned all claim to tax the Colonies. Win or lose, the total cost of the war would thus fall on the British taxpayer, which gave a further argument for winding up the American war as quickly as possible. To counter this peace maneuver, the government created the Loyalist myth. A parade of witnesses assured Parliament that the great majority of Americans were still loyal to the king. Britain could not honorably abandon them to their fate. The Loyalist myth further explained away any objection that still larger forces of British soldiers and sailors and still greater amounts of money would be needed to maintain British honor by protecting the Loyalists. These loyal subjects in America were so numerous and so devoted to the crown that, with only token support, they could take over the burden of defeating Washington and free British regulars for service in Europe. It was all nonsense, or nearly so, but it made an impressive case for renewed military efforts in North America.[15]

This changed climate made British commanders in the field more receptive to information from Loyalists like Rankin and Sauer and the importance given them subtly influenced the numbers found in their reports. The government wanted to believe that thousands of Loyalists were arming themselves in every corner of the American Colonies and reports began to come in, not of 50 or 60 joined in an Association to fight for king and country, but of 5,000 here and 7,000 there. In the earlier stages of the war a bold Loyalist might have led a handful of men into the British lines and small bodies of men did risk their lives all through the American Revolution to join the king's army. Their numbers had always been few. During the British occupation of Philadelphia from September 1777 to June 1778, for instance, no more than 1,000 men from Pennsylvania and New Jersey joined the British. Joseph Galloway put the figure at less than 1,000 in his testimony before Parliament in 1778, adding that at least 2,300 deserters from

Washington's army came into the British lines and these provided the greater number of enlistments.[16]

A Growing Number of Active Loyalists

Loyalist claims thus need to be taken cautiously. When Christopher Sauer wrote to Sir Henry Clinton on May 1, 1780, that "many of those who heretofore professed to be conscientiously scrupulous of bearing arms do now promise to exert themselves in seizing and securing the ringleading rebels," how seriously should we take his report? The same letter related that Rankin had 6,000 men "spread all over the country." In November 1779 Sauer had put Rankin's associated Loyalists at 1,800 on the basis of Andrew Furstner's report. This figure included 623 raised independently by Alexander MacDonald and a second party of 600 Roman Catholics recruited by one Scherrop in the vicinity of Hanover. This would indicate that Colonel Rankin's own force did not amount to more than 577 men. Had he actually recruited 5,500 men in five months? The suspicion that these figures are being inflated by the inclusion of anyone supposed mildly sympathetic to the cause is further deepened by Scherrop's claim to have raised 600 Roman Catholics in the Hanover area.[17]

Except for Sauer's assertion, possibly based on contacts with the Kauffmans and Melchior Brenneman, that "many" nonresistants were prepared to take an active part against the rebels, a statement contradicted by the report he made on Christian Mussleman's mission, there is little hard evidence linking Mennonites, Dunkers, Amish, Schwenkfelders, and Moravians to these Tory plots. Jacob Rowland, a Washington County, Maryland, Mennonite circulated Sir William Howe's promise of a general amnesty in 1777 (*Document 286*). Hugh Kelly, a Tory leader in western Maryland, claimed that 500 persons with conscientious scruples had promised in 1781 to help the British with wagons and teams.[18] But only Henry Newcomer, the Mennonite brother of Bishop Christian Newcomer of the United Brethren Church, took a leading role in the Maryland plot. Jacob LeFever, a Mennonite in York County, was arrested in 1781 apparently as implicated in some way in Colonel William Rankin's schemes.

Amish Prisoners in Berks County Jail

Amish tradition has preserved the memory of arrests and harsh sentences meted out by the Berks County authorities to conscientious objectors.

The Berks County Amishmen who were jailed in Reading more

likely faced charges of treason or the lesser offense of misprision of treason, the failure to report treasonable words or actions of another person to the authorities, rather than of simply neglecting to muster with their militia class when it was drafted. The Militia Act of 1777 authorized the drafting of men for active duty, class by class, and required those who refused to serve in person or by substitute to pay fines. But there was no legal basis for a death sentence on anyone who failed to answer a draft call. While it is always possible that the Berks County militia officers arrested and imprisoned men who refused to march with their units, as happened in Lancaster County, it is improbable that death sentences handed down by such a kangaroo court would have escaped the notice of the state authorities.

Treason, on the other hand, was a capital offense, and the wartime courts were inclined to give a broad definition of what constituted treason. The judges of the Pennsylvania Supreme Court tried a great many treason cases, particularly in the summer of 1778. The presence of a British army in the state from September 1777 to June 1778 had given Pennsylvania Loyalists an opportunity to join British military units, serve in civilian offices under the crown, or assist the king's cause in other ways. Many of these Tories fled to New York when the redcoats evacuated Philadelphia. But others, who had simply followed their trades as blacksmiths or millers or who had sent firewood or fresh eggs to the Philadelphia market, had also contributed to the British war effort. Where was the line to be drawn?

In passing sentence on John Roberts, a Quaker miller from Lower Merion Township in Philadelphia [present Montgomery] County who was hanged as a traitor in November 1778, the court declared that "it is in vain to plead that you have not personally acted in this wicked business; for all who countenance and assist are partakers in the guilt." In this interpretation, treason could include any word or act that gave aid and comfort to the enemy, even indirectly. Refusal to pay a fine or turn over a horse to some military officer, if accompanied by a remark critical of the Congress or a suggestion that the Americans were sure to be defeated, could, and did, bring treason charges. The details of Pennsylvania treason trials in 1777 and 1778 will never be known, for the Supreme Court records are missing for these years, probably lost when the state government moved from Lancaster back to Philadelphia after Sir William Howe retreated. A list of Philadelphia County cases heard in 1778 has been preserved, showing that treason charges were brought against a number of Quakers and at least one Mennonite, but that the greater number were acquitted. Jacob Clemens, a Mennonite from

Lower Salford Township, was one of those found innocent of treason, but the details of the charge are lost. If similar cases were heard in Berks County in the summer of 1778, not even a bare listing of names has survived.

The Berks County tax lists provide an important clue to the identity of the men from the Northkill Amish community who were brought to trial. On the returns for the State Supply Tax for 1779, some 32 persons have "Tory" written next to their names and no property of any kind recorded. Nearly half of these "Tories" are in Bern Township, the center of the Berks County Amish community. The "Tory" names are found in two distinct sections of Berks County: the townships at the foot of Blue Mountain in the westernmost part of the county and those bordering on Lancaster County in the southeastern corner of Berks. Both of these geographical areas included Amish settlements, and there were congregations of the Church of the Brethren and the Society of Friends in two of the townships where "Tories" resided. Two other townships were the homes of individual Mennonites. Almost half the Berks County "Tories" can be identified with high probability as members of one of the peace churches; of the 32 named as "Tories," 9 were Amish, 2 Brethren, 2 Quaker, and 1 Mennonite.

The Amish "Tories" came principally from Bern Township, where John Hochstetler, Isaac Kauffman, Stephen Kauffman, Henry Stayly, John Yoder, John Zuck, and Christian Zuck are among those named by the authorities, and Christian Kauffman, Jr., is listed as without property. Jacob Kurtz, a "Tory" listed on the Cumru Township tax list, and Joseph Hochstetler, whose name appears on the Heidelberg Township list, were probably also Amish. Only three of these men (Stephen Kauffman, John and Christian Zug) are named by the later tradition.

The indictment and trial of these men was necessarily in 1778, or more probably 1779, since they all appear on the earlier tax assessments with considerable property credited to their names. In the 1780 tax assessment, Stephen and Isaac Kauffman, Henry Stehly, Christian Zuck, Joseph Reno, Nicholas Miller, and George Edward are again listed with substantial property in Bern Township, and only John Hochstetler and William Tomlinson are still recorded as without property. Three of the others designated as "Tories" in the 1779 list are no longer living in Bern Township. The successful intervention of the Reformed pastor and other neighbors evidently secured the release of the Amish prisoners and won the restoration of their property sometime between 1779 and the 1780 tax assessments. These tax records tend to confirm the traditional account.[19]

Alleged Plots in Lancaster County

In January 1781, the authorities arrested two deserters from the Continental Army named Francis Steel and Peter Dill. They had been staying in Bart Township in Lancaster County, apparently undetected, and planned to get down Chesapeake Bay to join the British army. A mysterious person called "Roving John" was supposed to smuggle them into Maryland, but the plan went awry and they were caught.

Steel and Dill claimed that Abraham Beam (Boehm) of Bart Township had persuaded them to try to get to the British. They had certainly come to his farm with Jacob Barkman (Bargman) to help with the butchering and stayed as hired men. Beam admitted all of this, but denied any part in their escape plan. They also implicated Barkman and a Methodist preacher, John Thompson, who was staying with Beam.

Abraham Beam (Boehm) was arrested on January 19 at the home of his brother Martin Boehm in Conestoga Township. They were sons of Jacob Boehm, a pioneer Mennonite settler. Martin Boehm had been a Mennonite bishop in the Byerland and New Danville congregations from 1761. A third brother, Jacob Boehm, was a Byerland deacon. Martin Boehm, after being a center of controversy for years in the Mennonite Church, was excommunicated by his fellow Lancaster bishops probably in 1780 or 1781. As Abraham Boehm explained in his examination that Methodist preachers regularly stayed at his house, he probably shared his brother's views and may no longer have been associated with the Mennonite Church. When Boehm was tried in May 1781, John Grove, Martin Byers, Jacob Whistler, and Casper Shirk appeared as witnesses for the defense. The first three, presumbly Mennonites, affirmed in court. Henry Funk of Manor Township and Christian Yorty of Lampeter stood bail for Boehm, Barkman, and the Methodist preacher Thompson. The defendants always claimed their innocence, before and after the trial, and the testimony of two deserters from the 1st Pennsylvania Regiment, who faced a possible death sentence themselves and might attempt to win favor with the authorities by turning in dangerous Tories, ought to be suspect.

But a certain Alice Griffith gave information to a Lancaster County justice about a number of suspicious-looking incidents involving Boehm, the Methodist preachers Richard Webster and Robert Cloud, and others in giving aid and comfort to the enemy. The charge that Boehm and Jacob Whisler, who was evidently the same man who appeared as a witness at Boehm's trial, sent 12 oxen, 12 cows, 12 bulls and 12 sheep to the British on December 1, 1780, was mentioned in the trial proceedings and obviously gave some support to the deserters' story. Boehm was found guilty and sentenced to pay a fine of £750. As his petition to the Supreme Executive Council explained, passage of a bill that made greatly depreciated paper money no longer acceptable as legal tender threatened to make this equivalent to a life sentence in jail. The Council took action in October 1781 to permit Boehm to pay whatever Pennsylvania paper currency was worth at this time of his trial. The case is interesting because of its documentation of unsuspected links between the Mennonite community and the Methodist revival.[19a]

New British Efforts to Encourage the Tories

With the war threatening to stalemate on the Hudson River, where Washington's army watched Clinton's army in New York City, the British commander made a bold move in December 1779 loading his best troops on transports to begin a new campaign in Georgia and South Carolina. By May 1780 Sir Henry had achieved a stunning victory in the capture of Charleston, where American General Benjamin Lincoln surrendered not only his own garrison, but the entire state of South Carolina. Since every available Continental unit south of Philadelphia had been rushed to Charleston in the last stages of the campaign, there was no longer an American army in the Southern Colonies and in South Carolina every militiaman, every state and county official, every citizen was pledged as a prisoner of war to do nothing to oppose His Majesty's forces. Sir Henry promptly threw away his advantage, doubtless overestimating the number of actual Loyalists, by requiring every adult male to take an oath of allegiance to the king. Then he sailed back to New York, leaving Cornwallis with a token force to subdue the Carolinas. Instead of following up his victory with an immediate advance into North Carolina, Cornwallis waited for the Loyalists there to rise, exposing them to danger. Even with an inadequate army and South Carolina Patriots harassing British lines of communication and supply, Cornwallis routed the hastily assembled American army sent against him under Horatio Gates in a crushing victory at Camden in August 1780. Still he hung back, waiting for a Loyalist revolt that left the Tories defeated and disheartened by the time the redcoats made contact with them. Disasters at King's Mountain in October 1780, where Loyalist militia were slaughtered, and at Cowpens in January 1781, where Tarleton's command was wiped out, left Cornwallis' army weak, but not too weak to attempt to destroy the main American army under Nathanael Greene. A final bloodletting at Guilford Court House in March 1781 left Cornwallis with an army too decimated and too weary for further offensive operations. He marched north, virtually abandoning the Carolinas, to join a smaller British army at Petersburg, Virginia, in April 1781.

At that very moment Sir Henry Clinton had adopted Colonel William Rankin's plan "for subduing the Rebellion in the Provinces of Pennsylvania, Maryland and the three Lower Countys on the Delaware." Clinton wanted Cornwallis to abandon all plans for an offensive in the Chesapeake Bay region, leave only a small defensive force to keep a toehold there, and transfer all of his army to New York for a major operation against Pennsylvania and the neighboring states. There Clinton would put into practice the plan that Cornwallis had fumbled in the Carolinas, of putting legal government in the hands of Loyalists, establishing peace and order, and organizing a loyal militia for defensive purposes only.

American morale had rarely been lower than in 1781. Militia sent from Washington and Montgomery counties in southwestern Virginia for the North Carolina campaign mutinied and went home on the eve of the Guilford Court House battle. Rockbridge and Augusta County militia deserted Greene's army as soon as the battle was over. There were draft riots in these two Scotch-Irish counties when a new call for militia to repel Cornwallis came in April 1781. A Tory rising broke out in Rockingham County, fed by draft resistance and war-weariness. Demands for farm produce and clothing as well as the militia draft touched off a small-scale war in Hampshire County, (West) Virginia the same month, tying down militia from several Shenandoah Valley counties. British forces under Cornwallis and Benedict Arnold were meanwhile going where they would in eastern Virginia, driving the militia before them like sheep, and a British fleet sailed up the Potomac without opposition. It was little wonder that Henry Newcomer and John Caspar Fritchie were ready to play their part and looked anxiously for word that the British were landing at Georgetown (*Document 311*).

What would have happened if Cornwallis had followed Clinton's orders? Would 500 farm wagons driven by Dunkers and Mennonites and Quakers have carried British baggage along the dusty roads of Maryland and Pennsylvania that summer, as Kelly testified? Would many a member of the peace churches have joined the authorities in tracking down rebel committeemen and militia officers, as Sauer promised? Or would the peaceable sects have stood aside, as they always had, until the king or Congress was clearly established as the ruling power? When Cornwallis took the road to Yorktown, the peace churches escaped this last test of nonresistance.

DOCUMENTS

Howe's Promise of Pardon

Jacob Rowland, a Mennonite farmer in Washington County, Maryland, admitted to the members of the Committee of Observation at Hagerstown (then known as Elizabethtown), in January 1777, that he had a copy of Sir William Howe's promise of pardon to all who returned to their allegiance to the king and had evidently shown it to others.

Document 286

Wednesday Jany. 15th 1777

Jacob Rowland was brought before this Committee, accused that he had published Lord Howe's Declaration and other Reports inimical to the united States of America upon examination acknowledged the Charge, ordered that said Rowland be kept under safe Guard, untill he shall produce said Declaration and give Bond and sufficient security in the Penalty of £1,000 Conditioned that he shall well and truly make his personal appearance before this Committee at Elizabeth Town on Saturday the 25th day of this Instant Jany. then and there to answer such Charges as may be laid against him.

Saturday Jany 25th 1777

Jacob Rowland appeared before the Committee, agreeable to appointment. Ordered that said Rowland give Bond with sufficient Security in the Penalty of £2,000. Conditioned that he shall neither say nor do anything inimical to the united States of America, agreeable to the Resolves of the Convention of this State with which he has comply'd.[20]

Document 287

The Commonwealth of Pennsylvania
against
Jacob Clemens

Jacob Clemens bound in £1000
Jacob Uptygrave bound in £500
Jacob Pannebecker bound in £500

To be levied of their Goods and Chattels Lands and Tenements respectively for the Use of the Commonwealth of Pennsylvania Upon the Condition that if the above bounden Jacob Clemens shall be and appear at the next Court of Oyer and Terminer and General Goal Delivery to be held for the City and County of Philadelphia then and there to answer to such Matters and Things as shall be objected against him

on the Part of the said Commonwealth and shall not depart the Court without License then these Recognizances to be void else to remain in full Force. Taken & acknowledged this
17th day of July 1778.
Before Me *Zebn. Potts.*[21]

Farmers Supply British in Philadelphia

While the British occupied Philadelphia during the winter of 1777-1778, many farmers in the surrounding counties carried produce through the enemy lines to the city markets. George Washington saw this as direct aid to the British cause and ordered it stopped by force, stationing guards on all the main roads to arrest any one violating his orders. The farmers needed the market and many watched their opportunity to sneak into the city and supply their old customers. Some got off lightly. Abraham Hunsberger, a Mennonite farmer in Philadelphia County, was taken up by a patrol and kept under guard all night. Expecting the worst, Hunsberger sang hymns throughout the night in his excellent voice. His singing so charmed the soldiers that they released him the next morning.[22] Matthias Tyson of Bedminister Township in Bucks County, a member of the Deep Run Mennonite congregation, was arrested carrying butter and eggs to Philadelphia. Colonel Piper of the militia had him tied to a tree and let the soldiers pelt him with his own eggs, and sent him home with a warning.[23] Others were less fortunate.

A fragment of a court record kept by Justice Evans records the conviction of Mennonites and others for bringing farm products to market in Philadelphia during the British occupation. This is a loose page from a no longer extant court minute book, preserved among the files of the Pennsylvania Supreme Court, in the State Archives. John and Christian Benner of Franconia Township in Philadelphia (Montgomery) County were members of the Indian Creek Reformed Church in 1775, although many of their family were Mennonites.

Document 288

Judgment against Martin King for going in to Philadelphia and staying there while in the Possession of the British Army Entered the 8th day of August 1778.

Peter Evans.

Judgment against Christian Benner for Carry provisions to the British Army & for Refusing to take the Oath of Allegiance to the States Entered the 9th day of August 1778.

Peter Evans.

Judgment against Jacob Sowder for Carrying provisions to the British Army and for Refusing to take the Oath of Allegiance to the states Entered the 9th day of August 1778.

Peter Evans.

Judgment against John Benner for Carrying provisions to the British Army Entered the 10th day of Augt. 1778.

Peter Evans.

Judgment against John Hackman for Carrying provisions to the British Army Entered the 10th day of Augt. 1778.

Peter Evans.

Judgment against John Wright for going in to Philadelphia while in the Possession of the British Army and staying there while in their possession and going with the said Army to New York Entered the 5th day of Septr. 1778.

Whereas sundry persons propose giving Evidence said Wright that he hath been Guilty of Crime whilst with the British Army Inimical to the Commonwealth of this State

To stand the Judgment of the Court.

Peter Evans.[24]

Document 289

Headquarters, 8th Feb. 1778. Sir—The communication between the city and the country, in spite of every thing hitherto done, still continuing, and threatening the most pernicious consequences, I am induced to beg you will exert every possible expedient to put a stop to it. In order to this, to excite the zeal of the militia under your command, and make them more active in their duty, I would have you let everything actually taken from persons going into and coming out of the city, redound to the benefit of the parties who take them. At the same time it will be necessary to use great precaution to prevent an abuse of this privilege; since it may otherwise be made a pretext for plundering the innocent inhabitants. . . . I would recommend to you to remove to some nearer post, and not to depend upon fixed guards; but to keep out continual scouts and patroles, as near the city as possible,—to ramble through the woods and by-ways, as well as the great roads. The strictest orders should be given to the parties; even, when necessary, and the intention is evident, to fire upon those gangs of mercenary wretches who make a practice of resorting to the city with marketing.
George Washington.
To Brigadier General Lacey, near the Cross-roads, Bucks County.[25]

Document 290
Headquarters, Valley Forge, 2d March 1778.
Sir. . . .

I don't well know what to do with the great numbers of people taken going into Philadelphia. I have punished several very severely, fined others heavily, and some are sentenced to be imprisoned during the war. If the state would take them in hand, and deal properly with them, it would be more agreeable to me than to inflict military punishment upon them. . . .

George Washington.
To Brigadier General Lacey.[26]

Document 291
Camp, Crooked Billet, March 4th, 1778.
Sir—It is distressing to learn the numbers of people who flock to the enemy with marketing; amongst whom there are many young fellows who have fled from their homes to save their fines, and are carrying on a peddling trade between the city and country. I have taken several of them who were going to the enemy with parcels of meal on their backs. Some of them I am acquainted with and I do believe they were going to join the enemy.

I have written to his Excellency General Washington, concerning them. He is willing that they should be delivered up to the state, either to be punished as criminals, or kept to exchange for those inhabitants who have lately been taken from their families.

I wish most sincerely the state would adopt some plan of this sort; and designate some place where the villains might be sent for their confinement or punishment. Many have been shipped, their horses, marketing, and everything taken from them, yet they will not desist—and I am well convinced that nothing will stop them but confinement.
J. Lacey
To the President of Council.[27]

Document 292
Camp, March 19th, 1778.
Sir—You are to proceed with our troop towards the enemy's lines—to keep on the roads leading to Bristol, to Smithfield, the York, and the Whitemarsh roads. You will keep constant patroles on these roads, by night and by day; and if the enemy should come out, you will immediately send me notice. If your parties should meet with any people going to market, or any persons whatever going to the city, and they

endeavor to make their escape, you will order your men to fire upon the villains. You will leave such on the roads, their bodies and their marketing lying together. This I wish you to execute on the first offenders you meet, that they may be a warning to others. *J. Lacey*
To Mr. VanHorn, commanding Light Horse.[28]

Document 293
Headquarters, Valley Forge, April 13, 1778

The General Officers conducted a General Court Martial, whereof Col. Vose was President, 4th Inst., Philip Calp was tried for attempting to carry flour into Philadelphia—Found guilty, and sentenced to receive 50 lashes, and to be employed on some public works, for the use of the cantonment, while the British Army continues in this state, unless he should enlist into the service during the present war.[29]

Document 294

Whereas Isaac Penner and John Sowder are accused of trading to Philadelphia with provisions while the British army was in possession of the city, and have refused to take the Oath of Allegiance, these are therefore, in the name of the State of Pennsylvania, to charge and command you that presently upon sight hereof, you receive and take them into your custody and safe to keep until they shall be thence discharged by due process of law. Hereof fail you not! Given under my hand and seal the third day of July A.D. 1778
Peter Evans, Esq., Justice of the Peace, Philadelphia County[30]

Tory Hunter

Attorney General Jonathan D. Sergeant made a reputation as a Tory hunter during his term in office. One case he successfully prosecuted was that of Isaac Kauffman, an Amish farmer from Bern Township in Berks County who refused to give a horse to one George Berstler, evidently a militia officer.

Document 295

August Sessions MDCCLXXIX

Berks County ss.

The Grand Inquest that now is for Berks County aforesaid upon their Oath and Affirmation respectively do present that Isaac Kaufman late of the County aforesaid Yeoman the tenth day of July in the Year of our Lord 1779 at the County aforesaid and within the Jurisdiction of this Court then and there being a person of evil and seditious mind and disposition and being an Enemy to the Liberties and Independency of the united States and conspiring and intending and maliciously and advisedly contriving to disturb the peace of the Commonwealth and to aid and abet the King of Great Britain the declared Enemy thereof in his Attempts to conquer the same did then and there speak and utter publickly and advisedly the words following to wit *You* (one George Berstler and other liege Subjects of this Commonwealth meaning) *are Rebels and I will not give a horse to such blood spilling persons* thereby speaking against the publick Defence of America from the cruel Invasion of the King of Great Britain and his Armies and then and there endeavouring to prevent the Measures carrying on in Support of the Freedom and Independency of this Commonwealth contrary to the form of the Act of General Assembly in Such Case made and provided To the evil Example of all others in like Case offending and against the peace and Dignity of the Commonwealth of Pennsylvania.

Jona: D: Sergeant Atty. Genl.

Berks County ss.

I do hereby certify that the above is a true Copy of the Indictment found by the Grand Inquest against Isaac Kaufman and whereupon the said Isaac was convicted at the last Sessions held for the said County of Misprison of Treason for which Offence Judgement was given against him according to Law Witness my Hand and Seal of Office the 29th Day of September Anno Domini 1779

Danl. Levan Clk. Sess.[31]

Document 296

To the Honourable the President and Council of the State of Pennsylvania

The Petition of Frederick Koble and Isaac Kauffman both of Berks County in the said State

Humbly sheweth

That at the last Court of General Quarter Sessions of the Peace held at Reading in and for the said County your Petitioners were severally convicted of Misprison of Treason against this State. In Consequence of which they have been sentenced to Imprisonment during the present War and to the Forfeiture of One half their Lands and Tenements Goods & Chattels respectively.

That as your Petitioners have the greatest Confidence in the Justice and Humanity of your Honours, they have good Reason to believe that, upon examining into the Circumstances of their Case, You will be of Opinion that your Petitioners are proper Objects of Mercy, having been guilty of no other Offence than making use of some inconsiderate Expressions for which they are exceedingly sorry.

Your Petitioners therefore humbly pray your Honours to grant them your Pardon in the Premises and remit the Forfeitures they have incurred, but in Case that cannot be done, Then they humbly pray your Honours to mitigate the Severity of their Sentence by the Discharge of their Persons from Confinement.

And they will ever pray &c.

his
Frederick X *Koble*
mark

his
Isaac I K *Kauffman*
mark

Reading Goal 29th September 1779.[32]

Document 297

To the Honourable the President and Council of the State of Pennsylvania

The Petition of Isaac Kaufman a prisoner in the Goal of Berks County

Humbly Sheweth

That your Petitioner was at the last August Sessions convicted of Misprison of Treason whereby he hath incurred the Forfeiture of one half of his Estate and is become liable to the Continuance of his Imprisonment until the End of the present War.

That he hath a Wife and eight young Children dependent on him for Support who suffer exceedingly by his Imprisonment. And that the Offence of which he was convicted was the making use of some improper Expressions respecting the present Contest for which he is exceedingly sorry and willing to make every Atonement in his power.

He therefore humbly prays your Honours to take his distressed Situation into Consideration and grant him a pardon of his said Offence and that you would also be graciously pleased to remit his said Forfeiture & Imprisonment.

And he will ever pray &c.

Reading Decr. 18th 1779

his
Isaac IK *Kaufman*
mark

We the Subscribers Justices of the peace of the said County do hereby certify the Facts contained in the above petition, And beg Leave to recommend the petitioner as an object of Mercy to your Honours.

Decr. 18th 1779.

Peter Spycker *Henry Christ*
Jacob Weaver *Danl. Levan*
Jacob Shoemaker[33]

Speaking Treason

In October 1776 the Virginia Assembly passed a bill "for punishing certain offences" that included maintaining the authority of the king by words or using expressions that might "alienate the affections of the people from the present government" or "terrify or discourage them." Innocent grumbling and repeating of rumors came within the scope of this loosely drawn statute and virtually every session of the Virginia County courts heard cases related to this law. None of the many persons summoned on these charges in the Valley counties can be identified as Quaker, Mennonite, or Dunker, but two known Mennonites stood bond for a Christian Kibler accused in Shenandoah County Court of speaking treason.

Document 298
July 29, 1779

Christian Gibler [Kibler] being brought before the Court on suspicion of Speaking Treason against the United States of America and the Evidence being Sworn & examined it is the Opinion of the Court that he be bound over to the Next Grand Jury Court & that he enter into Security for the same he the said Christian in the Sum of ten thousand pounds and Jacob Heaston & Benj Shoe his Securities each in the Sum of five Thousand Pounds to be levied on their land Tenements &c.[34]

Resistance to Collection of Militia Fines

Resistance to the collection of militia fines in Lancaster County led to a threatened attack on Johannes Cline, the collector in Warwick Township, in 1780 as well as on Christian Hare and Christian Martin, who were collecting fines in Strasburg Township in 1781. The Strasburg collectors were clearly of Mennonite background, although collecting fines for failure to serve personally or by substitute in the militia. Their attackers can be positively identified as Peter Hummer, Sr. (d. 1784), minister of the White Oak congregation of the Church of the

Brethren; and his son, Peter Hummer, Jr. No one else of this name can be found in the tax records. Catherine Hummer, daughter of Peter Hummer, Sr., had created considerable stir in Dunker circles in 1762-1763 by relating visions she had received and Pastor Hummer made much of her in revival meetings at that time.

Document 299

Pennsylvania, to wit—

Whereas Johannes Cline of the Township of Warwick Yeoman hath made Oath before me that he being duly appointed to collect the Moneys assessed for the hire of Volunteers in the seventh Company of the third Battalion of Militia of the County of Lancaster did on the sixth Day of July instant go to the Houses of Jacob Bortner of the same Township, John Gromer of the same Township and Henry Mark of the same Township to collect and receive from them the Moneys assessed on them for the purposes aforesaid. That the said Jacob Bortner did beat him, drive him out of his House & threatened to take his life from him if he seized any of his Goods for the said Assessment. That the said John Gromer & Henry Mark also refused payment and threatened him, declaring that all those who laid the Taxes or were concerned in that business might be damned & that if they wanted fighting they might come to them & they would fight them. These are therefore to require & command you That you apprehend the said Jacob Bortner, John Gromer and Henry Mark and bring them before me to answer the premisses & that they may be dealt with according to Law. Given under my Hand & Seal at Lancaster the fifteenth Day of July in the Year of our Lord One thousand seven Hundred & eighty.

Willem. Atlee

To The Sheriff of the County of Lancaster
& to his Deputy & each & every of the
Constables in the same County.[35]

Document 300

Lancaster County ss.

May Sessions 1781

The Grand Inquest for this Commonwealth and for the Body of the County of Lancaster upon their Oath and Affirmation Do present that Peter Hummer of the said County Yeoman being a Person of disquiet evil and seditious Mind & Disposition and contriving, practicing and falsely, maliciously, turbulently and seditiously intending the Peace and common Tranquility of this Commonwealth of Pennsylvania to molest & disturb & the good and wholesome Laws for the Regulation of the same Commonwealth and for the defence & support of the Freedom & Independence thereof to obstruct & oppose and so terrify the Officers of the same Commonwealth from executing the same Laws & discharging their duty & that the said Peter Hummer his most wicked contrivances & Intentions to compleat, perfect & render effectual at the County aforesaid & within the jurisdiction of this Court on the 21st day of February in the Year of Our Lord 1781 having discourse then and there concerning Militia fines and a certain Christian Hare and Christian Martin Officers duly appointed according to Law for collecting the same in the Presence & hearing of divers liege Subjects of this Commonwealth publickly & deliberately, maliciously & advisedly did say & with a loud voice did publish & declare, the Words following, that is to say, we, (the said Peter Hummer and a certain Peter Hummer the Younger then present meaning,) must raise some Men & go to their Houses (the Houses of the said Christian Hare & Christian Martin meaning) and make them (meaning the said Christian Hare & Christian Martin) deliver up their Commissions (meaning the Commissions of the said Christian Hare and Christian Martin for Collecting Militia fines incurred under an Act of Assembly of this Commonwealth for the Regulation of the Militia) that they (the said Christian Hare and Christian Martin meaning) can collect no more Militia fines & as long as we (the said Peter Hummer & Peter Hummer the Younger) do not knock down some of them (the said Christian Hare & Christian Martin meaning) we (the said Peter Hummer & Petter Hummer the Younger) shall have no rest; contrary to the form of the Act of General Assembly in such case made & provided to the Evil Example of all others in the like Case offending & against the Peace & Tranquility of the Commonwealth of Pennsylvania.

William Bradford Jr.
Atty. Genl.

Test.
John Oswald Sworn[36]

Samuel Huber's Story

The Rev. Samuel Huber, who was born in Franklin County, Pennsylvania, in 1782, related in his *Autobiography* an incident involving his father, John Huber, and a recruiting officer. Huber declared that "my parents were members of the Mennonite Society" and "my father's house was the regular place for Mennonite preaching." John Huber and his neighbors did not apparently hesitate to use violent means to redress a wrong, however, and came after the officer, "with guns, pitch forks, axes, and other implements of destruction."

Document 301

According to the most correct information I can obtain, my Grand Father, Christian Huber, emigrated from the Palatinate, in Germany, between the years 1727 and 1736. He settled near New Holland, Lancaster county, Pa., from whence my father, John Huber, moved to the Rocky Spring, Franklin county, Pa., at the time the Indians lived near the North Mountain.

At one time during the Revolutionary war, my father hauled a load of wheat from his farm to Newport, near Philadelphia, where he sold it. On his return homeward through Shippensburg, an American recruiting officer took passage in his wagon to Chambersburg. When they came to Col. Crawford's farm at the Conococheague creek, the officer handed him a written paper. After reading it, he threw it away, upon which the officer clapped him upon the shoulder, saying, "I have pressed you for the army. You are my soldier." My father expostulated with him against the impropriety of his conduct, as it was not lawful to impress men in that way. The officer said: "You must either go with me, or pay so much money." In order to get clear, he gave him all the money he had, went home, and told the circumstance to his neighbors, Messrs. Grove, Burkholder, Culbertson, and others.

In the mean time, the officer went to Chambersburg, and took up his quarters in the house standing on the corner of Main and King streets, which was then kept as a tavern, and for many years after that was occupied by Peter Cook. The idea of a man being robbed in that way by an American officer, did not correspond with the notions of "liberty" these cultivators of the soil entertained at the time. Therefore, very soon, thirty or forty of them collected together, armed themselves with guns, pitch forks, axes, and other implements of destruction, and went to Chambersburg. It was in the night. They surrounded the tavern. The officer was in bed quietly *snoosing* at the time. One of the party fired a bullet into the gable end of the house, which awoke and alarmed him. He sprang out of bed, and, in his haste to escape, came running down stairs in his shirt, holding his pants in his hands. He was soon arrested, and returned to my father the money. He was then placed in irons and sent to the Carlisle jail, which was the last my father heard of him.[37]

Mennonites and Dunkers Seek British Stance on Religious Liberties

In 1780 Mennonites and Dunkers united in an address to the British government, asking if their religious liberties would be secure should the British reestablish their authority. Since Christian Musselman, their messenger to British headquarters in New York City, destroyed the original documents when he was captured by American soldiers, the incident is known only from a memo prepared by Christopher Sauer III for Maj. Oliver DeLancey, Jr., of Sir Henry Clinton's staff. No official comment or related document can be found in the William L. Clements Library in Ann Arbor, Michigan.

Document 302 [September 1, 1780]

That the Mennonites and German Baptists (the latter in derision called Dunckers) in the different parts of Pennsylvania, have long wished to know from authority how to conduct themselves during the present rebellion, that they might not give offence to His Majesty or his representative in America.

That at length some of the ministers and leading men of those two societies to wit: Michael Kauffmann, Senior and Junior, Philip Shoemaker, and Melchior Brennemann, all of Lancaster County drew an address and petition to the king in behalf of those two societies (which Musselmann destroyed when taken by the rebels coming in) setting forth their happiness while under his government, their desire to be reinstated in the enjoyment of their former blessings, and their readiness to assist with their goods and chattels to bring about so desirable an event; and praying that a general line of conduct might be pointed out to them, to conduct themselves by, etc. whether their sowing grain, planting corn, etc. was not in some measure considered as aiding and abetting the rebellion, and whether they would be suffered to enjoy their religious principles as heretofore. That he was directed to represent their request to the commander-in-chief and if he did not think himself authorized to answer it, he—Musselmann—was to forward the address to the throne.

I am well acquainted with almost all the leading men and with many of the laity of those two societies (it was my interest so to be) in Pennsylvania, and believe them to be the most loyal people in the world, and flatter myself that both the British and Hessian officers and soldiers, who were prisoners in the vicinity of those two sects will agree with me from experience. I judge the Mennonists in that province to consist of between two and three thousand families and from the Rev.

Mr. Edwards' Journal it appears that the German Baptists consist of about three thousand members of their church, the women in the latter included. In political matters they are ignorant to an extreme and glory in being so. The aged of both societies profess to be conscientiously scrupulous of bearing arms, but the young men of the former, are not so much contracted. They have ever since the beginning of this rebellion excommunicated every person that took up arms against the king, or otherwise voluntarily assisted the rebels.

I have known them to be very anxious on the first commencement of this contest, to have a line of conduct pointed out unto them by the general. They have had several meetings on this occasion at one of which I was present and have heard of such an address being intended early last spring. I wish their request could (in part if not in the whole) be granted, and think I could safely and privately convey any message unto them without any particular expense to government.

Major De Lancey[38]

Loyalist Recruiters

George Washington personally warned Pennsylvania authorities about the activities of Loyalist recruiters within the state. Andrew George Fustner (Furstner) had lived in Allen Township in Cumberland County until 1778, when he went to New York with the retreating British army. The man who called himself "John Staria" or "the Irish Dutchman" and his companion "John Smith" are more difficult to identify. But "the Irish Dutchman" is very likely the same person as "Roving John" whose alleged presence in Bart Township in Lancaster County on a recruiting mission involved Abraham Boehm and Jacob Bargman in charges of persuading two deserters from the Continental Army to go with "Roving John" to join the British.

Peter Dill and Francis Steel, apprehended as deserters from the Continental Army, gave evidence against Boehm and Bargman. They also implicated John Thompson, described as a Methodist preacher from Maryland. Curiously, no one of this name can be found in any extant Methodist records. A John Thompson of Upper Gunpowder Hundred in Baltimore County was charged in Baltimore County Court in 1777 with failure to take the oath of allegiance; as Baltimore County Methodists all refused to take the oath and Upper Gunpowder Hundred was a center of Methodist activity, this Thompson could well have been a Methodist layman.[39]

The presence of Methodist preachers at the home of Abraham Boehm and his better known brother, Martin Boehm, is understandable, although both men may have still been members of the Mennonite Church. Martin Boehm worked closely with visiting Methodist preachers in 1780-1781 in promoting what Methodist Bishop Francis Asbury termed "a great work among the Germans near Lancaster."

Document 303

Head Quarters, Prekaness, 4th Novem^{r}, 1780

Dear Sir,

I have received information from New York, that a person who is called Andrew George Fustner, and who is Brother in law to Rankin, formerly of York County, comes frequently out as a Spy by way of Stark River, thro' Jersey, and from thence to Lancaster.

He left New York the 27th ult^{o}, and is probably at this time upon that Business. Your Excellency may perhaps, from the foregoing Clue, have him intercepted upon some of his Visits.

There is also another person who goes by the feigned name of John Staria, or the Irish Dutchman, because he speaks both languages who goes constantly between New York and Lancaster, accompanied by a lusty old man called John Smith, who serves as a guide to him. They lately carried 12 or 14 Recruits from Lancaster.

I shall be happy should the above description be sufficient to lead to the discovery of another of the many Engines of this sort, which the enemy have at work against us.

I have the honor to be,
with great Regard, Dear Sir,
y^{r} most ob Servt,
G^{o} Washington

His Excellency Governor Reed.[40]

Document 304

The Examination of Abraham Beam of Lancaster County Yeoman taken the 19th Jany. 1781.

The sd. Abraham Beam says he cant tell what time or when Peter Dill and Francis Steel came to his House.

That he did not see them or either of them at Jacob Barkman's.

That Jacob Barkman never sent him any word of those two Persons being at his House & wanting to see him.

That Jacob Barkman did come with those Men when they came to his House; but came to Butcher for him the Examinant.

That those Men were strangers to him the Examinant, that he did not ask them where they came from & as they were strangers was afraid to have them in his House.

That those Men helped Barkman to butcher for him & afterwards staid at his the Examinant's House.

That some Days after the sd. Peter & Francis came to his House, he asked them where they came from & they told him they came from the American Army & that they had a pass & was not afraid but had not their discharge.

That the sd. Peter & Francis told him they once had a mind to go to Maryland but did not tell him why they did not go.

That the sd. Peter & Francis told him that they had heard there was one roving John about there who engaged People for the English to which Examinant answered that he knew nothing about it & did not know where he was.

That he did not tell the said Peter and Francis any thing about the said John.

That he did not tell them that sd. John would be back about Christmas, nor advise them to stay at his House till the sd. John should come there.

That he never knew of the sd. John's engaging any people to go to the English nor of his taking any people to them.

That he don't remember that sd. John ever told him that he had ever taken any People to the English.

That he never heard the said John say anything of his having assisted the Prisoners who escaped from Lancaster in their escape or his conducting them to the English.

That he never told John Thompson the Methodist preacher that the said Peter & Francis had agreed to go with the said John to the English.

That the said Peter was once bottoming chairs in his House, that he the Examinant was not in the House at the time; but was in the Still House & dont know who was in the room with him.

That he the said Examinant never saw John Thompson the methodist preacher & the said Person called roving John together in his own House nor elsewhere.

That he never was in company with them together.

That he never was in company with the said roving John or the sd. Thompson when it was mentioned that the Prisoners of the convention Troops were expected at Lancaster & when it was consulted how they should be assisted in their escape.

That he never heard the said roving John say he had provided or would provide Arms to assist the convention Troops in their Escape.

That he has heard that the sd. John should have said so; but did not believe it & dont know who mentioned it to him.

That one of those Men he dont recollect which threshed for him in his Barn.

That he dont know of Thompson the preachers going to the Barn & threshing with him.

That he dont know that the sd. roving John ever came to his the Examinants House, while the said Peter & Francis were there.

That he never saw the said Peter & Francis or either of them with the said roving John; nor never knew of their having any conversation with the said John.

That he dont remember the sd roving John's coming to his House, & his telling Peter or Francis that that was the Man who would take them to the English.

That he did not know that the said Peter & Francis were Deserters before the time that they were apprehended as such.

That the sd. John Thompson the methodist preacher has his home in Maryland, but when he came into these parts usually made his place of abode at his (the Examinants) House.

That he dont know of sd. Thompson ever encouraging sd. Peter & Francis or either of them or any other Persons to go to the English.

That he never told Peter Dill nor Francis Steel that the sd. roving John with five or six hundred Men under his command wou'd come after the seven months Men were discharged & make a sweep thro' the Country, or that those who wou'd go with him wou'd make their Sack[?].

That he never told Peter Dill nor Francis Steel that he wondered how the Rebels came on, or that they (the Rebels) never wou'd have any luck, or that the English wou'd gain the Country.

That he never told either the said Peter or Francis that if they stayed in the Country they wou'd be apprehended, nor ever advised either of them to go to the English.

That he knew nothing of a Warrants being out against him till Tuesday last & did not leave his home to be out of the way or avoid being taken.

That he went to his Brother Martin Beam's on Sunday morning last (the morning after roving John was apprehended) & staid at his Brothers till this morning where he was taken by the Undersheriff.

That he heard on Saturday Evening of roving John's being taken.

his
Abraham AB *Beam*
Mark

Taken & Subscribed the 19th of Jany. 1781
By & Before me
Wm. Atlee
Abraham Behm's Exn.[41]

Document 305

I do Certify that at a Court of Oyer & Terminer & General Gaol Delivery held at Lancaster for the County of Lancaster the Fourteenth Day of May in the Year of Our Lord One Thousand Seven Hundred and Eighty One Before the Honorable Thomas McKean, William Augustus Atlee and John Evans Esquires, Justices of the Supreme Court of Pennsylvania and Justices of the said Court of Oyer and Terminer and General Gaol Delivery, an Indictment was duly found by the Grand Inquest regularly Impanelled returned Sworn & Affirmed to Inquire for the Commonwealth and for the Body of the said County against a certain Abraham Beam late of the said County of Lancaster Yeoman for that the said Abraham Beam little regarding the Laws and Acts of Assembly of the said Commonwealth and not fearing the Pains and Penalties therein Contained on the First Day of January in the Year of Our Lord One Thousand Seven Hundred and Eighty One at the County aforesaid falsely and wickedly maliciously and advisedly did persuade and endeavour to bring Peter Dill and Francis Steel two of the people and Inhabitants of this Commonwealth of Pennsylvania then and there being to return to a dependence upon the Crown of Great Britain and did then and there falsely and wickedly maliciously and advisedly dispose the said Peter Dill and Francis Steel then being two of the People and Inhabitants of this Commonwealth to favour the Enemys of this State and of the United States of America then actually invading the United States aforesaid and did then and there falsely and wickedly maliciously and advisedly oppose and endeavour to prevent the measures carrying on in Support of the Freedom and the Independence of the said United States and did then and there falsely and wickedly maliciously and advisedly advise encourage and persuade the said Peter Dill and Francis Steel to Join the Armies of the King of Great Britain then at Open War with this State and the United States of America and did then & there in Order to effect his wicked and malicious attempts, designs endeavors and purposes aforesaid Publicly and deliberately maliciously and advisedly Speak against the Public Defence of this Commonwealth and did then and there publicly and Maliciously deliberately and Advisedly say and Affirm in the presence and hearing of the said Francis Steel and Peter Dill the following false and malicious words that is to say I wonder how the Rebels (the liege Subjects of this Commonwealth & of the United States aforesaid meaning) come on; they (the said Liege Subjects meaning) will never have any luck; but the English (the Armies of the King of Great Britain then at open War with this State meaning) will gain and Conquer this Country before long and You (the said Francis and Peter meaning) will be better with the English than with the Americans so the Jurors aforesaid upon their Oaths and Affirmations aforesaid do say that the said Abraham Beam in manner and form aforesaid the Misdemeanors aforesaid did Commit to the Evil Example of all others in like manner offending Against the form of the Act of Assembly in such Case made and provided and against the Peace and Dignity of the Commonwealth of Pennsylvania To which Indictment the said Abraham Beam pleaded that he was not guilty and for Tryal put himself upon the Country and the Attorney General in like manner and a Jury being called came to Wit, Alexander Scott, Hugh Pedan, William Kelly, Patrick Hay, William Hay, John Offner, Robert Craig, Samuel Woods, John Mease, Evan Evans, William Corren, and Samuel Robinson, who being duly Impanelled returned tried Sworn and Affirmed upon their Oath and Affirmation that the said Abraham Beam was guilty of the Misdemeanor whereof in manner & form &c. Whereupon It was Considered by the Court that the said Abraham Beam Should pay a Fine of Seven Hundred and Fifty Pounds to the State to be and remain in the Common Gaol of Lancaster County till the Fourth Day of July next the Anniversary of Independance Discharge the Costs of prosecution and be committed untill &c.

From the Records per
Edw. Burd Cl. Cur.

1781 October 3rd Lancaster Coy.
Copy record of Conviction of Abraham Beam
Read in Council same day and Ordered
that the fine be paid in State money of
the 7th of Aprl. 1781.[42]

Document 306

To his Excellency the President and the Supreme Executive Council of the Common Wealth of Pennsylvania.

The Petition of Abraham Beam and Jacob Barkman languishing Prisoners in the Gaol of Lancaster County

Most Humbly Sheweth

That your Petitioners were severally tried and convicted at the last Court of Oyer & Terminer & General Gaol Delivery held at Lancaster for the said County of Lancaster on the sixteenth Day of May last of a

Misdemeanor; when your Petitioner Abraham Beam was fined in the Sum of seven hundred & fifty Pounds in Specie, & your Petitioner Jacob Barkman was fined in the Sum of Two hundred & fifty Pounds in Specie & were respectively sentenced to Imprisonment for a certain Term by the Honorable the Judges of the said Court.

Your Petitioners with due Deference to the Verdict of a Jury humbly beg leave to protest their Innocence of the Facts charg'd against them:—It was their peculiar Misfortune, in these Times of public Danger, that infamous as the Character of their Accusers was proved to be, their Testimony received Credit from the Jury.

Your Petitioners pray the Liberty of suggesting to your Honorable Board, that their whole Estates real and personal, if sold at public Vendue, would not be sufficient to pay & satisfy their respective Fines:—They are advised, that by Magna Charta, amerciaments are to be laid "salvo contenemento sibi suo" and that it is a fundamental Part of the Constitution of this State, that "all Fines shall be moderate."

Your Petitioners have no Intention herein of insinuating any Reflections on the Conduct of the Judges, or of charging their peculiar Hardships on them:—They have heard from the best Information & verily believe, that, the Fines were imposed as aforesaid, having Respect to the Value of State Paper Money at the Time, which was then the Current Specie, and was in a State of Depretiation of at least six or seven for one, Compared with hard Cash. The late Law repealing the Tender of all Kinds of Paper Bills of Credit, however wise & politic in itself, subjects your Petitioners to the Difficulties they now labour under.

Of your Petitioners the former is in a very advanced age being Sixty one Years old and upwards; the latter has a Wife and four Infant Children depending on him for Support, who are now in the most distressed Situation: It is their inexpressible Misery to be fully assured that their Fines will amount to an Imprisonment for their several Lives, unless they shall receive Relief from the Mercy of the Supreme Executive Council.

Your Petitioners therefore most humbly pray the Interposition of the Honorable the Council in the Premises, & that they will be pleased at Least, to moderate the Fines according to the original Intention of the Judgments rendered against them, thereby in some small Degree proportioning them to the Circumstances of your Petitioners:—

And as in Duty bound, they shall ever pray &c.

The Mark of A B *Abraham Beam*

Jacob Bargman

Lancaster Gaol August 22d 1781.[43]

Accusations

Justice of the Peace Joseph Miller of Bart Township in Lancaster County followed up the arrest of Boehm, Bargman, and Thompson with further arrests based on the testimony of Alice Griffith of Coleraine Township, apparently a servant-girl as no one with this surname paid taxes in this township. Richard Webster and Robert Cloud, two well-known Methodist circuit riders, were charged with treasonable words and actions, along with several Lancaster County residents. Justice Miller, a member of the Octarora Presbyterian Church, a congregation of the Associated Church of Scotland or Seceders, decided that all Methodists were British agents and began to make life difficult for them, as a letter from Justice Richard Smith of Chester County and an entry from Francis Asbury's Journal confirm.

Document 307

Lancaster County.

The information of Ellice [Alice] Griffith of Colerain Township and County afsd. Taken upon oath before me the Subscriber one of the Justices of the peace for the Said County the 13th Day of Feby. 1781, That Jacob Whisler of Bart Township and County afsd. Did Some time in the Winter 1780 (in Company with Abraham Beam of said place) Ride to Maryland and stayed abrod about Two Weeks in which time they with the assistence of one Richard Web*e*ster (a Methodist preacher) Did Convey Twelve Cattel to the English. Taken the Date above before me.

Jos. Miller

Lancaster County.

The information of Ellice Griffeth of Colerain Township & County afsd. taken upon Oath before me the 13th Day of Feby. 1781, That William Fell of Drumore Township and County afsd. Did about the first of Jany. 1779 bring to the House of Abraham Beam of Bart Township & County afsd. in the Night time Eleven men appeared to be Soldiers by their Apparel, with blankets around them. She thought they were from the English. Stayed about one Hour at said Beams and then went away with Said Fell as he said to go to his House. Taken & acknowledged the Date above before me.

Jos. Miller

Lancaster County.

The information of Ellice Griffeth of Colerain Township and County afsd. Taken upon oath before me the Subscriber one of the Justices of the peace for the said County the 13th Day of Feby. 1781, That

John Griffeth of Sadesbury Township and County afsd. Did about the first week in March last (at the House of Abraham Beam of Bart Township & County afsd.) Say that if it was in his power he would Get to the English and he would make Somebody Rew it and that he had Two fatt Steers if it was in his power he would Send them to the English they better Deserved them than this Country if he Would keep them at home they would take them from him. Taken the Date above before me.

Jos. Miller

Lancaster County.

The information of Ellice Griffeth of Colerain Township and County afsd. Taken upon Oath before me the Subscriber one of the Justices of the peace for the said County the 13th Day of Feby. 1781, That James Marshall of Drumor Township and County afd. Did about Two months ago at the House of Abraham Beam of Bart Township and County afsd. Say that said Beam had a good Mare She would Make a good light Hors he would get her if Said Beam Would part with her and Send her to the English one of his Neighbours Designed to go with him and Said Marchell and Robert Cloud a Methodist preacher and Jacob Barkeman being together in the House of said Beams said Cloud and Barkeman Said to Said Ellice Griffeth if they Could Get her to Go to the English She would be a good Hand to Carry letters to them She would not be so Apt to be apprehended. They said they Would Give her a Horse and Saddle and free her of all Charges. Said Marchell then Said if She Would but Go he himself Would Give her a Hors. Taken and acknowledged before me the Date above.

Jos. Miller[44]

Document 308

Dear Sir,

Having not the least acquaintance with Mr. Reed, I hope the sending of this Letter may be no offence; I'm at present uneasy, understanding, that a Gentleman in Lancaster County known by the Name of Joseph Miller Esqr. Intends to get Mr. Reed to break or take my Commission which I have the Honour to hold (viz.) (that of a Magestrate,) for no other reason then a Methodist preached at my House one Evening, and two other times I went to hear them meaning no harm. But Squire Miller allows the Methodists to be Torify'd. Having heard that such people as the Methodists preached in the city of Philadelphia without any opposition, and being well informed by a Rev. Clergyman, that they had don a great deal of good among many wicked People, and having recourse to our Bill of Rights Tolorating a liberty of Conscience as was allways heretofore obtained in Sd. state of Pennsylvania I referd Squire Miller to the Bill of Rights, though he says it was Benjn. Franklin and two or three other Deists that obtained that liberty, in spite of Sd. Miller and some others of the Convention, I told the Squire it was a liberty I thought proceeded from a Christian love; by this shall all men know that ye are my Desiples if ye love one another. Squire Miller has sent all the Methodist preachers that he can catch to Lancaster Goal; whether or not them people deserves such treatment God only knows. It is reported by the society that Squire Miller adhers to (Called Soceadears) that the Methodists has been recruiting Men for the British Service if that is really so, I shall not Justify any People of that Stamp, for my own part (besides many others) thought them able preachers; and seed not the least sign of Recruiting Men for the British Service, only Recruiting Volunteers for the Kingdom of our Lord Jesus Christ, was their devouted study, & care to my view. Dear Sir, I shall conclude with the words of ye great Apostle Paul 25, C. Acts, 16, v. To whom I answered it is not the manner of the Romans to deliver any Man to die; before that he which is accused, have the accuser face to face Self praise is no Commondation, but as for whigasm I am now what I ever was since this present Contest Commenced, I have march'd out before and since the Law obliged; and on every Call I either went or sent, I make no doubt Sir, but it may be told you that I'm Toryfy'd, but it is very likely them or theirs that utters such News if any such be laid to my Charge—lived in Philadelphia that Campaign and not a man belonging to his Company of Trinton the day of the Canonade where I myself was present and in sd. Company a man killed and the hand shot off one other Man, this is the solid truth can be proven by many People

I am thy assured Friend,

R. Smith.

Chester County, Oxford Township, Feby. 24, 1781.

N. B. Sir, be plais'd to remember my love to Mr. Thos. McKain Esqr. and I shall ever be obledged.

R.S.

For Joseph Reed Esq. President Philadelphia.
favour WmBradfourd Esqur.[45]

Document 309
March 14, 1781.

I have heard of a great work among the Germans towards Lancaster. Certain opposing sectarians hunt our preachers like partridges upon the mountains; they are trying to stop, but they are going, I apprehend, the readiest way to establish us.[46]

Plans for a Tory Rising

Henry Newcomer, a Mennonite, was involved in a more serious accusation of treason when Christian Orendorff laid bare a widespread Loyalist plot in Frederick and Washington counties in western Maryland. Newcomer was the only one of the conspirators *known* to come from a peace church background, but Dunkers, Mennonites, and Quakers *may* have been involved in the movement in significant numbers. Hugh Kelly, one of the Loyalist leaders, reported to the British commander-in-chief that he had recruited 1,300 fighting men in Maryland, while nearly 500 others had taken either an affirmation intended specifically for "Menonists, German Baptists and Quakers" or one designed for persons whose age or other circumstances militated against their personally bearing arms. A report from Thomas Hagerty, a Frederick County Loyalist, to Lord Cornwallis in June 1781 makes clear that serious plans for a Tory rising in western Maryland were far advanced when Newcomer made the mistake of trusting Orendorff with the secret.

Document 310

Thomas Hagerty's Report

That he left the Shipping at Shirley's the 13th Instant with an intent to return to the Army, under Lord Cornwallis' Command, but falling in with 3 Deserters from the Queen's Rangers, who knew him, and caus'd him to be pursued, he alter'd his Course, and went to the vicinity of Fredericks Town in Maryland, the place of his former residence, w[h]ere he arrived the 16th and was informed as followeth.

That a certain Christian Orendorf of Sharpsburg, a Lieutenant in the Rebel Service, and a Prisoner on Parole from New York, had professed Friendship to the associated Loyalists, and after taking the usual Oath of Secrecy, was entrusted with the Combination and with the Names of the Officers and many Privates of the Association, their Intentions etc. and then went to Annapolis, discovered the whole Affair to the Governor and seized the Persons of many of them, before they could have any notice of his perfidy, all of whom he conveyed under a strong Guard to Fredericks Town and Hagers Town Jails, to the amount of upwards of 170—thirty of which were Officers from different Parts of Maryland and Pennsylvania. That Caspar Fritchy, Peter Sueman and Hugh Kelly, Captains, and George Poe, an Ensign, all of

Fredericks Town were condemned to suffer Death, as also Ten others at Hagers Town. That they are still going on with the Tryals of the remainder—seizing of others—and do declare that they have discovered 1500 of the Associators in Maryland, & a like number in Pennsylvania. That some of these unfortunate People are tryed by a Court Martial consisting of Militia officers, and others bv a Court of Oyer and Terminer. That the Loyalists are in great want of Arms and Ammunition, which keeps them from rising in Arms and risking [rescuing?] their imprisoned Confederates, a small number armed with Rifles are however determined to defend themselves, and have already revenged the injuries of their Friends on some of the Rebels. And that the Associators in Pennsylvania were also in great Confusion, several of them confined, and that particularly one of the Name of Rankin was mentioned to him, to be a Prisoner.

That the said Hagerty was desired by several of the principal Loyalists of the Vicinity of Frederickstown to haste his return to the Royal Army, to represent their Case to the Right Hon'ble the Earl of Cornwallis and to entreat his Lordship to send a Detachment of the King's Forces to take Post in some Part of Maryland and to supply them with Arms and Ammunition, that they may have it in their Power, to Stop that horrid Scene which is now opening.
Williamsburgh June 29, 1781.[47]

Document 311
Informa of Christian Orendorff.

about a Fortnit ago Henry Newcomer of Washington County came to him in Sharpsburgh and called him out of his Father's House and asked what he thought of these Times, answered the Times were very bad & precarious—he then asked if he thought the King would over-come this Country answered he thought he might. I'm sure he will overcome the Country and Orndorff if you will keep it a secret I lead you into a Matter of great Importance—answered he would he said we have raised a Body of Men for the Service of the King and we thought proper to make appln to you to go to N York for a Fleet, asked how many Men they had raised he said upwards of 6000—asked who was the Commanding officer of the Party, answered one Fritchy of Fred. Town a Dutch Man dont know his Christian name—ordered Orndorf to go to his House and he would shew him the Man went to his House and rode with him to Fred. Town but did not go to Fritchy's House. Newcomer informed him Fritchy would not see him in Town but would meet him ten Miles from Town—he met him and then took him aside and said he understood Orndorf was let in to a Matter that was carrying on now. Orndorf said to him I understood you are the commanding Officer—Fritchy said he was and told Orndorf the Name of the Man in Virginia from whom he received Instructions to recruit but has forgot the name—asked why they pitched upon him; said because he had been in N. York so long they thought he was the fittest Person if he would undertake it—though they were not quite ready for a Thing of that sort. Orndorf desired him to get the Names of all the Officers which he promised to do—before they parted Fritchy told him not to disclose what he had communicated Orndorf replied he would sooner sacrifice his Life than do it.

Orndorf told him to get ready as soon as he could and let him know it and he said he would & as soon as he was Orndorf should be informed of it—and then he said some of his officers were so violent for it that he was afraid it would be made public—asked who they were he said one Kelly a Lawyer & an Irishman who lives in the mountains about twelve or fourteen miles from Fred Town—had no further Conversation with Fritchy.

After Orndorf rode four or five miles along the main Road Newcomer said Orndorf you look so dead I'm afraid you ruin the matter; answered not at all Sir—says keep it a Secret whatever you do, for we will soon give these Fellows a damn Threshing—said as we are not ready I must send my Boy up to the South Mountain and let them know We are not ready yet. Our Boys are so violent we can hardly keep them in—said he sent an Express last week to Lancaster to hush them a little while longer—he slapt Orndorf on the shoulder and said I am so glad as if I had £10000 we have got you Orndorf for they could not get one so proper for the Expedition as you are—said we have consulted one another a great while and were afraid to mention the Matter on your Father's Account as we knew him to be a violent Rebel—and then they parted and Newcomer went towards Hagers Town. Newcomer lives within five or six Miles of Hagar's Town.

two or three Days after Orndorf got Home Bleacher one of the Captains came to him and called him out aside and said I understand you are let into a Secret that is going on now—answered he was—and said I suppose you are one of the Officers. Bleacher said he was Orndorf asked him what Rank he was—he answered a Captain. Orndorf asked how many men he had recruited he said he had fifty men. Orndorf asked him to let him look at his Warr^{t} he said he had it not about him and made it a Rule not to carry it about him. Orndorf asked him to put it in his pocket and bring it to his House and shew it to him, he said he would—then Orndorf asked him how he managed to make known his Doings to those he wanted to join him said he had applied to twenty that had refused him and asked Orndorf how he thot he must have felt after being refused—said to Orndorf you are acquainted with our Secrets and if you expose them you must abide by the Consequences. Orndorf asked him how he thought they would do if he went & brought the Fleet to George Town for you have no arms Bleacher said they would mount on Horses and ride down there and receive their arms for the Troops in the State could not hinder them—and further said he could take the Magazine in Fred. Town with their Men—and then they parted.

Orndorf was at one Tinkles (who lives nigh to Kelly) who told him Jacob Young was informed of the Matter—made answer and said why is Jacob Young informed of the Matter—he said he was—Orndorf said why Jacob Young will certainly expose the Matter for he is a Magistrate—he said he would not.[48]

More Details of Plot

Philip Replogle, who had earlier been arrested as a deserter from the Maryland militia and imprisoned in the Tory jail at Hagerstown in December 1777, revealed additional details of the plot, including the involvement of many people settled on the South Branch of the Potomac in present West Virginia.

Document 312

June 17th 1781

The deposition of Philip Replogle after being sworn saith that on the fourth day of this Instant he was Persuaded by Henry Claycom to go and Take protection that they went to Doctr. John Hose and that said Hose Administered an Oath to this Deponent not to bear Arms against the Brittish Army and to Supply them With Provisions and a Waggon or Horses if Called on that said Hose Told him that John Parks of Baltimore one of the Head men and Fritche in Frederick was Colonel—he further saith that John Gripe told him a few days after he was Sworn that if the Potomack was not as High that the people from the South Branch would Come down and rescue the prisoners from the fort and Take them to the English, that there was Two or Three thousand that had sworn in there, That the Head man at the south Branch wears a Long Beard but did not remember his name; he further Saith that Jno. Hose Came by his House the Friday after Whitsunday and Informed him he was going to Swear in Twenty at Jacques Furnau and that said Claycom Told him that George Stewart had Sworn in Twenty men right Jno Carpenter, Jno & James Blare, Jacob & Philip Lear, William Jones, Adam Risler, Jacob Easter, Peter & George Easter and Christian Livingston and a Weaver Living at Claycoms etc. Remainder he does not remember.

Philip Replogle

Copy R. Johnson[49]

Document 313

Saturday 9 June 1781

Whereas from Information given this Board have good reason to believe that Henry Newcomer and Bleachy of Washington County and Fritchy Kelly and Tinckles of Frederick County are disaffected and Dangerous Persons whose going at Large may be detrimental to the State. The Lieutenant of Washington is therefore ordered to arrest Henry Newcomer and Bleachy and the Lieutenant of Frederick to arrest Fritchy, Kelly and Tinckles without delay and have them before the Board forthwith that they may be dealth with according to Law.[50]

Document 314 June 9, 1781

[Council Circular to Lieu[ts] of Frederick and Washington Counties.]

Enclosed you have Warrants to apprehend Henry Newcomer of Washington County, Fritchy of Frederick Town. Kelly of Frederick County Bleachy of Washington and Tinkles near Kelly, whose going at large we have the strongest reason to believe from the Information of Cap[t] Orendorff is dangerous and may be detrimental to the State. The Capt. intends to have another Interview with them and converse fully on the Subject; he thinks they repose the utmost Confidence in him and will disclose all their Views and mention the Names of the principal Persons concerned in the Plot. If you think no bad Consequence will arise from your delaying to execute the warrants, we would have you do it, till the fullest Information can be obtained otherwise we would have them taken into Custody immediately and sent down, we wish you would see Capt. Orendorff and talk with him.[51]

Document 315

[Thomas Sprigg, Co[un]ty. Lt., Hagars Town, to the Council.]

(fav'd by Capt. Morgan)

June 17, 1781

I Rec[d] Your Hon[rs] favours by Capt[n] Ornorf of the 9th and 10th before his return the Conspiracy was discovered and several persons apprehended Among^{t} them the two persons mention'd in Yours of the 9th Henry Newcomer and Yost Pleacker, I've been busy exam^{g} evidences for several days and find A great N^{o} are concernded in this Co^{ty} Many in Virg^{a} some in Fred^{k} Co^{ty} there is about 30 in Goal and expect the Guards every moment that are detach'd for 50 or 60 more of those in prison their are 5 or 6 that Acknowledge themselves to be Captains that they have Inlisted and Admin'd the Oath of Allegeance to many persons, one of them to the Amo^{t} of 42 they Confess very freely they say they expect and deserve to be hang'd, and I pray God they may not be disappoint'd, I expect their will be a Considerable N^{o} more inform'd Ag^{t}, had the Law for trial by Court Marshall Pass'd last Session, I should not be at any loss to proceed, but at present I really am, Many of their Crimes have been Commitd before the Meet^{g} of the Assembly, some of them since, I would be Glad to be inform'd by Your hon^{rs} as soon as possible whether all Laws pass'd at the same Session are in force from the first day of the Session, if so I shall immy call a Court proceed to trial and Execution of those that Came under the Law, the Militia in General discover such a desire to appr^{d} the trators that I think very few will Escape, the Whigs are very desirous of hav^{g} a few of the principle persons Execut'd I believe it would have a very good Effect. I but this moment knew of this opp^{y} by Captn Morgan that I hope Your hon^{rs} will excuse my not giving a fuller Acc^{t} and the hurry in which I write, as soon as the Offenders are all Apprehend^{d} and Exam'd shall transmit the whole proceedings by Express, in the mean time shall be Glad to receive Your Hon^{rs} Instructions when I return'd from Annap^{s} I found one Comp^{y} of the select Mil^{a} had march'd to assist in Guarding the prisoners besides a N^{o} of the Other Mil^{a} from this Co^{ty} the whole of the prisoners Hessians and Brittish Consists of 15 or 1600 was guarded by this Co^{ty} to York, and also finding we were likely to be in much Confusion, and that a Guard would be necessary in Town, I Order'd the Other select Comp^{y} not to March until further Orders but to appear at This place to Guard the Goal which I hope will meet with Your hon^{rs} Approbation.

Aggreeable to Your directions I prov'd 20 four pound Guns at Mr Hughes works, empress'd 10 wagons to haul them to Balt they will set out to Morrow, of which please Advise Mr Hughes as I've not time to write him, they stood the first proof so well it induc'd me to give them something more than the usual proof in the second Charge, I believe them to be Extry Guns.

P.S. the Cloathing that your hon^{rs} propos'd sending up to the rec^{t} is not arriv'd, I wish could be sent as they might March.[52]

Loyalist Leaders Tell Their Story

Hugh Kelly and James Fleming, leaders of the Loyalist conspiracy in Frederick County, Maryland, later escaped to New York City where they presented a joint statement of their experiences to Sir Guy Carleton, British commander-in-chief, in 1782. According to their own account, both men had actively supported the Patriots in the early stages of the war. (Fleming was a militia officer and had charge of obtaining signatures to the Association in Upper Catoctin Hundred in Frederick County; Kelly's activities are less easily documented.) In 1779, when word spread of a British thrust at Pittsburgh, Kelly went to Red Stone Settlement (present Brownsville, Pa.) and recruited 175 men to join the king's troops. The following year British success in South Carolina inspired Kelly to contact British Brigadier General James Hamilton, then a prisoner in Frederick, with plans to raise a Loyalist force in Maryland. The remainder of the story is best told in their own words.

Document 316

. . . . That previous to June 1781, near Thirteen hundred fighting men had taken the annexed Oaths, No. 3 and 4 Under the Name or Appellation of the Maryland Royal Retaliators, and near five Hundred the Affirmation No. 1 and Oath No. 2

That in February 1781 Hugh Kelly and 27 of the Officers and privates were apprehended by the Rebels at which time, James Fleming made his escape, and joined Lord Cornwallis, near Guildford Court House in North Carolina, and informed him of the situation of the Kings friends in Maryland.

That after a few weeks Confinement, the said 27 men, were admitted to give bail for their future appearance, and Kelly without any mode of trial was condemned by Militia Officers to be Hanged, and in preparing for Execution, a dispute arose between the Civil and Military Officers, respecting their Prerogative of Tryal, And the civil Officers having the majority in their favour, reprieved Kelly and took bail for his future appearance, for tryal, by civil authority.

That in June 1781, a Discovery was made, and an information given against Kelly, Fleming and several Others, for enlisting men for his Majesty's Service, on which 170 Officers and privates were apprehended and seven of the Officers received Sentence of death, and most part of the remainder Sentenced to be confined, some for two months, and some for two Years, and pay fines from Twenty Pounds to One Thousand Pounds, in Gold or Silver.

That in the August following, Three of the Condemned Officers were Executed, in Frederick Town in Maryland, and the other Four reprieved, on Condition of Transportation to France for Life.

That said Kelly, with great difficulty escaped the hands of the rebels, and near Two Hundred of the men, who are now dispersed in the County and the families of all, left in a very distressed condition, the rebels having seized their Estates, real and personal. . . .[53]

Affirmation for Loyalist Sympathizers in Peace Churches

Kelly and Fleming included copies of several documents with their report, one of them the affirmation intended for Loyalist sympathizers in the peace churches.

Document 317
Copy of Instructions to the nominated Officers of the Maryland Royal Retaliators, with Copies of the Oaths to administer to the People.

Sir

Take notice that the following affirmation No. 1 is intended for Menonists, German Baptists and Quakers, and all others, who do not take an Oath or Personally bear Arms, Oath No. 2, is for aged and infirm people, and those, whose Circumstances frustrates their personally bear[ing] Arms. No. 3 is for those distinguished (non-jurist) Loyalists who will Voluntarily serve his Majesty during the Rebellion. No. 4 is for all those who have through Ignorance, Inadvertency or Oppression taken an Oath of Allegiance to the States, And those who freely and Voluntarily took said Oath, and are now come to a just sense of their duty, and has not Materially injured any of his Majesty's Leige Subjects and will Support his Majesty's interest in future.

You are likewise to keep a regular list of the names and Surnames of all who may swear, and affirm, with the dates of their Inlistment, and places of residence and annex to their names, the Number of the Oath taken.

I have the Hon'r to be Yr. &c.
H.[ugh] K.[elly]

No. 1 I, A.B., do freely and Voluntarily, solemnly and sincerely Affirm, in the presence of Almighty God, that I will bear true and faithful Allegiance, to the King of Great Britain, and that I will aid, abet, and assist, his said Majesty, against all enemies and Opposers whatsoever (so far as is consistant, with my religious principles) and that I will keep this, and every other secret Proceeding, relative to his Majesty's interest, a profound secret, during the rebellion.[53a]

Newcomer's Sentence

Henry Newcomer was sentenced by a special Court of Oyer and Terminer to imprisonment for two years and a fine of £1,000. Mild compared to the death sentences handed down in seven cases and even in comparison to life imprisonment on board a French warship to which the death sentence of four conspirators was commuted, the heavy fine was a crushing blow to Newcomer's family and many of his neighbors joined in petitioning for a reduction.

The Maryland authorities reduced Newcomer's fine to £150 in 1783. He was thus able to keep his farm and continued to live in Washington County, Maryland, after the war. His more famous brother, Bishop Christian Newcomer, was a close associate of Martin Boehm and Philip William Otterbein in the revival movement which resulted in the founding of the Church of the United Brethren.

Document 318
November 24, 1781
[Council to Alexander Clagett Esq[r] Sheriff of Washington County.]

A Petition signed by many respectable Inhabitants of Washington County in Favor of Henry Newcomer, requesting a Remission of the Fine lately imposed on him by the Special Court; but it being still undetermined by the General Assembly, whether that Power may be rightfully exercised by the Governor, we have not considered the Subject. To prevent the Hardship and Injustice which may arise from an immediate Sale of his Property, we think it adviseable to suspend the Sale thereof during the present Session of Assembly, or until some Order is taken therein, and do accordingly, require you to suspend the same.[53b]

Document 319 Saturday 23. November 1782

Present as on Yesterday except Jerem[a] T. Chase & John H. Stone Esq[rs.]
[Council to Upton Sheredine James Johnson Wm Murdock Beall & Philip Thomas, Esq[rs]]

Henry Newcomer has applied to this Board for a Remission of his Fines, on his Convictions in Frederick County. We have delayed determining on his Case, 'til we can be furnished with the Records of Conviction and a State of the Testimony, and therefore request you to favor us with a full State of the Evidence, and direct the Clerk to send Transcripts of the Convictions.[54]

Document 320
Monday January 27th 1783.
Present His Excellency the Governor.
Benj. Stoddert, G. Duvall, and John H. Stone Esquires

The Board took into Consideration the Case of Henry Newcomer of Washington County who had been tried and convicted on two several Indictments at a special Court held at Fredericktown on Friday the 6th of July 1781, charging the said Henry Newcomer with inticing and persuading a certain Andrew Horshman and a certain Gabriel Baker, Citizens of this State, to return to and acknowledge Dependence on the Crown and Parliament of Great Britain; and on each Indictment and Conviction aforesaid, adjudged to suffer one Years Imprisonment and to pay a fine of five hundred pounds: And it appearing from the Petition of Barbara Newcomer his Wife, and the Petition of a number of respectable Inhabitants of Frederick and Washington Counties that the said Newcomer has eleven small Children, who will be reduced to a State of Begging and Ruin, unless the whole or a part of the aforesaid Fines be remitted: And it also appearing from the Certificate of the Clerk of Washington County that the whole of the said Newcomers property was Assessed to no more than five hundred and sixty two pounds, ten shillings.—

Wherefore, and in Consideration of his having already suffered a severe Imprisonment, It is determined that four hundred and twenty five pounds of each of the said Fines be remitted.—*Benj Stoddert*
G. Duvall
J. H. Stone.—
Wm Paca[55]

LeFeber Charged with Recruiting for British

The diary of the York Moravian congregation records the arrest of a Mennonite named LeFeber on charges of recruiting for the British among prisoners of war confined in the vicinity of York. Jacob Lefevre, a farmer in York Township, owned 185 acres in 1779.[56] His connection, if any, with Colonel William Rankin's schemes is unknown.

Document 321
July 21, 1781

A traitor by the name of LeFeber, a Mennonite, was arrested on the accusation of a British deserter, that he had persuaded 40 men of General Howe's army to join the Tories and Indians to plunder the people living on the borders.[57]

Aid to Prisoners of War

An important aspect of the situation in western Maryland, York, and Lancaster was the presence of British and Hessian prisoners of war, guarded by American troops. Mennonites did not fail to show hospitality toward them whenever possible. A captured Hessian officer, Lieutenant August W. DuRoi, commented that "the great part of them (Germans) are Quakers and Anabaptists. . . . All of these sects are not much thought of by the other inhabitants of America, because they refuse to go to war or carry arms." He added, "We liked it best at the Quakers, Anabaptists, and other sects; they were the most hospitable to our men."[58]

It was not only Hessians who received succour from Mennonite inhabitants of Lancaster, but any person who stood in need, be he American soldier or British prisoner.

Sargeant Roger Lamb of the 23rd Royal Welch Fusiliers described how he and two other British prisoners escaped from York, Pennsylvania, in 1782 with the aid of unidentified "friends" in Lancaster County and Quakers closer to Philadelphia. Sergeant Lamb in later years conducted a school in Dublin, Ireland, and published *An Original and Authentic Journal of Occurrences during the late American War* in 1809. His "Sentimental Journal," written as a report to Sir Henry Clinton, has been preserved in the Clinton Papers.

Escapes like that of the three sergeants led to harsh reprisals on persons who knowingly or unknowingly aided fugitives on their way to the main British encampment at New York City. A number of Earl Township Mennonites suffered for their assistance to escaped prisoners. Peter Miller, Prior of Ephrata Cloister, interceded for them with the authorities.

Document 322

Journal of Three Serjeants of The 23rd Regiment, who made their escape from York, in Pennsylvania, the 1st March, and arrived at New York the 23rd March 1782.

A Sentimental Journal of 21 Days

Left our confinement 1st March and received from Captain Saumerez one dollar each, crossed the Susquehanna 2d March paid two dollars to our Guide that conducted us over the ice. 3d March crossed

Conastoga Creek & paid one dollar. 4th March changed our cloathing among friends—read His Majesty's Speech to them which we Coppy'd from the Pennsilvania Journal, the [y] seem'd rejoiced being afraid of a general evacuation of His Majesty's Troops from America. 5th March conducted us 25 Miles to the cross keys 30 miles from Philadelphia expected a friend in the Landlord but happen'd to prove otherwise having discovered ourselves he seem'd cautious & told us our affairs was Desperate & that we need not expect any indulgence from him. we reasoned in a Politick manner & enlarged upon the Success that would attend his Majesty's Arms the ensuing Campagne. he was often bouyed he said with that hopes but seen no prospect in the accomplishment & that our former friends in that state was almost diminished to a Cypher as for his part he had entirely chang'd his principles seeing such a Gloomy prospect of success—finding him so hardned we beged him to direct us to a friend, he would not. we told him if he would do us no good we hoped he would do us no harm. as their was at that time Continental officers in the house, he seem'd uneasy at our stay in his house being on the Public road. we set of very much down hearted and kept the road but unfortunately met a party of militia that was returning from conducting a party of prisoners to Philadelphia, examined us & fetch us back to Lancaster & put us in Jail. 11th March made our escape & proceeded through the woods directing our course to Valley forge, where our worthy friends the Quakers are thickly Settled the[y] received us with the greatest cordiality expressing the greatest veneration & Loyalty to His Majesty and assisted us in our distress and hoped we would mentioned their attachment & zeal to the Commander in Chief if we arrived safe in N. York. the are Greivously oppressed and pays more taxes in one year now than in 21 years before. the conducted us across Schuykill four miles above Sweads ford and directed us to friends which are numerous between the two rivers, in Short whole townships are attached to Government. 15th March crossed Delaware four miles above Trenton, found our friends greatly diminished in the Jerseys & very difficult to march upon the account of the swamps. as we were obliged to Steer through the woods, lay in the woods Several days for want of a Guide. came to Princetown & pass for deserters from Staten Island. found friends in Hopewell township five miles from princetown, remain'd among them till we could procure a Guide to carry us to N. York. we got a man that generally carried prisoners to our lines, but was affraid at that time to come with us, as Captain Hyler was in Brunswick & kept a Guard on the bridge as a Gunboat was building their—however we gave him what money we had which had a great effect upon him. 17th March at night came to a town & loss'd our Guide. our affairs being desperate we resolved to Guide ourselves, came to a house and obliged the man to put us on the right road or death should be his portion—however he happened to be a friend and was Suprized he said at our boldness but knew the British was always intreped in any dangerous enterprize. 18th March directed us to a friend which conducted us & avoided Brunswick. 19th March left destitute of friends we proceeded to South Amboy rambl'd along shore all night but could not find a craft. 20th Concealed ourselves in the woods 3 Miles from S. Amboy up Brunswick river, Seen Captain Skinners Galley in the river. 21st Hungar making us desperate came to a house on the Shore Side and discovered our intention, proved to be good friends & put us aboard the Galley—beg'd us to mention'd their names at Head Quarters—we told them their was numbers more on the road if the would assist them the might be assured of a bounty from the Commander in Chief.

Johnson
Calver

the mens Names that fetch'd us to the Galley lives 3 miles from S. Amboy up Brunswick River

Our Total expence £9.15.9.

R. Lamb
Serjt. R. W. Fuziliers[59]

Document 323

I Edward Burd Prothonotary of the Supreme Court and of the Courts of Oyer and Terminer and General Goal Delivery for the State of Pennsylvania do hereby certify that at a Court of Oyer and Terminer and General Goal Delivery held at Lancaster for the County of Lancaster the fifteenth day of October in the year of our Lord one thousand seven hundred and eighty two before the honorable Thomas McKean Esquire and his Associate Justices of the said courts, Mark Groves, Christian Martin, Peter Summey, Christian Weaver, Christian Carpenter, and Henry Martin all late of the township of Earl in the county afsd. . Yeomen were indicted and convicted by a Jury of the county for that James Bart being a subject of the King of Great Britain and serving in his armies than actually invading the United States of America on the seventeenth day of January in the year of our Lord one thousand seven hundred and eighty one was taken in arms and made a prisoner of war by the troops and armies of the said United States and was fully within the power custody and possession of the armies last afsd. at the county of Lancaster in this commonwealth and that the soldier James Bart afterwards to wit on the seventh day of September in the year of our Lord one thousand seven hundred eighty two at the county aforesaid did make his escape from the Armies last afsd. and out of the custody power and possession of the same armies did go at large. The said Mark Groves Christian Martin Peter Summey Christian Weaver Christian Carpenter and Henry Martin not being ingnorant of the premises but well knowing and each of them well knowing the same James Bart so to have made his escape in manner and form afsd. afterwards to wit on the day and year last afsd. at the township and county last afsd. unlawfully basely seditiously and treacherously did and each of them did abet aid and assist the said James Bart in making his escape from the Custody and Possession of the armies last afsd. contrary to the form of the Act of Assembly in such Case made and provided and against the peace band dignity of the Commonwealth of Pennsylvania and the said Mark Groves Christian Martin Peter Summey Christian Weaver Christian Carpenter and Henry Martin were then and there further indicted and convicted for that they on the sixth day of September in the year last afsd. at the township and county last afsd. did and each of them unlawfully did basely and treacherously advise counsel aid encourage incite and endeavour to persuade the said James Bart so being a prisoner of war to the armies of the said United States to make his escape from the custody of the same armies and to join the armies of the King of Great Britain the open and cruel Enemy of this State and of the said United States of America and then and there did and each of them did harbour the said James Bart and with meat Drink lodging cloathing and other necessaries for his aid and comfort the said James Bart and each of them did then and there furnish and supply with the wicked Intention to enable and assist the said James Bart to make his escape from the Custody of the armies of the said United States and to join the armies of the said King of Great Britain they the said Mark Groves Christian Martin Peter Summey Christian Weaver Christian Carpenter and Henry Martin then and there well knowing and each of them then and there well knowing the same James Bart to be a prisoner of War to the armies of the said United States to the Evil Example of all others in the like case offending and against the peace dignity of the commonwealth of Pennsylvania whereupon it was considered by the said Justices that the said Mark Groves Christian Martin Peter Summey Christian Weaver Christian Carpenter and Henry Martin severally pay a fine of fifty pounds one moiety thereof to the use of General Moses Hazen the prosecutor or in case the same by not respectively paid before the twentyfifth day of March next that each delinquent shall then be whipped at the public whipping post of Lancaster County with thirty nine Lashes that they severally discharge the costs of Prosecution and ramain in the custody of the Sherrif of the said county in the mean time, witness my hand this seventeenth day of December 1782, *Edward Burd*,[60]

Document 324

In Council, Philadelphia, Monday, December 2, 1782.

The petition of Jacob Grove and Christian Grove, convicted of harboring and aiding British prisoners to escape, at a Court of Oyer and Terminer held at Lancaster the eighteenth day of October 1782, and sentenced to pay the sum of one hundred and fifty pounds, were read, praying remission of same; and the said Jacob Grove and Christian Grove being recommended to this Board by the judges of the Supreme Court, and a number of the inhabitants of the county of Lancaster; on consideration, Ordered, that two thirds parts of the fines adjudged to be paid to the use of the State by the said Jacob Grove and Christian Grove, be remitted.[61]

Document 325

To his excellency the President of the Supreme Executive Council of the Commonwealth of Pennsylvania, The petition of Mark Grove, Most Humbly Showeth, That your petitioner was convicted at the last court of Oyer and Terminer and General Goal Delivery held at Lancaster for the County of Lancaster of aiding and abetting Ebenezer Archibald, James Bart and Walter Miller, British prisoners of War, to join the Enemys of the United States of America.

That your petitioner is possessed of no property, but what he procures by daily labor, which is not more than sufficient to support him and to borrow so large a sum is not in petitioners power as is has not property to secure the repayment.

Your petitioner therefore implores the mercy of this honourable board to protect him from the ruin that must follow carrying the judgment pronounced against him into execution, and he hopes to convince his fellow citizens by his future conduct that Mercy extended to him was not improper and that want of Gratitude is not amongst the number of his faults. . . .

Read in Council, December 24, 1782. Ordered that the fine due to the Commonwealth must be remitted.

Mark Grove was tryed and court of Oyer and Terminer Lancaster

October 18, 1782 for harbouring and aiding fugitives of war to escape. He was convicted and fined 150 pounds for assisting prisoners, on the act of Assembly. He pretends he was ignorant who they were, but he told them that 3 others in red-coats had passed lately. He fed these men and put his son along with them as a guide,—He is however as far as is appeared a person less able to pay than others. Could the court have regulated their sentences by equity, his fine might probably have been lessened.— 30th December 1782.

George Bryan What is above recited respecting Mark Grove appears to be in case of Jacob Grove or Groff by my notes, and therefore I am inclined to think the name of Mark has been mistaken by Judge Bryan. *Tho. McKean.*
To His Excellency the President and the Supreme Executive Council
of the Commonwealth of Pennsylvania
The Petition of Jacob Grove
Most Humbly Sheweth
That your petitioner was convicted at the last court of Oyer and Terminer and General Goal Delivery held at Lancaster for the County of Lancaster of aiding and abetting Ebenezer Archibald, James Bart and Walter Miller, British Prisoners of War, to join the enemies of the United States of America.

Your petitioner humbly begs leave to respect this, he can scarcely understand one word of the English language much less speak it, and therefore he cannot be supposed to be informed of any Declaration of the Prisoners aforesaid respecting their intended escape.

That he is an aged and infirm man, living on a poor place and having a numerous Family of Children depending on him for support.

That the levying of fines imposed on him by the court will end in the total ruin of himself and family.

Your petitioner not being conscious of any intentional offense he has committed against his country Humbly supplicates your Honourable Board to remit such part of the fine laid on him as you in your mercy and compassion deem fit and proper.[62]

Document 326
To His excellency the President and the Supreme Executive Council of the Commonwealth of Pennsylvania. The petition of Christian Martin. Most humbly sheweth, That your petitioner was convicted at the last court of oyer and terminer and General Goal Delivery held at Lancaster for the county of Lancaster of aiding and abetting Ebenezer Archibald,

James Burd, and Walter Mills, British prisoners of War, to join the Enemys of the United States of America.

That your petitioner has no real property, but depends upon his labour to support his Family, this circumstance he begs leave to assure your honourable board that all he is possessed of is not sufficient to pay the Fines imposed on him, and utter ruin must be the consequcne of his paying them.

Your petitioner implores your Mercy which if extended to him will raise him and his family from the utmost distress, and gratitude for this goodness will induce your petitioner to render every service to his country that is in his power and at the same time convince him and others that that government which is merciful must be good.

Your petitioner therefore humbly supplicates your honorable board to remit such part of the Fines laid on him as you in your Mercy and Compassion shall deem fit and proper.[63]

Document 327

To His excellency the President and the Supreme Executive
Council of the Commonwealth of Pennsylvania
The petition of Henry Martin, most humbly sheweth,
That your petitioner was convicted at the last court of Oyer and Terminer and General Goal Delivery held at Lancaster for the County of Lancaster of aiding and abetting Ebenezer Archibald James Bart and Walter Mills British Prisoners of War to join the Enemies of the United States of America.

Your petitioner has cheerfully shared all the public assessments and has at all times paid due obedience to the Laws of His Country: his character as an inoffensive Man he trusts was most fully proved by his neighbors at his trial and he begs leave to assure your Honourable Board that he never harbored a thought injurious to the true interests of America.

Your petitioner therefore most humbly requests your Honorable Board to remit such part of the Fines laid on him as you in your Mercy and compassion shall deem fit and proper.[64]

Document 328

Sir, Having lately been solicited by some Menists who were fined for not apprehending British deserters, to intercede for them, I have ventured to lay their case before his Excellency, your President. Since that time I have heard that their fine was considerably lessened, which was an Act worthy of your honourable Council and must needs draw upon you the Affection of the Good People of State. The Bearer hereof, Henry Martin, and another Christian Weaver, who intend at present to address themselves to your honorable Board, have also sent down their Petition, attested by sundry worthy freeholders,; but have hither to miscarried in their humble expectation. As they are equally entangled with the others in the Guilt, it is not probably that their Petition should have been rejected, at the same time the Council hath extended its mercy over the others. And therefore, at their Desire, I took the Freedom to Recommend their Case by means of your Person, to His Excellency and the Council. If you think it proper to lay this letter before the President, I desire you to mention my humble respects to Him and Family.

I humbly am of opinion that all rulers of Governments should be invested with Power, to mitigate the Rigour of the Law by the Interposition of Mercy, when necessary; at least we find thereof many remarkable instances in the Jewish Dispensation. And if this People must pay so great a Fine, it is certain that they will be ruined, and that for no other Crime but neglect of Duty in Matters which they were not permitted to do by their Principles and Conscience. You had always been considered as an accomplished Politician: and therefore I propose to you the most perfect Pattern of sound Policy, of a Woman, which was employed by Joab to intercede before King David for Absalom, 2 Sam. 14, 11, when she prayed that the King would not suffer to multiply in the Country the Revengers of Blood, or, as we say now, the Informers, for thereby the Evil is more increased, than lessened. I have no more to add, but that, besides my Humble Respect to You, I am, Sir,
Ephrata, the 9th of Feb. 18, 1783 *Peter Miller*
Read in Council Feb. 18, 1783.
Directed, Timothy Matlack, Esquire, Philadelphia[65]

Document 329
In Council Philadelphia, February 20th 1783
The petition of Henry Martin convicted of a misdemeanor upon three indictments in the County of Lancaster, for aiding British prisoners to escape was read. The record of his conviction and a recommendation in his behalf were also read, and the council having considered his case.

Ordered that two thirds of the fines adjudged to be paid to the use of the state by the said Henry Martin be remitted.

The petition of Christian Weaver convicted of the like offence in the said county praying remission of his fines was read, together with the record of his conviction and recommendation in his behalf,

On consideration, ordered That two thirds of the fines adjudged to be paid to the use of the State of the said Christian Weaver be remitted;

The petition of Christian Carpenter convicted of the like offenses in the said county praying remission of his fines was read, together with the record of his conviction and recommendation in his behalf,

On consideration, Ordered that one third of the Fines adjudged to be paid to the use of the State by the said Christian Carpenter be remitted.[66]

Document 330

To his Excellency the President and the Supreme Executive Council of the Commonwealth of Pennsylvania

The petition of Christian Weaver most humbly sheweth

That your petitioner was convicted at the last Court of Oyer and Terminer and General Goal Delivery held at Lancaster for the County of Lancaster of aiding and abetting Ebenezer Archibald, James Bart and Walter Mills, British prisoners of War, to join the Enemies of the United States of America.

Your petitioner flatters himself that he has ever supported a fair and honest character and that of a peaceable and inoffensive man. While the continental Army was encamping at the Valley Forge the House of your petitioner was open at all times to both Officers and Soldiers in the Service of the United States; when the enemy was about to possess themselves of Philadelphia his wagon was sent down chearfully for the Removal of the public stores. To this he begs leave to add that he understands but little of the English language and is hard of Hearing, so that whatever passed in conversation with the prisoners aforesaid at his House he was totally ignorant of.

Your petitioner therefore most Humbly requests your Honourable Board to remit such part of the Fines laid on Him as you in your Mercy and compassion shall deem fit and proper.[67]

Document 331

To His Excellency the President and the Supreme Executive Council of the Commonwealth of Pennsylvania

The Petition of Jacob Myer, most Humbly Sheweth

That your Petitioner was convicted at the last court of Oyer and Terminer and General Goal Delivery held at Lancaster for the county of Lancaster of aiding Richard Lillico, James Bart and Ebenezer Archibald British Prisoners of War to make their escape.

That your petitioner lives within two miles of the Borough of

Lancaster the bounds then prescribed by the Commisary for British and Other Prisoners out of the Stockade, and that many of the prisoners frequently came to his house for the purpose of procuring provisions for themselves and comrades. That the criminal conversation supposed to have happened between your petitioner and one of the prisoners at his trial was sworn to by them alone, and contradicted by two Witnesses, and that the Witnesses, and that the testimony of the prisoners themselves was variant and repugnant.

Your petitioner therefore prays your honourable Body to take his Case into Consideration and afford him such relief as to your Honours shall seem meet.[68] And your Petitioner as in duty bound will ever pray, *Jacob Mayer.*

Document 332

In Council Philadelphia March 18th 1783

A Petition from Jacob C. Myers convicted of Misdemeanors upon two indictments in the county of Lancaster for aiding British prisoners to escape, praying remission of his fines was read, the record of his conviction being also read, On Consideration, Ordered, That the fines due to the States be remitted.

A petition from Martin Meyers convicted of the like offence in the said county was read praying remission of his fines. The record of his conviction being also read On consideration, Ordered, that one moiety of the fines due to the state be remitted.

A petition from Abraham Myers convicted for the like offence upon three indictments in the said county—was read praying remission of his fines. A record of his Conviction being also read,

On consideration Ordered That two thirds of the fines due to the State be remitted.[69]

Document 333

To His Excellency the President and Supreme Executive Council of the State of Pennsylvania. The petition of Martin Myer, Most Humbly Sheweth,

That your Petitioner was Indicted and Convicted at the last Court of Oyer and Terminer and General Goal Delivery held at Lancaster for the County of Lancaster the Sixteenth day of October 1782 for a misdemeanor in encouraging James Bart and Ebenezar Archibald Prisoners of War to make their escape.

James Bart and Ebenezar Archibald who Swore that the first time they were in company with Petitioner that Petitioner had informed them that he has harboured many prisoners of war, and that they without any previous introduction or acquaintance with petitioner informed him that they are to make their Escape to New York, and that petitioner by his Conduct encouraged their going, the petitioner did not assist.—The improbability of this account is very evidant, for surely on business of so dangerous a nature both sides would observe some caution. Which they said they did not. But it is a remarkable circumstance that they swore they had no intention then to go to New York and that when they went in Company with Captain Lee they did not call at Petitioners house or make any inquiry about him. Surely if they had such an opinion of petitioners attachments to them they would have required his advice.

Your petitioner does not wish to offer the most distant reflection on the jury, as he is convinced they gave their verdict from a belief that the witnesses swore the truth, but your petitioner does declare he is innocent of the Offence of which he was convicted.

Your petitioner therefore prays the Honorable Board to take the Circumstances of his Case into their consideration and grant him such relief as to them shall appear just and reasonable under the circumstances in his case. *Martin Mayer*[70]

Document 334

To his Excellency the president and Supreme Executive
Council of the State of Pennsylvania
The Humble Petition of Benjamin Bowman
Most Humbly Sheweth

That your petitioner was indicted at the last court of Oyer and Terminer and General Goal Delivery held in and for the county of Lancaster the sixteenth day of Oct. 1782 for harbouring and concealing Joseph Turner a British prisoner of war and aiding him to make his escape upon which indiictment your petitioner was convicted and fined the sum of fifty pounds.

That the above Joseph Turner was not confined as a prisoner of War but permitted by General Hazen to go at large through the Borough of Lancaster and did for many months work at his trade as a Carpenter in the Town and that at the time it was pretended that he made his Escape he had a (pass?) from General Hazen to go into the country as a prisoner of war, but with private instructions as appear'd in Evidence on the Tryal, to discover any person who assist or give anything to British prisoners, at this period he was at your petitioners house but he doth most solemnly declare no such conversation passed between them as the said Turner swore on the Trial indeed one Truth he did swear, that he neither went to New York nor intended to go there.

That by this representation your petitioner does not mean to reflect on either the court or jury, not does he think it the only ground upon which he can ask the mercy—full interposition of the Honourable board, for he begs leave to mention that he has a Family depending on him for support, they can (Live?) only by his industry and labour, and from the great want of money in the country he is barely able to do, he therefore hopes when this Honourable Board considers of how much consequence the sum of fifty pounds is to a poor farmer and how trifling to the Publick that they will relieve your petitioner from distress for which he will be bound in gratitude to Love and serve them.[71]

Deliberate Entrapments

Rev. Martin Urner, pastor of the Coventry Church of the Brethren in Chester County, was the victim of deliberate entrapment by American soldiers sent out in rags to pretend to be escaped prisoners. Urner insisted he gave them food, not because they were British, but because they were men. Susanna Longacre, an elderly woman in the same community, was also given a harsh sentence for offering food to those same pretended deserters.

Document 335

April the first 1783. Honourable Gentlemen of the Council President and all of you who have the Honour to be assistant thereunto my humble petition shoewth that at a court held of oyer and terminer I Martin Urner and several other fellows cittysens where made guilty of a misdemeanor for aiding three prisners of war and the honourable court fines mee one hundred and fifty pounds to be paid on or before the first day of April 1783 or els to receive thritynine lashes for three offences separately. Now honorable councilors I pray you might consider my circumstances that I am old and have been unwell this great wile and have a week family to maintain and am much incumbered with debts and have not been a will full offender but desired the prisoners to return and give themselves up until exchange could be made I have been a great sufferer these many years and always paid my taxes and furnished the army with grain and provender and pasture which if I had time could show certificates for Butt worthy gentlemen I begg your pardon to Act according to the Golden Rule Hence I shall always acknowledge it thankful as your humble petitioner and well wisher of liberty. *Martin Urner Senr.*[72]

Document 336

To the Honorable the President and Executive Council of the Commonwealth of Pennsylvania

The petition of Martin Urner of the Township of Coventry in the County of Chester Humbly Sheweth

That your petitioner was prosecuted at the last court of Oyer and Terminer held at Chester for giving food and drink to some travelers who called at his house pleading necessity for refreshment, and thereupon adjudged to pay the sum of one hundred and fifty pounds.

That your petitioner was then entirely ignorant of any Act of Assembly against feeding the hungry, even if they were British prisoners—so far was he from apprehending that he had offended against any law, that he believed he had only performed an act of hospitality, as he did it not because they were British, but because they were men.

That when your petitioner was given to understand that the above persons were British prisoners endevoring to get to New York, he endeavoured to dissuade them from their purpose and to prevail with them to return to Lancaster and deliver themselves up, which he probably would have effected, had they been in reality what they pretended.

That as your petitioner has not been a willful offender against the laws of his country, as he has been much injured in his property by the present unhappy contest, as he has had considerable sum of money due to him these four or five years past for forage for the use of the Continental Army, and as the raising the said heavy fine at this time of scarcity of cash, and at a time when so many of his countrymen and fellow citizens are by the same means brought into the same predicament, will be very difficult Your petitioner prays the Honourable the President and Council will take his Case into their Consideration and grant such relief as to them in their wisdom shall seem expedient, and your petitioner as in duty bound shall pray.[73]

Coventry, February 4th 1783 *Martin Urner*

Document 337

September the 2d day 1783. Honourable Gentlemen and worthy Councilors. I return your kine thankes for your good will and mercy which you shewed me the first day of April last when as it has pleased you to consider my distressed condition of paying one hundred and fifty pounds fine for giving three men a breakfast who said they were prisoners of War. When two of them complaint of being sick they discovered their matter chiefly while they sat at meat and obtained the mercy of you to take of one hundred dollars and now am very much concerned how to pay the remainder three hundred dollars I petitioned to General Hazen and got no answer the sherif John Gardner hath patiently trusted me hitherto I am old and weakly and have had a son and daughter in law who have been very expencif this summer for they where likely to die and I have served the dood of my country and been a great sufferer during the War having my plantation ruined by General Smallwoods brigade lost a good waggon and horses and supplyed our army with many articles which may appear if required I pray your pardon gentlemen to consider me once more in my distressed estate I will acknowledge it very thankfull as your Humble Petitioner *Martin Urner.*[74]

Document 338

To the Honourable the President and Executive Council of the Commonwealth of Pennsylvania

The petition of Susanna Longacre, wife of Jacob Longacre of the Township of Coventry in the County of Chester Humbly Sheweth

That your petitioner on a late prosecution in the Court of Oyer and Terminer held at Chester has been adjudged to pay a fine of one hundred and fifty pounds or in default of payment to receive one hundred and seventeen lashes on her bareback at the public post, for giving some victuals and drink to four travelers, and directing them along the Great Road to the house of a person for whom they inquired.

That your petitioner is near seventy years of age, and laboring under great bodily infirmity, that at the time of the above transaction your petitioners husband was many miles from home, and no other person about the house but your petitioner and a girl of about eight or nine years old.

That your petitioners place of dwelling is by the side of a public road, where the needy traveler has generally partaken of such refreshment as the House afforded. That the persons above mentioned did not give the least intimation of their being British prisoners until the Victuals was before them on the Table, She therefore conceives that what she gave them cannot with justice or propriety be considered as given to such, but as an act of hospitality corresponding with her general conduct for many years past.

That your petitioner was totally ignorant of any Act of Assembly of other law, against giving food or directions to British Prisoners, so that if they had more early explained themselves, and your petitioner (either from motives of humanity and compassion, or from motives of fear, considering her then helpless situation) had given them food and directions, she hopes the President and Council would not have deemed it a crime deserving so heavy a sentence.

Your petitioner therefore prays the Honourable the President and Council will take her unhappy case into their consideration, and grant such relief as to them in their Wisdom shall seem expedient, and your petitioner as in duty bound shall every pray. Coventry Feb 4th 1783 *Susanna* her mark *Longeneker*[75]

Late Hopes for British Victory

According to Henry Dulhauer, who came to Pennsylvania as an agent for Mennonites in East Friesland and elsewhere in Europe seeking a grant of land in the wilderness of the Ohio country, many Mennonites in Lancaster County were reluctant to believe that the United States had been victorious and entertained hopes even in 1784 that a British Army would yet liberate them. With this hope still alive, he claimed, they were reluctant to affirm their allegiance to the new government.

Document 339 Lancaster County the 12 Day of April 1784

To the Honourable Congress

I hope you will not take it Miss, that your Memorialist coms to you with this Lines. I am oblig'd to do it upon account of my German Breathern, so very Desirous, Since peace is publish'd in Europe, that America for free independend States proclaimed is, this Europeans Breathern, to Settle, that till this Time unsetled yet not Inhabited Country from the Mouth of Ohio Rivier up by 240 Miles Long and 120 Broad under certain Conditions as Sub No. 1 in copia enclosed, in German Language. I would have translated it into the English Tongue while I am not Scholar enough to do it. I hope you will Execuse me; I Live in hopes that Congress will take in Consideration, what Benefit it will be for the Country when such Wild Countrys with Such Laborous Platers will be Settled, Remarqueable florishing will overpower you to believe their Industry to give the Right Thine one of the best Country's. Therefore I Expect if Congress is intended to See, that a country is popular and florishing in Trade to give Grace to your petitioners to look in their poverty, and for the Benefit of the country and Grant their Desire to give them priviliges and Record'd that Such Wild countrys may be Inhabited. Further I cane not See it longer, like you will find in the German Copia which is Enclosed, that the German Breathern of the Menonist Religion, to Shew them American Breathern their Desire, but I found no Audience, because they will not believe, that it is peace, their Reason is while the King of Britton had not published in this Country, and such News was only from France and Congress. I Defended and Contradicted their foolish Notions without any Satisfaction, but I take the Liberty not to hide it longer like a Anonimy that my Name upon no Way Shall publish'd about this it is Such: So much I cane find out and See, that they are Encouraged from some English because while their is a great difficulty between the Majority and Minority of censers in the state of Pensilvani and that they all should give their Votes to the Majority, they are in Such hopes Blindfooled, the Minority would take up Arms and than they English would come in the midle to make peace betwixt them, whil America has Dispersed all the Soldiers upon Such Terms would the King Win the Country yeat. This is the Fault and the Surely hopes most tro the hohl Country's, the Right Author of it I cane not Denounciat while it is a Common Speech of the Country amongst the Thorries. Therefore, Congress may Consider it well, when their will not be a great Rebellion in the Country, my Sentiment is this: that Congress most take the Sharpest Measures at hand in Time,/: while peace is publish'd, they are oblig'd to take the Oath of fidelity and Liberty according their Conscience of Religion:/no Man has a Right to Execuse himself no More; It is a impossibility tha Stop their Thories Kind when Congress dos not immediatly expedit a Mandat to the Governeurs and Counsils or Assemblys at every State, that all Inhabitans without Regard any Exception, Shall be oblig'd every Man, Since peace in every State proclaimed, to take the Oath of Fiedlity and Liberty to the united States in less than 3 Days under the poenalty that all their Estate Shall be forfeited and Confiscated after this Mannor them So has not took the Oath, their Mouth will be Stoped and will be peacibler in the Country, &, but I leave it to the Congress own Consideration and Ientention, but the Cause is a Realy the truth.

Further, I hope for what I was Deputised in the Name of the European Menonist, to take Reflection to Grand their petition, if Congress Considered what Benefit it will be to the Country, that the inhabited Country will be Settled upon Such Conditions, popular, thick in plantations will to be Seen in a very Short Time, Trade and

Florishing of the Desirous Petitioners will Sound tro all the World, but Suppose Congress would give the Land to Some Frish Gentlemen, Some 10 or 15 Thousand acres, that never would be florishing, their would be no Incouragement the thinking was we are Servants, that is no Liberty, we are Slaves to the Rich; but I am Surely Convinced if it was in the Kingdom of Prussia where I come from and their would be petitioners to Inhabit upon Such Conditions the Wild Country's it would be Granted and upon Some Years more Liberty than your petitioners Desired, and would have a Compleat Resolution Send in 30 Days, but while they Expect this Liberty would be ever for their Heirs and wate dayly for their Redeeming answer from me, how they themselfes shall prepare and Sell their Estats for Money. I think Congress could make no objection, than they Desires no more, what after a great Concluding and Considering would according the Confession of Religion will be granted. In Such hopes I look upon a granting Answer of Privilege for my Desirous Breathern and petitioners and I have the Answer to Remain

Your most obedient Svt
Henry Dulhire Deputy of
European Menonists

P.S. My Address is to Henry Dulhire living by Peter Musselman Senior near Lancaster.

To the Honourable Congress of the united States at thees Annapolis[76]

Notes for Chapter 7

1. Egerton, 380.

2. Donald F. Durnbaugh, *The Brethren in Colonial America* (Elgin, Illinois, 1967), 387.

3. *Ibid.*, 396.

4. The full text with introductory notes is given in Durnbaugh, *The Brethren in Colonial America,* 408-419, and in M.R.J., X (January 1969), 1-8.

5. Charles F. Kauffman, *A Genealogy and History of the Kauffman-Coffman Families* (York, Pa., 1940), 66, 500, and 547-549. He follows the late Ira Landis' identification of Michael Kauffman, Sr., but it is to be noted that his son Jacob Kauffman (1752-1840), a miller in Manor Township, was an active Patriot and served as a commissary officer.

6. Durnbaugh, *Brethren,* 407. Albert H. Gerberich, *The Brenneman History* (Scottdale, Pa., 1938), 41-43.

7. Conestoga and Donegal Tax Lists, Lancaster County Historical Society, Lancaster, Pa.

8. Egerton, 381.

9. Donald Baker, "Charles Wesley and the American War of Independence," Proceedings of the Wesley Historical Society, XL (October 1976), 175.

10. *Colonial Records*, XI, 307.

11. *Pennsylvania Archives,* 2nd Series, III, 109-111.

12. *Ibid.*, 8th Series, VIII, 7437 and 7453.

13. Mary Jean Kraybill, Gerald R. Brunk, and James O. Lehman, *A Guide to Select Revolutionary War Records Pertaining to Mennonites and Other Pacifist Groups in Southeastern Pennsylvania and Maryland 1775-1880,* No. 2 (Harrisonburg, Va., 1974), 41.

14. Carl Van Doren, *Secret History of the American Revolution* (New York, 1941), 129-134.

15. Paul H. Smith, *Loyalists and Redcoats* (Chapel Hill, N.C., 1964), 94-99.

16. Wilbur H. Siebert, *The Loyalists of Pennsylvania* (Boston, 1972), 42-43.

17. Van Doren, 221.

18. Richard A. Overfield, "The Loyalists of Maryland During the Revolution" (PhD dissertation, University of Maryland, 1968), 277.

19. Unfortunately, the records of the Berks County Court of Quarter Sessions and Oyer and Terminer cannot be located for any earlier date than the February 1780 term of the court, although they were deposited in the Berks County Historical Society many years ago, complete from 1773 through 1781. The record of the Berks County Tory trials is probably to be found there, rather than in the records of the Supreme Court. Although treason cases were normally heard by the Supreme Court, cases of misprision of treason were normally settled in the county court. Since the Supreme Court records are extant from November 1778, we know that none of these Berks County "Tories" appeared in that court after that date and we know from another source that one of the imprisoned Berks County Amishmen was not indicted for misprision of treason until August 1779.

19a. Records of the trial were found in the Lancaster County Indictments in the Lancaster Court House, now in the Lancaster County Historical Society, and in the Records of the Supreme Court of the Commonwealth of Pennsylvania in the State Archives. The petition and the accompanying transcript of the trial and sentence were found in the Clemency File of the Supreme Executive Council in the State Archives. The spelling used in all these records for the defendant's surname is *Beam,* but, as he did not sign his own name, this is obviously a phonetic spelling by a court clerk.

20. "Proceedings of the Committee of Observation for Elizabeth Town District (Washington County)," *M.H.M.*, XIII (March 1918), 39 and 51.

21. Records of the Supreme Court, *Pennsylvania State Archives,* Harrisburg, Pa.
22. N. B. Grubb, "Mennonite Reminiscences," *The Mennonite,* XXXVIII (June 15, 1922), 3.
23. *Bucks County Bulletin,* V (1875), 268-269.
24. Records of the Supreme Court, *P.S.A.*, Harrisburg, Pa.
25. *Hazard's Register,* May 1829, "Revolutionary Letters and Papers," 305.
26. *Ibid.*, 306.
27. *Ibid.*, 307.
28. *Ibid.*, 308.
29. John Whiting, *Revolutionary Orders of General Washington* (Philadelphia, 1844), 59-60.
30. "Detective Work Among the Benners," *Montgomery County Bulletin,* VII, No. 2, 134-135.
31. Clemency File, Records of Supreme Executive Council, P.H.M.C.
32. *Ibid.*
33. *Ibid.*
34. Shenandoah County Court Minute Book, 1774-1780, fol. 108. Shenandoah County Court House, Woodstock, Va.
35. Records of the Supreme Court, P.S.A.
36. Lancaster County Indictments, Lancaster County Court House, Lancaster, Pa.
37. *Autobiography of the Rev. Samuel Huber, Elder in the Church of the United Brethren in Christ* (Chambersburg, Pa., 1858), 9-11.
38. Sir Henry Clinton Papers, W. L. Clements Library, Ann Arbor, Michigan.
39. Baltimore County Court Minute Book, 1772-1781, fol. 305, Md.H.R. Three other John Thompsons, in Cecil, Prince Georges, and Ann Arundel counties are even less likely to have been Methodists.
40. *Pennsylvania Archives,* 1st Series, VIII, 598.
41. Records of the Supreme Court, P.H.M.C
42. Clemency File, Records of the Supreme Executive Council, P.H.M.C.
43. *Ibid.*
44. Lancaster County Indictments, Lancaster County Court House, Lancaster, Pa.
45. *Pennsylvania Archives,* 1st Series, VIII, 740-741.
46. Elmer E. Clark, ed., *Journal and Letters of Francis Asbury* (Nashville, Tenn., 1958), I, 401.
47. Cornwallis Papers, Public Record Office, London, 30/11/6/270-271. Microfilm, Alderman Library, University of Virginia, Charlottesville, Va.
48. *Archives of Maryland,* XLVII, 328-330.
49. Replogle's deposition is in the Executive Correspondence, Md.H.R., 6636-30-132. Details of his earlier brush with Patriots can be found in "Proceedings of the Committee of Observation for Elizabeth Town District (Washington County)," *M.H.M.*, XIII (March 1918), 231. *cf.* Klaus Wust, "Disaffection in the Rear: German Tories in the West Virginia Mountains," *The Report,* XXXVI (1975), pp. 66-74.
50. *Archives of Maryland,* XLV, 467.
51. *Ibid.*, 469.
52. *Ibid.*, XLVII, 298-299.
53. Sir Guy Carleton Papers, Colonial Williamsburg Foundation, Research Archives, Williamsburg, Va., 5178(1)

53a. Carleton Papers, Colonial Williamsburg, 88(3) and 89(2).

53b. *Archives of Maryland,* XLVIII, 3.

54. *Ibid.*, 307-308.
55. *Ibid.*, 350
56. *Pennsylvania Archives,* 3rd Series, XXI, 143.
57. *P.M.H.B.*, XLIV (1920), 323.
58. W. H. Reed, "The Pennsylvania Militia and the Convention Troops,"

Montgomery County Historical Society Sketches, Vol. 5 (1925), 3400-1.

59. Sir Henry Clinton Papers, W. L. Clements Library, Ann Arbor, Michigan.

60. R.G., #27, P.H.M.C.

61. *Colonial Records*, XIII, 441-442.

62. R.G. #27, P.H.M.C. Also in the collections at the Archives are the petitions which were filed by their friends and neighbors.

63. R.G., #27, P.H.M.C.

64. *Ibid.*

65. Peter Miller was the prior at the Ephrata community of Seventh Day Baptists; The letter is from the *Pennsylvania Archives*, 1st Series, IX, 751-752.

66. Extract from the Minutes R.G. #27, P.H.M.C. A petition of neighbors in support of Martin is also found at this location.

67. P.H.M.C. R. G. #27.

68. *Ibid.* A petition of neighbors in support of Myers is also found at this location.

69. Extract from Minutes found in R.G. 27, P.H.M.C.

70. *Pennsylvania State Archives*, R.G. 27. A petition.

71. *Ibid.* There is in the same location a petition of neighbors in support of Bowman.

72. *Ibid.*

73. *Ibid.*

74. *Ibid.*

75. *Ibid.* Petitions signed by 54 neighbors supported her.

76. Papers of Continental Congress, Microfilm 247, Reel 94, Item 78, Vol. 8, 74-79. National Archives, Washington, D.C. Cf. Donald F. Durnbaugh, "Religion and Revolution: Options in 1776," *Pennsylvania Mennonite Heritage*, I (July, 1978), 8-9.

EPILOGUE

Renewed Sense of Separateness

The searing experience of the American Revolution had many profound effects on the historic peace churches, but none was more important than the renewed sense of separateness among Mennonites, Quakers, Brethren, and Schwenkfelders. Sometime before his death in 1760, Mennonite Bishop Henry Funk had written of persecution as the normal relationship between the state and the individual Christian. To Funk's way of thinking, the freedom that Mennonites shared with the other sects in his lifetime was the root of their decay, as they adopted "the ways of the world" and sought to escape the consequences of their faith. Funk had only disapproval for those in the "nonresistant churches who make an effort to elect officials or magistrates according to their own wishes and ideas", and for those who "seek these offices themselves and serve in them in order that they may assure not only those in our own time, but also our children, exemption from the feast of affliction as kept by Jesus."[1] The war had swept away the security of the Proprietary regime and with it any temptation for the sects to seek protection by political action. In Pennsylvania and North Carolina the Mennonites and Quakers lost the right to vote or hold office for more than a decade; in other states their civil rights were restored more quickly. Fines, imprisonment, double and triple taxes became part of the daily experience of all conscientious objectors.

Although the response of the peace churches was far more uniform than it would be in any later American war, local and regional differences marked the response of Mennonites, Quakers, and other nonresistants to the wartime situation. The Franconia and Lancaster

Mennonites approached such issues as affirming allegiance and paying taxes to the new government from different vantage points. Christian Funk's movement had no apparent echo in the other Pennsylvania Mennonite communities, but the attitudes of the majority of Franconia ministers on war taxes may also reflect a closer relationship with Friends who felt strongly on this point.

The Quaker response also differed to some degree from meeting to meeting. William Matthews, who visited the meetings at West River, Herring Creek, and the Cliffs in Ann Arundel County, Maryland, in 1781 found "there is not more than 3 or 4 Men at all them Meetings that retains a Right of Membership with us," since "the Love of the world & friendship thereof hath destroyed the pure life of Religion."[2] Hugh Judge found all in order in Hopewell Monthly Meeting in Frederick County, Virginia, on a religious visit in 1782, as well he might, for this meeting had been winnowed by suffering, with five members imprisoned for refusing to do militia duty.[3]

Variations in response to the crisis may represent honest differences of opinion on religious questions or reflect varying degrees of fervor or commitment to the brotherhood, but there is little evidence to link these variations to social or economic differences. Wealthy Mennonite farmers and their poorest brethren behaved much the same way. Urban Friends and members of rural meetings do not exhibit distinct patterns. Nor can any one pattern of response be found for those Mennonites whose command of the English language might suggest a greater degree of assimilation; although many who took a more active part in the war were fluent in English, the more conservative Franconia bishops were also bilingual.

The wartime experience of the peace churches proved a vehicle for reform and renewal because the implications of nonresistant discipleship were the real issues and not merely incidental to some other division. One major effect of the war on the Society of Friends, for instance, is exemplified in the dispute between the Free Quakers and the Meeting for Sufferings of Philadelphia Yearly Meeting, which was aired before the Pennsylvania legislature and in the Philadelphia newspapers in 1783. The Free Quakers, compromised by military service during the Revolution, argued that they had a birthright to membership in the Society of Friends. The Meeting for Sufferings replied that the Society of Friends had an undoubted right to require standards of conduct of its members and to exclude any who did not accept these standards.[4] The drift from sect to church had been successfully reversed. Slave-owning, dancing, swearing, use of tobacco or alcoholic beverages, as well as violations of the peace testimony were among the many causes for disownment in this period of Quaker history, as Friends deliberately chose once again to be a separate people called out to exemplify in their lives the teachings of Jesus Christ.

The relatively few Quakers disowned for offenses against the peace testimony and the even fewer Mennonite compromised by wartime activities stand in sharp contrast to the enormous numbers who "married out" or otherwise separated themselves from the religious community in these decades of revival. So far as Quakers are concerned, most of those disowned for military service or similar offenses did not compound their wrongdoing with other unrelated offenses.[5] But they were a distinct minority in every local meeting. In comparison to those who carried their birthright membership so lightly that they refused to unite with Friends after marrying someone from a different background, the military offenders were an insignificant minority.

Nonresistance was a deeply ingrained and "popular" doctrine among Mennonites, Quakers, Brethren, and Schwenkfelders. There were few waverers. Those Mennonites and Quakers who took an active part with the Americans were generally serving on committees and drilling with the Associators in May 1775 and even earlier. Taxes, test oaths, militia fines, and official pressure did almost nothing to increase their number. (Nor did the presence of a British army in eastern Pennsylvania in 1777, in the Carolinas in 1780, and in Virginia in 1781 stimulate more than a handful of Friends, Mennonites, and Dunkers to give aid and comfort to the king's forces.) But official persecution obviously increased the sense of alienation from the larger society and of belonging to a close community. What reformers within the peace churches could not do, the government did for them.

The American Revolution strengthened the resolve of each of the nonresistant sects to tighten membership standards, to cast off the half-committed, and to withdraw from contact with outsiders. Over the next decade or two a great many Mennonites and Quakers were formally disowned by the brotherhood or drifted away voluntarily.

Quaker meetings disowned a few members for "joining the Methodists" or "joining the Baptists," but the impact of the evangelical revival was greater, and hence more threatening, among the Mennonites. Between 1780 and 1800 Mennonite congregations in several Pennsylvania counties, in western Maryland and in the Shenandoah Valley of Virginia either disappeared entirely or were greatly diminished in number. Until about 1780, the Mennonite Church had successfully absorbed the revival. The Lancaster Conference leaders had "borne and forborne" with preachers who emphasized the need to repent and be born again, sometimes downgrading every other aspect of Christian nurture. Bishop Martin Boehm of the Byerland congregation was long a controversial figure among Lancaster Mennonites and some meetinghouses were closed to him, but he preached the new birth as a Mennonite for more than twenty years.

Martin Boehm's own account suggests that it was his association with Methodist preachers that provoked the break between him and the Lancaster bench. The carefully worded statement drawn up by the Lancaster Mennonite leaders cited exaggerated phrases used in his preaching and his readiness to reconcile persons under the ban in their own congregations. The two are not incompatible. Both point to the closing years of the American Revolution as the date of Boehm's excommunication. Boehm's house first became a preaching station for visiting Methodists in 1780, so any earlier date would have to be ruled out.[6]

Boehm continued to preach in churches, private homes, and in the open air, drawing into closer fellowship not only with Methodists, but especially with Reformed Church pietists, such as Philip William Otterbein. It is suggestive that one of Boehm's early converts, Dr. Peter Senseny, a Mennonite physician of York, Pennsylvania, who heard Boehm preach in an open field sometime between 1781 and 1783, sent a troubled patient to a Reformed pastor in western Maryland for spiritual advice, rather than to any Mennonite or Methodist.[7]

The 1780s witnessed the growth of an informal fellowship of Reformed and Mennonite preachers who were fully committed to the revival movement. These nondenominational (*unparteische*) evangelists had no formal organization until 1800, when they began to hold annual conferences and chose Otterbein and Boehm as their overseers.[8]

They had close ties to the Methodists. Otterbein attended the 1784 Baltimore Conference that began the formal organization of the Methodist Church in the United States. Methodist circuit riders regularly preached in Martin Boehm's house, until his sons built Boehm's Chapel for Lancaster County Methodists in 1791. His influence contributed to the number of former Mennonites who helped Methodism take root in Lancaster County in these years, while they in turn brought Mennonite doctrines and practices that can still be recognized in some Methodist congregations.[9]

Although Otterbein gave the Reformed Synod in 1788 a written statement that included views contrary to the traditional Reformed Church understanding of atonement, he remained a Reformed minister in good standing until his death in 1813.[10] The Reformed leaders took no steps to dismiss any of Otterbein's associates until long after the United Brethren had become a separate denomination. Others among the "nondenominational preachers," like the Lutheran schoolmaster Simon Harr, considered themselves members of their former church and had no wish to separate.[11]

The Mennonites who were drawn into this revival movement were more likely to cut themselves off from the Mennonite brotherhood. Christian Newcomer, who looked to Otterbein and George Adam Geeting as his spiritual fathers, described what may have been a more common experience. He was disappointed on a visit to friends and relatives in Lancaster County to find that the preachers in his home congregation "still continued in the same inexperience of religion as when I left them." The contrast to the German Reformed preachers he had heard in western Maryland was so great that Newcomer testified, "I withdrew myself from the Mennonite Society on account of the want of the life and power of religion among them." Since Otterbein and Geeting "preached the same doctrine which I had experienced," Newcomer "associated with them and joined their Society."[12]

This was the crux of the problem presented by the Great Awakening to the Mennonite community. Emphasis on personal conversion, the new birth, and repentance could be readily absorbed into the life of the congregation, but a community based on nonconformity, nonresistance, and daily discipleship could not accept religious experience as the only basis of Christian fellowship.

Martin Boehm's association with the Methodists after 1780 and Christian Newcomer's discovery of "the life and power of religion" among German Reformed pietists as early as 1777 challenged the Mennonite community at such a fundamental level that they could not continue to function within it. They were not alone in their course of action. Martin Crider, John and Christian Hershey, John Neidig, Abraham Histand, and other former Mennonite preachers encouraged whole congregations to move in the direction of independent evangelical churches and finally to unite with the Church of the United Brethren in Christ.[13] At about the same time, Jacob Engle and other former Mennonites united with others of different background, baptizing each other in the first instance and later adopting a Confession of Faith that shows marked pietist influence. They came to be known as the River Brethren and later as the Brethren in Christ Church.[14]

Nonresistance was never an issue in the rise of these new religious fellowships. An independent church formed under Baptist influence in present Page County, Virginia, by former Mennonites led by Martin Kaufman could not enter into fellowship with any Baptist Association because of its stands on nonresistance and anti-slavery.[15] Nevertheless these and other strongly held doctrine and modes of worship were considered of secondary importance to the experience of conversion.

The Mennonite response to this challenge was explained in a pamphlet written in 1792 by Christian Burkholder, a preacher in Earl Township in Lancaster County, Pennsylvania. Intended for those who might be "confused by so many calls at the present time" by Christians who disagreed one with another, Christian Burkholder's *Useful and Edifying Address to the Young on True Repentance* dealt with controversial subjects in such a loving spirit that no one could take offense at his words. He answered the objection that the church was in a declining state, very destitute of love, by admitting its imperfections. The search for "a church that consisted of none but awakened, enlightened, and regenerated persons standing in the bond of pure love" was doomed to failure, for Christians were but imperfect followers of their divine Master. Burkholder recognized the importance of conversion and repentance. But the new birth was effected by God and could not be forced into the mold of a particular conversion experience. "My experience can help you nothing."[16]

Nonresistance and Civil Government

Christian Burkholder emphasized nonresistance and the peaceable kingdom in his writings. "Nature and mere human reason cannot comprehend the doctrine of loving our enemies with a true heart." Nonresistance only made sense within the context of servanthood developed in such New Testament passages as Luke 22:25, 26, Mark 10:43, 44, and 1 Peter 5:3. "But as the whole doctrine of Christ leads into a course of self-denial, and separation from the world, Christ makes a distinction between the practice of worldly government and that of his true followers." Government is not instituted for Christians to exercise power. "But that they should be 'servants' and 'ministers' is in accordance with the doctrine of Christ, as well as with his course of life; as also that of a pilgrim on earth." Christians owe Caesar his tribute money, but they cannot use civil government to force others to do their will. "Indeed I would rather lose something, than to use force against anyone by law."[17]

Burkholder did not explicitly forbid voting or holding civil office as he did lawsuits, but his treatment of the subject could easily be taken to exclude office holding. Another Lancaster County Mennonite, Francis

Herr, writing in 1790, argued against participation in any way in civil government. "If we for the gospel and Christ's sake cannot hold any office, how should we be capable to elect others into office?"[18]

Francis Herr represented a conservative element in the Lancaster Mennonite community who were convinced that the church as a whole had slipped from the standard of the past. His comment, like Bishop Henry Funk's more than a generation earlier, may well reflect the ideal, rather than the reality of contemporary Mennonite practice. It was certainly a deliberate rejection of the political activities of members of his immediate family, Herrs and Carpenters.

The same strain of withdrawal from public life was strong in the writings of Quaker reformers and in the epistles sent by several Yearly Meetings. Friends were discouraged from holding office, "rather let us by our peaceable lives & good Conversation evidence to the world our Attachment to the real Welfare of our Country."[19] There was nothing new about this attitude. The Meeting for Sufferings of Philadelphia Yearly Meeting had urged total Quaker withdrawal from the Pennsylvania Assembly in the French and Indian War crisis and in the more peaceful 1760s and 1770s.

What was new about the situation of the peace churches in Pennsylvania and North Carolina was the result of the harsh Test Acts adopted in 1777. Under provisions of these laws, the great majority of Mennonites, Quakers, and Dunkers had lost the right to vote or hold office. They did not have full civil rights restored until 1787 in North Carolina and 1789 in Pennsylvania. The political alliance of the peaceable sects that had functioned so well until the election of 1776 was dead and many Quakers and Mennonites were reluctant to see their brethren attempt to revive it.

Francis Herr's pamphlet, which appeared in both English and German editions, illustrated a tendency among at least some Mennonites not only to withdraw from political activity but to put greater distance between themselves and their longtime friends the Quakers. Herr criticized the Society of Friends for its failure to practice water baptism and to give primacy to the Holy Scriptures. He also took Quakers to task for involving themselves in lawsuits, seeking public office, and sending formal addresses to rulers that appeared to have no other purpose than currying favor with them. Herr asked "where war is more earnestly forbidden as going to law, resist force by force and to be elected into office?"[20] Benjamin Mason, a Pennsylvania Friend, responded to Herr's criticism in a pamphlet of his own, dealing, as Herr did, mainly with the question of baptism and the Scriptures. He replied to Herr's objections to Quaker practice with regard to the courts and to addressing rulers, but had no comment on the question of office-holding. Quite likely he agreed with Herr on this point.[21]

Separation from the world meant for all of the nonresistant sects separation from weaker brethren within their own communities and from other Christian groups. They virtually abandoned all efforts to influence the larger society in which they lived and became "the quiet in the land."

Private Benevolence and Public Virtue

Throughout their wartime trials, the peace churches had all justified their nonresistant stand, in part, by pointing to mutual aid within their own group and widespread charitable efforts outside it. They not only took care of their own poor, but organized relief efforts for victims of Indian raids and refugees from the fighting around Boston. They had insisted in the early days of the Revolution on their readiness to give generous support to any sort of relief work, while refusing to contribute anything to destroy lives.[22]

It was a natural response to the charge that they were unwilling to contribute their just share to the common burdens of the community and one that would recur many times thereafter in legislative petitions.

Internal reform had important social consequences in the postwar decade, as Quakers and others began to deal with the problem of slavery. The earliest American protest against slavery had been the joint effort of Mennonites and Quakers in Germantown in 1688, but it had no long-lasting effect. Many Quakers owned slaves by the middle years of the eighteenth century and some were involved in the slave trade. African slavery was not unknown among Mennonites. Tax lists in Philadelphia (present Montgomery) and Berks counties reveal a few Franconia Mennonite slaveowners. Lancaster Mennonites do not appear to have owned slaves and the anti-slavery stand of Martin Kaufman's "Menno-Baptists" in Virginia suggests that it was from conviction.[23]

John Woolman, Anthony Benezet, and other reformers in the Society of Friends pressed their fellow Quakers to consider freeing their slaves and by 1775 the cause of the oppressed blacks had taken deep root in Quakerism. The limited number of sources for the German-speaking peace churches in comparison to Quaker records make it impossible to trace the growth of anti-slavery sentiment. Woolman gave a story of a York County Mennonite who slept in the fields rather than be served by his friend's ill-treated slaves, but an anecdote is no proof that slavery was condemned by Mennonites as a whole in 1758.[24] Christopher Sauer II put items critical of slavery in his Germantown paper and the Annual Meeting of the Church of the Brethren in 1782 put its condemnation of the slave trade in no uncertain terms.[25] The Schwenkfelder elder Christopher Schultz saw slavery as one of the sins of the Americans in a sermon preached in 1776.[26]

The idea that the American Revolution was a just punishment for the sins of the people and particularly for the sin of slavery was a commonplace by 1776. New England Congregationalists, Quakers, and Methodists in the Middle Colonies issued pamphlets and published sermons to the same effect.[27]

With the war over and the national shame still visible on every side, some Friends turned the rhetoric of the American Revolution into an argument for a general emancipation.[28] But it was the Methodists who carried this argument to the Virginia Assembly, while Friends in the same state sought no more than a manumission act that would let them free their own slaves.[29] Thomas Nicholson and other North Carolina Friends made a bold stand involving civil disobedience when the North Carolina Assembly not only refused to enact a manumission bill, but authorized sheriffs to take up and sell any slaves freed by Quakers contrary to the law. Nicholson took a leaf from the Patriot pamphleteers in arguing that an unjust law had no binding power on the citizen and defied the Perquimans County justices. He had the full support of North Carolina Yearly Meeting who agreed to protect the former slaves in every way possible.[30] As in the war tax and conscription issue, the right of the sects to *live* in accordance with conscience would not be readily granted by the new republic.

Continuing Problems After 1783

The end of the war did not mean the end of the difficulties it had created for the nonresistant sects. Americans were in general agreement that government could lawfully require citizens to perform some manner of military service, sometimes with allowance for alternative service or, more commonly, monetary payments.[31] The doctrine of the Pennsylvania Bill of Rights of 1776 that made the right to claim the protection of society in the enjoyment of life, liberty, and property dependent on personal military service, or an equivalent, had not only gained wide acceptance during the war years, but found a place in nearly every state constitution adopted in wartime. The constitutions of New Hampshire, Massachusetts, New York, and Pennsylvania made it most explicit. This was in sharp contrast to eighteenth-century British practice which made military service voluntary, in the militia as well as in the regular army.

Mennonites, Brethren, and Quakers did not hesitate to protest against both compulsory militia service and the need to pay a substantial fine as the price of exemption. When the Virginia General Assembly debated a new Militia Act in November 1784, Mennonites and Brethren in Rockingham County joined in petitioning the legislature, while another petition came from representatives of the Mennonite Church in Virginia. The bill passed by the Virginia Assembly exempted members of the peace churches from personal service, but retained the requirement that they pay a fine as an equivalent to military duty. Other provisions that took the power to appoint officers from the county court and centralized it in the governor's hands created a good deal of opposition to the militia system in many parts of the Old Dominion. But the citizens of Virginia generally saw no injustice in making conscientious objectors pay for their privilege of exemption. The protests of Shenandoah Valley Mennonites and Dunkers did not enter into the debate at all.[32]

Did the lawmakers act in the mistaken belief that the Mennonites, Dunkers, Quakers, and the other nonresistant sects had no objection to paying a fine in lieu of personal service? The debates over the Federal Constitution and the Bill of Rights suggest that the case was quite the contrary. Roger Sherman of Connecticut declared in Congress in 1789 that "it is well known that those who are religiously scrupulous of bearing arms, are equally scrupulous of getting substitutes or paying an equivalent. Many of them would rather die than do either one or the other." The previous year Samuel Jones, who represented a Long Island district with many Quakers, had reminded the New York State Ratifying Convention that "those who are scrupulous to bear arms object to pay the fine" and no one had risen to contradict him.[33]

The failure of the United States Constitution to include a specific provision granting exemption from military service to the members of the nonresistant sects was one of the many points discussed and debated in the different state conventions that met in 1787 and 1788 to decide whether or not to adopt the document drafted by the delegates in Philadelphia. These debates shed light on the prevailing attitude toward conscientious objection and the reasoning process behind it. The Anti-Federalist minority in the Pennsylvania Ratifying Convention first raised the question in December 1787. They observed that the omission was "the more remarkable, because even when the distresses of the late war, and the evident disaffection of many citizens of that description, inflamed our passions, and when every person who was obliged to risk his own life, must have been exasperated against such as on any account kept back from the common danger, yet even then, when outrage and violence might have been expected, the rights of conscience were held sacred." Among the 21 signers of the minority protest were Joseph Hiester, Adam Orth and Nicholas Lutz, who had firsthand knowledge of the wartime experience of Mennonites, Schwenkfelders, Dunkers, Moravians, and Quakers. Their view is doubly interesting as a summary of their own understanding of the operation of the Pennsylvania Militia Act.[34]

Other state ratifying conventions took up this challenge and proposed amendments to answer the need. Maryland suggested an amendment declaring flatly "that no person conscientiously scrupulous of bearing arms, in any case, shall be compelled personally to serve as a soldier." Virginia and North Carolina qualified their conscientious objector amendments by adding, "upon payment of an equivalent to bear arms in his stead." A similar proposal came from Rhode Island.[35]

We can only guess at the arguments put forward by the supporters of these proposed amendments, but the points made on each side of the debate in the New York State Ratifying Convention have survived. They give an insight into the motives of the men who argued for and against the amendment. John Jay expressed satisfaction with the proposal, if it could be limited to Quakers, but he said he would have to oppose it, "if it will comprehend every person who in time of War will declare they are conscientious about it." Melancton Smith suggested the amendment name the sects whose members would be exempted, "as there are more sects than one which are scrupulous." It was left for Alexander Hamilton to sum up what can fairly be considered the consensus of the meeting. He agreed that "those who are now scrupulous may be exempted." but at the same time nothing should be done "to encourage this idea" among others. In other words, the small number of persons who could claim exemption on the basis of membership in one of the nonresistant sects alone made the idea palatable. The possibility of selective conscientious objection or even a refusal to fight based on personal moral conviction, apart from one of the peace church traditions, was rejected out of hand.[36]

These same objections were raised again, when James Madison introduced Article II of the Bill of Rights in Congress.[37] Madison's draft survived both committee revisions and a general debate in the House of Representatives sitting as a committee of the whole, with one important exception. He had proposed as part of Article II, "but no one religiously scrupulous of bearing arms shall be compelled to render military service." One Congressman objected that "if this becomes part of the constitution, we can neither call upon such persons for services, nor an equivalent." The same speaker acknowledged that "there are many sects religiously scrupulous in this respect" and "I am not for abridging them of any indulgence by law." The words "in person" were then added on the motion of Congressmen Vining of Delaware and Jackson of Georgia.[38]

Even with this important verbal change, the Madison amendment barely survived in the House. Elbridge Gerry argued against giving "a discretionary power to exclude those from militia duty who have religious scruples" and wanted exemption limited to named sects. Roger Sherman quickly pointed out that many Quakers had fought in the Revolution, despite the official stand of the Society of Friends on war, so that exempting the whole sect would free men from militia service who would otherwise defend their country. Fear of too sweeping an exemption made others hesitate. With religion said to be on the decline, all the greater was the need "to guard against those who are of no religion." But Judge Egbert Benson of New York had the last word in the congressional debate on conscientious objection. "It may be a religious persuasion, but it is no natural right, and therefore ought to be left to the discretion of the government." Provision for conscientious objectors would turn the militia laws of every state into a mare's nest of conflicting legal opinions that could never be resolved. The national and state governments could be trusted to have "sufficient humanity" to deal fairly with the sects without a specific guarantee in the Constitution. His motion to strike the entire clause failed in the House by only two votes. When the Senate took up Article II, they struck out the conscientious objector clause without debate.[39]

The lawmakers were reluctant to appear in the role of religious persecutors. Elias Boudinot of New Jersey had reminded Congress of "several instances of oppression in the case which occured during the war."[40] But they were firmly of the opinion that military service was an obligation of every citizen. If some citizens could not fulfil their military obligation because they saw participation in war as inconsistent with the teachings of Jesus, their protest could be dismissed as no more than "a religious persuasion." The argument for freedom of conscience that the nonresistant sects had presented again and again for more than 50 years was inadmissible. No man had a natural right to *live* by his conscience. The best he could hope for would be that government would be disposed to tolerate his peculiar opinions. It was a far cry from the liberty of conscience the peaceable sects had enjoyed under William Penn's Charter.

With the debates over the Federal Constitution as background to their own deliberations, Pennsylvanians adopted a new state constitution in December 1789. Article XX of the Pennsylvania Bill of Rights provided simply "That those who conscientiously scruple to bear arms shall not be compellable to do so, but shall pay an equivalent for personal service."[41] In November 1793 Maryland's General Assembly passed "An Act to regulate and discipline the militia of this state," which to serve in the militia, "upon condition of paying two dollars yearly towards defraying the expenses of civil government." It was a neat compromise with the sectarian obligation to support civil government by the payment of taxes, but Philadelphia Yearly Meeting decided in 1790 that "no Friend can pay such fine or tax, consistent with our religious testimony and principle, it being a fine in lieu of personal service."[42]

The Maryland General Assembly adopted a similar militia act in the November 1793 session, which allowed "quakers, menonists and tunkers, and persons conscientiously scrupulous of bearing arms" to be "excused from militia duty (except when called into actual service) on the payment of two dollars each."[43]

Militia records and petitions to the legislature provide ample testimony that Quakers, Mennonites, and Dunkers absented themselves from militia drills and training days. Fine books record the individual protests of members of all the historic peace churches in Maryland and Pennsylvania against paying fines since they were "scrupulous of bearing arms."

Some historians, even among their own denominations, have seen too great a difference between the Friends and the Mennonites and Dunkers on the payment of militia fines.[44] It is obvious from the extant records that all three groups had remarkably similar attitudes. A petition from Botetourt County Dunkers to the Virginia Assembly in 1799 requested exemption from militia fines as well as militia duty, hoping that "in this our country, the boast of which is the uninterrupted enjoyment of civil & religious Liberty" they might not be impoverished by fines and penalties handed down by the courts for nonpayment of fines.[45] This petition protested that, despite fines and amercements, the Brethren had steadfastly refused all militia duties.

Time was on the side of the authorities. What was abhorrent to the sectarian conscience in 1775 and remained unacceptable in 1799 became eventually the accepted way of life for the nonresistant churches.

If many Mennonites, Quakers, Dunkers, and Schwenkfelders readily paid militia fines, while others protested, the time would come when protest would be forgotten and the sects considered fines the inescapable companion of their nonresistant faith.

Embracing the Sectarian Vision

Their experience in the American Revolution thus reaffirmed Mennonites, Brethren, and Quakers in their belief that faithful discipleship meant separation from the norms of the larger society and a willingness to suffer for their fidelity. They discovered that the promise of Jesus, "Whosoever will save his life shall lose it; but whosoever shall lose his life for my sake and the gospel's, the same shall save it" (Mark 8:35), has application to the corporate life of the church as well as the individual.

The faithful following of Christ brought different challenges to different men and women in that generation, as in our own, but His pattern of nonresistant love remains the same for each one. We need not sentimentalize the eighteenth-century Mennonites, Quakers, and Brethren or make them more or less than human to acknowledge the testimony of their lives. After two hundred years their witness is still fresh and they challenge us to follow them as they followed Christ and to bear our testimony to Him whose kingdom is in peace and righteousness.

Notes for Epilogue

1. Henry Funk, *Restitution or an Explanation of Several Principal Points of the Law* (Elkhart, Ind., 1915), p. 269. This work was originally published in Philadelphia in 1763 in the German language.

2. William Matthews, Journal, May 2, 1781. M.H.S.

3. *Memoirs and Journal of Hugh Judge; A Member of the Society of Friends, and Minister of the Gospel* (Byberry, Pa., 1841), pp. 16-19.

4. Philadelphia Yearly Meeting, Minutes of the Meeting for Sufferings, 1775-1785, fols. 335-337 and 346. Quaker Collection, Haverford College Library.

5. Morse, pp. 51-53. Kenneth Radbill, "Socioeconomic Background of Nonpacifist Quakers during the American Revolution" PhD dissertation, University of Arizona, 1971 pp. 54-58.

6. Abram W. Sangrey, *Martin Boehm* (Ephrata, Pa., 1976), p. 14 dates the first Methodist class at Boehm's in 1775. Martin Boehm's own account of his experiences, given in the form of answers to questions by his son Henry, was printed in a free paraphrase in *The Methodist Magazine,* VI (1823), pp. 210-212. It was published for the first time from the original manuscript in Kenneth Rowe, "Martin Boehm and the Methodists," *Methodist History,* VIII (July 1970), pp. 49-53. John F. Funk published an English translation of the greater part of the Lancaster bishops' statement in *The Herald of Truth,* XIV (March 1877), pp. 33-37 and later reprinted it in his *The Mennonite Church and Her Accusers* (Elkhart, Ind., 1878), pp. 42-56. The original is not known to be in existence.

7. Huber, pp. 129-132.

8. A. W. Drury, ed., *Minutes of the Annual and General Conferences of the United Brethren in Christ 1800-1818* (Dayton, Ohio, 1897), pp. 9-10. Phares B. Gibble, *History of the East Pennsylvania Conference of the Church of the United Brethren in Christ* (Dayton, Ohio, 1951), pp. 30-31.

9. Sangrey, pp. 17-20. Earl H. Kauffman, "Anabaptist Influence on United Methodism in Central Pennsylvania," *M.H.B.*, XXXVIII (July 1977), pp. 4-5.

10. William J. Hinke, *Ministers of the German Reformed Congregations in Pennsylvania and Other Colonies in the Eighteenth Century* (Lancaster, Pa., 1951), pp. 71-79. J. Steven O'Malley, *Pilgrimage of Faith: The Legacy of the Otterbeins* (Metuchen, N.J., 1973) puts Otterbein in his full context, while Arthur C. Core, *Philip William Otterbein: Pastor, Ecumenist* (Dayton, Ohio, 1968) makes available the known writings of Otterbein. *Minutes and Letters of the Coetus of the German Reformed Church 1747-1792* (Philadelphia, 1903), p. 240.

11. George Adam Geeting (Gueting) was expelled by the Reformed Synod in 1804 by a vote of 20-17. Hinke, pp. 230-231. John Ernst, another of Otterbein's associates, died as pastor of the East Berlin Reformed congregation in York County, Pennsylvania, the same year, although some Reformed churches were locked against him. *Ibid.*, pp. 415-416. Simon Harr (Herr), often identified in United Brethren sources as a former Mennonite, was a lifelong Lutheran, residing at Strasburg, Shenandoah County, Virginia where he died in 1794.

12. John Hildt, ed., *The Life and Journal of the Rev'd. Christian Newcomer* (Hagerstown, Md., 1834), pp. 6-7.

13. Sem Sutter, "Mennonites and the Pennsylvania German Revival," *M.Q.R.*, L (January 1976), pp. 37-57.

14. Carlton O. Wittlinger, "The Origin of the Brethren in Christ," *M.Q.R.*, XLVIII (January 1974), pp. 55-72. Stoeffler, pp. 92-94.

15. Robert B. Semple, *History of Virginia Baptists* (Richmond, 1894), pp. 247-249.

16. Christian Burkholder, *Christian Spiritual Conversation on Saving Faith for the Young* (Lancaster, Pa., 1857) pp. 219-221 and 227. Robert Friedmann, *Mennonite Piety*

Through the Centuries: Its Genius and Its Literature (Goshen, Ind., 1949), pp. 238-244.

17. Burkholder, pp. 213 and 251.

18. Francis Herr, *A Short Explication of the Written Word of God; Likewise of the Christian Baptism, and the Peaceable Kingdom of Christ, Against the People Called Quakers* (Lancaster, Pa., 1790), p. 40. Daniel Musser, *The Reformed Mennonite Church, Its Rise and Progress* (Lancaster Pa., 1878), pp. 295-297. Theodore W. Herr, *Genealogical Record of Reverend Hans Herr and His Direct Lineal Descendants* (Lancaster, Pa., 1908), pp. 28-29.

19. Sydney V. James, *A People Among Peoples: Quaker Benevolence in Eighteenth-Century America* (Cambridge, Mass., 1963), pp. 268-269.

20. Herr, p. 40. He undoubtedly had in mind the "Address of the People called Quakers" to President George Washington, rather than any Quaker petition for redress of grievances. Both the "Address" and Washington's reply were published in *Pennsylvania Gazette*, Oct. 21, 1789. The 1789 Annual Meeting of the Church of the Brethren discouraged even township officeholding. *Minutes of Annual Meetings, 1778-1908, p. 13.*

21. Benjamin Mason, *Light Rising Out of Obscurity* (Philadelphia, 1790), pp. 42-45

22. James, *W.M.Q.*, 3rd series, XIX (July 1962), p. 375.

23. Semple, pp. 247-249.

24. *A Journal of the Life, Gospel Labours, and Christian Experiences of That Faithful Minister of Jesus Christ, John Woolman* (Dublin, 1794), pp. 78-79. Robert Ulle has located a clear statement of the Mennonite anti-slavery position in "John Hunt's Diary," *Proceedings of the New Jersey Historical Society*, LIII (January 1935), pp. 28-29.

25. Durnbaugh, *Brethren in Colonial America, p. 209.*

26. Christopher Schultz, Ms. Sermon, June 18, 1776. Another indication of Schwenkfelder anti-slavery interest is in Anthony Benezet to Christopher Schultz, 15th 7 Month July 1783. Schwenkfelder, Library, Pennsburg, Pa.

27. Daniel Byrnes, *A Short Address to the English Colonies, in North America* (Wilmington, Del., 1775) is a fair example, written by a Quaker. Richard K. MacMaster, "Anti-Slavery and the American Revolution," *History Today*, XXI (October 1971), pp. 715-723.

28. David Cooper, *A Serious Address to the Rulers of America* (Trenton, N.J., 1783), pp. 4-5.

29. Religious Petitions, *V.S.L.* Virginia Quakers petitioned for a manumission act in 1780 and in 1782. The Methodist petitions for a general emancipation were sent to the General Assembly in 1785.

30. Thomas Nicholson Papers, Philadelphia Yearly Meeting, Quaker Collection, Haverford College Library. Hiram Hilty, "North Carolina Quakers and Slavery," PhD dissertation, Duke University, 1968, pp. 43-50.

31. Charles A. Lofgren, "Compulsory Military Service under the Constitution: The Original Understanding," *W.M.Q.*, 3rd ser., XXXIII (January 1976), pp. 61-62.

32. Hening, *Statutes*, XI, pp. 18 and 477-484. Harrison M. Ethridge, "Governor Patrick Henry and the Reorganization of the Virginia Militia, 1784-1786," *V.M.H.B.*, LXXXV (October 1977), pp. 427-439.

33. Bernard Schwartz, *The Bill of Rights: A Documentary History* (New York, 1971), pp. 898 and 1052.

34. *Ibid.*, p. 672.

35. *Ibid.*, pp. 735, 842 and 968.

36. *Ibid.*, p. 898.

37. Robert A. Rutland, *The Birth of the Bill of Rights 1776-1791* (New York, 1966), pp. 201-203.

38. *Pennsylvania Gazette*, September 2, 1789.

39. Schwartz, p. 1052. *Pennsylvania Gazette*, October 7, 1789.

40. *Pennsylvania Gazette*, September 2, 1789, September 9, 1789.

41. *Pennsylvania Gazette*, December 30, 1789.

42. Ezra Michener, ed., *A Retrospect of Early Quakerism; Being Extracts from the Records of Philadelphia Yearly Meeting and the Meetings Comprising It* (Philadelphia, 1860), p. 306.

43. Kilty, *Laws of Maryland,* October 1793, Chapter XXXI.

44. Brock, pp. 335, 390-391, and 409.

45. Legislative Petitions, Botetourt County, V.S.L. On the background of the petition, see Robert Douthat Stoner, *A Seed-Bed of the Republic; A Study of the Pioneers in the Upper (Southern) Valley of Virginia* (Roanoke, Va., 1962), p. 387.

A NOTE ON SOURCES

Without primary sources, history would be unthinkable, and, without the generous cooperation of archivists, librarians, state and county officials, access to the raw materials of this history would have been all but impossible. The results of our research into the experience of the peace churches in North America in a turbulent half-century are presented with a deep sense of gratitude to the many individuals and institutions who made our research possible in the first place.

Official Records: State and Local Records

The State Archives Division of the Pennsylvania Historical and Museum Commission provided many collections of major importance to this study, as the footnotes amply attest. The Records of the Council of Safety and the Records of the Supreme Executive Council, notably the Clemency File (Record Group 27), included much unpublished material on the nonresistant sects, as did the Records of the Pennsylvania Supreme Court, especially the Records of the Courts of Oyer and Terminer (Record Group 33). The Forfeited Estates Accounts and Militia Fine Exonerations in the Records of the Office of Comptroller General (Record Group 4) and the Minute Books and General Assembly File in the Records of the General Assembly (Record Group 7) had far fewer items of use to this study. Other materials in Record Group 4 proved of very great importance to an understanding of the Revolutionary War experience of the sects. These are the Military Accounts, Associators, and Military Accounts, Militia, in the Records of the Office of Comptroller General. The usefulness of these last named collections has been greatly increased by the publication of *A Guide to Select*

Revolutionary War Records pertaining to Mennonites and other Pacifist Groups in Southeastern Pennsylvania by Gerald R. Brunk, Mary Jean Kraybill, and James O. Lehman (Harrisonburg, Va., 1974).

These manuscript materials provided a supplement to the invaluable printed sources for the official records of Pennsylvania as proprietary colony and state in the series of *Colonial Records* and the nine series of *Pennsylvania Archives*.

Official records of Maryland are also readily accessible through the ongoing series of published *Archives of Maryland* and the excellent *Calendar of Maryland State Papers*, almost entirely devoted to Revolutionary War materials in the "Rainbow Books" in the Maryland Hall of Records at Annapolis, published between 1943 and 1958. The Records of the General Court for the Western Shore and the microfilmed House and Senate Journals, as well as the Records of the Commissioners for Confiscated Estates, all in the Hall of Records, added additional details. Some militia records, tax lists, and the important Frederick County Treason Papers are in the Maryland Historical Society in Baltimore.

A great many official Virginia records were lost, when much of Richmond was laid in ashes in 1865. Two important exceptions in the Archives Division of the Virginia State Library at Richmond are the Legislative Petitions, arranged by counties, and the Religious Petitions. Much of the surviving material has been published, including the *Journals of the House of Burgesses of Virginia 1619-1776* (Richmond, 1905-1915), the *Journals of the House of Delegates of the Commonwealth of Virginia 1776-1790* (Richmond, 1827), and the *Calendar of Virginia State Papers and Other Manuscripts, Preserved in the Capitol at Richmond* (Richmond, 1875-1894) devoted almost entirely to Revolutionary War period Executive Correspondence files.

North Carolina official records have been made readily accessible in the *Colonial Records of North Carolina* series published by the state (Raleigh, 1886-1890).

Legislation affecting the peace churches can be easily traced in printed collections of state laws. William Kilty's compilation of *The Laws of Maryland* (Annapolis, 1799) and William Waller Hening's *The Statutes at Large; Being a Collection of all the Laws of Virginia* (Richmond, 1819-1823) have not been superseded. No less important is the compilation of *The Statutes at Large of Pennsylvania from 1682 to 1801* by James T. Mitchell and Henry Flanders (Harrisburg, 1896-1915).

Fortunately for the researcher interested in the Mennonites and other peace churches, the local records of Lancaster County, Pennsylvania, are among the best preserved county records. Original tax lists and some militia records are in the Lancaster County Historical Society. John W. Aungst, director of the Lancaster County Historical Society, and Mrs. Charles W. Lundgren, librarian, made available to us records from the Lancaster County Court House, temporarily closed to researchers for microfilming. In addition to court minute books and other county records, the extensive file of original indictments and related papers provided a rich vein of material on the wartime experiences of Loyalists, pacifists, and British prisoners. The Records of the Lancaster County Commissioners gave special insight on tax problems.

Lancaster County tax lists were not unique in identifying Non-Associators and persons who refused to take an oath or affirmation of allegiance. York County, Pennsylvania, records made these identifications possible for at least some townships, while card indices in the Historical Society of York County added to the ease of using these sources. The Chester County Historical Society in West Chester has custody of early court and tax records.

Berks County, Pennsylvania, court records and tax lists have been deposited in the Berks County Historical Society in Reading for many years, but only the tax lists are readily accessible and many court records could not be located at all. Court minute books and a separate record of defaulting tax collectors provided useful material for at least the last year of the American Revolution.

Court records in the Cumberland County, Pennsylvania, Court House at Carlisle and the Bucks County, Pennsylvania, Court House at Doylestown proved disappointing. Philadelphia County court records and tax lists, few earlier than 1780, in the Municipal Archives in Philadelphia shed light on townships now included in Montgomery County. The Northampton County Court House in Easton provided some details on the Mennonite community in what is now Lehigh County.

The Maryland Hall of Records in Annapolis is a central depository for all Maryland county records prior to 1788. Two important exceptions for this study are the court minute books in the Washington County Court House in Hagerstown and the files of original court papers in the Montgomery County Court House at Rockville, each dating from 1776 when these two counties were created by the Maryland Convention.

Court minute books in the Shenandoah Valley counties of Virginia revealed the large amount of grain, livestock, and wagons requisitioned from individuals for the government service in the last years of the

American Revolution and an occasional tax problem surfaced among the hundreds of routine cases. With these exceptions, the county records in the Rockingham County Court House in Harrisonburg, Virginia; the Shenandoah County Court House in Woodstock, Virginia; the Frederick County Court House in Winchester, Virginia; and the Berkeley County Court House in Martinsburg, West Virginia; shed little light on the wartime experience of the sects. The Frederick County Clerk helped us locate court martial records, dating from 1755-1761, preserved in a later deed book.

Official Records: Revolutionary Bodies

The records of the Continental Congress, state conventions, and many local committees have survived. Worthington C. Ford's edition of *The Journals of the Continental Congress, 1774-1789* (Washington, D.C., 1904) must be supplemented by the voluminous collection of Papers of the Continental Congress in the National Archives at Washington, D.C. Completion of a superb index to these documents has made it possible to retrieve every reference to Quaker prisoners in Winchester, Virginia, or wagons requisitioned in Lancaster County, Pennsylvania, in a matter of minutes. The proceedings of provincial and state conventions have long been in print. The published *Pennsylvania Archives* include the records of the Convention and the Council of Safety, both journals and correspondence, and much material from County Committees. *The Proceedings of the Conventions of the Province of Maryland, Held at Annapolis, in 1774, 1775, and 1776* (Baltimore, 1836) is still useful, although the journal of the 1775 Convention, the journals and correspondence of the Council of Safety and the later State Council have all been published in the *Archives of Maryland* series. The Virginia Convention published its own proceedings in 1775 and 1776, while the manuscript record is extant in the Library of Congress. The "Proceedings of the Virginia Committee of Correspondence" was published in the *Virginia Magazine of History and Biography* between 1902 and 1905. North Carolina records were published in the *Colonial Records* series.

By far the most important collection of records of a county or town committee is the Lancaster County Committee of Safety and Observation journal and related correspondence in the Peter Force Collection in the Library of Congress. For some reason, *a portion* of the Lancaster County Committee minutes for 1774-1775 was published in the *Pennsylvania Archives,* but the greater part of both minutes and correspondence remains in manuscript. The Library of Congress has a rich collection of printed broadsides issued by the Lancaster County Committee. The minutes of the Bucks County Committee of Observation in the Bucks County Historical Society in Doylestown, Pennsylvania, and the Northampton County Committee of Observation minutes in the Easton Public Library were very useful. The Maryland Historical Society in Baltimore has in its collections both the "Proceedings of the Committee of Observation for Elizabeth Town District," the present Washington County, Maryland, and the "Journal of the Committee of Observation of the Middle District of Frederick County," which were both printed in accurate transcription in the *Maryland Historical Magazine* between 1915 and 1918. Since these areas contained the only substantial population of "Menonists and Dunkards" in Maryland, their survival filled in many gaps in this study. A fragmentary collection of minutes, collection papers, and muster rolls from Dunmore (present Shenandoah) County, Virginia in the Twyman Williams Papers at Hampden-Sydney College (photostats at the Virginia State Library) is the only extant record of a Shenandoah Valley committee.

Official Records: British Headquarters

The Sir Henry Clinton Papers, actually the files from British Headquarters in New York 1778-1782, in the William L. Clements Library, University of Michigan, Ann Arbor, Michigan, contain a valuable collection of correspondence from Christopher Sauer III, William Rankin, and the Tory leaders in Pennsylvania and reports from British prisoners confined in Lancaster and York. The Papers of Sir Guy Carleton, Clinton's successor, available in photostatic form in the Research Department of Colonial Williamsburg, Williamsburg, Virginia, shed important light on Loyalist activities in western Maryland. The Cornwallis papers, available on microfilm in the Alderman Library, University of Virginia, Charlottesville, Virginia, also revealed details of the Tory Plot in Maryland, but otherwise yielded only a vague reference to German Loyalists in a region of South Carolina settled in part by members of the Church of the Brethren. All three collections are supplied with thorough indices.

Church Records

Alms books, records of deacons' fund distributions, and school accounts make up nearly the whole of extant eighteenth-century records from Mennonite and Amish congregations. Two sermons or religious writings from 1770 and 1782 respectively survive in the John F. Funk Papers in the Mennonite Archives in Goshen, Indiana, which also contains correspondence of Isaac Gross from the 1760s. Records of the Church of the Brethren annual meetings from 1778 on have been published several times in translation, most recently by Donald F. Durnbaugh. The Brethren Germantown congregation was apparently unique in preserving any record of its activities. A few devotional writings and personal letters in the Cassel Collection in Juniata College Library, Juniata, Pennsylvania, completes the list of contemporary manuscript material. Morgan Edwards included Mennonites and Brethren in his *Materials Toward a History of the American Baptists*, but they are secondhand and for the Mennonites extremely sketchy. Edwards published his volume of Pennsylvania data in 1770; the rest of his study remained in manuscript. The Historical Commission of the Southern Baptist Convention has microfilmed the entire work.

The Schwenkfelder Library, Pennsburg, Pennsylvania, has a rich collection of primary sources from this small religious body, including letters from Schwenkfelders in Pennsylvania to friends in Saxony and correspondence of eighteenth-century leaders, notably Christopher Schultz. Andrew S. Berky initiated a program of translating and publishing these American sources, including some in his *The Journals and Papers of David Schultz* (Pennsburg, 1952) and *Christopher Schultz and the American Revolution* (Pennsburg, 1952), the latter a translation of reports to European Schwenkfelders down to April 1775.

The Moravian Archives in Bethlehem, Pennsylvania, are also a rich storehouse of church records. The John Ettwein Papers, described and calendared by Kenneth Hamilton, were especially valuable. The diaries of Moravian congregations at Lititz, Hebron, York, and Emmaus are available in English translation.

Quaker records provided an embarrassment of riches in contrast to Mennonite and Brethren sources. The minutes and boxes of related papers of the Meeting for Sufferings of Philadelphia Yearly Meeting in the Quaker Collection at Haverford College Library, Haverford, Pennsylvania, proved of primary importance, as did the Papers of the Friendly Association in the same place. Records of individual meetings, used selectively, varied very much in their value for the wartime experience of Friends. The Minutes of the Meeting for Sufferings of Maryland Yearly Meeting, which began only in 1778, was useful for the Revolutionary War period. Records of meetings in Virginia, Maryland, and Pennsylvania, on deposit in the Friends Historical Library at Swarthmore College, Swarthmore, Pennsylvania, was microfilmed for the Maryland Hall of Records. Phebe R. Jacobsen, who directed the project, prepared a convenient guide, *Quaker Records in Maryland*

(Annapolis, 1967). Records of the North Carolina Yearly Meeting and its constituent bodies are on deposit in the Quaker Collection at Guilford College Library, Guilford, North Carolina.

Personal Papers

The Pemberton Family Papers in the Historical Society of Pennsylvania Library in Philadelphia provided much valuable information, as did the Curtis Grubb Papers, the William Henry Papers, the Shippen Family Papers, the Christopher Marshall Diary and Letterbooks, the Penn Manuscripts: Official Correspondence, the Conrad Weiser Papers, and a large number of individual items in the Etting, Gratz, and Parrish Collections and in several smaller collections, all in the same institution. Documents relating to the Friendly Association were found in both the Historical Society of Pennsylvania and the American Philosophical Society Library in Philadelphia. The Henry Drinker Papers in the custody of Haverford College were helpful. The Slaymaker Family Papers on microfilm in the Lancaster County Historical Society were also useful. The William Matthews Papers in the Maryland Historical Society included the wartime diaries of a traveling Friend.

Newspapers

Newspapers published in Philadelphia and Germantown provided a major source, particularly for the years of the American Revolution. We consulted the Germantown *Pennsylvanische Berichte*, 1754-1762 and scattered issues before that date; the Philadelphia *Pennsylvania Gazette*, 1754-1789; the *Pennsylvania Packet*, 1774-1784; the *Pennsylvania Evening Post*, 1775-1779; the *Pennsylvania Ledger*, 1775-1778; the *Freeman's Journal*, 1781-1783; the *Pennsylvania Chronicle*, 1767-1774; the *Philadelphische Staatsbote*, 1775-1777 and 1778-1779; the *Pennsylvania Journal and Weekly Advertiser*, 1775-1783; and the short-lived Lancaster *Pennsylvanische Zeitungs-Blat*, published for a few months in 1778. All of these papers were available on microfilm from the Pennsylvania Historical and Museum Commission. The Annapolis *Maryland Gazette* and the Baltimore *Maryland Gazette and Baltimore* provided a few items from the war years. The Williamsburg *Virginia Gazette*, despite a complete index prepared by Colonial Williamsburg, had little to our purpose, partly because of the very few issues that have survived from certain years. This newspaper's account of the Indian massacres in the Shenandoah Valley in 1758 is extant only in the *Pennsylvania Gazette's* reprint of news from Virginia, for example.

The German language press was surprisingly derivative. The *Philadelphische Staatsbote* translated items from the English language Philadelphia papers to the exclusion of any original news or comments and the others relied heavily on this source.

Pamphlets and Other Printed Sources

Mennonites published a variety of devotional, controversial, and educational works in the eighteenth-century, but only two pamphlets from Mennonite sources were germane to our subject. Christian Funk published *A Mirror for All Mankind* (Norristown, Pa., 1814) as a defense of his own conduct during the American Revolution and incorporated in it a pamphlet he had published in 1785, of which no copy is known to be extant. Francis Herr's *A Short Explication of the Written Word of God; Likewise of the Christian Baptism, and the Peaceable Kingdom of Christ, Against the People Called Quakers* (Lancaster, Pa., 1790) included a discussion of nonresistance. Benjamin Mason replied for the Society of Friends in *Light Rising Out of Obscurity* (Philadelphia, 1790).

The extensive pamphlet literature on the Paxton massacre and its aftermath is readily accessible in John R. Dunbar, ed., *The Paxton Papers* (The Hague, 1957).

Among other modern editions of primary material that proved particularly helpful, the following need to be mentioned. Hugh Edward Egerton, ed., *The Royal Commission on the Losses and Services of the American Loyalists 1783 to 1785* (New York, 1971); Howard Peckham, ed., *Memoirs of the Life of John Adlum* (Chicago, 1965); Johann David Schoepf, *Travels in the Confederation* (New York, 1968); Sylvester K. Stevens and Donald H. Kent, eds., *The Papers of Colonel Henry Bouquet* (Harrisburg, Pa., 1940-1943) and *Wilderness Chronicles of Northwestern Pennsylvania* (Harrisburg, Pa., 1941); Theodore G. Tappert and John W. Doberstein, eds., *The Journals of Henry Melchior Muhlenberg* (Philadelphia, 1942-1958); and William B. Willcox, ed., *The American Revolution: Sir Henry Clinton's Narrative of His Campaigns, 1775-1782* (New Haven, Conn., 1954).

BIBLIOGRAPHY

Printed Works

Ahlstrom, Sydney E. *A Religious History of the American People*. New Haven, Conn.: Yale University Press, 1972.

Alexander, Arthur J. "Exemptions from Military Service in the Old Dominion During the American Revolution." *V.M.H.B.*, LIII (July 1945), 163-171.

__________. "Service by Substitute in the Militia of Lancaster and Northampton Counties." *Military Affairs*, IX (1945), 278-282.

Ammerman, David. *In the Common Cause: American Response to the Coercive Acts of 1774*. Charlottesville: University Press of Va., 1974.

Ankrum, Freeman. *Alexander Mack the Tunker and Descendants*. Masontown, Pa.: The Author, 1943.

Archer, Adair Pleasants. "The Quaker's Attitude Towards the American Revolution." *W.M.Q.*, 2nd Ser., I (July 1921), 167-182.

Bainton, Roland H. *Christian Attitudes Toward War and Peace*. Nashville, Tenn.: Abingdon Press, 1960.

Baker, Donald S. "Charles Wesley and the American War of Independence." *Proceedings of the Wesley Historical Society*, XL (June 1976), 125-134, (October 1976), 165-182.

Baker, Frank. *From Wesley to Asbury: Studies in Early American Methodism*. Durham, N.C.: Duke University Press, 1976.

Baker, Gordon Pratt, ed. *Those Incredible Methodists*. Baltimore, Md.: Commission on Archives and History, Baltimore Conference, 1972.

Barba, Preston A. *They Came to Emmaus*. Emmaus, Pa.: Privately Printed, 1959.

Barker, Charles Albro. *The Background of the Revolution in Maryland*. New Haven, Conn.: Yale University Press, 1940.

Bauman, Richard. *For the Reputation of Truth: Politics, Religion, and Conflict Among the Pennsylvania Quakers, 1750-1800*. Baltimore: Johns Hopkins University Press, 1971.

Bell, Whitfield J. "Physicians and Politics in the Revolution: The Case of Adam Simon Kuhn." *Transactions and Studies of the College of Physicians of Philadelphia*, 4th Series, XII (1954) 25-31.

Bemesderfer, James O. *Pietism and Its Influence upon the Evangelical United Brethren Church*. Harrisburg, Pa.: Privately Printed, 1966.

Bender, Harold S. *Two Centuries of American Mennonite Literature*. Goshen, Ind.: Mennonite Historical Society, 1929.

Bender, Wilbur J. *Nonresistance in Colonial Pennsylvania*. Scottdale, Pa.: Mennonite Publishing House, 1934.

_______________. "Pacifism Among the Mennonites, Amish Mennonites, and Schwenkfelders of Pennsylvania to 1783." *M.Q.R.*, I (July 1927), 23-40.

Berky, Andrew S. *Practitioner of Physick*. Pennsburg, Pa.: Schwenkfelder Library, 1954.

Bockleman, Wayne L. and Ireland, Owen S. "The Internal Revolution in Pennsylvania: An Ethnic-Religious Interpretation" *Pennsylvania History* XLI (April 1974), 125-160.

Bowman, Rufus. *The Church of the Brethren and War 1708-1941*. Elgin, Ill.: Brethren Publishing House, 1944.

Bradley, A. Day. "Joshua Brown, Prisoner for Conscience Sake." *Journal of the Lancaster County Historical Society* 81 (Hilarymas, 1977), 25-29.

_______________. "New York Friends and the Loyalty Oath of 1778." *Quaker History*. XLVII (Autumn 1968), 112-114.

Braithwaite, William C. *The Second Period of Quakerism*. Cambridge: Cambridge University Press, 1961.

Bridenbaugh, Carl. *Mitre and Sceptre*. New York: Oxford University Press, 1962.

_______________. *Rebels and Gentlemen: Philadelphia in the Age of Franklin*. New York: Reynal, 1942.

Brock, Peter. *Pacifism in the United States: From the Colonial Era to the First World War*. Princeton, N.J.: Princeton University Press, 1968.

Bronner, Edwin B. "The Disgrace of John Kinsey, Quaker Politician." *P.M.H.B.*, LXXV (October 1951), 400-415.

_______________. "The Quakers and Non-Violence in Pennsylvania," *Pennsylvania History*, XXXV (March 1968), 1-22

Brookes, George. *Friend Anthony Benezet*. Philadelphia: University Press, 1937.

Brown, Wallace, *The Good Americans: The Loyalists in the American Revolution*. N.Y.: William Morrow & Co., 1969.

_______________. *The King's Friends: The Composition and Motives or the American Loyalist Claims*. Providence, R.I.: Brown University Press, 1966.

Brumbaugh, Martin Grove. *History of the German Baptist Brethren*. Mt. Morris, Ill.: Brethren Publishing House, 1899.

Brunhouse, Robert L. *Counter-Revolution in Pennsylvania 1776-1790*. Harrisburg, Pa.: P.H.M.C., 1442.

Brunk, Harry A. *History of Mennonites in Virginia 1727-1900*. Staunton, Va.: McClure Press, 1959.

Cadbury, Henry J. "Nonpayment of Provincial War Tax." *Friends Journal* XII (September 1, 1966), 440-441.

_______________. "Quaker Relief during the Siege of Boston." *Colonial Society Publications*, XXIV (1943), 39-179.

Calhoon, Robert McCluer. *The Loyalists in Revolutionary America 1760-1781*. N.Y.: Harcourt, Brace Jovanovich, Inc., 1973.

Carroll, Kenneth L. "A Look at the 'Quaker Revival of 1756.'" *Quaker History*, LXV (Autumn 1976), 63-80.
Cassel, Daniel Kolb. *History of the Mennonites*. Philadelphia: Daniel Cassel, 1888.
Clarkson, Paul S. and Jett, R. Samuel. *Luther Martin of Maryland*. Baltimore: Johns Hopkins University Press, 1970.
Claussen, W. E. "The Impact of the Revolutionary War Upon Exeter Friends." *Historical Review of Berks County*, XXXVIII (Spring 1972), 52-53.
Cohen, Norman S. "The Philadelphia Election Riot of 1742." *P.M.H.B.*, XCII (July 1968), 306-319.
Core, Arthur C. *Philip William Otterbein Pastor, Ecumenist*. Dayton, Ohio: Board of Publication or the Evangelical United Brethren Church, 1968.
Cummings, Hubertis M. "The Paxton Killings." *Journal of Presbyterian History*, XLIV (December 1966), 219-243.
Cunz, Dieter. *The Maryland Germans*. Princeton, N.J.: Princeton University Press, 1948.
Currey, Cecil B. "Eighteenth-Century Evangelical Opposition to the American Revolution: The Case of the Quakers." *Fides et Historia* IV (Fall 1971) 17-35.
____________. *Road to Revolution: Benjamin Franklin in England 1765-1775*. N.Y.: Doubleday & Co., 1968.
Davenport, John Scott. "The Brethren in North Carolina During the Revolution." *Brethren Life and Thought*, XXII (Winter 1977), 25-32.
Davidson, Robert L. D. *War Comes to Quaker Pennsylvania, 1682-1756*. N.Y.: Columbia University Press, 1957.
Doherty, Robert W. "Sociology, Religion and Historians." *Historical Methods Newsletter*, VI (September 1973), 161-169.
Dunkelberger, George Franklin. *The Story of Snyder County*. Selinsgrove, Pa.: Snyder County Historical Society, 1948.
Durnbaugh, Donald F. *The Believers' Church: The History and Character of Radical Protestantism*. N.Y.: The Macmillan Company, 1968.
____________. "The Brethren and the Revolution: Neutrals or Tories?" *Brethren Life and Thought*, XXII (Winter 1977), 13-23.
____________. *The Brethren in Colonial America*. Elgin, Ill.: The Brethren Press, 1967.
____________. *The Church of the Brethren Past and Present*. Elgin, Ill.: Brethren Press, 1971.
____________. "Relationships of the Brethren with the Mennonites and Quakers." *Church History* XXXV (March 1966), 35-59.
____________. "Religion and Revolution: Options in 1776, *Pennsylvania Mennonite Heritage*, I (July, 1978), 2-9.
Eisenberg, J. Linwood. *A History of the Church of the Brethren in Southern District of Pennsylvania*. Quincy, Pa.: Quincy Orphanage Press, 1941.
Eller, Paul Himmel. *Revivalism and the German Churches in Pennsylvania 1783-1816*. Chicago: Univ. of Chicago Libraries, 1935.
____________. *These Evangelical United Brethren*. Dayton, Ohio: Otterbein Press, 1950.
Eller, Vernand. "Friends, Brethren, Separatists." *Brethren Life and Thought*, VII (Autumn 1962), 47-56.

———. "A Tale of Two Printers—One City." *Brethren Life and Thought,* XVI (Winter 1971), 49-57.

Ellis, Franklin and Samuel Evans. *History of Lancaster County.* Philadelphia: Everts and Peck. 1883.

Epp, Frank H. *The Mennonites in Canada, 1786-1920.* Toronto: Macmillan, 1974.

Erb, Peter C. "Dialogue Under Duress: Schwenkfelder-Mennonite Contact in the Eighteenth Century." *M.Q.R.* L (July 1976), 181-199.

Eshleman, H. Frank. *Historic Background and Annals of the Swiss and German Pioneer Settlers of South-Eastern Pennsylvania.* Lancaster, Pa., 1917.

Flory, John S. *Literary Activity of the German Baptist Brethren in the Eighteenth Century.* Elgin, Ill.: Brethren Publishing House, 1908.

Frantz, John B. "The Awakening of Religion Among the German Settlers in the Middle Colonies," *W.M.Q.,* 3rd Series, XXXIII (April 1976), 266-288.

Funk, John F. *The Mennonite Church and Her Accusers.* Elkhart, Ind.: Mennonite Publishing Co., 1878.

Funkhouser, Jacob. *A Historical Sketch of the Funkhouser Family.* Harrisonburg, Va.: The Author, 1902.

Futhey, J. S. and Gilbert Cope. *History of Chester County, Pennsylvania.* Philadelphia, 1881.

Gegenheimer, Albert P. *William Smith, Educator and Churchman.* Philadelphia: University of Pennsylvania Press, 1943.

Gehman, Amy Histand and Bower, Mary Latshaw. *History of the Hereford Mennonite Congregation at Bally, Pennsylvania.* No publisher, 1936.

Gergerich, Albert H. *The Brenneman History.* Scottdale, Pa.: Mennonite Publishing House, 1938.

Gewehr, Wesley M. *The Great Awakening in Virginia.* Durham, N.C.: Duke University Press, 1930.

Gilpin, Thomas. *Exiles in Virginia.* Philadelphia: Printed for the Subscribers, 1848.

Gipson, Lawrence H. *Lewis Evans.* Philadelphia: The Historical Society of Pa., 1939.

Gleason, J. Philip. "A Scurrilous Colonial Election and Franklin's Reputation." *W.M.Q.,* 3rd Series, II (January 1961), 68-84.

Graeff, Arthur. *The Relations Between the Pennsylvania Germans and the British Authorities.* Norristown, Pa.: Pennsylvania German Society, 1939.

Gratz, Delbert A. *Bernese Anabaptists and Their American Descendants, Studies in Anabaptist and Mennonite History, 8.* Goshen, Indiana: Mennonite Historical Society, 1953.

Hamilton, Kenneth G. *John Ettwein and the Moravian Church During the Revolutionary Period.* Bethlehem, Pa.: Times Pub. Co., 1940.

Hammer, Carl. *Rhinelanders on the Yadkin: The Story of the Pennsylvania Germans in Rowan and Cabarrus Counties, N.C.* Salisbury, N.C.: Rowan Printing Co., 1943.

Handy, Robert T. *Religion in the American Experience: The Pluralistic Style.* Columbia, S.C.: University of S.C. Press, 1972.

Hanley, Thomas O'Brien. *The American Revolution and Religion: Maryland 1770-1800.* Washington, D.C.: Catholic University Press, 1971.

Hanna, William S. *Benjamin Franklin and Pennsylvania Politics.* Stanford,

Calif.; Stanford University Press, 1964.

Hansen, Marcus L. and John B. Brebner, *The Mingling of the Canadian and American Peoples* New Haven, Conn: Yale Univerity Press, 1940.

Harbaugh, Henry. *The Life of Rev. Michael Schlatter*. Philadelphia: Lindsay, 1857.

Hawke, David. *In the Midst of a Revolution*. Philadelphia: University of Pennsylvania Press, 1961.

Harrell, Isaac S. *Loyalism in Virginia*. Durham, N.C.: Duke University Press, 1926.

Henry, J. Maurice, *History of the Church of the Brethren in Maryland*. Elgin, Ill.: Brethren Publishing House, 1936.

Hershberger, Guy F. *Nonresistance and the State: The Pennsylvania Quaker Experiment in Politics, 1682-1756*. Scottdale, Pa.: Mennonite Publishing House, 1936.

———. "Pacifism and the State in Colonial Pennsylvania." *Church History*, VIII (March 1939), 54-74.

———. "The Pennsylvania Quaker Experiment in Politics, 1682-1756." M.Q.R. X (October 1936), 187-221.

———. *War, Peace, and Nonresistance*. Scottdale, Pa.: Mennonite Publishing House, 1969.

Hindle, Brooke. "The March of the Paxton Boys." *W.M.Q.*, 3rd Series, 3 (1946), 461-486.

Hirst, Margaret E. *The Quakers in Peace and War*. N.Y.: E. P. Dutton, 1923.

History of the Church of the Brethren of the Eastern District of Pennsylvania. Lancaster, Pa.: New Era Printing Co., 1915.

Hocker, Edward W. *The Sower Printing House of Colonial Times Pa. German Society, Proceedings and Addresses*, LIII, 1944-1946, Norristown, Pa.: The Pa. German Society, 1948.

Huber, Samuel. *Autobiography of the Rev. Samuel Huber, Elder in the Church of the United Brethren in Christ*. Chambersburg, Pa.: M. Kieffer, 1858.

Hudson, Winthrop S. *Religion in America*. New York: Charles Scribner's Sons, 1965.

Hunter, William A. *Forts on the Pennsylvania Frontier, 1753-1758*. Harrisburg, Pa.: P.H.M.C., 1960.

Hutson, James H. "Benjamin Franklin and Pennsylvania Politics, 1751-1755: A Reappraisal." *P.M.H.B.* 93 (July 1969), 303-371.

———. "The Campaign to Make Pennsylvania a Royal Province, 1764-1770." *P.M.H.B.* 94 (October 1970) 427-463, 95 (January 1971), 28-49.

———. *Pennsylvania Politics, 1746-1770*. Princeton, N.J.: Princeton, N.J.: Princeton University Press, 1972.

Illick, Joseph E. *Colonial Pennsylvania, A History*. New York: Charles Scribner's Sons, 1976.

Ireland, Owen S. "The Ethnic-Religious Dimension of Pennsylvania Politics, 1778-1779." W.M.Q., 3rd series, XXX (July 1973), 423-448.

Jacobson, David L. *John Dickinson and the Revolution in Pennsylvania*. Berkeley: University of California Press, 1965.

James, Sydney V. "The Impact of the American Revolution on Quakers' Ideas about Their Sect." *W.M.Q.*, 3rd Ser., XIX (July 1962), 360-382.

__________. *A People Among Peoples: Quaker Benevolence in Eighteenth Century America.* Cambridge, Mass.: Harvard University Press, 1963.

Jennings, Francis. "Thomas Penn's Loyalty Oath." *American Journal of Legal History,* 8 (October 1964), 303-313.

Johnson, Elmer. E. S. "Christopher Schultz in Public Life." *Schwenkfeldiana,* I (September 1940), 15-20.

Jones, Rufus. *The Quakers in the American Colonies.* New York: W. W. Norton & Co., 1966.

Kauffman, Charles F. *A Genealogy and History of the Kauffman-Coffman Families.* York, Pa.: Privately Printed, 1940.

Kercheval, Samuel. *A History of the Valley of Virginia.* Strasburg, Va.: Shenandoah Pub. House, 1925.

Ketcham, Ralph L. "Benjamin Franklin and William Smith: New Light on an Old Philadelphia Quarrel." *P.M.H.B.* 88 (April 1964), 142-163.

__________. "Conscience, War, and Politics in Colonial Pennsylvania," *W.M.Q.,* 3rd Ser. 20 (October 1963), 412-439.

Keyser, Charles S., comp. *The Keyser Family.* Philadelphia: Privately Printed, 1889.

Klaassen, Walter "Mennonites and War Taxes," *Pennsylvania Mennonite Heritage,* I (April, 1978), 17-23.

Knauss, James O. "Christopher Saur the Third." *Proceedings of the American Antiquarian Society,* N.S., XLI, Part 1 (Worcester, Mass., 1931), 235-253.

Knollengerg, Bernhard. *Growth of the American Revolution 1766-1775.* N.Y.: The Free Press, 1975.

Konkle, Burton Alva. *George Bryan and the Constitution of Pennsylvania 1731-1791.* Philadelphia: William J. Campbell, 1922.

Kriebel, Howard Wiegner. *The Schwenkfelders in Pennsylvania.* Lancaster, Pa.: Pennsylvania German Society, 1904.

Landis, Ira D. "Mennonites in Lancaster County, Pa.: The Hammer Creek Ebys." *Youth's Christian Companion* (September 30, 1945), 648.

__________. "The Origins of the Brethren in Christ Church and Its Later Divisions." *M.Q.R.,* XXXIV (October 1960), 290-307.

Lapp, Dorothy B. "Union Hall." *Chester County Collections,* XVI (October 1939), 489-495.

Lehman, James O. "The Mennonites of Maryland During the Revolutionary War." *M.Q.R.* L (July 1976), 200-229.

Lemon, James T. *The Best Poor Man's Country: A Geographical Study of Early Southeastern Pennsylvania.* Baltimore, Md.: Johns Hopkins Press, 1972.

Lemon, James T. and Nash, Gary B. "The Distribution of Wealth in Eighteenth-Century America. A Century of Change in Chester County, Pennsylvania, 1693-1802" *Journal of Social History,* II (1968-1969), 1-24.

Leonard, Sister Joan De Lourdes. "Elections in Colonial Pennsylvania." *W.M.Q.,* 3rd Series, XI (July 1954), 385-401.

Lincoln, Charles H. *The Revolutionary Movement in Pennsylvania.* Philadelphia: University of Pa. Press, 1901.

Littell, Franklin H. *From State Church to Pluralism.* Garden City, N.Y.: Anchor Books, 1962.

Lodge, Martin E. "The Crisis of the Churches in the Middle Colonies, 1720-

1750." *P.M.H.B.*, XCV (April 1971), 195-220.

Lofgren, Charles A. "Compulsory Military Service under the Constitution: The Original Understanding." *W.M.Q.*, 3rd Series, XXXIII (January 1976).

Lyman, Richard M. "Mennonites or German Friends." *Papers Read Before the Bucks County Historical Society*, I (1882), 39-44.

MacMaster, Richard K. "Thomas Rankin and the American Colonists." *Proceedings of the Wesley Historical Society*, XXXIX (June 1973), 3-26.

Marietta, Jack D. "Conscience, the Quaker Community, and the French and Indian War." *P.M.H.B.*, XCV (January 1971), 3-27.

________________. "A Note on Quaker Membership." *Quaker History*, LIX (Spring 1970), 40-43.

________________. "Quaker Family Education in Historical Perspective." *Quaker History*, LXIII (Spring 1974), 3-16.

________________. "Wealth, War and Religion: The Perfecting of Quaker Asceticism 1740-1783." *Church History*, XLIII (June 1974), 230-241.

Martin, C. H. "Two Delaware Indians Who Lived on Farm of Christian Hershey." *Papers Read Before the Lancaster County Historical Society*, XXXIV (October 1930), 217-220.

Martin, E. K. *The Mennonites*. Philadelphia: Everts & Peck, 1883.

Mast, C. Z. and Simpson, Robert E. *Annals of the Conestoga Valley in Lancaster, Berks, and Chester Counties, Pennsylvania*. Elverson, Pa., Privately Printed, 1942.

Maxson, Charles H. *The Great Awakening in the Middle Colonies*. Chicago: University of Chicago Press, 1920.

Mead, Sidney E. *The Lively Experiment: The Shaping of Christianity in America*. N.Y.: Harper and Row, 1963.

Mekeel, Arthur. "The Free Quaker Movement in New England During the American Revolution." *Bulletin of Friends Historical Association*, XXVII (1938), 72-82.

________________. "The Relation of the Quakers to the American Revolution." *Quaker History*, LXV (Spring 1976), 3-18.

Mishoff, Willard O. "Business in Philadelphia During the British Occupation, 1777-1778." *P.M.H.B.* 61 (April 1937), 165-181.

Morse, Kenneth S.P. *Baltimore Yearly Meeting 1672-1830*. Barnesville, Ohio: Friends Boarding School, 1961.

Müller, Ernst. *Geschichte Der Bernischen Taufer Nach Den Urkunden Da Gestellt*. Nieukoop: B. DeGraff, 1972.

Musser, Daniel. *The Reformed Mennonite Church, Its Rise and Progress*. Lancaster, Pa.: Inquirer Publishing Co., 1878.

Nead, Daniel Wunderlich. *The Pennsylvania-German in the Settlement of Maryland*. Lancaster, Pa.: Penna. German Society, 1914.

Neuenschwanger, John A. *The Middle Colonies and the Coming of the American Revolution*. Port Washington, N.Y.: Kennikat Press, 1974.

Newcomb, Benjamin H. "Effects of the Stamp Act on Colonial Pennsylvania Politics." *W.M.Q.*, 3rd Series, XXIII (April 1966), 257-272.

________________. *Franklin and Galloway: A Political Partnership*. New Haven: Yale University Press, 1972.

Nixon, Lily Lee. *James Burd, Frontier Defender, 1726-1793*. Philadelphia: Univ. of Pennsylvania Press, 1941.

Oaks, Robert F. "Philadelphians in Exile; The Problem of Loyalty During the American Revolution." *P.M.H.B.*, 96 (July 1972), 298-325.

Olson, Alison Gilbert. "Penn, Parliament, and Proprietary Government," *W.M.Q.*, 3rd Series, XVIII (April 1961), 176-193.

O'Malley, J. Steven. *Pilgrimage of Faith: The Legacy of the Otterbeins.* Metuchen, N.J.: The Scarecrow Press, 1973.

Overfield, Richard A. "A Patriot Dilemma: The Treatment of Passive Loyalists and Neutrals in Revolutionary Maryland." *M.H.M.*, LXVIII (Summer 1973), pp. 140-159.

Pennypacker, Samuel W. *Historical and Biographical Sketches.* Philadelphia: Robert A. Tripple, 1883.

Perry, William Stevens. *Historical Collections Relating to the American Colonial Church.* N.Y.: A.M.S. Press, 1969.

Reed, W. H. "The Pennsylvania Militia and the Convention Troops." *Montgomery County Historical Society Sketches,* V (1925), 340-341.

Reichel, Levin T. *The Early History of the Church of the United Brethren in North America.* Bethlehem, Pa.: Moravian Historical Society, 1888.

Reichmann, Felix and Doll, Eugene E. *Ephrata, As Seen by Contemporaries.* Allentown, Pa.: Pa. German Folklore Society, 1952.

Richards, H. M. M. "The Pennsylvania Germans in the French and Indian War." *Proceedings of the Pennsylvania German Society,* XV, Lancaster, Pa.: Penna. German Society, 1906.

Rosenberger, E. D. "The Funkites." *Penn-Germania,* XIII (Nov.-Dec., 1912), 829-830.

Rothermund, Dietmar. "The German Problem of Colonial Pennsylvania." *P. M. H. B.*, LXXXIV (January 1960), 3-21.

__________. *The Layman's Progress: Religious and Political Experience in Colonial Pennsylvania 1740-1770.* Philadelphia: University of Pennsylvania Press, 1961.

__________. "Mennonites, Moravians and Salvation in Colonial America." *M.Q.R.* 32 (January 1958), 70-73.

__________. "Political Factions and the Great Awakening." *Pennsylvania History* XXVI (October 1959), 317-331.

Rowe, Kenneth E. "Martin Boehm and the Methodists." *Methodist History* VIII (July 1970), 49-53.

Rupp, I. Daniel. *History of Lancaster County.* Lancaster: G. Hills, 1844.

Ryland, Garnett. *The Baptists of Virginia 1699-1926.* Richmond, Va.: Baptist Board of Missions, 1955.

Sabine, Lorenzo. *Biographical Sketches of Loyalists of the American Revolution.* Port Washington, N.Y.: Kennikat Press, 1966.

Sangrey, Abram W. *Martin Boehm.* Ephrata, Pa.: Science Press, 1976.

Sappington, Roger E. *The Brethren in Virginia.* Harrisonburg, Va.: Park View Press, 1973.

__________. "Dunker Beginnings in North Carolina in the Eighteenth Century." *N. C. Historical Review*, XLVI (July 1969), 214, 238.

__________. "The Mennonites in the Carolinas." *M.Q.R.*, XLII (April 1968), 96-116.

__________. "Two Eighteenth Century Dunker Congregations in North Carolina." *N. C. Historical Review* XLVII (April 1970), 176-204.

________________. "North Carolina and the Non-Resistant Sects During the American War of Independence." *Quaker History* LX (Spring 1971), 29-47.

Schaff, Philip. *Anglo-Germanism or the Significance of the German Nationality in the United States.* Chambersburg, Pa.: Publication Office of the German Reformed Church, 1846.

Schrag, Martin H. *The First Brethren in Christ Confession of Faith.* Grantham, Pa.: Privately Printed, 1975.

________________. "Influences Contributing to an Early River Brethren Confession of Faith." *M.Q.R.*, (October 1964), 344-353.

Schultz, Selina Gerhard. *A Course of Study in the Life and Teachings of Caspar Schwenkfeld Von Ossig (1489-1561) and the History of the Schwenkfelder Religious Movement (1518-1964).* Pennsburg, Pa.: Schwenkfelder Library, 1964.

Semple, Robert B. *History of the Rise and Progress of the Baptists in Virginia.* Richmond, 1810.

Seidensticker, Oswald. *First Century of German Printing in America.* Philadelphia: Schaefer and Koradi, 1893.

Sharpless, Isaac. *A History of Quaker Government in Pennsylvania.* Philadelphia: Leach, 1899.

Shy, John. "A New Look at Colonial Militia." *W.M.Q.*, 3rd Series, XX (April 1963), 175-185.

Siebert, Wilbur Henry. *The Loyalists of Pennsylvania.* Columbus, Ohio: Ohio State University Press, 1920.

Skaggs, David Curtis. "Maryland's Impulse Toward Social Revolution." *J.A.H.*, LIV (March 1968), 771-786.

Skizzen Aus Dem Lecha-Thale. Allentown, Pa.: Trexler & Hartzell, 1886.

Sloan, David. " 'A Time of Sifting and Winnowing:' The Paxton Riots and Quaker Non-Violence in Pennsylvania." *Quaker History*, 66 (Spring 1977), 3-22.

Smith, C. Henry. "The Mennonite Immigration to Pennsylvania in the Eighteenth Century." *Penna. German Society Proceedings*, XXXV, Norristown, Pa.: The Pennsylvania German Society, 1929.

Smith, Elmer L., *et al. The Pennsylvania Germans of the Shenandoah Valley.* Allentown, Pa.: The Pa. German Folklore Society, 1964.

Smith, Horace W. *Life and Correspondence of the Reverend William Smith, D.D.*, 2 vols. Philadelphia: S. A. George, 1879.

Smith, Paul H. *Loyalists and Redcoats: A Study in British Revolutionary Policy.* Chapel Hill: University of North Carolina Press, 1964.

Steiner, Bernard C. "Western Maryland in the Revolution." *Johns Hopkins Studies in History and Political Science,* XX, Baltimore: Johns Hopkins University Press, 1902.

Steinmetz, Rollin C. *Loyalists, Pacifists and Prisoners.* Lancaster, Pa.: Lancaster County Bicentennial Committee, 1976.

Stoeffler, F. Ernest. *Continental Pietism and Early American Christianity.* Grand Rapids, Mich.: William B. Eerdmans Publishing Company, 1976.

Stoltzfus, Grant M. *History of the First Amish Mennonite Communities in America.* Harrisonburg, Va.: E.M.C., 1958.

Stout, Harry S. and Taylor, Robert. "Sociology, Religion and Historians

Revisited: Towards an Historical Sociology of Religion." *Historical Methods Newsletter*, VIII (December 1974), 29-38.

Strickler, Harry M. *Massanutten*. Strasburg, Va., Shenandoah Printing House, 1924.

________________. *A Short History of Page County, Virginia*. Richmond: The Dietz Press, Inc., 1952.

Sutter, Sem C. "Mennonites and the Pennsylvania German Revival." *M.Q.R.*, (January 1976), 37-57.

Sweet, William Warren. *Religion in Colonial America*. N.Y.: Charles Scribner's Sons, 1942.

Thayer, Theodore. "The Friendly Association." *P.M.H.B.*, LXVII (October 1943), 356-376.

________________. *Israel Pemberton, King of the Quakers*. Philadelphia: Historical Society of Pennsylvania, 1943.

________________. *Pennsylvania Politics and the Growth of Democracy 1740-1776*. Harrisburg: P.H.M.C., 1953.

Thom, William Taylor. *The Struggle for Religious Freedom in Virginia: The Baptists*. Baltimore: Johns Hopkins, 1900.

Thompson, Mack. *Moses Brown, Reluctant Reformer*. Chapel Hill: U. of North Carolina Press, 1962.

Thorne, Dorothy Gilbert. "North Carolina Friends and the Revolution." *N.C.H.R.*, XXXVIII (July 1961), 323-340.

Tolles, Frederick B. *Meetinghouse and Countinghouse, The Quaker Merchants of Colonial Philadelphia, 1682-1763*. Chapel Hill, N.C.: U. of N.C. Press, 1948.

________________. "Quietism Versus Enthusiasm: The Philadelphia Quakers and the Great Awakening." *P.M.H.B.*, LXIX (January 1945), 26-49.

________________. "The Twilight of the Holy Experiment: A Contemporary View, *Quaker History* 45 (1956).

Tully, Alan "Englishmen and Germans: National Group Contact in Colonial Pennsylvania 1700-1755," *Pennsylvania History*, XLV (July 1978), 237-256.

____________. *William Penn's Legacy: Politics and Social Structure, in Provincial Pennsylvania, 1726-1755*, Baltimore, Md. Johns Hopkins Press, 1978.

Urner, Isaac N. *A History of the Coventry Brethren Church in Chester County, Pennsylvania*. Philadelphia: Privately Printed, 1898.

VanDoren, Carol. *Secret History of the American Revolution*. N.Y.: The Viking Press, 1941.

Wallace, Paul A. W. *Conrad Weiser: Friend of Colonist and Mohawk*. Philadelphia: U. of Pennsylvania Press, 1945.

Walsh, Richard and Fox, William Lloyd. *Maryland: A History 1632-1974*. Baltimore, Md.: Md. Historical Soc., 1974.

Warden, G. B. "The Proprietary Group in Pa., 1754-1764." *W.M.Q.*, 3rd Series, 21 (October 1964), 367-389.

Washington and Franklin County Mennonite Historical Committee. *A Record of Mennonite Bishops, Ministers and Deacons That Served and Are Serving in the Washington County, Maryland, and Franklin County, Pennsylvania Conference Area*. N.P., 1968.

Wayland, John W. *Twenty-Five Chapters on the Shenandoah Valley.* Strasburg, Va.: The Shenandoah Pub. House, Ind., 1957.
Weaver, Glenn. "Benjamin Franklin and the Pennsylvania Germans." *W.M.Q.*, 3rd Series, (October 1957), 539-559.
_______________. "German Reformed Church During French and Indian War." *Journal of Presbyterian History*, XXV (December 1957), 265-277.
_______________. "Mennonites During the French and Indian War." *M.H.B.*, XVI (April 1955), 2-3.
_______________. *The Schwenkfelders During the French and Indian War.* Pennsburg, Pa.: Society of Descendants of Schwenkfelder Exiles, 1955.
Weber, Edwin S. *The Charity School Movement in Colonial Pennsylvania.* Philadelphia: Campbell, 1905.
Wellenreuther, Hermann. *Glaube und Politik in Pennsylvania 1681-1776: Die Wandlungen der Obrigkeitsdoktrin und des "Peace Testimony" der Quaker.* Köln: Böhlau Verlag, 1972.
_______________. "The Political Dilemma of the Quakers in Pennsylvania 1681-1748." *P.M.H.B.*, XCIV (April 1970), 135-172.
Wenger, John C. "Franconia Mennonites and Military Service." *M.Q.R.*, X (October 1936), 222-245.
_______________. *History of the Mennonites of the Franconia Conference.* Telford, Pa.: Franconia Mennonite Historical Soc., 1937.
_______________. *The Mennonite Church in America.* Scottdale, Pa.: Herald Press, 1966.
Western, J. R. *The English Militia in the Eighteenth Century, The Story of a Political Issue 1660-1802.* London: Routledge & Kiegan Paul, 1965.
_______________. *William Penn's Legacy: Politics and Social Structure in Provincial Pennsylvania, 1726-1755.* Baltimore, Md., Johns Hopkins Press, 1978.
Wittlinger, Carlton O. "The Origin of the Brethren in Christ." *M.Q.R.*, (January 1974), 55-74.
Wolff, Mabel Pauline. *The Colonial Agency of Pennsylvania 1712-1757.* Philadelphia, Pa.: For Bryn Mawr College, 1933.
Wust, Klaus. "The Books of the Immigrants of the 18th Century," *Rockingham Recorder*, II (1958), 24-29.
_______________. "Disaffection in the Rear: German Tories in the West Virginia Mountains," *The Report*, XXXVI (1975), pp. 66-74.
_______________. *The Virginia Germans.* Charlottesville: Univ. Press of Va., 1969.
Young, Henry J. "Agrarian Reactions to the Stamp Act in Pennsylvania." *Pennsylvania History*, XXIV (January 1967), 25-30.
_______________. "Treason and its Punishment in Revolutionary Pennsylvania." P.M.H.B., 90 (July 1966), 278-291.
Zimmerman, John J. "Benjamin Franklin and the Quaker Party." *W.M.Q.*, 3rd Ser., 17 (July 1960), 291-313.

Unpublished Dissertations and Theses

Arnold, Douglas McNeil. "Political Ideology and the Internal Revolution in Pennsylvania, 1776-1790." PhD dissertation, Princeton University, 1976.
Guidas, John Thomas. "The Maryland Quakers in the Era of the American

Revolution." MA Thesis, Georgetown University, 1969.

Kobrin, David R. "The Saving Remnant: Intellectual Sources of Change and Decline in Colonial Quakerism 1690-1810." PhD dissertation, U. of Pennsylvania, 1968.

Lodge, Martin. "The Great Awakening in the Middle Colonies." PhD Dissertation, U. of California, Berkeley, 1951.

Marietta, Jack D. "Ecclesiastical Discipline in the Society of Friends." PhD Dissertation, Stanford University, 1968.

Mekeel, Arthur J. "The Society of Friends (Quakers) and the American Revolution." PhD Dissertation, Harvard, 1940.

Overfield, Richard A. "The Loyalists of Maryland During the American Revolution." PhD Dissertation, U. of Maryland, 1968.

Radbill, Kenneth A. "Socioeconomic Background of Nonpacifist Quakers During the American Revolution." PhD Dissertation, University of Arizona, 1971.

Schrag, Martin H. "The Brethren in Christ Attitude Toward the World." PhD Dissertation, Temple University, 1967.

Steckel, William R. "Pietist in Colonial Pennsylvania: Christopher Sauer, Printer, 1738-1758." PhD Dissertation, Stanford University, 1949.

Wood, Jerome H. "Conestoga Crossroads." PhD Dissertation, Brown University, 1969.

Young, Henry J. "The Treatment of Loyalists in Pennsylvania." PhD Dissertation, Johns Hopkins University, 1955.

INDEX

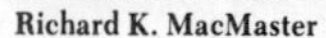

Richard K. MacMaster

Samuel L. Horst

Robert F. Ulle

Richard K. MacMaster, Bridgewater, Virginia, is Associate Professor of History at James Madison University, Harrisonburg.

He received his formal training in history at Georgetown University (PhD, 1968) and Fordham University (MA, 1962, and BA, 1958).

Since 1976 MacMaster has served as Field Representative for Mennonite Mutual Aid.

He is married to Eve R. Bowers. They are members of Park View Mennonite Church, Harrisonburg, and are the parents of three young children: Samuel, Thomas, and Sarah.

Among other published books and articles, he is author of *Christian Obedience in Revolutionary Times* (Mennonite Central Committee, 1976).

Samuel L. Horst is Associate Professor of History at Eastern Mennonite College, Harrisonburg, Virginia.

He holds degrees from the University of Virginia (PhD, 1977; MEd, 1957), American University (MA, 1965), Goshen College (BA, 1949), and was a Johns Hopkins University Fellow (1967-68).

He is the author of *Mennonites in the Confederacy: A Study in Civil War Pacifism* (Herald Press, 1967).

Robert F. Ulle is administrator of the Germantown Mennonite Church Corporation in the Germantown section of Philadelphia.

He is a doctoral candidate at the University of Pennsylvania, researching the growth of the black church in Philadelphia to the Civil War. He holds the BA degree in history from Eastern Baptist College.

His articles have appeared in *Afro-American*, *Pennsylvania Heritage*, *Pennsylvania Folklife*, *Mennonite Historical Bulletin*, and *Pennsylvania Mennonite Heritage*.